THE COMPLETE BOOK OF PERSONAL FINANCE

BOARDROOM® CLASSICS

330 West 42 Street, New York, NY 10036

Copyright©1987, 1988, 1989 Boardroom® Reports, Inc.

Second Completely Revised Edition
Including The Tax Reform Act of 1986
10 9 8 7 6 5 4 3 2 1

Boardroom® Classics publishes the advice of expert authorities in
many fields. But the use of a book is not a substitute for legal,
accounting, or other professional services. Consult a competent
professional for answers to your specific questions.

Library of Congress Cataloging in Publication Data
Main entry under title:

The Complete Book of Personal Finance.

Includes index.
1. Finance, Personal.   I. Boardroom Books (Firm)
HG179.C323   1987   332.024   87-30948
ISBN 0-88723-013-X

Boardroom® Classics is a registered trademark of
Boardroom® Reports, Inc.
330 W. 42nd Street, New York, NY 10036

Printed in the United States of America

Contents

iv

3 • FIGHTING THE IRS

Cutting Through Red Tape

Audits

What To Do Next

4 • FOR BUSINESSPEOPLE ONLY

5 • DEALING WITH BANKS, CREDIT, & DEBT

6 • HOLDING THE LINE ON MEDICAL COSTS

10 • INSURANCE TACTICS & STRATEGIES

Life Insurance

Health Insurance

Disability Insurance

Home Insurance

11 • ESTATE PLANNING

12 • INVESTING TO WIN

Investment Advice

Stocks

Bonds, Options, Commodities

Funds

Other Investment Vehicles

13 • MAKING MONEY WITH REAL ESTATE

14 • BUYING & SELLING A HOUSE, CONDO, OR CO-OP

Before Buying A Home

1 SMART MONEY MANAGEMENT

The Most Common Mistakes in Personal Financial Planning

More families should note Ben Franklin's observation that "in this world nothing is certain but death and taxes." An amazingly large number of intelligent people don't know how to achieve their life goals, provide for their families, or plan for the death of the main income earner.

Take full control of your life—before you begin to invest. Of the many errors families make in money management, 12 are repeated constantly:

- Only one family member is involved in financial affairs. Give one spouse ultimate responsibility for decision making, but both should be involved in financial planning and in meetings with accountants and lawyers. Bonus: Goals are more easily met if both partners pull in the same direction.

- Life goals are not on paper. Write down your goals, attach a dollar amount to them, and weigh their relative importance.

- There is no family budget. Budget carefully, so you know what you're spending. It's easier to change what you spend than what you earn.

- The family has no excess liability (umbrella) insurance. For only about $100 per year, a family can get $1 million in excess liability coverage. It could be one of the wisest investments you ever make.

- The contents of your home are not insured up to their replacement value. To maintain your standard of living, buy replacement-cost coverage. The premium costs only about $25 extra per year to cover almost everything you own. Discuss exceptions with your insurance agent.

- There is insufficient liquidity to handle emergencies or opportunities. Create a war chest. Have available for emergencies funds equal to six months' of spending money. Use your budget to arrive at an exact figure.

- Tax reduction is used as a goal. People devote too much attention to reducing taxes

1

when they should be concentrating on accumulating wealth.

• Employee benefits are poorly understood. Maximize your contributions to payroll savings and 401(k) plans with corporate matching. They are the best tax deferral mechanisms among voluntary retirement programs. Also, make sure your group disability plan is adequate. Check for inflation protection, partial disability coverage, lifetime benefits, and "own occupation" definition of disability—all of which most plans exclude. You can purchase a residual wrap policy that fills in some of the holes.

• Investments are not diversified. Buy non-specialty mutual funds, such as index funds. They are a relatively inexpensive way to play the market while making your first significant investment step a diversified one.

• A general-practice attorney drafts the family's wills, trusts, and durable powers-of-attorney. Important: Consult an estate-planning specialist, especially if your life insurance and death benefits equal $600,000 or more.

• No tax projections are made. Know the tax weather so you can better decide which "investment clothes" to wear. Read the financial pages regularly and consult with professionals.

• Income earners have no disability insurance. Know your disability coverage needs and seek adequate protection. It is well worth your time and effort to do so. Most insurance agents do not push this type of policy (because it's hard to explain the importance of it or because the commissions are lower than those on whole life insurance). Generally, you should get as much disability coverage as the insurance company will let you have. Disability differs from life insurance in that companies are reluctant to sell you so much coverage that you would have no incentive to return to work.

Source: Charles Haines, president, Haines Financial Advisors, 302 Ash Place, 2100 16 Ave. S, Birmingham, AL 35205. The fee-only firm specializes in financial planning for families, professionals, and small-business owners.

How To Apply Sophisticated Business Financial Techniques to Personal Finances

When finances become complicated, they often become clouded as well. When you're dealing with a variety of assets, investments, and income sources, it can be hard to focus clearly on how well things are really going.

The wizards who run the financial affairs of large corporations have developed analytical tools to deal with this problem by providing clear answers in crucial areas. These tools are just as useful for diagnosing your personal financial health.

In order to get valid and useful figures, you must begin with accurate data. A net worth statement, a cash-flow analysis, and a taxable income statement should contain all the numbers you need. Simply plug the appropriate figures into the following formulas.

Tool	Formula	What it shows
Liquidity Ratio	$\dfrac{\text{Liquid Assets}}{\text{Current Liabilities}}$	Are liquid assets sufficient to meet short-term obligations?
Expense Coverage Ratio	$\dfrac{\text{Liquid Assets}}{\text{Monthly Expenses}}$	How many months' expenses will your liquid assets cover?
Debt Ratio	$\dfrac{\text{Total Assets}}{\text{Total Debt}}$	How aggressive is your balance sheet?
Working Assets Ratio	$\dfrac{\text{Investment Assets}}{\text{Total Assets}}$	How much of your net worth is working for you?
Marginal Tax Rate	Tax rate (federal) paid on your last-earned dollar.	What percentage of each additional dollar will go for taxes?
Work ratio	$\dfrac{\text{Earned income}}{\text{Total Income}}$	How dependent are you on your job to meet income needs?
Fixed Expenses as Percentage of Total Income	$\dfrac{\text{Fixed Expenses}}{\text{Total Income}}$	How much of your income goes to cover expenses over which you have no control?

After-tax Return on Investment Assets

(See formula below.)

$$\frac{[\text{Taxable Investment Income} \times (1 - \text{Marginal Tax Rate})] + \text{Nontaxable Income}}{\text{Total Investment Assets}}$$

These tools should help you put your personal financial picture in perspective, but keep in mind that, unlike a business, there are no "objective" guidelines to follow in shaping your personal financial future. Only you can accurately assess the weight you give to factors of personal circumstance.

For example, a married couple with a taxable income in 1988 of $90,000 would have a federal marginal tax rate of 33%. This is the percent of each investment dollar they are paying in federal taxes. At present, they have $100,000 in a taxable money-market account earning 7% ($7,000 annual income). Their after-tax return is 4.69% $\frac{[\$7,000 \times (1-.33)] + 0}{\$100,000}$. They can then use this figure and compare it with tax-free money-market yields to determine which has a better after-tax return.

The same couple has monthly expenses of $5,000 and their Expense Coverage Ratio is:

$$\frac{\$100,000}{\$5,000} = 20 \text{ months}$$

This should highlight to them that they are being overly conservative and can invest the funds (within their risk tolerance) at a higher return. (Note: Many financial advisers use a rule of thumb of keeping enough liquid funds to cover six months' expenses. Since many factors, including your disability coverage and attitude, must be taken into account, be careful of rules of thumb).

Source: Joel S. Isaacson, CPA, MBA, Manager of the Personal Financial Planning Department at Weber, Lipshie & Co., 1430 Broadway, New York 10018. He is also adjunct professor in Iona College's Certificate in Financial Management Program, a member of the Financial Planning Advisory Board, Golden Gate University, and a member of the board of directors for the New York Chapter of the International Association for Financial Planning.

A Net Worth Calculation

Calculating your net worth is the basic method of determing if you're getting ahead or behind in the struggle for financial health. Those who like to keep close tabs on their progress may want to do this frequently; most ought to do it annually. January is a convenient time, since you receive year-end statements and have to do much of this work for your taxes anyway. Hopefully, each year will show you are closer to financial independence—whatever that dollar amount is for you.

Assets

Item 1: Cash. Total the contents of your checking and savings accounts, money-market funds, and certificates of deposit.

Item 2: Non-income-producing assets. These include the value of your home (tax assessments or local real estate ads should help you determine this if you're in doubt), vacation home (if you have one—and don't rent it out for part of the year), jewelry, automobiles, home furnishings, art, and the like.

Item 3: Insurance. Determine the cash value of all insurance policies. If you haven't checked recently, it is definitely a good idea to write to your insurers and find out.

Item 4: Investments. Check the current value of your stocks and bonds, any rental properties, real estate partnerships (the amount of your investment; you won't know the value of your share until the partnership is dissolved), oil and gas partnerships (which may have no current value), gold and silver (and other personal commodities), municipal bonds, company stock options, personal collections (stamps, coins, antiques, etc.), notes receivable, and the book value of your business.

Item 5: Retirement assets. Add in IRA, Keogh, pension and profit-sharing plans, 401(k), any deferred compensation, and company savings plans. Be sure to count only the amount you could take from your company if you left tomorrow.

Liabilities

Liabilities include mortgages, bank loans, credit card and any other trade debit balances, and notes due.

Total up the assets. Total up the liabilities. Subtract the liabilities from the assets. That's your net worth—the figure that can help you estimate when to retire or the progress you are making each year to increase your wealth.

Source: Alexandra Armstrong, CFP, president of the independent financial-planning firm, Alexandra Armstrong Advisors, Inc., 1140 Connecticut Ave. NW, Washington, DC 20036.

How Much of Your Wealth Should Be Kept Liquid?

Determining the best size of liquid monetary reserves (checking, savings, money-market funds) is largely a matter of psychology: What do you feel comfortable with? Depending on the individual, this may vary from practically nothing to $50,000.

To put the question in perspective, remember that the purpose of keeping liquid assets is to avoid having to disturb your long-term investments in the event you need money. In fact, cash reserves are seen by most people primarily as an emergency hedge. What fewer people see is that you can hold a larger amount so this money can also serve as an opportunity reserve, making it easy to take advantage of investment opportunities that come along.

With this in mind, then, figure that adequate liquid reserves should be between three and six months' expenses—not income. When adding up your liquid assets, you may want to include your certificates of deposit, which could be liquidated prior to maturity with the loss of only part of the interest. The possibility of borrowing against the value of your life insurance is another plus. If you're accustomed to the fast lane, you may be perfectly happy with a lower total, but three months' expenses is a realistically comfortable margin for most people.

Source: Alexandra Armstrong, CFP, president of the independent financial-planning firm, Alexandra Armstrong Advisors, Inc., 1140 Connecticut Ave. NW, Washington, DC 20036.

A Plan To Double Your Wealth

The concept of doubling your wealth has little meaning without a specific time frame. If you have any income-producing investments, they will eventually double your wealth without your having to do anything. But doubling your wealth within a target time period calls for some planning.

If invested capital remains constant, the return on investment needed to accomplish your goal can be figured by the "rule of 72": Divide the number 72 by the number of years within which you aim to double your worth. The resulting number is the percentage you must earn on invested capital. Doubling in 10 years will require investments to yield 7.2%; in five years, 14.4%; in two years, 36%.

To find out if your current investment portfolio is producing up to your expectation, do a careful review. Consider liquidating poorly performing investments and reinvesting the capital. A good rule of thumb in deciding whether to keep or sell an investment is: "If I had the cash, would I make this investment now?"

A good wealth-building portfolio is diversified and balanced. A good balance would be about one-third in stocks, one-third in income-producing real estate, one-third "other" (which includes municipals, annuities, and precious metals).

Regardless of how well balanced your portfolio is, your wealth will grow far more rapidly if you augment it with a regular and ongoing program of new investment. This will require some self-education in investment matters to help you work more effectively with your financial adviser. Careful investigation of each new asset prior to purchase reduces your risk. Emphasize updates, too: Regular review of your portfolio on at least an annual basis will give you a better picture of how well your plan is working.

Source: Alexandra Armstrong, CFP, president of the independent financial-planning firm, Alexandra Armstrong Advisors, Inc., 1140 Connecticut Ave. NW, Washington, DC 20036.

Cash Flow

Positive cash flow is what counts. You can be getting rich on paper and still not be able to meet your bills—unless you have a positive cash flow. Fortunately, it is not difficult to make a reasonably accurate annual projection of where you stand.

Step 1

Itemize every source of income you have. This will include base salary, any bonuses, commissions, self-employment income, Social Security and pension or other retirement income (if any). Add to that any capital gains you anticipate for the year. Add any interest, dividend, trust fund, or other investment income.

Step 2

Figure your yearly expenses. The following spending schedule should cover all of most people's categories of expenditure. If you have others, you can add more headings. The schedule includes this year and next so you can record the past and plan for the future. This way you can avoid the emergency expense—because you will have planned for it. Total your expenses and subtract from income. If you come up with a positive number, congratulations—you are accumulating wealth. If the bottom line comes up negative, it's time to trim some of your voluntary (non-fixed) expenditures. Recommended: Consider your retirement contributions and annual investments as expenses to include.

Annual Spending Schedule

These annual figures are for the current year. If you expect next year's expenditures or deductions to vary greatly, indicate them in the second column.

	This Year	Next Year
Food/Groceries		
Clothing		
Mortgage Payment(s)		
Utilities		
Telephone		
Cleaners, Drugstore, Hairdresser		
New Household Purchases		
Real Estate Taxes		
Auto Maintenance (gas, repairs, etc.)		
Transportation (cabs, bus, etc.)		
Car Payments		
Entertainment		
Club Dues		
Vacation Trips, Camp		
Domestic Help		
Child Care (deductible)		
Home Maintenance		
Yard/Pool Maintenance		
Subscriptions/Books		
Gifts/Birthdays, Etc.		
Medical Expenses (not reimbursed)		
Insurance Premiums		
—Life		
—Disability		
—Medical		
—Auto		
—Personal Liability		
Alimony		
Child Support		
Regular Allotments to Savings		
Retirement Contributions		
Stock Purchase Plans		
Personal Property Taxes		
Charitable Contributions		
Unreimbursed Business Expenses		
Tax Preparation Fees		
Education		
Legal Fees		
Federal Estimated Tax Payments		
State/Local Estimated Tax Payments		

Other—Source:

_____ _____ _____
_____ _____ _____
_____ _____ _____
_____ _____ _____

Source: Alexandra Armstrong, CFP, president of the independent financial-planning firm, Alexandra Armstrong Advisors, Inc., 1140 Connecticut Ave. NW, Washington, DC 20036.

Finding a Financial Planner

Most successful people are too busy being successful to spend any serious time analyzing their financial situation, establishing goals, and structuring and executing a financial plan that will enable them to achieve those goals. That is what a good financial planner should be able to do—alleviate the time burden on the very people who have the least amount of time to spare.

What to Expect

Financial-planning firms assume responsibility for coordinating your financial affairs—balance your investments, manage your taxes, plan for retirement, plan your estate, and above all protect your assets. What they will require of you is that you take an inventory of your assets and gather every conceivable kind of financial paper. Once you've provided the necessary information, a planner will analyze your financial profile and issue a comprehensive plan for achieving your major financial objectives. The plan will make recommendations and organize follow-through.

You should receive periodic reports of your financial condition to help you adjust your decisions over time. With a good financial planner, there is no such thing as "one size fits all." A quality planning firm will help you develop the perspective needed to make intelligent financial choices.

What to Look For

Over the past several years, it seems everyone has become a "financial planner." That can make your search a little tricky, but looking for the following characteristics should provide some help.

Professional expertise: Credentials are important. The best credentials in the field are the Chartered Financial Consultant (ChFC) and the Certified Financial Planner (CFP) designations. Some attorneys and accountants also specialize in financial planning.

Resources: Financial planners should work closely with other professionals—attorneys, accountants, tax experts, investment specialists—to cover all of the important financial-planning areas for the client. State-of-the-art computer facilities are almost essential to the firm's ability to work out the tax and other consequences of various planning proposals. Also, a reliable network of contacts throughout major financial circles is an important but sometimes intangible asset.

Range of offerings: A financial-planning firm should be licensed to offer securities, limited partnerships, and insurance—a full range of products to support the plans and strategies of all its clients.

Affiliation with a major institution: Many financial institutions, including banks and investment houses, are now offering financial planning in the same manner that life insurance companies have been doing for many years. A company with a strong long-term reputation can be your best guarantee of superior service.

Source: Randy Breidbart, J.D., regional director, Mutual Benefit Financial Service Co., 633 Third Ave., New York 10017.

Choosing the Best Financial Planner

A sound professional relationship with a financial planner is vital in today's increasingly complex financial world. A financial planner will help you: analyze your current financial situation, define your financial goals, develop a specific plan to achieve those goals, and implement the plan.

The first step in choosing a financial planner is familiarizing yourself with the field in general. Read. Talk to knowledgeable friends and professionals. Financial planning is a partnership, and the more knowledgeable the client-partner, the more effective the partnership will be. Furthermore, you will be better able to evaluate the quality of service you are getting.

The next step is to begin interviewing planners. If you need help in getting names, obtain references from friends or other financial advisers whom you trust. Other possible sources: The *Better Business Bureau's Consumer Resource Book*, the International Association for Financial Planning (IAFP), and the Institute of Certified Financial Planners (ICFP).

Interview a number of practitioners over the telephone. You will soon get a feel for the ones who are likely to be suitable for you. Plan to narrow your choices to three or four and schedule an interview with each. In the interview you will want to inquire about: Professional credentials, scope of services, areas of specialization, and compensation (fees and/or commissions).

Credentials

Two types of certification are available to financial-planning professionals, indicating rigorous courses of professional training. The Certified Financial Planner (CFP) designation is awarded to those who successfully complete the comprehensive six-part curriculum of the College for Financial Planning in Denver, CO. The Chartered Financial Consultant (ChFC) designation is awarded by the American College, Bryn Mawr, PA, following successful completion of its 10-course program. Both certifications include adherence to a strict code of ethics. The CFP also indicates commitment to a plan of continuing education—very important in the financial-planning field, due to the changing nature of many areas of finance, including investments, insurance, and taxes. Planners who offer investment advice must be registered with the Securities and Exchange Commission.

Continuing educational activities should be on the roster of interview questions. Three organizations sponsor major continuing education programs in financial planning: The College for Financial Planning, the ICFP, and the IAFP, mentioned above. All three issue certificates of completion for programs attended.

Scope of Services

Does this planner develop a plan on a one-time basis, or are plans reviewed and updated periodically? Is contact limited to an annual office visit, or is there continual contact and interaction as investment opportunities arise? How specific is the advice offered? Does your planner suggest particular investments that may be appropriate for you? What is the planner's role in actually purchasing investments?

Different levels of service may be appropriate to your needs, depending on the size and the activity of your portfolio, your degree of personal involvement, your work situation, etc. For example, many people have done a fine basic job of structuring their investments and may simply need some overall strategic advice, or merely the peace of mind that comes from confirmation of the value of their efforts.

Areas of Specialization

Look for a planner who serves clients whose needs are similar to yours. Such a person, thoroughly familiar with your type of situation, will be able to give you more insightful service. A financial planner who claims to be an expert in many fields should be regarded with a degree of skepticism. A competent planner should have working relationships with other financial services professionals and be willing to work with the financial advisers you are already using.

Compensation

Find out how much the services are going to cost. On what basis is the planner compensated? Hourly fee? Commissions on financial products sold? Or a combination of the two? The advice of a fee-only planner is generally free from any conflict of interest. When working with a commission-compensated planner, make sure that a variety of financial instruments and products is being offered for your consideration, not just the ones on which the planner stands to make the largest commission. Investigate the fee-and-commission alternative; it may provide the most flexible solution for both parties.

One final qualification is personal compatibility. Your financial planner should be someone whose philosophy and background you respect and with whom you feel comfortable personally. Clients who have selected carefully can be rewarded with a financial-planning partnership well suited to meeting their personal goals.

Source: Jan Walsh, MBA, an academic associate at the College for Financial Planning, 9725 E. Hampden Ave., Denver, CO 80231. A Certified Financial Planner, she holds memberships in the ICFP and IAFP, in addition to serving on the board of directors of the Rocky Mountain Chapter of the IAFP.

Checklist for Interviewing Financial Planners

When interviewing a prospective financial planner, make sure to cover these vital points:
• Experience. Three years' track record as a professional financial planner should be considered a minimum. A related financial background in accounting, brokerage, insurance, etc., is a plus.
• Credentials. CFP (Certified Financial Planner) and ChFC (Chartered Financial Consultant) credentials indicate extensive education. Admission to the Registry of Practicing Financial Planning Practitioners (maintained by the International Association for Financial Planning) indicates experience as well as expertise.
• Support. Make sure your planner has full computer services and adequate support staff. A solo practitioner is at a distinct disadvantage today. Many planners are teaming up to offer broader, better service.
• Clients. How many and what type. Favor a planner who has clients like you. A planner with more than 150 clients is spread too thin.

Also find out how many of them renew each year. A 75% client renewal rate is minimum.
• Reviews. Are ongoing reviews provided to make the plan current? How does the planner keep clients up-to-date? A regular newsletter and periodic seminars are customary.
• Fees. Don't expect a personalized plan for less than about $1,500. Fees can go up to many times this figure, consistent with the complexity of your particular situation. Ask beforehand.
• Above all, be sure you are comfortable with this person. Trust is an essential factor in producing meaningful results.

Source: Alexandra Armstrong, CFP, president of the independent financial-planning firm, Alexandra Armstrong Advisors, Inc., 1140 Connecticut Ave. NW, Washington, DC 20036.

Make an Asset Inventory

If something should happen to you, would your family know how to locate your important papers and assets? Here's an asset inventory form that will make this important job easy. Give copies to your spouse, perhaps another relative outside your home, any outside executor, and, of course, to your attorney. It will make many of their jobs much easier—and you might locate some neglected assets. Keep some blank copies of the form on hand and update your inventory when significant changes take place.

Presumably you have a fireproof lockbox at home that holds your important (nonnegotiable) papers. This is a good place to store your asset inventory. Your spouse (or whomever you designate) knows where this box is and has access to it. Alternatively you could put this asset inventory in your safe-deposit box, assuming your state does not seal this box upon your death.

Asset Inventory

For_____

Social Security number_____–_____–_____

Employer_____

My valuable papers and assets are stored in these locations:

A. Residence (address and where to look)

_____

_____

_____

B. Safe-deposit box (bank and address)

_____

_____

_____

C. Office (address)

_____

_____

D. _____

_____

E. _____

_____

F. _____

_____

Item	Location					
	A	B	C	D	E	F
My will (original)	☐	☐	☐	☐	☐	☐
My will (copy)	☐	☐	☐	☐	☐	☐
Powers of attorney	☐	☐	☐	☐	☐	☐
My burial instructions	☐	☐	☐	☐	☐	☐
Cemetery plot deed	☐	☐	☐	☐	☐	☐
Spouse's will (original)	☐	☐	☐	☐	☐	☐
Spouse's will (copy)	☐	☐	☐	☐	☐	☐
Spouse's burial instructions	☐	☐	☐	☐	☐	☐
Document appointing children's guardian	☐	☐	☐	☐	☐	☐
Handwritten list of special bequests	☐	☐	☐	☐	☐	☐
Safe combination, business	☐	☐	☐	☐	☐	☐
Safe combination, home	☐	☐	☐	☐	☐	☐
Trust agreements	☐	☐	☐	☐	☐	☐
Life insurance, group	☐	☐	☐	☐	☐	☐
Life insurance, individual	☐	☐	☐	☐	☐	☐
Other death benefits	☐	☐	☐	☐	☐	☐
Property and casualty insurance	☐	☐	☐	☐	☐	☐
Health insurance policy	☐	☐	☐	☐	☐	☐
Homeowners insurance policy	☐	☐	☐	☐	☐	☐
Car insurance policy	☐	☐	☐	☐	☐	☐

Item	A	B	C	D	E	F
Employment contracts	☐	☐	☐	☐	☐	☐
Partnership agreements	☐	☐	☐	☐	☐	☐
List of checking and savings accounts	☐	☐	☐	☐	☐	☐
Bank statements, canceled checks	☐	☐	☐	☐	☐	☐
List of credit cards	☐	☐	☐	☐	☐	☐
Certificates of deposit	☐	☐	☐	☐	☐	☐
Checkbooks	☐	☐	☐	☐	☐	☐
Savings passbooks	☐	☐	☐	☐	☐	☐
Record of investment securities	☐	☐	☐	☐	☐	☐
Brokerage account record	☐	☐	☐	☐	☐	☐
Stock certificates	☐	☐	☐	☐	☐	☐
Mutual fund shares	☐	☐	☐	☐	☐	☐
Bonds	☐	☐	☐	☐	☐	☐
Other securities	☐	☐	☐	☐	☐	☐
Corporate retirement plan	☐	☐	☐	☐	☐	☐
Keogh or IRA plan	☐	☐	☐	☐	☐	☐
Annuity contracts	☐	☐	☐	☐	☐	☐
Stock option plan	☐	☐	☐	☐	☐	☐
Stock purchase plan	☐	☐	☐	☐	☐	☐
Profit-sharing plan	☐	☐	☐	☐	☐	☐
Income and gift tax returns	☐	☐	☐	☐	☐	
Titles and deeds to real estate and land	☐	☐	☐	☐	☐	☐
Title insurance	☐	☐	☐	☐	☐	☐
Rental property records	☐	☐	☐	☐	☐	
Notes and other loan agreements including mortgages	☐	☐	☐	☐	☐	☐
List of stored and loaned valuable possessions	☐	☐	☐	☐	☐	☐
Auto ownership records	☐	☐	☐	☐	☐	☐
Boat ownership records	☐	☐	☐	☐	☐	☐
Birth certificates	☐	☐	☐	☐	☐	☐
Citizenship papers	☐	☐	☐	☐	☐	☐
My adoption papers	☐	☐	☐	☐	☐	☐
Military discharge papers	☐	☐	☐	☐	☐	☐
Marriage certificates	☐	☐	☐	☐	☐	
Children's birth certificates	☐	☐	☐	☐	☐	☐
Children's adoption papers	☐	☐	☐	☐	☐	☐
Divorce/separation records	☐	☐	☐	☐	☐	☐
Names and addresses of relatives and friends	☐	☐	☐	☐	☐	☐

Listing of professional
memberships ☐ ☐ ☐ ☐ ☐ ☐
Listing of fraternal organization memberships ☐ ☐ ☐ ☐ ☐ ☐
Other:

_____ ☐ ☐ ☐ ☐ ☐ ☐
_____ ☐ ☐ ☐ ☐ ☐ ☐
_____ ☐ ☐ ☐ ☐ ☐ ☐
_____ ☐ ☐ ☐ ☐ ☐ ☐
_____ ☐ ☐ ☐ ☐ ☐ ☐
_____ ☐ ☐ ☐ ☐ ☐ ☐

Important Names, Addresses, and Phone Numbers

Lawyer_____
Accountant_____
Stockbroker_____
Insurance agent_____
Date prepared_____
Copies given to:

_____
_____
_____

Source: Alexandra Armstrong, CFP, president of the independent financial-planning firm, Alexandra Armstrong Advisors, Inc., 1140 Connecticut Ave. NW, Washington, DC 20036.

How To Build Private Wealth—Secretly

There have never been more legitimate reasons for wanting financial privacy. These days, the more the IRS knows you have, the greater the chances of expensive, time-consuming tax audits. And when other people know how much you're worth, you're more likely to become a target of lawsuits, theft, and con artists.

Yet building wealth privately has never been harder. Several laws have tightened government reporting requirements. Insurance companies, credit bureaus, and major corporations keep detailed dossiers on people's personal affairs. And tax returns, once regarded as confidential documents, are becoming much more available.

The higher your net worth, the more effort you should make to put money away in private places. Best privacy vehicles: Precious metals, diamonds, collectibles, and offshore bank and brokerage accounts.

Moving Money Quietly

In moving funds into private investments, maintain a low profile. Avoid government reporting requirements whenever it's legal.

Banks have to file a report with the government every time you deposit or withdraw more than $10,000 in "cash" (loosely defined as any financial instrument that doesn't bear the name of the payee—cash, traveler's checks, checks made out to "cash," etc.), and the federal government has gotten stricter about enforcing this requirement. Under the tax law, banks must also report smaller cash transactions if they seem suspicious.

So if you withdraw $50,000 in cash (or traveler's checks) to buy gold coins—or $8,300 a day for six days in a row—your bank may report the withdrawal(s).

Best way to move large amounts of money: Have your bank wire it. This generates a record but attracts less attention because bank wire transfers have become routine.

If you have cash that you don't want to send by mail, or deposit in your checking account and write a check against, or use to buy a cashier's check, you may want to purchase a postal money order and send that. These are sold anonymously in amounts up to $700.

Private Stash

The surest way to invest invisibly in this country is to buy gold coins and store them in a safe-deposit box held in the name of an *inter vivos* trust—an entity that avoids probate at the time of death (a lawyer can create one easily). Buy the coins with cash or a money order a few hundred dollars worth at a time—never more because coin dealers are required to report suspicious cash payments to the government, just like banks and brokerage houses. Also, pay for the safe-deposit box in cash. This way, your name isn't attached to the purchase of the coins, to the coins themselves, to the rental of the safe-deposit box, or to the safe-deposit box.

Another good option is to buy warehouse certificates for precious metals stored in Zurich, Switzerland, through Mocatta metals, a well-known international metals wholesaler. The certificates are registered in your name, and you may take delivery of your gold or silver in Switzerland at any time. Certificates are sold by retail metals brokers nationwide.

Collectibles—stamps, antiques, art, wine—are excellent private stores of value, but they aren't as liquid as precious metals and they are less durable and more difficult to conceal. Investment-grade diamonds are small, durable, and relatively liquid, but it's hard for a novice diamond investor to know the quality of the purchase.

Offshore Investing

Many countries don't have the massive cash-reporting requirements for financial institutions that the United States has. Dividends, interest, and capital gains aren't reported to the government in Canada, Hong Kong, Japan, Australia, Britain, Switzerland, and most other Western European nations unless the receiver is suspected of breaking the law.

A US citizen may put up to $10,000 worth of currency and securities in foreign bank or brokerage accounts legally without having to report their existence to the US government. If you fail to report foreign accounts that are worth over $10,000, you've committed a felony.

If you have multiple foreign accounts whose total value exceeds $10,000, you must report them to the IRS, but it is legal to set up accounts worth $10,000 or less for each member of your family and not report them to the IRS.

Example: A couple with three children decides to put 15% of its $250,000 investment portfolio abroad. So it opens five $7,500 Swiss bank accounts—one for each family member —for a total of $37,500.

Trap: You deposit just a little less than $10,000 in foreign accounts, but the dollar falls—not unlikely—and the value of your account rises above $10,000, subjecting you to the reporting requirement. To avoid this problem, invest somewhat less than $10,000 abroad (as in the example above) and monitor the value of your foreign accounts carefully.

What Doesn't Work

Bearer municipal bonds. They don't carry the owner's name, and interest goes unreported because it's exempt from federal tax and state and local tax where the bonds were issued. But in 1982 the government outlawed the issuing of these bonds, and now you can buy only leftover issues that haven't matured or been called yet. You may still deposit coupons in a bank account without it being reported, but when you redeem a bearer bond at a bank or brokerage house, a Form 1099-B is sent to the IRS.

• Buying stocks with cash. Most brokers won't take cash, and those who do must report any cash purchase over $10,000 to the government.

• Carrying or sending bearer instruments abroad (cash, traveler's checks, cashier's checks made out to "cash," etc.). The transfer of bearer instruments worth more than $10,000 to a foreign country must be reported to the US Customs Service. Failure to do so constitutes a felony.

However, bank-to-bank wire tranfers, checks made out to a specific person or entity, and other types of transfers in which a bank record of payer and payee is created need not be reported, no matter what the amount.

Source: Mark Skousen, author of *The Complete Guide to Financial Privacy*, and editor of *Forecasts & Strategies*, Winter Park, FL.

Keeping Your Financial Records Private

Banking within the US banking system pretty much guarantees the availability of your financial records to the IRS, should it ever want to requisition them. By opening an account in a bank outside the jurisdiction of the US banking system and its laws, rules, and regulations, you can (under normal circumstances) keep your files and records well away from the scrutiny of US government agencies.

The only way the IRS or any other agency can find out about your transactions in an "offshore" bank is if you tell them.

What is an offshore bank? An offshore bank is simply any bank outside the country in which the depositor lives. For example, any Canadian bank is "offshore" to a depositor living in the US. Banking rules, regulations, and customs vary from country to country, and you may be more comfortable with one jurisdiction than another, but the confidentiality of your records is protected anywhere, as long as the bank is outside the US.

Is it legal to bank outside the US? Yes it is. The only legal stricture operating on offshore banking is the obligation of all US citizens to make a declaration any time they transfer funds outside the country in the amount of $5,000 or more. (You are, of course, still obligated to pay income tax on all income earned from your accounts, regardless of the location of the bank.)

Is it hard to open an offshore bank account? No, it is quite simple—roughly equivalent to opening a money-market account by mail in another city. The one difficulty is getting the necessary information, since it is against the law for any bank to advertise in the US unless it complies with US banking regulations. If the confidentiality of your banking records is important to you, it will be well worth the minimal detective work involved in finding an offshore bank.

Where do I find information about offshore banks? You can start by visiting your local library and looking through the various directories of international banks. Then, write to those in the jurisdictions you choose for more information, current rates, and opening account forms.

But will I have access to my money? Yes. Your checks may take longer to clear and you may have to wait a few extra days for withdrawals by mail, but in other respects, an offshore account is really no different from a normal account.

Are collection fees charged on money in overseas banks? Collection fees are charged when your offshore bank account is denominated in a currency other than US dollars. To circumvent the collection fees, simply have your offshore bank send you your money in US dollar instruments payable through one of the bank's correspondents or agencies in the US. Collection fees are collected by your bank based upon the amount it is charged by the international clearinghouse. If your money is paid in US dollars, through a US institution, there are no collection fees.

What "creative" options does offshore banking offer me? Well, probably most important, payments into your account of less than $5,000 will be undocumented (by the US government, anyway). You are still obligated under the tax laws to declare all income, but you will be the one to decide what information goes to the IRS. This opens up some interesting possibilities. Suppose you sell an asset, for example, and instruct the purchaser to remit directly to your offshore account. If you should later spend that money outside the US (on a vacation, say), the only way the IRS is ever going to find out about the transaction is if you tell them.

Are there any other benefits? Yes. While many people would pay a little more to get the confidentiality that offshore banking provides, the fact is that most offshore banks, not being subject to the "protectionist" regulation of interest rates, offer substantially higher returns on deposits than US banks.

Source: J.F. (Jim) Straw, publisher and editor of *Offshore Banking News*, 301 Plymouth Dr. NE, Dalton, GA 30720. He also owns an offshore bank based in the Northern Marianas Islands (a US commonwealth) that has approximately $3 million in deposits.

Protect Your Assets from Personal Financial Crisis

These days, most professionals and businesspeople can easily and unexpectedly find themselves embroiled in a financial conflict that could cost them most of their assets: Doctors, lawyers, and other professionals sued for malpractice or misconduct; business owners who must fight liability suits; anyone dealing with whopping medical bills to cover a long-term illness; people who can't get enough insurance or can't afford to pay for the coverage they need.

In this escalating crisis, the best self-defense is to get assets out of your name far in advance of any trouble with creditors. Although judges don't look kindly on people who transfer their assets in order to defraud creditors, the longer the time between a transfer and a court judgment, the less likely the transfer will be deemed fraudulent. (Once you're involved in a suit or have been dunned by creditors, all transfers—no matter what the purpose—are considered fraudulent and can be reversed.)

Caution: Don't overdo it. If you impoverish yourself, the transfers won't stand up in court as estate and tax-planning measures, and you'll run into serious financial difficulties even if you're never sued.

Effective Strategies

• Setting up a "family personal holding company" lets you keep control of your assets while transfering ownership of most of them out of your name. How it works: You establish a corporation, giving yourself a relative majority of the stock and dividing the rest among family members.

Example: You issue 100 shares: 30 for you, 25 for your spouse, and 15 for each of your three children. You then give your assets to the corporation as a gift, managing them yourself as chairman of the board. If you're sued, creditors can only get hold of your 30 shares, a minority interest in a private company, which isn't very useful. In many cases, creditors will be willing to settle for much less than originally demanded if it's in a more liquid form (cash, publicly traded stocks, bonds, etc.). Drawback: You must pay gift tax on transfers of more than $10,000 to family members other than your spouse. (You're allowed to give away up to $600,000 tax-free in your lifetime, but that includes the estate you leave to heirs.)

Since this type of asset transfer is a legitimate estate-planning tool (it helps lower inheritance taxes), a judge is unlikely to invalidate the transfer as long as it's done in advance of creditor troubles.

• Spendthrift trusts are an effecitve way to protect inheritances and other windfalls from ending up in your creditor's hands. How it works: A trust is set up with you as beneficiary and another party—spouse, lawyer, close friend—as trustee. Wording in the trust states that its assets can't be used to pay creditors. People who intend to will or to give you money—for example, your parents—then give it to the trust instead. Drawback: You lose control of your money to the trustee, although you can, of course, have the trustee removed if he violates the rules of the trust.

• Giving away assets to family members is simple and effective, as long as the giveaways aren't used to defraud someone. Guidelines: Gift must be given well in advance of credit difficulties, and the receiver has to exercise control over the gift—and be able to prove it—not merely serve as a front.

Drawbacks: Possible gift tax and complete loss of control over the assets you give away. In the event of a falling-out with the receiver (such as a divorce), you may regret the gift.

Alternative: Transferring assets into either an irrevocable or a reversionary trust, of which your heirs are the beneficiaries and a trusted third party is named trustee. Advantages: With both types of trusts, you can give assets to family members even if you can't trust them to manage the assets wisely. With a reversionary trust, the assets are returned to you at a prearranged date in the future. Trap: Once back in your name, the assets are again fair game for creditors.

• Company pension plans are one of the easiest ways to sequester funds from creditors. If you don't have access to the funds, neither does anyone else. However, creditors can attach distributions from the plan. Unprotected: Retirement plans in which you do have access to the money, such as an IRA (but not a Keogh).

• Gift-leasebacks can be used to give property to an individual, trust, or corporation, which then leases it back to you for your use, but not for your control.

• Life insurance policy cash values can't be touched by creditors. Trap: Investment-advantaged insurance, such as single premium annuities, isn't protected.

Less Effective Strategies

• Joint ownership. In most states, judges will trace assets held jointly to see which party contributed them and then determine the portion that can be attached by creditors. Avoid moving your assets into a joint bank or brokerage account with someone who contributes little or nothing. You might, however, be slightly better off with assets in joint ownership than in your own name, because getting assets from a joint account requires extra legal proceedings which might encourage creditors to settle for a lesser amount.

• Power-of-attorney accounts. Transferring your assets to an account in a relative's name —while retaining control yourself—is better than leaving them in your own name, but it's certainly not safe. A judge will probably rule that the account is de facto yours. The earlier you set up such an arrangement, the more likely it will survive a court test.

• Home ownership. Your family's residence is protected from creditors by state law, but only up to a relatively small size or value.

After the Fact

Once you've been sued by a creditor, there's little you can do to protect your assets. Misguided temptation: To liquidate your assets for cash, gold coin, or precious gems and hide them in a cookie jar or foreign bank. Such schemes are illegal and dangerous.

What can happen: The court can dig into your financial records—as far back as it wants to go. If the reords show that you once had $1 million and now have nothing, you'll be asked, under oath, what happened to it. Refuse to tell and you're on your way to jail for contempt of court. Lie and get caught and you've perjured yourself into jail.

Strong defense: You might be able to substantially limit damage to your finances by setting up a variation on the family personal holding company described above. Set up the corporation, but give all of its stock to family members. The corporation then issues shares of preferred stock equal in value to your assets, and you exchange your assets for that preferred stock, tax-free. The preferred stock pays, say, 6% interest a year. Result: The holding company now owns your assets, and the transfer is unlikely to be considered fraudulent because you didn't really give away your assets—you exchanged them for something of equal fair market value (the preferred stock). And that's all creditors can get from you. That might be all it takes to convince the creditors to settle for less.

Source: Attorneys Mark N. Kaplan, partner, Skadden, Arps, Slate, Meagher & Flom, New York, and Peter J. Strauss, senior partner, Strauss & Wolf, New York.

Savings Are Coming Back into Style

The US has one of the lowest savings rates in the world, placing us at the bottom of the list of industrialized nations. We save only 2% of our income each year, compared with 12% in Germany and 20% in Japan.

In the short run, our penchant to spend rather than save isn't all negative. High consumer spending ultimately translates into a growing economy. The danger: Over time, a low savings rate means less money is available for businesses to borrow and to invest in new plant and equipment. That means a decrease in the amount of capital goods created each year. When a nation's capital creation declines, so does its standard of living.

Who's to blame? The baby boomers—those age 30 to 40, who make up the largest component of our population. They are spending like crazy and saving next to nothing. With their rising salaries and easy credit, most are spending beyond their means, digging into debt, and saving very little.

Problem: The baby boomers are not planning for the future. Most don't even know what it will take to achieve their most basic goals: Buying a home, sending their kids to college, retiring without depending on other people or the government for assistance.

Typical example

Bob and Helen have a combined salary of $50,000 and two children ages 7 and 10. They have no savings and no debt, and they want to send their children to $10,000-per-year colleges. Bob and Helen figure that if they save 5% of their income they will have plenty of money for retirement. Harsh reality: When retirement time rolls around, Bob and Helen will be $31,000 in debt.

The situation is far from hopeless. By making some small adjustments, Bob and Helen can get themselves back on sound financial footing.

• First, they must take steps to reduce the educational expenses for their children. By choosing less expensive schools, taking out student loans, and sending the children to work during the summer, Bob and Helen can scale back anticipated college costs from $10,000 per year to $3,000. If they save the difference and invest it at a modest tax-deferred rate of 3% (after inflation), they will have accumulated a net worth of $70,000 by retirement time.

• Simply by selling a rarely used boat and trailer (nonearning assets) for $10,000 and investing the money, they can boost their retirement nest egg to $94,000.

• If they can manage to save 10% of their income rather than only 5%, their net worth will go up to $207,000.

• If they put some of their passbook-account savings into safe stocks, increasing their real overall return from 3% to 5%, their net worth at retirement will increase to $293,000.

Although these steps are small, it takes planning and discipline to execute them effectively.

The Sooner, the Better

The earlier you start, the easier it is to save what you need for retirement. The magic of compound interest makes smaller savings grow faster over long periods of time.

Example: Let's say your goal is to have $500,000 by the time you retire. If you start saving at age 20, you will have to put away only $650 a year at a 10% average return to reach your goal by age 65. If you don't start until you are 35, you will need to put away $2,750 per year. At age 50, you will have to save $14,000 per year. And at age 55, you will need to save a whopping $27,500 per year.

Prediction

In the next five to 10 years, many couples will realize that they're going to come up short at retirement. They will then change their habits—swiftly and dramatically.

For the past two decades we have been enjoying the present by sacrificing the future. The time has come to start sacrificing in the present so we can enjoy the future. This is what Japan did after World War II, and it's one of the major reasons for that country's current economic success.

Source: John Rutledge, Ph.D., chairman, and Deborah Allen Olivier, Ph.D., president, Claremont Economics Institute (which publishes *The Main Street Journal*). Dr. Rutledge is also president of The Claremont Fund, a family of no-load mutual funds. Both are located in Claremont, CA.

Which Kind of Personal Loan Is Best

Best Places to Borrow

• Broker loans. Though they don't often advertise them, brokerage houses offer some of the best loan deals around. If you open a margin account with a brokerage house, you can borrow up to 50% of the value of your stocks or bonds. In effect, you're using your own investment as collateral and are borrowing against the equity of the portfolio. The interest is deductible if you pay it monthly. However, it's not deductible if you let it accumulate in the debit account.

Drawback: If the value of your portfolio declines to a point below the brokerage house's margin limit, you'll be subjected to a margin call and be required to add money to the account to bring it back up to the acceptable level.

• Credit-union loans. If your company has a credit union, it makes sense to join if you're looking for low-cost credit. Most credit unions allow you to borrow at rates as low as two to four percentage points below commercial rates. Repayment is convenient because it's handled through payroll deduction.

Drawback: Under tax reform the deduction for interest on credit-union loans is phased out.

• Home equity loans. Tax reform made home equity loans even more attractive by leaving the deduction for interest on such loans intact while eliminating deductions for interest on other major forms of consumer debt such as bank and department store credit cards.

There are two types of home equity loans—a second mortgage and a line of credit. In order to find the best home equity loan, look at three sources—commercial banks, savings and loan associations, and most of the large brokerage houses. Rates and repayment terms vary from one lender to another, but most of them will let you borrow up to 75% of the appraised value of your home that exceeds the amount of your first mortgage.

Example: If you bought your house five years ago for $100,000 and have a $75,000 mortgage on it and the appraised value today is $125,000, you can get an equity loan of up to $37,500 (75% of the $50,000 in equity).

Most lenders offer a choice of a fixed-rate loan or a variable-rate line of credit. Most people choose 30-year equity loans, though 15-year terms are also widely available.

For many individuals, variable-rate home equity loans have big advantages, including low interest rates. If rates remain stable or decline, these loans are less costly than most other alternatives. If rates do rise, you can always refinance.

If you take out a credit-line type of home equity loan, you pay interest only on the amount you withdraw.

Example: You can take out a $50,000 home equity credit line and actually use only $10,000 of it now. Until you borrow more, you pay interest only on that $10,000.

Caution: Most banks charge an origination fee of 1%–4% of the loan amount. The lower the interest rate, the higher the origination fee.

Add that amount to the interest rate when calculating the real cost of the loan. Moreover, under tax reform, there's a limit on how much of the interest you may deduct. Check with your tax consultant.

Also Worth Considering

• Loans against your pension plan. Subject to certain stringent limitations, you may be able to borrow up to $50,000 against the vested amount in your qualified plan, whether you work for a company or are self-employed. Under tax reform you must repay these loans with interest on at least a quarterly basis for a period that can't exceed five years.

However, a longer repayment period may be permissible if the loan is applied to a down payment on the purchase of a primary residence or to paying for certain hardships. Rates are set by the plan's trustees and are usually pegged to the prime rate.

• Secured consumer loans. Most banks will extend loans collateralized by assets such as certificates of deposit, stock, or bonds. You can usually get a one-year renewable credit of up to 75% of the value of the collateral pledged. Caution: If you need credit for more than a year, consider a secured consumer loan only if you expect interest rates to remain stable or decline. Once you renew the loan, the rate is adjusted, and if rates have risen, you're worse off than if you had taken a longer-term fixed-rate credit such as a home equity or credit-union loan.

Loans to Avoid

• Loans against life insurance policies. Though many insurance companies are aggressively selling fancy life insurance policies that allow you to borrow at very low interest rates, don't buy one unless you're also in the market for insurance protection. Reason: You're mortgaging your own death proceeds. For instance, if at the time of your death you have a $25,000 loan against a $100,000 policy, your heirs will receive only $75,000. Since there may also be more tax liability than you realized, it's essential to check with your tax consultant when you borrow against a life insurance policy. It makes no sense to pay a life insurance company just for the privilege of borrowing.

However, if you already have a life insurance policy, consider using its borrowing privileges if you need a loan. Many older policies can be borrowed against for as little as 4½ % a year.

• Credit card debt. Though some banks have succumbed to consumer pressure to reduce their exorbitant finance charges, most haven't. Most credit card holders are still subject to charges of 16%–20% a year.

Those were outrageous rates while the interest was still deductible, but now they make even less sense. If you have a large balance on your credit cards, your best strategy would be to get a home equity loan or brokerage loan and use the money to pay off credit card balances. If you're paying 19% a year on the outstanding credit card balance and you pay it off with a 9½ % home equity loan, you cut your annual interest in half. Plus you have a full tax deduction for the interest payments.

Source: Connie S. P. Chen, president, Chen Planning Consultants, financial planners, 515 Madison Ave., New York 10022.

Borrowing Without Reducing Your Insurance Coverage

A loan on your life insurance policy can be particularly attractive if you have an old policy that provides for low-interest-rate loans. However, many people fear—with good reason—that borrowing on their life insurance policies will reduce their coverage in case of death. Solution: Use the dividends or part of the loan on the policy to buy inexpensive term insurance to keep your coverage level at the face value of your original policy. That will permit you to borrow without endangering your beneficiary's financial well-being.

Source: Thomas Lynch, senior vice president, Ayco/American Express, a consulting group that advises corporate personnel about financial and tax matters.

Keeping Tabs on the Fed

For many years, economists have been trying to figure out when the Federal Reserve Board will raise or lower interest rates. Although the Fed keeps its policies secret, David M. Jones, chief economist at Aubrey G. Lanston & Co., has figured out its basic guidelines.

The Fed manipulates interest so that growth in the Gross National Product stays in the 3%–4% range. It lowers rates if GNP growth approaches 2% and raises them if growth gets near 6%. Even though this is the Fed's target, Jones warns that it will still change rates to counter bursts of inflation or fluctuations in the value of the dollar.

What Part of a Greenback Is Worth

Worn and torn paper money will be replaced by the Department of the Treasury if three-fifths or more of the bill remains intact. If less than three-fifths but more than two-fifths exists, the bill is worth one-half its face value. For redemption of a smaller fragment, proof must be offered that the missing portion is destroyed. Such bills will be replaced at face value by your local bank.

A Shopper's Guide to Bargaining

The biggest problem most shoppers have with bargaining is a feeling that nice people don't do it. Before you can negotiate, you have to get over this attitude. Some ammunition:

Bargaining will not turn you into a social outcast. All shopkeepers see when you walk in is dollar signs. If you are willing to spend, they will probably be willing to make a deal. They

17

know that everybody is trying to save money.

Bargaining is a business transaction. You are not trying to cheat the merchant or get something for nothing. You are trying to agree on a fair price. You expect to negotiate for a house or a car—why not for a refrigerator or a winter coat?

You have a right to bargain, particularly in small stores that don't discount. Reasoning: Department stores, which won't bargain as a rule, mark up prices 100%–150% to cover high overhead costs. Small stores should charge lower prices because their costs are less.

The Savvy Approach

Set yourself a price limit for a particular item before you approach the storekeepers. Be prepared to walk out if they don't meet your limit. (You can always change your mind later.) Make them believe you really won't buy unless they come down.

Be discreet in your negotiations. If other customers can overhear your dickering, the shop owner must stay firm.

Be respectful of the merchandise and the storekeeper. Don't manhandle the goods that you inspect. Address salespeople in a polite, friendly manner. Assume that they will want to do their best for you.

Shop at off hours. You will have more luck if business is slow.

Look for unmarked merchandise. If there is no price tag, you are invited to bargain.

Tactics That Work

Negotiate with cash. In a store that takes credit cards, request a discount for paying in cash. (Charging entails overhead costs that the store must absorb.)

Buy in quantity. A customer who is committed to a number of purchases has more bargaining power. When everything is picked out, approach the owner and suggest a total price about 20% less than the actual total. Or, if you are buying more than one of an item, offer to pay full price on the first one if the owner will give you a break on the others. Storekeeper's alternative: You spent $500 on clothing and asked for a better price. The owner couldn't charge you less, but threw in a belt priced at $35 as a bonus.

Look for flawed merchandise. This is the only acceptable bargaining point in department stores, but it also can save you money in small shops. If there's a spot, a split seam, or a missing button, estimate what it would cost to have the garment fixed commercially, and ask for a discount based on that figure. Variation: You find a chipped hairdryer. When you ask for a discount, the manager says he will return it to the manufacturer and find you an undamaged one. Your reply: "Sell it to me for a little less and save yourself the trouble."

Adapt your haggling to the realities of the situation. A true discount house has a low profit margin and depends on volume to make its money. Don't ask for more than 5% off in such a store. A boutique that charges what the traffic will bear has more leeway. Start by asking for 25% off, and dicker from there.

Buy at the end of the season, when new stock is being put out. Offer to buy older goods at a discount.

Neighborhood stores: Push the local television or appliance dealer to give you a break so you can keep your service business in the community.

Source: Sharon Dunn Greene, coauthor of *The Lower East Side Shopping Guide*, Brooklyn, NY.

What Goes on Sale When

Here is a month-by-month schedule for dedicated bargain hunters.

January:
After-Christmas sales.
Appliances.
Baby carriages.
Books.
Carpets and rugs.
China and glassware.
Christmas cards.
Costume jewelry.
Furniture.
Furs.
Lingerie.

Men's overcoats.
Pocketbooks.
Preinventory sales.
Shoes.
Toys.
White goods (sheets, towels, etc.).
  February:
Air conditioners.
Art supplies.
Bedding.
Cars (used).
Curtains.
Furniture.
Glassware and china.
Housewares.
Lamps.
Men's apparel.
Radios, TV sets, and stereos.
Silverware.
Sportswear and equipment.
Storm windows.
Toys.
  March:
Boys' and girls' shoes.
Garden supplies.
Housewares.
Ice skates.
Infants' clothing.
Laundry equipment.
Luggage.
Ski equipment.
  April:
Fabrics.
Hosiery.
Lingerie.
Painting supplies.
Women's shoes.
  May:
Handbags.
Housecoats.
Household linens.
Jewelry.
Luggage.
Mother's Day specials.
Outdoor furniture.
Rugs.
Shoes.
Sportswear.
Tires and auto accessories.
TV sets.

  June:
Bedding.
Boys' clothing.
Fabrics.
Father's Day specials.
Floor coverings.
Lingerie, sleepwear, and hosiery.
Men's clothing.
Women's shoes.
  July:
Air conditioners and other appliances.
Bathing suits.
Children's clothes.
Electronic equipment.
Fuel.
Furniture.
Handbags.
Lingerie and sleepwear.
Luggage.
Men's shirts.
Men's shoes.
Rugs.
Sportswear.
Summer clothes.
Summer sports equipment.
  August:
Back-to-school specials.
Bathing suits.
Carpeting.
Cosmetics.
Curtains and drapes.
Electric fans and air conditioners.
Furniture.
Furs.
Men's coats.
Silver.
Tires.
White goods.
Women's coats.
  September:
Bicycles.
Cars (outgoing models).
China and glassware.
Fabrics.
Fall fashions.
Garden equipment.
Hardware.
Lamps.
Paints.

October:
Cars (outgoing models).
China and glassware.
Fall/winter clothing.
Fishing equipment.
Furniture.
Lingerie and hosiery.
Major appliances.
School supplies.
Silver.
Storewide clearances.
Women's coats.
November:
Blankets and quilts.
Boys' suits and coats.
Cars (used).
Lingerie.
Major appliances.
Men's suits and coats.
Shoes.
White goods.
Winter clothing.
December:
Blankets and quilts.
Cards, gifts, toys (after Christmas).
Cars (used).
Children's clothes.
Christmas promotions.
Coats and hats.
Men's furnishings.
Resort and cruise wear.
Shoes.

Get Out Your Scissors

When is the best time to hunt for coupons in newspapers, magazines, store circulars, etc.? Coupon clipping is most profitable in June and October. Next best: May, September, and November. Poorest months: July and December. (But even then, you can still save.)

Source: *The Frugal Shopper* by Marion Joyce, published by Perigee Books.

How To Buy a Car Without Getting Taken For a Ride

Just Any Dealership Won't Do

There's more to buying a car than price. Where you buy it counts, too. Take the time to evaluate different dealerships. Go to a few and walk around. When a salesperson comes up to you—and one will—say, "I'm just looking around. I'll come to you when I'm ready." Don't let any of them intimidate you.

Walk through the service area and sit down. Stay for about a half hour. Observe:

Is it orderly and run efficiently?

Is the manager there and working?

Are the customers treated with respect?

Proceed into the service lot and look at the license plate frames. In a good dealership, you'll see frames from competing dealerships, too.

Don't choose a dealership that's out of the way. The salespeople know that they have just one chance to make a sale, and they lean hard on you. Also avoid multifranchise dealerships. Too many people run different parts of the operation, causing confusion in service.

Choose your salespeople—don't let them choose you. Speak with several. Ask:

• How long have you been at this dealership? (The longer, the better.)

• Where else have you worked? For how long?

• May I get the name and number of a recent customer? (Follow up with a phone call.)

If there's a lot of turnover, leave—the dealership is unstable. Trap: Looking for a salesperson who's a member of your ethnic group because you think you'll get special treatment. You won't, and you'll be letting your guard down.

Knowledge Is Power

Educate yourself. Get as much information as possible about a car before you sit down with the salesperson. Collect brochures (dealers don't usually keep them on display, because they want you to approach the salespeople) and read consumer magazines that rate autos.

Don't let salespeople woo you into trusting them with their "impressive" knowledge of a car. That's how they try to establish authority and take control of the sale.

Know the competition, too. If you say that you're considering a competing brand, the salesperson will knock it and be very convincing if you're uninformed.

Know What You Want

If you're not firm about what you want, you could easily end up with what the salesperson wants to sell you—the most expensive model, with the most extravagant options, at the highest price.

Once you show serious intentions of buying, the salesperson will offer you a test drive, during which he will talk glowingly about the car to get you to take mental ownership of it. He is seducing you. Resist.

Trap: Negotiating to buy when you're tired of shopping. Salespeople are attracted to this kind of customer like bees to honey. They know that if they promise you what you've been looking for—whether they have it or not—you'll probably buy on the spot. Buy only in an energetic mood.

Few salespeople ask idle questions. Seemingly irrelevant questions are actually attempts to find out about your lifestyle, income, driving habits, etc. Avoid answering these questions.

Unscrupulous Tricks

Options are where dealers make their money. Common tactic: The dealer says, "Sorry, but all the cars arrive with power windows. If you don't want them, I'll have to make a special order. It could take several months." Result: You end up paying for an option that you don't want. But if you stand firm, he'll work something out—he wants the sale.

Another trick: Cars for the lot are ordered without carpeting, and customers are told that carpeting is extra, when it's really standard. Read the dealer's brochure carefully. It lists every standard option and every extra.

Also make sure every option has the car's name on it: That means the dealership is responsible for it if it breaks. For example, Honda uses Alpine brand radios, but Honda's name is on the faceplate—which means Honda is responsible.

To get the best price, get a range of prices from several dealerships, and write them down. When you're at the first one, don't let the salesperson know it. When he asks what other dealers have quoted, say, "Why don't you give me your best deal and we'll take it from there."

Read the sticker carefully. D.A.P. stands for Dealer Added Profit. Locator Cost means the dealer located the car. Procurement Cost means the dealer procured the car. All these charges are negotiable.

Take particular note of a common price-padding tactic: A prep fee of $100 or more (whatever the dealership thinks it can get away with). The cost of preparing your car for delivery is already included in the manufacturer's sticker price.

Salespeople's trick: Constantly consulting with the manager and pretending that they're really on your side. They aren't—they work on commission.

Don't shop for price by phone because salespeople will quote anything just to get you into the dealership. Shop for financing in advance so you'll know a good deal when you hear one. Don't believe salespeople who claim that they can get you good insurance rates—they can't.

Trap: Accepting a trade-in price for your old car that you know is too high. The dealership will make up the difference on the price of the new car or on the options.

Being "Turned Over"

Don't let yourself get "turned over." If a salesperson feels that he's not in control of the sale, he'll say that he's going on coffee break and will "turn you over" to another salesperson. In a high-pressure operation, this could happen three or four times, until they wear you down. How to resist: Go out for a walk, have a cup of coffee at a nearby diner, say that you need to think about it. Get away from the salespeople so you can think clearly.

Now You Own It

When the deed is done, inspect your new car thoroughly before you leave the dealership. Make sure everything is working correctly.

Final dirty trick: The car was dented in transport, so the dealer parks it close to a wall to hide the damage—which greets you when you arrive home.

Source: Two veteran car salesmen who asked to remain anonymous.

Determining the Dealer's Cost

To determine dealer cost and bargain for a fair price on a new car, subtract markup from the base sticker price (before options are added on), then subtract markup on the options. A rough guide to figure the markup on base sticker prices follows.

Small cars: 8%—Sprint; 9%—Colt, Omni; 10%—Escort, Nova, Spectrum.

Sporty cars: 10%—Mustang, Escort EXP; 11%—Camaro, Merkur XR4Ti; 16%—Corvette.

Compact cars: 8%—Skyhawk, Cavalier; 10%—AMC Eagle, Tempo; 11%—Aries, Grand Am.

Intermediates: 11%—Le Baron GTS, Lancer; 13%—Le Baron, Caravelle; 14%—Century, Regal, Cutless Supreme, Toronado, Riviera, Celebrity, Monte Carlo, Grand Prix, Le Baron Coupe, Taurus, Cougar, Thunderbird; 15%—Eldorado, Seville.

Large cars: 14%—Electra, 98 Regency, Le Sabre, Caprice, LTD Crown Victoria, Grand Marquis; 15%—Lincoln Town Car.

Vans: 11%—Astro, Caravan, Voyager, Aerostar.

Markups on options vary. In general, figure 15% of the total options package on the sticker. For the Lincoln Town car, Eldorado, and Seville, figure 16%; for the Corvette and the AMC Eagle, figure 17%.

After subtracting the markups to determine dealer cost, add $175 for dealer overhead. Add on freight charges (itemized on the sticker) and also $100 profit for the dealer (he'll still get an additional 2% rebate from the manufacturer). The final figure is what you should pay for the car you want. Shop around until you find a dealer who will sell it for that price (give or take $100). Don't be pressured into buying a loaded car.

Win Bigger and Cut Your Losses

There are two kinds of odds you've got to beat to have a successful day at the casinos. Numerical odds for each game are set by the casinos, and you have little chance of controlling them. All you can do is play the games and bet the combinations that offer the best odds.

Behavioral odds, however, are what really give the casinos the winning edge over most players. Few casino visitors are practiced or skilled enough to make the best bets every time. The casinos count on most players making the dumb mistakes over and over again. When the house holds, say, a 2% edge in a particular game, that's the numerical edge and tells only part of the story. The behavioral edge is much, much greater.

Players can turn the behavioral edge to their favor. Professional gamblers know how, and so do casino insiders.

Biggest edge: All casinos aren't alike in the odds they offer, and there can even be important differences among neighboring tables in the same house. Nevada casinos vary widely from one another—more than do houses in Atlantic City.

Example: In Vegas, craps tables might list the odds on a "2 or 12" roll as 30 to 1—on a $1 bet, the croupier will return to you $31. Or the odds might be listed as 30 for 1—a winning bet of $1 returns only $30. The odds are clearly marked on the table, but the casinos count on you to not read the fine print so they can earn what amounts to a free dollar on the 30 for 1 odds.

Las Vegas

In Vegas, the best deals are usually found in the smaller casinos in the Fremont Street-downtown area, away from the fabled Strip. Big caution: The more out-of-the-way casino, the greater your chances of being cheated by crooked dealers. Be especially wary of blackjack games, because in Nevada all cards are dealt by hand.

In Vegas craps, steer clear of the "Big 6" and "Big 8" sucker bets. The odds might look attractive, but an identical wager of place bets on the 6 or 8 gives a higher payoff. Better: Look for craps tables that offer triple odds bets after the come-out roll. This shaves the casino edge to well under 1%.

On the Vegas Strip, the best place to play blackjack allows you to double down on a 9, as well as on 10 and 11. All Strip casinos stymie card counters, however, by dealing players' cards face down. The less you can see, the less you can count.

Downtown Vegas rules are less strict than those on the strip. Some houses allow for six-card Charlies, where player wins by taking six cards totaling 21 or less. If you can count cards: Look for a two-deck game with player cards dealt face up. The rules in any given casino can–and do–change frequently. You're allowed to ask about the details before you sit down.

Blackjack variation to avoid: "Double exposure," in which player and dealer cards are dealt face up. Trade-off: House wins all ties, instead of having to push the bet to the next hand. Overall, the odds are worse than in conventional blackjack.

Another Nevada variation is minibaccarat, played at conventional blackjack tables. It attracts many players because of the low $2 minimum bet. Drawback: Some casinos take out a minimum 25¢ commission on bets on the banker. On a $2 wager, that amounts to a 12.5% built-in loss, as compared to the traditional house edge of 5%. If you like the game, look for a Vegas casino that plays it with four, rather than eight, decks. The fewer the decks,

the better the odds when betting the player position.

In Nevada poker games, you're playing against the house. Problem: High-stakes poker attracts pros, hustlers, and cheats. Safest: Stick to $5-limit games.

Playing slots: Vegas rules are most chaotic for slot machines. In Atlantic City, all machines must return at least 83% of the amount wagered, and a few return even more than 83%. But in Nevada, one machine might pay back 99% while the one right next to it pays back only 60%. The bettor's problem is that it's impossible to identify the hot machines. Their placement is the casino's most private and closely guarded secret.

Atlantic City

Among Atlantic City's casinos, the variations are narrower than in Vegas, but they can still be worked for or against you.

Look for a single-zero roulette game instead of one that uses a wheel with two zeros. Since the house always wins when the roulette ball lands on 0 or 00, a single-zero game halves the house edge.

In blackjack or baccarat, seek games with the lowest minimum bets.

If you are a slot player, stick to the so-called "progressive" slot machines, because the jackpots can build indefinitely. The best casino for slots in Atlantic City offers both liberal payoffs and coupons to exchange for prizes or hotel discounts.

Source: Lee Pantano, a professional gambler, teacher, and consultant.

Enjoy a Day at The Races Without Going Broke

The aim of a day at the track should be to enjoy every race while controlling your losses. Fifty dollars lost out of a hundred dollars played could be considered a highly satisfactory day.

• When betting, begin with the choices of

the handicappers. Handicapping—the prediction of likely winners—is done by a track official who assigns odds to the horses in the morning races. Handicapping is also done by bettors in the course of the day (which causes the odds to change). One-third of the favorites chosen by handicappers win their races.

• Decide on the amount of money you are willing to lose. Set aside one-fifth of it for entertainment betting. The rest should be spent on serious betting. For about $20 you can bet on every race plus the daily double.

• Avoid the temptation to increase bets when losing in order to catch up. Also avoid the trap of betting more when winning to try to make a killing.

• To control spending, bet just 20% of your remaining capital each time you bet, whether your capital goes up or down.

• For fun betting, choose horses by name, jockey, appearance, or any means you wish. You may get lucky and win one out of 10 bets this way.

• For serious betting, pick the appropriate races to bet on. Always eliminate maiden races (the horse's first year of racing), two-year-old races, and races where it's indicated that the horses chosen won no race but their maiden race.

• To pick the two or three likeliest winners in the race, check handicappers' choices in local newspapers, racing forms, and tip sheets sold at the track. Look especially for handicappers who predict in great detail how the race will be run, and those who tell you the front runners and the come-from-behind horse as well as the outcome.

• Late scratches (the elimination of contenders) can very much change the projected script of a race. If one of the two predicted front-runners is scratched, the remaining front-runner's chance is increased.

• Rain. In the racing charts, "mudders" (horses that have a history of doing well in the rain) are indicated with an asterisk. As the track is progressively softened by rain, the chances of mudders improve. The horse in the most adverse position on a rain-sodden track is a speed horse—a front-runner in the post position.

• Shifts in odds. Lengthening (higher) odds on a horse increase your chance of a good return. Observe the physical condition of your horse during the viewing ritual, when the horses are paraded at the rear of the track before each race.

You can place several types of bets:

• To win: Pays only if the horse comes in first.

• To place: Pays if the horse comes in first or second.

• To show: Pays if the horse comes in first, second, or third. A combination of bets, such as a win and place, or a win and a show, increases your chances of a payoff. But the return will be smaller.

Source: Peter Shaw, cultural critic, historian, college professor, and occasional bettor.

Picking Harness Winners

Harness racing is far easier to handicap than thoroughbred ("flat") racing: The bettor has fewer variables to take into consideration.

Harness races are almost always at a mile and on the dirt. The fields are more manageable, with rarely more than nine entries. And, since the horses carry no weight on their backs, there are no weight differences to compensate for. (Thanks to the laws of physics, the sulky pulled by the horse actually adds momentum, rather than drag.)

Standardbred harness horses are calmer, tougher, and more dependable than thoroughbreds. The favorites win more often than thoroughbred favorites—about 36% of the time. Still, most bettors are chronic losers, in part because they ignore the most important betting factors.

Post Position
Most decisive of all is post position, especially on short half-mile or five-eighths-mile tracks. The nearer the rail, the less distance the horse must travel, both at the start and around a turn. The horse in the number one post (at the far inside) has a tremendous advantage.

Since he's already at the rail, he doesn't need to spend energy to get there. Even if he doesn't make the lead, he will likely be close enough to make a move in the stretch.

Conversely, if a horse draws an outside post (number six or higher), the driver will either have to "park" outside other horses while contending for the lead or take back to the rear. Later on, he may be boxed in with no racing room. To mount a stretch drive, he will have to return outside, losing at least one and a half lengths around the final turn. And given the width of the other sulkies, there may be no convenient holes to burst through. All in all, it's tough to catch the leader.

Post positions are also a key to interpreting past performances. Example: In his last outing, your pick raced from the eight post and finished a distant sixth. But in the race before that, starting from the one post, he led the way and won handily. If he's returning to an inside post, you can expect the horse to improve, perhaps at good odds.

The Driver

The other underrated factor: The driver's ability. Every track has a few leading drivers; check their names in your program and remember them. Steer clear of any drivers who fail to win at least 10% of their starts. And you should never bet on a novice or provisional driver.

Positive sign: A switch from a trainer-driver to a leading full-time driver. This often means the trainer believes the horse is now at his best, ready to win.

But even the best driver can't help a slow starter from an outside post. Check each race (consult the track program) for horses with good early speed. There are no Silky Sullivans in harness racing—no champions who consistently come from last place to take the purse. You'll find that the winner is usually among the first four horses at the half-mile.

Pluses and Minuses

In weighing past performances, the horse's time in the final quarter mile is more revealing than his overall time. Most promising: A fast final quarter (under 31 seconds) following a fast first half-mile.

It's also positive if the horse:

• Won his last race (unless he won by a small margin that was less than the last time).

• Is going off at lower odds than in his last race.

• Raced steadily last time while parked (indicated by a small "o" in the program) for one or more calls. (Parked means outside one or more other horses.)

But don't bet heavily if the horse:

• Is moving up steeply in class (signified by purse money or claiming price).

• Hasn't been in a race for more than two weeks.

• Seems clearly superior in the program but is going off at odds of 5–2 or greater. (The horse's handlers don't think he can win.)

• Broke stride in his last race (check in your track program).

• Has pinned ears (ears are back flat against his head) or is nervous or sweating in prerace warmups.

Source: Don Valliere, manager of the Ontario Jockey Club's track in Fort Erie, and author of *Betting Winners: A Guide for the Harness Fan,* published by Gambling Book Club Press.

The Truth about State Lotteries

State lotteries are one of the worst bets around. They claim that about 50% of the money wagered is returned as prizes. In fact, considering the lotteries' deferred-payment schedules (a $1 million prize is awarded as $50,000 a year for 20 years), the payout actually comes to less than 25%. Comparison: In Nevada or Atlantic City, the payout in roulette is about 94%.

Source: *The Wall Street Journal.*

Contest Winners: Secrets of Success

Cash, vacations, houses, cars, electronic equipment, cameras, and much, much more are the dream prizes that keep millions of Americans doggedly filling out entry blanks for contests. More than $100 million in prize money and goods are dispensed annually through an estimated 500 promotional competitions and drawings.

Dedicated hobbyists know that there is an advantage of a planned approach to overcome the heavy odds against each entrant. Here are some winning strategies:

• Use your talents. If you can write, cook, or take photographs, put your energy into entering contests rather than sweepstakes. Contests take skill, so fewer people are likely to compete—improving your chances. Photography contests have the fewest average entries.

• Follow the rules precisely. If the instructions say to print your name, don't write it in longhand. If a three-inch by five-inch piece of paper is called for, measure your entry exactly. The slightest variation can disqualify you.

• Enter often. Always be on the lookout for new sweepstakes and contests to enter. Sources: Magazines, newspapers, radio, television, store shelves and bulletin boards, product packaging.

• Make multiple entries. The more entries you send in, the more you tip the odds in your favor.

• For large sweepstakes, spread out your entries over the length of the contest—one a week for five weeks, for example. When the volume of entries is big enough, they will be delivered to the judges in a number of different sacks. The theory is that judges will pick from each sack, and your chances go up if you have an entry in each of several different mailbags.

• Keep informed. Join a local contest club or subscribe to a contest newsletter. Either source will help you to learn contest traps, problems, and solutions. They'll alert you, too, to new competitions.

• Be selective. You must pay taxes on items that you win, so be sure the prizes are appropriate for you. If you don't live near the water, winning an expensive boat could be a headache. (Some contests offer cash equivalents, but not all do.)

• If you do win, check with your CPA or tax lawyer immediately. You must report the fair market value of items that you win, whether you keep them, sell them, or give them away. This can be tricky. Also, if you win, you can deduct the expenses of postage, stationery, etc., that you have used to enter this and other sweepstakes and contests in the same year. These costs are not deductible if you don't win.

• Most contests and sweepstakes ask you to enclose some proof of purchase or a plain piece of paper with a product name or number written on it. Many people assume that a real proof of purchase will improve their chances of winning. Fact: In a survey, more than half the winners or major prizes reported that they had not bought the sponsor's product.

Source: Roger Tyndall, coeditor with his wife, Carolyn, of the country's largest-circulation newsletter, *Contest Newsletter*, Fern Beach, FL.

2 TAX TACTICS, STRATEGIES, & OPPORTUNITIES

Ten Big Loopholes

Tax reform took dead aim at tax shelters and eliminated many deductions and tax-planning strategies that Congress perceived as abusive. But tax planning wasn't killed by tax reform, nor was the business of finding loopholes. The best loopholes to date:

Dramatically lower individual tax rates. This is the biggest new loophole of all—the best news for taxpayers in many, many years. Sharply lower rates will eliminate the need for tax shelters. Taxpayers will feel less pressure to stretch for dubious deductions.

Income-shifting loophole. Tax reform preserves a window of opportunity to shift income to young children so it will be taxed at a lower rate. The first $500 of annual investment income of a child under age 14 is completely tax-free. The next $500 is taxed at the child's low rate. A child's investment income above $1,000 is taxed at the parent's top rate. Strategy: Put enough assets in your children's names to give each child at least $1,000 of investment income a year.

S corporation loophole. Virtually every newly formed, closely held company should be set up as an S corporation. An S corporation avoids the double tax that regular corporations pay: The income of an S corporation is taxed only when it is passed through to the shareholders on their personal tax returns. Now that the top individual tax rates are lower than the top corporate tax rates, S corporations make even more sense. Loophole: When an S corporation liquidates its assets, only one tax has to be paid on gain from the sale.

Capital losses loophole. All capital losses are fully deductible. As under the old law, however, only $3,000 of ordinary income (e.g., salary) can be offset by capital losses in any one year. Also, as before, unused losses can be carried over into future years. Old law: Only 50% of net long-term capital losses were deductible. So it took $6,000 of long-term losses to offset the limit of $3,000 of ordinary income.

Taking money out of the company. When the top individual tax rate was 50%, it was prohibitive to take money out of a closely held company in the form of dividends. But this prohibition disappears as the top tax rate falls. Owners of closely held corporations with

27

accumulated retained earnings that are not needed in the corporation can now pay out dividends with the income taxed at a top rate of only 28% (33% for some taxpayers). Caution: Watch out for state tax on dividends, which could boost the total tax bill.

Itemizers' loophole. If your total deductions are below the standard deduction, you must take it; you can't itemize. Strategy: Beat the limit by bunching two years' worth of deductions into one. If your deductions average $4,000 a year, arrange to pay $2,000 in one year, and $6,000 the following year. You would then get the standard deduction in year one and $6,000 of itemized deductions in year two. Deductions susceptible to bunching: Charity, medical expenses, miscellaneous business expenses, real estate taxes, state income taxes.

Alimony loophole. Under the old law, alimony payments (exceeding $10,000 a year) had to be spread out over at least six years in order to be fully deductible. Payments now only have to be made for three years. This will mean bigger tax deductions for alimony payers.

Rental property loophole. All rentals are treated as "passive" activity under the rule that makes passive losses deductible only against passive income. But there's an important exception to the rule for taxpayers whose adjusted gross income is under $100,000 and who actively participate in the management of rental property. They can deduct up to $25,000 of rental losses each year even if they have no passive income. (The deduction is phased out for taxpayers whose AGI is between $100,000 and $150,000.)

401(k) loophole. The amount you can put into a 401(k) plan has been cut from $30,000 a year to $7,000. But a $7,000 "deduction" is one of the biggest you're going to get. It's an especially important tax break for people who can't make deductible contributions to IRAs because of the restrictions. Plan to make the maximum contribution to your company's 401(k) plan this year.

Categories-of-income loophole. There are three kinds of income (and losses)—portfolio income, passive income, and active income. A situation to avoid is involvement in an S corporation that throws off taxable portfolio income and passive operating losses. This could happen, for instance, if you did not materially participate in the business. If the corporation had investment income, you would have to pay tax on it, and you would not be able to write off the corporation's operating losses unless you had passive income. Strategy: Either be active in the business or avoid having portfolio income.

Source: Edward Mendlowitz, partner, Siegel, Mendlowitz & Rich, CPAs, 310 Madison Ave., New York 10017.

Tax Breaks That Survived Reform

Many important tax breaks have not been eliminated by tax reform, and others have been changed only slightly. When overhauling your tax-planning strategies, keep these valuable breaks in mind.

Intact Breaks

• State and local income taxes and real- and personal-property taxes are still fully deductible on federal returns.

• Home mortgage interest: Fully deductible on your personal residence and one other residence to the extent that the mortgage loan does not exceed $1 million in *acquisition debt* (borrowed to purchase, build, or improve the residence) plus $100,000 in *home equity debt* (borrowed for any purpose whatsoever). However, under any circumstances, the loan can't exceed the present market value of the residence. Special break: The limitations are not applied retroactively. If you took a mortgage or refinanced your home before October 14, 1987, your interest deduction is not limited by the above. Interest on a mortgage remains deductible up to the fair market value of your home, even if you borrowed more than the dollar limits listed above.

• Second-residence interest on one other home you own, such as a vacation home, is deductible even if you don't use that home during the year. Special rules apply if you rent that home to others during the year. You must personally use the vacation home for 14 days or 10% of the number of days the home is rented, whichever is greater.

• Gain on the sale of your home remains tax-free, if you reinvest the full selling price of your old home into your new home.

• The $125,000 exclusion on the gain from the sale of a home by a taxpayer over age 55 is still in effect.

• Social Security income is treated as before. You can still receive at least half of these benefits tax-free.

• Gifts and inheritances aren't taxable income to the recipient. (The estate or donor pays the tax at rates that were not changed by tax reform.)

• Property that you inherit continues to get a big tax break. You can take the property at its value as of the date of death of the original owner. Example: You inherit your mother's diamond ring, which was originally purchased for $1,000. At the time of her death, its value has appreciated to $6,000. If you sell the ring for $8,000, you have to pay tax only on your gain of $2,000—that is, the difference between the value on the date of her death and the selling price.

Tax-Free Income That Survived

• Life insurance proceeds that you receive as a result of the death of the insured.

• Cash-value buildup of life insurance policies and most deferred annuities.

• Contributions to qualified retirement plans made by your employer, plus the earnings on those contributions.

• Employer-paid health insurance.

• Employer-provided group term life insurance policies up to $50,000.

• Interest and dividends earned by your existing Individual Retirement Accounts, Keoghs, 401(k)s, simplified employee pension plans, etc. (tax-deferred).

• Vacation home rental if your property is rented out for 14 days or fewer.

• Scholarships and fellowships if used to cover tuition and course equipment.

Deductions and Credits That Survived

• Charitable contribution deductions, if you itemize.

• Credit for child-care and dependent-care expenses.

• Moving expenses that are job-related (but you must itemize to deduct them).

• Gambling losses up to the amount of gambling winnings for the year.

• Alimony payments.

• Small-business operating expenses that result from the cost of doing business (rent, salaries, postage, taxes, etc.).

• Business gifts of up to $25 per recipient per year, if you itemize.

• Car expenses for the use of your personal car for business purposes. Take the IRS standard mileage allowance or your total actual expenses.

Source: Sidney Kess, partner and director of tax planning and policy, Peat Marwick Main & Co., 55 E. 52 St., New York 10055.

Big Hidden Benefits of Tax Reform

The Tax Reform Act of 1986 will be maligned because so many people will be paying more income tax rather than less, and because Congress clearly failed in its announced goal of simplifying our tax system. But Congress did put into the new law a number of little-publicized provisions that are favorable to taxpayers in general.

The IRS was given the authority to abate interest charges that are generated by its own errors or delays. Before this change in the law, taxpayers had to pay the interest that piled up on tax assessments even if the cause of the extra interest was that the IRS had messed up its own bookkeeping. For example, if it took the IRS a year to get around to issuing a deficiency notice, after efforts to resolve the tax dispute had been completed, the taxpayer was liable for an additional year's interest. Now, if the IRS is to blame for the delay, it can erase the extra interest charges. Important: This new IRS power to abate interest charges is retroactive to payments made after 1978. Taxpayers who paid interest because of bureaucratic error or delay should claim refunds by filing amended returns.

Sales tax remains in the tax-planning picture. The sales tax you pay when you buy investment property, such as art or jewelry, is added to the original cost of the property. This addition reduces your taxable profit when you sell the property. Be sure to keep a record of the sales tax you pay when you acquire investment property.

Penalty-free withdrawals from Individual Retirement Accounts. Although the Tax Reform Act clobbered the IRA deduction for many taxpayers, it created a penalty-free way to withdraw money from the account before you reach age 59½. Old law: You had to pay an additional 10% penalty tax on distributions from IRA accounts before age 59½. New law: You won't pay the extra 10% penalty tax if you convert the account to an annuity and receive the money in a scheduled series of substantially equal payments over your life or your life expectancy.

The tax treatment of loan origination fees, or "points," charged by banks for the use of money borrowed to buy your principal home was not altered by the Tax Reform Act. The points are fully deductible in the year you pay them. Key requirements: The points must be paid separately and not simply deducted from the loan proceeds. (The best thing is to write a check on separate funds for the points.) Also, to be deductible, the points can't be fees for specific services provided by the lender, such as mortgage preparation costs, appraisal fees, notary fees, etc.

Fewer Audits

Perhaps the biggest hidden benefit of tax reform for taxpayers will be fewer IRS audits. The Tax Reform Act of 1986 is the most comprehensive revision of the Internal Revenue Code since 1954. IRS employees must learn the new law and then learn how to enforce it. Unless Congress comes up with money for a

significant increase in staff, the training problem facing the IRS is bound to result in fewer audits.

Steps the IRS will likely take to shore up its audit power:

• Eliminate unnecessary training programs, such as management training and training in audit technique. This will mitigate the short-run problem of less available examination time. But in the long run, the IRS will pay dearly for this, in reduced effectiveness of its audit personnel.

• Reassign personnel from low-income taxpayers (many of whom will be off the tax rolls because of tax reform) to more complex returns. This would be an expensive switch in staff because of the heavy training cost involved.

• Apply more sophisticated selection techniques to examine fewer returns overall but more of those returns that are most vulnerable to audit assessments. Problem: The audit-selection criteria presently used by the IRS come from audits of returns filed under the old tax law. The Tax Reform Act has diluted the validity of the current data base. Although competent statisticians may indeed build an interim workable model for the IRS to use, without validation by testing it's just a shot in the dark.

Don't rejoice too soon. The IRS has many ways to keep taxpayers honest:

• All taxpayers continue to be vulnerable to TCMP audits (the Taxpayer Compliance Measurement Program). Returns are picked at random for these audits. And if your return is selected, you will be asked to verify every item on it.

• All information returns (Forms 1099) will be matched by IRS computers with the income figures taxpayers report on their returns.

• Certain businesses, professions, and occupations will continue to be IRS audit targets. The IRS knows from experience the types of businesses to audit for the greatest financial return.

The bottom line: While taxpayers as a whole may be confident that a smaller number of returns will be audited, individuals can't be certain that they won't be audited. So, enjoy the knowledge that there will be less likelihood of an IRS examination, but file honestly and carefully so that if you are picked in the audit lottery, you can successfully defend your return.

Source: George S. Alberts, former head of the Albany and Brooklyn IRS District Offices.

What Do You Need from A Tax Preparer?

Aside from the first requirement—honesty—what do you look for in a tax preparer and adviser? The answer depends on your needs.

The Options

For most taxpayers, the IRS itself can supply some appropriate help. Its many instructional booklets are useful, though they may take the tax collector's side in arguable matters. The booklets cover subjects from record-keeping requirements to moving expenses, deductions for bad debts to tax information for homeowners, charitable contributions to self-employment tax. The IRS will also answer tax questions over the telephone, in person, or by mail; millions make inquiry each year. There are even volunteer programs located in public libraries each tax season. The problem: You can't expect to rely on volunteer advice or even advice from the IRS. If you get into trouble, you're on your own.

A step up from free tax advice are commercial tax preparers. They will use the proper forms and fill out your return based on the information you give them. It's usually all done correctly and inexpensively, but even at best the service is not very sophisticated.

You may have heard of some independent tax practitioner who has been helpful to a colleague or business associate. That's not a bad way to find tax help, as long as you remember that ability and experience vary greatly. Find out if the recommended tax adviser is either an attorney, a certified public accountant, or an "enrolled agent." In order to become enrolled agents, qualified to practice before the IRS, tax practitioners must pass a government examination and keep up their expertise. Anyone may prepare tax returns, but enrolled agents, like lawyers and CPAs, are specialists.

CPAs can usually be relied upon when they tell you they know about taxes. Like most other professional tax preparers, they are likely to use an independent computerized service bureau for the actual preparation of returns, but CPAs will do more: They can diagnose a current tax problem and advise on its cure, and assist you with tax planning.

The most sophisticated—and expensive—tax advice usually emanates from law offices. Unless you are already a valued client, it isn't likely that your attorney will welcome a simple tax preparation job from you. Seek a tax attorney's assistance only in extreme circumstances.

The Interview

Interview any tax adviser before signing on. Of course you will want someone with a permanent address. But also ask about credentials and experience. Feel free to inquire about fees.

If a preparer asks you to sign a blank return, guarantees a refund, refuses to sign the return as preparer, or won't use his identification number, look elsewhere.

Source: Robert A. Garber, vice president of a major investment-banking house. He writes frequently on tax matters, is the author of several books, and has over 25 years' experience in trusts and estates, and as a tax attorney.

How To Pick the Shrewdest Tax Adviser

The shrewdest tax adviser (preparer, practitioner, etc.) is the one who can minimize your *overall expenditures for taxes* (your tax bill plus his bill plus any expenses connected with audits, etc.).

Finding the best tax adviser for you is a search for a marriage of true minds. The first requirement is that your tax professional offer the services you need. Then, in addition to being prompt, courteous, diligent, organized, thorough, and well versed in new developments, the best tax adviser will be inquisitive, innovative, and sensitive to your situation, temperament, and outlook.

The relationship will be personal as well as professional, so plan to devote as much time and effort as necessary. It will pay off. The most effective procedure is to first solicit recommendations and referrals from friends and business acquaintances whose business acumen you respect, and to follow up with in-depth interviews.

Here's a checklist of points to consider.

• Technical competence. Is this person able to field most of your questions with ease and confidence? If he has to grope for answers or look everything up in a book, you can conclude that knowledge is weak in areas of importance to you. If, on the other hand, you find yourself being told about new developments in tax laws in your areas of interest, consider this a strongly positive indication.

• Organization and interview depth. Does this professional provide an organized worksheet prior to the interview to help you gather your materials effectively and efficiently? Offer advice on record-keeping procedures that speeds and clarifies your work together? Go through your checkbook register, discuss your investments with you, pore through your records and receipts for overlooked deductions?

• Comprehensive analysis. In the initial interview, a top-notch tax adviser will do all of the following: Review all your financial activities for their tax impact; review your three prior years' returns looking for tax breaks you might have missed; spend time discussing ways to cut your tax bill for the coming year. The only way to save on taxes is by year-round planning. This is what you pay a tax adviser for. If your adviser isn't inclined to probe, ask questions, and offer advice, you should definitely consider a change. Filling in the forms is something you can learn to do yourself.

• Audit compatibility. A vital point. While we would all love to pay the lowest possible tax bill and never be audited, the fact is that to save tax dollars, you must take aggressive positions on your financial dealings—which makes it much more likely your returns are going to be audited. If you want to cut your audit risk, you must take a more conservative approach. You can't have it both ways. What's important is that you and your adviser agree on your audit tolerance.

• Audit representation. Will this professional represent you at an audit? Will there be an extra fee for this? Will he be able to strongly argue the positions you took on your return, especially where the tax law isn't clear?

• Support network. Is the adviser in question a member of a firm that includes resident specialist/experts, attorneys, accountants? Such support personnel provide more comprehensive service.

• Silent partner. Even the shrewdest tax adviser is only as strong as his silent partner—the client. To get the most from your tax advice, you must take an active role—the more active the better. If you are careful to bring to your adviser's attention any potential out-of-the-way deductions, present your records in an organized way, make sure records are complete at interview time, keep your expert informed about changes in essential personal and financial matters, and make your own tax education an ongoing concern, your relationship with any tax adviser you choose will be that much more fruitful.

Source: Paul N. Strassels, a tax-law specialist, Money Matters, Inc., Box 195, Burke, VA 22015.

Getting the Best from Your Tax Preparer

Familiarize yourself with the tax law. By being knowledgeable, you won't waste anyone's time or your own money. There are many tax-preparation guides on the market, and the IRS itself provides plenty of free basic filing information. At the very least, review both the tax forms and the accompanying instructions so you'll understand the basic concepts and have an idea of the information your preparer will need to know to fill out your return.

Organize your materials. Don't show up at your preparer's office with a briefcase full of tax-related paper work that you expect him to sort out. If your preparer has to muddle through the papers, it will cut into the time that should be spent figuring out the best tax strategy.

Bring the right information to the meeting. Once you've organized your records, bring the necessary information, such as:

• Past tax returns. If this is the first time you are working with this tax preparer, or if you've always prepared your own returns, it's especially important to bring old returns. It will give your new preparer valuable information about your tax history—and he can review your past three returns to see if you missed any tax breaks in those years (they can still be claimed). If you have worked with this preparer before, he should have copies of your old returns in his file.

• Tax statements. Bring your W-2 form and all 1099 forms, showing income and proceeds from security transactions.

• Expense diary. This will help your preparer determine the deductibility of your expenses. He will also be able to tell you if it meets the stringent record-keeping requirements of the IRS. If it's not in good enough shape for use on this year's return, he should be able to advise you about making it audit-proof for next year's return.

• Canceled checks. Bring all your checks, even those not written for deductible items. Helpful: Categorizing the checks (travel, etc.). Your accountant will probably find some deductions that you didn't know about. Nondeductible expenses may trigger deductions —for example, on a new car. Of course, the purchase price is nondeductible, but if you used the car for business, there may be some deductions. Had you not brought that check to the interview, the whole issue might never have come up.

• Preparer worksheets. Many firms send out detailed worksheets for you to fill out long before your actual appointment. Bring that worksheet with you, and be sure you've filled it out with scrupulous care.

Never jump to tax conclusions. Many taxpayers don't bother mentioning some financial matters to their accountant because they have already made a decision on its tax status. Yet taxpayers often reach the wrong conclusions and lose out on deductions. Tell your preparer everything, and let him make the final decision. Even if an item isn't deductible this year, you may get some good advice about how to make it deductible for next year.

Get a tax projection. Ask your preparer to look at next year's taxes while he's doing your return. You'll see early in the year where you stand, and you'll know what to expect.

Source: Edward Mendlowitz, partner, Siegel, Mendlowitz & Rich, CPAs, 310 Madison Ave., New York 10017.

The IRS's Current Hot Topics

The best way to head off unwanted problems with the IRS is to know in advance what areas on your return are likely to get the most scrutiny. Here's a list of the IRS's current hot topics and the steps that you can take to handle them and avoid a tax dispute before troubles arise.

Home refinancings. As is well known, tax reform phases out the deduction for interest on consumer loans. However, it allows a deduction for interest on a loan secured by a primary residence or second home, to the extent that the amount of the loan doesn't exceed $1 million in acquisition debt (borrowed to purchase, construct, or improve the residence) plus $100,000 in home equity debt (borrowed for any purpose whatsoever).

In addition, interest is deductible in full on mortgages obtained before October 14, 1987, even if the mortgage exceeds the dollar limits. The amount of this mortgage will be subtracted from the amount of acquisition debt still available to the taxpayer. However, it does not affect the $100,000 allowable home equity loan, which is still available, no matter how large the mortgage.

Information returns. The IRS has made a great effort to increase the number of Form 1099 information returns (received from banks, brokerage houses, insurance companies, etc.) that it's able to match against individual taxpayer returns. Today the IRS claims that it successfully matches more than 90% of the 1099s it receives, so a taxpayer shouldn't assume that if something isn't reported to the IRS, the IRS will never know of it. Of course, a tremendous amount of paper work is involved in the IRS return-matching program, and mistakes do occur. Most common:

• The wrong Social Security number on a 1099 causes somebody else's income to be matched against your return.

• Your broker reports the dividends paid to you through your dividend account. At the same time the individual companies that you've invested in report the dividends that they've paid in your name. Result: The same dividends may be double-counted.

• Because of a clerical error, a bank or broker reports tax-exempt income as taxable or attributes income to the wrong time period.

What to do: When a discrepancy is found, you'll receive a computer-generated notice of the error from the IRS service center. Make a copy of the notice and mail the copy back to the IRS service center along with your explanation of the discrepancy.

If a mistake was made in the issuance of the 1099 (by your bank, broker, etc.), include a letter from that issuer explaining the error. In most cases a straightforward explanation of an error on a 1099 will settle matters satisfactorily and quickly.

Understatement penalties. The IRS is cracking down on persons who understate the tax due on their returns: The penalty on a substantial tax understatement has doubled from 10% to 20% of the understated tax.

A substantial understatement is deemed to occur when the amount of the understatement exceeds $5,000 (generally $10,000 for corporations) or 10% of your total tax bill for the year, whichever is greater.

Strategy: The tax law contains many gray areas that are subject to uncertain interpretation by the IRS and the courts. If you claim large deductions that are grounded in one of these gray areas (and which don't involve a tax shelter), you can protect yourself from the substantial underpayment penalty by making an adequate disclosure of all the facts. File Form 8275, Disclosure Statement Under Section 6661.

You should also be able to cite a credible authority (such as a court decision, published IRS ruling, Treasury regulation, etc.) in support of your reading of the law. After making such a disclosure, you'll be safe from the 20% penalty even if the IRS and Tax Court finally rule against your position.

Retirement plan rollovers. Individual Retirement Accounts and other retirement programs are an increasingly popular investment tool for high-tax-bracket individuals. Transfers and rollovers of funds between accounts have become common as persons change investment selections.

Trap: When funds are taken out of a retirement account, the account trustee will issue a Form 1099-R reporting the withdrawal to the IRS—even if the withdrawal is part of a tax-free transfer of funds between plans. Thus, the IRS will know about the withdrawal, and if it doesn't see a transfer of funds reported properly on your return, it may assume that you kept the withdrawn money for personal use.

What to do: Include the amount shown on the 1099-R in your gross income, as reported in line 16a of your form 1040 tax return. Then, on line 16b of your 1040, report zero as the amount of the distribution that was taxable, if properly rolled over.

Simplest mistakes. The most common tax return filing errors are also the simplest: Forgetting to sign a return, making math errors, and omitting necessary IRS forms.

If you forget to sign, the IRS will notify you and send you a form to sign and send back for attachment to your return. If you make an arithmetic mistake, the IRS will correct it and notify you, even if it's in your favor. If after mailing in your return, you discover that you left out a necessary document, such as a W-2 form, you'll do best to wait until the IRS notifies you of the omission and then send in the missing form. The omitted W-2 is much more likely to get lost if the IRS receives it in a separate mailing without having asked for it. In some cases, if a return requires a correction, an amended tax return (Form 1040X) should be filed.

Source: Charles Pomo, former IRS appeals officer, now tax principal with Arthur Young & Co., 277 Park Ave., New York 10172.

How To Get More Time To File Your Return

If you need extra time to prepare your tax return, you can get it automatically: Just file Form 4868 with your local IRS Service Center by April 15. The deadline for filing your return will be pushed back four months to August 15. If you're self-employed, the extension gives you four more months in which to make contributions to a Keogh plan (if the plan was set up by December 31 of the preceding year).

Caution: A filing extension does not extend the time for paying your tax. The instructions on Form 4868 tell you how to estimate your tax; if you don't send in a check for the estimated tax due, the extension will not be valid.

Never simply file a late return without getting an extension. The penalty for filing late without an extension is 5% of the unpaid tax per month, up to a maximum penalty of 25%. There's also a minimum penalty for not getting your tax return in within 60 days of its due date—$100 or 100% of the tax due, whichever is less. You'll also be penalized for paying your taxes late, and you'll be charged interest on the late-paid tax.

Second extensions: It is possible to get a second filing extension from the IRS by filing Form 2688. But the second extension isn't automatic. You must have a valid reason for requesting it, such as a death in the family or loss of your records. A second extension, if granted, gives you an extra two months—until October 15—to file your return.

Checklist: Before Mailing Your Return

Check to make sure you've completed everything on this list. A slipup can cause delays and inconvenience. Moreover, every time you draw attention to your return, you increase the chance of audit. Checklist:

• Do your name, address, and Social Security number appear on page 1? If you used the IRS address label, be sure you have made any necessary corrections.

• Have you put your Social Security number on every page, every document, and every check to be sent to the IRS?

• Are all Form W-2s attached?

• Are all other necessary forms and schedules attached?

• Have you checked and rechecked your arithmetic?

• Is the form signed and dated? Both husband and wife must sign a joint return.

• If you owe money, is your check or money order attached to the return? Have you written your Social Security number on the check? Have you written the year and "Form 1040" on it?

• Is the return addressed to the correct IRS office?

• Have you made a copy of the return for your own records?

Source: Florence B. Donohue, a tax attorney with offices at 3846-B Bailey Ave., Bronx, NY 10463.

Big Tax Refund? You've Done Something Wrong

If you got a fat tax refund this year, don't feel too happy about it. It means you overpaid your estimated taxes or had too much withheld from your salary. In effect, you made an interest-free loan to the government, when you could have been using the money for yourself—in an interest-paying bank account.

Trap: The IRS can withhold all or part of your refund to offset a tax liability, a debt to a government agency (for instance, a student loan), or unpaid child support.

What to do: File a new Form W-4 or W-4A to reduce the amount withheld from your salary. If you pay estimated tax, reduce your quarterly payments.

Caution: Don't overdo it. You can be hit with underpayment penalties unless withholding taxes plus estimated tax payments amount to at least 90% of your total tax bill.

Tax Refunds: The Second Time Around

It's not too late to get a cash refund for past years by filing a Form 1040X with the IRS. Take the time to review old tax returns to see if you overlooked anything that may lead to getting money back.

The time limit for amending your original tax return is three years from the date you filed the original return or two years from the date you actually paid the tax, whichever is later. Early filers are treated as though they had filed on the actual due date of the return.

Caution: Filing an amended return may invite the IRS to take a second look at your original return. If there's anything on it that you think may not pass this additional IRS scrutiny, you should be wary about amending. On the other hand, if you'll get back a significantly larger refund by amending, or you know the IRS can't challenge anything on the original return, it may be worth the risk.

What You Can Amend

The most common oversights that eventually lead to an additional refund:

• Filing the wrong form. Short-form filers might well have been able to file a long form and get the benefit of a lower tax bill. But you're not stuck with your original choice. Perhaps you used the short form because you were in a last-minute rush to file the return, or you thought the long form was too difficult. If you file a long form this year but filed a short form for the past two years, check your earlier returns to see if you missed anything.

No matter what your original reason for filing the short form, it is worth taking the time now to see how much you would save by filing the long form.

• Overlooking deductions. As you fill out your return this year, perhaps you will remember deductions that you should have taken in the past. If you forgot to claim an item to which you were entitled, consider amending that year's return.

• Overlooking credits. Taxpayers often forget about or miscalculate certain tax credits. Carefully review the following on your past returns:

Excess Social Security tax paid.

Child care credit.

Earned income credit.

• Using the wrong filing status. When a married couple files separately, the overall tax bill is usually larger. If you would have saved taxes by filing jointly, you are allowed to amend your return. However, it doesn't work the other way: Once you've filed a joint return and the due date of the return has passed, you can't change the filing status to married filing separately.

• Overlooking exemptions. If you were supporting a parent who didn't live with you during the year, you may have forgotten to claim him or her as an exemption on your return.

• Neglecting to do five- or 10-year averaging on lump-sum distributions. Many taxpayers forget this special tax saver when they receive a lump sum from their retirement plan and don't expect to roll it over into another plan. If you received such a distribution, make sure you compared your tax liability with five- or 10-year averaging and without it, to see which one produced the lower tax.

• Overpaying Social Security. If you worked for more than one employer in a single year, you may have paid too much Social Security tax. The maximum you must pay changes from year to year, but you can find out the amount by looking at your old returns.

• Neglecting to check for retroactive tax changes. Sometimes the IRS, Congress, and the courts make retroactive decisions that may allow you to take a deduction for something that was disallowed in the past. Keep informed about all tax changes to see if any of them affect your past returns.

Source: John L. Withers, special consultant for IRS regulations and procedures, Touche Ross & Co., Washington Service Center, 1900 M St. NW, Washington, DC 20036.

What To Do When the IRS Places a Lien on Your Home

People who owe money to the IRS often find that a tax lien has been placed on their home. The IRS files the lien to get a preferential interest in the proceeds from the sale of the house. Catch 22: Banks usually won't lend money to homeowners while an IRS lien is outstanding. And the IRS won't release the lien until the taxes are paid.

Inside information: You can remedy this situation by taking advantage of a little-known IRS procedure. Ask for a Certificate of Discharge of Property from Federal Tax Lien. Under this procedure the IRS agrees to release the lien simultaneously with the payment of the money you owe it. The bank can then register a mortgage that takes priority over the interests of all other creditors, including the IRS. The mortgage will give you the money you need to pay the back taxes.

Free Information from the IRS

The IRS publishes a wealth of material on virtually every subject taxpayers have to grapple with. The publications are all free for the asking.

The IRS updates its general tax guides every year. They are indispensable.

Most Helpful
• Publication 17, Your Federal Income Tax (approximately 200 pages).
• Publication 334, Tax Guide for Small Businesses.
• Publication 910, Guide to Free Tax Services.
• Publication 920, Explanation of the Tax Reform Act of 1986 for Individuals.
• Publication 921, Explanation of the Tax Reform Act of 1986 for Small Businesses.

Specialized Publications
These publications contain in-depth explanations of a wide variety of tax-related subjects. Among the publications are:
• Publication 523, Selling Your Home.
• Publication 915, Social Security Benefits.
• Publication 575, Pension and Annuity Income.
• Publication 587, Business Use of Your Home.
• Publication 526, Charitable Contributions.
• Publication 590, Individual Retirement Arrangements (IRAs).
• Publication 917, Business Use of a Car.
• Publication 907, Tax Information for Handicapped and Disabled Individuals.

• Publication 530, Tax Information for Owners of Homes, Condominiums, and Cooperative Apartments.

• Publication 548, Deduction for Bad Debts.

• Publication 552, Recordkeeping for Individuals and a List of Tax Publications.

• Publication 554, Tax Information for Older Americans.

• Publication 521, Moving Expenses.

• Publication 547, Nonbusiness Disasters, Casualties, and Thefts.

To get these publications: Call the IRS toll-free number, 1-800-424-FORM.

More Facts on Amended Returns

You can file an amended return or claim a refund on Form 1040X within three years after the original return was due or two years after you actually paid the tax, whichever is later.

The time limits are absolute. If you're even one day late, your claim must be disallowed. Use Form 1040X if you file early and discover an error before April 15. You'll get faster handling.

You can use Form 1045 for claims based on carrybacks (net operating losses, certain credits). This will get you a fast refund, as the IRS must act within 90 days. But the action isn't final. The claim can be disallowed later. Time limits on these claims are figured from the year the carryback arose.

Form 1040X has space to write your income, deductions, and credits as you reported them on your original return and the changes you want to make for those amounts. Important: Include explanations for the changes you are making and the year you are amending on page 2. You must calculate the new tax on the corrected amount, just as you would on your regular return.

State all possible grounds. If the matter ever reaches court, you may be limited to the exact claim stated on the form. If, for example, you're not sure whether an item should be

claimed as a business loss, a casualty loss, or a bad debt, state all three grounds in the alternative. You can even assert inconsistent grounds.

Where to send it: Mail the amended return to the IRS Service Center where you now live. If you moved during the year, mail it to the Service Center at your new address. Be sure to complete the information on the front of the 1040X about where your original return was processed in order to expedite your return.

Caution: When you amend your federal tax return, your state tax liability from that year may be affected, too.

It's important to assess your audit risk before you amend your return. It depends on how much you'll get back by amending, why you're amending, and the safety of your original return.

Question: Is the amount that you are getting back worth the risk for what you might possibly lose?

Safer amendments:

• Changes of very small dollar amounts, especially where the amount on the original return is very small, too.

• Mathematical changes.

Not-so-safe amendments:

• Any change that has huge tax consequences on your return.

• Tax-shelter losses.

• Losses from business activity.

• Reclassifying ordinary income to capital gain.

How Long Should Tax File Documents Be Kept?

• Normally, tax returns and supporting documents should be kept for three years from date of filing.

• If income previously has been underreported by 25% or more: Six years.

• In cases of previous failure to file or serious suspicion of criminal fraud: Indefinitely.

Suggestion: Put canceled checks and supporting documents into a manila envelope, mark with the tax year and the discard date, and put it on the top shelf of your highest closet. You'll only need this material if you're audited. Returns should be kept in an accessible file drawer.

Source: Stephanie Winston, president of The Organizing Principle, 461 Park Ave. South, New York 10016, and the author of *The Organized Executive,* Warner Books.

Don't Pay More Than the Law Demands

Thirty years ago Judge Learned Hand of the US Court of Appeals said: "There is nothing sinister in so arranging one's affairs as to keep taxes as low as possible. Everybody does so, rich or poor; and all do right, for nobody owes any public duty to pay more than the law demands."*

Here are the best ways I know of to keep your taxes as low as possible under the tax law we have today.

Be aggressive both in setting strategies that save taxes and in preparing your return. Too many people deny themselves the full tax breaks they're entitled to because they're afraid they'll be audited. They take overly conservative positions on their returns and scale back unusually large deductions that they think the IRS will disallow. In effect, these people are auditing themselves. The IRS never gets a chance to review the item. Better way: Take the full deduction no matter how high it is in relation to your income. Write "See substantiation attached" beside the item and attach photocopies of the bills, receipts, canceled checks, etc., that prove you paid the amount you're deducting. Don't audit yourself; let the IRS do it.

Buy a vacation home. The problem with renting a vacation home is that you get no tax break from it. But when you buy one, the carrying charges—mortgage interest and property taxes—are deductible. (Mortgage interest on one second home is fully deductible, as long as the loan doesn't exceed the cost of the home plus improvements.) Also, the appreciation in the property's value goes untaxed until you sell it, and you can earn tax-free income by renting out the place each year for two weeks or less. The rent is not taxable.

Hire the best tax preparer and planner you can find. Don't let the fee stop you from getting sound professional advice. To really save taxes, you need a specialist who can guide you through financial transactions. Most tax professionals will save you far more money than they will charge.

Buy single premium deferred annuities (SPDAs) or universal life insurance. Interest earnings on your investment in these insurance company products accumulate tax-deferred until you cash them in. And these investments pay relatively high interest—more than 10% in some cases. With an SPDA, you have a choice of taking out the money you've invested (plus earnings) in a lump sum or in a series of payments over a number of years. Caution: Most companies charge penalties for early withdrawal of SPDAs and universal life. Interest rates, fees, and penalty structures vary widely, so it's important to shop around for the best deal.

Make the maximum contribution to your company's 401(k) plan. Earnings on your investment are tax-deferred—and you get the equivalent of a deduction for the contribution, since you don't pay tax on the salary that goes into the plan. That's one of the biggest deductions you're going to get.

Keep a diary of all tax-deductible expenses. Record the details of travel and entertainment expenses at or near the time you incurred them. Keep track of business expenses that your company doesn't reimburse you for. Keep a list of gifts you make to charity, especially the unusual ones that you might not remember when it comes time to do your return, such as donations of old clothes and expenses of volunteer work. Also keep a list of unreimbursed medical expenses, including out-of-pocket transportation costs.

Create your own venture partnership. Form

a limited partnership to finance a new business that needs money up front for deductible expenses. The partnership can be structured so that income and losses are allocated differently than the individual investor's actual capital contributions. A higher share of the losses can go to the person investing the money. If the person who has the losses also has income from other types of passive investments, the partnership losses will shelter that income.

Invest in rental real estate, a house or small apartment building that you actively manage. If your write-offs for depreciation, taxes, etc., exceed the rent, and your adjusted gross income is under $100,000, you can deduct up to $25,000 of losses against your salary and other taxable income. If your AGI is between $100,000 and $150,000, you can deduct some of your losses against taxable income. (If your AGI is above $150,000, the deduction is lost.)

Let family members inherit assets that have appreciated in value. If you sell the assets before you die, the full increase in value will be taxed. But if you let your beneficiaries inherit the property, they receive it at its stepped-up, date-of-death value, and income tax is forgiven on the appreciation. If you need cash before your death, borrow against the assets, rather than selling them.

Find out now whether you're going to be subject to the alternative minimum tax this year. If you are, plan to take advantage of the AMT. Instead of deferring income and accelerating deductions, do the exact opposite: Accelerate income and defer deductions. Income brought into an AMT year is taxed at only 21% (the AMT tax rate). This is considerably lower than the top regular tax rate. Deductions should be shifted into next year, where, assuming it's a non-AMT year, they will give you greater tax benefits. But don't go overboard. Accelerate only enough income so that you're at your "AMT break-even point"— just short of the level at which you must pay regular tax.

Commissioner v. Newman, 159 F2d 848.

Source: Edward Mendlowitz, partner, Siegel, Mendlowitz & Rich, CPAs, 310 Madison Ave., New York 10017.

Tax-Free Income Checklist

The IRS isn't allowed to put the bite on every dollar that finds its way into a taxpayer's pocket. The following is a list of what's exempt from taxation.

• Gain on the sale of your home. If you buy a new home within two years before or after you sell the old one, no tax is generally owed on the gain if the new home costs at least as much as the amount you got for the old one. If you (or your spouse) are at least 55 years old, any gain up to $125,000 is tax-free. (You must have owned and lived in the home for at least three years out of the last five.)

• Gifts you receive. Any gift tax is payable by the person who makes the gift. The recipient gets the gift free and clear of tax.

• Money you borrow. Normally, borrowing is not a taxable transaction. But you'll be taxed if you borrow from your IRA, if you borrow more than $50,000 (or half your account) from your company pension fund, or, in some cases, if you get an interest-free loan from your company or a family member.

• IRA rollovers. No tax is payable on a lump-sum distribution that is received from a company pension plan if you put it into an IRA within 60 days. You can also take money tax-free from your IRA if you roll it over within 60 days into another IRA.

• Inheritances. Beneficiaries don't pay federal income tax on anything they inherit. Moreover, if you inherit property that has increased in value, you receive it at its "stepped-up" estate value. You would then use this value, rather than the original cost, to calculate your taxable gain if you sold the property.

• Life insurance proceeds. The beneficiary gets the full amount income-tax-free. But the estate may be liable for estate tax on the proceeds.

• Property settlements between spouses in divorce or separation proceedings. The recipient owes no tax at the time property is transferred. (There may be a tax later if property is sold at a gain.)

• Child-support payments. They are tax-free to the recipient. Alimony payments to a spouse or ex-spouse, however, are taxable to the recipient.

• Money recovered in lawsuits for personal injuries or defamation of character. But money recovered to compensate you for lost wages or other income is taxable.

• Workers Compensation payments.

• Disability payments from accident and health insurance plans. The payments are tax-free if you paid for the insurance, but taxable if your employer paid the premiums.

• Federal income tax refunds. (But any interest the IRS pays you on a late refund is taxable.)

• State income tax refunds, provided you didn't itemize deductions on your federal return for that year.

• Municipal bond interest. Generally, it's exempt from federal income tax and sometimes from state and local tax as well. However, interest from some "private purpose" municipal bonds is subject to the alternative minimum tax. And, municipal bond interest is taken into account in figuring your income level to determine whether any of your Social Security benefits are taxable.

• "Like-kind" property exchanges—swaps of tangible property or real estate are tax-free if the properties are of similar nature.

• Vacation home rental. If you rent your vacation place out for 14 days or less, the income is not taxed.

• Kids' wages. Dependent children can earn up to $3,000 tax-free.

• Kids' investment income. Dependent children can receive up to $500 of unearned income tax-free (dividends, interest, etc.).

• Scholarships and fellowships granted on or before August 16, 1986, to candidates for degrees, are tax-free. But if granted after that date they are tax-free only to the extent they are used to cover tuition, fees, books, and course equipment. Grants for room and board, etc., are taxable.

• Fringe benefits from your employer. Examples: Health insurance, pension contributions, up to $50,000 of life insurance coverage, up to $5,000 of death benefits, certain child and dependent care, legal services under group plans, and supper money.

• Meals and lodging, if furnished by your employer for the employer's convenience—for example, to enable the employee to remain at the workplace.

• Private annuities. The payments are partially excludable from tax based on an interest-rate factor, the asset exchanged, and the life expectancy of the person receiving the asset. How they work: They are usually arranged by individuals who are not in the business of issuing annuities. One person makes periodic annuity payments in exchange for the other person's assets. Example: A father owns a business worth $2 million. He wants to transfer the business to his daughter. So, he sells the business to his daughter and the daughter promises to pay a certain amount (based on IRS tables) to her father for the rest of his life, no matter how long he lives. Loophole: On the father's death, the unpaid portion of the purchase price is not taxed.

Source: Edward Mendlowitz, partner, Siegel, Mendlowitz & Rich, CPAs, 310 Madison Ave., New York 10017.

Frequently Overlooked Deductions

"Points" paid for mortgage on purchase or improvement of principal residence.

State unemployment and disability taxes withheld.

Expenses related to seminars attended for business purposes. Deductible items include registration fees, travel, lodging, and 80% of the cost of meals.

Investment-related expenses:

• Travel expenses to check on income-producing property.

• Cost of telephone, postage, office supplies, and automobile operation (trips to and from broker).

• Books, magazines, and newsletters on investment, financial, or tax matters, including appropriate daily papers (e.g., *Wall Street Journal, New York Times*).

• Insurance and storage charges for merchandise held as a speculative investment.

Spouse's expenses on business travel—if spouse's presence has a bona fide business purpose.

Out-of-pocket expenses incurred in providing charitable services. May deduct actual cost of auto usage, tolls, and parking.

Out-of-pocket expenses incurred in changing jobs. Include the cost of printing resumes or traveling to an interview.

A portion of health insurance for the self-employed.

Charitable contributions made through payroll withholdings (e.g., United Way).

Deductible items on December credit card statement, even if paid in the following year, including:
  • Medical expenses.
  • Charitable contributions.
  • Miscellaneous business expenses.

Tax reform note: Employee business expenses and miscellaneous deductions are allowed only to the extent they exceed 2% of adjusted gross income.

Source: Barry Salzberg, CPA, partner in charge of Executive Financing Counseling services with the firm of Deloitte Haskins & Sells, 1 World Trade Center, New York 10048.

Tax Credit Checklist

The following is a checklist of tax credits available under current tax laws. Unlike deductions, which merely reduce your taxable income, credits reduce your tax liability, dollar for dollar.

• Targeted jobs credit. Available for taxpayers who employ individuals from certain designated groups. In addition, there is a youth summer jobs credit.

• Foreign tax credit. An individual or corporation may deduct foreign income taxes paid or accrued, or may take such taxes as a credit against US income taxes paid.

• Credit for increased research expenditures. A credit is available against tax paid for research expenditures incurred after June 30, 1981, and before 1989. The credit is equal to 20% of the excess of qualified research expenses for the current year over the average base period expenses for the three immediately preceding years.

• Regulated investment company credit. The taxpayer receives as a credit the tax a regulated investment company pays on retained long-term capital gains.

• Investment credit for business energy property. The business energy investment credit is equal to various percentages between 10% and 15% of the taxpayer's qualified properties which include alternative energy property: Solar, geothermal, ocean thermal, or biomass energy property.

• Child- and dependent-care credit. Permitted for a portion of qualifying expenditures incurred for the purpose of allowing the payor to be gainfully employed. The amount of credit depends on the taxpayer's adjusted gross income.

• Earned income credit. Generally, available to low-income workers maintaining a household that is the principal place of abode of a child.

• Alternative fuels credit. A nonrefundable credit allowed for domestic production of oil, gas, and synthetic fuels derived from nonconventional sources, such as shale.

• Credit for federal tax on gasoline and special fuels. Credit available where fuel is used for farming, nonhighway purposes, buses.

• Credit for diesel-fueled vehicles. Credit available for a 1979 or newer diesel-powered auto, van, or light truck.

• Windfall profit tax credit. Credit can be taken by taxpayers who overpay such tax from domestically produced crude oil.

• Credit for testing certain drugs (orphan drugs credit). A tax credit is available for 50% of the qualified testing expenditures for drugs created for rare diseases.

• Alcohol fuel credit. Per gallon credit for certain alcohols, produced or used in a trade or business.

• Credits for the elderly and the permanently and totally disabled. A 15% credit based on age and adjusted gross income and type of income.

• Credit for interest on certain home mortgages. For low-income homeowners who obtain qualified mortgage credit certificates from state or local governments.

• Credits for taxes withheld. For example, from salaries and wages.

• Credit for excess Social Security tax withheld. Usually arising when an employee works for more than one employer and has total Social Security taxes withheld in excess of the maximum FICA limit.

• Rehabilitation credit. Credit allowed for expenses related to the rehabilitation of certain buildings. The credit is 10% for qualified buildings placed in service after 1986 and 20% for certified historic structures.

• Low-interest housing credit. Allowed for residential buildings placed in service after 1987 where a designated percentage of tenants qualify as low-income earners. The credit is claimed over 10 years at a rate of 4% or 9% of qualified basis depending on whether the building is new and/or federally subsidized.

Source: Lester A. Marks, tax partner in Ernst & Whinney, 787 Seventh Ave., New York 10019, who has an extensive practice related to taxation. He is a frequent contributor to professional journals and is often quoted in business publications.

Easy Tests for Dependency

To be claimed as a dependent for the purposes of the income tax exemption, a person must meet five sets of criteria.

1. The dependent must be related to you or be a member of your household. The individual must fall within one of the following categories:

Child, grandchild, adopted child, stepchild, etc.

Brother, sister, half brother, stepbrother, etc.
Parent, grandparent, but not foster parent.
Stepfather, stepmother.
Brother or sister of your father or mother.
Son or daughter of your brother or sister.
Father-in-law, mother-in-law, etc.
Persons you claim as dependents who are unrelated to you must live with you the entire year as members of your household. Temporary absences, such as hospital stays or vacations, are allowed.

Can a foster child be claimed as a dependent? Only if your home is the child's principal home and the child is a member of your household for the entire year. However, if you are receiving payments from a child placement agency or a state agency, the payments are considered reimbursements for expenses incurred and you are not allowed to claim the exemption.

In a divorce situation, the dependency exemption for a child normally goes to the parent having custody.

There are instances in which a noncustodial parent can claim a child as an exemption: When there is a multiple support agreement that allows the child to be claimed by a taxpayer other than the custodial parent; when a signed release from the custodial parent gives the right to someone else; where a pre-1985 divorce decree grants the exemption to the noncustodial parent, who provides at least $600 support in the year the exemption is claimed.

2. The dependent must meet the gross income test. The person you claim as a dependent in any year must earn less than the exemption amount. However, the earned income test does not apply if the dependent is your child and is either under 19 or a full-time student.

3. The individual must meet the support test. You must provide more than one-half of the dependent's support for the calendar year in which you take the exemption. Total support includes money spent on food, clothing, education, medical and dental care, recreation, transportation, and similar items.

There are two exceptions to the one-half support rule. The first—support is provided by several taxpayers, as in the case of caring for an aging parent. Under these circumstances, all taxpayers who contribute 10% or more to that parent's support must sign a multiple support agreement. Then, one of those taxpayers is entitled to the exemption. The second exception to the support rule applies to children whose parents are divorced or separated, as discussed above.

4. The individual must be a citizen of the US. Only persons who are US citizens, residents, or nationals, or are residents of Canada or Mexico for some part of the calendar year, are eligible to be claimed as dependents.

5. The dependent cannot file a joint return. You cannot claim as an exemption a person who has filed a joint return with a spouse. The only exception is when the joint return was filed merely to claim a refund and no tax was due.

Note: As a result of the Tax Reform Act of 1986, beginning in 1988, personal exemptions are phased out for certain high-income taxpayers. For instance, in 1988, the phase-out of the $1,950 exemption starts for taxable income above the following breakpoints: $149,250 for joint returns, $123,790 for heads of households, and $89,560 for single individuals. Beginning in 1989, these breakpoints will be indexed for inflation. Also, under the act, an individual who is eligible to be claimed as a dependent on another taxpayer's return, usually the parent's, may not claim a personal exemption on his own return.

Source: David L. Nelson, tax partner in charge of personal financial planning, Ernst & Whinney, 333 Clay St., Suite 3100, Houston, TX 77002.

The Tricky Alternative Minimum Tax

A hidden danger that may unexpectedly increase the tax bills owed by many high-income individuals is the expanded and toughened alternative minimum tax. Prior to tax reform, the AMT applied primarily to people with large tax-shelter losses or unusually large capital gains. Now, however, most upper-income individuals, when devising year-ahead tax-planning strategies, will have to think about how to avoid falling into the AMT trap. Dangers:

• While tax reform reduced normal tax rates, it increased the bite of the AMT by both increasing the AMT tax rate and adding to the list of items that can produce AMT liability.

• Under tax reform many more people will be liable for the tax.

• Many high-income executives have entered into income-deferral programs (through salary-deferral agreements and the like). But for a person who's subject to the AMT, income deferral may be the worst strategy.

If, however, you are subject to the AMT, smart tax planning can cut your liability, and maybe even make the AMT work for you.

How the Tax Works

The AMT must be worked out—in addition to your regular tax bill. If it produces a tax liability that's larger than that derived under the regular rules, you must pay this increased amount instead of your regular tax bill.

Under tax reform, income that's subject to the AMT is taxed at a flat rate of 21%. This is less than the normal top tax rate, but when computing the amount of income that's subject to the AMT, you lose the benefit of many deductions and credits that serve to cut your regular tax bill.

When figuring the amount of income subject to the AMT, you start with your adjusted gross income as reported on your normal return. To this amount you must add certain "tax preference items," namely:

• Profits received from the exercise of incentive stock options. That is the difference between the value of the stock you acquire and the price paid for it.

• The accelerated depreciation that you claim on property or equipment. This is depreciation that exceeds the amount you would be entitled to claim if you were taking depreciation on a straight-line basis.

• Gifts to charity of appreciated property. Under normal rules, the full market value of property that you've donated to charity is deductible. But under AMT rules, the amount by which such property has increased in value since you acquired it is added to your income.

• Interest paid on certain tax-exempt bonds, defined as private activity bonds, which are issued by local governments on behalf of private companies. Ask your broker about the status of the bonds in your portfolio.

• Excess intangible drilling costs, such as those attributable to an investment in an oil or gas tax shelter.

After you total up your AMT income, you subtract your deductions. However, under AMT rules, many deductions that are allowed under normal rules are prohibited, while other deductions are limited.

No AMT deductions are allowed for:

• State and local taxes.
• Consumer interest expense.
• Tax-shelter losses.
• Miscellaneous deductions, such as tax preparation fees, investment advisory fees, membership dues paid to professional organizations, and the like.

Limited AMT deductions are allowed for:

• Medical expenses. Under normal rules, these are deductible to the extent that they're in excess of 7.5% of your AGI. But to be deductible for the AMT, medical expenses must exceed 10% of AGI.

• Home financings. Under a complicated set of rules, the AMT deduction for interest expense may be limited when a house was refinanced in 1982 or later. Check with your tax adviser for details.

After your net AMT income (AGI, plus preference items, minus deductions) is figured out, you're entitled to claim a personal exemption. This exemption is $40,000 on a joint return and $30,000 on a single return, but it's phased out as income rises. No exemption exists when net AMT income exceeds $310,000 on a joint return or $232,500 on a single return.

After subtracting your personal exemption from your net AMT income, multiply the resulting figure by the AMT tax rate of 21%. This is your AMT liability. It's what you owe the IRS for the year if it's larger than your regular tax bill as computed under normal rules.

Looking Ahead

It's essential that you determine your potential AMT liability early in the year. Conventional tax-planning strategies that are used to reduce the normal tax bill may increase your AMT liability. Therefore, it's imperative to adopt the right strategies now. Also, individuals are required to pay their estimated tax liabilities through quarterly estimated tax payments. If the AMT liability isn't discovered until year-end, underpayment penalties may arise.

To figure out your potential AMT liability for next year, start by looking at the tax return you've just prepared. Adjust it by estimating the amount of income you expect to earn and by factoring in the deductions you plan to take and the tax-cutting strategies you intend to use. Come to an estimate of AGI, then apply the AMT rules. Get a copy of IRS Form 6251, Computation of Alternative Minimum Tax, to help you with the figuring. You'll get a good picture of whether you'll owe the AMT.

Cutting the Tax

When you're planning to face the AMT, the key is that the 21% AMT tax rate is lower than the top regular tax rate. The goal is to make this fact work for you. Strategies:

• Accelerate the receipt of income. Conventional wisdom calls for taxpayers to defer the receipt of income to postpone tax. But if you know that you'll be subject to the AMT this year but not next year, it makes sense to take as much income as possible now. Consider exchanging tax-exempt bonds for taxable bonds that pay interest at a higher rate, cashing in savings bonds and paying tax on their appreciation, or arranging to receive bonuses and other forms of taxable income before year-end.

• Be selective with your deductions. Again, because of the AMT's low tax rate, you may want to save your deductions for a later year when they'll be more valuable. But if you're going to take deductions, take those that provide you with some benefit under the AMT (such as most charitable deductions). Do not incur expenses that are deductible under normal rules but not under AMT rules. Thus, you'll want to postpone the payment of items such as local property or income taxes until after year-end, whenever possible.

• Time your tax moves carefully. You may be able to maximize the benefit you receive from certain tax moves by careful timing. For example, if you own valuable incentive stock options, you may be able to avoid AMT liability by simply postponing your exercise of them or by exercising only a limited amount. Similarly, the donation of a valuable appreciated property to charity may be made at a selected time for the best effect.

The only way to find out if the AMT poses a problem for you is to work through the figures. Ask your tax adviser to help you do this while there's still plenty of time to adopt the appropriate strategies for the upcoming year.

Source: Howard A. Rabinowitz, tax partner, and Lawrence W. Goldstein, tax manager, Arthur Young & Co., 277 Park Ave., New York 10172.

Tax Breaks on US Securities

US government securities offer tax-saving opportunities that are perfectly safe and legal. They're exempt from state and local income tax—a big saving for individuals in high-tax states. Some kinds of US securities offer federal tax advantages as well.

Treasury bills are issued at a discount for periods of up to one year. You pay less than the bill's face value when you buy it, then redeem the bill for its full face value when it matures. Your gain isn't taxed until you cash in the bill. This means you can defer taxes to next year by buying a bill that matures after year-end. By contrast, if you invested the same money in a bank account or corporate bond, you'd owe tax this year on the interest earned before year-end.

Series EE savings bonds let you choose how you'll be taxed. You can pay tax on your income from the bonds each year. Or you can defer paying tax on the bonds until some date between now and the time the bonds mature—an option that makes sense if you expect to have offsetting deductions or to be in a lower tax bracket in the future.

When Series EE bonds mature, you can elect to further defer tax on them by converting them into Series HH bonds. Planning option: Supplement your retirement income by buying EE bonds until you retire, deferring the tax on them, then convert them into HH bonds to collect extra cash income after you retire, all without paying tax on the increase in the bonds' value.

Tax Sheltering a Windfall

Want to bet on a sure thing? It's certain that we all want to keep as much as we can of any windfall we get. Another sure bet is that taxes can devour a large chunk. But you may be able to substantially reduce your tax liability with a little planning. After all, a windfall usually isn't as unexpected as it appears to be: You buy a lottery ticket, or bet on a horse, or take legal action; you believe you will win or at least have a chance to win.

At one time, windfalls often did not get taxed—not so much because of active cheating, but because no effective reporting system existed and the lucky recipients didn't know, or care, that their new wealth might be taxable. Now the IRS and many state tax agencies have improved reporting systems, and tax awareness is definitely on the upswing. Most windfalls are subject to income taxes, sharing a windfall with friends and family can generate gift taxes, and what you don't spend may be hit with estate taxes when you die.

The next time you enter a sweepstakes that gives a choice between a lump-sum payment or annuity payments, consider the following points.

• A lump sum draws the higher income tax rate. Giving some of it away can result in gift taxes. Any portion you still have when you die is includable in your estate. On the other hand, you may be able to invest a lump sum at earnings comparable to the annuity payments and keep the after-tax principal intact.

• An annuity is subject to income tax each year as payments are received by you or your heirs, with generally fewer worries about gift taxes (since gifts would be smaller). The present value of future payments on the date of your death is includable in your estate. Of course, an annuity also provides some protection from spendthrift tendencies.

Gambling Winnings

All gambling winnings are taxable. In fact, federal income tax is withheld at a rate of 20% from some types of winnings—for example, a state lottery win of $5,000 or more or a jai alai win of $600 or more. To soften the tax blow, you can deduct your losses, limited to the winnings reported on your tax return, but only as an itemized deduction unless you are in the business of gambling. Deductions for losses are not subject to the 2% limitation placed on deductions for miscellaneous expenses.

Records that document your losses are essential. The IRS does not take kindly to estimates of gambling losses or to records showing lots of losses and no wins but the big one. So, keep written records (an accurate diary is recommended), and receipts when available (wagering tickets, canceled checks, credit records, bank withdrawal statements, and credit receipts), of every dollar you spend and of all of your wins and losses. All kinds of gambling fall into the same pot, from bingo to bets on races and athletic events, to a state lottery.

As another tax saver, you might consider sharing the chance for wealth with family or friends. Sharing ownership of a chance to win will cut the tax bite. Sharing your winnings won't. For example, if you win $1 million and give part of it to friends and relatives, you still pay the income tax on the full amount, and maybe some gift taxes as well. But if you can list yourself and one or more buddies on a chance to win, each winner will be taxed on his share of the winnings, generally resulting in a lower total tax.

Insurance or Damages Awards

Are damages taxable? It depends. The Supreme Court says it is necessary to look to the source of an award to determine whether it is taxable. Thus awards for lost wages or business profits are taxable. Punitive damages—that is, amounts specified to punish a person who has injured you—are taxable too.

On the other hand, awards for personal injuries—physical, mental, and emotional—are not taxable. Nor are awards for current and future medical expenses. (However, medical expenses covered by an award are not deductible.)

Some awards are partly taxable. For example, an award for lost wages and emotional stress due to on-the-job harassment is not taxable to the extent allocated to emotional stress. And an award for property damages is taxable only to the extent it exceeds your basis in the property.

In any legal action, to avoid unnecessary taxes, insist that the injury be called by its correct name.

You can claim an itemized deduction for expenses, such as legal fees and court costs, to obtain a taxable award. Expenses related to a partly taxable award are partly deductible. Legal fees and court costs to obtain a taxable award must be combined with tax determination expenses, investment expenses, and unreimbursed employment expenses. The total of these expenses, reduced by 2% of your adjusted gross income, is then deductible as an itemized deduction.

Source: Nancy A. Anderson, tax research and training specialist, H&R Block, Inc., 4410 Main St., Kansas City, MO 64111, and writer-editor of H&R Block/Macmillan Publishing Company tax publications.

Tax-Deferred Income— Checklist

Deferring taxation of a portion of your income until a year in which your income will be lower can save you a bundle on your tax bill. Here's a list of the kinds of income eligible for deferral—starting with the one that no one should overlook.

• Income from an IRA account, Keogh or qualified corporate pension, SEP (simplified employee pension), or profit-sharing plan is tax-deferred until time of withdrawal. (Note:

You're not taxed on the money invested *or* the earnings!)

• Interest on single-payment deferred annuities is tax-deferred until withdrawn.

• Income from US Series EE savings bonds is tax-deferred if you do not elect to be taxed on them annually.

• Income from the exercise of incentive stock option plans is tax-deferred until the stock is liquidated. (But it may trigger the alternative minimum tax.)

• Income deferred under a section 401(k) plan.

• Income earned pursuant to an "unfunded deferred compensation" plan (i.e., deferred pay) is tax-deferred until actually received.

• Security deposits received are not taxable unless and until they are deemed unreturnable (forfeited).

• Receipts from the sale of stock options are not taxable until the options are exercised or expire, or the position is closed.

• Capital appreciation is tax-deferred up to the point when you sell.

Source: Edward Mendlowitz, partner, Siegel, Mendlowitz & Rich, CPAs, 310 Madison Ave., New York 10017.

AMT Avoidance Tactics

Strategies that can keep you out of the AMT:

• Find investments that produce passive income to offset your passive tax-shelter losses. Reducing your net deductible passive losses may keep you out of the AMT. Consider income-producing limited partnerships and rental properties, such as office buildings, parking lots, etc., which throw off passive income.

• Exercise incentive stock options with care. Exercise only a limited amount or postpone your exercise of options to avoid AMT liability.

• Put off giving appreciated property to charity until a year when you won't be subject to the AMT. Or, spread the gift over a number of years.

• Avoid prepaying state and local income tax, if paying it early throws you into the AMT.

• Unload "private activity" municipal bonds if the interest income makes you liable for the AMT. See your broker.

Sales Tax Can Add Up— To Savings

Sales taxes no longer qualify as itemized deductions. They are absolutely out—but not always (because we are talking about taxes, after all).

If you buy a big-ticket item you will not be able to claim an itemized deduction for the state or local levy on the new purchase. But don't throw away the receipt—add the sales tax to your cost basis.

For property used in your trade or business, you will be able to increase your depreciation deductions. For other assets, adding the sales tax to your cost will reduce any eventual gain you might have to report on a subsequent sale.

For example, suppose you buy a delivery truck to be used exclusively in your business. The purchase price is $25,000 plus an additional $1,500 in state sales taxes. The whole $26,500 is depreciable. Suppose, further, that you buy a painting for $25,000 plus $1,500 for the sales levy. When, after the artist has passed on, you sell the work for $30,000, your taxable gain will not be $5,000 but only $3,500. Keep records: They'll save you money.

Source: Special report, *New Tax Loopholes for Investors,* written for Boardroom Reports by Robert A. Garber, a tax attorney and vice president of a major investment-banking house. He writes frequently on tax matters and is the author of several books.

Loopholes for Working Families

Very few working families take advantage of all the tax breaks they're entitled to. It seems the harder they work, the more taxes they pay. But the loopholes are there—for spouses who have separate jobs or separate businesses, and for those who work together in a family business.

Separate Corporations

When a husband and wife own separate corporations, great care must be taken that one spouse is not a shareholder, officer, director, employee, or check signer of the other spouse's corporation. Trap: Such involvement by one spouse in the other's corporation will cause the loss of the full tax benefits that separate corporations are entitled to. For one thing, the corporations will be required to split the benefit of graduated income tax rates. For instance, instead of each corporation having its first $50,000 of taxable income taxed at 15%, the two companies will have to divide that amount—only $25,000 of each company's taxable income will be taxed at 15%. The other brackets will also have to be split.

This is a very important planning item. Don't be a shareholder, employee, officer, etc., of your spouse's corporation if you, too, own a corporation.

One Business

• Tax advantages of operating the business as a sole proprietorship, rather than a partnership or a corporation. You can hire your spouse as an employee and your spouse's salary, which is deductible by the business, reduces the amount of self-employment income that you have to pay Social Security tax on.

Trap: If you set up the business as a partnership with your spouse, you will both be subject to self-employment tax on your income from the business.

• Why to pay your spouse a salary. One reason is to increase the family's deductible pension-plan contributions. If you make over $200,000, say, you may be contributing the maximum deductible amount to a Keogh or simplified employee pension plan. But your spouse's salary can be the basis of additional deductible retirement-plan contributions.

Paying your spouse a salary also may actually reduce the total amount of state tax the family pays. You may be able to split your income on state income tax returns, thus reducing the tax. Some states allow a husband and wife to file separate returns for state taxes, even though they file a joint federal income tax return.

• Write off working vacations with your spouse. The extra cost of taking your spouse along on a business trip isn't ordinarily deductible unless the spouse's services are essential to the business. But when the spouse is an employee of the business, it's much easier to make the case that his or her services are essential to the overall business purpose of the trip.

• Hire your children. Instead of giving them allowances, find them real work to do in your business. Pay them reasonable salaries and deduct the salaries as a business expense. Tax savings: If your business is unincorporated, you don't pay Social Security tax on wages paid to a child who is under 18. Also, a child can earn $3,000 totally tax-free; an additional $2,000 of a child's salary would escape tax if it was put into an Individual Retirement Account.

Loophole: Pay the children a salary while they are going to college. Give them jobs doing market research for your business, product testing, sales, etc.

• Medical insurance. If your business is incorporated as a C corporation, the full amount you pay for medical insurance for you and your family is deductible. (But then you're subject to the extra costs of being a corporation—accounting, legal fees, FICA, unemployment insurance, additional bookkeeping costs, etc.)

Tax reform benefit for sole proprietors: Self-employed taxpayers can deduct 25% of their medical insurance premiums. The remaining

75% of premium payments are included in medical expenses (subject to the floor of 7.5% of adjusted gross income).

• Avoiding probate. You can avoid the hassle of probate by setting up a revocable living trust and having the trust own the business, rather than yourself, under terms that pass ownership to your spouse when you die. This has no tax effect but it facilitates transferring ownership of the business to your spouse—who won't have to wait until the probate process is completed to assume ownership.

The working couple's deduction was repealed by tax reform. But the child-care credit was retained.

You may be eligible for the child-care credit even if your spouse doesn't work. The tax law's definition of a working spouse includes a spouse who is a full-time student for at least five months during the year. So if you hire someone to look after the children while your spouse goes to school and you work, that person's wages qualify for the credit.

Downside: If you hire baby-sitters, you must pay Social Security taxes for them, and in some states you must pay for their unemployment insurance. This could negate part of the benefit you get from the child-care credit.

Underwithholding trap: When both spouses work it is easy to have too little tax withheld by your employer. You could end up paying the IRS a penalty for being underwithheld. To avoid this, fill out your W-4 forms very, very carefully and completely. Keep in mind that the form is designed to figure tax withholding from the start of the year. (You may want to take fewer withholding allowances than you're entitled to.)

Source: Edward Mendlowitz, partner, Siegel, Mendlowitz & Rich, CPAs, 310 Madison Ave., New York 10017.

Joint Versus Separate Returns

Married couples can file a joint return or separate returns. Usually, a joint return works out better, especially if one spouse has appreciably higher income than the other. Nevertheless, filing separately can be advantageous in some situations:

• Deductions for casualty losses must be reduced by 10% of adjusted gross income. On a joint return, the casualty loss is reduced by 10% of the *combined* AGI, even if only one spouse suffered the loss. If separate returns are filed, the loss is reduced only by 10% of that spouse's income.

Example: A husband has AGI of $70,000; his wife, $20,000. The wife's jewelry, worth $25,000, is stolen. On a joint return, the loss must be reduced by $9,000 (10% of combined income); on a separate return, by only $2,000 (10% of the wife's income).

• The same considerations apply if only one spouse has heavy medical expenses, since only expenses in excess of 7½% of AGI are deductible.

Caution: The only way to tell for sure whether it's better to file jointly or separately is to take pencil and paper and figure the tax both ways.

Source: Herbert M. Paul, a tax attorney with the firm of Herbert Paul, P.C., 805 Third Ave., New York 10022.

Divorce Is Tougher after Tax Reform

The complicated tax reform law has profound implications for divorcing couples. The law makes it more important than ever for couples involved in a matrimonial dispute to seek the advice of a knowledgeable tax professional. Tax considerations:

• Changing tax rates. While alimony will still be fully deductible by the spouse who pays it, lower income tax rates will diminish the value of the deduction. Husbands, who traditionally pay alimony, may balk at making alimony a big part of the divorce settlement. And because of the increased tax on capital gains, they may be more disposed to give low-basis, appreciated property, such as the family home, stock, an interest in a business, etc., to the other spouse as part of the settlement. Reason: The spouse who gives the property would avoid paying increased tax on the gain; the spouse who receives the property could sell it and have the gain taxed in her lower bracket. The tax saving would then be factored into the amount of the settlement.

• Reduced value of home-mortgage interest deductions, caused by lower income tax rates, may be an additional incentive for one spouse to give up his or her interest in the family home.

• Increased exemptions for dependents will make the right to claim children as dependents after a divorce a more valuable bargaining chip. Tax reform raised substantially the amount of the dependency exemption and permitted exemptions to be signed over to the noncustodial spouse. Spouses may consider trading dependency exemptions for increased child support. Flip side: High-income spouses may not want dependency exemptions, since the exemptions could cause the spouse to pay more income tax. (The benefit of the exemptions is phased out for taxable income above certain breakpoints.)

• Medical expenses. Tax reform increases the floor on medical expense deductions to 7.5% of adjusted gross income (from 5%). Planning point: Have the low-bracket spouse pay the medical expenses. That way, more of the expenses are likely to be deductible.

• Legal fees. The portion of a divorce lawyer's fee that is for tax advice is deductible (if separately stated on the bill) as a miscellaneous deduction. But you can claim miscellaneous deductions only to the extent they exceed 2% of your AGI. Planning point: Bunch your miscellaneous deductions into the year you pay the divorce lawyer, so that as much as possible of the bill will be deductible.

• Alimony complication. The 1984 tax act imposed recapture rules to prevent nondeductible property settlement payments from being deducted as alimony. Excess upfront alimony payments (those that exceed the limits set by the law) must be added back into income by the spouse who paid them. These complicated recapture rules have been com-

pletely revised. Bottom line: This change in the law is reason in itself to get expert tax advice on your divorce settlement.

Source: Sidney Kess, partner and director of tax planning, Peat Marwick Main & Co., 55 E. 52 St., New York 10055.

Alimony and the IRS

A property settlement made after a divorce is not tax deductible, but alimony payments are fully deductible. Tax reform has made it easier to have your payments categorized as tax-deductible alimony. Here's how:

• The length of time that alimony payments must continue has been shortened to three years after separation rather than six years after separation under the old law.

• The recapture rules, which under old law penalized those who paid much larger amounts in the first year or years and smaller amounts in the last years have been liberalized. The first-year payment can exceed the average of the second- and third-year payments by up to $15,000 under tax reform before the recapture rules come into play. The second-year payment can exceed the third-year payment by $15,000.

If the husband deducts the alimony, the wife must declare it as income. Child support, lump-sum payments, wife's legal fees, premiums on life insurance policies owned by the husband—all these are not deductible by the spouse paying them. And they need not be reported as income by the spouse who receives the payments.

In the still common case among executives where the husband has a large taxable income and the nonworking wife has little or none, it probably makes sense to make all the payments as alimony rather than something else. The result is to shift income from the husband's high bracket to the wife's lower bracket. It's essential to prepare carefully several alternative plans, varying the mix among alimony and other types of payments, and figuring the available income from each after taxes.

The dependency exemptions for children of divorced or separated parents are given to the custodial parent unless he or she agrees in writing to waive the exemptions.

A parent having a child living with him or her may be able to file as a (tax-favored) head of household. Conceivably, both parents might have head-of-household status. This could happen if the younger children stayed with the mother, but an older child—away at college full-time—stayed with the father when home on vacation.

Child support normally stops when the children become independent. Alimony often goes on until the wife remarries.

If it's agreed that the husband will pay for the wife's divorce lawyer, estimate the fee and add this amount to the alimony that has been negotiated. Then get a deduction for the amount. But don't forget it's income to the wife in that case.

How To File as Head of Household— Even When You're Not

Head-of-household rates are much lower than "married filing separately" rates. If you're married and have children, but lived apart from your spouse for the last six months of the taxable year, you may file as head of household if:

• Your home was the principal abode for your dependent children for over half the year (the full year if the children are foster children).

• You provided more than half the cost of supporting the household.

• You or your spouse can claim your children as dependents.

If each spouse maintained a household for one or more dependent children, both are eligible for head-of-household status. If only one qualifies, the other must file as "married filing separately." There's no rule for determin-

ing whether this would result in lower taxes than a joint return; that has to be calculated for each individual case.

How Much Can Your Child Earn and Not Pay Taxes?

How much income can your minor (i.e., dependent) child have in any given year without having to pay income tax? First, the IRS makes a distinction between earned and unearned income and children under 14 and those 14 years of age and over. There are different rates for each.

Earned income (wages, salaries, fees, tips, etc.). First of all, the standard deduction can offset the earned income of a child who is a dependent on the parents' return. The amount: $3,000. Second, the child may open an IRA with a maximum contribution of $2,000.

Unearned income (dividends and interest). Each child gets a standard deduction that cannot exceed $500 (or the child's earned income).

So, what is the maximum income your child can make without being subject to income tax? A child of any age can have earned income of up to $5,000 and pay no tax:

Wages	$5,000
IRA contribution	(2,000)
Standard deduction	(3,000)
Taxable income	$ –0–

The Tax Reform Act of 1986 generally eliminates the benefit of parental income shifting to children under age 14 by taxing investment income in excess of $1,000 at the higher of the parents' tax rate or the child's tax rate. A child under 14 years of age with only unearned income is entitled to a standard deduction of $500. In addition, the next $500 of unearned income is taxed at the child's rate of 15%. Any amount of unearned income in excess of $1,000 is taxed at the parents' rate. To avoid taxation of the income of a child who is under 14 years of age at the parents' rate, the child's principal should be invested in income-deferral investments such as Series EE bonds or growth securities.

The major difference between children 14 years of age and over and those under 14 is that the older children pay tax on their unearned income in excess of $500 at their own bracket, which begins at 15%. If the child is under 14, the child gets a $500 standard deduction and the next $500 is taxable at 15%. After this $1,000, the under-14-year-old child pays tax at the higher of his own or his parents' rate.

Source: Lester A. Marks, tax partner in Ernst & Whinney, 787 Seventh Ave., New York 10019, who has an extensive practice related to taxation. He is a frequent contributor to professional journals and is often quoted in business publications.

Checklist of Tax Tips for Retirees

• Check applicability of credit for the elderly.

• Make sure to use any state exclusions available for pension payments.

• Check for special state credits. There are many.

• Move to a low-tax state such as Florida, Texas, Nevada, or possibly Connecticut, New Jersey, or New Hampshire, depending upon individual circumstances.

• Take advantage of the one-time $125,000 exclusion from income of the gain on the sale of a principal residence for individuals over 55.

• Take advantage of tax benefits for tax-free rollovers of pension-plan distributions.

• Use five-year averaging for lump-sum distributions from pension/profit-sharing plans. A person who was born before 1936 can elect to use 10-year averaging if it is more beneficial.

• Make gifts to children of income-producing property if the children are 14 or older.

• Establish irrevocable trusts to shift income to grandchildren, to other lower-bracket individuals, or to a lower-bracket trust.

• Make charitable gifts of appreciated property. Such appreciation is a preference item for alternative minimum tax purposes.

Source: Lester A. Marks, tax partner in Ernst & Whinney, 787 Seventh Ave., New York 10019, who has an extensive practice related to taxation. He is a frequent contributor to professional journals and is often quoted in business publications.

A Wedding Gift from the IRS

A parent who provides over half of a child's support can claim a dependency exemption if the child is under 19 or a full-time student. The cost of a child's wedding is considered support. So even if the child lives with a spouse after marriage, the wedding may push the parent's support cost over the 50% mark and entitle the parent to the exemption. Drawback: The newlyweds cannot file a joint return for the year, nor can the child claim the personal exemption.

Source: Revenue Ruling 76–184.

Use Your In-Laws To Cut Your Tax Bill

If you've suffered a loss on an investment property, you can't deduct it while keeping the property in the family by selling it to your spouse, brother, sister, parent, grandparent, child, or grandchild. It doesn't matter if the sale is perfectly legitimate. The Tax Code prohibits any loss deduction from a sale to one of these relatives.

Loophole: The Tax Code does *not* consider in-laws to be relatives under this rule. So don't sell to your son or daughter—sell instead to your son-in-law or daughter-in-law (or some other in-law). You'll keep the property in the family and get a deduction too.

Student Exemption Trap

A taxpayer can claim an exemption for a dependent child over 19, even if the child earns over the exemption amount, provided the child is a full-time student for at least five calendar months during the year.

Trap: The five-month rule is interpreted strictly. The IRS has denied an exemption for a child who was a full-time student for four months but then left school when she fell ill and was hospitalized for the rest of the year.
Source: IRS Letter Ruling 8623050.

Income-Shifting Checklist

• Gifts of income-producing property to children, so that income on the gifted principal is taxable to children who are in a lower tax bracket. This benefit is limited to the tax savings on $1,000, if the child is under age 14.

• Gifts of income-producing property to parents, if they are in a lower tax bracket.

• Irrevocable trusts for the benefit of children, parents, or others.

• Children of parents can work for and get paid from the family business.

• An S corporation can be formed for splitting income among family members.

• Gifts of appreciated property to children, parents, or grandchildren. (They can sell and the gain will be taxed at a lower rate.)

• Estates in administration become, in effect, new taxpayers and may be able to take advantage of graduated tax brackets.

• Make an interest-free loan of up to $10,000. The transaction will not be taxed as long as the borrower does not use the proceeds to purchase income-producing assets. (The borrower could use the money to purchase a car, for example.)

• Make an interest-free loan for up to $100,000 (to a child, for example). The transaction is tax-free if the borrower has investment income of less than $1,000. Typical use

of the funds would be the purchase of a house.
Source: Lester A. Marks, tax partner in Ernst & Whinney, 787 Seventh Ave., New York 10019, who has an extensive practice related to taxation. He is a frequent contributor to professional journals and is often quoted in business publications.

Great Tax Benefits in Single Premium Life Policies

Single premium life is a hybrid investment vehicle with tax advantages peculiar to life insurance products. But not everyone who should know about the main tax benefits of single premium life actually knows about them.

You pay no income tax on the interest, dividends, or capital gains earned on your initial investment—the single premium payment. As long as the policy remains in force, your investment gains accumulate free of current tax.

You can borrow money from the policy, usually at very little or no cost. The loans are, in effect, tax-free income, since borrowing is not treated by the IRS as a taxable transaction. (Loan interest payments, however, are not tax-deductible.)

The beneficiary you name on the policy receives an insurance benefit on your death free of federal income tax. By contrast, a single premium annuity triggers income tax when you die.

Additional, not-so-obvious tax advantages to single premium life insurance:

• Tax-free investment switches. Single premium variable life insurance policies offer a number of investment options, rather like a family of mutual funds. You can put your money in one or a combination of investment funds, and you can switch the money from one fund to another. When you change your investment decision (switch) in a regular mutual fund, any profit you make in the fund you switch out of is taxable at that point. But gains on investment switches in single premium variable policies are not taxable currently.

• Tax-free income to your spouse. A single premium life policy can be set up to provide tax-free income, through borrowing, to your surviving spouse. This can be accomplished by making your spouse the contingent owner of the policy. On your death, the ownership passes to your spouse, who takes over the policy with the same rights as you had. If you had been receiving tax-free income from the policy by borrowing the annual earnings, your spouse would be able to continue to do the exact same thing. This would give your spouse tax-free income for life.

• Social Security break. Amounts you borrow from the policy are not included in the calculations that tax up to half of your Social Security benefits. By contrast, earnings from tax-free municipal bonds, even though they are not subject to income tax, are included in the Social Security benefits tax calculations and can trigger tax on half of your Social Security. By switching from municipal bonds to single premium life and getting retirement income from borrowing, you can avoid tax on any part of your Social Security.

• No increased audit risk. Investment in a single premium life policy does not increase your risk of an audit. Purchase of the policy isn't reported to the IRS, nor are loans reported. Only if you terminate the policy will the IRS be put on notice.

Advice to Investors

Avoid surrendering the contract. If you do surrender it, you will trigger very adverse tax results.

Don't put all of what you plan to invest in single premium life into one contract. Build a portfolio of policies so you're not at the mercy of one insurance company's investment decisions.

For security's sake, the company issuing the policy should be rated A+ by A.M. Best Company, the insurance industry analysts.

Source: Alan R. Nadolna, president, Financial Planning Associates, c/o Pacific Financial Associates, 135 S. LaSalle St., Chicago 60603.

Using Single Premium Insurance To Shift Income to Children

Income shifting is still possible under tax reform if you plan carefully. One smart way of beating the law is through the purchase of life insurance. How it works: Buy single premium life insurance policies on the lives of your children under age 14 and give it to them. Drawback: There are gift tax consequences on this gift if the value of the life insurance is more than $10,000 ($20,000 if you're married) per child. But once the children own the policies, you won't have to pay gift tax on the inside buildup in the policies. Advantages:

• The cash-value buildup over the years is tax-deferred. So even though this income is actually earned by children under age 14, it won't be taxed at all until the policies are cashed in.

• Children over age 14 can cash in the policies and pay tax in their low tax bracket. The children avoid paying tax at the parents' high tax bracket, even though more than $1,000 of income may have accumulated per year when they were under age 14.

• Your children can borrow against the cash value of the policies without triggering any tax. The policies increase in value over the years and at the same time the children have use of the money.

• Parents who want to control the life insurance policies can own the policies themselves, and give them to the children when they are older.

Source: Craig D. Stepnicka, tax partner and head of the personal and financial tax-planning practice in the Chicago office of Arthur Young & Co., 1 IBM Plaza, Chicago 60611.

Income-Producing Property to Children

Tax reform has severely limited a family's ability to shift income—and taxes on that income—from high-bracket family members to those in lower tax brackets. Biggest changes: Clifford trusts are no longer effective. And large gifts of income-producing assets to children under age 14 won't cut the family's tax bill the way they used to. But it would be a mistake to write off income shifting completely. Opportunities still exist for parents to transfer taxable income to low-bracket children.

If you want to give income-producing property to a minor, make sure the income is deferred until the child reaches 14. Suggestions:

• US Series EE savings bonds, which are free from tax until cashed in at maturity. If you choose, the proceeds can be rolled over into Series HH savings bonds—deferring tax on the EE bonds still further.

• Growth stocks or real estate that don't produce current income but increase in value as time goes by. After the child reaches 14, the property can be sold if cash is needed (e.g., for college).

• Single premium life insurance, which builds up in value, but isn't taxed until the policy is cashed in. If necessary, money can be borrowed against the policy tax-free, at extremely low interest.

Source: Philip B. Kimmel, partner, Hertz, Herson & Co., 2 Park Ave., New York 10016.

Appreciated Securities: Shifting Capital Gains

Give appreciated securities to your parents instead of cash if you are supporting them. They can cash in the securities and pay tax on the appreciation in their low tax bracket. You'll avoid paying tax in your high tax bracket.

Caution: A large gain could push your parents into a higher bracket. Of course, if you and your parents are in the same tax bracket, this ploy won't help you (nor will it hurt).

Tax Advantages of Filing for Personal Bankruptcy

Tax considerations are hardly ever the main reason an individual files for bankruptcy. But the tax aspects of personal bankruptcy can be very favorable, especially for taxpayers who are heavily in debt to their employers or to their own closely held corporations. Main benefits:

• Cancellation of indebtedness. As a general rule, when a debt is forgiven, the debtor must report the amount forgiven as income. But a debt canceled in bankruptcy is not treated as income.

Example: Among other debts, a financially troubled taxpayer owes his employer $25,000. If the debt is simply forgiven by the employer, the employee must report the $25,000 as income. If, however, the employee files for bankruptcy and the debt is canceled, he does not have to treat it as income.

Example: An individual had credit card charges of $10,000 last year. This year the credit card debt is discharged in bankruptcy. If any of the credit card charges were previously deducted (e.g., as a business entertainment deduction) they would have to be reported as income. But the other part of the discharged debt wouldn't have to be reported.

Example: Five years ago, an individual borrowed heavily from his closely held corporation. For other reasons business is now so bad that the corporation must file for bankruptcy. If the individual also declares bankruptcy and the loan is discharged, he has a big tax windfall. He will not have to pick up the money he borrowed from the company as income.

• Cancellation of back taxes. Unpaid federal income taxes are canceled in bankruptcy if they become due more than three years before the bankruptcy filing.

• Deductible expenses. Fees paid to an accountant to prepare an individual's personal records for Bankruptcy Court are tax-deductible (subject to the 2% of AGI limit on miscellaneous deductions). So are legal fees, to the extent they involve the tax aspects of bankruptcy.

• Carryovers. Some carryovers are retained by the individual after bankruptcy. Included: Net operating loss carryovers (business losses), capital loss carryovers, tax credit carryovers, and charitable contribution carryovers. Limit: Net operating loss carryovers must be adjusted downward to the extent that the debt giving rise to the carryovers is canceled in bankruptcy.

The negative tax consequences of personal bankruptcy:

• Recapture of credits. Any investment credit taken on an asset that is disposed of in the course of the bankruptcy proceeding must be recaptured (that is, added back to the tax due on the individual's postbankruptcy tax return).

• Payroll taxes. Individuals who are personally responsible for payroll taxes (e.g., officers of a company) cannot cancel their liability for those taxes in bankruptcy.

• Tax refunds are payable to the trustee in bankruptcy, not to the individual who files for bankruptcy. Loophole: Taxpayers who expect to file for bankruptcy next year should arrange payroll withholding this year so that no tax refunds will be coming from the government. Alternative: If large refunds are expected, file for bankruptcy prior to December 31, before the refund becomes an asset payable to the bankruptcy trustee.

Source: Edward Mendlowitz, partner, Siegel, Mendlowitz & Rich, CPAs, 310 Madison Ave., New York 10017.

Buying Relatives' Investment Losses

If you are a high-bracket taxpayer and have a relative with little or no taxable income, consider taking advantage of a tax law provision that allows you, in effect, to acquire your immediate relatives' deductible losses.

How it works: If a member of your immediate family sells property to you at a loss, that loss can't be deducted. But, when you turn around and sell that property, you don't have to pay tax on any gain unless the gain is more than your family member's loss. Even then, only the portion of the gain that exceeds the previous loss is taxable.

Example: John White's mother is very ill. She has some income from dividends and a modest pension. But her deductible medical expenses are so high that her taxable income is zero. Her portfolio includes 100 shares of Consolidated Conglomerate that she bought at $35 a share. The current price is $11. If Mrs. White sells on the open market, she'll have a $2,400 loss that won't save a penny in taxes. If John buys the stock, he can hold on to it until the price recovers. And although he bought the shares at $11, he won't have a taxable gain until the stock hits $35 again.

In addition, John can give his mother a note for the purchase price of the stock with a reasonable interest rate. The money can help defray Mrs. White's medical costs, while John gets an interest deduction.

This special rule applies on any transaction between you and your parents, grandparents, children, grandchildren, brother, sister, or any corporation in which you own more than 50% (by value) of the shares.

Charitable Giving: Good News

Smart giving strategies can let a top-bracket individual cut income taxes and estate taxes while retaining economic benefits from an appreciated investment.

Opportunities

The typical estate tax deduction results from a gift to charity made through a will. If you're planning to make such a gift, it may be better to make a deferred gift to charity now.

You can do this by establishing a trust and donating to it property that will pass to a named charity when you die. Until then, the trust will pay cash income to you. Two kinds of trust:

• Annuity trust. The property that you place in the trust is used to buy an annuity that will provide you with specified annual cash payments for the rest of your life.

• Unitrust. This kind of trust pays you a percentage of its total value each year. Thus, if the trust remains invested in the stock market and the market booms, the payment you receive from the trust will increase each year.

Benefits from trusts:

• You get an income tax deduction now for the present value of your gift to charity.

• If you make your gift with appreciated securities, you avoid paying tax on your capital gains.

• Because the amount of the property you place in trust is removed from your estate, you get the benefit of an estate tax deduction without having to claim one. Thus, you preserve your $600,000 estate tax credit to shelter your other property.

Low-cost alternative: If the size of your gift doesn't justify the cost of setting up your own trust, you can make your gift to a pooled income fund. These funds are trusts that are run by major charities. You make a donation to the fund, get an income tax deduction now, and receive annual payments for the rest of your life.

Whether you contribute to an annuity trust, unitrust, or pooled income fund, the result is the same. The charity in the end receives the same gift that you would have made through your will, but you receive benefits that are much greater.

Big-Dollar Deductions

A shareowner in a profitable privately held corporation has a unique opportunity to claim a deduction on his personal return for a charitable gift that's paid for by the company. The device to use is a charitable bailout.

Here, the owner donates some of his shares in the company to a charity, claiming a deduction for their full value. The company then redeems the shares for cash. Results:

• The owner pays nothing out of pocket to get the deduction, since the cash payout is made by the company.

• The owner avoids ever having to pay cap-ital gains tax on the shares, while getting a deduction for their full appreciated value.

• The current owners retain full control over the business because the donated shares, once redeemed, return to the company.

Another idea for an individual who wishes to make a large contribution that will provide lasting benefits is to set up a private foundation.

A private foundation is a corporation that's required to operate for charitable purposes. While a private foundation can't be run to benefit its creator directly, a person who sets up a foundation can retain influence over its operation by naming its directors and serving as a director himself.

Of course, the foundation may bear the donor's name, so it may generate favorable publicity and goodwill for its creator, in addition to providing an opportunity for a large tax deduction. Again, when the foundation is funded with appreciated securities, the donor gets a deduction for their full value while avoiding capital gains tax.

Inexpensive variation: While administration costs and reporting requirements may make the creation of a private foundation impractical for the average taxpayer, similar benefits can be obtained from a contribution to a local community trust.

Community trusts are organizations that solicit contributions from the public. And while a contributor has no legal right to direct how a donation is spent, a community trust usually will make an expenditure according to a donor's request and in the donor's name. A gift to a community trust makes particular sense when a person wants to get a deduction for a large gift now, while retaining some say over how the gift will be spent in future years.

Grandchild's Tax

A new trap established by tax reform is the generation-skipping transfer tax. It applies to any large gift (exceeding certain specified exemptions) that's made to a grandchild or great-grandchild. The tax is a steep one—50%—and it applies in addition to any regular gift or estate tax. However, it's possible to beat the tax with smart giving strategies.

For example, say you have a grandchild to whom you want to pass a large amount of money. You don't want the child to get the money immediately because he's not old enough to handle it. You also don't want to pay heavy estate or gift taxes when you pass the money to the child by will or gift several years from now.

What to do: Give a charity the right to receive an annuity earned from funds that you wish to pass to the grandchild until the transfer takes place. The present value of your gift to charity will reduce the value that will be assigned to your future gift to your grandchild, according to IRS valuation tables. By having your tax adviser carefully structure your arrangement, you can eliminate both estate tax and generation-skipping tax on your future gift to your grandchild. The amount after taxes that's left to pass to your grandchild won't be increased, but money that would have gone to the IRS will go to your favorite charity instead, and you'll get a gift tax deduction now.

Final Word

Under tax reform the technical rules involved with charitable giving are more complicated than ever before. Gifts of appreciated property may make the donor subject to the alternative minimum tax. Although this provision should affect only people making very large gifts, it should be considered by your adviser when planning contributions. Also, all arrangements involving trusts or private foundations should be examined by an expert, to be sure that they meet both tax rules and the requirements of local law.

Source: David S. Rhine, partner, Seidman & Seidman/BDO, 15 Columbus Circle, New York 10023.

Giving Doesn't Have To Hurt

The easiest way to make a charitable donation is by a check. But other kinds of gifts to public charities can also produce large tax sav-

ings and may accomplish the same charitable objectives at less cost.

Donate appreciated assets (stocks, bonds, real estate) rather than cash. If you've held the property for more than a year, you're entitled to a double tax benefit. You can deduct the full market value of the property as a charitable contribution, and you avoid paying capital gains tax on the appreciation. Trap: The appreciation in donated property is a tax preference item that may subject you to the alternative minimum tax. Deduction limit: 30% of your adjusted gross income. Any excess is deductible in the five succeeding tax years.

Set up a charitable remainder trust, preferably with securities that have gone up in value. Most commonly, this kind of trust pays you a fixed amount of income each year until your death and then distributes the remaining assets to charity. You get a tax deduction now for a gift the charity won't receive until some time in the future. In the meantime, you continue to have the use of the money.

Example: A man of 55 sets up a charitable remainder trust with securities that cost him $25,000 but which are now worth $50,000. He reserves an income of $3,000 a year for life. Tax benefits: An immediate charitable deduction for the present value of the charity's remainder interest. And even though this deduction is based on the stock's current value, no regular income tax has to be paid on the appreciation.

Fund the trust with municipal bonds and you will also avoid paying tax on the income you receive from the trust. If you set up the trust with very long-term municipal bonds, your yield might well exceed current money-market rates. And it's completely tax-free.

Contribute to a pooled income fund. Many charities maintain investment funds called pooled income funds. The fund pools the contributions of individual donors, each of whom has retained the right to receive an income for life from his contributions. Tax loopholes: Similar to those of a charitable remainder trust. The investment benefits are that funds are diversified. You get the benefit of professional management without having to pay for establishing and administering a trust. Drawback: Pooled income funds are not permitted to invest in municipal bonds or other tax-exempt securities.

Charitable lead trusts are the reverse of charitable remainder trusts. Instead of providing you with an income, the charity gets the income from the trust assets for a number of years, usually eight to ten. When the trust's term is over, the assets are returned to you. Loophole: You get a big up-front tax deduction for the value of the charity's income interest.

Lead trusts make a lot of sense for high-earning taxpayers who intend to retire in a few years. The trust gives them a big tax deduction in an earning year, lets them continue to provide for their favorite charity, and gives them the security of knowing that the trust assets will be available for their own use in retirement.

Community trusts. Another way to get maximum tax benefits from your charitable donations is to set up a fund in your own name through a recognized public charity that will serve as a conduit to other charities that you recommend. You get a deduction when you set up the fund without the pressure of having to name specific charities at that time. Set up the fund and get big tax deductions in high-income years—for example, the years just before retirement. In the years after your retirement, the fund will make donations in your name to the various charities that you suggest. Problem: You can't order the charity that is administering the fund to make donations. You can only suggest the beneficiaries. But the administering charities usually do follow a donor's suggestions.

Gifts of life insurance. The mere naming of a charity as the beneficiary of a policy on your life will not provide you with an income tax deduction. To guarantee a deduction you must give up all ownership rights in the policy. Loophole: Have the charity own the policy. Make annual contributions to the charity. The charity will use its own money to pay the premiums. You will get a current income tax deduction for your annual gifts and you will have given the charity a very large gift—the proceeds payable on your death.

Source: Edward Mendlowitz, partner in Siegel, Mendlowitz & Rich, CPAs, 310 Madison Ave., New York 10017.

Making the Most of Medical Deductions

You can only deduct medical expenses that exceed 7½% of your adjusted gross income, but the IRS and court decisions have expanded the definition of deductible medical costs. Plan ahead to take advantage of as many medical expenses as possible.

Medical deductions can be taken for the costs of diagnosis, the treatment or prevention of a disease, or for affecting any structure or function of the body. Limitation: Treatment must be specific and not just for general health improvement.

Weight-Control Programs

The IRS successfully denied taxpayers deductions for the cost of weight-control and stop-smoking classes that were designed to improve general health, not to treat a specific ailment or disease. On the other hand, a person with a health problem specifically related to being overweight, such as high blood pressure, might be allowed the deduction.

If an employer tells an overweight employee to lose weight or leave, and the boss has previously enforced such a rule, the plump employee can deduct the cost of a weight-loss program, because money spent to help keep a taxpayer's job is deductible. The IRS says it will allow a deduction if a physician prescribes a weight-reduction program for the treatment of hypertension, obesity, or hearing problems. The same could go for a person whose doctor certifies that a stop to cigarette smoking is necessary for a specific medical reason (such as emphysema).

Other Deductions

• Because medical costs are deductible only after they exceed 7½% of a taxpayer's AGI, it is tempting to declare them as business expenses. The IRS rarely allows those business deductions, but there is a sizable gray area. A professional singer was once not allowed to deduct the cost of throat treatments as a business expense, but an IRS agent did allow a deduction for a dancer who found it necessary to her career to have silicone breast implants.

• Medically unproven treatment is generally deductible, since the IRS has taken the position that it cannot make judgments in the medical field. For example, Laetrile treatments are deductible if the taxpayer receives them legally.

• Over a two-year period, an ailing taxpayer and his wife consumed $2,700 worth of vitamins under their doctor's prescription. The IRS said that the vitamins were not deductible medical expenses. Tax Court: The IRS was wrong. Where a doctor prescribes vitamins to treat specific ailments, those vitamins fall within the definition of medical expenses.

• Deductions for nondependents are sometimes possible. How it works: The daughter of a highly paid executive ran up medical bills of more than $5,000. She married later that year and filed a joint return with her husband. Nevertheless, her father was allowed to deduct the cost of treatment on his return for the year, even though the daughter didn't qualify as a dependent.

Education

The IRS draws a hard line on deductibility of special schooling for children with medical problems. Not deductible: The cost of attending a school with smaller classes, even for a child with hearing or sight problems. To be eligible to make such a claim, the school would have to offer special programs for the children with specific disabilities. Deductible: The full cost of sending a child to a boarding school equipped to handle deaf children with emotional problems. Not deductible: Extra costs, including travel, claimed by a parent who sent his deaf child to a distant public school that was better equipped than the local public school to handle such students.

Special care for the handicapped may be deductible, however. An eight-year-old child was blind, retarded, and asthmatic, and required constant care and attention. The child lived with an attendant who was paid $400 a week, plus $60 for the child's food and clothing. IRS ruling: The entire amount was deductible, except for the clothing costs not related to medical care.

Source: Sidney Kess, tax partner, Peat Marwick Main & Co., 55 E. 52 St., New York 10055.

Neglected Medical Deductions

• You can deduct medical bills paid for another person, provided that you paid more than half that person's support in either the year the bills were run up or the year they were paid. A similar rule applies to married couples. You can deduct bills paid now for a former spouse, so long as you were married when the bills were incurred.

• A transplant donor can deduct surgical, hospital, and laboratory costs and transportation expenses. So can a prospective donor, even if found to be unacceptable. If the recipient pays the expenses, the recipient gets the deduction.

• Removing lead-based paint and covering areas within a child's reach with wallboard, to help prevent and cure further lead poisoning, are deductible expenses. But paint removal and wallboard for areas beyond the reach of the child are not—nor is the cost of repainting.

• A clarinet and lessons are deductible medical expenses when prescribed to cure teeth defects.

• A hypoglycemia patient was put on a special diet requiring six to eight small, high-protein meals daily. The Tax Court allowed a deduction of 30% of her grocery bills—the amount spent in excess of the cost of her normal diet.

• A taxpayer who was given power of attorney over his mother's bank account had all of her funds deposited into his own account. He used the funds for her support and claimed her medical expenses on his return. The IRS and the Tax Court claimed that he shouldn't be allowed the deduction because the money belonged to his mother. Court of Appeals: For the son. His mother had made a gift under state law, and the money belonged to him.

• Other deductibles: Birth-control pills and other prescription drugs, face lifts, hair transplants, vasectomies, legal abortions.

Tax Breaks for the Handicapped

The Tax Reform Act permanently restored the deduction for expenses incurred to make life easier for the disabled. Taxpayers who furnish special parking spaces for the physically handicapped (ramps, wider doorways, enlarged bathroom spaces, etc.) can deduct up to $35,000 a year of the construction costs.

Another break: Structural changes that physically handicapped individuals make to their houses automatically qualify as a deductible medical expense. And since the kinds of changes handicapped persons would make to houses do not normally increase their value, the cost is usually fully deductible as a medical expense. There is no increase in the property's value to be subtracted from the cost of the home improvement.

Medical Deductions for Homeowners

You may be able to deduct at least part of the cost of capital improvements you make to your home for medical reasons. Of course, you must be able to prove that you have a medical reason for making the improvement.

Your deduction will be limited to the cost of the improvement minus any increase in the value of your property that may result from it. To determine the value, have the property assessed before and after the improvement. (The appraisal fees are deductible.) Moreover, you can only deduct that portion of your total medical expenses for the year that exceeds 7½% of your adjusted gross income.

Examples of deductible medical home improvements:

• An elevator installed for a person with a heart condition.

• Central air conditioning when a member of the family suffers from a respiratory ailment.

• A swimming pool installed after a doctor advises swimming as therapy for an illness or handicap and public swimming facilities are not accessible.

The Best Shelter You'll Ever Have

The best tax shelter you'll ever have is very likely to be your own home. The major costs of carrying a house as an investment—mortgage interest and property taxes—are tax-deductible. And the appreciation in the property's value continues to qualify for a number of very special tax breaks:

• Tax on the gain from the sale of a residence is deferred, provided you buy another, more expensive, residence within two years of the sale.

• Up to $125,000 of gain can be permanently excluded from tax if you're age 55 or older when you sell your house.

• The entire appreciation in value escapes income tax if you own the house when you die (although it may be subject to estate tax). For income tax purposes your beneficiaries inherit the place at what is called its "stepped-up basis." They inherit the property at its value on the date of your death, and income tax on the appreciation is forgiven. If your beneficiaries later sell the house, only the difference between the selling price and the date-of-death value is taxed.

To make the most of homeowner's tax breaks:

Let your beneficiaries inherit the house. Many elderly people sell their houses to their children for $1 to keep the property out of their estate. Trap: The IRS treats these deals as gifts of property rather than sales. And because it is a gift, the children assume the tax cost the parents had in the house. When the children sell the house they have to pay income tax on the full appreciation in value.

Better way: Let the children inherit the house. That gives them a stepped-up, date-of-death basis, and income tax is forgiven on the appreciation.

Another problem with $1 sales to children: Depreciation deductions are severely limited if the children decide to rent the house back to the parents. The depreciation is not based on the property's current value but on the parents' tax basis in it.

Buy your parents' home and rent it back to them. This transaction will convert payments that you make toward your parents' support into a perfectly legal tax shelter. How it works: Buy the house from your parents on the installment method, making monthly payments on the purchase price, then rent it back to them at fair market rent. Make the installment payments equal to the rent plus the amount you had been giving for support.

The rent you receive from your parents is sheltered from tax by depreciation deductions, property taxes, upkeep, etc. And if the write-offs exceed the rent—and your adjusted gross income is under $100,000—you may deduct up to $25,000 of losses against your salary and other taxable income. (If your AGI is between $100,000 and $150,000, you may deduct some of your losses against taxable income.) Additional benefit: Your parents' gain on the sale may be tax-free because of the $125,000 exclusion.

Buy a house or an apartment for a college-age child who is living in another city while attending school. Charge the child a fair rent and rent extra space to other students. Now you own rental property and you get all the tax-shelter benefits it produces—you can write off up to $25,000 of losses on the property if your AGI is under $100,000. Bonus: You will have an attractive investment that will appreciate in value while your child is going to school.

Take back a note or a mortgage if you sell the house when you are under 55 and do not intend to reinvest the proceeds in another house. This will defer tax on a portion of your gain (the portion that relates to the amount of money you did not receive immediately because you took a mortgage back). You only pay tax on the gain as you collect principal payments under the mortgage. (A 10-year mortgage would spread the tax on your gain over 10 years.) Bonus: You collect interest on the full mortgage principal.

Take out your own mortgage on the house, rent it out, and move into a rented apartment. You might do this to keep the appreciation value of the house. (You can use the mortgage proceeds for investment.) The rent income you receive will be offset by mortgage interest and depreciation deductions. If your AGI is less than $100,000, you can write off losses of up to $25,000. You don't have to pay any tax on the gain—since you haven't sold the house.

You can still qualify for the $125,000 lifetime exclusion if you sell the house within two years and are over 55 at the time. (The house qualifies for the exclusion if you owned and lived in it as your principal home for at least three years out of the five-year period ending on the date of the sale.)

Convert nondeductible interest payments into deductible interest. Aim: To increase mortgage interest, which is deductible, and decrease other interest that is not deductible. The Tax Reform Act eliminates deductions for interest paid on personal loans, car loans, credit-card balances, etc. And it limits deductions for investment interest to the amount of investment income you earn during the year. But the law permits full deductions for mortgage interest on your house and on one second home. Limit: The mortgage can't exceed $1 million in acquisition debt (borrowed to buy, build, or improve the residence) plus $100,000 in home equity debt (borrowed for any purpose).

The dollar limits don't apply to mortgages taken out before October 14, 1987, provided the mortgage doesn't exceed the current market value of the home.

Source: Edward Mendlowitz, partner, Siegel, Mendlowitz & Rich, CPAs, 310 Madison Ave., New York 10017.

Homeowners' Tax Breaks

For the alert taxpayer, the family home can be a major source of tax savings. Federal tax law is studded with provisions that encourage and enhance home ownership, as opposed to other forms of investment.

• Mortgage points. For borrowers other than homeowners, mortgage points (a prepayment of interest represented by a percentage of the loan) have to be capitalized and deducted over the life of the loan. But points charged on money borrowed to buy or improve a principal residence are fully deductible by homeowners in the year they're paid. The points must be paid out of the homeowner's own funds and not simply deducted by the lender from the loan proceeds.

Warning: Pay the points by separate check. When negotiating a mortgage for a new house, make sure you tell the bank you intend to do this. If you don't tell them, they'll automatically take the points out of the funding, and you'll lose the big up-front tax deduction you're entitled to.

• The glories of giving. Homeowners who take advantage of a technique known as deferred giving can get a large immediate income tax deduction that will produce cash flow now without giving up their right to live in the house. How it works: The owners, a husband and wife, say, give what is called remainder interest in their house to charity. This is the right the charity has to take over the house on the owners' death. But the owners reserve the right to live in the house until the survivor of them dies. The owners get a current charitable deduction for the value of the charity's interest. This is computed from IRS tables and depends on how long the charity is expected to wait before taking over the house.

• Joint property ownership. The tax law encourages couples to own the family home in the name of the spouse most likely to die first. Statistically, that's the husband.

The unlimited marital deduction means that the first spouse to die can leave the house to the surviving spouse without incurring any tax at all on his death. Yet the property will get a stepped-up tax basis (its cost for tax purposes) to the fair market value at the date of death. No estate tax will have to be paid on the house's appreciated value. When the surviving spouse sells, since she inherited the house at the increased value, the gains tax she will have to pay will be reduced. If the house remains in joint ownership, the widow's tax on sale will be much higher.

Source: Ivan Faggen, a tax partner with Arthur Andersen & Co., in charge of the Tax Division for the South Florida offices, 1 Biscayne Tower, Suite 2100, Miami 33131. Mr. Faggen is coauthor of *Federal Taxes Affecting Real Estate,* published by Mathew Bender.

Home Improvements That Provide Big Tax Savings

It has always been important to keep careful records of home improvements. The cost of capital improvements—even small ones—increases your tax basis in the house so that when you eventually sell the place, your taxable gain is lower.

Caution: Keep invoices and contracts that specify the work done—canceled checks may not be enough to convince the IRS that the money was spent on legitimate improvements.

Improvements Versus Repairs

As a general rule, additions and improvements will be included in your tax basis if they are intended to be permanent. Repairs and maintenancc, on the other hand (repainting, replastering, fixing leaks, and the like), are not included in basis. Fine line: The distinction between an improvement and a repair is not always clear. For example, the cost of painting a room for the first time would be an improvement, but the cost of repainting that room would be a repair.

Often the deciding factor for including an item in basis is whether it can be removed if the home is sold. For example, a bookcase unit that is built into a wall would be included in basis. But a freestanding bookcase that could be taken with you if you moved could not be included.

Checklist of costs that will generally be included in basis, by category:

• Appliances, major household: Clothes drier, freezer, room air conditioner, stove, washing machine—provided they will be sold with the house and not removed.

• Bathrooms: Bathtub sliding doors, faucets, medicine cabinets, mirrors, shower controls, toilets, towel racks, etc.

• Building improvements: New siding, deck, fireplace, mantel, garage, gutters, drainpipes, porch, screen and storm doors, tool shed, new roof or extensive improvements, termite inspection, waterproofing.

• Communications: Call bells, chimes, fire or burglar alarms, intercoms, cable installation, permanent telephone outlets.

• Electricity and lighting: Replacement of fuses with circuit breakers, floodlights, lighting fixtures, rooftop TV antenna and wiring.

• Flooring: Wall-to-wall carpeting, tiles, linoleum, wood floors.

• Furniture and fixtures: Built-in bookcases, built-in cabinets, closet shelves, curtains and drapes (which are not removed when the house is sold).

• Garden, grounds, outdoor additions: Barbecue pit, birdbath, fences and gates, greenhouse, landscaping, mailbox, swimming pool, terraces and patios, trees and shrubs, underground sprinkler system.

• Kitchen: Built-in dishwasher, garbage disposal, range hood, countertops, etc.

• Laundry: Laundry tub, laundry chute, ventilator.

• Mechanical equipment: Attic fan, central air conditioner, furnace, hot-water heater, radiators.

• Paving: Blacktop or gravel driveway, cement walks and steps.

• Plumbing and sanitation: Copper tubing, sump pump, water pipes, water supply system, septic system.

• Renovation: Conversion of unfinished basement or attic into areas such as recreation rooms or bedrooms.

• Walls and ceilings: Insulation, wallpapering (first time only), wood paneling.

• Windows and doors: Screens, storm windows and doors, weather stripping.

If you have a question about what qualifies, call your tax adviser.

Source: Lawrence M. Axelrod, partner, and Richard A. Bockman, supervisor, in the Washington office, Touche Ross, Washington Service Center, 1900 M St. NW, Washington, DC 20036.

Your Vacation Home

Owning a vacation home may no longer be considered one of the best investment strategies around: Advantageous tax write-offs may be limited in their application by the new passive activity rules. But the news isn't all bad.

A choice now needs to be made as to whether the vacation home is to be treated as either rental real estate or as a second residence. For the taxpayer to classify the vacation home as a second residence, the extent of personal usage must be greater than the greater of 14 days or 10% of the number of days actually rented. Losses in excess of rental income are never deductible. Disallowed losses cannot be carried over to succeeding taxable years. However, mortgage interest and real estate taxes are deductible without limit. Real property which is neither rented nor occupied by the owner during a year may be claimed as a second residence.

To be considered rental real estate, the taxpayer must own 10% or more interest in such property, actively participate in its operation, and the amount of personal usage must be less than the greater of 14 days or 10% of days actually rented. Active participation requires the taxpayer or spouse to participate in a bona fide sense. For example, management decisions which involve approving tenants, lease terms, and repairs would be sufficient to satisfy the active participation requirement.

Passive-activity loss limitations apply to the vacation home rental. Losses (including interest expense) incurred through such rental property are added to other passive losses and are only deductible against passive income from that or another passive activity. Any losses not allowed in one tax year may be carried over indefinitely to succeeding tax years, subject to the income limitation. Upon a taxable disposition of the specific activity property, previously disallowed losses from that activity are allowed in full. In a case where net passive income exists, passive activity credits may be applied exclusively to the amount of tax attributable to such passive income.

There is some relief for an individual who actively participates in rental real estate activity. The taxpayer can offset nonpassive income with up to $25,000 of losses and credits (in deductible equivalents) from "active" real estate interests. The deduction equivalent of credits is the amount that, if allowed as a deduction, would reduce tax by an amount equal to the credit. The $25,000 relief provision is phased out by 50% of adjusted gross income between $100,000 and $150,000 without regard to the IRA deduction, any net passive losses, and taxable Social Security benefits.

In making the choice between a second residence or rental real estate, the length of time the property is to be held should be a consideration. Keeping the home long-term as a second residence would entitle the taxpayer to continuous deductions for mortgage interest and real estate taxes, but other expenses might never be deductible. On the other hand, if the property is kept short-term, as rental real estate, the taxpayer may suspend any losses until the time of sale, whereby all passive disallowed losses are allowed in full.

Source: Thomas L. LoCicero, former IRS branch manager and presently senior tax manager and executive tax-planning specialist with the firm of Deloitte Haskins & Sells, 1 World Trade Center, New York 10048.

Traps in Owning Vacation Property

Many people have invested in vacation properties that are leased out to others during the year. Examples: An apartment at a ski resort, or a beachfront cottage. Danger: Such investors may fall into a number of traps set by the Tax Reform Act.

Trap: Mortgage interest on such a property is no longer automatically deductible. Generally, the interest is deductible only if, after taking taxes and casualty losses into account, the rental activity results in a profit. If the property generates a loss during the year, your deduction for the loss (including interest costs) is limited to $25,000. Even this deduction is cut back for persons with adjusted gross income exceeding $100,000, and eliminated for persons with AGI over $150,000.

Trap: If the average stay in your leased-out property is less than 30 days, transient rental rules may apply. If these rules do apply, you can claim no losses incurred by the property unless you manage it yourself and provide substantial services. Thus, if you hire someone else to manage the property for you (as is typically the case), you get no loss deduction.

Ways around these traps:

• Consider increasing your personal use of

the vacation property. Under old law, people minimized personal use of vacation property to maximize business deductions. But if tax reform's passive loss rules cut your business deductions, you may want the property to qualify as a second residence to obtain full mortgage interest deductions that would otherwise be limited. Rule: A property generally qualifies as a residence if you use it during the year for more than the greater of 14 days, or 10% of the days you've rented it to outsiders. But, then other deductions are limited to net rental income after the interest, taxes, and casualty loss deductions.

• Lease out the property for periods that are longer than 30 days to avoid the deduction limits that are imposed on properties used for transient lodging.

Source: Thomas P. Ochsenschlager, partner, Grant Thornton, CPAs, 1850 M St. NW, Washington, DC 20036.

Tax Loopholes for Salaried Executives

One of the major income tax problems facing salaried executives is having to pay taxes currently on their salaries. Generally, executives will be better off financially if a portion of those taxes can be deferred until a later date. If your employer will cooperate, there are various methods available to structure compensation arrangements to minimize their tax impact. These generally involve the use of noncash compensation arrangements or unfunded deferred compensation arrangements.

Caution: Many experts are wary of deferred compensation arrangements because they expect tax rates to rise sharply in the future. Result: The compensation you defer will be taxed at a higher rate than if you received it now.

Cash must be included in income in the year received, but this is not always the rule for noncash compensation. There are two common noncash arrangements that can defer income significantly: Nonstatutory stock options and restricted property.

Some corporations provide executives with compensatory nonqualified stock options, if permitted by state corporate law. These are stock options granted to an individual for services rendered. Such options differ from incentive stock options, which are a form of statutory stock options. In general, the compensatory portion of the nonqualified options is not included in income until the options are exercised. And, when income finally is recognized, the only amount that constitutes ordinary income is the excess of the fair market value of the stock at the date of exercise over the option price.

Corporations also have provided executives with noncash compensation in the form of "restricted property." Restricted property is property received for services, such as stock, which is not freely transferable and is subject to a substantial risk of forfeiture. For example, a corporation may stipulate that stock transferred to executives is subject to forfeiture if the executives choose not to serve out their terms of office and leave the corporation. Further, if the sale of stock at a profit could subject an executive to suit under section 16(b) of the Securities Exchange Act of 1934, the executive's rights in that property are subject to a substantial risk of forfeiture and are not transferable.

The tax consequences associated with receiving restricted property are determined under specific rules. Assume you receive stock which, on the date of issuance, is not freely transferable and is subject to a substantial risk of forfeiture. You may elect to recognize compensation income when the stock is issued—if you do so within 30 days after the stock is issued. Otherwise, compensation income is recognized when the stock becomes transferable or free from risk of forfeiture. The amount of compensation recognized—ordinary income— is equal to the fair market value of the stock on the applicable recognition date less any amount paid for such stock.

Many corporations provide executives the opportunity to defer compensation through the use of an unfunded deferred compensation arrangement. While these arrangements work in various ways, basically executives elect to defer all or part of their salaries, and the corporation agrees to pay deferred amounts in later years. Amounts deferred are not currently taxable to the executives.

For example, an executive might merely accept a reduced amount of cash now in return for the corporation's promise to pay the amount deferred (perhaps with an interest factor) at a later date. As another alternative, the executive might agree to receive a reduced amount of cash now if, in return, the corporation promises to pay a certain amount per year, starting at a set date, for as long as the executive lives. This is an annuity-type deferred compensation arrangement. The corporation generally protects itself by purchasing a commercial annuity with the corporation as beneficiary.

For these arrangements to be effective, the deferred funds cannot be made available to the executives currently. Thus, the corporation generally should not set aside funds specifically for the executives to cover the compensation deferred. This means that, until they receive payment, the executives are unsecured creditors of the corporation. However, there are ways to further assure payment beyond merely relying upon the creditworthiness of the company.

The unfunded arrangement can be coupled with a third-party guarantee. Under such an arrangement, the corporation promises to pay the executive cash in the future. In addition, the executive may obtain a guarantee from a third party (e.g., a surety bond issued by an insurance company) to pay the executive should the company default on its payment. However, if the corporation purchases the third-party guarantee, the premiums will be taxed to the executive.

Many executives are not satisfied with merely having a bare corporate promise to pay in the future. The IRS has allowed a corporation to establish an irrevocable trust to administer the unfunded arrangement. Under the terms of the trust agreement, the trustee will make distributions of the principal and income to the executive or designated beneficiary on the executive's death, disability, retirement, or termination of services, or in the event of financial hardship. But the trust's assets are the corporation's and remain subject to the claims of the corporation's creditors. Further, the executive's interest in the trust may not be assigned, alienated, pledged, attached, or made subject to the executive's creditors.

The IRS has issued private letter rulings approving the third-party guarantee and the irrevocable trust arrangements. While both of the arrangements should continue to work, the IRS may decide to contest them in the future.

Source: David L. Nelson, tax partner in charge of personal financial planning, Ernst & Whinney, 333 Clay St., Suite 3100, Houston, TX 77002.

A Checklist of Deductions for Salaried Executives

Many executives have been duped into believing that they are entitled to few, if any, job-related deductions. Not true! Job-related expenses are deductible as miscellaneous itemized deductions. *Note:* Under tax reform, total miscellaneous deductions must be reduced by 2% of your adjusted gross income. Here's a comprehensive list.

• Dues for professional organizations, associations.

• Professional publications: Periodical subscriptions, journals, books.

• Personal equipment: Attache case, pens and pencils, calculators, diaries.

• Fees for credit card accounts used strictly for business.

• Costs of looking for a new job in your field of work.

• Educational expenses, if incurred for the purpose of maintaining or improving skills needed in your current position or occupation.

The following *unreimbursed* expenses are also deductible, or partially deductible to the extent that they are unreimbursed.

- Cost of fixing up or decorating your office (including perishable items such as flowers).
- Gifts to business associates (limited to $25 per person per year).
- 80% of the cost of entertainment of business associates, people with whom you have business dealings.
- 80% of the cost of entertainment at home, provided the function's primary purpose is business; e.g., if you invite business associates to your daughter's wedding, that expense is not deductible, as the primary purpose of the event is clearly not to discuss business.
- Local transportation (taxis, buses) used in the course of business (but *not* to and from work).
- Use of your own automobile. (The unreimbursed portion is deductible.)
- Business use of pay phones and home phone.
- Unreimbursed cost of stationery, office supplies, photocopies, photography, etc., used in connection with your work.
- Unreimbursed business transportation (air fares, cabs, etc.).
- Lodging and living expenses on a business trip, including getting your suit pressed, your shoes shined, tipping the doorman or bellhop, etc., *plus* 80% of the cost of food and drink.

Source: Edward Mendlowitz, partner, Siegel, Mendlowitz & Rich, CPAs, 310 Madison Ave., New York 10017.

Bigger and Better Business Deductions on Personal Tax Returns

For executives who want to claim business deductions on their personal returns, it's more important than ever to seek out every deduction opportunity. That's because under tax reform, the deduction for employee business expenses is allowed only to the extent that such costs exceed 2% of adjusted gross income. An executive who overlooks a deductible item and fails to reach the 2% limit will get no deduction at all.

There are many unusual and unexpected deductions available to executives. Here's a rundown of what's been allowed.

Legal Bills

Legal costs are deductible when they are job-related, even for those accused of a criminal act and convicted; in fact, business expense deductions have been allowed even when the business itself was illegal:

- Executive was sued for an accounting by investors who accused him of misappropriating company funds.
Harold K. Hochschild, 161 F2d 817.

- Company president was sued by a shareholder for making fraudulent misrepresentations.
Bernard A. Mitchell, 408 F2d 435.

- Company officer became involved in a dispute concerning control of a family business, and some of the shareholders tried to remove him from his job.
Stanley Waldheim, 25 TC 839.

- President of a company was charged with criminal antitrust violations. His legal fees were deductible even though he was sent to jail.
Central Coat, Apron and Linen, 298 F Supp 1201.

- Purchasing agent was convicted of extortion in a kickback scheme. His bail bond fees were deductible as well.
Bernard G. Murphy, TC Memo 1980-25.

- Government successfully held a corporate officer liable for the company's income tax evasion.
Revenue Ruling 68-662.

- Electronics expert, who was involved with organized crime, was accused of installing illegal wiretaps.
Bernard B. Spindel, TC Memo 1965-164.

Deductible Damages

When an executive *loses* a case that arises

69

from business, he may even be able to deduct the damages that he has to pay:

- Company president who was found to have defrauded investors was allowed to deduct his payment of damages, because he commited the fraud to further the company's interests.

C.A. Ostrum, 77 TC 608.

- When an auto accident occurred while a person was driving on the job, the driver could deduct the resulting damages as being business-related.

Harold Dancer, 73 TC 1103.

Plaintiffs—Right or Wrong

Persons who bring suits as plaintiffs may also be able to deduct legal costs:

- Job candidate sued to be reinstated at the top of the candidate list, which would have enabled him to fill a vacancy.

Caruso, 236 F Supp 88.

- An executive was summarily replaced, given a desk in an isolated location, and paid to do nothing. He sued his employer, claiming to be a victim of bias. The IRS ruled the executive could deduct the cost of the lawsuit as a business expense, even though he lost the case.

IRS Letter Ruling 8712009.

- Person sued to prevent publication of an article. He was entitled to the deduction even though he lost his case and the article was ruled not libelous. The fact that he thought the article could hurt his business reputation was enough to justify the deduction.

J. Raymond Dyer, 36 TC 456.

Charity and Business

It's sometimes possible to get around the charitable contribution deduction limits (50% of AGI on a personal return, 10% of AGI on a corporate return) and boost business deductions by claiming payments made to charity as a business expense:

- Payments were made to a charity in order to secure the goodwill of a customer who was heading its fund-raising drive.

Adeline Marcelle, 8 AFTR2d 5344.

- Contributions were made to a local organization that was fighting pollution. The pol-

lution had hurt tourism and thus hurt the donor's business.

Revenue Ruling 73-113.

- Travel agent made large contributions to charities that booked trips through her agency.

Sarah Marquis, 49 TC 695.

- Person donated turkeys and entertainment tickets to the poor through a Lions Club, which was not a qualified charity. The donations were intended to obtain favorable publicity for the taxpayer's business.

William H. Limerick, TC Memo 6/8/50.

For the Unemployed

Business expense deductions have been allowed even for people who are unemployed. That's because, once you're in business, the IRS considers that you remain in business through any period of temporary unemployment. Unemployment is generally considered temporary if it lasts for less than one year, though the specific facts of the case may lead to a different conclusion. Business expense deductions were allowed when:

- Unemployed salesman continued to entertain persons who had been customers in the past. The salesman was looking for a new job, and it was important that he retain the customers' goodwill.

Harold Haft, 40 TC 2.

- Business manager quit his job and deducted the cost of taking a full-time MBA program. On getting his degree, he took another management job with another firm.

Steven G. Sherman, TC Memo 1977-301.

- Unemployed person looked for a new job in the same line of work as his old one. All the costs of the job search were deductible, including the cost of travel, printing and mailing resumes, taking out newspaper advertisements, getting career counseling, and hiring executive recruiters.

Revenue Ruling 75-120.

Home Deductions

Unique home deductions were allowed when:

- Person who managed a family business was required to be on the premises around the clock to handle operations. He incorporated the business and then signed an employment contract under which the company provided him with a house and paid his utility bills. Since the Tax Code says that lodging given to an employee for the benefit of an employer is tax-exempt, he was able to take the house and utility payments tax-free. And the company got to deduct the expense payments and depreciate the home.

Jim Grant Farms, TC Memo 1985-174.

• Executive owned vacation property on which he had a vacation home. He further improved the property by building a separate office on it. Because the office was a separate structure it did not fall under normal home-office rules, and the executive was able to fully depreciate it and to deduct related costs.

Ben W. Heineman, 82 TC 538.

Travel Deductions

Employee travel deductions were upheld when:

• Salesman had to cover the entire state of Ohio and was not reimbursed for his meals, lodging, or auto costs by his company. He had receipts, canceled checks, and notes showing how much he spent on his trips, but did not have records indicating the business purpose of specific expenditures. The trips themselves were clearly business-motivated, so the expenses incurred on them were business-related and deductible.

Michael J. Bernard, Cl Ct, No. 205-84T.

• A taxpayer regularly drove between several job sites for business, but didn't keep good records. The IRS disallowed his deduction for auto costs. Tax Court: It was clear that it was necessary to drive between these sites for work. Further, the cost could be estimated by measuring the distance between work sites and the number of trips he had to make. The taxpayer, therefore, was entitled to a deduction, but because he didn't have any records of his travels, the court allowed him only the minimum deduction that was reasonable under the circumstances.

Rudolph J. Barnes, TC Memo 1986-585.

• Employer had a formal policy of reimbursing workers for job-related expenses. However, the taxpayer's boss had a personal policy of not approving reimbursements for car expenses.

The taxpayer didn't want to get into trouble by going over his boss's head, so he deducted his car costs on his own return. Reimbursable expenses normally aren't deductible, but here there was a good business reason for not asking for reimbursement. Thus the car costs were ruled deductible.

George Kessler, TC Memo 1985-254.

Personal Deductions

Business expense deductions were allowed for:

• Office furnishings bought by an executive with his own funds in order to maintain his image as a successful district sales manager.

Leroy Gillis, TC Memo 1973-96.

• The cost of enrolling in an advanced degree program concentrating on taxes and financial planning, even though the financial consultant involved was not required to take the courses for work. The education was job-related because it enhanced the skills used by the consultant in his current job.

IRS Letter Ruling 8706048.

• Briefcase bought for use on the job.

Stanley Bailey, TC Memo 1971-107.

• Calculator used by a salesman for business.

Robert G. Galazin, TC Memo 1979-206.

• Office supplies that were bought by an insurance salesman.

George Blood Enterprises, TC Memo 1976-102.

• Part of the basic charge for a home phone, when an employee had to be reachable at home, even though he would have had a phone anyway.

Robert H. Lee, TC Memo 1960-58.

• Medical checkups, when proof of fitness was a job requirement.

Revenue Ruling 58-382.

Better Than a Raise

Employee business expenses, along with the cost of investment advice, tax preparation fees, and other miscellaneous items (such as the cost of subscribing to business or investment publications) are deductible, under tax reform, only to the extent that their total exceeds 2% of adjusted gross income. Thus a person with adjusted gross income of $50,000 can get no deduction for the first $1,000 worth of such items.

When executives have large unreimbursed business expenses, they may do better by negotiating with their employers for an increase in their reimbursements instead of a raise. If the executive gets a raise, it will be taxed, while the executive will lose at least part of the deduction for the unreimbursed expenses. On the other hand, an increase in reimbursements will be tax-free and completely cover the cost of expenses.

Deducting a Company Car— And Chauffeur

The use of a company car can be a valuable fringe benefit. The expenses of the car, including depreciation, are deductible by the corporation and not taxable to the shareholder-employee if it is used exclusively on company business.

One way to get around the rules taxing employees for personal use of company-owned automobiles is to have a second car available for personal use. Agents are reporting cases of taxpayers buying small used cars to substantiate the fact that they have another car available for weekend and after-hours use.

If a shareholder-executive is given the use of two cars, and it is clear that one of them is being used by a spouse for nonbusiness purposes, the employee will be taxed on the value of the use of the car. But the tax liability will be less than the cost of renting a car, and most likely less than it would cost to buy, finance, and maintain the car. If the extra car is treated as extra compensation, the attending expenses are deductible by the corporation as compensation,

subject to the overall limitation of reasonableness. If treated as dividend income to the shareholder, it is not deductible by the corporation.

The cost of a chauffeur may be deductible by the corporation and not taxable to the shareholder-employee if deemed an "ordinary and necessary expense," sometimes translated as "appropriate and helpful."

Commuting Costs Can Be Deductible

Most commuting expenses aren't deductible. But if a person works at least two jobs in the same day, the cost of traveling from the first job to the second job is deductible as a business expense to the extent that when added to all your other business expenses, they exceed 2% of your adjusted gross income. (You still can't deduct travel from home to your first job or from your second job back home.)

Similarly, customer visits made on your way to work are partially tax deductible. The deductible portion: The distance between the customer's place of business and your office (or the next customer, etc.).

Job-Hunting Expenses (Whether You Get the Job Or Not)

If you change jobs, keep track of your job-hunting expenses. The costs of looking for a new job in your present line of work are tax deductible (subject to the 2% of adjusted gross income limit on miscellaneous deductions), even if you don't get a new job. However, you can't deduct expenses of looking for a new job in a new trade or business even if you get the job.

Deductible job-hunting expenses include:

• Fees paid to employment agencies and executive recruiters.

• Cost of typing, printing, and mailing resumes to prospective employers.

• Career counseling to improve your position in your present trade.

• Advertising for a new job in your present field.

• Cab fares to job interviews, car expenses, and other transportation costs.

• Phone calls to prospective employers.

• Newspapers and business publications that you buy for employment ads.

• Entertainment expenses directly related to your job search.

• Out-of-town travel expenses, including lodging, local transportation, and 80% of the cost of meals, if the trip is primarily to look for a new job. If the main purpose of the trip is personal, your travel costs are not deductible. But you can deduct out-of-pocket job-hunting expenses at your destination.

• The cost of drumming up business by a taxpayer who is an employee but who wants to become self-employed in the same trade has been held by the Tax Court to be deductible.* The court disagreed with the IRS's position that self-employment in a person's present line of work is really a new job.

Howard L. Cornutt, TC Memo 1983-24.

Tax-Free Severance Pay

When top executives lose their jobs, it is important that any severance or termination payments receive the most favorable tax treatment possible. Key: Severance pay is taxable as ordinary salary. But payments made to compensate ex-employees for damages are tax-free.

Assuming they have grounds to sue, dismissed employees can bring suit against their former employers in court, or before a federal agency (such as the Equal Employment Opportunity Commission), alleging that they suffered damages as a result of wrongful dismissal. (The dismissals may have harmed their business or personal reputations, caused embarrassment, or resulted in physical or emotional harm.)

The objective: A settlement can be reached with the company that allocates part of the termination payment as compensation for harm. What would have been taxable severance pay is converted into tax-free damages. Extra benefit: The company can profit from this sort of agreement as well. Since it is paying its former employee in tax-free dollars, it may be able to negotiate a smaller settlement that gives the employee more in the end.

Deducting Vacation Costs as a Business Expense

Combining a tax-deductible business trip with a short vacation, perhaps with a spouse and family, can be quite attractive. It is important to keep expense categories straight, since different tests apply for deductibility.

You can deduct the cost of traveling in the US for business or professional purposes. But you must be able to show that the primary purpose of the trip was business. This does not mean that you cannot combine business with pleasure, only that the primary purpose is business. Best way to satisfy the IRS: Prove that more than half of your time at the destination was spent on business.

The all-or-nothing test for travel: Your transportation expenses are either fully deductible to the extent they exceed 2% of your adjusted gross income (when added together with your other business expenses because they meet the test), or they cannot be deducted at all. On the other hand, meal and entertainment expenses at your destination are 80% deductible and should be separated into business and nonbusiness categories.

Do not count on deducting the full cost of a trip with your spouse. It is not enough for the IRS that a spouse's presence is a big help to you. Only your expenses at the meeting site are deductible, but you are not limited to half of the total costs there. You can still deduct the full amount of what it would cost you to attend alone at the single-room hotel rate, for instance. You can deduct the full cost of services where your spouse's presence does not boost the charge, say, for the taxi from the airport. If you drive to the meeting site, you can deduct almost the full transportation cost. If you fly or take the train, only your ticket is deductible.

For business-vacation combinations of seven days or less to spots outside the US, the regular rules on business travel, explained above, apply. But if you are gone more than seven days and you spend more than 25% of your total time vacationing, you lose a deduction for the portion of your transportation costs equal to the number of nonbusiness days divided by the total number of days outside the US.

Ship travel can be an asset on a combined business-vacation trip. Reason: Days spent in transit count as business days in the allocations formula.

The rules are tighter for conventions outside the North American area. No costs can be deducted for such a business meeting unless the IRS can be convinced that the selection of the meeting site is reasonable. (In practice, it probably is better to be able to prove that it is more reasonable to hold the convention at the foreign site than in the US.)

No deduction is permitted for a convention or related expenses incurred in connection with investments, financial planning, or income-producing activities.

Both directly related and associated entertainment expenses are 80% deductible on a working vacation, if you follow the rules. Associated entertainment expenses cover nights on the town, box seats at a game, etc. A specific business discussion must occur before or after the entertainment.

Business gifts are deductible, subject to a $25 limit. So if you give theater tickets worth more than $25 to a client, you can't deduct the excess. Suggestion: Go to the show with the client, and you can write off the whole evening as business entertainment.

Good records are essential to justify your deductions. Keep a diary in which you record expenses and their business purpose. You must also keep receipts for expenses of $25 or more. The diary alone is sufficient proof for smaller amounts.

Source: Edward Mendlowitz, partner, Siegel, Mendlowitz & Rich, CPAs, 310 Madison Ave., New York 10017, and author of *Successful Tax Planning*, published by Boardroom Books.

Imaginative Travel Deductions

Traveling for Education

Traveling costs to educational seminars are still deductible if you are in the trade or business that is the subject of the seminar. The cost of attending a general seminar on how to improve your dealings with your broker is not deductible, even if you have many investments. But stockbrokers who attend the same seminar would be entitled to a deduction because that's their trade or business.

Teachers can no longer deduct the cost of travel to a foreign country to enhance their general understanding of the culture and language of that country. Before tax reform, this expense was deductible for teachers who wished to improve their teaching skills.

Traveling for Charity

You can deduct the cost of traveling with a charitable group if you serve as an escort or chaperone. You must have some kind of responsibility for the group, such as helping the handicapped to travel or assisting as a Scout leader where you are assigned the task of supervising a specific number of children in the group.

All the related travel costs can be taken as a charitable deduction, such as the cost of your meals (100% is deductible for charity) while away from home, lodging, and other out-of-pocket costs. However, no deductions are permitted for family members who accompany you.

Traveling for Medical Reasons

If you must travel for medical reasons you can deduct the cost of getting there. In addition, deductions can be taken if travel expenses are incurred for a traveling companion needed for the trip. This could happen where the person getting the medical treatment is too ill or too young to travel the distance alone.

However, meals are not deductible during your medical stay. Lodging expenses are limited to $50 per night if it is absolutely essential that you stay overnight to receive the medical treatment.

Note: Tax reform has greatly limited medical expense deductions by allowing them only to the extent they exceed 7.5% of your adjusted gross income.

Source: David S. Rhine, tax partner, Seidman & Seidman/BDO, 15 Columbus Circle, New York 10023.

Deduction Checklist for Business Owners

More than ever, the best source of tax breaks is running your own business. Business owner's tax advantages:

• Fully deductible business expenses. For the self-employed, business expenses are deductible in full directly from gross income.

• Full home-office expense write-off. If you run a business from your home, you may deduct not only property taxes and mortgage interest, but also a percentage of depreciation, utilities, insurance, repairs, and any other costs. Your home-office deductions may *not* exceed your net income from the business. You can't use them to show a tax loss. However, you can carry over any unused deductions and take them in future years, when you have income from the business.

• Greater tax-deferred retirement savings. Tax reform severely limited IRAs and capped 401(k) contributions at $7,000 a year. But Keogh plans for the self-employed were left practically untouched.

Potential drawback: If you have employees, you must include them in your plan on a nondiscriminatory basis.

• Hiring your kids. Their wages are deductible business expenses. And you may still claim them as dependents. Bonus: children under 18 who work for a parent are exempt from Social Security tax. (The exemption doesn't apply if the parent's business is incorporated.)

Caution: Kids must perform actual services for reasonable compensation. Phony jobs and inflated wages don't stand up to IRS scrutiny.

• Hiring your spouse. Your spouse may participate in any retirement plans that you have for employees (pension, 401(k), etc.). In some cases he or she may qualify for deductible IRA contributions. Finally, if your spouse accompanies you on a business trip as an assistant or colleague, you may write off travel expenses for both of you.

• Timing income. If you use the cash accounting method, you can easily defer income from one year into the next. You just don't send out bills late in the year—you wait until January.

• More deductible transportation expenses. Going to work and coming home are nondeductible commutation expenses. But if you work out of your home, you're already at your place of business when you get up in the morning. So all travel costs are deductible. Justifying transportation deductions is also easier for business owners.

• Fully deductible casualty losses. Business casualty losses (from fire, theft, accident, natural disaster, etc.) may be written off in full against business income.

• Full write-offs for bad debts. Bad business debts may be deducted in full in the year in which they become uncollectible.

• Operating losses. If your business loses money—as many do at first—you may write off the loss against your other income. If the loss exceeds income, you may carry the excess up to three years into the past to get a refund for those years. If there's still any excess loss, you may carry it forward for the next 15 years.

Source: Philip Kimmel, partner, Hertz, Herson & Co., CPAs, 2 Park Ave., New York 10016.

A Sideline Business: The Best Tax Shelter

Even under tax reform the best tax shelter still remains. With it you can generate large paper losses, claim deductions for personal or hobby-like expenses, and legally shift income to your low-tax bracket minor children.

The best tax shelter is a sideline business.

Here's how a sideline business can be used to get big tax-shelter-type deductions, along with winning examples of taxpayers who have already done it.

Income Shifting

Under tax reform, investment income exceeding $1,000 for a child under age 14 is taxed at the rate paid by the child's parents. But this rule does not apply to the earned income of a child.

Result: A child who works for a parent's sideline business can take up to $3,000 tax-free, and earnings in excess of this amount are taxed at the child's own low tax rate. Since the parent deducts the salary paid to the child as a business expense, the family's tax bill is lowered by the difference between the parent's high tax rate and the low or zero rate on the child's salary.

Of course, this income-shifting technique is also available for children over age 14 and other family members. And even greater tax benefits can be obtained when family members use the salary you pay to make deductible IRA retirement contributions, or when the business pays for deductible benefits.

The only rule that governs paying salaries to family members is that they must actually earn their salaries. Salary deductions have been allowed when:

• A business owner hired his wife to act as the company's official hostess.
Clement J. Duffey, 11 AFTR2d 1317.

• The owner of a trailer park paid his children, ages seven to 12, to perform cleaning chores, landscaping, and office work.
Walt Eller, 77 TC 934.

• A doctor paid his four children, ages 13 to 16, to answer telephone calls, take messages, and prepare insurance forms.
James Moriarity, TC Memo 1984-249.

• The owner of a rental property hired his teenage sons to maintain and clean the building.
Charles Tschupp, TC Memo 1963-98.

What Qualifies

A part-time activity can easily qualify as a business. The only requirement is that you operate your activity with the objective of making a profit. You don't actually have to make a profit, nor do you have to expect to make a profit in the near future. Winning examples:

• Eugene Feistman, a probation officer, collected and traded stamps for many years. The Tax Court initially refused to let him deduct his costs, saying his collecting was merely a hobby. So he filed a business registration certificate with the local government, opened an account that let him make sales by charge card, set up an inventory, and started keeping good business records concerning purchases and sales. New ruling: Now Eugene could deduct his costs because he was operating in a businesslike manner. The Tax Court let him deduct $9,000 over two years.
Eugene Feistman, TC Memo 1982-306.

• Gloria Churchman, a housewife, admitted that she painted for pleasure, but she also was able to show that she had made a serious effort to sell her works at shows and galleries. The Tax Court let her deduct her expenses and losses, including the cost of a studio in her home.
Gloria Churchman, 68 TC 696.

• Melvin Nickerson, an executive who lived in the city, bought a farm and began renovating it on weekends. He intended to retire to it in the future. Although Melvin didn't expect to make a profit from the farm for another 10 years, the Court of Appeals let him deduct his renovation costs right away. It said that his expectation of future profits, combined with the real work he put in, sufficed to justify a deduction now.

Melvin Nickerson, 700 F2D 402.

• Bernard Wagner, an accountant, fancied himself a songwriter and music promoter. He hired a band, rehearsed it, booked it, and copyrighted the songs he wrote. Although his chances of success were slight, he intended to succeed, so the Tax Court let him deduct his costs and losses.

Bernard Wagner, TC Memo 1983-606

• J.V. Keenon bought a house, moved into it, then rented an apartment in the house to his own daughter. The Tax Court agreed that he was not in the real estate rental business, so he could deduct depreciation on the rented apartment, along with utilities, insurance, and related expenses. And this was in spite of the fact that he charged his daughter a below-market rent. The court felt that the rent was fair because it's safer to rent to a family member than to a stranger.

J.V. Keenon, TC Memo 1982-144.

Home Deductions

A major benefit of running a sideline business out of your home is the possibility of claiming a home office deduction. This entitles you to deduct expenses that were formerly personal in nature, such as rent, utility, insurance, and maintenance costs attributable to the office. Even better: You can depreciate the part of your home that's used as an office, getting large paper deductions that cost you nothing out-of-pocket.

To qualify for the deduction, you must have a part of your home that's used exclusively for business and is the primary place where you conduct the sideline business. Winning examples:

• A doctor who owned and managed rental properties to get extra income could deduct one bedroom in his two-bedroom apartment as an office.

Edwin R. Cruphey, 73 TC 766.

• A woman who ran a laundromat two hours a day could deduct a home office since she spent more time at home doing paper work for the laundromat than she spent at the laundromat itself.

Sally Meiers, 782 F2d 75.

• A woman who did economic consulting work out of a home office could deduct it even though her husband, a famous newspaper editor, used the same office for nondeductible activities. The Tax Court did not reduce her deduction because her husband shared the office.

Max Frankel, 82 TC 318.

Big Dollar Deductions

Tax reform prohibits taxpayers from offsetting their salary and investment income with losses from businesses in which they participate as passive investors (as shareholders or limited partners without management duties). But if you actively manage your own sideline business, it's still possible to claim big loss deductions. Important: Tax losses do not necessarily mean cash losses. Items such as depreciation on cars, equipment, and real estate can result in deductible tax losses while the business is earning a cash-flow profit.

A sideline business is presumed to have a profit objective if it has reported a profit in three out of five years (two out of seven years for horse breeders). But such a business may be deemed to have a profit objective even after reporting many years of continuous losses. Winning examples:

• A real estate operator tried to develop and market an automatic garage door opener. He was entitled to deduct $355,000 over 11 years, because he had made a sincere effort to sell the door openers.

Frederick A. Purdy, TC Memo 1967-82.

• A horse farm incurred 20 straight years of losses totaling over $700,000. During the next seven years it lost another $119,000, but in two of those years it had profits totaling $17,000. Since the two-out-of-seven-years test had been met, the farm was ruled to be a profit-motivated business and all of its losses were deductible.

Hunter Faulconer, 748 F2d 890.

• A corporate vice president and management expert ran a breeding farm as a sideline and lost $450,000 over 12 years. The loss was deductible because evidence indicated that it often takes eight to 12 years to establish an acceptable bloodline for the animals involved. *Lawrence Appley*, TC Memo 1979-433.

Start-up Tactic

When starting a new sideline business, you can protect your deductions by electing to have the IRS postpone its examination of your business status until after you've been operating for four years (six years in the case of a horse farm). You'll be able to treat your sideline as a business during that period, even if it earns continuous losses. But if you can't demonstrate a profit objective at the end of that period, you'll owe back taxes. Make the election by filing IRS Form 5213, Election to Postpone Determination that Activity is for Profit.

How To Deduct Your Hobby

For your own bottom line, it can make a huge difference whether you operate a hobby as a hobby or a sideline business. As a hobbyist, your tax deductions are pretty much limited to the amount of income the activity generates. But if you run the hobby as a business, all your expenses are deductible to the extent that when they are added to your other business expenses the total exceeds 2% of AGI—even if they exceed business income.

Problem: The distinction between a hobby and a business is very fine. When you deduct losses from a business that the IRS could label as a hobby, you must be able to prove that you intended to make a profit.

Hobby or Business

As far as the IRS is concerned, a business is an activity engaged in for profit. There's no law, however, that says you must actually make a profit. The only rule is that you must intend to make a profit.

Presumption of law that aids taxpayers: If you show a profit in three of any five consecutive years (two out of seven for breeding, showing, training, or racing horses), it is presumed you are engaged in an activity for profit. Although the IRS can challenge the presumption, normally it will not.

Profit Motive

If you don't meet the presumption, the IRS may challenge your deductions as hobby losses. It will be necessary for you to prove your good intentions. Checklist of things you should be prepared to show the IRS if your business losses are challenged:

• You operate in a businesslike manner. Keep accurate books and records.

• You instituted new operating procedures to correct past business practices that resulted in losses.

• You act professionally. Show that you hired or consulted with recognized experts in the field, and that you followed their advice.

• You made a serious effort. Show that you hired qualified people to run your day-to-day operation. Remember, no rule says you must devote 40 hours a week to your sideline business.

• There is a profit potential. Even if your business continually produces losses, you can still prove a profit motive by showing that assets you have acquired are expected to appreciate.

• You have had past successes. It may help establish a profit motive if you show that in the past you were successfully involved in your current activity.

Doing Business

The IRS will look for tangible indications that you have really embarked on a business enterprise. Suggestions:

• Register your business name by filing a "doing business as" statement with your local county clerk.

• Use business cards and stationery.

• Take out a company listing in the Yellow Pages.

• Keep a log of the business contacts you've seen during the year.

• Send promotional mailings to prospective customers.

- Advertise in local papers.
- Set up a business bank account.
- Get a business telephone.
- Buy a postage meter and a copying machine.
- Hire at least some part-time help.

Tougher Questions

The IRS will argue that, since you had other sources of income and could afford to lose money, you could not have had a profit motive. Your defense: Nobody goes into business expecting to lose money. Even with your tax deductions, you would have been better off had you done nothing and never started the venture in the first place.

Suppose your business occasionally generates small amounts of income. You can prove a profit motive if you can also show an opportunity to earn a substantial ultimate profit in a highly speculative business.

If the IRS can show that you derive personal pleasure from your business, it will count this against you. Businesses that involve horse racing, farming, car racing, and antiques are particularly vulnerable to this kind of attack. Don't let the IRS bulldoze you. The courts have consistently held that enjoying what you do is not, by itself, proof that you lack a profit motive.

Source: Randy Bruce Blaustein, Esq., a former IRS agent now with Seigel, Mendlowitz & Rich, CPAs, 310 Madison Ave., New York 10017. He is author of *How to Do Business With the IRS*, published by Prentice-Hall, and of *Tax Shelters: Shrewd Insights*, published by Boardroom Books.

Special Advice for Self-Employeds and Moonlighters

Those already in business for themselves know that the IRS is a reality—and those just starting their own business will soon learn it. The IRS is a partner and overseer and it cannot be ignored. Mistakes are costly. Even if your accountant makes the mistake on your return, you pay. To avoid trouble with the IRS:

- Be prepared to explain your style of living. The IRS knows that it takes time to build a growing business. The IRS also knows that some people fraudulently underreport their income. If the circumstances of your enterprise dictate that you report low income or even a loss, be prepared to answer the question "What did you live on?" Trap: If you are unable to answer to the satisfaction of an IRS examining officer, you may find yourself involved in a costly investigation or be assessed with a heavy tax.

Cost of living for an individual is derived from one or more of the following sources:
Current income.
Borrowing.
Repayment of money lent to others.
Gifts and inheritances.
Support from others.
Accumulated assets (savings accounts, securities, house, car, cash on hand, etc.).
Caution: The source of assets accumulated before you launched your business may also be questioned.

Your accountant will urge you to keep track of business transactions. Equally important is the need to keep track of your personal expenses, including the source of funds for payment of living expenses.

- Keep separate bank accounts for business transactions. This will simplify record keeping. Note: It is inevitable that there will be some cross-flow of funds between business and personal accounts. Pay special attention to documenting this flow of funds. Without adequate documentation the IRS will suspect, and may allege, additional taxable business income.

- Have separate credit cards for business transactions. This too will simplify your record keeping. At times, certain expenditures will be a mixture of business and personal expense. For example, your spouse may accompany you on a business trip. Advice: Keep a diary keyed to your business credit card use and all cash expenditures for business.

The combination of receipts, credit card vouchers, canceled checks, and a diary is strong enough proof to deter the most zealous IRS examiner.

• Have separate equipment, etc., for business use. If the nature of your business requires that you make and receive business calls at home, install a separate telephone for that purpose. If you drive a significant number of business miles, keep a separate automobile for that purpose. If your business requires that you do substantial work at home, set aside a room or area of your home as an office. Furnish the area exclusively with office furniture, equipment, and business materials, and use it exclusively for business purposes.

• Know your tax responsibilities. Even if you leave the matter of taxes largely to your accountant and bookkeeper, take the time and trouble to educate yourself on the subject. The penalties for slipping are prohibitively high. Learn your personal responsibility for income tax, self-employment tax, and estimated tax payments. Then be sure to have some understanding of your responsibility in the area of employment taxes. Helpful: IRS Publication 15, commonly known as Circular E (Employer's Tax Guide), available free of charge from the IRS. You should also be aware of state and local tax requirements.

Caution: In the past, some employers used government trust funds (taxes withheld from employees' wages) to tide the company over periods of weak cash flow. Be advised that the IRS has little patience with such methods. It has an ever-increasing policy of cracking down fast and forcefully on employers who don't follow the letter of the law in handling withheld payroll taxes. If you are in a pinch, ask your accountant to locate an alternate source of funds.

• Keep good records. Your accountant has primary responsibility to provide you with a system that clearly and properly reflects your business income and transactions. A simple method of record keeping that works is one that is organized to reflect tax return items line by line. For example, if you are a sole proprietorship, set up your accounts according to the line items on Form 1040, Schedule C. Mark your checks, credit card receipts, and diary entries with the appropriate type of expense or line number.

For more complex and/or active business enterprises, you would be wise to rely on the expertise of a reputable accountant familiar with your type of business. Expect your accountant to set up a record keeping-system, give business advice, and represent you at the IRS if necessary. It will be money well spent.

Source: George S. Alberts, former head of the Albany and Brooklyn IRS District Offices.

The Home Office

Using a part of your home in your business may enable you to deduct certain expenses if you satisfy specific tests. To take this deduction, that portion of your home must be used exclusively and regularly:

as the principal place of business for any trade or business in which you engage;

as a place to meet or deal with your trade or business; or

in connection with your trade or business, if you are using a separate structure that is not attached to your house or residence.

"Exclusive use" means that you must use that specific part of your home only for the purpose of carrying on your trade or business. Any personal use will prevent you from claiming the deduction. "Regular use" means that you use the exclusive business part of your home on a continuing basis, not just occasionally.

As an employee you must be using your home for the convenience of your employer in addition to satisfying these three tests. Just being helpful to your work will not qualify you for a home office deduction.

To deduct the expenses for the business use of your home office, the use must be connected with a trade or business, not just a profit-seeking activity. For example, if you use part of your home to carry on personal investment activities, not as a broker or dealer, expenses cannot be deducted since you are not in that trade or business.

The allowable deductions attributable to the business use of the home are limited to the net income from the business activity. Income is reduced first by deductions from the home office business and mortgage interest and real estate taxes. Any loss *at this point* is deductible in the year incurred with other expenses (i.e., insurance, maintenance, utilities, and depreciation) being carried forward, as a net operating loss from the home office business, to be used against future years' home office income. Net income *at this point* would then be reduced by other expenses to the extent it did not fall below zero.

An exception to the home office rules exists where an employee leases a portion of the home to the employer and subsequently collects rental income. In this case the home office deductions are disallowed. The only deductions allowable are those attributable to the home itself, such as mortgage interest, real estate taxes, and casualty losses.

Source: Thomas L. LoCicero, former IRS branch manager and presently senior tax manager and executive tax-planning specialist with the firm of Deloitte Haskins & Sells, 1 World Trade Center, New York 10048.

Escaping the Penalties on Estimated Tax

Under tax reform, your estimated tax payments, plus the taxes withheld from your salary, must equal 90% (old law, 80%) of the total tax due or you'll be hit with a penalty on the underpayment. Moreover, the penalty is imposed on a quarterly basis; if your first estimated tax payment is too small, you can't make up for it by bigger estimated payments later. There are, however, ways to avoid the penalty:

• Increase withholding. If it looks like your payments will fall short, file a new Form W-4, claiming fewer withholding allowances, to increase the amount withheld from your salary. Or ask your employer to withhold more. Withheld taxes are presumed to be paid equally throughout the year so larger withholding payments late in the year can be applied retroactively to wipe out any earlier underpayments.

• Penalty exceptions. The tax law still pro-

vides two "safe harbors" that protect you from penalties even if you don't meet the 90% test. The first is to pay last year's tax. If your estimated tax payments, plus withholding taxes, are at least equal to the tax shown on last year's return, you're safe from penalties no matter how high your taxes may be this year.

The second safe harbor is through annualization. If most of your income is derived late in the year, you can take advantage of the "annualization" rules, but you'll probably need an accountant to make the calculations. Basically, it works like this: On any estimated payment date, you figure your income up to that point, "annualize" it, and base your payment on the annualized figure. Here's a simplified example of how the rules work.

Example: Your income during the first quarter of the year is only $5,000, so your "annualized" income is $20,000. You pay only the estimated tax that would be due from a person with an income of $20,000 a year. Of course, you have to recompute the figures on each payment date and recalculate your payments accordingly.

A Great Tax Shelter That Isn't a Tax Shelter

If you own your business, you can take advantage of certain tax strategies to substantially improve your cash flow and the quality of your life. For example, you can have your company start a medical reimbursement plan for employees. Rationale: The only medical expenses you can deduct on your personal tax return are those that exceed 7.5% of adjusted gross income. So if your AGI is $40,000 and you have medical expenses of $1,000, you're $1,000 out-of-pocket—with no tax benefit whatsoever. But if your company reimburses you, it can deduct the $1,000.

This strategy works only if the plan applies equally to all employees. If it is limited to top officers, they will be taxed as though the reimbursements were salary income. Caution: In the case of shareholders, dividend treatment may result (see below). But even that isn't necessarily terrible. You're still better off paying the taxes than $1,000 in medical bills.

Salary Versus Dividends

The way you take money out of your company makes a difference in your taxes. Dividends are taxed twice—once to your company (because they aren't deductible) and once to you. Salaries are taxed only once. Obviously, the more of your total compensation you take in salary, the better.

There's a limit, though—your salary must be "reasonable." Guidelines: Your education, knowledge, expertise, and what top executives in similar companies make. If it appears to the IRS that the reason for the compensation is your ownership interest, it's probably a dividend. If, on the other hand, the reason appears to be the blood, sweat, and tears you put into the company, it's probably salary.

S corporations are a way around the whole salary versus dividends problem. An S corporation pays no taxes itself. Instead, the owners pay taxes on their proportionate share of the company's income. For tax purposes, ⌐his is really equivalent to receiving all salary and no dividends. Drawback: You have to pay the tax on your share of income whether or not you take any money out of the company. If your company has loan covenants that restrict payment to owners (as many small businesses do), you could have trouble coming up with the cash for taxes.

Useful Perks

Perks are another way to use your business to improve your standard of living, and they are nontaxable if you can show they are necessary to your business. That can be tricky. For company cars, you must charge employees fair rental value for any personal use of the car. But the amount you charge can be less than what Hertz charges.

Of course, if a perk fails the necessity test, you can still take an unreimbursed business expense deduction to the extent your business expenses exceed 2% of AGI for whatever part of the expenses is attributable to business. Example: Membership dues for a club at

which you do a lot of business entertaining. Be sure you have good documentation for any such claims.

Source: Jack Salomon, partner in charge of state tax services at Peat Marwick Main & Co., 55 E. 52 St., New York 10055.

S Corporation Magic

The number of ways in which Subchapter S corporations can be used to cut business and personal taxes has been greatly expanded. It is now possible to use S corporations:

• in syndications and other money-raising ventures;

• in tax-shelter arrangements, subject to passive loss rules;

• as a tax-cutting tool for personal investments.

An S corporation combines the tax benefits of personally owning a business with the legal protection of the corporate form. The income and deductions of the firm flow directly to the shareholders, in proportion to their stockholdings, to be claimed on their personal tax returns.

For example, business losses can be used to cut the tax on shareholder salaries. But, at the same time, shareholders have personal protection from corporate liabilities (such as lawsuits and unsecured debts).

It now is possible for an S corporation to receive most of its income from investments in the form of rents, dividends, and interest. Changes in the law also allow different shares of an S corporation's stock to bear different voting rights. These changes create many new tax-saving opportunities.

Tax shelters: Until now, the typical tax shelter has been arranged as a limited partnership. The shelter business (such as oil drilling or equipment leasing) incurs losses in its early years, which flow through to the partners and offset other passive income.

Drawback: Each limited partnership must have at least one general partner who has unlimited liability for the shelter's debts. The remaining partners are limited partners who are liable only up to the amount they invest. But, since limited partners can't have any regular input into the management of the business, they have little say as to how their money is being spent. Furthermore, it's difficult to get out of a partnership because partnership interests aren't freely transferable.

S corporation advantages: Tax benefits flow through to investors in much the same way as in a partnership, and the same shelter advantages (subject to passive loss rules) result. But in addition:

• The corporation protects all the investors from personal liability.

• Since shareholders can be executives and managers of the firm, they can control how their money is spent.

• Shares of stock may be much easier to sell or give away if the investor wants to get out.

Business opportunities: Because most businesses incur tax losses during their start-up phase, syndicators and entrepreneurs can attract investors by starting up a new business in the S corporation form. The flow-through of losses will offset income from other shelters.

Similarly, a large, established business that wishes to expand (by purchasing new equipment or real estate, for example) can have some of its executives and shareholders form an independent S corporation to acquire the new property on terms that are arranged to be advantageous to it and the new firm's shareholders.

Personal tax planning: Because an S corporation may now have investment income, it's possible for a top-bracket investor to incorporate his personal portfolio. Shares of stock without voting rights may then be given to (or placed in trust for) other family members. At the same time, by keeping all the voting shares of the S corporation's stock, the taxpayer retains complete control over the investments. Of course, the same tactic is available to the top-tax-bracket owner of a family business.

Restrictions: There's no limit to the size of a company that elects S corporation status. But the company can have no more than 35 shareholders (with husband and wife counting as one). Another corporation can't be a shareholder.

While an S corporation's losses flow through to its shareholders, the amount of losses a shareholder can claim is generally limited to the amount he paid for his stock plus the amount of any loans he has made to the company. Excess losses can be carried forward and deducted from the company's future income.

The loss limitation rule means that S corporation status may not be best when company losses result from heavy interest payments on borrowings for which the shareholders aren't personally liable—for example, real estate tax shelters, when a mortgage is secured by the property alone. Tactic: Shareholders can increase their deduction limit by substituting themselves for the company as the party primarily liable on the loan. (They're then assumed to have reloaned the borrowed amount to the company.) If the business is successful, they will never have to pay off the loan out-of-pocket. And since the owners of a closely held company are usually required to guarantee its major debts personally anyway, the substitution doesn't really increase their liability, even in the worst case.

There are other technical rules that apply to S corporations, making it necessary to consult with a tax professional to see if an S corporation election is a good idea in your case. But don't overlook the flexible planning opportunities that result from the liberalized law.

Even an established company that's highly profitable may gain by electing S status:

• The election eliminates corporate income tax at the federal level, and sometimes at the state level as well.

• Income can be collected by shareholders at favorable rates if they have tax benefits or offsetting losses from other investments (such as tax shelters).

• The election eliminates the risk of two common IRS challenges, namely, that the company pays unreasonably large salaries or has accumulated too much in earnings in the business.

A firm that expects to lose money can elect S corporation status to pass its losses through to its owners. It can then return to regular corporate status when it returns to profitability.

Normally, S corporation status can't be elected more than once every five years. But the new law allows the company to reelect S corporation status now if it ended its previous election under prior law.

Source: Barry D. Sussman and Martin Galuskin, partners, Milgrom, Sussman, Galuskin & Co., CPAs, New York.

Tax Havens: What They Offer; What They Don't

"Tax haven" is probably one of the most misunderstood terms in investment jargon. Despite the visions it conjures up of tax-free investments and avoidance of a host of other taxes, so-called tax havens have relatively little potential for tax savings for US residents. Nor do they offer (in any meaningful way) much-vaunted privacy or confidentiality of business records. But they do offer some real benefits to investors.

A tax haven is not a type of investment (like a "tax shelter"). It is a political jurisdiction: A state or nation in which the local government has elected not to levy taxes—on income, inheritance, property, or whatever. The tax-free status, however, exists only in that particular jurisdiction. US residents with accounts, investments, trusts, or other business structures in tax havens still have to pay income tax on all earnings derived therefrom; to the IRS it's income, period.

A tax haven is also not a means to privacy. Although it's true that your investments are confidential in most tax haven jurisdictions, you will keep evidence of those investments in personal records and files. No matter how or where they are maintained, the records effectively void any privacy to be gained from a tax haven the first time they are found. The only way to achieve total privacy would be to keep no records—in which case it wouldn't matter where your investments were located.

So, what is the advantage of an investment in a tax haven jurisdiction? A big one: Higher earnings.

One of the highest nonrecoverable costs of business in the US is taxes (income, property, ad valorem, etc.). Obviously, the more a business has to pay the government, the less there is to distribute to stockholders. In effect, private investors in US business enterprises are taxed twice: Once on the income to the business, once on dividends paid to them. A tax haven investment eliminates (or significantly reduces) that double taxation, and the investors reap the benefit.

Business investors may be able to defer a substantial amount of taxes by utilizing business structures in tax haven jurisdictions. By owning less than 50% of the voting stock of the foreign company, doing business in the international marketplace, and meeting certain other requirements, business investors can effectively defer US taxation until earnings are repatriated and thereby become reportable and taxable as ordinary income, not capital gains.

If you are inspired to become a business investor for the purpose of deferring US taxes, be forewarned. Owning and operating a business in a tax haven jurisdiction requires business management skills far exceeding those needed for a domestic business. While the possibility of deferring US taxes may be enticing, the costs (and almost assured losses) will more than outweigh any savings unless you are an international entrepreneur with proven skills.

Investors, then, should remember these rules when evaluating a tax haven opportunity:

- Do not invest just because the asset is located in a tax haven; your income is still taxable under the Internal Revenue Code.

- Examine the opportunity—not its location—for tax advantages.

- Do not buy or establish a business structure in a tax haven jurisdiction unless you have the exceptional business skills necessary to operate it.

- Privacy is not a sufficient reason for investing in a tax haven.

- If the investment wouldn't be an attractive one in the US, then its location in a tax haven jurisdiction holds no advantage for you.

Source: J.F. (Jim) Straw, publisher and editor of *Offshore Banking News*, 301 Plymouth Dr. NE, Dalton, GA 30720. Mr. Straw also owns an offshore bank based in the Northern Marianas Islands (a US commonwealth) that has approximately $3 million in deposits.

How To Hold on to Meal And Entertainment Deductions

Meal and entertainment deductions have been drastically changed by tax reform. In most cases you can now only deduct 80% of cost (rather than 100%). Also, the rules of proof are stricter. It's essential to comply with these rules or the whole deduction could be lost.

Tougher substantiation rules for business meals over $25. Substantiation requirements which used to apply only to entertainment expenses have been extended to cover meal expenses, too. Under old law, as long as you had some way of proving the expense, you could deduct it. Sufficient in the past: Proving meal expenses over $25 by a credit card receipt, canceled check, or restaurant check stub plus some other proof such as a diary entry.

After tax reform: There is a specific checklist of information you must have for each business meal in order to deduct it. This checklist was always necessary for entertainment, but now you'll need it for both entertainment and meals. Be prepared to prove:

• The amount of the expenditure.
• The time, date, and place of the expenditure.
• The nature of the business discussion, and the business reason for the expense or the nature of the business benefit to be derived as a result of the expense.
• Identification of the people who participated in the business discussion.

Discussing business now required. If a meal had a business purpose and took place in surroundings conducive to business, it was fully deductible under old law. It was not essential that a business discussion actually took place if the main purpose was business rather than social.

After tax reform: The cost of a meal is deductible only if it occurs directly before, during, or after a substantial business discussion. If a business meal occurs before or after a substantial business discussion, the taxpayer must show that the expense was associated with the active conduct of his trade or business. The cost of taking a customer to dinner for the purpose of retaining his goodwill, for example, is no longer tax-deductible unless business is actually discussed.

Special substantiation rules for business meals under $25. Business meal expenditures that total under $25 are not subject to the strict rules above. While you still must have records of who you entertained and why, you don't need a receipt to substantiate a meal less than $25. Example: A diary that you keep which shows the details of these meals. Better, but not absolutely necessary: A restaurant receipt that shows the amount, date, location, and name of the restaurant. It's always best to have as much proof as you can to nail down a deduction.

Source: Lawrence W. Goldstein, tax manager, and Howard A. Rabinowitz, tax partner, Arthur Young & Co., 277 Park Ave., New York 10172.

Four Ways To Beat the "Only 80% of a Business Meal Is Deductible" Rule

• Company dining rooms, employee cafeterias, and other "eating facilities" operated by an employer for employees are not subject to the 80% rule if the facility is located on the business premises of the employer, brings in revenue that normally equals or exceeds its direct operating costs, and does not discriminate in favor of highly compensated employees.

• Company parties. The 80% rule does not apply to certain traditional employer-paid social or recreational activities that are primarily for the benefit of the employees. Holiday parties and annual summer outings continue to be fully deductible.

• Banquets. Meals provided as an integral part of a "qualified banquet meeting" are not subject to the 80% rule until January 1, 1989. A qualified meeting is a convention, seminar, annual meeting, or similar business program that includes a meal, where more than 50% of the participants are away from home, at least 40 people attend, and the event includes a speaker.

• Reimbursement angle. Employees are not subject to the 80% rule if their company reimburses them for business meal and entertainment expenses. It's the company that's subject to the rule—the company must limit the amount of deduction it claims on its tax return to 80% of the amount given to the employee. Bottom line: The tax law has no adverse effect for an employee on an expense account who is reimbursed in full for business meal and entertainment costs. It may be more desirable to have your employer reimburse you than for you to receive an expense allowance and deduct meal and entertainment expenses on your own return, where they will be limited to 80%.

Escaping IRS Limits on Investment Losses

At the heart of the Tax Reform Act is the anti-tax-shelter provision called the passive loss rule. Although the purpose of the rule is to curtail tax-shelter abuses, it reaches far beyond those investments that are usually thought of as tax shelters. Trap: Investors who don't fully understand the rule are almost certain to be caught in its net.

The Passive Loss Rule
The law requires you to separate your income and investment losses into two categories: One for "passive activities" and one for "nonpassive activities." It then prohibits you from offsetting income from nonpassive activities, such as salary, with losses from passive activities, such as tax-shelter investments. Passive activity losses may offset only passive activity income.

Passive activities:
• Limited partnership interests of all kinds (i.e., tax shelters).
• All rental activities.
• Business activities in which the taxpayer does not materially participate, including sole proprietorships, S corporations, and general partnerships. "Materially" means being involved year-round on a regular, continuous, and substantial basis.

Nonpassive activities:
• Work that pays wages, salary, or commissions.
• Investing that yields "portfolio income" such as dividends, capital gains, interest, or royalties.
• Business activities in which there is material participation by the taxpayer.

Who's affected: The passive loss rule applies to individuals, trusts and estates, personal-service corporations (self-incorporated doctors, dentists, lawyers, etc.) and S corporations. It does not apply to regular "C" corporations. Closely held C corporations are subject to the rule in a modified form (see below). At greatest risk: High-income taxpayers who have invested heavily in tax shelters.

Softening the Blow
Some types of investment activity are exempt from the passive loss rule. And to cushion the impact of the rule:

• There is a phase-in period. Passive losses from investments acquired before October 22, 1986 (the date on which the president signed the Tax Reform Act), will be partially deductible against nonpassive income for four years following this date.

Problem: If you acquired your interest in a passive activity after October 22, 1986, none of your losses from that activity will be deductible against nonpassive income. The phase-in rule does not apply to these losses.

Carryovers
• Unused passive losses may be carried indefinitely into future years when they may be used to offset future passive income. The

accumulated unused losses on a property may generally be used to offset the gain when the property is sold. And if the unused losses are more than the gain, the excess may be written off against nonpassive income. Trap: This break does not apply to property that is sold to a family member.

Troubleshooting

Individuals who are locked into investments that throw off large passive losses must use new strategies to deal with their losses. Recommended:

• Find investments that produce passive income, which will absorb the passive losses. Trap: Income from a mutual fund is not considered passive. Only investments that fit the new law's definition of a passive activity will generate passive income, for example, income-producing limited partnerships and rental properties.

Income-producing limited partnerships: Unfortunately, in many parts of the country there are very few passive income deals available. Demand is great, so expect to pay a premium. Caution: Under 1987 tax amendments, income from many publicly traded limited partnerships, such as master limited partnerships (MLPs), is no longer considered passive income and cannot be used to offset passive losses.

Rental properties such as occupied apartments, office buildings, parking lots, and shopping centers. You don't have to be a limited partner in these deals to get passive income, because all rental activity is considered passive under the new law, whether it's in the form of a limited partnership or not.

• Convert nonpassive income into passive income. You might do this by converting a corporation that is not subject to the passive loss rules into a corporation that is subject to the rules.

Example: Convert a regular corporation that is throwing off a great deal of taxable nonpassive income into an S corporation, and then hire a manager to run the S corporation. Income from an S corporation in which the owner does not materially participate (that is, in which he is not involved year-round on a regular, continuous, and substantial basis) is

passive income.

• Restructure leasing arrangements with your business. Suppose you are currently leasing a building that you own to a manufacturing company that you own. You've been renting the building to the company at a rate of only $100,000 a year. Your depreciation deductions on the building give you a tax loss, which you needed and could use under the old law. But under the new law, you can't use the loss. What you need now is passive income.

What to do: Increase the rent to $300,000 a year, which is the building's fair market rent today. This will give you net income (above the depreciation deductions), and it will be passive income, because it comes from rental activity.

Break for Closely Held Corporations

Closely held corporations that are not personal-service corporations are subject to the passive loss rule in a modified form.

Losses from a closely held corporation's passive activities may be used to offset the business income of the corporation. For example, a small manufacturing firm could offset net income from its operations with losses from tax-shelter investments. While the owner of a closely held corporation, as an individual taxpayer, will probably not wish to continue to invest in tax shelters, his corporation might very well want to.

Added incentive: Corporate rates are higher than individual rates. That makes tax-shelter losses more valuable to a corporation than to individual owners (assuming they could use the losses). Restriction: The corporation may not use passive losses to offset portfolio income (dividends, investment interest, etc.).

Source: Jerry Williford, partner, Grant Thornton, CPAs, 2800 Citicorp Center, Houston, TX 77002.

Tax Shelters: Still Alive And Kicking . . . Sort Of

Although tax reform has made the traditional tax shelter an endangered species, it has not yet made it extinct. For investors with adjusted gross income of less than $250,000 a year, there are still a few interesting ways to reduce taxes on nonpassive income (salaries, wages, dividends and interest). It's important to be very careful, however, because Congress has placed strict limits on the use and viability of these shelters.

Surviving Shelters

Real estate: For individuals with AGI below $150,000, rental real estate investments can still produce losses to offset nonpassive income. However, the investor must have a direct interest in the rental property (own 10% or more) and must be actively involved in its management.

The size of the deduction varies with the taxpayer's income. Taxpayers whose AGI is less than $100,000 each year may deduct losses of up to $25,000 from their nonpassive income. As taxable income increases to $150,000, the $25,000 deduction declines gradually to $0.

Rehabilitated housing: If you rehabilitate a certified historic structure (listed in the national register) or a building put into service before 1936, you can claim a percentage of the annual rehabilitation expense as a credit against your tax bill. The credit equals 20% of expenses for certified historic structures and 10% for structures put into service before 1936. It applies only to the cost of the structure and its rehabilitation—not to the cost of the land.

Again, the size of the deduction taxpayers can claim against nonpassive income is limited by their AGI. Taxpayers whose AGI is $200,000 or less can claim enough rehabilitation credits to offset the tax on up to $25,000. As income increases to $250,000, the deduction gradually declines to $0.

Low-income housing: A generous annual tax credit is now available to taxpayers who buy, build, or rehabilitate property classified as low-income housing. It is based on a percentage of total costs (excluding the cost of the land) and can be applied each year for 10 years. There are two different credits:

• For newly constructed or rehabilitated properties not federally subsidized, an annual credit equal to 9% of the total costs of the project can be claimed against income.

• For the acquisition of existing buildings and/or where federal subsidies or tax-exempt financing is used, a 4% annual credit is available each year for 10 years.

Example: A taxpayer who spends $100,000 to rehabilitate a low-income property will be eligible for a $9,000 credit each year for 10 years, a total of $90,000 in credits.

Only a portion of this credit can be used to offset taxes on nonpassive income. To qualify, a taxpayer's income cannot exceed $250,000. A maximum credit equal to the tax on $25,000 can be taken by individuals who make less than $200,000 a year. The size of the credit gradually declines to $0 as an individual's income increases to $250,000.

The annual credit means sizable deductions over an extended period of time—sometimes over the life of the project. Also, unlike other real estate investments, the tax credit does not reduce the depreciable basis of the property: You can deduct for depreciation each year in addition to taking the credit.

Caution: Although the tax credits on low-income housing are generous, the risk can be significant. Rules regarding what constitutes low-income housing are strict. For example, for the project to qualify for the tax status, a set percentage of tenants must earn less than the median income of the surrounding area for a period of at least 15 years. (This means an investor could not invest in a low-income property, rehabilitate it, kick the poor people out, and turn it into a high-rent apartment building.)

With so few shelters left, an increasing number of syndicators will be trying to sell tax-loss deals for low-income housing. Problem: No one has a long enough track record in this area to prove that these deals can work economically over an extended period of time. Also, the secondary market will be limited—once you are in a low-income-housing deal, you're in it for good.

Source: William Brennan, editor and publisher, *The Brennan Reports*, Valley Forge, PA.

Don't Rush into Shelters

The passive loss rules enacted by tax reform have wiped out most conventional tax shelters. Yet many opportunities still exist. Some individuals have rushed into them without understanding the limitations or dangers involved. Here's a rundown of what you need to know.

Oil and Gas

This is the last of the old-time tax shelters that still lets you deduct large passive losses against ordinary income. Large current deductions are available here as before, but at a price.

Before tax reform, a typical investor would buy into an oil-drilling deal by obtaining a limited partnership interest that restricted his financial liability to the face amount of his investment. Now, however, to obtain deductible losses from an oil well an investor must acquire a working interest. And such investors are fully liable personally to the business's creditors. In the event of an underinsured casualty (such as a fire), a lawsuit, or some other unexpected liability, the investor's personal assets (such as a bank account, car, home, etc.) may be attached by creditors.

Bottom line: Tax benefits are still there, but the risk of claiming them is far greater. The professional skill and responsibility of the shelter's management team is more important than ever.

Life Insurance

Since the passage of tax reform, life insurance products have been all the rage among financial planners. Single premium life insurance in particular has been cited for its tax advantages.

How it works: An investor buys a policy, paying one large premium up front. The policy's cash value increases at a specific rate. The policy owner can then borrow against the policy, taking out the earnings on a tax-free basis. The owner doesn't pay back the borrowed amounts until he dies, when they are subtracted from the policy proceeds.

By borrowing the earnings each year, the owner gets a tax-free income stream, much as he'd get from a municipal bond, but without incurring the same risk (a bond can go down in value).

While single premium life insurance is being aggressively sold by insurance companies, it is not for everyone:

• Single premium insurance is often sold as an investment, but you'll be paying for its insurance aspect. Don't buy it unless you need the insurance it provides.

• There's talk in Congress about changing the law so that borrowing against such a policy will no longer be tax-free, thus defeating the purpose of the investment.

• Once you buy a policy, there's no escape. If for any reason you ever decide to surrender the policy (perhaps simply because you no longer need insurance), all outstanding loans against it will immediately become fully taxable. Similarly, all outstanding loans will become taxable when the policy matures.

For these reasons, single premium life insurance probably is not a good device to use for long-term savings. If you plan to let earnings pile up in the policy for several years, intending to borrow them when, say, a child goes to college, you'll be out of luck if the law changes and borrowing becomes taxable.

On the other hand, a policy can be a good investment if you need both life insurance coverage and current income. You can borrow the policy earnings each year tax-free. If the law changes, you simply stop borrowing.

Annuities

Also sold by insurance companies, deferred annuities provide the opportunity to obtain tax-deferred earnings on an investment. You make a payment to an insurance company, and in turn receive the right to take either a series of annual payments or a distribution of your account balance at a future date. In the meantime, earnings accrue in your account on a tax-deferred basis, and are taxed only when they are finally paid to you.

Two kinds of annuities:

• Fixed annuities. Your payment accrues earnings at a fixed rate, and the size of the annuity payment is determined in advance.

• Variable annuities. Earnings depend on the result of the investment. You typically have the choice of investing your account in a stock, bond, or money-market fund, and may switch from one to another. The size of the annuity you receive depends on the success of your investments.

While many people are attracted to the idea of being able to manage their investments through a variable annuity, management charges usually amount to 2% annually or more. A person who wants investment flexibility will usually do better to invest through a taxable mutual fund, where charges typically run at about ¾ of 1% annually. The difference in charges more than offsets the tax-deferral benefit of the variable annuity. A variable annuity becomes a better investment than a taxable mutual fund only when the annuity's annual service charge is 1.5% per year or less.

Ginnie Mae Securities

Government National Mortgage Association securities (Ginnie Maes) have become very popular in the last couple of years because of the government-guaranteed interest they pay, and because many states exempt them from state tax. But Ginnie Maes are seriously misunderstood by many investors and pose dangerous traps for the unwary:

• While the interest paid on a Ginnie Mae is guaranteed by the federal government, the principal amount of your investment is not. Ginnie Maes represent mortgage commitments, and when interest rates drop, mortgage holders are likely to refinance, paying off their loans at face value. Many investors who thought they were buying securities that were fully US guaranteed have lost large amounts of money after investing in a fund that bought Ginnie Maes at a steep premium, only to have them redeemed at face value.

• The US Supreme Court has recently ruled that Ginnie Maes, while federally guaranteed, are not securities issued by the US government. That gives states and local governments the right to tax them. Be sure to check the policy that will be followed in your state.

Tax-Exempt Bonds

Municipal bonds are still an attractive investment. However, the municipal bond market can be extremely volatile. Because of the risk, it's probably best to invest in short-term bonds—those with maturities of three to five years—in an uncertain market.

Overlooked Shelters

• Tax-exempt money-market funds. They exist in many states and offer a tax-free return without the commitment of time and money that's required by a bond investment. Check with your broker.

• Savings bonds. These are no longer just for the small savers. Many smart top-bracket investors buy $15,000 worth of Series EE bonds each year, the maximum investment allowed by law. The bonds are exempt from state tax and give you a choice as to how they're taxed under federal law. You can defer the tax until a future year. Or if you're in a low tax bracket or have offsetting deductions, you can elect in any year to have them taxed immediately.

The 6% yield on these bonds is a guaranteed minimum. Since the yield will always match 85% of the five-year Treasury note rate, EE bonds offer protection against inflation and high interest rates that can't be obtained from most other investments.

Finally, on maturity, EE bonds can be converted on a tax-deferred basis into Series HH bonds, providing cash income. The appreciation on the EE bonds will remain untaxed—an ideal retirement tactic.

Source: Steven B. Enright, director of financial planning, Seidman Financial Services, Seidman & Seidman/BDO, 15 Columbus Circle, New York 10023.

More Tax Shelters That Survived Reform

Buying your parents' home and renting it back to them can produce deductible tax losses. The transaction converts payments that you make toward your parents' support into a perfectly legal tax shelter. How it works: You buy the house from your parents on the installment method and rent it back to them for fair market rent. Make the installment payments equal to the rent plus the amount you had been giving for support. Shelter: The rental income is sheltered from tax by depreciation deductions, property taxes, etc. And if the write-offs exceed the rent—and your adjusted gross income is under $100,000—you may deduct up to $25,000 of losses against your taxable income.

Offsetting properties. Under the new rules, passive losses are deductible only from passive income. If you have a piece of real estate with a very low mortgage that is producing a positive cash flow, you might consider buying a second property with a high mortgage that causes the property to generate losses. Shelter: The losses on the second property will shelter the income from the first.

Conventional write-off shelters, such as cattle breeding, newsletter publishing, research and development and venture partnerships, are of no use to taxpayers who do not have passive income. But for taxpayers who have passive income, traditional limited partnership investments may make some sense. Reason: The losses may be written off against passive income. A conventional shelter also makes sense if you hold a burned-out tax shelter that is about to generate passive taxable income. A conventional shelter's passive losses will absorb the passive income from the burned-out shelter. Caution: Don't invest in a conventional shelter only for passive tax losses. Look for economically sound deals. The alternative minimum tax now includes tax-shelter items that previously escaped this tax.

Company pension and profit-sharing plans are great tax shelters, particularly for owners of family businesses. The amounts they put into their company's plan are deductible by the business. Tax is deferred, and neither the original amount contributed nor any earnings are taxed until actually paid out to the individual. This is a bonanza for business owners, who can put a share of the business profits aside for retirement and see the government contribute a sizable additional amount (equal to the taxes saved by deducting the contributions).

IRAs can still be a good tax shelter even if the law prevents you from making tax-deductible contributions. Earnings on non-deductible IRA contributions are tax-deferred.
Source: Edward Mendlowitz, partner, Siegel, Mendlowitz & Rich, CPAs, 310 Madison Ave., New York 10017.

The Scoop on Capital Losses

Most people realize that the maximum tax rate paid on long-term capital gains has risen from 20% to the same rate as ordinary income (up to 33%). What many people don't realize is that the deduction for capital losses remains sharply restricted. How it works:

• Capital losses must still be divided into long-term losses (on assets held for longer than six months) and short-term losses (on assets held less than six months). *Note:* For assets purchased on or after January 1, 1988, the long-term holding period is one year, rather than six months.

• No more than $3,000 of capital losses in excess of capital gains may be deducted on a personal return in any one year (although excess losses may be carried forward and deducted in future years).

• Long-term losses are deductible dollar for dollar in offsetting capital gain income.

Planning point. Capital losses are often best used to offset capital gains. This tactic is even more important under tax reform, since the tax rate on gains has gone up, while the deductibility of losses remains limited. Consider this when forming investment strategies and time your gains and losses for the most advantageous impact. Also: Long-term capital gains are now considered investment income for purposes of limiting interest expense deductions.
Source: James Conley, partner, and Rick Miller, tax manager, Arthur Young & Co., 300 K St. NW, Washington, DC 20007.

Tax Break for Closely Held Corporations

An opportunity exists for closely held corporations to shelter taxable income. Here's how: Invest in office buildings, shopping centers, equipment rentals and limited partnerships, or other tax shelters that produce passive losses.

Reason: Closely held corporations that aren't S corporations can use the tax losses from investments in passive activities to offset operating income—unlike most taxpayers, who are allowed to deduct passive losses only from passive income.

Important restriction: The corporation may not use passive losses to offset portfolio income (dividends, investment interest, capital gains, etc.).

Passive activities include:
- Limited partnership interests of all kinds.
- Business activities in which the taxpayer (individual or corporation) does not materially participate.
- All rental activities, whether the taxpayer materially participates or not.

Kinds of investments likely to generate passive losses:
- Commercial real estate—office buildings, shopping centers, warehouses, parking lots, etc.
- Residential real estate, such as apartment buildings.
- Equipment leasing. For instance, the company buys computers and rents them out to other companies.
- Limited partnerships (e.g., tax shelters), such as oil and gas.
- An interest in a business in which the company doesn't materially participate.

Companies that are eligible for this tax break: A corporation is defined in the new tax law as a closely held corporation if, during the last half of the taxable year, more than 50% of the value of its stock is owned by five or fewer individuals.

Not eligible: Closely held corporations that are personal service corporations (incorporated doctors, dentists, lawyers, etc.) and S corporations. They don't qualify for this exception to the passive loss rule. Totally exempt from the passive loss rule: Regular C corporations that are not closely held. They can use passive losses against any type of income, including portfolio income.

Among the factors to consider before investing:
- There are bargains to be picked up in real estate, both commercial and residential, in many parts of the country.
- You may need "holding power," that is, the ability to carry the property for a few years. In depressed markets, where the good deals are, the cash flow on the property probably won't be quite enough to service the debt. The company may have to come up with a little of its own money for a few years. But when the real estate market turns around, the company will have a valuable investment.

Best: An investment that has a stable positive cash flow and produces tax losses.

The bottom line: While the owner of a closely held corporation, as an individual taxpayer, will probably not wish to continue to invest in passive activity investments (because he can't get any tax benefit from the investment), his corporation might very well want to. Closely held corporations can get tax benefits from passive activity investments.

Source: Jerry S. Williford, partner, Grant Thornton, CPAs, 2800 Citicorp Center, Houston 77002.

3 FIGHTING THE IRS

What the IRS Already Knows About You

The IRS gets information from third parties and matches this information to you through its computers. Stay one step ahead. . .by being extra careful to report on your tax return what the IRS already knows about you. (You should receive from the third parties copies of all the information that they send to the IRS.) What the IRS knows and how:

Your income. The IRS knows, of course, if you have been paid over $600. The payer must report this payment to the IRS on Form 1099-MISC, Statement for Recipients of Miscellaneous Income. Included in this category:

- Free-lance income.
- Rent or royalty payments.
- Prizes and awards that are not for services.
- Payments made by medical and health-care insurers to a doctor or other supplier of medical services under an insurance program.
- Attorney's and accountant's fees for professional services.
- Witness or expert fees paid by a lawyer during a legal proceeding.
- Payments made to entertainers for their services.

Your wages. And the IRS knows from your W-2 Form exactly how much you earned in regular income, bonuses, vacation allowances, severance pay, moving-expense payments, and travel allowances. Your W-2 must be attached to your return.

Interest income. The IRS knows if you've been paid any interest. Banks and financial institutions must report these payments to the IRS on Form 1099-INT, Statement for Recipients of Interest Income. Trap: Some interest income is reported to the IRS even though you haven't received it yet. It must be reported as part of your income. All that matters is that you are entitled to it.

Dividend income. The IRS knows if you received over $10 in money, stock, capital-gain distributions, or property from a corporation. The corporation must report these payments to the IRS on Form 1099-DIV, Statement for Recipients of Dividends and Distributions. Important: Make sure the report agrees with your records.

Tax-refund income. The IRS knows about tax refunds you receive. State and local governments must report such payments of over $10 on Form 1099-G, Statement for Recipients of Certain Government Payments. Important exception: If you didn't claim the state and local taxes that you paid as itemized deductions on your federal return, you don't have to report these refunds as income. If you receive a Form 1099-G, analyze it carefully to see whether you must include it in income or if you qualify under this exception.

Gambling winnings. The IRS knows about money you won from horse racing, dog racing, jai alai, lotteries, raffles, drawings, Bingo, slot machines, and Keno. It's all reported to the IRS on Form W-2G, Statement for Recipients of Certain Gambling Winnings. The general rule: Payments of $600 or more must be reported by the payer. Exceptions: Bingo payments of $1,200 or more and Keno payments of $1,500 or more will be reported.

Other income the IRS knows about:
- Original-issue discounts.
- Mortgage interest received from individuals in the course of a trade or business.
- Money received from broker and barter exchanges.
- Distributions from pension and profit-sharing plans, IRAs, etc.
- Cash payments of over $10,000 received in a trade or business.
- Cash deposits of over $10,000 made to your bank account.
- Fringe benefits received from your company.
- Social Security benefits.
- Tax shelter participation.
- Unemployment income.

Source: John L. Withers, special consultant for IRS regulations and procedures, Touche Ross & Co., Washington Service Center, 1900 M St. NW, Washington, DC 20036.

Tax Return Completion Checklist

In dealings with the IRS, no news is good news. More precisely, in this case, no *mail* is good news. Every time the IRS sends a letter to a taxpayer, it means that someone within the service has taken another look at the return in question. Every look taken increases the chance that "problems" will come to light (if they haven't already).

There are a number of simple steps you can take to minimize the risk of ongoing activity with your tax return.

- Before filing, make sure your return is complete. Check to see that all necessary forms and schedules are present and accounted for. This includes any and all attachments (e.g., if you donate common stock to a charitable organization, you must attach a statement of certain information regarding the gift. Staple your return together securely. Missing pages generate correspondence.
- Make sure the return is accurate: Check, double-check, and recheck all arithmetic.
- Make sure your reporting is consistent with the information the IRS receives. For example, if you have invested in IBM and General Motors stock through *XYZ* Brokerage, your return should list dividends paid to you by *XYZ*, not IBM or GM, because the IRS will receive a 1099 form from *XYZ*.
- Double-check to see that the return is signed by all necessary parties.
- Finally, file your return on time. By all means request an extension if you need one, but mail your return well before the expiration date. In the event you must file at the last minute, use registered mail in order to have evidence of timely filing.

Source: Ralph C. Ganswindt, partner specializing in closely held businesses, with Arthur Andersen & Company, 777 East Wisconsin Avenue, Milwaukee, WI 53201.

Unanswered Questions Cause Problems

Income tax returns with unanswered questions are considered no returns. That means the statute of limitations never expires and you can be audited no matter how many years have passed. Unanswered questions can also delay refunds, result in interest charges, and call attention to your return by IRS agents (since the computer automatically spits out the return). If a question doesn't seem to apply to you (Do you have any foreign bank accounts? Do you claim a deduction for an office in your home?), just answer no—but answer.

What To Do if You've Forgotten To Send in all The Forms

If you file your return and then realize you left out your W-2 or some other necessary form, wait until the IRS contacts you about it before sending it in. The form is more likely to be lost if you just stick it in an envelope and send it to a service center before you receive an IRS notice.

Source: *IRS Publication No. 17.*

When It's Safe To Ignore Your April 15 Deadline

You are legally required to file a tax return (or extension request) by April 15, whether you owe extra tax or not. But since the civil penalty for late filing is generally a percentage of the tax still owed (5% per month, up to 25%), there's no penalty unless you owe the government money. And you have two years to file for your refund.

Nevertheless, it's advisable to file on time for these reasons:

• You get your refund faster.
• It may turn out that you miscalculated and actually owe taxes instead of having a refund coming. In that case, you'll be charged

penalties and interest for late filing.
• If you want to file an amended return later, you'll have three years to do it in, instead of two.
• If the IRS concludes that you are willfully refusing to file a return, you may be hit with criminal penalties.

How To Get Late-Filing Penalties Eliminated

Penalties for filing your tax return late without getting a valid extension may be forgiven by the IRS if you show that you had reasonable cause for filing late.

Although the IRS cannot be required to waive late-filing penalties, it often does so when convinced that the late filing was not the taxpayer's fault.

Among the excuses the IRS may accept as reasonable cause for late filing:

• Death or serious illness of the taxpayer or a member of his immediate family.
• Unavoidable absence of the taxpayer.
• Destruction of records in a fire or other casualty.
• Delay due to erroneous information given the taxpayer by the IRS.
• A timely request for needed tax forms wasn't answered by the IRS.
• The return was filed on time but was sent to the wrong IRS service center.
• The taxpayer was filing for the first time and was ignorant of the law.

Encouraging: Close to 50% of the total dollar amount of penalties the IRS assessed in 1985 for all infractions, including late filing, was excused. Bottom line: You have a relatively good chance of avoiding a late-filing penalty if you can convince the IRS that the delay was not your fault.

Late-Filing Excuse That Worked

When the IRS tried to penalize William Haden for not filing a tax return, he claimed that he had filed a return at the Post Office on April 15. He said that the Post Office was so crowded on filing day that he had given the return to a postal worker who had been stationed on the street to accept returns, and concluded that the worker must have lost the return. Both Haden's wife and a friend supported his story as witnesses. Tax Court: Although Haden's story was "shaky" on a few details, it was believable overall. The penalty was set aside.

Source: *William F. Haden,* TC Memo 1986-539.

If Your Lawyer Forgets To File

If you sign your tax return in time, give it to your lawyer and he forgets to file it, who's responsible?

You are. It's your responsibility to see that the return is filed. Even though it's your lawyer's fault, you pay the penalty.

How To Extend the Float On Tax Checks

The IRS Service Centers are quick to get your check into their bank. During tax filing season, when thousands of envelopes are received every day, the IRS strives for what it calls "zero day deposit". . . all checks are deposited within 24 hours. Computerized mail processing machines can tell which envelopes contain checks by detecting, through the envelope, the magnetic ink on the check inside. To extend the float: Mail your check in an over-sized envelope. The machines can only process standard, letter-sized envelopes; oversized ones must be handled individually. Human processing, especially during busy periods, can add as much as 10 days to your float.

Never Let the IRS Apply Refund to Next Year's Tax Bill

If you file the short form, 1040A or 1040EZ, and claim a refund, the IRS will send you a check for that amount (provided you haven't made any errors on your return). But if you file the long form, 1040, you are offered an alternative to getting a check. The back of the form, down at the bottom, asks if you want to let the IRS keep your refund and apply it to your next year's estimated tax bill.

Advice: Don't do it! Never, ever let the IRS hold on to your refund.

Why not? Because it won't really help you in the long run—and it may end up hurting you.

Example: You fill out your return and discover that you had a $900 refund coming. You decide to let the IRS hold on to it and apply it to your next year's estimated tax bill.

But what if the IRS finds a math error on your return? Or your employer made a mistake on your wage statement? Or you forgot to include in your income the interest you earned on a bank account?

These things happen all the time. And any one of them would affect your tax return.

Let's suppose that the bottom line is this: After correcting your return, the IRS sends you a bill for an additional $400. You already have $900 sitting in your estimated tax account. As far as you're concerned, the IRS can go ahead and take the $400 out of that. Right?

Wrong. You told it to credit the $900 to your estimated tax account, and you're stuck with that decision. In other words, you'll have to come up with the extra $400 on your own.

What if the IRS audits a recent return and finds that you owe additional taxes plus interest? You still can't touch your $900.

To make matters worse, the money you left in your estimated tax account doesn't even earn any interest.

If you really want to earmark your refund for your future tax bill, let the IRS send you your check. Then deposit the money in a savings account or invest it for a year. Don't let the IRS have it for nothing.

Tracking Down Your Refund

If it's been at least 10 weeks since you filed your tax return and you still haven't received your refund, you can do something about it.

Step 1. Get out the copy you kept of your tax return. Be sure you know your Social Security number, your filing status, the exact amount of the refund you claimed and the service center to which you sent your return.

Step 2. Call the IRS's automated refund information service to find out the current status of your refund check. Use the number for your area that's listed below. If no number is listed for your area, call the IRS Federal Tax Questions telephone number for your area that's listed in the back of the Form 1040 instruction booklet. Or call 800-424-1040, a national toll-free number for taxpayer assistance.

Step 3. If there's still a problem write to the IRS service center where you filed your return. Include your name, address, Social Security number, the tax year involved and an explanation of your problem. Keep copies of the letters you send.

Step 4. If you've done all of the above and still haven't gotten your refund, it's time to call the IRS's Problems Resolution Office (PRO). The telephone number of the local PRO can be obtained from the governmental listings in the phone book, or from the local IRS district office. To get help from the PRO you must show that you first tried to resolve your problem through normal channels. Have a record of the names of IRS agents you've talked with, along with copies of all your correspondence with the IRS. Shortly after a PRO officer is assigned to your case, you'll get either your refund or a full explanation of what's holding it up.

IRS automated refund information phone numbers can be found in Form 1040.

Missing Refund

Irene Crosby *thought* she had filed an income tax return for 1979, but she never received her refund, and the IRS finally told her that it had never received her return. When she refiled to get the refund, the IRS said it was too late—the statute of limitations had run out. Irene protested. *District Court:* Irene had a long history of filing on time. Moreover, during 1979 she was the sole support of six children, one of whom was gravely ill. It was reasonable to conclude that she *had* filed a return which the IRS had lost, and understandable that she hadn't noticed the IRS's failure to reply. Therefore she *was* entitled to her refund.

Source: Irene O. Crosby, ND Ca., No. C-85-20331-RPA.

Unclaimed Refunds

The IRS is sitting on millions of dollars in unclaimed tax refunds. According to the IRS, the addresses listed under taxpayer's Social Security numbers are no good. Those likely to be affected: Anyone who has moved during the year, a surviving spouse who filed a joint return; unmarried taxpayers who later marry and change their names. Tax returns are identified by Social Security number, joint returns by the first Social Security number listed. If you marry and are listed second on the return, you disappear from the IRS files. Suggestion: If you move send the IRS a formal change-of-address letter.

Taxpayer Penalizes IRS For Lateness

You file your tax return in February, and get a refund check in May—but no interest. Does the government owe you interest on the money?

No. The government doesn't have to pay interest if it sends your refund within 45 days of the date the return was due—April 15—not 45 days from the date you filed it. But if it doesn't get the refund out within the 45 days, it has to pay interest all the way back to April 15, even if it's only one day late.

Best Time To File for a Refund

Suppose you discover, about a year after filing your return, that you omitted a sizable deduction. You immediately file a claim for a refund, only to find out that the refund claim triggers an audit. The good news is that your claim is allowed in full by the auditor. The bad news is that during the audit he probes other areas of your return where your proof is weak, and you end up owing the IRS additional tax.

Loophole: File your refund claim just a few days before the statute of limitations expires—three years from the due date of the return or two years from the date you actually paid the tax, whichever is later. If the last day for filing a claim is April 15, then file your claim on April 12.

Problem for the IRS: The limitation period that applies to your refund claim also applies to the IRS's ability to assess extra tax. Once that April 15 has gone by, the IRS may consider other items to offset your claim but may not assess additional tax (except in some very specialized situations). What's more, because the year involved is an "old" year, in IRS jargon, unless your claim is for a very large

amount, the chance of it triggering an audit is remote.

Source: George S. Alberts, former IRS Director of the Brooklyn and Albany District Offices.

Winning the Refund Game

• The IRS said it hadn't received a taxpayer's 1978 return . . .so she refiled in 1982, claiming a refund. The IRS argued the statute of limitations had expired. Court: The taxpayer gets her refund. She had a long history of filing on time and getting refunds—in all probability, she filed in 1978 and the IRS lost the return.

Source: *Irene O. Crosby,* ND CA, No. C-85-20331—RPA.

• A misplaced comma in the IRS computer resulted in the Bruces' getting a tax refund of over $49,000 instead of $4,900. They notified the IRS of its mistake, but were assured that they were entitled to the money. Over two years after the Bruces got the check, the IRS tried to get the money back. District court: The IRS had two years from the date it made the mistake to correct its error. Since it waited so long, the Bruces were allowed to keep the money.

Source: *Alice A. Bruce,* SD TX, G-84-220.

How To Answer When The IRS Writes

The Internal Revenue Service is sending notices demanding money to more taxpayers than ever before.

By responding shrewdly to IRS notices, taxpayers can often reduce the amount they owe. . .and sometimes pay nothing. Keys to success:

• Never blindly pay what the notice claims you owe without first checking facts and figures. Don't assume that the bill is correct just because it came from the IRS. It's imperative that you review the notice, line by line, and understand exactly how the IRS arrived at each figure. Only after you fully understand the notice will you be in a position to respond effectively.

• Always ask that penalties be excused. Negligence penalties are now automatically included in notices for unreported income. . . and other types of notices carry other penalties, such as those for late filing and late payment.

To get penalties dropped: You must show there was "reasonable cause" (that is, a good excuse) for your alleged misdeed (misreporting income, filing late, paying late, etc.). Encouraging statistic: Of the $5.7 billion in penalties assessed by the IRS in its 1985 fiscal year, $2.6 billion (46%) was excused.

If You Receive a Notice

• Answer promptly—within one week of the day that you receive the notice—regardless of the deadline specified (usually 30 days out). Reason: The earlier you respond to the notice, the less likely is the possibility that you will receive computer-generated follow-up notices and that correspondence between you and the IRS will cross in the mail.

• Keep your letter succinct and to the point. Your response should be no more than three paragraphs long, and no paragraph should have more than three sentences. Reason: Brevity and directness increase the chances that the matter will be settled quickly. . .and not snowball into a full-scale investigation.

• Back up your response with documentation. For instance, if you are claiming that you already paid the amount of tax that the IRS says you owe, attach a photocopy of your cancelled check (both sides) proving the tax payment.

• Mail your response by certified mail, return receipt requested. Keep the receipt in case the IRS "loses" your letter.

Shrewd Answers

Types of IRS notices and sample letters of response:

• Penalty notices for filing a tax return late,

paying taxes late or failing to pay the correct amount of estimated taxes.

Sample response:

Gentlemen:

I am in receipt of your letter dated April 26, a copy of which is enclosed, which reflects that a late-filing penalty has been assessed in the amount of $561. Given that reasonable cause exists, the penalty should be abated.

Although I had obtained an extension that permitted me to file my tax return up until October 15, it was impossible to obtain the information needed to complete my return until the middle of November. As soon as the information was made available to me, the tax return was completed and filed. The missing information was a K-1 form that reflects the amount of income I had earned as a partner in *ABC* limited partnership.

Because the late filing was caused by circumstances beyond my control, it is requested that the late-filing penalty be abated. In the event of an unfavorable determination, it is requested that this matter be forwarded to the Regional Director of Appeals for consideration.

• You-owe-us-more-tax notices that indicate that you made a mathematical error on your return or that the IRS did not give you credit for tax withheld or for estimated tax payments.

Sample response:

Gentlemen:

Enclosed is a copy of your notice dated May 15, which indicates an amount due of $300.

Your notice fails to give me credit for estimated tax payments that I made during last year. Enclosed are photocopies of both sides of my cancelled checks for payment of estimated tax. Accordingly, no money is owed.

Thank you for your prompt attention to this matter.

• Unreported-income notices that demand additional tax, interest, and a penalty because—the IRS claims—income paid to you was not reported on your return.

Sample response:

Gentlemen:

I am in receipt of your May 3 notice, a copy

of which is attached. Please be advised that your notice is incorrect.

Enclosed is a copy of a corrected Form 1099 issued by *XYZ* bank in the amount of $3,124 taxable interest. The information previously furnished to you was incorrect.

Kindly correct your records.

• No-return notices that indicate that the IRS has no record of a tax return, which it claims you were required to file.

Sample response:

Gentlemen:

I am in receipt of your May 12 notice, a copy of which is enclosed, which indicates you have no record of my tax return.

Enclosed is a copy of my 1986 tax return, which was filed on or about April 15, 1987. Also enclosed is a copy of both sides of my cancelled check for the balance of 1986 tax paid with that return.

How To Not Get a Notice

• Report dividend and interest income in the same amounts and under the same payer names as appear on your 1099 forms. If you lump several separately reported interest payments together, even if they're from the same bank, the IRS computer won't be able to find them. Result: You'll get a notice from the IRS claiming that you failed to report any of that income on your return.

• Mail your return at least one full week before the due date, even if you've gotten an extension. Returns received by the IRS after the due date, even though mailed on or before that date, are more likely to trigger an erroneous assessment for late filing penalties than those received by the due date. Since the IRS often misplaces the envelopes in which returns are mailed, it may be impossible to prove that a return was filed on time.

Source: Randy Bruce Blaustein, principal, Siegel, Mendlowitz & Rich, CPAs, 310 Madison Ave., New York 10017, and author of *How to Do Business with the IRS*, Prentice-Hall, Old Tappan, NJ.

Answering Unreported Income Notices

The IRS mailed over 1.6 million computer-generated notices to taxpayers whose 1984 returns did not show dividend or interest income as it was reported to the IRS by banks and financial institutions. The notice recalculated the tax due, added interest charges. . .and imposed a negligence penalty.

How should taxpayers handle such notices? What can they learn from them that will help in preparing future returns? Here's the procedure:

First step: Study the notice carefully and define the problem. Discover precisely which item, or items, of income the IRS says you did not report. You'll find this information on a separate page of the multipage notice.

Second step: Review your copy of the return and the 1099 forms you used to fill it out. Determine whether the IRS notice is right or wrong. Never automatically write out a check for the amount the IRS says you owe. The notice could be dead wrong—many are.

Third step: Answer the notice, in writing, within the time limit given—usually 30 days. Write to the IRS Service Center at the address given in the notice.

• If the IRS is right and you did accidentally fail to report an item of income: Pay the tax and interest but ask that the negligence penalty be waived.

Sample letter:
IRS Service Center
City, State
  Re: John and Sally Connell
  Social Security Nos. . .
  Form 1040-1984
Gentlemen:

In response to your notice, a copy of which is attached, you will find enclosed a check payable to the IRS in the amount of $x, consisting of tax of $y and interest of $z.

The item in question was inadvertently omitted from our return as filed under the following circumstances: [Give the reason for the accidental omission of the income.] It is contended that this constitutes reasonable cause for the inadvertent omission of this item. It is respectfully requested that the negligence penalty assessed in your notice be abated.

Sincerely yours,
John & Sally Connell

• When you did report the income or the notice is otherwise wrong:

Review the notice and your return to discover the cause of the discrepancy. One of several things may have happened. The IRS may be working with an incorrect 1099. Or the 1099 may be right and you reported the income but not as you should have.

Sample letter:
Gentlemen:

In response to your notice, a copy of which is enclosed, I am submitting the following in explanation of the alleged omission. [Examples follow.]

1. The dividend of $1,200 reported on my return as being received from General Motors should have been reported as being received from Merrill Lynch as nominee. A copy of my 1984 Schedule B is enclosed. [Circle the item where it appears on your Schedule B to show that you reported it.]

Lesson: Report dividends from stock held in street name by your broker as dividends received from the broker as nominee and not from the company. That's the way the 1099 will show them.

2. Dividend of $400 from Dreyfus Liquid Assets Fund was reported as interest income of $400 from Dreyfus. A copy of my Schedule B is enclosed. [Circle the item.]

Lesson: Most money-market funds report their income as dividends and not as interest. Report the income as it is reported to the IRS on the fund's 1099.

3. Interest of $600 from Citibank was on an account owned jointly by myself and my brother. I reported only one half of the interest—$300. A copy of my Schedule B is enclosed.

Lesson: The correct way to report interest from a joint account would be: "Interest, Citi-

bank, $600, less amount reported by others, $300. Net amount: $300."

4. Interest of $500 from Wells Fargo Bank was reported on my return as $100, per corrected Form 1099, a copy of which is enclosed.

Lesson: Review all 1099s when you receive them. Immediately request corrected copies of any that are wrong. Report the correct information on your return. If the IRS doesn't pick up the correction, you'll have it in your files should you need it.

5. Interest of $2,140 from American National Bank was nontaxable income distributed from my IRA account and immediately reinvested in another IRA. I enclose a copy of a corrected 1099 from American National showing $0 taxable interest in this account.

How to end the letter: If there are any further questions, please contact me.

• If you get a second notice that seems to have ignored your letter:
Gentlemen:

In response to your notice dated March 28, I received a similar notice dated February 23. I answered the first notice with the enclosed letter. It would appear that my response was not received in time to prevent the second request for payment from being issued. [Enclose photocopies of both notices and a copy of your original letter.]

Sincerely yours,
John & Sally Connell

Source: Philip B. Kimmel, partner, Hertz, Herson & Co., 2 Park Ave., New York 10016.

Some Excuses That Work And Some That Don't

Taxpayers who face penalties for misfiling returns or misreporting income will do the best they can to come up with a good explanation. Some excuses work—others don't.

Excuses That Work
• Reliance on bad IRS advice from an IRS employee or an IRS publication. If the advice

came from an employee, you must show that it was his job to advise taxpayers and that you gave him all the facts.

• Bad advice from a tax professional can excuse a mistake if you fully disclosed the facts to the adviser. You must also show that he was a competent professional, experienced in federal tax matters.

• Lost or unavailable records will excuse a mistake if the loss wasn't the taxpayer's fault and he makes a genuine attempt to recover or reconstruct the records.

• Incapacity of a key person can be a legitimate excuse. Examples: Serious illness of the taxpayer or a death in his immediate family.

Excuses That Don't Work

• Pleading ignorance or misunderstanding of the law generally does not excuse a mistake. Exception: Where a tax expert might have made the same mistake.

• Someone else slipped up. You are personally responsible for filing your tax return correctly. You can't delegate that responsibility to anyone else. If your accountant or lawyer files late, for example, you pay the penalty.

• Personal problems don't carry much weight with the IRS. For example, don't expect to avoid a penalty by pleading severe emotional strain brought on by a divorce.

Perils of a Joint Return

Filing a joint tax return creates "joint and several liability." This simply means that each spouse is liable for the entire amount of tax, interest and penalties ever assessed by the IRS on that return. When the IRS discovers that one spouse has understated income, it may be possible for the other spouse to avoid liability for the extra assessment by claiming protection under the "innocent spouse" provision of Tax Code Section 6013(e). To qualify for this relief, the innocent spouse must generally prove that he or she didn't know of the understatement and had no reason to know of it under the circumstances.

Strategy in negotiating a settlement with a revenue agent: Convince him to include the innocent spouse relief in the settlement. Then, if it later proves impossible for you to pay the tax and penalties, one spouse will have been able to accumulate assets that are immune from IRS collection methods.

How To Take Advantage Of IRS Mistakes

A few years back more than a million taxpayers benefited financially from a major IRS blunder. A computer foul-up at filing time caused unprecedented delays in mailing out refund checks. Taxpayer advantage: When the Service doesn't mail a refund check in the time provided by the tax law—within 45 days after April 15 in most cases—it must pay interest on the refund.

Other, less obvious tax law requirements that the Service sometimes slips up on:

Deficiency Notices

The IRS can't assess extra tax until it has sent you a statutory notice of deficiency, also known as a 90-day letter. You have 90 days to contest the amount of additional tax levied against you by filing a petition with the Tax Court. If you don't file a petition within 90 days, the Service may, without further notice, assess and begin to collect the tax.

Look for possible defects in a 90-day letter:

IRS notice wasn't mailed within the three-year limitation period. Ordinarily, the IRS has only three years from the return filing date to send a 90-day letter. One mailed on April 17 of the third year after you filed your return is no good, and any subsequent IRS attempts to collect tax are void.

Catch: You're not necessarily home free if you don't receive a 90-day letter by April 15 of the third year. Reasons:

• 90-day letters mailed on April 15 of Year Three are good.

• The Service has six years to assess tax against persons who have underreported their income by more than 25%.

• If the Service is alleging fraud, there is no limitation period—the extra tax can be assessed and billed at any time.

The 90-day letter was mailed on time but wasn't sent to your last known address. This is the address shown on your tax return unless the Service has reason to know (or should have known) that your address has changed since the return was filed.

What frequently happens is that a taxpayer moves, files tax returns showing his new address, and then is audited on an old return. The IRS sends the 90-day letter to the address on the old return. Is this notice good? Probably not. The courts are showing increasing impatience with the Service on this issue.

Developing rule: If the filing division of the IRS is dealing with you at your new address, the 90-day letter should go to your new address. If the auditing division happens to send it to your old address and you don't receive it, and the Service knows that you haven't received it because it is returned to them by the Post Office, then the 90-day letter is invalid.

If the letter was mailed at the last minute, the three-year limitation period will have expired and the IRS won't be able to collect either the outstanding tax or any penalties you may have accrued.

The IRS is also subject to a limitation period on collecting tax. They must start collection proceedings within six years after tax has been formally assessed, unless . . . they get you to sign a waiver of the limitation period. Key: They only have to begin an action in court to collect the tax. The moment the action starts, the limitation period is put on hold.

Defects in Liens

Before the IRS can put a lien on your property, they must follow the collection procedure set down in the tax law. Checklist of possible defects in tax liens:

• The original assessment of tax was made at a time prohibited by law. Assessments can't be made during the 90-day period after the date of a deficiency notice, nor can they be made while a Tax Court proceeding is pending.

• The Service failed to send you a notice of the assessment and a demand for payment.

• You received the notice and demand . . . but weren't given 10 days to pay, as required by law.

• The notice and demand wasn't sent to your last known address.

• The IRS didn't begin collection proceedings within the six-year limitation period.

Audit Errors

Audits must be completed within the three-year limitation period. The IRS watches the time limit closely and almost always gets taxpayers to sign a waiver extending the limitation period. Inside information: Agents can be fired for not getting a waiver of the limitation period, so the chance of a slipup is slim. It's most likely to happen when the taxpayer has moved out of state and the audit is transferred to another jurisdiction.

Taxpayers should be aware that it's not always in their interest to play hardball with the IRS over the waiver. Trap: If you refuse to sign a waiver, you could lose your right to appeal the agent's findings to the appeals division. Service policy: They won't let you take your case to the appeals division unless there is at least six months left in the limitation period. Carefully weigh your chance of negotiating a favorable settlement in the appeals division before you refuse to sign a waiver. Policy on waivers: Don't give long-term waivers. If the agent has already begun the audit, don't give more than an extra six months.

Source: Michael I. Saltzman, tax attorney with Saltzman & Holloran, 1 Rockefeller Plaza, New York 10020. He is the author of *IRS Practice and Procedure,* Warren, Gorham & Lamont, Inc., Boston.

Every Taxpayer's Dream: Catching the IRS in A Mistake

All in all, the IRS's accuracy rate is good. But the IRS is far from infallible. In many cases, its approach is to shoot first and ask questions later. The burden is on you, the taxpayer, to prove the government wrong. Some areas of IRS attack:

• Unallowable items: A legitimate deduction may be disallowed with no elaboration simply because it was screened out by the IRS's "unallowable items program." Defense: Immediately write to the Service Center, explaining in detail why the disallowed item is deductible.

• Automatic penalties: If your withholding and estimated-tax payments don't equal at least 90% of the tax owed, you're liable for a penalty unless you fall within one of the safe harbors that lets you avoid the underpayment penalty. The IRS won't go out of its way to see if you qualify for one of the exceptions. It will automatically assess the penalty and let you explain. Defense: File Form 2210 (Underpayment of Estimated Tax by Individuals), showing which of the exceptions applies to you.

• Mistaken information returns: The reporting of interest and dividends by banks and brokerage companies is not always right. The IRS approach: The information return is correct and the taxpayer is wrong. If the interest and dividends you declare are less than what is reported on the information return, the IRS will invariably assess more tax. Defense: If you come up with different figures from those on the information returns, be prepared to defend your numbers with copies of bank and brokerage account statements, for example.

The following are some common off-the-wall mistakes:

• Misplaced estimated-tax checks: You get a letter from the IRS saying your estimated payments don't show up on its computers. Essential: Send in photocopies of both sides of canceled checks used to make estimated payments. The reverse side of the check notifies the IRS which account it deposited the checks in.

• No return filed: Sometimes the IRS may say it has no record that you filed a return at all. Precaution: Always send tax returns by certified mail, with a return receipt requested.

This receipt is your best proof that the return was actually filed. If you have that receipt, send a copy of it in immediately. If you don't have one, send in a copy of your return.

• Interest errors: It's easy for the IRS to make a mistake in calculating interest on deficiencies and refunds. The question of when interest on a deficiency ends is governed by very complex rules. Defense: Make your own calculations before paying interest on a deficiency. Always check to see that the IRS is paying you the right amount of interest on a refund.

• Ignored refund claims: The IRS often has to be prodded into sending a refund. If you apply for a refund by filing an amended return (Form 1040X), send it by certified mail, with a return receipt requested. There's a three-year limitation period on refund claims. If you're close to the three-year limit, the government may well disallow the claim as being statute-barred. You have to prove that it was filed on time. Best proof: A certified mail receipt slip.

Getting Help

If you can't get action from the IRS Service Center or District Office, take the matter to the IRS's Problems Resolution Office (PRO). This section of the IRS is staffed with people whose job is to cut through IRS red tape.

Problems Resolution officers are not advocates for the taxpayer. They're expediters. Their job is to unearth a problem that may be buried in the IRS archives and get the right people to act. The PRO won't fight the battle for you, but in these days of red tape and bureaucracy, it can help.

IRS forms and publications:

Don't blindly rely on instructions given in IRS forms and information publications. The tax law has become so complicated that the government itself makes mistakes in its own publications.

IRS information booklets are often outdated. It takes a while for the booklets to catch up with changes in the law. On debatable issues, IRS instructions almost always take the government's side of the case. Rarely will the information booklet say: The issue is still open. Here's the government's position, but you have a right to disagree.

Source: Leon M. Nad, national director, technical tax services, Price Waterhouse, New York.

How To Get the IRS To Solve Your Tax Problems

The safest way to play the IRS game is to stay anonymous. The less contact you have, the better. But there comes a time for almost all taxpayers when they have to confront the IRS. How to safely handle some typical predicaments:

IRS Mistakes

• Computer matching notice. This is the most common IRS mistake. You get a computer-generated automatic tax assessment from the IRS. It claims that you didn't list an item of income on your return and now you owe more taxes.

It often turns out that you did list that item on your return. It's just that the IRS can't find it. This mistake happens because the IRS gets its information from the source of the income on a Form 1099, and sometimes the amount or some other information doesn't exactly match what you reported.

Example: You correctly reported the amount of dividends you received from a company, but the IRS got the 1099 information in your broker's name rather than the company name. When it looked for the dividend income from "Broker *X*" on your 1040, Schedule D, all it found was income from "Company *Y*." Solution: Send copies of all relevant papers with a letter of explanation to the IRS. Avoid this situation in the future by reporting your income exactly as it appears on the 1099. If the 1099 is incorrect, be sure to get it corrected through the source.

• IRS loses your return. This is really no problem if you prepare in advance by keeping copies of all forms and schedules that you send to the IRS. Keep a copy of any checks sent to satisfy your tax liability. Make sure your Social Security number is on every single piece of correspondence you send.

• IRS sends you a refund for your overpayment, but you had asked them to apply the refund to your estimated taxes. Solution: To avoid a bureaucratic mess, just keep the check and pay your estimated taxes separately. Key: If the IRS's mistake will subject you to a penalty, get it straightened out. Send a copy of your return showing that you checked off the proper boxes and return the uncashed checks to the IRS. Keep copies of everything you send.

• IRS doesn't send your refund. Wait at least 10 weeks from the date you filed your return. If you still haven't gotten your refund, get the IRS to check its status. Call the automated refund information number set up by the IRS (look in your 1040 instructions to find the correct number to call in your area).

Any taxpayer who has tried knows it can be frustrating to call the IRS. The numbers are often busy. Recommendation: If you're having trouble getting through, write to the IRS. It may take longer, but it's likely to increase your chances of getting action.

More Problems

• You can't pay your tax bill. Get in touch with the collection division at your local IRS office before April 15. It's almost always possible to work out an installment plan for paying your taxes. Be prepared to prove that you can't pay your taxes and need this "loan" from the IRS. Don't ignore the fact that you can't pay your taxes; the IRS won't.

• You are unsure of the tax law. The IRS publishes a wealth of material on almost every tax subject. Look in the back of your tax instructions for a list of these publications and where to get them.

If you are still unsure, favorable tax results can be guaranteed by asking the IRS for a private letter ruling on the subject. If the IRS decides in your favor, you can go ahead with your transaction knowing the law is on your side.

Private letter rulings are only effective for the specific taxpayer who asked for the ruling. Ask your tax adviser for help if you think a private letter ruling would resolve your uncertainty about the requirements of the law. The

IRS is now required to charge for letter rulings. Fees: $50–$400.

• You can't get a problem solved. Let the IRS solve it for you through the Problems Resolution Office (PRO). This is a branch of the IRS that may be able to help you when all else fails. Each IRS district has its own PRO, and you should use it if you can't get satisfaction elsewhere at the IRS. Get the phone number from your District Office. Prerequisite: Prior attempts at solving the problem through regular IRS channels.

Source: Michele R. Bourgerie, tax partner, Arthur Young & Co., 277 Park Ave., New York 10172.

How To Cut Through IRS Red Tape

The frustration of getting a problem straightened out at the IRS is enough to make most taxpayers despair. But don't give up if you get bogged down in the IRS bureaucracy. . . when the regular channels of communication have broken down, there is a way of cutting through the red tape.

Where To Turn

The IRS Problems Resolution Office (PRO) was created so taxpayers will have somewhere to turn when the system fails. It is the one office at the IRS where your problem will not be overlooked. Where to find the PRO: You can call or write to the Problem Resolution Office at your IRS District Office or your Taxpayer Service Center. Sample problems for the PRO:

• Your tax refund is missing.

• The IRS 1099 matching program mismatched your income. Example: Your bank account earned $300 in interest and the IRS mistakenly claims that the account earned $3,000.

• Tax deposits or payments you made were incorrectly posted by the IRS to the wrong year or the wrong taxpayer.

• You can't get other paperwork or bureaucratic mix-ups straightened out.

What you can't do: The PRO can't be used to resolve legal questions with the IRS such as a dispute over your tax liability or interpretation of the tax law.

PRO Prerequisites

Before the PRO will take your case, you must have attempted to solve the problem through the normal IRS channels without success. Be ready to explain to the IRS what you have already done to try to solve your case. You must have allowed sufficient time for the IRS to act on your problem through its regular channels. Depending on the type of problem you have, there are different prerequisites for getting a case accepted at the PRO.

• Refund problems: First, you have to wait 90 days from the date you filed your refund claim. After the 90 days have passed, you have to make two inquiries at the IRS about your refund. Prior to making the second inquiry, a taxpayer should wait at least 10 workdays for a response. When these attempts have been unsuccessful, the PRO will then accept your case and find out quickly where your refund is.

Example: Ninety days have passed since you filed and you haven't got your refund. You call the regular IRS channels and are told that you will get your refund in three weeks. You call three weeks later, because you still haven't gotten the refund, and the IRS tells you to wait another three weeks. Three weeks pass and you still don't have your refund.

• IRS notices: If you have received three or more notices from the IRS, and have replied to at least one of them without results, the PRO will take your case and resolve the problem.

• Inquiries: If you wrote a letter to the IRS requesting information about a tax-related issue and 45 days have passed without a response, the PRO will take on your problem. Also: The PRO will take your case if the IRS acknowledged your letter, promised to respond by a certain date and that date has passed without a response.

• Other: Whenever the normal IRS channels have not been successful in resolving your complaint or inquiry, you should contact the PRO.

Speedy Results

Once your case is accepted by the PRO, it should be quickly resolved. You will be advised of the progress on your case and the expected resolution date.

The average time it will take in most cases is 15 to 25 days. The majority of cases will be closed within 30 days, because any case that isn't closed in this time period is brought to the attention of IRS management. Highest priority at the PRO: Cases that are reopened at the PRO for a second time due to prior IRS mishandling.

Source: Charles Pomo, tax principal, Arthur Young & Co., 277 Park Ave., New York 10172. He is a former IRS agent and appeals officer.

Secrets of Getting Fast Action at the IRS

• Making waves at the IRS is an effective way to move a case along. Often, the hardest part of dealing with the IRS is getting an IRS employee to do his job. The thing to do if you suspect an employee is taking too long to complete a task, is to confront the employee and, if necessary speak to his supervisor. Don't be too concerned that you are alienating the employee. The threat to go over the employee's head may be enough to get action.

• When Congress criticizes the IRS, the IRS takes notice. Recent hearings on the subject of IRS abuses and the need for legislation to protect taxpayer rights has made higher-level management personnel sensitive to irate taxpayers who are being frustrated by the system. If you feel you're being treated unfairly by lower-level IRS employees, get in touch with the chief of the examination or collection division in your local IRS district office. There's a good chance the chief will attempt to accommodate you.

• Finding the right person at the IRS to solve your problem is often the biggest problem. Many taxpayer difficulties occur at the regional service centers where tax returns and tax payments are processed. Suggestion: If you don't know who to write to, address your letter to Chief, Taxpayer Service. If you are responding to correspondence received from the service center, put the stop number on the envelope. (The stop number appears after the zip code in the service center's address; for example, IRS Service Center, Holtsville, NY 00501, STOP: 422.) The stop number will direct your letter to the right area in the service center complex.

• Sometimes it's necessary to fight fire with fire. There are rare situations when an IRS agent will use his position to intimidate a taxpayer or intimidate his representative. A taxpayer can be intimidated by an agent who threatens to disallow all the deductions on his tax return. A tax accountant or attorney can be intimidated by an agent who threatens disciplinary action for delay or procrastination. The best defense in these situations is to take an offensive position. Immediately write to the agent's group manager setting forth all the facts and requesting that the intimidation cease. Such letters get immediate attention and are generally made part of the agent's permanent personnel file.

IRS Audit Triggers

If you know what makes the IRS decide to audit your return, you should be able to avoid audits entirely, right? Well, yes and no.

Approximately 70% of all returns audited are chosen through a top-secret grading process designed to indicate the probability that an audit will produce money for the government. Every tax return is reviewed and scored by this process, in which a number of DIF (Discriminant Income Function) points are assigned to key items listed on (or omitted from) the return. The higher the DIF score, the greater the likelihood of audit.

The DIF scoring process is a closely

guarded secret, but experience indicates a number of red flags that may cause the IRS to scrutinize your return.

Most provocative:

• Unusually large deductions in relation to income.

• Unusually large refunds (which you should avoid anyway, unless you enjoy subsidizing the government with interest-free loans).

• Missing forms or schedules. Always staple your return securely after making sure all required elements are present.

Discrepancies, including . . .

• Reporting the sale of a dividend-paying stock, but failing to report any dividend income.

• Reporting the installment sale of property, but failing to report interest income.

• Married couples filing separately and claiming the same deductions.

The higher your income and the more complex your return, the greater the likelihood that you'll be audited.

Other factors that could lead to an audit:

• A taxpayer's past history with the IRS. Some taxpayers may be audited regularly, particularly if a tax deficiency has been found in the first audit year.

• In any given year, the IRS will target certain types of businesses and financial dealings for intensified audit activity (for example, large corporations, small proprietorships, investors in abusive tax shelters, etc.).

Trap: The IRS maintains a list of unscrupulous tax return preparers and audits a much higher proportion of returns prepared by these persons.

Unavoidable: There is one audit trigger that you cannot avoid, regardless of how scrupulous you are in preparing your return and no matter what your income and expenses may be. It is the Taxpayer Compliance Measurement Program (TCMP) audit, an entirely random selection process. If your return is selected by this program, every item on it is subject to scrutiny. In a normal audit only certain areas of the return are examined.

Source: Michael H. Frankel, partner in the international public accounting and consulting firm of Peat Marwick Main & Co. and director of the firm's Washington National Tax Office, 1990 K St. NW, Washington, DC 20006. Author of many publications, he has lectured at several tax conferences and has been widely quoted in the newspapers.

Reduce Audit Risk

You may have the impression that the IRS computers are quite sophisticated and that it is virtually impossible to do anything legally to divert their eagle eye from your tax return. By and large this is true, but there are at least two things that may help minimize the effect of the IRS's high-tech capabilities.

First, how income is reported on the return may make a difference. Suppose you have freelance income. If it is merely reported as "Other Income" with an appropriate description as to its source, chances of having the return selected for audit may be smaller than if the same income is reported as business income on Schedule C (Income from a Sole Proprietorship).

Second, you can minimize your chances of being audited by filing as late as legally permissible. A tax return filed around April 15 generally has a greater chance of being audited than one filed on October 15 (the latest possible date). This is because the IRS schedules audits more than a year in advance. As returns are filed and scored by the computer, local IRS districts submit their forecasted requirements for returns with audit potential. The fulfillment is made from returns already on hand. If your return is filed on October 15, there is a smaller chance that it will be among the returns shipped out to the district office in the first batch. As a result of scheduling and budget problems that are likely to develop in the two years after your return has been filed, it may never find its way into the second batch slated for examination.

Although the IRS is wise to this ploy and has taken steps to make sure that the selection process is as fair as possible, inequities invariably result. Why not try to be part of the group that has the smallest chance of being audited?

The best way to reduce your chances of being audited is to avoid certain items universally thought to trigger special IRS scrutiny. There are also some common-sense considerations that should be thought about before you mail in your return. They are often overlooked by the very people who can least afford to be the subject of an audit. Here are a few examples:

Some people who are in cash businesses are not content with merely skimming some of their income. They also want to get every possible tax deduction—which is where the potential for audit comes in. When a business owner reports only a modest income, the IRS naturally becomes suspicious if that person also claims many business expenses and has high interest expense deductions. Two immediate questions are raised in the mind of the IRS examiner: Where does this person get money for personal living expenses and how is he or she able to make the principal repayments to justify the interest expense? When you are preparing your return, step back and think like an IRS auditor. If you can spot questions, so can the IRS.

What else can be done to minimize the chances of being audited? The following items should be reviewed carefully:

• Choose your return preparer carefully. When the IRS suspects return preparers of incompetence or misconduct, it can force them to produce a list of all their clients—all of whom may face further IRS examination, regardless of their personal honesty.

• Avoid problem tax shelters. Many tax shelters are perfectly legitimate, but many have been identified by the IRS as abuses. If you really want to avoid any chance of an audit, steer clear of all but the most conservative tax-shelter investments.

• Avoid formal membership in barter clubs. Members of these clubs trade goods and services on a cashless basis. The club keeps track of all transactions between members. Although no cash changes hands, these trades are taxable like any other profitable deal. Very often, however, they are not reported to the IRS. The IRS can force such clubs to produce membership lists, so that the returns of all club members can be examined.

• Answer all questions on the return. IRS computers generally flag returns with unanswered questions. For example, there is a question asking if you maintain funds in a foreign bank account. Even if you do not, you should answer no to the question.

• Fill in the return carefully. A sloppy return may indicate a careless taxpayer. The IRS may examine the return to be sure the carelessness did not lead to any mistakes.

• Categorize each deduction. Don't place deductions under headings such as miscellaneous or sundry. If you can't categorize a deduction, the IRS may decide you can't prove it.

• Avoid round numbers. A deduction that's rounded off to the nearest hundred or thousand dollars will raise IRS suspicions. It makes it look as though the taxpayer is guessing at the deduction's size, rather than determining it from accurate records.

• Limit deductions for unreimbursed business expenses and casualty losses. These deductions typically trigger audits. Try to have as many business expenses as possible reimbursed by your employer rather than taking them as tax deductions. It's cheaper for you and will not make your tax return stand out. Make sure that casualty losses can be properly documented and be aware that the IRS may be able to make a case that you actually realized a gain from the receipt of insurance proceeds, even though you think you had a loss. Insist that your tax adviser check this out carefully before taking a deduction.

Source: *How to Beat the IRS* by Ms. X, Esq., a former IRS agent, Boardroom Books, Millburn, NJ.

How Risk of Audit Varies Geographically

The IRS district you live in may affect the odds of being audited. In the Manhattan district, for example, 1.98% of all individual income tax returns filed are audited, whereas in Dallas, the rate is only 1.20%. The following table shows the percentage of returns audited in various IRS districts. It will give you an idea of which areas are the most audit prone in the country.

IRS District	Percent of Returns Audited
Albany	.88
Anchorage	2.48
Atlanta	1.21
Baltimore	.99
Boston	.69
Chicago	.98
Cincinnati	.75
Dallas	1.20
Denver	1.37
Detroit	.90
Jacksonville	1.36
Los Angeles	1.88
Manhattan	1.98
Nashville	1.14
Newark	1.34
New Orleans	1.30
Philadelphia	.82
Phoenix	1.44
Salt Lake City	1.97
San Francisco	2.17

Source: *IRS Commissioner's Annual Report.*

IRS Hit List

Doctors and dentists are high-priority targets. Items IRS agents look for: Dubious promotional expenses. If the same four people take turns having lunch together once a week and take turns picking up the tab, a close examination of diaries and logbooks will show this. Agents also take a close look at limited partnership investments, seeking signs of abusive tax shelters. And they take a dim view of fellowship exclusions claimed by medical residents.

Other target occupations:

• Salespeople: Outside and auto salespeople are particular favorites. Agents look for, and often find, poorly documented travel expenses and padded promotional figures.

• Airline pilots: High incomes, a propensity to invest in questionable tax shelters, and commuting expenses claimed as business travel make them inviting prospects.

• Flight attendants: Travel expenses are usually a high percentage of their total income and often aren't well documented. Some persist in trying to deduct pantyhose, permanents, cosmetics and similar items that the courts have repeatedly ruled are personal rather than business expenses.

• Executives: As a group they are not usually singled out. But if the return includes a Form 2106, showing a sizable sum for unreimbursed employee business expenses, an audit is more likely. Of course, anyone whose income is over $100,000 a year is a high-priority target just because of the sums involved.

• Teachers and college professors: Agents pounce on returns claiming office at home deductions. They are also wary of educational expense deductions because they may turn out to be vacations in disguise.

• Clergymen: Bona fide priests, ministers, and rabbis aren't considered a problem group. But if W-2s show income from nonchurch employers, IRS will be on the alert for mail-order ministry scams.

• Waitresses, cabdrivers, etc. Anyone in an occupation where tips are a significant factor is likely to get a closer look from IRS nowadays.

Many people, aware their profession subjects them to IRS scrutiny, use nebulous terms to describe what they do. Professionals in private practice may list themselves as simply "self-employed." Waitresses become "culinary employees," pilots list themselves as "transportation executives." But there's a fine line here. Truly deceptive descriptions could trigger penalties. And if the return is chosen for audit, an unorthodox job title for a mundane profession could convince the agent you have something to hide. Then he'll dig all the deeper.

Source: Ralph J. Pribble, a former IRS field agent, president of Tax Corporation of California, 5420 Geary Blvd., San Francisco 94121.

You're Always Safe Taking the Standard Deduction, Right? Wrong

Self-employed people are likely to have their returns audited if they take the standard deduction instead of itemizing personal non-business deductions, especially if their business shows a high gross and a low net. The IRS will suspect that personal deductions have been charged to the business.

When It's Smart To Ask For a Tax Audit

• When a business is closed down, the records and key personnel who can provide tax explanations may disappear. A subsequent IRS examination could prove very costly to the business's former owners.

• When someone dies, the heirs can count only on sharing in the after-tax size of the estate. So the sooner the IRS examines matters to settle things, the better.

When a taxpayer requests a prompt assessment of taxes due, the IRS must act within 18 months. Otherwise, the IRS has three years to conduct an examination. Use Form 4810 to ask for the prompt assessment. You don't have to use this form, but if you don't use it, eliminate any uncertainty on the part of the IRS by having your letter mention that the request is being made under Code Section 6501(d).

When You Can Decline An Audit

Under its own rules, the IRS will not audit you if the same item was examined in the past two years and no change was made by the auditor. Problem: Audit invitations are computer-generated. If you get an audit notice but you fall within the two-year rule, call the IRS and request cancellation of the audit.

Source: Louis Lieberman, former IRS agent, Great Neck, NY.

Audits the IRS Forgets To Do

Asking the IRS to transfer your case to another district may be the key to avoiding an audit. Don't expect the IRS to admit it, but transferred cases often fall between the cracks and never get worked on even though the taxpayer has been notified of the examination. Delays caused in processing the case file between districts, combined with the fact that the case is likely to go to the bottom of the pile when it is assigned to a new agent, may bring help from the statute of limitations. Rather than asking the taxpayer to extend the statute of limitations, as is the usual practice, many agents are inclined to take the easy way out and close transferred cases without auditing them.

Source: Ms. X, a former IRS agent, still well-connected.

Types of IRS Audits

There are several different types of audits . . .

• Office audit. The IRS sends you a letter asking you to come in for an audit. The items in question are listed, and you are asked to bring in substantiation for these items.

• Field audit. The IRS conducts this audit at *your* home or office. You don't know in advance what will be questioned, and the scope of the audit is unlimited. Have everything in order before the agent arrives to conclude the audit as fast as possible.

• Correspondence audit. You are asked to mail information or proof, or to sign a form and mail it back if you agree with the IRS's conclusions. These audits often result from the IRS's 1099 computer-matching program. Read the letter very carefully, and make sure the IRS has matched the correct 1099 to your Social Security number. The IRS frequently makes mistakes. Don't agree to anything until you are satisfied that the IRS is correct.

• Taxpayer compliance audit (TCMP). This is the most dreaded of all audits. The IRS randomly selects a percentage of returns and asks the taxpayer to prove, in detail, virtually every item on the return. The IRS does this to measure the effectiveness of the system and to see if taxpayers are complying with the law. Luckily, very few returns are chosen for this scrutiny.

If IRS Agent Comes to Your Door

The IRS has issued new instructions to be followed by auditors making field visits to a taxpayer's home or place of business. New rules: Agents may enter private premises "only when invited in by the rightful occupant." The IRS is concerned about the growing number of taxpayer lawsuits for violation of privacy rights.

Source: *Manual Transmittal* 4200–471.

Scheduling an Audit

Knowing how the system at the IRS works gives an experienced practitioner an advantage when it comes to representing a client at an audit. Here are some of the truly "inside" things that go on:

• Postponing appointments: It is possible, though not likely, that the IRS will actually change its mind about auditing you if you have postponed the appointment enough times. The IRS is constantly under pressure to start and finish tax examinations. If the return selected for an audit becomes "old" (i.e., more than two years have passed since the return was filed), the IRS may not want to start the audit. This situation may develop if you are notified of an audit about 15 to 16 months after filing. By the time you have cancelled one or two appointments, the 24-month cutoff period may have been reached.

When is the best time to cancel? The day before the appointment. By that time, the next available appointment will probably not be for six to eight weeks.

• Best time to schedule an audit: To someone uninitiated, it may seem ridiculous that one time of the day or month is better than another to have your tax return audited. However, a real advantage can be gained by following some simple tips. Try to schedule an audit before a three-day weekend. The auditor may be less interested in the audit and more interested in the holiday. Another excellent time to schedule an appointment is at the end of the month. If an auditor has not "closed" enough cases that month, he or she may be inclined to go easy on you to gain a quick agreement and another closed case. As for the best time of the day, most pros like to start an audit at about 10 o'clock in the morning. By the time it comes to discussing adjustments with the auditor, it will be close to lunch time. If you are persistent, the auditor may be willing to make concessions just to get rid of you so as not to interfere with lunch plans.

Source: *How to Beat the IRS* by Ms. X, Esq., a former IRS agent, Boardroom Books, Millburn, NJ.

How To Protect Yourself

Knowing what to do if you receive notification of an IRS office audit makes all the difference in whether or not you survive it. Crucial:

• Read the notice thoroughly. It tells you

which items are being questioned and what you should bring to the audit. Sometimes the IRS is just questioning one or two items on your return. If you have the records and the items are allowable, simply show that proof at the audit.

• Respond to the notice. If you ignore it, the IRS may automatically adjust your bill—in its favor. You usually have 10 days from the date of the notice to answer it.

• Prepare carefully. Review the return for the year to be audited, and gather your evidence and documentation from your files.

• Avoid a second appearance at the IRS office. IRS auditors don't work under a quota system, but the more time they spend on your case, the harder they will try to find adjustments. Find out the office's working hours, and if the office closes at 4:30, don't make an appointment for 4:00. The audit may not be concluded in half an hour, and the last thing you want is to drag it out until the next day. Best time for an audit: In the morning, so the auditor can finish your case and start the next one.

• Bring only relevant material to the audit. If you include extra items of proof about other matters on your return, you open yourself to the danger of an expansion of the audit. Frequently, your arrival at the IRS office coincides with the first time the auditor sees your file. He probably won't be interested in anything beyond the original matters unless you bring it up. Just deal with the items at hand as quickly and in the most organized way that you can. Where appropriate, provide adding machine tapes of checks or invoices that show grand totals agreeing with the line items on your return.

• Don't give the IRS original receipts or proofs. The IRS is notorious for misplacing paperwork. Make a photocopy of everything you need, and give the copies to the agent.

• Replace any lost records right away, if it's possible. Get a copy or statement from the original source verifying the deductions in question.

Example: If your medical bills are being questioned and you've lost your receipts, ask your doctor to provide you with copies of them or a statement of what you paid for the year in question.

• Be cooperative. The IRS auditor is only doing his job. Starting the whole process with a surly attitude will work against you, making the auditor much less willing to compromise. He will certainly rule against you whenever he has to make a decision. Your courtesy may mean a more favorable decision.

• Avoid arguments with an unreasonable auditor. You may be confronted by an auditor who is discourteous or just plain unreasonable. Ask to see the auditor's supervisor if you feel you are being mistreated. You should also ask to speak to a supervisor if you and the auditor reach an impasse on proposed disallowances. Discuss the situation with the supervisor calmly. Drawback: The auditor has no authority to broaden the scope of the audit without the permission of his supervisor. You may not want to draw the attention of the supervisor to your return.

• Don't give in to pressure. Get professional tax assistance if the audit is too overwhelming. If the auditor is obstinate about a deduction to which you are sure you are entitled, and you are sure there are no other questionable items on your return, don't give up. Rather, stop the action and tell the auditor you would rather wait until your tax professional can be present. Remember, however, that this will increase your exposure because of the second visit. If you have any doubts, ask your professional to go to the first interview.

• Don't volunteer any information. Otherwise, the auditor may introduce a whole new line of questions about another item on your return. Don't make "small talk" with the auditor.

• Be truthful. Lying or giving misleading information to the auditor is a criminal offense. If you find yourself in a sticky situation that you can't handle (that is, the auditor uses an indirect method and claims you have omitted income), terminate the audit right then and there. Bring in an experienced tax professional. Also, if the IRS auditor sees that you are a truthful person in general, he is more likely to accept your explanations of deductions. Another plus for truth: The auditor could be testing you by asking questions to which he already knows the answers.

• Check to see if the IRS's policy against repetitive audits applies. Have you been questioned in the two previous years about the same issue? If so, and there was no change in tax on that item either time, the IRS has a policy not to audit you on that item for the third year in a row. Get out your letters from the IRS stating that there was no tax change on that item. Then . . . call the IRS office and tell them you want the repetitive audit procedures applied.

• Know your appeal rights. Although in general it's better to get your tax liability settled at the audit level, you don't have to accept an auditor's decision. You are entitled to a conference with the IRS Appeals Division if you think the auditor has made a mistake. If you can't come to an agreement with the Appeals Division, you can go to court.

Source: Walter T. Coppinger, tax partner and special consultant in tax practice and procedure, Arthur Young & Co., 2121 San Jacinto St., Dallas 75201. He is a former IRS regional commissioner.

When and Why You May Need Your Accountant

Call your accountant if the IRS is proposing a sizable adjustment of the monies that you owe. Ask your accountant to call the IRS and handle the audit for you.

Strategy: By insulating yourself from the auditor in this way, you can't say the wrong things. Also, your accountant will gain more time to think about answers to complex questions, since he will have to get more information from you and then get back to the auditor.

Point: Weigh the cost of bringing in your accountant against the amount of any potential tax assessment. If the tax is relatively small, it

may not be worth it to pay for an accountant.

Source: Thomas LoCicero, senior tax manager and executive tax planning specialist, Deloitte, Haskins & Sells, New York.

How To Survive an Audit

When you receive notice that your tax return has been selected for an audit, take a deep breath, count to 10—and then take note of what items are being questioned, and whether the audit is to be conducted through the mail, at the local IRS office, or "in the field" (i.e., at your residence or your principal place of business). Note: If your return was selected at random by the Taxpayer Compliance Measurement Program, all items are subject to examination.

Whatever the case, the first step is to get organized. If you have proof of all items of income and deductions, the audit should proceed quickly. Organize your documentation and make it as complete as possible. For items that are not fully supported, determine what evidence you can produce that will corroborate the position you've taken on your return. Painstaking preparation will help *you* to control the flow of the audit and may well prevent a tax deficiency assessment.

Once the meeting with the IRS agent gets under way, be polite and businesslike. If the audit takes place in your home or office, try to find the agent a private place to work. While it is important to be cooperative, you do not have to do the agent's work.

Some Basic Don'ts
• *Don't volunteer information,* unless it is advantageous to you or unless the agent has made such a glaring error that he is sure to discover it.

• *Don't give the agent unlimited access to records and information;* if the audit is extensive, the agent should submit written questions or lists of needed information. Even if the audit takes place at an IRS office, it is wiser, tactically, to bring only the information required to support the items in question. By bringing additional information, you may draw the agent's attention to an issue he may not have focused on.

• *Don't permit an agent to remove any books or records from your office;* a request to do so may signal a potential investigation of fraud.

Some Important Do's

• If the examination is conducted at your place of business, caution all employees to avoid speaking to—or within earshot of—the examining agent about company matters.

• Do designate one person to have all contact with the agent. Safeguard the originals of all your records, receipts, and checks. If the agent needs physical records, make sure only copies are taken.

• Consider calling in your accountant, attorney, or other tax preparer. These professionals can steer you clear of mistakes and represent your interests to the IRS.

After the Examination

Once the examination is complete, the agent has three options: Acccpt the return as filed, find an overpayment, or propose additional taxes. If the agent proposes a deficiency, this is an opportunity to negotiate. On legal matters, the agent is bound by IRS rules and regulations, but factual determinations are to some extent discretionary. Since agents often have an incentive to settle as many cases as possible on the audit level, your powers of persuasion may help arrive at a compromise proposal.

If the agent proposes an adjustment, you have the option of accepting the agent's findings or appealing the case. Before you make this decision, consider the fact that on an appeal the IRS can dispute *any* item on a return, not just those already scrutinized. Thus, if there is an undiscovered issue that you know about but the IRS has not raised, it may be to your advantage to settle.

Source: Michael H. Frankel, partner in the international public accounting and consulting firm of Peat Marwick Main & Co. and director of the firm's Washington National Tax Office, 1990 K St. NW, Washington, DC 20006. Author of many publications, he has lectured at several tax conferences and has been widely quoted in the newspapers.

Preparing To Face the Auditor

Before facing the IRS auditor yourself, the most productive way to spend your time and energy is in gathering and organizing documentation of your deductions and exclusions.

The process includes preparation of schedules of the items involved. In the case of charitable contributions, for example, list dates, amounts, relevant check numbers, and make notations of receipts in your possession. Such preparation will save time during the audit and may encourage the revenue agent to do a spot check rather than tying in all documentation to the amounts claimed on the return.

If you anticipate disputes over certain deductions and exclusions, a valuable added weapon is a memorandum from your accountant. It should contain:

• A statement which shows that you understand the law involved.

• A corroborating statement on how and why you fit the particular provision in question or how specific circumstances warrant the position taken on the return.

• Citations of recent relevant court cases.

Source: Ralph C. Ganswindt, partner specializing in closely held businesses, Arthur Andersen & Co., 777 E. Wisconsin Ave., Milwaukee, WI 53201.

How Long Should You Keep Your Tax Records?

Always keep them longer than the three-year limitation period that the IRS has to audit your return. Recent case: During an audit, a taxpayer's carryover losses were approved by the revenue agent. After the audit, he continued carrying over the approved losses but threw out the proof because he thought he didn't need it anymore. Tax Court: Not so. When the IRS audited him for the next few years he lost the carryover deduction. He could no longer prove it.

Source: *Robert F. Neece,* TC Memo 1986-121.

What To Do if You Haven't Kept Good Records

Under the law, a taxpayer has the burden of proving his deductions. If you haven't kept good records, get duplicate receipts from the people you paid money to. Alternatives: Sworn affidavits, copies of canceled checks from your bank (usually available for a fee).

Under IRS guidelines, agents generally will give you adequate time to come up with proof if they believe you're making a good faith effort to cooperate.

Most agents will allow only what you can substantiate under the circumstances. The balance is negotiable. Always present a plausible story to explain your lack of records. Example:

"I realize I didn't follow the law 100% but I couldn't because I had to do so much traveling and there was so much illness at home that I had to take care of. I'm willing to take a reasonable disallowance and prove the illnesses."

Records You Should Have

Itemized deductions are a common IRS target. Here's the information you'll need to support your numbers:

Medical expenses:
- Doctor and dentist bills
- Copies of prescriptions
- Doctor's letter describing the illness and treatment to justify travel costs
- Copies of premium invoices and policies to prove medical insurance coverage

Taxes:
- Copies of state and local returns
- Tax bills and receipts (property tax)

Interest:
- Copies of promissory notes
- Mortgage amortization tables
- Year-end credit-card statements

Contributions:
- Letters from the organization that prove the donation
- Appraisals or other proof of value

Casualty losses:
- Police or fire department reports
- Description of property and proof of ownership
- Appraisals to establish value
- Itemized list of stolen/destroyed items
- Documented insurance recovery

Professional fees:
- Invoices or letters itemizing services and detailing percentage of tax-deductible work.

Source: Stuart R. Josephs, tax partner, Seidman & Seidman/BDO, San Diego, CA.

Preparation Is the Key To Winning a Case

The weaker the case, the better must be the preparation and presentation. Always present your case as attractively as possible. Organize the material in a binder complete with a cover, table of contents, and index tabs. Address every negative point the IRS could raise and reach a favorable conclusion to those points whenever possible. Make your presentation to the IRS in person . . . literally read your material out loud, cover to cover, to the IRS agent.

Second Best Evidence

Just because you can't prove something to the IRS auditor while you're sitting at his desk, doesn't mean that you should pay more tax right then and there. Taxpayers often show up for audits with inadequate or incomplete proof of their deductions. The auditor's initial reaction is to disallow the deduction, in the belief that the taxpayer would have brought the complete documentation if it existed. Strategy: Ask the auditor to tell you exactly what he would accept as satisfactory documentation. If he demands proof that you can't possibly obtain, negotiate for second best, but still satisfactory proof that you will be able to get. Suppose you can't find the canceled checks the auditor wants to see, but you will be able to get an affidavit from the person you paid the money to. Get the auditor to agree that the affidavit will be acceptable proof of your deductions.

Fighting a Bank Deposit Analysis

A routine audit procedure used by IRS agents is a bank deposit analysis. Deposits in all of a taxpayer's accounts are added up and then compared to the amount of income reported on the tax return. What if you don't think that a particular deposit was income, but you can't remember the source of the deposit? Ask your bank to supply you with a copy of the check that was deposited. Most banks keep these records for five years. The person who wrote the check can then furnish you with an affidavit explaining the reason for issuing the check.

Audit-Proof Your Cost of Living

On occasion, the IRS will attempt to reconstruct a taxpayer's income by estimating his cost of living. The IRS does this by adding up all living expenses paid for throughout the year by check then adding to this figure an amount it feels is reasonable for other living expenses it assumes have been paid for with cash. Tip: Make sure to pay for expenses such as food, medical expenses, automobile costs,

mortgage payments, and credit-card payments by check. This should head off an agent's contention that you had "hidden" living expenses.

Source: Ms. X, a former IRS agent, still well-connected.

How To Handle an IRS Auditor

Prepare meticulously for the audit. Gather all your receipts for the deductions the IRS has questioned. List each, in detail, on a sheet of paper. Also, meticulously reconstruct cash expenditures for which you don't have receipts. Explain exactly how and when you made those expenditures.

By presenting your case in factual detail, you establish your credibility. And credibility is everything at an audit. It will be easier for the auditor to allow nondocumented items if you can show him that you kept some receipts, that you made an effort to comply with IRS rules and regulations, and that you've reconstructed, as best you could, your cash outlays.

T & E Audits

Travel and entertainment is the most commonly audited deduction. Your goal: To limit the items the agent examines by persuading him to do a test check of your expenses. Let the auditor choose a three-month period for detailed examination. Or talk him into limiting the audit to items over, say, $100. Make sure you can document all items in the test-check period or in the amount. Double benefit: A test check cuts down your work in assembling backup data, and it prevents the agent from rummaging through all your travel and entertainment expenses.

Keep Talking

Don't expect to walk out of an audit not owing a dime. Your objective is to strike the best possible deal. To get an auditor to see things your way: Keep harping on the items he says must be adjusted. Keep talking. Don't give up until he reduces the adjustment. Even the most hardnosed agent will ultimately concede some proposed adjustments if you're stubborn enough. But you must be prepared to give a little, too—to concede items you're weak on, to bargain. Keep in mind that the agent's goal is to close the case and move on to his next audit.

Special Problems

• Business audits. If your business is being audited, have it done at your accountant's office, not at your home or your place of business. You don't want the auditor to see your standard of living nor run the risk that an employee will say something to the auditor that could hurt you.

• Unreported income. Generally required to be asked at IRS audits is Have you reported all your income? Never answer this or other potentially embarrassing questions with a lie. Deliberately failing to report all your income is a crime. So is lying to an IRS employee. To avoid incriminating yourself, deflect the question with, "Why do you want to know that?" or "I'll get back to you on that later." The question may not come up again. Another way to avoid answering this question is to not show up for the audit. Then the deductions you've been asked to prove will be automatically disallowed. But you can appeal the agent's disallowance at the appeals level of the IRS. At the appeals level, you're generally not asked whether you've reported all your income.

• Special agents. Their job is to develop evidence for criminal tax cases. If they show up at your door, don't answer any of their questions, even seemingly innocuous ones. Tell them to talk with your lawyer. Then retain a lawyer who is knowledgeable in criminal tax matters. Best: A former assistant US attorney.

Source: Randy Bruce Blaustein, Esq., a former IRS agent, now tax manager of the New York CPA firm, Siegel, Mendlowitz & Rich, 310 Madison Ave., New York 10017. He is author of *How To Do Business With the IRS*, Prentice-Hall, Englewood Cliffs, NJ.

At the Audit— When To Talk and When To Keep Quiet

If you've decided to handle an IRS audit yourself, the sound policy is to make as little sound as possible. You never can tell when some thoughtless remark will draw the agent's attention to something you want ignored.

The first step in keeping quiet is preparation. Prior to the audit, try to think of all the questions you might be asked. Go over them in your head until you're satisfied with your answers. Do not plan to lie.

During the audit itself, be on guard for seemingly innocent questions or other conversational gambits that pry into your family affairs or lifestyle.

For example, the "innocent" question, "How old are your children?" clearly has nothing to do with the business at hand. Moreover, if you're not fully on your guard you might find yourself responding, "Well, one is nine and the other is 11. The 11 year old goes to private school, and boy is *that* expensive!"

While questions about your upcoming vacation plans may make pleasant conversation, they can have no possible relevance to the issues at hand. But your answers are likely to be quite revealing about your lifestyle.

Also be on the lookout for trick questions. An example might be, "How many miles is your trip to work each day?" Here the agent may be looking to disallow some of your travel costs as nondeductible commuting expenses.

For questions that do legitimately relate to the audit process, take all the time you need to think through your answers. It is prudent to say no more than the minimum required to answer the question. In other words, supply only requested information. The agent can always ask for more information if you haven't provided enough.

Finally, and most important, do not, under any circumstances, answer an incriminating question. If the agent asks, "Did you report all of your income?" for example, what do you say? If you have reported all your income, you can, of course, say yes. If you haven't and you lie (by saying yes) you face even more trouble. But you don't have to say either. One evasion tactic is to pose a counterquestion: "What makes you think I haven't declared all my income?"

If you can't deter the agent and you find yourself being backed into a corner, you can always terminate the audit. This is your right. You can invoke it at any time. Simply tell the agent you need the assistance of your lawyer or tax professional. Flight may go against all your instincts, but conceding the opening skirmish still gives you a chance of winning the war.

Source: Mark A. Levinson, tax manager, Edward Isaacs & Co., 380 Madison Ave., New York 10017.

How To Beat the IRS at its Own Game

People at the IRS choose their words carefully when they want you to help them make a better case against you. They choose words that intimidate, convince, or cajole someone into doing something he or she otherwise wouldn't do.

To beat the IRS at this game, you must know what the agents mean when they talk tough. You must know what to expect if you call their bluff. Examples:

• Game One: An IRS agent asks you to produce all of your books and records for a tax examination. More often than not, the agent doesn't want every single record you maintain. He may only be interested in your bank statements, or in one or two unusually large items you deducted on your tax return.

Respond to the agent's request for all books and records by simply asking, "Exactly which records do you want?" Or, "What items are you really interested in checking?" Chances are he'll tell you, and it won't be every record you kept for the year.

• Game Two: The official line at the IRS is that agents do not negotiate proposed audit adjustments. Real life: Everything is subject to "discussion." Many agents will try to bulldoze their way through a case by taking a position and not budging from it. They will come right out and tell you that they don't bargain. But what they really mean is that they will not bargain unless they have to. If they feel they have a chance of closing the case on an agreed basis (you and the IRS agree on the extra tax owed), they will become more receptive to your proposals. The lesson: Be persistent. This will give you an excellent chance of meeting the agent on some reasonable middle ground.

• Game Three: You're in the middle of an audit and the agent asks you to supply him with a copy of the tax return you filed in a prior year. Perhaps the agent wants to review it to determine if it contains anything worth looking into in greater depth. Technically, you don't have to supply it since the IRS already has a copy in its possession. The problem, which the agent generally fails to tell the taxpayer, is that it takes forever for an agent to get a copy through normal IRS channels. If you don't supply a copy, most agents won't bother to pursue the matter. Suggestion: Make a deal with the agent to let him see a copy of the tax return only after you're satisfied that the audit has been concluded.

• Game Four: Revenue officers who are in the final stages of preparing for a seizure of a taxpayer's home or business will generally request consent from the taxpayer. Consent allows the IRS to enter private premises for purposes of conducting the seizure. Complications: What the revenue officer usually neglects to tell the taxpayer is that, if consent is not given, the IRS must go through the trouble of obtaining a court order authorizing the seizure. This can take up to six weeks. Taxpayers who refuse to give their consent can use this time to make a last effort to raise the money they need to pay the outstanding tax bill.

• Game Five: Special agents handling criminal investigations often approach people they suspect of wrongdoing and try to solicit incriminating information from them. If the people are reluctant to cooperate, the special agent will usually explain that if they don't answer the questions now, the agent will have no choice but to serve a summons and the questions will have to be answered down at his office. Privileged information: This is not 100% true—you can always claim your Fifth Amendment rights by refusing to answer any questions on the grounds that you might incriminate yourself. Taking the Fifth doesn't give a special agent any ammunition that can be used against you in court.

Source: Randy Bruce Blaustein, Esq., a former IRS agent, now tax manager of the New York CPA firm, Siegel, Mendlowitz & Rich, PC, 310 Madison Ave., New York 10017. He is the author of *How To Do Business With the IRS,* Prentice-Hall, Englewood Cliffs, NJ.

Making a Deal

• What do you do when the IRS asks for information that's already in its possession? It's not unusual for an IRS agent to ask a taxpayer to provide a copy of his return for the year prior to the one being audited and for the year subsequent to the audit. The agent wants the returns so that he can make comparisons of income and expense items. Even though the IRS already has copies of the returns in its files, the agent has to go to a lot of trouble to get them from the service center. It's much easier to get them directly from the taxpayers. Strategy: Tell the agent that you will give him copies of the returns, but only after he has concluded his examination and presented you with the items he feels should be adjusted. The agent will probably agree. By not giving copies of the two returns until the adjustments have been settled, you will prevent the agent from making potentially damaging comparisons.

• During an audit, the agent may ask you for a copy of a prior year's tax return. The agent can always requisition the original return from the service center, but that takes months. Strategy: Tell the agent you'll make his life easier by giving him a copy of the

return, but only if he, in turn, makes a concession. For instance, get him to agree to entirely avoid one of the issues he wants to examine.

Helping Novice Auditors

One way to resolve an audit in your favor is to write up the agent's workpapers (the forms he prepares on the audit) yourself. Sounds ridiculous, doesn't it? But it can be done in some circumstances by seasoned tax professionals. Many newly hired IRS agents simply do not have enough experience to know how to set up audit workpapers in a way that won't be criticized by their bosses. If your adviser knows what to put in the workpapers, and what to leave out, he can coach the agent accordingly. Many novice agents are receptive to a helping hand.

Psychological Warfare

How do you make an IRS agent see something your way when the agent continues to hold a position that you believe is unreasonable? One technique is to try to make the agent feel guilty that if he doesn't budge you'll have to take the case to court and that will cause you an unreasonable amount of anxiety and cost a lot of money. By getting the agent to feel sympathetic and guilty at the same time, you may be able to work toward a negotiated settlement.

What Happens if You Drag an Audit On and On And On

Contrary to what is generally thought, your odds of settling are actually increased if an IRS agent has been holding your case for a long time—over one year. Although tax professionals who intentially procrastinate can be barred from practice before the IRS, the Service is, for all practical purposes, helpless against taxpayers who procrastinate.

Source: Ms. X, a former IRS agent, still well-connected.

Extending the Statute of Limitations

It is not unusual for an audit to stretch out beyond the normal three-year limitation period. When this happens, the agent will ask the taxpayer to sign Form 872 consenting to extend the period during which the IRS may propose additional tax assessments. Many times it is in the taxpayer's best interest to give his consent, since withholding it will only result in the agent's coming up with an arbitrary assessment in an effort to protect the government's interest. Strategy: Agree to extend the statute for only six months rather than the one-year period the IRS normally asks for. This will put a degree of pressure on the agent to close your case. Also, a short extension gives the agent less time to develop tax issues that you would rather not be pursued.

Source: Ms. X, a former IRS agent, still well-connected.

When Not To Waive

It's common practice for an IRS auditor to ask you to waive the statute of limitations to give him more time to work on your case. If you refuse to sign the waiver, the examiner will generally disallow all the items he wanted to audit and issue a Notice of Deficiency. The Notice of Deficiency requires you to file a peti-

tion with the Tax Court within 90 days to avoid having to pay the tax until the merits of your case are considered by the court. Important: It may be to your advantage not to sign the waiver if there are items on your return that you would rather the agent not dig into at an audit. At Tax Court, you will still have to prove your deductions. But you won't be subject to the kind of probing that can open up other items that you prefer not opened.

When To Negotiate— When To Litigate

Unless you are prepared to cave in to the judgment of the agent on every issue, any tax audit is likely to turn into a negotiation. In disputes with the IRS, the outcome of the controversy depends not only upon the nature of the items at issue, but also to a large extent upon the level at which settlement is reached.

Where To Negotiate
Generally, a taxpayer's chance for success at negotiating questionable items is directly proportional to the bureaucratic level at which settlement is achieved. Your chance of success is *lowest* at the lowest level—the audit. Since the function of the IRS is to raise revenue, it's no surprise that examining agents do not readily concede a deduction or exclude an item of income subject to debate.

The taxpayer's position and outlook improve somewhat, however, at the conference level, where the case is reviewed for technical propriety and where arguments involving precedent (such as litigation on similar issues, Treasury Department rulings, or announced policy of the Revenue Service, etc.) may become the focal point of the discussion.

If the controversy is sufficiently serious, both in terms of the nature of the item and the dollar amount, litigation may be considered. Cases docketed for Tax Court generally involve a semiformal pretrial conference with a government attorney in which the Service's decision to press on is governed largely by its perceived chances of winning, a concern *not* permitted at lower levels. So there is a chance it may abandon the field to you at this stage.

In deciding whether to litigate in the regular Tax Court or the Tax Court for small claims, keep in mind the following: If the amount under dispute exceeds $10,000, you have no choice; the regular court is the only option. If you choose "small" Tax Court, remember that while proceedings are more informal, the rulings of this court are final. There is no further appeal.

Who Should Negotiate?

We all applaud the harassed taxpayer who defends himself in court and whips the IRS. Unfortunately, such cases are few and far between. At the prelitigation stages, however, the situation is different. Many reasonably sophisticated taxpayers can adequately represent themselves across the table from an examining agent, or even at the conference level—and do. In many instances, only the person who must eventually sign the check to pay the tax deficiency (if any) can bring to bear the requisite amount of enthusiasm to press his point.

On the other hand, representation by a specialist (an attorney, accountant, or enrolled agent) has much to recommend it.

• First, the representative can be expected to have an adequate grasp of the technical aspects.

• Second, a specialist is generally more objective and less likely to be distracted by emotional considerations, discussing only the facts at issue, and never volunteering more than the necessary amount of information.

• Third, a representative acting in the absence of the taxpayer offers an additional layer of negotiating space. The representative may tentatively agree with a settlement offer but will have to confer with his client, thus buying additional time to evaluate the proposal.

• Clearly, if a situation is serious enough to litigate, it is also serious enough to justify the cost of a tax attorney.

Note: Keep in mind that a representative need not be present at the outset. A taxpayer is not obligated to agree to the IRS settlement offer at the initial meeting. A specialist may be brought in at a later time without prejudicing his case. This strategy may be advisable if you detect a losing situation during or after the initial confrontation.

Source: Richard D. Lehmbeck and Henry J. Murphy, partners, Peat Marwick Main & Co., 150 JFK Pkwy., Short Hills, NJ 07078.

A Look at Tax Litigation And Appeals Procedures

Is it a good or bad idea to appeal an IRS decision that you owe more tax? The following list of steps in the appeals process will help answer the questions you'll have when the IRS contacts you.

• Audit. If the IRS questions or takes exception to any portion of your tax return, you will be notified of an examination or audit, to be held either "in the field" (on your premises) or in the local IRS offices. Following the conclusion of the audit, you will receive a notification of the Service's findings and proposed adjustments. The letter of notification gives you 30 days in which to appeal an agent's decision.

• IRS appeal. An IRS conference at the appellate level is initiated by filing a protest ("informal," if the disputed amount is under $2,500; "formal," if over that amount) with the regional director of appeals. A formal protest—a very simple document despite its name—includes the taxpayer's position on the disputed item as supported by some type of authority. The informal protest is just a short note requesting a review by the appeals division.

If the appeal decision goes against you (or if you did not appeal or otherwise respond to the "30-day letter"), you will receive a deficiency notice or "90-day letter" specifying the amount of additional tax, interest, penalties, etc., that the Service contends you owe.

• Tax Court. A deficiency notice allows you 90 days in which to file a petition to have your case heard in Tax Court. Within the Tax Court there is a special division for small claims (under $10,000). Its proceedings are relatively informal and litigating here is considerably less costly and time-consuming than in the "regular" Tax Court. However, its judgments are not subject to appeal elsewhere. Decisions of the "regular" Tax Court can be appealed.

If you fail to *properly* file within the 90-day time limit, you forfeit the right to have your case heard in Tax Court (although alternatives remain). Then, once the 90-day period has expired, the disputed tax is due and payable, regardless of whatever alternative you choose to pursue. You can file a claim with the IRS for a refund. If that claim is disallowed, your next step is an appeal to a higher court.

Source: Mark A. Levinson, tax manager, Edward Isaacs & Co., 380 Madison Ave., New York 10017.

How To Win the Fight After You Lose the Audit

Taxpayers who disagree with an auditor's findings can appeal the decision both within the IRS and beyond . . . to the courts. The end of the audit may, if you choose, just be the beginning of your fight with the IRS.

Round One

Actually, it's the IRS that really starts the fight—with what is called its 30-day letter. That contains a copy of the audit report showing the examiner's proposed adjustments to your tax bill. You have 30 days to respond or request an extension.

Important: Never ignore a 30-day letter. If you don't respond in time you'll get a notice of deficiency (a 90-day letter) and you'll have to file a court petition to continue your fight. Best: Try to settle the case without going to court. It's quicker that way and much cheaper.

How to get to the IRS appeals office: Send a protest letter. This will move your case from the audit division to the IRS appeals office. Advantages: The hearings officers at the appeals office have more authority to settle a case than the IRS auditor did. They can use their discretion to judge by the facts and circumstances of the case what the chances are of each side winning in court.

Example: If the hearing officer thinks that you have a 60% chance of winning your argument about the disallowance of a certain deduction, he can decide to allow you to take 60% of the deduction.

If you haven't had one before, it's a good idea to get a tax professional to help you at this stage. He will know what the best legal arguments are in support of your case. He will also know what information to include in your protest letter. A protest letter should include:

• A statement that you want to appeal the findings of the examiner to the appeals office.

• Your name and address.

• The date and symbols from the letter transmitting the proposed adjustments and findings you are protesting.

• The tax periods or years involved.

• An itemized schedule of the adjustments with which you do not agree.

• A statement of facts supporting your position in any contested factual issue, declared true under penalty of perjury.

• A statement outlining the law or other authority on which you rely.

Appeals Conference

You will be notified by the IRS when the appeals conference will take place. You may have to wait six months to one year. While you can represent yourself at this conference, it's a better idea to be represented by a professional who is qualified to practice before the IRS. These experts have experience in presenting your side of the issue to the IRS.

There is a very high rate of settling cases at this point. Usually the cases that aren't settled involve issues that the IRS has decided it isn't going to compromise, such as abusive tax shelter cases. On these issues, the IRS usually wants to test the cases in court in order to set a precedent for the future rather than settle at appeals. Advantage of settling at this point:

Court proceedings are costly, time consuming, and should be conducted with legal counsel.

Continuing the Fight

If you can't reach agreement with the IRS at the appeals level, you don't have to give up. You have the option of fighting it out in court. The IRS at this point will send you a notice of deficiency (also known as a 90-day letter). You have 90 days from the date of the notice to file a petition with the Tax Court.

Important: Never ignore a notice of deficiency—or fail to answer it within the 90-day period. If you do ignore it, the IRS will automatically make an assessment and bill you for what it thinks you owe. You will forever lose your right to argue your case in Tax Court.

Major disadvantage: If you lose your right to go to Tax Court, you can still sue in district court or claims court. However, for either of these two courts, you must pay the tax first, and then sue. In Tax Court, you don't have to pay the tax until the trial is over.

Source: Arthur S. Hoffman, tax partner, and Evette S. Weinberg, tax manager, Oppenheim, Appel, Dixon & Co., 101 Park Ave., New York 10178.

Appealing IRS Audit Conclusions

The best forum to fight in, after the audit or examiner level, is the IRS's own Appellate Division. There, taxpayers who disagree with IRS audit conclusions and who can document their position with sound facts have a good chance of getting at least part of what they're asking for, without going to court.

An appeal to the appellate level of the IRS is handled by highly trained IRS personnel called appeals officers. It is the appeals officers' job to settle cases, to see that they don't go to court, while still getting the most they can for the government.

Unlike auditors, who are bound by the regulations and rulings of the IRS, the appeals officer is entitled to consider the hazards of litigation. That is, the chance that the government might lose in court if it litigates a case. If the officer feels that the government has a weak position on the facts, or there are cases in the taxpayer's jurisdiction against the government, odds are that he will concede or agree to a settlement.

The officer has a great deal of leeway. It is possible for a taxpayer to horse-trade and negotiate on individual items with conferees. Typical is for the officer to concede half the tax bill (or a third of the bill) as being deductible. The taxpayer will have to concede the other half or two-thirds.

Some issues that are not likely to be settled at the audit level, but which taxpayers have a good chance of resolving at appeal, are:

• Cash expenditures that the auditor has disallowed for lack of documentation where those expenditures are common in the taxpayer's business.

• Travel and entertainment deductions that are disallowed because the taxpayer does not have all the support the tax law requires. These disallowances can normally be settled on appeal if the amounts are reasonable.

• Business use of property. A taxpayer uses his car in business 75% of the time, say. But the auditor says he hasn't supported his deduction. If the taxpayer can show that he normally uses his car in business, an appeal should be successful.

• Charitable contributions. Large deductions and those involving hard-to-value gifts, such as stock in a closely held business, become battles of appraisals. These often need to be settled on appeal.

• Constructive dividends. Are items of expense paid by a closely held company to an officer-shareholder deductible, or are they a nondeductible preferential dividend?

But do not go up through the appeal process on a lark, hoping for the best outcome. Prepare a decent case. Get sound professional advice. The appeals officers are technically competent people. They are not likely to let anything slip by them.

Do not expect to get 100% of what you ask for. If several issues are taken to appeal, be prepared to concede some as part of the give-and-take negotiations.

Cases that involve questions of fact rather than law have the best chance of being settled because facts lend themselves to compromise. On legal issues, there's less room for negotiation. For every six cases the taxpayer can come up with in support of a legal position, the appeals officer will have six for the government. There's a standoff, which the officer will have no choice but to resolve on the principal of hazards of litigation.

The best approach in dealing with an appeals officer (or an auditor, for that matter) is to give as much factual background as possible. Point out where the auditor was wrong. Support that position with facts. What prevails is a strong factual presentation, forcefully argued.

Source: David E. Lipson, partner in charge of the tax division of the Chicago office of Arthur Andersen & Co.

Tax Court Vs. District Court

The two most popular courts for pursuing tax cases are Tax Court and federal district court. The difference: Tax Court decisions are rendered by judges who are tax specialists. If you want a jury trial, you've got to go to district court. Catch: District courts only hear tax refund cases. So you have to pay the tax first to get your jury trial. If you win, you get your refund plus interest. Recent ruling: A person who had not filed a valid refund request could not have his tax dispute tried before a jury.

Source: *Kevin E. Krzyske,* E.D. Mich., No. 81-60223.

If You're Out of the Country

A Tax Court petition usually has to be filed within 90 days after the taxpayer receives a notice of deficiency. However, Mrs. Mohamed was out of the country when the IRS mailed the notice. Tax Court: Taxpayers who are out of the country when the notice is mailed have 150 days to answer a notice of deficiency. Mr. and Mrs. Mohamed filed within 139 days so their petition was valid.

Source: *Zaid A. Muthala Mohamed,* TC Memo 1987-132.

Winning in Tax Court

You've taken your case to the IRS appeals office and they have upheld the determination of the original examining agent. You still think you're right, but you don't want to go broke proving it. Does it make sense to take your fight to the next stage—the court?

If your case is strong on the facts but weak on the law, it might be advisable to pay the tax and sue for a refund in the district court. This would give you an opportunity to be heard by a jury of fellow taxpayers. (The court of claims is an alternative, but does not provide for a jury and has no apparent advantages.) For less subjective issues, Tax Court offers one enormous advantage: A taxpayer can dispute an IRS assessment without prior payment of the disputed tax.

Two Tax Courts

There are, in fact, not one but two tax courts: The tax court for small claims ("small" Tax Court) and the tax court ("regular" Tax Court). Which you choose will depend on which arena you think you can win in.

If you qualify, it may be to your advantage to have your case heard in "small" Tax Court. This forum is relatively informal—strict rules of evidence are not in force and the taxpayer can plead his or her own case. If the claimed deficiency plus penalties are under $10,000 for any one taxable year for income taxes, or $10,000 for estate or gift taxes, you can take your case to "small" Tax Court.

Advantage: This court saves you the cost of an attorney or tax practitioner and extensive preparation, if you have a fairly simple, one-issue case. Disadvantage: The decision of the court is not subject to appeal. You'll have to live with the ruling.

When you do not qualify for "small" Tax Court, you are in for a more elaborate and expensive effort. If the issues are complex, involving some of the more arcane provisions of the Tax Code, and the proposed additional tax is more than $10,000, the "regular" Tax Court will be where you make your case. Here it's wise to retain experienced tax counsel.

How To File

Once you decide to pursue your case in one of the tax courts, you must file a petition within 90 days of receiving your deficiency notice from the IRS (filing fee: $10). Information requested in the petition includes a statement in "clear and concise" terms of the errors the IRS made in determining the tax deficiency. You are also asked to state the facts upon which you base your belief that the assessment is wrong and unfair.

Your petition must be filed with the tax court in Washington, DC (400 Second Street, NW, Washington, DC 20217). Remember, if you file anywhere else, or if you file after the 90 days are up, the petition will be held invalid, and unless you refile properly and in time, you will lose forever your right and opportunity to have this case heard before the tax court.

Source: Raymond Polen, attorney-at-law in private practice at 60 E. 42 St., New York 10165. He specializes in estate and tax planning, and was formerly an estate tax attorney with the Internal Revenue Service, where he worked for more than 10 years.

Getting the Government To Pay Your Legal Fees

A recent Tax Court opinion provides insight into the factors that must exist before a taxpayer can get the government to pay his attorney's fees under Section 7430 of the Tax Code. (A taxpayer who beats the IRS in Tax Court can recover legal costs if he can establish that the IRS took an unreasonable position against him.) Factors favoring the taxpayer include: Did the IRS continue to pursue the case even though it had been aware that the case was defective? Did it send the taxpayer a long list of questions that were unrelated to the issues in the case? Did it adopt an inflexible attitude in rejecting the taxpayer's attempt to engage in settlement negotiations? Above all, the courts will not permit the IRS to wear down a taxpayer financially as a tactic to win its case.

Source: Ms. X, a former IRS agent, still well-connected.

When Not To Trust a Bill You Get from IRS

When the IRS comes up with a deficiency as the result of an audit, the taxpayer is given a waiver to sign and mail back to the Service. According to the tax law, if the IRS doesn't demand payment of the tax bill 30 days after the waiver was executed, interest on the deficiency stops running.

Problem: The IRS has been charging some taxpayers interest right up to the date of billing, which is often several months after the waiver was signed and returned. This extra interest can be several hundred dollars more than you should pay.

What to do: Carefully check interest charges before paying the deficiency bill. Interest should be charged for the period beginning with the due date of the return and ending 30 days after you sign the waiver and mail it back to the IRS. Pay the tax you owe and the interest that you determine to be correct. Clearly explain in an accompanying letter how you arrived at your figures, including a detailed computation of the correct interest. *Note:* Pay the deficiency bill within 10 days after you get it. If you don't, interest will start running again.

Source: Peter A. Weitsen, a former IRS agent, now with Laventhol & Horwath, CPAs, Box 11, East Brunswick, NJ 08816.

Stopping IRS Interest

Audited taxpayers can stop interest from building up on proposed tax liabilities (while preserving their right to contest the auditor's findings in Tax Court) by depositing the contested amount with the IRS. Conditions: The deposit must be made before the IRS sends a statutory notice of deficiency—a 90-day letter. The taxpayer must say in writing that the payment is "a deposit in the nature of a cash bond." Drawback: If the taxpayer wins in court, the IRS doesn't have to pay interest on the refunded deposit.

Source: IRS Revenue Procedure 82-51.

What Do You Do if You Can't Pay Your Taxes?

Can the IRS put you in jail because you owe it money and have failed to pay, even though the debt has been outstanding for years? The answer is no. Unless you fraudulently conceal your assets or otherwise conspire to beat the government out of its money, no crime has been committed merely because you can't afford to pay your taxes.

The best way to approach the situation of having fallen behind in the payment of taxes is to respond immediately to all notices sent you requesting payment. Make every attempt to speak to someone at the IRS and follow up the conversation with a confirming letter. Depending upon the facts and circumstances involved, the IRS may be willing to enter into an installment agreement for payment of the outstanding taxes. Usually, such a part payment agreement requires a down payment, followed by monthly payments over a year or 18 months. If you fail to comply with the terms of the part payment agreement, which also requires that all current taxes be paid on time, the agreement becomes void and your property is then subject to levy seizure.

The best time to try to get the IRS to offer you an installment agreement is at the beginning of the collection process. If you have ignored IRS attempts to work out an arrangement and it is now at your door with a Notice of Seizure, it is extremely unlikely that a part payment agreement will be offered.

Don't Let the Collection Division Near Your Bank Account

Suppose a person voluntarily files two or three years of delinquent tax returns on which he owes the IRS money that he simply can't pay. What can he expect from the Collection Division? Answer: Very little sympathy. An installment plan can be arranged, but the terms will be tough. Usually the entire amount of back taxes plus interest and penalties must be paid in no more than 18 months. Strategy: If you find yourself in this situation, empty your bank accounts fast before the Collection Division has a chance to seize them. Then try to work out a reasonable installment plan. If it gets to the money first, the Collection Division will not give it back even if you later work out a payment plan.

Advantage of Informal Payment Arrangements

Entering into an informal arrangement to pay your tax over a number of months may be the way to buy extra time from the IRS. The Collection Division has a formal procedure whereby a taxpayer must submit a financial statement and formally request permission to pay his tax liability in installments over a period of time. If your financial statement shows that you own assets, the IRS will generally request that you sell them. By avoiding

127

the formal route of an official installment plan, you may be able to gain the time you need to gather enough money together to pay the tax bill without having to sell or liquidate assets you would rather keep. Suggestion: Tell the revenue officer that you will pay at least 40% of the bill immediately and the balance in equal payments over two or three months. His initial reaction may be negative, but his bark may be worse than his bite. Give him the down payment anyway. He will privately be happy that your case can be closed in so short a time without extra work on his part.

Payment Strategy

The collection division usually holds all the cards in negotiations with taxpayers who owe the IRS money. But you may be able to gain some bargaining power by using a technique that has worked well in the past. Real case: A client owed the IRS more than $100,000. His accountant came into the revenue officer's office with a $25,000 check made payable to the IRS. He put the check on the agent's desk and said "It's yours. . .just let my client pay the rest in reasonable installments." A large up-front payment has a real impact. Most revenue officers won't want to see it slip through their fingers.

Buying Time

Just because a case has been assigned to the Collection Division, it does not necessarily mean that collection activity will begin right away. In a great many cases enforcement action will not start until after the taxpayer has failed to respond to a series of letters from the Collection Division requesting payment. Even after personal contact has been made by a revenue officer, it is still possible to squeeze out a few more months before you are in seri-

ous jeopardy of losing your house and business. The way you can really get in trouble with the IRS is to completely ignore the Collection Division. Sooner or later, time will run out.

Collection Tactic

Here's a strategy to use when the Collection Division is threatening to seize a home. The owner may not be in a position to refinance his home because the bank isn't satisfied of his ability to repay the loan. Helpful: Present the revenue officer with this proposal: "Until such time as I can refinance my house, I'll increase my monthly payments to the IRS by the amount that I would have otherwise paid to the bank had they granted me a mortgage." Keep in mind that the revenue officer won't be interested in a 20-year payment arrangement. Impress on the officer that you'll try to refinance your home again in six months when, hopefully, your financial situation will have improved.

How To Negotiate a Settlement When You Owe Money

The first step in negotiating a settlement of taxes owed is to provide the IRS with a current financial statement. Without a statement it can verify, the IRS will not even consider a settlement. What should you do if you don't want the IRS to know about certain assets you own? Just don't furnish the financial statement. It's better to offer no statement at all than offer one that is misleading or fraudulent.

If the IRS already knows about all of your assets, and there is no disadvantage in providing a financial statement, then go ahead and submit the statement. The IRS will be interested in knowing how much money you receive each month, how much is spent, and where. When you complete the personal living expense portion of the form, it is generally a good idea to arrange for some money to be left over each month to pay taxes. The IRS is more inclined to go along with a part payment offer if it feels confident there is money available to make the agreement work.

If you have assets and no income, there is nothing the IRS can levy. If you are in this desperate predicament, it does provide an opportunity to discuss an Offer in Compromise with the IRS.

An Offer in Compromise is a little-publicized procedure whereby the IRS will accept a one-time payment of as little as 10¢ for each $1 owed in settlement of your tax debt. If the IRS feels it will receive more money from you in the long run by entering into an Offer in Compromise and a collateral agreement (an agreement whereby you agree to pay a certain percentage of your income for 5 to 10 years), it may agree to the compromise.

The best chance of successfully using the Offer in Compromise route is when the tax debt has been on the books for a number of years. The IRS must be convinced that conventional collection procedures won't work. That's why a relatively recent tax obligation will not be settled this way. But if the IRS has had a chance to collect and hasn't succeeded, it is likely to accept your compromise offer.

Here's a suggestion you should bear in mind: Always use a tax pro to get you through the Offer in Compromise procedure.

Source: *How to Beat the IRS* by Ms. X, Esq., a former IRS agent, Boardroom Books, Millburn, NJ.

Tax Fraud: Who Gets Caught?

Executives, lawyers, doctors, and other high-income professionals are accused of tax fraud more often than the general population. Charges stem from IRS challenges that there

was willful or intentional failure to file, understatement of income, or claiming of fraudulent deductions. About one out of every five charges brought by the IRS in one recent year involved a professional or business executive. The average claim for back taxes is nearly $70,000.

	Investigations	Convictions
Total	**8,901**	**1,476**
Of which:		
Business owners	2,059	328
Other executives	485	94
Company officers	438	94
Attorneys	299	46
Dentists & doctors	199	33
Non-CPA accountants	164	40
CPAs	89	13

Less than 20% of IRS fraud investigations end in convictions. Other cases are dropped, the Justice Department refuses to prosecute, or they end with acquittal or dismissal.

Negligence or Tax Fraud?

Failure to report income deposited in a bank could be considered careless. That is punishable, at most, by a 5% negligence penalty. But when the omitted income represented deposits made in a bank in a different state, one court regarded the omission as a fraudulent, willful attempt to conceal income.

Source: *Candella et al. vs. United States*, USDC, E. Dist. WI.

Fraud Defense

• Albert Friedman was an independent insurance agent. On his tax return he reported commission income tax that was much less than the amount reported as being paid to him on 1099 forms filed by the insurance compa-

129

nies he dealt with. When the IRS discovered the discrepancy, it charged him with tax fraud. Tax Court: Understating income by itself is not fraud. Friedman hadn't acted to hide his income, and the IRS was bound to find out about it because of the 1099s. Thus, there was no fraud.

Source: *Albert C. Friedman,* TC Memo 1987-6.

• By having your tax return prepared by a competent professional and disclosing all necessary information to him, you can protect yourself from charges of tax fraud even if you greatly underpay your taxes by mistake. Recent case: The Borowieckis were charged with fraud when they moved $50,000 from their business to their personal account without reporting it as income on their tax return. They said they hadn't reported the money because their return preparer told them that no tax was due on it. Tax Court: Fraud occurs only when a person hides income. The Borowieckis had disclosed all their income to the return preparer. Thus, they couldn't be guilty of fraud even though the preparer had made a mistake.

Source: *Robert Borowiecki,* TC Memo 1987-23.

• The IRS tried to assess the fraud penalty against a contractor who didn't report all his income. He relied totally on others to keep his books and prepare his tax returns. He never examined them carefully. And, he never questioned the fact that his business receipts were sometimes deposited into his personal savings account and weren't taxed. Tax Court: The intentional wrongdoing necessary for fraud wasn't proved.

Source: *Wendell W. Vaughn,* TC Memo 1986-578.

• Charlie filed a tax-protest return which didn't include any income information. He didn't cooperate with the IRS during the audit, either. Tax Court: The IRS was wrong to try to assess the fraud penalty, because he didn't try to conceal his identity or his address. Clark, however, did have to pay the negligence penalty.

Source: *Charles Thomas Clark,* TC Memo 1986-586.

About Fraudulent Conveyance

When you owe the IRS money and then make a gift or transfer of an asset to another person for less than its fair market value, the IRS will claim that you have made a fraudulent conveyance. The IRS can take the property from the person you gave it to. One way to avoid this is to negotiate the property's fair market value with the revenue officer and agree to pay that amount to settle the case. Caution: Make sure that the IRS gives a release to the person you gave the property to. Otherwise it may go back later and assert its claim that the transfer was fraudulent.

How the IRS Gets Inside Information

• The IRS has the power to summons whatever information may be relevant to the audit of your tax return. The most commonly summoned records are bank and brokerage firm records. But the courts have also ordered a department store to turn over to the IRS copies of a taxpayer's monthly statements. Presumably, these spending records would help the examiners determine whether the taxpayer was reporting all his income by enabling them to estimate his cash flow and the extent of his wealth.

Source: *US v. Lazarus Department Stores,* DCSD, Ohio.

• The auditor can ask to see car repair bills even though you took the IRS allowed per mile deduction and didn't itemize car expenses. The reason: Repair bills often show the odometer reading on the car being serviced. By comparing readings at various dates, the auditor gets an idea of how far the car has been driven.

Suppose a bill in January showed an odometer reading of 10,000 miles and a December bill showed only 20,000. A taxpayer would have a hard time claiming a deduction for 50,000 miles driven during the year.

• Some of the country's biggest data marketing firms have refused to participate in the IRS's scheme to track down cheats by matching "lifestyle" information collected by the companies with IRS taxpayer lists. The companies say the information they gather couldn't help the IRS because it can't accurately predict a taxpayer's income.

• Local federal attorneys have been given authority to seek search warrants in connection with criminal tax cases without prior approval of the Justice Department in Washington. The number of warrants is expected to rise markedly above the handful that are currently issued each year. Reason for the policy: The dramatic rise in the number of fraudulent tax-avoidance schemes.

• The IRS was investigating a taxpayer and ordered his bank to produce the records of his account. The bank refused because it was a joint account, and the IRS hadn't sent notice to the account's co-owner. The district court ruled for the bank, and the IRS appealed. Court of appeals: There's no requirement that the account's co-owner be warned of the disclosure. Produce the records.
Source: *First Bank,* CA-2. No. 83-6350.

• Accountant-client privilege does not exist. That's what the Supreme Court held while ordering a private accounting firm to turn over to the IRS its confidential assessment of a taxpayer's tax strategies.
Source: *US v. Arthur Young & Co.,* S. Ct., No. 82-687.

• Informant danger. If a trusted friend, or relative or employer turns on you, steals your personal financial records and delivers them to the IRS, there's nothing you can do to keep the IRS from using them against you. Key: The IRS didn't take the records from you illegally, the person you trusted did.
Source: *Resmondo v. US,* DCSD Fla, No. 79-8166.

• Pressure is on Caribbean tax havens to provide the IRS with criminal and civil tax information. The bait: Liberal rules will permit business expense deductions for people attending conventions in Caribbean countries that cooperate. Eligible islands include: Anguilla, The Bahamas, Barbados, Cayman Islands, Grenada, Netherlands Antilles, British Virgin Islands.
Source: *Interest and Dividend Tax Compliance Act.*

4 FOR BUSINESSPEOPLE ONLY

What Should Be in Your Employment Contract?

Movement from job to job has become today's prevailing career strategy. One result of this change has been the development of increasingly complex employment contracts aimed at helping companies hold onto and motivate managers, and at protecting executives' benefits, and even their jobs.

Who Benefits from a Contract?

Employment contracts offer advantages and disadvantages to both employer and executive, but overall, a well-rounded agreement favors the interests of the employee. Here are the pros and cons.

Disadvantages to employer:

• Employers don't like employment contracts for managers generally, since they limit the freedom to fire employees at will. The cost to an employer of terminating the contractual relationship can be steep, measured in terms of severance payments.

• Employers resent broad use of employ-ment contracts because they establish prece-dents.

• Employers fear that executives protected by contracts may not show the desired amount of drive.

Advantages to employer:

• A contract locks in the executive for the life of the agreement at the terms specified.

• Annual bargaining and divisiveness over salary and bonuses are eliminated.

• Contracts may protect the employer and contain a covenant that the employee will not compete for a specified period after leaving the organization.

• The employee's use of confidential or secret information (important in certain indus-tries: fashion, high technology, etc.) may be barred.

Disadvantages to employee:

• The employee is tied down to the com-pany for the life of the contract (although if another company wants him badly enough, it will offer compensation for the loss in the form of up-front bonuses, enhanced benefits, accelerated vesting in the pension plan, etc.).

• Noncompete clauses may be enforced, although courts tend to look askance at these provisions if they are too restrictive of the employee's ability to earn his livelihood.

Typical Contract Elements

• Term. This clause spells out when the contract is to begin and end. Most employment agreements run three to five years.

• Duties. Description of the job and status. This clause is important, as it would be the basis of any employer's claim of termination "for cause." It is often very general, but should be specific.

• Compensation. The focal point of most agreements. Usually spells out minimum salary without limitation on the upside amount, and includes bonuses, stock options, etc.

• Vacation. How long each year, whether it can be accrued, and the availability of payment in lieu of vacation.

• Benefits. Life and health insurance, retirement plans, etc. Can include one-time relocation expenses; can call for an up-front bonus for signing the contract, for example.

• Place of performance. Spells out where the employee will be performing his duties (corporate headquarters, subsidiary or field offices, city, state, and country).

• Termination. Under what circumstances parties can discontinue the agreement.

• Severance. What compensation is due an executive upon firing. May include special provisions (e.g., "golden parachute" package, triggered automatically in the event of a change of ownership).

• In event of death. Can provide that the "fruits of the agreement" are assured for the employee's heirs if he dies and for those persons entitled to receive them if the employee is incapacitated.

• Disability provision. Can specify that disability of the employee does not constitute breach of the contract.

• Options of perks. For example, an expense account (standard), limousine, club membership, financial counseling, consulting provisions, noncompete provision, arbitration clause, purchase of old and/or new residence.

• Amendments. Provide for continuing the agreement unchanged for an additional period.

• Mutual assent. The best practice is for both parties to the employment contract to sign the document.

Source: Sandra E. Rapoport, attorney and managing consultant with William M. Mercer-Meidinger, Inc., 1211 Ave. of the Americas, New York 10036. Her specialty is consulting to management on labor and employment relations, including reductions-in-force, communications strategy during labor negotiations, executive compensation, employment contracts, and equal employment planning.

Your Perk Shopping List

The following is a list of perks commonly offered to valued executives by American corporations. Of course, no list of perks can be definitive. Perks are special by nature, and you might think of one or two more you'd like— and that are appropriate to your situation.

Remember, when negotiating for perks, that the most important ones permit the accumulation of wealth. They allow you to build for the future rather than just live off your paycheck and after-tax earnings.

• Use of company aircraft.
• Executive apartments and suites.
• Company-provided cars (with or without chauffeurs).
• Country club memberships.
• Deferred compensation plans.
• Discounts on products or services.
• Educational programs.
• Employment contracts.
• Large expense account.
• Health club membership.
• Home entertainment allowances.
• Incentive stock options.
• Group life insurance.
• Added life, health, and disability benefits.
• Loans or mortgages at low or no interest.
• Luncheon club memberships.
• Medical expense reimbursement.
• Lavish offices.
• Special parking privileges.
• Personal computers.

- Personal financial, legal, and tax services.
- Preretirement counseling.
- Private secretaries.
- Resort or convention accommodations.
- Supplemental retirement plans.
- Severance payment plans.
- Signing bonuses (usually 10% to 15% of base salary).
- Tickets to theater or sports events.
- First-class travel.
- Extra vacation time.

Source: Andrew Sherwood, founder, chairman, and CEO of the nation's largest full-service human resources management consulting firm, Goodrich & Sherwood Company, 521 Fifth Ave., New York 10017.

Salary Negotiating Tactics

Negotiating salary with a prospective employer is, and probably always will be, the most awkward phase of the hiring process. Keep in mind, however, you will probably never again have as good an opportunity to get what you want from your employer. As in any negotiation, you cannot hope to succeed unless you know what you want and what you can realistically hope to get.

Proven Strategies

The single most important bargaining tactic is to hold off the salary discussion until you know you have the job. This swings considerable weight in your direction.

Explanation: Once you are offered the job, it usually means that other candidates have been disregarded. Most companies don't pursue runner-up applicants if their primary choice turns them down. Further, a company knows that if it must start over to fill a position, it will probably find less qualified people on the second pass through the marketplace. The company wants *you,* and that gives you an advantage when the question of money comes up.

If the prospective employer raises the salary question early in the interview process, do your best to evade the issue. A good way to handle this is to mention your current salary, then add, "I'm really more interested in the career opportunities for me here."

Once you've been offered the job (and assuming you've been able to delay the salary question), present your salary demands with confidence. After all, you're the one they've chosen.

Trap: Don't blow your new job by asking for the moon. There has to be some give and take on both sides of the desk. Going for every last nickel can only create resentment and an adversarial atmosphere, which is not what you want when starting a new position.

If you and your new employer reach a true standoff on the salary question, and you're unemployed, try this novel approach: Make him an offer he can't refuse. Offer to work for a month at the minimum wage. At the end of the month, your boss has the option either to fire you or to give you the salary you are asking for. Chances are the firm won't take you up on your offer to work at the minimum wage, and may agree to your initial salary demands.

Source: Robert Half, president, Robert Half International, 522 Fifth Ave., New York 10036, a personnel recruiting firm with over 100 offices specializing in financial and data processing positions. He is also an author and columnist on the subjects of hiring and career planning.

Raising the Odds in Salary Negotiations

Most executives pride themselves on their negotiating skills in complex, high-pressure bargaining sessions. Yet it is not unusual for normally polished performances to falter badly when the issue being negotiated is as basic and personal as pay or status.

The temptation to hire a proxy to represent you in raise negotiations can be almost overwhelming. Unfortunately, this is one situation in which no one can do the job as effectively as you can. In fact, the mere presence of a third-party representative will usually create an adversarial situation.

135

For Businesspeople Only

Basic Strategies

If you dread salary discussions, you'll find that by applying business strategies to raise negotiations you can turn a negative prospect into a positive outcome. The basics of these strategies never change.

• Be fully informed in advance on the details of your own desired result and on the nuances of the situation of the other party.

• Insure the strength of your position before you enter the arena; you cannot negotiate from weakness.

• Apply the same rules you would use in a business situation: Both parties must perceive and achieve benefits; avoid cornering the other party or being cornered—ultimatums are a mistake; and begin by being sure the needs of the other party are understood.

Two Realities

Getting the raise or title you want involves taking a very close look at two realities. First, you. What do you do best? What do you enjoy doing most? What do you want to learn to do? Under what conditions do you wish to work? What are you aiming for in the company—or outside of it?

Second, the reality of your company and the position you hold in it. How is your company positioned in the market? What is its need for new products? How important is service to the buyer? Is the company in a field with growth opportunity? What is the importance of your present function to the profitability of the company? (In the case of a not-for-profit, your role in the value of its service.) How is your boss positioned politically in the organization?

When there's a good match between the needs and wants of both parties, the probability of raises and promotions rises dramatically. Successful negotiations therefore rest on informing yourself of these two realities in advance.

Swing into Action

Make the first move. Rarely do people get the best opportunities by waiting to be asked—initiate an appraisal discussion. Pro-

pose a new product or service, with an appropriate raise and change in title for you incorporated in the proposal. Volunteer when you would like to help meet a need expressed by the company.

Present your proposal with company politics in mind. Know who is politically disposed to accept or reject you and your ideas. Peers, who may feel threatened, or superiors who may be displaced, should be sidestepped. The party with whom you negotiate must be able to see the personal benefit of your actions.

Always begin negotiations orally, rather than with written communiques. This enables you to test reactions, modify your proposal, if necessary, and follow it up in writing. Since timing is very important, a conversation will aid your judgment. Then persevere. One turndown doesn't mean a permanent no.

Alternate Rewards

Consider a performance-based raise or bonus. If resources for an early monetary reward seem scarce, don't overlook the long-term monetary value of a more elevated title should you choose to leave the company. At least get that. You can also arrange for other rewards, such as time, different working space, etc. If you know in advance what you want, you'll be able to present your case as to how these rewards are appropriate to your responsibilities.

Be wary of holding up your superior for more than the situation warrants, however. It may be tempting or even easy to do this if you appear indispensable to a project, but ultimately you will suffer for it.

Finally, be willing and prepared to move out of your present organization if your needs aren't met over time. If you don't see yourself as able to move, you can't negotiate as a free agent.

Source: Nella G. Barkley, president and founding member, Crystal-Barkley Corporation, 111 E. 31 St., New York 10016. She was formerly a private consultant to industry and nonprofit organizations on management planning and start-up projects. She has completed the Advanced Management Program at Harvard University's School of Business Administration.

Alternatives to a Straight Salary

The main purpose of alternate compensation should be for executives to build up their investments, accumulate an estate, or pay for major expenses such as college costs for children. In essence, regular salary should pay the bills, extra compensation should be geared toward achievement of specific financial planning objectives.

The most common alternatives to a straight salary:

- Bonuses.

- Stock options.

- Employee benefits.

- Company car or limousine.

- Club memberships.

- Loans.

- Financial planning.

Since executives rarely have the time to fully explore all these alternatives, concentrating on two or three forms of extra compensation is usually the most effective planning method.

Bonuses

Bonuses are commonly paid as immediate cash, but can also be paid as cash in the future, or deferred compensation. Sometimes part of the bonus will be paid immediately and part deferred, with the executive deciding how much to receive and when; this decision will depend partly on the fact that bonuses are taxed as ordinary income upon receipt. Tax reform made cash bonuses something to be highly prized.

Most bonuses are based on some formula of performance geared to how well the company, division, or department did and the role of the executive in that performance. Study the formula and conservatively predict your next five years' payouts.

What makes deferred compensation unique is that it is only a *promise* of payment. There is no funding of payments, otherwise the executive would have to report them as current income (although a fairly new technique called a Rabbi Trust approached funding). This may present a problem only to executives of new or unstable firms. In these cases, recipients should consider opting for immediate cash over deferred compensation.

Stock Options

Many executives are not as enthusiastic about stock options as they are about straight cash bonuses. That's because stock prices don't always reflect the company's earnings—the stock price may remain stable or even decline despite increases in earnings. By the same token, executives working for firms whose stock prices experience dramatic increases in value are very fortunate, though this number tends to be exceptionally small.

Stock options primarily come in three varieties: Incentive stock options (ISOs), non-qualified stock options (NQSOs), and various forms of hypothetical stock, usually called stock appreciation rights or phantom stock plans. The first two varieties are actual stock, the third is primarily paper transactions which may not involve real stock. In all cases, only an increase over the initial stock price (i.e., the price at the time the option was issued) allows the executive to exercise the option and to benefit financially from it. One of the main differences between the first two plans is that with an ISO you only pay the company the stock option price. No immediate taxes are due for any increase in the stock price when you exercise the option. With NQSOs, however, you pay the company the option price plus you must pay taxes on the stock increase at the time of the option's exercise.

A frequently overlooked strategy is a stock-for-stock swap. Instead of paying for a stock option with cash, you may be able to pay for it with other company stock. Not all companies permit this type of transaction and it may not be advantageous for all executives, but for those who already hold stock and are tight on cash, stock-for-stock swaps are well worth exploring. Because of the elimination of long-term capital gains in tax reform, there is a de-emphasis on stock options, especially the ISOs and NQSOs. These forms of options were designed to take advantage of the maximum 20% long-term capital gains rate. With the highest tax bracket at 28% (actually 33%) the emphasis is now on current cash rewards.

Employee Benefits

Pensions and savings plans are among the most important compensation alternatives for most executives. Pension plans generally involve complicated formulas and payout options; it's a mistake to wait until retirement to investigate them. Instead, carefully study the plans offered several years before retirement, devoting special attention to lump-sum versus annuity plans.

Lump sums are primarily for executives who don't immediately need the money at retirement because of other income sources. The executive can roll the lump sum over into an IRA where the sum can grow on a tax-deferred basis until needed. Deferred compensation and consultancy arrangements are often the income sources that can make this possible. After the five or ten years payouts of these other sources, then the lump sum could have grown to a considerably larger sum, permitting the executive to either buy a larger pension from an insurance company than was available from the company at retirement, or use only earnings from the lump sum for needed retirement income. Annuities, however, can be best for executives who do not have other significant income and will need to rely primarily on the annuity for retirement income. The annuity lasts for the executive's lifetime whereas the lump sum could run out during retirement.

Savings plans are huge pluses—especially if they are 401(k) plans—because they can be an even better means than outside investments to accumulate money. 401(k) plans are so attractive because earnings can be used to save directly without being taxed first. Limit: A $7,000 contribution each year.

Discipline yourself to save as much as possible on a regular basis. In as few as five or ten years you'll be well on your way toward your financial planning goals.

Source: Paul R. Westbrook, national director, financial and retirement planning, Buck Consultants, Inc., 2 Pennsylvania Plaza, New York 10121, one of the largest employee-benefit consulting firms in the country. He is also a frequent lecturer and writer on financial and retirement planning, and has been widely quoted in financial publications.

Deferred-Compensation Rule

Deferred-compensation agreements make sense for executives, even under tax reform, because interest on the deferred compensation accumulates tax free until finally paid. Rule of thumb: An arrangement is attractive if your company credits you with interest equal to at least the prime rate plus 1%, or the going rate on Treasury bills. Drawbacks: You have to rely on the company's staying solvent.

Executive Pension Planning

Tax reform had a big impact on executive pension planning—by both increasing the cost of qualified retirement programs to the company and reducing the amount of benefits that top executives can claim through such programs.

Now's the time for the company and its executives to start considering alternatives to conventional pension programs that may provide greater benefits at less cost.

The Basics

There are two basic kinds of retirement programs:

• Pension plans, also known as defined-benefit plans. With these an employee receives a specified annual pension payment, usually equal to a percentage of his salary. The company is required to make whatever contributions are necessary to pay for this benefit. Result: An employee can be sure of what his pension will be, relative to his final salary, at retirement age.

• Profit-sharing plans, also known as defined-contribution plans. Here the company's plan contributions are usually based on a percentage of an employee's salary. Whether a contribution is made in a year is often up to the employer, and thus contributions can vary from year to year. Result: The employee can't be sure of the specific amount of benefits he'll receive several years from now. The value of his benefits will simply equal the amount that's accrued in his profit-sharing account.

A company can have both kinds of retirement programs.

Today's Rules

Starting in 1987, distributions from qualified retirement programs were subject to a range of new restrictions:

Pension-plan limits. The maximum benefit that can be paid out under a defined-benefit pension program was reduced from $136,000 per year to $90,000 per year by the 1982 tax bill. Tax reform further reduced the limit when a pension is received before age 65. Under tax reform such a pension must be reduced to the actuarial equivalent of a pension, beginning at age 65. The formula involved is complicated, but the result can be a dramatic reduction in pension benefits. Examples:

• Under old law a person retiring at age 62 could receive a pension as large as $90,000 per year. Under tax reform the maximum pension would be $63,000–$72,000 per year (the exact amount depending on the actuarial assumptions used and the recipient's date of birth).

• A person retiring at age 55 under old law could have had a pension as large as $75,000 per year. Under tax reform such a person's maximum pension would be only $28,000–$44,000 annually.

Advice: Before counting on pension benefits that were set up under old tax rules, double-check with your accountant or actuary to make sure that your benefits will be as large as you've been expecting them to be under tax reform.

Combined payouts. Tax reform imposed a 15% excise tax on annuity benefits exceeding $150,000 per year paid to an individual. When computing the $150,000 limit, payouts received from all qualified benefit programs and IRA accounts are combined.

This $150,000 limit may sound generous, but a surprising number of retiring executives may find themselves confronted by this tax. Typical situation: An executive who's been with a company for many years is covered by both a pension plan and a profit-sharing plan, and the profit-sharing plan has earned big gains from investments during a recent stock market run-up.

What to do: Postpone taking payouts from one of the plans to stay below the $150,000 limit. Or take a distribution from one of the plans in the form of a lump-sum payment, since lump-sum payments may be subject to higher limits.

Advice: Individuals with significant retirement benefits should seek professional advice before receiving a distribution.

Income averaging. A person who receives a lump-sum distribution from a qualified plan can cut the tax bite by forward averaging—treating the distribution as if it were received over a period of several years. Snag: Tax reform repealed the old law's 10-year averaging rules and replaces them with generally less-favorable five-year averaging.

Special benefit: A person who reached age 50 before January 1, 1986, can choose to have a distribution taxed under either the old law's 10-year rule or the new law's five-year rule. Usually, 10-year averaging will result in a lower tax bill. However, because the top tax rate imposed by tax reform is lower than the top rate imposed by old law, five-year averaging may be advantageous on very large distributions (those exceeding approximately $473,700).

Early payouts. In recent years many executives have used their retirement programs as investment accounts. Often they'd leave the company at an early age, take a lump-sum distribution of benefits, and use the benefit money to make further investments (such as the financing of a new business). New trap: Under tax reform an executive who leaves the company and receives a distribution of plan benefits before age 59½ will find his benefits subject to a 10% penalty tax.

Exceptions: Since this penalty doesn't apply to payments made as a result of formal early retirement at or after age 55, companies can amend their qualified programs to allow for this. Also, the penalty doesn't apply to annuity payments, death or disability payments, or amounts that are rolled over into an IRA.

Alternatives

Nonqualified plans. These are simply contractual arrangements under which the company agrees to provide benefits to key executives on an individual basis. Nonqualified plans are not subject to the distribution rules and limits that apply to qualified plans. And since a plan can be designed to meet a single executive's specific needs, it's likely to be more valuable to him.

Pitfalls:

• Employee benefits aren't funded by a trust, as is the case with qualified plans. The employee's benefits are part of the company's general liability. And even seemingly secure businesses can incur sudden unexpected hardships—as the Texaco case demonstrates.

• The company can't deduct employee benefits until they're actually paid. Deductions may be available more quickly with a qualified plan.

• The company must be careful not to provide nonqualified benefits to too many employees, or the nondiscrimination rules of the pension law may come into play. The rules here are complicated, so expert advice is a must.

401(k) plans. These are now perhaps the most attractive company plans. They let executives take up to $7,000 of salary on a tax-deferred basis and deposit it in a retirement account. This gets the equivalent of a $7,000 IRA deduction, which is even more valuable now that IRA deductions have been curtailed for many high-income executives. And since the company is not required to contribute cash to an employee's 401(k) account, it may incur only administration costs while providing a valuable benefit.

IRAs. Of course, deductible IRA contributions are available to persons not covered by qualified plans, and to persons who are covered by qualified plans but who report less than $40,000 of adjusted gross income ($50,000 on a joint return). And an IRA contribution is among the best tax-sheltered investments.

Overlooked: Persons who no longer qualify for deductible IRA contributions can still make nondeductible contributions to an IRA account and accrue investment earnings in the account that will not be subject to tax until withdrawn. Thus, IRAs can continue to serve as an effective tax-shelter device even for high-income individuals.

Annuities and life insurance products. With an annuity, you make payments now that will be invested and used to fund annual payments to you at some future date. With life insurance, your invested funds increase the cash value of your policy. In each case, you obtain tax-shelter benefits because earnings on your investment are not taxed until you withdraw them. With many insurance products you can borrow against the earnings, thus obtaining the use of the money tax free.

Source: David Kautter, partner, and Maria Stefanis, tax manager, Arthur Young & Co., 3000 K St. NW, Washington, DC 20007.

Borrowing Against Your Retirement Plan

Borrowing pitfall: Tax reform created several new pitfalls for the many executives who have borrowed against their retirement plan accounts. In recent years such borrowing has become a popular way to raise cash, and many executives have outstanding loan balances of as much as $50,000 (the limit under the old law). Now, however, these executives must beware of these new traps:

• Permanent loan balances of $50,000 are no longer allowed. All loans must be paid off at a level rate over a period of five years or less. Loans with a longer term are allowed only in connection with the financing of a principal residence.

• No interest deduction is allowed on loans extended to the company's key employees.

• No interest deduction is allowed on loans secured by an employee's elective 401(k) plan account.

• When an interest deduction is allowed, it will be limited by tax reform's general phaseout of the deduction for all consumer interest. In 1987 only 65% of such interest is deductible. The percentage drops to 40% in 1988, 20% in 1989. . .and to only 10% in 1990.

Planning: These new rules (except for the general deduction limit on consumer interest) do not apply to loans that were made before 1987. But they do apply to pre-1987 loans that are modified, renewed, or extended in 1987 or subsequent years. Thus, to avoid falling under the new rules, an executive will want to leave alone all old loans that are currently outstanding.

Trap: An executive has been carrying forward a loan balance of $50,000. He can continue to do so under the old rules as long as the loan terms aren't modified. But if he extends the loan or lowers the interest rate, he'll have to provide for repayment of the loan over five years.

Special trap: In 1987 many regular corporations elected S corporation status in order to make use of several benefits provided to S corporations by tax reform. A danger that's often overlooked exists when the owner-employees of such a corporation have borrowed against their retirement plan accounts. Such individuals are prohibited from borrowing from a qualified plan maintained by an S corporation. Thus, the S election may result in a law

violation and the imposition of penalty taxes.

Source: William E. Offutt III, partner, Grant Thornton, 1850 M St. NW, Washington, DC 20036.

When an Employment Agreement Goes Sour

Being one of the growing number of executives who demand that the employer "put it in writing," you have a written employment agreement. At the time the contract was signed, everything was rosy. Neither party thought the termination provisions of the contract would come into play. But now the relationship has gone sour. What do you do?

• Review your employment contract. Some people make the mistake of merely looking over the severance clause, which specifies what the company must pay if the employer terminates the agreement. Look instead for loopholes the employer might use to withhold severance pay or force you into a bad bargaining position from which you'll have to take less than you're entitled to. The key lies in the "for cause" provision, which describes the conditions under which you can be held in violation of the contract, making it unnecessary for the employer to pay you anything.

• Fulfill the contract provisions meticulously. You know you're already in trouble. Do not give the employer any pretext for refusing your severance pay. Follow the terms of the agreement in detail. Work a full day. Make all meetings. Don't violate any company policy, major or trivial. (Don't even bring home a scratch pad.)

• Collect proof. Build a file that gives evidence of your service to the company: Appreciative memos, reports, documents showing you have achieved goals, etc.— whatever you can get that shows the employer has recognized your worth to the organization. Then, if told you've been doing a poor job, produce the evidence.

• Request an evaluation of your work. Get on record as giving your boss a chance to criticize your work. Send a memo reviewing your progress on a particular project. Add something like, "As I see it, this fulfills all of the conditions of the assignment, and substantially achieves the stated goals." The worst that can happen is that the employer disagrees. If your document is accepted, actively or tacitly, you have evidence that you've been doing a reasonably good job.

None of this is calculated to keep your head from rolling. But it can help you get the full severance pay and benefits called for in your contract.

Planning for the Worst

If you're lucky enough to be reading this before the crunch and you don't have a contract, ask for one. This may be easier than you think—if the company values your work and wants to keep you around. Negotiate a good severance agreement and a tight "for cause" provision. Some such provisions are drawn so broadly as to cover almost anything: "'For cause' shall mean failure to carry out assigned duties. . ."

Make this provision in your contract as narrow and specific as possible, e.g., "The company may terminate this agreement for cause in the event of gross, repeated, and demonstrable failure to carry out reasonable instructions, if such failure is not remedied within a reasonable time after written notice. . ."

Also include a clause that submits disagreements over the contract to binding arbitration. This will keep you from being forced to negotiate your severance under the threat of a long and costly lawsuit.

An employment contract can be the best protection against being fired with minimum severance. It is much better, obviously, to have a strong contract in place than to try to make up for weaknesses in the contract when the agreement goes sour—or to have nothing in writing at all.

Source: John Tarrant, 167 S. Compo Rd., Westport, CT 06880, author of more than a dozen business books, including *Perks and Parachutes—Negotiating Your Executive Employment Contract; Drucker: The Man Who Invented the Corporate Society;* and *How To Negotiate a Raise.*

What To Do When the Ax Begins To Fall

Scores of bright, competent, but unhappy managers have come to us over the years saying that if they did not quit soon they knew they would be fired. We managed to convince a great number of these people that despite their distress, the situation contained great potential for positive change. The key to opening that door was a change in attitude—from locked in, angry, and frustrated to "private entrepreneur." The new attitude made an enormous difference in their lives and it can in yours, too.

If you find yourself stuck in a bad work situation and know there's trouble ahead, take action now, before the ax falls. Try the strategy we recommended to the executives mentioned above. Imagine yourself a free agent, determined to find the way you can best put your abilities to work for your company. Then turn your insights into business proposals and take them to the people in your company who could actually implement them (regardless of titles or company policy). This can be the best defense against being fired, because no company wants to lose its star performers.

The success of this strategy hinges on a willingness to open up to different thought patterns and to accept responsibility for planning and managing your own life. It works equally well whether or not you decide to stay with the same organization. If you should decide to leave, spend some time analyzing what you prefer doing and do best. When you know what this is (it may not be as obvious as you think), pick your own preferred career and job target and *go after it* as any intelligent private entrepreneur would. It may sound terribly risky, but so is having your neck on the block. Moreover, your chances are probably a great deal better than you think.

There's nothing like true motivation to make things happen. The fact is that thousands of people are risking such changes and are not doing too badly. Of one such group studied, 95% wishing to change job or career did so successfully, getting the job they decided they *really* wanted after their careful research. Further, these private entrepreneurs did not have to drop to the bottom of the career ladder and start all over again; 18% stayed at the same salary level in their new jobs, 77% won *increases.* Of these, nearly half received increases averaging $12,800, and 18% nearly tripled their incomes.

The final alternative to hanging in there in a deteriorating work situation is leaving the employee scene altogether and starting a business. This is increasingly popular, and the odds of succeeding will be increased immeasurably by following the same entrepreneurial planning principles.

Source: John C. Crystal, an internationally recognized life and career planning authority. He is chairman of Crystal-Barkley Corporation, 111 E. 31 St., New York 10016. He is the originator of the Crystal Life/Work Planning Process and a consultant to corporations, government agencies, universities, and professional associations.

How To Get Fired Profitably

Anyone can get fired. This risk is an integral part of work life. Like any other normal risk, it should be factored into your own long-range life and career plans and reduced to manageable proportions by intelligent planning. In combination with a little assertiveness, realistic planning allows you to turn a potential disaster into a positive opportunity.

Preparing for risk allows you to be alert to any early warning signs. And, unlikely as it may sound, reading the handwriting on the wall early gives you a substantial measure of control over the progress of events. Most important, it gives you time to make preparations to move smoothly on to another—and better—job or into your own business. (Note: Don't concentrate all your attention on finding a new job; take whatever time is necessary to familiarize yourself with company policy on termination and with your rights under the law.)

Making a Forceful Exit

You have picked up warning signs and have begun your preparations. Here's an approach that may well turn the situation to your advantage: Preempt the decision making by arranging a meeting and calmly asserting that you have read the signs and would like to make things easier for all concerned by asking for your own dismissal—under certain terms, of course—thus saving emotional wear and tear on all sides.

It does not take as much courage to do this as you might think: Just hardheaded realism. In some cases, the reaction may be quite surprising. The impression you create by being very professional about the situation may stimulate your superior to revise earlier opinions of you. Once in a while this can lead to a real opening in which you can (if you wish) offer your own proposal as to how you could serve that same employer far better in a position much more to your liking. Your proposal might just be accepted; it has happened.

If, instead, your proposed self-dismissal is accepted, these are terms you should negotiate for (as needed):

- Full severance pay.
- Use of corporate "outplacement."
- Use of your office for several months.
- Secretarial and other support help.
- A recommendation (specific form to be mutually agreed upon).
- Opportunities to meet other potential employers.
- Permanent or temporary use of your car or other perks.

You may not win on every point, but you will probably win on a significant number. Realize that corporations will go to surprising lengths to avoid the unpleasantness associated with terminating highly placed employees—and make this work for you.

Source: John C. Crystal, an internationally recognized life and career planning authority. He is chairman of Crystal-Barkley Corporation, 111 E. 31 St., New York 10016. He is the originator of the Crystal Life/Work Planning Process and a consultant to corporations, government agencies, universities, and professional associations.

How To Change a Job or Career After 40

When you're in your twenties, changing jobs within the same field, or even changing to another field, is relatively easy. But it gets progressively more difficult after 35 and becomes just about impossible after 40. The first thing that an over-40 job changer is questioned about is his track record.

Employment agencies and personnel people will tell you that your experience and credentials are nontransferable. So, unless you stay away from the conventional system, it's almost certain that you'll get absolutely nowhere.

Understanding the Realities

The usual reaction of people who are trying to change careers or jobs is simply to keep trying. If 1,000 resumes don't work, they send out 3,000. By the time they realize that this isn't getting results, they're in a syndrome of rejection and depression. And once you're in that self-defeating cycle, it's extremely difficult to escape.

The right approach:

• Don't even think about looking for a job through employment agencies or personnel departments, sending resumes, or answering newspaper ads. Decide beforehand to forget that route.

• Think of yourself as a product that you have to market. If you've been in management, you've been trained and are experienced in analyzing your company's problems. This is the time to use those abilities in analyzing your own situation.

Marketing Yourself

• Do research and development on yourself. You must figure out who you are, what your skills are, and what you really most want to do. This should include considerations such as where you want to live and intermediate goals versus long-term goals. See yourself as a whole person with skills, interests, and goals that may have nothing to do with your past employment. Be specific. A vague goal such as "I'd like to be a teacher" is meaningless. "I want to teach music on the high-school level in San Francisco" is much better.

• Do market research for yourself. Find out exactly who would be interested in the product you're selling—yourself. How to do this: Talk with people to find out what's available in your area of interest. Don't look for a job. Simply survey the situation and find out what the needs are. This takes the pressure off, and you make valuable contacts.

• Meet with contacts. Personal and business contacts are all-important. You'll make some contacts while surveying your interest area. But don't hesitate to survey friends, relatives, or current business associates.

• Go with your heart. Radiate enthusiasm about your goal. A positive attitude is crucial and comes only from doing what you really want to do, not what you think you should do, or what seems sensible, or what someone else wants you to do. If your proposal turns you on, it will have the same effect on your potential buyers.

• Go to the right person with your proposal. Approach the person who has the power to accept or reject it. Find this person through your contacts.

Example: A 42-year-old graphic artist was interested in getting into the television field but had no TV experience. She talked with a number of people in various aspects of television and found there was a need for artists to do on-screen computer graphics and animation. One broadcasting company was hiring artists who had taken a particular manufacturer's three-day course. She took the course and got the job. She's now making triple her previous salary.

• Make them an offer they can't refuse. Figure out not only what you can contribute but also the best method of reaching your potential market with a strong sales message. Recommended: The business proposal. Work up a proposal identifying a need in a particular area. Then outline and explain how you think it can be filled by using your services.

Source: John C. Crystal, chairman, and Nella G. Barkley, president and founding member, Crystal-Barkley Corporation, 111 E. 31 St., New York 10016.

Own-Business Basics

Launch a new business only after you have formulated a complete business plan. The plan should include careful projections of your monthly cash needs and available income for the first three to five years. Rarely does a new enterprise produce positive cash flow early on.

Questions to answer first:

• Is the money to be invested in the new business money that you can afford to lose?

• Are you young enough to get another job and build another career if the new venture fails?

• Can you afford to replace the insurance coverage you may have now as an employee?

• Do you need a bank loan to start? If so, would you be wise to apply for it before you quit your present job?

Source: Edward Mendlowitz, partner, Siegel, Mendlowitz & Rich, CPAs, 310 Madison Ave., New York 10017.

How To Make Money as a Consultant

At one time or another, most executives consider selling their expertise on their own, as consultants. The majority are at least moderately successful, but many fail. Most commonly, they overestimate the salability of their services and underestimate the effort needed to sell them.

How to find out if your service will sell: There is no fail-safe method. A talk with several potential clients will tell you if you are headed in the right direction. The big sellers: Services that help companies keep up with change, whether it is in technology, marketing, personnel relations, or other areas that business needs to know about.

Pitfalls for New Consultants

• Not realizing that consultants, especially new ones, spend more time selling their services than performing them.

• Wasting time on unproductive prospects.

• Choosing too broad a field in which to consult.

• Not learning to talk the client's language. This is essential because many consultants sell a highly specialized service with its own vocabulary to an equally specialized customer who uses a completely different language. Example: A computer expert who is hired to automate market research for a diaper manufacturer.

New consultants are also faced with the temptation to sell their services cheaply at first in order to build up a good track record. Do not underprice. Clients are reluctant to establish a good working relationship with a bargain-basement consultant. And without that, the job is likely to be a failure.

It is also unnecessary to hire a public relations firm at the outset because a PR campaign will not have anything to talk about. Using a part-time consultant could be helpful, however, in planning a credentials brochure.

To sell their services, successful consultants:

• Maintain pressure by keeping in touch with clients and prospects.

• Master such sales and marketing methods as the art of writing letters, making convincing phone calls, and developing presentations.

• Start at the top, contacting the chief executives of the Fortune 1000 companies. Send individually typed letters and follow up with phone calls.

Source: Charles Moldenhauer, vice president, Lefkowith, Inc., marketing and corporate communications consultants, New York.

To Start a Business on a Shoestring

Shoestring businesses aren't limited to small ventures tucked away in the dusty corner of someone's garage. Many are capitalized at hundreds of thousands of dollars. They're called "shoestring" because the owner has invested little—if any—of his own cash.

Shoestring businesses are more a state of mind than a modus operandi. They work only if the owner is willing to adhere to the One-tenth Principle. Starting a business with one-tenth of the required capital demands that you exert ten times the effort.

Planning Comes First

Don't fall into the trap of thinking that the smaller a business, the less risk involved. Starting too small is actually more of a risk than starting too big. If you're starting a service business, microscopic beginnings might work. But new retail and manufacturing ventures require some more to begin—and enough to internally generate profits.

Careful planning and well-researched start-up costs are the keys to attracting financing. Helpful: Get a copy of the Small Business Administration's excellent cost worksheet. It's invaluable in pinpointing frequently overlooked cost items.

Once you've identified costs, the next crucial step is figuring out how to slash them. Don't emulate the small journal publisher who struggled in his plush $66,000-a-year offices when a $10,000 facility would have sufficed... and would have produced profits instead of red ink.

If your shoestring business does require extensive quarters, however, look for retail basement space or space in a large, older home. Both are usually priced well below conventional commercial property.

Retail businesses must focus on location. These businesses need immediate cash flow, and that means a high-traffic, high-rent location. Bad alternative: Low-rent space that will force you to plow rent savings into advertising to attract customers.

Better: Negotiate with the landlord to pay partial rent early in the lease and a higher rent later when cash flow is likely to be more substantial. Or, negotiate to pass renovation costs on to the landlord. Keep in mind that a landlord who pays for your new ceilings, carpets, and air-conditioning is going to charge a higher rent. But this can save you as much as $100,000 in initial costs.

Equipment bargains are next on the shoe-stringer's cost-slashing list. In fact, it should be part of every entrepreneur's game plan to scour auctions, chain stores, equipment supply houses, classified ads, bankruptcy sales, and trade journals for secondhand equipment and fixtures.

Nothing Down . . . The Smart Way

One-hundred-percent financing is plentiful. . . if you know where to look. Although banks and finance companies aren't prime lending sources for shoestring businesses, they'll usually consider full financing on bargain-priced equipment with established collateral value. And equipment sellers are often more interested in unloading unneeded equipment than in getting immediate cash.

Manufacturer financing can also be arranged. Trade-off: Manufacturers' lending standards are more lenient than banks'. . .but you'll have to pay two or three percentage points more.

Leasing is often a wiser choice than buying, especially for motor vehicles, computers, carpets, and cash registers. Rule of thumb: If it will last more than five years, buy. If it will wear out or become obsolete within five years, lease wherever possible.

Inside idea: Whether buying or leasing, negotiate with the equipment manufacturer for a 30- to 60-day trial run. If you've planned well, your business should be generating enough cash flow to complete the buy or lease agreement by the end of the trial. If it isn't, return the equipment. . .and you've spent nothing.

Look to suppliers for financial support. Big suppliers can usually afford to let you defer payment for a while if they see the possibility of more and more business from you down the road. And, if your business looks like it will do well in the future, small suppliers might offer price breaks or better terms.

Example: A small enterprising baked-goods manufacturer convinced his flour supplier to buy him $40,000 of baking equipment against $800,000 in flour purchases over four years. The deal amounted to nothing-down equipment and a 5% discount for the baker, and a long-term customer for the supplier.

If you can't offer good collateral to a lender, you'll have to look to nontraditional financing sources. Best bets: Friends, relatives, high-tax-bracket investors, and the SBA.

And while you're abandoning the idea of conventional sources, you might as well discard thoughts of conventional terms. Your best deal is whatever you can bargain for. Private backers generally want 24%–26% of your business, sometimes with a percentage of profits as well.

Seeking 100% financing when you have personal funds safely stashed away can cause potential lenders to back off. Suspicions arise when investors sense that you're playing only with other people's money.

The Shoestring Corporation

Incorporating your venture is essential. But don't buy shares with all of your investment funds. Instead: Use a small portion for share-buying and loan the balance to a friend or relative who, in turn, loans the money to the new corporation in exchange for a mortgage. In the event of a failure, your friend or relative will be a preferred creditor. . .when he gets his money back, so will you. By contrast, if you loan directly to the corporation as a share-holder, repayment may be disallowed by a bankruptcy decision.

Source: Arnold S. Goldstein, partner, Meyer, Goldstein, Chyten and Kosberg, 850 Boylston St., Chestnut Hill, MA 02167.

Smart Investing

Putting your money where your business plan is makes you likely to get backing for that plan. Venture capitalists look favorably on managers who make significant investments (relative to their personal wealth) in their own companies.

Source: *Financing and Managing Fast-Growth Companies* by Teledyne, Inc. co-founder George Kozmetsky, Lexington Books, Lexington, MA.

Use Accrued Pension To Start Your Own Business

Employee Getum has "had it" working for his present boss. He wants out now, he has $100,000 coming from his employer's qualified plan, and he is entitled to and qualifies for lump-sum treatment. Getum finds out the tax bite on the $100,000, if distributed this year, would be $35,000; he needs $50,000 to finance his new business. What to do?

The steps would be as follows:

1. Getum forms a new corporation, Go-Getum Co.

2. Go-Getum Co. adopts a qualified profit-sharing plan.

3. The distribution—the full $100,000—from Getum's former employer's qualified plan is rolled over to the new Go-Getum plan.

4. The new plan would have a provision to allow loans to be made to participants in an amount not to exceed 50% of the participant's vested interest, or $50,000.

5. The new profit-sharing plan would loan $50,000 to Getum to be repaid over five years at 11% interest per annum.

Obviously, the documentation from the new plan itself, the plan administrator's minutes describing and approving the loan, and the note payable by Getum to the profit-sharing trust must be impeccable in every detail.

Source: Irving L. Blackman, CPA, senior partner, Blackman, Kallick & Bartelstein, 300 S. Riverside Plaza, Chicago, IL.

The Basics of Using Other People's Money

Other than your own pockets, where do you go for business financing? Trends in the popularity of different types of financing vary from season to season, but the sources all fall into two categories: Debt and equity. The following summary covers a few of these sources along with their respective criteria.

Debt

• Banks. Short- or long-term, secured or unsecured, bank loans are the traditional form of financing for all types of business needs. Banks typically make lending decisions based on a company's operating history and potential cash flow; they analyze the past few years' financial statements, requesting that they be audited, reviewed, or compiled, and examine projected cash flow, income statements, and balance sheets for the next few years. Banks look at a number of key financial ratios, including receivables and inventory turnover, liquidity, debt/equity, and profit margins. Their emphasis is on historic trends of the business and comparable industry averages.

Recent changes in the banking industry have increased competition, making new sources of financing available for small and medium-sized businesses. These include large commercial banks, most of which have established market divisions to service smaller companies (generally, those with less than $100 million in revenues), and savings and loans, which are now permitted to make a limited amount of business loans.

• Finance companies. Small businesses with less stable operating histories can turn to finance companies for funding. Finance companies offer many of the same forms of asset-based lending as banks, but focus more on a company's collateral than its operating record or potential profits, and are often willing to lend to less stable businesses. The cost of these loans typically is higher than that of bank loans, because of the greater risk assumed and the cost of monitoring the collateral. However, the true differential may not be as great as it appears, once all the hidden costs of bank loans (compensating balances, commitment and other fees, prepayment penalties, etc.) are factored in.

Equity

• Venture capital. While venture funds are not as plentiful as they were, venture capital firms continue to make strategic investments.

Unlike sources of debt financing, venture capitalists place less emphasis on a company's stable financial track record; financial history and projects are important, but secondary to management, market, and product. Venture capitalists are more inclined to look for medium-term payoff from a new venture's management-team strength, identification of a strong market need, and ability to satisfy that need with a unique product.

• Regulation D. "Reg D" represents a relatively recent change in the requirements of the Securities & Exchange Commission (SEC). Under Reg D, smaller businesses can issue securities without SEC registration. The amount of the eligible offering is generally dependent upon the number of investors. Form D, which must be filed with the SEC, is relatively straightforward to prepare.

• R&D partnerships. This form of financing involves investors willing to fund product research and development in return for tax and other benefits. Typically, investors look for businesses in a well-developed technological area, plans for rapid expenditure of funds to yield immediate tax deductions, and prospects for near-term revenues. As a result of the Tax Reform Act of 1986, the tax breaks from such partnerships have all but been eliminated so investors will be seeking other benefits.

Successful Financing

Here are three important rules of seeking financing, regardless of its form or source:

1. Keep your proposal presentation clear, concise yet informative, and easy to absorb. A potential funding source should be able to quickly understand your business, your reason for requesting funding, and the benefits of providing that funding.

2. Don't sign away too much in your effort to obtain financing. In equity financing, be cautious about the amount of control you relinquish. When taking on debt backed by personal guarantees, try to exempt certain assets, such as your home.

3. If you're turned down, find out why—in writing, if possible. Then, if feasible, rework

your financing proposal to meet the objections and either resubmit it or try a new source.

Source: Jacob Weichholz, partner in the tax department of the metropolitan office of Arthur Young & Company, 277 Park Ave., New York 10172, specializing in the tax and organization needs of small and medium-sized businesses.

Unconventional Ways of Raising Capital

When companies need cash to grow, the vast majority turn to proven sources: Family and friends, commercial banks, and venture capital funds. The choice depends on the amount of money needed, their stage in the corporate life cycle, and how fast they plan to expand. But other capital avenues are open to the shrewd entrepreneur that may suit the company's needs better than the traditional ones. These include corporate ventures, joint ventures, R&D limited partnerships, and marketing partnerships. It may even be possible to combine two or more of these sources in a total funding package.

Corporate ventures: The corporate venture, a direct equity investment by a large corporation in a smaller entrepreneurial company, is becoming a popular alternative to traditional venture capital investing. Corporate ventures are generally not entered into for the sake of profit alone. The investing business also may have an interest in identifying windows into new technology, screening potential acquisitions, leveraging available skills, or enhancing a staid corporate image.

By the same token, the entrepreneurial company generally receives more than just cash: Its corporate partner may provide additional value in the form of credibility, a built-in customer-supplier relationship, or expertise in planning, marketing, R&D, or distribution. Further, entrepreneurs entering into these strategic alliances generally don't need to give up as much equity as they would to a venture capitalist. Finally, corporate partners can offer deep pockets for later-stage financing.

Businesses likely to receive this type of investment are often smaller, technology-driven companies that have a logical "fit" with the sponsoring companies. However, unless you have a corporate partner experienced in this type of investment, you run a much higher risk of clashing corporate and entrepreneurial cultures.

Joint ventures. Joint ventures pair companies with complementary strengths on specific projects. For instance, a company that has designed a salable product may lack the cash to manufacture it. If the company can identify a partner with the right manufacturing capabilities, the two then can form a joint venture, divide the profits, and eliminate the need for cash exchange.

Joint venture financing holds promise for the future in terms of providing emerging companies with a way of achieving the financial weight necessary to compete with larger corporate entities. There is plenty of room for imagination in setting up business arrangements of this type. One company, for example, developed a software program for farmers and is now successfully marketing it through booths in feedstores.

R&D limited partnerships. Specific projects are financed and investors receive attractive tax shelter, through R&D limited partnerships. The sponsoring company provides project management, while the investors provide capital in exchange for tax benefits and the rights to the technology developed. It is generally agreed that when the R&D work is successfully completed, the company will exercise its option to acquire the rights to the technology from the partnership through royalty, equity, or joint venture.

Some of the benefits to the sponsoring company of an R&D partnership include:

• The financial risks are borne by the limited partners.

• The sponsoring company retains full control over product development.

• The sponsoring company has the right to acquire the successful technology.

149

IRS rules for R&D limited partnerships are changing and have become very complicated in certain situations. In addition, the Tax Reform Act of 1986 effectively eliminated the ability of individual limited partners to offset against all but certain other income losses generated by R&D partnerships. For these reasons, it's important to get expert financial counsel to sort out the details.

Marketing partnerships. In a variation on the R&D limited partnership—the marketing partnership—the limited partners put up cash to market an existing product or service. In exchange, the company gives them a percentage of each sales dollar. The partners don't receive tax advantages in this arrangement, but if the product is successful, the return on investment can be very high.

Source: David T. Thompson, partner, Deloitte Haskins & Sells, Crocker Center, 333 S. Grand Ave., Los Angeles 90071, an international accounting and consulting firm. He is the national coordinator for venture financing in the firm's emerging business services practice.

How To Find a Venture Capitalist

Are you looking for venture capital? Don't reach for the Yellow Pages. The goal is not just to find a venture capital firm, but to identify the right one for you. After a successful funding, your company will be married to the firm—in spirit as well as in equity. Finding the perfect match takes research, contacts, and patience.

Anxious about the prospect of raising capital, entrepreneurs are often tempted to use the "shotgun" approach: Printing up hundreds of copies of the company's business plan and distributing them to anyone wearing a suit. Unfortunately, this method wastes time and money and can damage the reputation of the company.

A targeted approach can improve your chances. The majority of venture capital firms specialize in particular types of deals. Some

look only at high tech, others won't touch it. Some prefer leveraged buyouts, others work strictly with start-ups. High- versus low-tech preferences are important to determine, as well as discriminations on the basis of geographic area, industry, company growth stage, or amount of money sought. Like any other professionals, venture capitalists tend to stick with what they know best.

After you've figured out what kind of firm specializes in your kind of deal, the next step is to locate them. An authoritative resource is *Pratt's Guide to Venture Capital Sources,* published annually by Capital Publishing Corp. in Wellesley Hills, MA. Another good listing can be found in the *Venture* magazine annual venture capital directory. Both publications list firms all over the country and include addresses, staff, and areas of interest and specialization.

It's a good idea to read articles in business or trade magazines for news of venture firms; take special note of deals in your industry or area. You may also want to subscribe to the monthly *Venture Capital Journal,* widely considered to be the industry bible.

You already should be in continuing contact with your accountant, lawyer, and banker, having relied on their counsel to develop a sound business plan and financial projections. Remind them that you're interested in meeting venture capitalists. People whose businesses are already venture-backed can be particularly helpful. They've been through the process and may know venture capitalists looking for a deal like yours. One steadfast rule: A personal referral is infinitely preferable to a blind letter; it will get you and your venture more attention.

Is there a venture capital club in your area? Over 50 clubs have been established across the country, with more added every year. They offer entrepreneurs and investors a place to meet and exchange ideas. For beginners, this is a good way to learn the rules of the game and the buzzwords. In the best situation, you can meet people who are willing to support your company—either with money or experience—or to tell you honestly that it isn't likely to take off.

Venture capital clubs can be difficult to find, because they want to attract only serious entrepreneurs and investors, not hucksters. Contact the Association of Venture Capital Clubs in Stamford, CT (203-323-3143), to find out if there's a member club in your area. Again, it's always best to get involved with an organization like this through a friend or business associate.

While the "who do you know" side of the process may be frustrating to an eager entrepreneur, don't despair. The creative and managerial synergy produced by a well-matched venture capital firm and entrepreneurial company is well worth the trouble it takes to find a mate.

Source: Michael A. Reagan, partner, Deloitte Haskins & Sells, 695 Town Center Dr., Suite 1200, Costa Mesa, CA 92626. He is a member of the firm's emerging business services practice. He specializes in the high-tech industry, working with companies seeking growth financing.

How To Appeal to Investors

To be a successful entrepreneur you need more than a good idea. Among other things, you need money. One option is to raise the funds from family, friends, and other personal sources (second mortgages, insurance policies...). But if such funds are either unavailable or inadequate, you'll have to know where to find other avenues of financial backing.

Investment Sources

• Informal investors: These wealthy groups or individuals generally put up $10,000–$25,000 (but sometimes as much as $100,000) per investment. These investors can be found through the "in" accounting or law firms.

• Early-stage venture-capital funds: These lend $50,000–$250,000 per investment. They look for young companies that have products ready for market and demand a substantial chunk (up to 50%) of the company's ownership. For help in locating these funds, call Venture Resource Associates, (603) 863-6024.

• Traditional venture capitalists: These include private firms supported by insurance companies, pension funds or wealthy families...small business investment companies (SBICs) funded by a combination of Small Business Administration loans and private funds ...and corporate venture-capital firms. The best reference book is *Guide to Venture Capital Sources*, by Stanley Pratt, Venture Economics, Wellesley Hills, MA.

• Investment bankers: This group includes small local firms and the giants—Merrill Lynch, Paine Webber, etc. They aid young companies that can't get venture capital by helping them go public. Some firms have both a venture-capital and an investment-banking arm.

Your Next Move

Entrepreneurs see all the possibilities for making money and usually downplay the risks. Investors, on the other hand, focus more on risk than on opportunity. They know there are more losers than winners among new businesses. Therefore, before approaching investors, it is critical to draft a detailed business plan. The plan should be 20–40 pages long, complete with a table of contents and summary (which includes the highlights of the plan). Without such a written plan, submitted in advance, few investment groups will grant an interview.

The plan should include:

• A clear description, of course, of the product or service.

• Hard evidence of the marketability of the product or service and the benefits to users.

• Financial justification of the chosen means of selling or distributing the product or service.

• An explanation of product development and the manufacturing process and their associated costs.

• The qualifications of each member of the management team.

• Believable financial projections that are not out of line with industry norms.

• A statement of what the founders expect to have accomplished three to seven years into the future.

The aspiring entrepreneur must also be prepared to give a concise and thorough oral presentation and to answer potential investors' questions.

What Turns Investors On

The best way to impress investors is to bring them around to see your product in use by a satisfied customer. This is so important that it is worth begging, borrowing, or stealing funds to at least get your product assembled and into the hands of customers on a trial-demonstration basis.

Venture capitalists will want evidence that you know which one or two things your company does best and are prepared to focus on those things. They will also want to know what your company wants to be when it grows up. Will it be a cash cow, generating income for years to come? Do you expect to go public? Sell the company? Buy investors out? What is your timetable?

Investors also look more favorably on companies that have a proprietary position. Though patent, copyright, or trademark protection doesn't guarantee success, it does limit competition at least for a while. It may also suggest potential profits from licensing. And companies with proprietary products are apt to be more attractive acquisition candidates when it comes time to sell out.

What Turns Investors Off

- Too much product orientation. Entrepreneurs are often so obsessed with their product or technology that they talk too much about that instead of about who will be the user and what the user wants.
- Insufficient attention to budgeting and finance. There must be someone who is watching every penny and who is knowledgeable about matters such as when the company needs a loan and whether it should go public.
- Too much custom engineering. When investors see that a company's product must be specially designed or altered for each individual customer, a red flag goes up. Standard problems: High costs and low profits. Investors also shy away from products that simply don't promise enough volume.

- A one-man band. Venture capitalists like to see a well-rounded management team of at least three players, encompassing marketing, finance, production, and research. You should have the team players outlined on paper, even if the slots have not yet been filled.

The least risky venture, from an investor's point of view, is a going concern with an established market and satisfied users. At the other end of the spectrum is a start-up venture whose single founder has an idea and whose market is assumed but not yet proved. Investors are especially leery of putting in money that will be used for unproductive research or development. And . . . the greater the risk the investor perceives, the greater the ownership interest he will insist on.

Source: Stanley R. Rich, a founder of MIT Enterprise Forum, coauthor of *Business Plans That Win $$$*, Harper & Row, New York, and an entrepreneur who has started nine ventures.

When To Incorporate And When Not To

Enormous confusion surrounds the question of the best way to organize a business—as a proprietorship, partnership, or corporation. Yet it is possible to make some sense out of the issue by examining the potential advantages and disadvantages of incorporating in light of specific tax and business considerations. Here are some basic rules.

When To Incorporate

- If you, as owner, wish to enjoy tax-free fringe benefits. A proprietor or partner is not an employee of a company and therefore can't participate in tax-free fringe benefit programs enjoyed by employees.
- If you are trying to build working capital in the business. This may be the best single reason for a profitable company in the growth stage to incorporate. You can conserve cash by saving tax dollars, since part of your total income will be taxed at corporate rates rather than personal rates.

• If you want to divert income to dependent family members. Gifts of business property can be made to family members in lower tax brackets through a trust; the business then can lease the property back from the trust. This type of arrangement virtually requires the use of a corporation.

• Forming multiple corporations offers substantial tax advantages. Income can be split among multiple entities if the venture can truly be divided into separate businesses and the partners are not related. Check with a competent tax adviser before trying this tactic.

When Not To Incorporate

• If both spouses are active in the business. For the small family business in which husband and wife work, it is usually best to operate as a proprietorship for payroll tax savings.

• If you want to take money out of a profitable business. When you reach the stage of life where you want to draw out the maximum amount from a business in the form of salaries and retirement benefits, the corporate form becomes a disadvantage due to IRS limitations on "reasonable compensation."

• If you want to maximize deductible retirement plan contributions. Since it is no longer necessary to use the corporate form to obtain the maximum deductions for pension and profit-sharing plans, this should not be your sole reason for incorporating.

• If you expect losses in early years that you can offset with other personal income. When you operate a new business as a partnership, proprietorship, or S corporation, start-up losses can be deducted from other taxable income.

Taxes Aren't Everything

There are two further considerations that may override strictly tax-oriented factors when determining whether to incorporate.

• Overall, management and administrative considerations favor use of a corporation. The bigger the business, the greater the administrative advantages.

• Personal legal considerations favor the corporate form. While benefits are not as marked for an active owner as for a passive investor, incorporation will secure some protection from personal liability. The protection is greater than that in a general partnership, but about the same as in a limited partnership.

Something Else To Consider

The top tax rates on individuals are lower than the top tax rates on corporations. Where corporate profits exceed $75,000 per year, it may be worthwhile to do business as an S corporation, which is sometimes referred to as a "tax-free" corporation.

Source: Vernon K. Jacobs, CPA, CLU, tax and financial adviser, 4500 W. 72 Terrace, Prairie Village, KS 66208. He is the author of *Taxwise Investing* and has written more than 300 articles about legal methods of tax avoidance.

Four Ways To Take Money Out of a Closely Held Business

If you're the president and sole or part owner of an incorporated business and you want to take money out of the business, you really have only four options. The one you choose may be largely determined by the varying tax implications. Here are the possibilities.

1. Sell the business. The first and most obvious method is to sell all or part of the business. Under the tax law the gain from the sale of capital assets is taxed as ordinary income—albeit at a presumably lower rate. While the 1986 law eliminated the capital gains rate, it continued to allow the offsetting of capital gains with capital losses. Short of this offsetting provision (requiring a capital loss), selling a piece of the business is not a more tax-effective device than straight salary for taking money out of the business.

2. Take a large salary or bonus. A simpler route—assuming you don't want to sell and the business generates the necessary cash—is to pay yourself a generous salary or bonus.

This money is deductible from the corporation's earnings and taxed as ordinary income to you. This is not the most tax-effective alternative, but it is a direct way to get cash with no strings attached. Beware, however, of excessive generosity: The IRS monitors closely held firms for "unreasonable compensation" and may assess excessive amounts as dividends.

3. Take advantage of perquisites, benefits, and amenities. Another alternative is to let the company pay for business-related meals, parking, and other executive perks. Again, caution is in order. The IRS has cracked down on all benefits and perquisites that are not: Minimal or incidental (e.g., occasional personal use of a copier or secretarial services, holiday gifts); qualified employee discounts (e.g., limited discounts on company products); or working condition fringes (e.g., business use of company car, cost of business periodicals).

Generally, the IRS holds that executives cannot receive company-provided amenities tax free, especially when the perks are not available to all employees. But under IRS guidelines, a company can pay for such job-related expenses as entertaining clients and parking. These costs are deductible by the company and tax free to the executive if various substantiation, discrimination, and other IRS tests are met.

4. Pay dividends. The final way to get money from a closely held business is to declare and pay substantial dividends to the shareholder(s)—in this case, you. However, this is the most inefficient alternative because it involves double taxation. You must pay dividends after corporate income taxes have been paid and declare them as personal income at ordinary rates.

Clearly, there is no perfect way of taking money out of a business. But if you decide to do it, keep three basic rules in mind:

• Sell any portion(s) of the business that will not dilute your control.

• Take "reasonable" salary and bonuses instead of dividends—it's more tax-efficient.

• Take advantage of all IRS-allowed benefits and perks.

Source: Brian D. Dunn, principal with Towers, Perrin, Forster & Crosby, 245 Park Ave., New York 10167, specializing in incentive compensation and organizational design. He has been published and widely quoted in professional journals and newspapers, and has spoken before the Human Resources Planning Society, the American Society of Personnel Administrators, and the New York Chamber of Commerce.

Buying Out a Partner

There are basically two ways to buy out a partner. Either the remaining partners can purchase equal shares of the departing partner's interest ("sale") or the partnership itself can purchase the interest ("liquidation"). The two methods have the same economic effect—the remaining partners' respective interests in the partnership are increased proportionately and each bears a proportionate share of the cost of the purchase. What differs in each case are the tax consequences of the transaction.

When selling his interest to the remaining partners, a selling partner recognizes a gain or loss equal to the amount of the sale less his basis in the partnership interest. Note: The seller's basis generally equals his contributions, increased or decreased each year by his share of the partnership's taxable income or loss, less any distributions by the partnership.

Gains or losses from the sale are treated as long-term capital gains or losses except for the partner's share of "hot assets" such as unrealized receivables and substantially appreciated inventory, assuming the interest has been held for at least six months and the holder is not a "dealer" in partnership interests.

"Unrealized receivables" are generally accounts receivable if such amounts have not previously been included in income and depreciation recapture. "Substantially appreciated inventory" is partnership inventory which has a market value in excess of 120% of its cost basis, if such inventory represents at least 10% of all partnership property other than cash.

The partnership has no gain or loss upon the sale since it is not a party to the transaction. However, if the selling partner has an interest of 50% or more in the partnership, the sale will terminate the partnership.

The purchasing partners, if they so elect, can now increase their basis in the newly purchased partnership property up to the amount paid to the departing partner. This could enable them to take larger depreciation deductions.

The Internal Revenue Code is more flexible when it comes to the liquidation of partner's interest. Liquidation transactions allow the remaining partners to deduct the departing partner's interest in the partnership's unrealized receivables. In the sale scenario, the remaining partners' share of unrealized receivables would have to be capitalized by the partnership.

The liquidation scenario also enables the parties to determine the tax treatment of the goodwill associated with the departing partner's interest in the partnership. The parties can agree to either treat the goodwill as ordinary income to the selling partner, which would result in a corresponding deduction for the partnership, or treat the goodwill as a capital gain to the selling partner, which would result in no current tax benefit to the partnership. (The latter will always be the result of the sale scenario.)

In 1986, the selling partner in the liquidation scenario generally preferred to choose capital gains treatment due to the large disparity in maximum federal tax rates between capital gains and other forms of income (20% versus 50%). However, the decision to choose ordinary income or capital gains should be made after weighing the relative tax benefits to all parties. In 1987, the maximum rate differential declined (28% to 38.5%).

Beginning in 1988, the choice became even more significant as the Internal Revenue Code provided for similar tax rates between capital gains and other forms of income. The liquidation scenario became even more attractive because while the selling partner received the same treatment as under the sale option (due to the tax rate being the same for capital gains and ordinary income), the partnership was entitled to more beneficial tax treatment if the value of goodwill was treated as ordinary income.

Buying out a partner through liquidation is often preferable to the sale transaction because it permits the partnership to accelerate the write-off of the departing partner's interest in unrealized receivables, including depreciated recapture. Additionally, in a liquidation, the partnership has flexibility in determining the tax treatment of goodwill. The selling partner will recognize the same amount and character of income under either method, unless he agrees to treat the goodwill as ordinary income. In such case, that partner will presumably be compensated for the tax advantage this provides to the remaining partners. This option became even more beneficial in 1988 when the disparity in rates between capital gains and other forms of income was fully phased out, leaving a clear benefit to the remaining partners in the liquidation scenario.

Source: Philip Tretiak, Esq., attorney, Summit Robins and Feldesman, 445 Park Ave., New York 10022.

How To Profit From a Merger or Acquisition

The thousands of mergers and acquisitions announced each year are only the tip of an enormous economic iceberg: For every deal we read about, several others take place more quietly. Mergers and acquisitions are almost considered routine, yet the rewards are not always worth the risks. Participants on both sides of the deal need to sharpen their strategies.

The Buyer's Strategy

Most acquisitions don't work out, because buyers outnumber sellers, giving sellers the edge, and because it's almost impossible to predict all of the problems involved in combining two companies. Also, diversification per se is not a sufficient reason to acquire. Most companies can't handle a totally new business.

To improve the odds of making an acquisition successful, make sure you first have a clear understanding of your own company:

- What do you do well—or badly?
- Do you undermarket your products or services?
- Do you challenge your managers sufficiently?
- Has technology begun to pass you by?
- Will selling new products and services help your sales force?
- How much of your own capital can you really spare for acquisition?
- How do your shareholders feel about risk?

Self-analysis helps you decide when to acquire; you may decide that now is not the time. An acquisition will quickly put you into new products, services, or markets, but is speed worth the risk and disruption? Acquisition makes the most sense when you have the resources to succeed, the opportunity to add something you're lacking, and the chance that you'll suffer if you move too slowly.

Self-analysis also helps you develop general acquisition criteria: Industry, company size, location, growth history and prospects, profitability, debt leverage, management objectives, and purchase price. More specific criteria can include union status, customer profile, competitive posture, technology levels, and image. Combining your criteria with a weighting system saves time and further reduces the risk of a poor acquisition.

Identifying Candidates

How you apply your acquisition criteria depends on how you identify candidates. The two search strategies are the passive, or "shotgun," approach and the active, or "rifle," approach. The former involves networking in the business community, especially among investment bankers, business brokers, lenders, accountants, and the like, with the goal of uncovering owners who have decided to sell

or at least to think about it. The active approach involves identifying, screening, and contacting companies whose owners don't yet plan to sell. The search can be conducted by your own staff, consultants, or intermediaries. Which method you use to identify candidates depends on your management depth. If your management team is "thin," the active approach usually won't work unless you hire outsiders.

If the companies on your list aren't yet for sale, it's especially important that actual contacts be made discreetly, possibly by a third party. Prepare for this by trying to answer these key questions: Who controls the stock? What are the current "hot buttons" ("clean up your estate"; "preserve company's existence"; "add to your marketing clout"; etc.)? Who should make each approach? How? How much are you willing to say about your own company? What must you learn? And, what should the next step be?

The passive approach to identifying candidates costs less, but can involve spending a great deal of time fielding calls without seeing the best targets—the ones on the market may not be right for you. The active method, on the other hand, focuses on the best corporate fits, but they have to be convinced to sell. This can be an emotional process.

The Seller's Strategy

Sellers obviously have a very different view of the acquisition process. As the owner of a company, you are probably under no pressure to sell, and the years you've spent building up the business can keep you from pricing it rationally. If you want to sell and you've minimized taxes, rather than maximized earnings, your company may not even be an attractive target.

In at least one way, selling a business does resemble buying one: Both require preliminary self-analysis. Do your shareholders need liquidity? Is selling to outsiders the only way to get it? Does the company need more growth capital than your current owners can provide? Are there other gaps, in production, marketing, or management, that can't be closed except by selling? Is the future rosy enough to attract a buyer at the right price?

One way to attract buyers is to prepare a well-organized corporate profile containing: An executive summary, a financial history, adjustments to show true asset values and earning power, an industry survey, the position of your company in the industry, your products or services, marketing methods, management resumes, your labor environment, brochures, etc. Such a profile can deflect casual buyers. Once they've read it, you can insist that their next step be a bid. (This also will reduce onsite "tire kicking" and employee rumors.)

Another way to identify potential acquirers is to consider your current customers, competitors, and suppliers. You may find you already know good contacts. Intermediaries may be useful, too.

Intermediaries and Confidentiality

Whether you are a buyer or seller, intermediaries can be used as a buffer and to maintain secrecy. Most intermediaries charge nonrefundable retainer fees, along with commissions or "success fees," with total charges computed as a percentage of the purchase price—often 1% to 5% for smaller businesses. Check on the intermediary's charges, terms, and credentials before making a commitment. Intermediaries can be paid by either party, or at closing. Most intermediaries prefer to be paid by the seller, since that symbolizes the seller's commitment to sell. Above all, keep in mind that most intermediaries are transaction-oriented and will push hard to close a deal quickly, even if you haven't made up your mind.

There are several ways an intermediary can help a seller maintain secrecy. He can provide you with background information on each potential buyer, use an anonymous fact sheet for each first approach, limit the number of potential buyers approached simultaneously, have each prospect sign and return a confidentiality letter before you send your profile, and provide you with a weekly status report. However, these steps can delay the selling process, so you may need to balance your desires for secrecy and speed.

Valuing the Target

How does each side arrive at a price? This is particularly difficult if the target is privately held or part of a larger company, but three valuation methods are generally used:

1. Asset appraisal, which assumes that a business derives more value from assets than from earnings or cash flow.

2. Discounted cash flow, which assumes that a business's value is attributable to its cash flow.

3. Comparable-company multiples, which assumes that the best way to decide what a company is worth is to examine what investors have paid for similar companies.

The seller and buyer independently use these valuation methods to arrive at their assessments. Negotiations typically proceed from that point.

The seller's minimum price depends on the seller's alternatives. For example, if the company has shareholders' equity of $6 million and net earnings of $1 million, a buyer might bid $8 million–$10 million. But if the current owners collectively take out $1 million or more each year—while retaining control—this offer might not give the owners as much as they already have.

The buyer's maximum price depends on synergies and other changes that could improve the target's earning potential. This requires the buyer to make two calculations: How much is the target worth, on a stand-alone basis? And, how much more can the buyer offer, if necessary, to reflect the company's potential value?

The result of the negotiations will depend more on the people involved than even these calculations of maximum and minimum price. (This is why the initial contact between companies is always a challenge.) The negotiating process underscores how important people are to the acquisition process as a whole. Many times, one party will walk away from a perfectly reasonable offer because he simply doesn't want to deal with the other party. At times like these, or when such a problem seems likely to arise, intermediaries can be helpful in buffering the parties from one another. However, whether you are the buyer or seller, remember that any merger or acquisition involves people; no price can make up entirely for ill will.

Source: Stephen Bennett Blum, CPA, co-director of the merger and acquisition department, Peat Marwick Main & Co., 345 Park Ave., New York 10145.

Eight Ways To Evaluate a Business Before You Buy It

Emotional and other less-than-pragmatic considerations often play major roles in deciding how much a business is worth. For buyers who want to rely on more logical techniques, there are eight basic methods for evaluating a closely held business with no publicly traded stock and owners who are near retirement:

• Capitalized earnings. The value is judged according to the previous year's earnings, income over the last few years, or projected earnings.

• Corporate and shareholder earnings. Both of these are capitalized. This amount is paid out over a period that is usually two to four times the capitalization period. Example: If earnings were capitalized for the previous two years, payment could be over the next four to eight years.

• Percentages of future profits. The definition of profit can include any items that management determines. Payments can be spread over a number of years and arranged in diminishing stages.

• Book value. The sum of assets as they appear on the books (excluding goodwill) less liabilities.

• Adjusted book value. Current values are applied to the balance sheet. Example: Fixed assets are valued at either their replacement or knockdown value rather than as they appear on the books.

• Book value plus pensions. Consideration is given to retirement plans in effect at similar companies and an equitable compensation program for the retiring sellers.

• Start-up cost. A buyer who wants to enter an industry will often pay more than a business is actually worth. Reason: The price may still be less than the cost of entering the field from scratch.

• Industry custom. Some types of businesses are valued on the basis of historic formulas. Examples: Dental practices may sell for the previous year's gross income. Insurance brokerages can sell for a price equal to the first year's retained renewals.

Source: Edward Mendlowitz, a partner with Siegel, Mendlowitz & Rich, CPAs, 310 Madison Ave., New York 10017.

Something for Nothing—How a Leveraged Buyout Works

Any investor who has participated in a successful leveraged buyout (LBO) may have reason to question the age-old axiom, you can't get something for nothing.

In a typical LBO, the amount of cash the investors put into the venture in the form of equity is a small percentage of the total acquisition cost. Most of the purchase price is financed through debt, secured by the company's assets and cash flow. The cash flow of the business is used to pay interest and debt amortization; also, less profitable segments of the business are sold to pay down the debt. At the conclusion of the transaction, the investors have something—ownership of an operating company, for next to nothing—their initial investment.

Since operating management usually obtains an equity position in the ongoing venture, increased productivity and profits often result from the entrepreneurial spirit of the new owners. If everything goes well, it may be possible to return the investors' original investment in the form of fees or proceeds from the sale of new stock (often a public offering). When this happens, the investors can find themselves with an ongoing business that has cost them nothing.

Minimizing the Risks

Obviously, not every company can provide investors with a windfall. To minimize the risks, look for the following general indicators of a good LBO candidate:

• Strong, predictable operating cash flow that is neither cyclical nor affected by interest rates.

• The potential to reduce costs by eliminating unnecessary overheads.

• Assets with fair market values in excess of net book values.

• Management with a strong entrepreneurial spirit.

Once you've chosen an LBO venture, there are still risks involved in making it pay for itself. Since the LBO is heavily dependent on debt financing, interest rate movements can have a significant impact on the company's ability to service its debt. One way to reduce this risk is to negotiate an interest rate cap with the financing sources. Another is to arrange to have interest charges in excess of a certain percentage deferred for a period of time.

In case profit increases don't materialize as quickly as originally planned, investors can keep a cash reserve available for future investment in the company. Sometimes a small additional investment is all it takes to put the company over the top.

Although LBOs involving millions of dollars of investment get most of the attention from the business press, smaller LBOs continue to be a strong investment opportunity. You may need to take some high short-term risks, but prudent analysis of cash flows and proper attention to management can help you get something for nothing.

Source: Kevin M. Smith, partner and director of entrepreneurial services for the New York metropolitan office of Arthur Young & Company, 277 Park Ave., New York 10172. He is responsible for providing financial accounting and consulting services to middle-market companies.

Selling an Unprofitable Business

There are four kinds of potential buyers for money-losing assets.

• Large public companies with a specific need for products or assets.

• Risk-playing entrepreneurs with expertise in the industry.

• Foreign companies looking for a toehold in a particular market in the US.

• The business's own management, backed by venture capital.

To find a buyer: Figure out which one of these groups will most logically profit from acquiring the business. Then quietly send out feelers to candidates within that group to see if they express interest in acquiring.

If word gets out that the business is for sale, capitalize on the publicity. Use it to flush out as many potential buyers as possible, then pit them against each other.

Caution: Publicly putting a business on the block hurts employee morale. If a business is labor-intensive, it's generally best not to publicize the intended sale. Labor-intensive companies on the block get raided. The loss of their top talent depresses the business's value.

Sales strategy: Know the strengths and weaknesses of the business. Address both of them openly when negotiating. Important: Don't spread false turnaround tales. When an owner tells a prospective buyer that the business is about to turn around, the buyer will wonder why the owner wants to sell it. This casts doubt on the owner's credibility.

Pricing strategy:

• Price the business at least 30% higher than the final acceptable figure. Warning: Don't overbluff.

• Keep marginal prospects in the picture to foster competition with serious potential buyers.

Choices if the sale is not made:

• Liquidate.

• Remove the business from the market for the time it takes to revive it and increase its salability.

• When to sell an entrepreneurial start-up: After the business makes a 40% return on the owner's equity.

Source: *The Profit Line,* Durkee, Sharlit Associates, Los Angeles.

What You May Not Know About Franchises

If you're considering the purchase of a franchise, you should understand first that franchises are not typically the bargains they once were. The costs and risks have increased and the payback periods are longer than they were in the past.

You also should be aware of the trap that lies in the common business cycle of heavily franchised industries. In the initial phase of the cycle—launching the new product or service, or entering the new geographic area—competition and pricing pressure are generally quite low. Franchise fees may not seem like a burden to the operation experiencing rapid sales growth and strong cash flow.

As business lines mature and new competition enters the field, bringing downward pressures on profit margins, the franchise operation may be at a disadvantage compared to the independent competitor. With equal sales and gross profit margins, the nonfranchised business should make more money; franchise fees limit a franchisee's ability to meet price competition and still make a profit, unless the franchise provides some unique competitive advantage.

Very important here are the franchisor's experience and attitude. Some franchisors not only are conscientious about helping franchisees who are in trouble, but also have the experience to anticipate and avoid problems of this sort. Unscrupulous franchisors, on the other hand, may simply let individual franchises fail and then resell them.

Aside from larger economic questions, specific difficulties and pitfalls can arise in franchise schemes. Here's what you should know about:

• Hidden costs. Not all franchise agreements clearly spell out the full fees the operator will be called on to pay. To avoid unpleasant surprises when the franchisor assesses fees for national advertising, administration, group accounting, and the like, be sure to find out about all costs ahead of time. Total fees paid to the franchisor could be as much as the net earnings of the franchisee.

• Product exclusivity. If you are paying for the right to sell a unique product or service, will it remain unique? Early in the game, buying a franchise may be the only way to obtain the right to sell a particular product. But in our free market system, it doesn't usually remain this way very long. Typical complaints from franchisees in this situation are that not enough is spent on advertising the franchise name; that anyone can get the product; that the franchisees pay a higher price because they are locked into buying from the franchisor; and that they cannot get the latest or enough merchandise.

• Location. Selection and provision of a business location are often the purview of the franchisor. Can you count on the franchisor to provide a good location? Are the best locations reserved for company ownership rather than franchise operations? Will the franchisor refrain from selling other franchises close enough to compete with yours? These are important questions to have answered.

• Standards. Are standards of quality, appearance of premises, levels of service, etc. detailed in the franchise agreement? Are they enforced? A poorly run franchise in your area may reflect badly on your operation and the rest of the system. A franchisor needs to be able to identify these problems and take corrective action before other franchise locations are adversely affected.

• Business and management assistance. Theoretically, this is part of the package with almost all franchise operations, but in practice the assistance may have little value. Good franchisors hold regular training sessions and have experienced and knowledgeable corporate personnel to assist individual franchisees. Some bring in successful franchisees to help in this area. However, in other instances, assistance may be limited to printed manuals or forms backed up by little or no hands-on help. For a first-time business owner, this may be inadequate.

• Stability of the franchisor. It may not matter how successful an individual franchisee is, if the franchisor fails. For example, a clothing store franchisor who restricted franchisees from carrying other brands of merchandise failed. Most of the successful franchises failed, in turn, since they had no existing relations with other vendors.

• Power of the lease. Who holds the lease to the franchise location? If the franchisor owns the lease, a franchisee who gets in trouble and misses a payment may be evicted instead of getting expected help and support from the organization.

All in all, it is an excellent idea to investigate and evaluate the experience and reputation of the franchisor when considering buying a franchise system. Talk to other franchise owners and obtain a copy of the Uniform Franchise Offering Circular from your state's record office. For assistance in finding reputable franchisors, contact the International Franchise Association, a trade group in Washington, DC, that provides a list of established companies. An individual franchisor's registration statement can be obtained from the state; it includes information on financial history and strength, litigation history (especially with franchisees and suppliers), and amounts it receives from franchisees. All of these sources will help you to know whether you'll get what you'll be paying for.

Source: Donald Murray, partner and director of the enterprise and retail group, Touche Ross & Company, 1000 Wilshire Blvd., Los Angeles 90010. He has published several articles on retailing and frequently lectures at universities and to business groups.

The Many Benefits of Franchising

Much of the risk involved in going into business on your own can be avoided through franchising. For an establishment fee and continuing royalties, you can purchase a franchise offering benefits that are unobtainable via other business routes.

• A franchise is your own business—preplanned, prestructured, preestablished, and pretested.

• A franchise is based on more than "a good idea"; it involves the previous establishment of pilot operations that have proved successful.

• You are in business for yourself, but not by yourself, since the franchise organization is behind you. The franchisor has extensive experience in implementing the business and can effectively guide you along the right path.

• In-depth training is available to you at the outset, with refresher training at subsequent periods. Workshops on management, communications, and personal finances also may be offered.

• The program is thoroughly documented—manuals cover all aspects of the operation.

• Selection of an effective site for your business is based on standardized marketing procedures.

• Economies are achieved from group advertising and purchases, accelerating as the franchise system grows.

• Each individual benefits from the whole. As the network expands, the value of the individual franchise grows too.

• The franchisor provides services that you often cannot afford, because they require either too much time or too much money. These services include researching and developing new products, ideas, and promotions, and the tools to help implement them.

The franchisor's staff also can assist in problem solving.

Source: David D. Seltz, president, Seltz Franchising Developments, Inc., 30 Ridge Rd., New Rochelle, NY 10804, an authority on and spokesman for the franchising and marketing fields. He has served as chairman of the International Franchise Congress, has conducted seminars, and is a prolific writer.

Lawsuit Guidelines

There are many exceptions, but as a rule:
1. Don't sue for less than $25,000. A lawsuit will cost so much that even if you win, you can only break even.

2. Keep in mind that the legal bills may cripple or kill your company.

3. Remember that if your company is sued by a determined one that's much bigger than yours, your company doesn't stand much of a chance. The legal help your company receives depends on the size of its bankroll—the facts of the case are only incidental.

4. Don't be the first to suggest a settlement. The unreasonable party usually wins.

Source: David W. Swanson, president, Daavlin Co., Box 626, Bryan, OH 43506.

5 DEALING WITH BANKS, CREDIT, & DEBT

How Safe Is Your Bank?

Banks don't have to fail in order to hurt the customers with whom they do business. Even as financial problems are just beginning to develop, the bank's operations may begin to deteriorate, and ultimately the bank may need to rein in its growth.

When banks run into financial problems, they behave like any other troubled company. They sometimes try to hide problems and limp along the best they can. For the customer, services can quickly deteriorate. Growing companies can be especially hurt because most rely on their banks to expand credit lines. On the contrary, too often a troubled bank will call in its loans because the bank needs the money—not because the customer is at any growth risk.

Ironically, thousands of customers are unnecessarily hurt. Many could have avoided problems by watching for early-warning signals of bank weakness. Typically, these distress signals show up as early as two years before an outright failure.

Chances are good, of course, that your bank is among the vast majority of healthy ones in the US. But ignoring the signs of problems now adds to your future risks.

Most recent bank problems stem from decisions to grow aggressively. Some banks that failed funded an ambitious growth strategy with "purchased" funds (such as large CDs), as opposed to deposits from their local customer base. That strategy puts them on shaky ground.

Customers who have dealt for some time with banks in this situation usually sense something is wrong:

• There's high turnover among the officers.

• Paperwork and record-keeping become sloppy.

• The bank encourages customers to extend credit when officers know it really isn't necessary.

But even when customers suspect that a bank is going through some sort of change, they rarely take the trouble to find out if it's merely because of routine personnel problems, for instance, or because of more serious financial trouble.

Essential steps: If a friendly bank officer has recently quit, invite him to lunch and ask him tough questions about his former employer.

If you think there's a problem, get a copy of the bank's Call Report. This twice-a-year document has the data that tell the financial conditions of a bank. (In fact, regardless of whether a customer senses trouble, his finance officer should routinely get Call Reports for banks with which the company does business.)

Although Call Reports are public documents, not all banks make copies available (usually obtainable from the bank's shareholder relations department). But if a bank balks, copies are available from the state agency that regulates banks or from the federal agency under whose jurisdiction it falls (Comptroller of the Currency, Federal Reserve Board or the Federal Deposit Insurance Corp).

What to look for: By comparing figures of Call Reports over time, a customer can read the warning signals. According to Cates Consulting Analysts, Inc., the signals include:

• Rapid expansion as reflected in a big increase in loan yield relative to other similarly sized banks.

• Loan recovery rate of less than 20%. This is the percentage of written-off bad loans that a bank is ultimately able to recover. It should be well over 20% and is an excellent indication of how riskily the bank is willing to operate.

• Low return on assets for a bank its size (can range from 0.6% for large banks like Citibank and Chase Manhattan to over 1.0% for a small bank).

• High overhead ratio. Failed banks had overhead expenses that amounted to nearly 80% of their income base, compared with a nationwide average of 56%.

How To Protect Yourself Against Bank Failure

Banks in many areas may continue to have financial problems but no companies or individuals should lose money if they understand how the banking system works. In order to protect against the possibility of bank failure, depositors must know how to:

• Judge the different types of insurance that banks can have.

• Spread deposits legally to maximize insurance coverage.

• Evaluate a bank's financial data for early-warning signs of trouble.

Insurance Quality
In view of bank difficulties such as those experienced in Ohio, be very cautious about doing business with financial institutions (usually thrifts) whose deposits are insured by private insurance, even though administered by state rather than federal agencies. State-administered insurance funds that don't have the full backing of the state's treasury run the risk of being depleted if even one bank gets into trouble.

Other problems: State insurance is often less than the $100,000 federal level and it frequently takes many months to collect, unlike federal insurance, which pays depositors within days of a bank failure.

Beyond the Limit
Surprise: With careful management of accounts it's possible to go far beyond the $100,000 insurance limit offered by the Federal Deposit Insurance Corp. for commercial banks and the Federal Savings & Loan Insurance Corp. for thrift institutions. Basic rules:

• Each depositor is insured up to $100,000 at each institution, including its branches.

• All time, savings and checking accounts owned by the same person, with the exception of IRAs and Keoghs, are lumped together to reach the $100,000 limit.

• Sole proprietorship business accounts are added to the same person's individual accounts for the $100,000 insurance limit.

• All valid joint accounts are separately insured from individual accounts.

These rules still leave a lot of leeway. Deposits owned jointly under such conditions as joint tenancy or community property are insured separately from deposit accounts individually owned by the co-owners.

Example: A couple can insure up to $500,000 by opening five $100,000 accounts—one in each spouse's name, one in a joint name and two retirement accounts.

Opportunity: Another simple way to expand insurance coverage at the same bank is to open revocable testamentary or trust accounts that name specific beneficiaries in case of death. In some legal arrangements, such as a Totten trust, the beneficiary must be a spouse, child or grandchild. Benefit: There's a $100,000 insurance maximum on these accounts for each beneficiary.

Pension Strategy

Similarly, a company's pension and profit-sharing deposits are considered to be trust funds. If they meet certain conditions and recordkeeping requirements, these pension and profit-sharing accounts are separately insured for up to $100,000 per participant at each depository bank. Check with bank officers to make sure the company meets FDIC regulations governing such accounts.

The most common insurance traps:

• Believing that securities held by a bank in IRAs and other accounts come under insurance plans. They don't.

• Creating a corporation or other type of organization with the sole purpose of using it to get more deposit insurance. Federal rules say that an organization must be engaged in "independent activity" in order for it to qualify for deposit insurance.

• Using a variation of your name to open another account in the hope of getting more insurance. Varying names or Social Security numbers on joint accounts usually isn't illegal. However, it won't get you more deposit insurance.

Safety Checks

Just as a business would check the financial health of a supplier or customer, it's a sound practice to keep a running check on the viability of the company's banks. Check on:

• Liquidity. Look at the bank's cash and securities that are readily convertible into cash as a percent of total deposits. A one-to-four or one-to-five ratio is pretty good. A lower ratio could signal trouble.

• Capital requirements. Total primary equity at commercial banks should be 5½%–6% of total assets, slightly lower at S&Ls.

• Loan losses. These shouldn't exceed 1% of a bank's total loan portfolio on an annual basis.

• Net interest margin. This is simply the difference between what the bank pays for funds and what it must pay out in interest.

• Bond portfolio. Compare current market value with the book value of bonds carried on the bank's financial statements. With many of these bonds, the actual liquidation value could be substantially less than book value.

Source: Herbert F. Mueller, president, North Valley Bancorp, 1377 South St., Redding, CA 96001. He has been a member of the American Bankers Association's advisory panel that explains banking practices to bank customers.

How To Question Your Banker

If you are concerned about the safety of the bank or thrift, there are things you can look for.

• Any bank or thrift should be able to give you its financial statement. Most banks publish them semiannually or annually.

• Read the statement, looking at the net worth, the number of "workouts" (situations in which bank officers are helping troubled companies get back on their feet), and the amount of real estate owned.

What you're trying to determine is the quality of the bank's investments. This is easier if the bank or thrift is a publicly traded company. These companies must file documents with the Securities & Exchange Commission.

• Look at the bank's track record over time. If the bank or thrift has gone through extraordinary growth, it means that the institution has put out a lot of money, and it may have taken more risk.

• If you are depositing more than $100,000, you should be able to discuss the kind of investments the institution has made.

• You should also look at the accountant's report. Each institution has one. Be sure to read the "exceptions" to the accountant's statement.

• Ask about the bank's "at risk" loans or "scheduled items" (loans that have been in default for 60–120 days).

• And, of course, be sure that your bank is insured by the FDIC or the FSLIC.

Source: Franklin H. Ornstein, chairman, Central Federal Savings Bank of Long Beach, Long Beach, NY. He is author of *Savings Banking: An Industry in Change*, Prentice-Hall, Englewood Cliffs, NJ

Can You Bank On Your Bank?

To check out the financial stability of your bank—or to find a bank in your area that's in top fiscal condition—contact VERIBANC, a banking research firm that publishes financial reports on banks, S&Ls, and credit unions.

• *Short Form Reports* provide equity, assets, their ratio, net income and projected months until equity will reach zero if the institution is unprofitable. Graphs relate these measures to the entire industry. Special factors and color classification based on capital strength and profitability are also included—"green" indicates safety, "yellow" caution, "red" danger.

• *Bank* and *S&L Research Reports* are much more detailed, giving data and analyses of 17–18 different financial measures.

• *Blue Bank Reports* list all the commercial banks in a particular geographic region that meet very high standards. Criteria include size, profitability, capital strength, and liquidity.

• *City Five Reports* give, for the city or county of your choice, the five commercial banks or S&Ls with the most assets, that are the most profitable, that have the largest equity/assets ratio, that are the most liquid.

Note: VERIBANC develops its data from the regulatory filings of federally insured lending institutions.

Source: VERIBANC, Box 2963, Woburn, MA 01888, (617) 245-8370.

Protect Yourself from Troubled Banks

When American banks are in big trouble, companies doing business with these banks may also suffer—unless they take defensive measures.

The threat to borrowers occurs when the government tries to get another bank to take over loans of a troubled bank. Trap: A bank that takes over a loan may require an accelerated payment schedule or demand more collateral. In some cases the loan may be called immediately. Best defense:

• Talk with bank officers around town. It's usually easy to pick up rumors about a problem bank.

• If your lender is on the verge of trouble, look immediately for alternative loan sources.

• Boost your credit rating and financial strength whenever possible. A bank that takes over loans usually won't change the terms of loans for borrowers with solid credit ratings.

Banking for the Privileged

The carpets are thick and lush. No fluorescent lights here—the chandelier is worthy of an elegant Swiss hotel or a stately New England townhouse. Fine china gleams as morning coffee is served.

But this is not a resort or a swank private parlor. It is the new hushed, unhurried environment a growing number of big-city banks (and some suburban ones) are pushing to attract affluent individual customers. Banks want to insure that wealthy customers have an image of themselves as a breed apart from the lowly weekly-check cashers lined up outside. So they are treating them—or giving some semblance of treating them—with the deference and elegance investment banks have lavished on important clients for years. However, in many cases such customers may be getting only a touch of the kind of personalized services that have been available to the super-rich (such as home visits, theater tickets, and handling allowances for children).

The personalized service goes by a variety of names. Bank of America and Bankers Trust call it "Private Banking." Bank of New York's special service is "Custom Banking," and at Chase Manhattan it's known as "Personal Banking."

In each case the intent is the same: To treat the customer's ordinary transactions and checking with class and care so that the customer will retain the bank as his or her custodian for trusts...borrow large sums from the bank when needed...and use its brokerage estate services.

Another intention: To insure that its well-established, well-heeled customers are not insulted by the indignities of having to deal with know-nothing tellers.

The main benefit: The customer gradually develops a "relationship" with a real human being—generally one who is far more knowledgeable and courteous than the average bank teller. For the customer, that's parallel to the advantages of being known at a fine restaurant.

This doesn't mean that private-banking customers never have to wait in line to cash a check. Most privileged customers actually bank by mail or have automatic deposit of dividends. But they also have a personal banker with a private telephone number if a foul-up occurs.

Who Qualifies?

Different banks have different rules about who qualifies.

At Bank of New York, for example, the custom-banking customer must have a minimum net worth of at least $500,000, excluding the value of his private real estate, and income of at least $150,000 per year. In addition, according to the program's administrator, "We like to see potential for using our lending products—the ability to borrow more than $50,000. And we like to see the potential for needing trusts to pass assets to the next generation."

At Chase Manhattan Bank, the personal-banking relationship will be extended to people with a minimum annual income of $250,000 and invested assets of over $500,000, excluding their home. To prove it, the potential customer must make available either last year's tax return or a financial statement. At Bank of America, the private-banking customer is required to have $1 million in invested assets beyond the value of his home.

Once the potential customer has established his impressive credentials, he is generally required to open a checking account. At Bank of New York, for example, a minimum of $10,000 is required for a noninterest-bearing account...and $25,000–$50,000 is required for an interest-bearing account.

The Bank's Motivation

Check cashing is not the crux of the bank's interest in the customer, however. Instead, it is on the loan and service side of the business that the true personal touch is offered. Once the customer has proved to have the required substantial liquidity, the bank is less rigorous about procedures when the customer requests a loan. Loans or overdraft privileges can be automatic, since the banks are willing to lend up to 50% of marginal securities held in the bank's trust department.

For larger loans, the customer's personal banker is available for private discussions at the special custom-banking office, at the client's office, or even at the client's home, if the potential loan is large enough. In any case, the luxury-carpeted private meeting rooms of the institution are available to aid in confidentiality of the transaction. The customer is spared having to discuss intimate financial matters on an open banking floor.

Although psychologically custom banking is a more soothing and personalized way of doing banking business, not all private-banking customers are treated equally. A client who keeps a million dollars at a bank may have a private banker at his beck and call to deliver money or even to walk his dog. But the less fortunate customer who maintains an account of merely $25,000 or $50,000....

Free Help from the FDIC

• FDIC insurance is carried by almost all commercial banks in the US. But surprisingly few depositors know just what is does—and doesn't do. Information: FDIC, 550 17 St. NW, Washington, DC 20429. Ask for a free copy of *Your Insured Deposit*.

• Trouble with your bank? The new Federal Deposit Insurance Corporation's hotline will answer questions and take complaints. It deals only with banks supervised by the FDIC, which include federal institutions but not all state-chartered banks. Call (800) 424-5488, or 898-3536 in Washington, DC. The hotline operates from 9 a.m. to 4 p.m. EDT, Monday through Friday.

How To Beat the Banks Before They Beat You

Since deregulation, banks vary widely in their services and in the costs of those services. In order to turn the best profit, banks depend on the fact that customers don't know what to ask for. How you can get the most for your banking dollar:

Deal with the smallest bank you can find. After deregulation, most large banks decided to get rid of smaller depositors. They find it cheaper to serve one corporate account than 10 individual accounts. Smaller banks, on the other hand, are more responsive to individual depositors because they need this business.

Ask about checking accounts.

• What is the minimum-balance requirement? How does the bank calculate it? Watch out for a minimum-balance calculation that uses the lowest balance for the month. A figure based on the average daily balance is best.

• Does the balance on other accounts count toward the checking-account minimum balance?

• What is the clearing policy for deposits? This is especially important if you have a

NOW account. Most banks hold checks 10 to 14 days, which means you lose interest and may be stuck with overdrafts.

• What is the overdraft charge? Often it is outrageous. In parts of the Midwest, for example, most banks charge $20.

Don't buy loan insurance from a bank. Credit life or disability insurance is often routinely included on loan forms and added to the cost of your loan. Don't sign any such policy when you take out a loan. This insurance benefits the bank—not you. It covers the bank for the balance of your loan should you die or become disabled. You can get more coverage from an insurance agent for half (or even less) of what the bank charges.

Avoid installment loans. These loans are front-end loaded: Even though your balance is declining, you're still paying interest on the original balance throughout the term of the loan. Ask for a single-payment note with simple interest and monthly payments. If you do have an installment loan, don't pay it off early—this actually adds to its real cost.

Pay attention to interest computations. Most people compare rates and assume higher is better. But it's conceivable that with certain methods 9.75% will actually earn more interest than 10%. Look for interest figured on a day-of-deposit-to-day-of-withdrawal basis, compounded daily.

Avoid cash machines. The farther bankers can keep you from their tellers and loan officers, the more money they'll make and the less responsive they'll be to your needs. Bankers like machines because people can't argue with them.

Negotiate interest rates. This sounds simple, but it means combating banks' tendencies to lump loans in categories—commercial, mortgage, retail, etc. For example, banks offer a long-time depositor the same interest rate on a car loan as they do a complete newcomer. But often all it takes to get a better rate is to say, "I think my car loan should be 2% lower. I've been banking here for 15 years and I have $10,000 in my savings account."

Forget FDIC security. Given the option of a higher interest rate investment with a secure major corporation that probably has more reserves than the FDIC, many people will still automatically opt for the bank investment because of FDIC insurance. But the FDIC has only $16 billion in reserves. That's a minuscule portion of the money it's insuring. Now that more and more banks are closing every year, the FDIC may soon find itself in big trouble.

Ignore the banks' amortization schedule for mortgages. When you make your monthly payment, especially in the early part of your mortgage, very little goes toward the principal. However, if you choose to pay a small amount extra every month, this will go toward the principal and save you an enormous amount of money.

Don't put all your money in one certificate of deposit. Now that you can deposit as little as $1,000 for the money-market rate, split your deposits so that you get the same interest rate and more liquidity. If you put your money into a $10,000 or $20,000 CD and then find you need to take out $1,000 or $2,000, you will have to pay a horrendous penalty. Instead buy 10 or 20 $1,000 CDs.

Source: Edward F. Mrkvicka Jr., president, Reliance Enterprises, Inc., Box 413, Marengo, IL 60152.

Picking the Bank That's Right for You

• Banks are suppliers and should be evaluated as such. Judge a bank's performance as you would that of a vital supplier—in terms of tangible factors (pricing, satisfactory performance, etc.) and intangible ones (loyalty, dependability and a willingness to be flexible).
Source: *Cash Management* by business journalist John M. Kelly, Franklin Watts, New York 10016.

• Shop for a bank before deciding where to keep your personal savings. Check to see: (1) How rush-hour traffic is handled. (2) If there are express lines. (3) If there are branches near your home and your work. (4) If bank officers are accessible. (5) If all types of services are offered.
Source: *How to Invest $50–$5,000* by financial analyst Nancy Dunnan, Harper & Row, New York 10022.

Choosing a Bank Account

Banks offer a bewildering array of accounts and rates to choose from. In order to compare, ask:
• What are the base rate and the annual effective yield after compounding?
• Is the account tiered? Are there different rates for higher balances?
• What are the fees and charges if the account balance drops below a minimum?
• What are the monthly maintenance fees?
• What are the transaction fees? How many checks can be written at no charge? What is the cost per check beyond a certain number a month? Is there a charge for using the automated teller machine?
• Is there a penalty for closing the account early? (At some banks you can be hit with a charge if you close a new account within the first 90 days.)
• How is the account insured? (FDIC or FSLIC insurance provides $100,000 per person, including principal and interest.)
• Am I eligible for a low-cost "life-line" account?
Source: *Investor's Daily*, New York 10038.

How To Protect Yourself From Your Banker

The average family overpays its bank more than $100,000 over the course of a 40-year relationship. . . borrowing money for mortgages, home improvements and auto purchases, and using checking and savings accounts. But any knowledgeable customer—large or small—can easily and effectively beat the banking system.

What the banks don't want you to know:

• Once you make a deposit, few banks immediately credit the funds to your account. That means you're giving the bank an interest-free loan, even though the bank generally has use of your funds within 48 hours. They're pocketing huge amounts in interest they earn on your money.

• Most loans, whether for mortgages, property insurance or car purchases, are negotiable. . .and it does not matter how much or how little you've deposited with the loaning bank. You will have to push for a better deal. No bank will simply volunteer one.

• Single-payment notes are much less expensive than installment loans. Banks strongly encourage the latter.

• Bank safe-deposit boxes aren't as safe as you've been led to believe. Although you'll be told that the boxes are fully insured, unless you take one simple step on your own, it's unlikely that you'll collect on losses if the bank is robbed or burns down. (All you need to do is prove your loss.)

Not like the Good Old Days

People used to view their bank as a partner in financial dealings. Common wisdom said that if you bundled all your business at one bank, you'd have a friend for life. The loyalty of a personal relationship would be there to help when the need arose. No longer.

Today's bankers are concerned with only one thing: the bottom line. The so-called "Five-C's" by which banks used to determine creditworthiness—collateral, capital, condition, character, and capacity—are now "Three C's." They no longer care about character and capacity. Even if you once starved so that you could pay off a note, your past performance will mean nothing when you apply for a new loan.

Checking and Savings Accounts

The best checking account is a NOW (negotiable order of withdrawal) account because it pays interest on outstanding balances. But when you choose the bank where you'll open the account, ignore the advertised interest rate.

More important: How interest is computed, when it accrues and at what point you can write checks against deposits.

Best: Interest should be figured on a day-of-deposit-to-day-of-withdrawal basis, compounded and paid daily. You should be able to write checks against deposits within two business days.

It's almost impossible to reach a decision by comparing the offerings of all banks in your area. Helpful: Ask officers at several banks, If I put $1,000 in my account at the beginning of a quarter and write ten checks totaling $750, how much would I have—after adding interest and subtracting bank fees (charges, per-check fees, charges for deposits)—at the end?"

Overdraft: If you write a check that can't be covered by your account, the bank will usually return the check unpaid and charge you for the trouble. Some banks charge as much as $50 for an overdraft. Real out-of-pocket cost for the bank: About $1. To beat the overdraft system, negotiate with the bank for your own personal overdraft policy. You can often convince a bank officer to cover the check with funds from, for example, your savings account and reduce the overdraft charge to a nominal fee.

Negotiating a Loan

Research the total cost of a loan at a minimum of three banks. Let each bank know that you're investigating others at the same time. Compare every aspect of each bank's deal. . . interest rates, legal fees, points, etc. Then, visit the president of the one offering the best deal. Explain that in addition to opening an account, you'll also be interested in borrowing some money. Ask for an introduction—by the president—to the chief loan officer. Benefit: When you're ready to take out the loan, you'll have access to the one person who can adjust the rules to your advantage.

Keep in mind that no matter how hard-nosed the bank seems, it's more profitable for the bank to knock a half-percent off the loan than to have you walk out the door, especially if it believes you'll take your other accounts with you.

• Mortgage loans. The bank calculates a fixed monthly figure to cover your repayment over the term of the loan. Early payments usually cover only the interest. As the loan matures, payments begin to reduce the amount of principal you owe. Surefire way to cut your costs: Deliberately overpay each month, even by just a few dollars. Benefit: Extra payments are automatically used to repay part of the principal . . . and the less principal outstanding, the less you'll pay in interest on it.

Example: Paying off a $100,000, 29-year loan at 15% by adding to the monthly payment an extra $50/month gets the loan paid in 20 years, saving $122,000 in interest charges.

The bank might refuse to accept the extra payments. Discuss it with the president. If you get nowhere, take it up with the state or federal agency that regulates your bank. You're sure to get your way.

• Installment loans. You pay interest on the full amount of the installment loan even though you pay it off bit by bit and therefore don't have full use of the money during the life of the loan. That's costly compared with a loan you pay off all at once at the end of the term (a "single-payment note").

Not all banks are willing to provide single-payment notes . . . installments are much more profitable. But shopping around can save you hundreds on a typical auto loan.

Safe-Deposit Boxes

Plenty of them have been robbed, burned or otherwise compromised. Banks assure customers that with the bank's millions in insurance, the customer's valuables will be covered. Trap: If you can't prove your loss—and most people can't—you won't collect a penny.

Self-defense: You'll have to forego secrecy about the contents of the box. Appraise valuables and take the appraisal to the bank. A bank officer will then verify that the appraised items are in the box. Next, request from the bank a "safe-keeping receipt" and list all the valuables . . . jewels, bearer bonds, cash, etc. Each time you open the box, take a bank officer with you to note on the receipt the removal or addition of any items. The receipt will guarantee reimbursement in the event of a loss.

Source: Edward F. Mrkvicka Jr., president of Reliance Enterprises, Box 413, Marengo, IL 60152, a consumer-oriented financial consulting company. He is also publisher of the monthly newsletter, *Inside Financial* and author of *Battle Your Bank—and Win!*, William Morrow & Co., New York.

What Banks Don't Tell You

• Banks like to advertise their effective annual yield, whereas money-market funds are legally permitted to advertise only the simple interest rates. The long-standing rule inadvertently conceals the fact that money-market funds do compound interest on a daily basis. If a bank and a money-market fund pay the same rate, the bank will appear to offer more by advertising the effective rate.

• Some banks say they let you draw on all checks immediately, provided you put up another bank account as collateral. Catch: If a check backed by a six-month certificate bounces, the bank can break into the certificate before maturity. If this happens, you will have to pay an interest penalty. Protection: Pick a bank that will allow you time to cover a bounced check before it takes any money from your time deposit. Be sure your bank has this policy before you decide to use a time deposit as collateral.

• Don't bite if the bank offers you a big saving in return for a lump-sum payoff of the old low-interest mortgage on your home. The catch: The discount "bonus" comes from principal—not interest—and is taxable income. You will gain a greater return on your money if you set aside the amount sought by the bank and invest it yourself.

• Checks dated more than six months ago are usually not cashable, no matter how much money the issuer has in the bank. (Exception: U.S. Treasury checks are valid indefinitely.)

• If the amount written on the check in words is different from the amount written in numbers, the bank will pay the sum shown in words.

• Be careful when endorsing checks. To prevent loss of money, when sending checks by mail for deposit, write "For Deposit Only" above your signature on the back. That limits the endorsement. An endorsed check with nothing but a signature is the same as cash and may be used by anybody if it's lost or stolen.

Beware of Banks Bearing Gifts

"Free" gifts from banks are usually included on year-end interest statements. If the gift is generous (say, a free vacation for opening a CD), it may saddle you with considerable extra taxable income.

Source: *Putting Your Money to Work* by Lana J. Chandler, Betterway Publications, White Hall, VA.

Interest Rates Aren't Always What They Seem

One of the banker's lucrative stocks in trade is the average customer's innocent belief that 10% is always 10%. Would that it were so, but like so many aspects of the financial business, it's not that simple.

As IRS regulations allow a business to elect from the various available accounting methods, the banking laws allow financial institutions to use varying methods of computing interest—both interest charged and interest paid. This means that in shopping for the best deal, either on a loan or on a savings account or other deposit vehicle, the customer must be aware of the method of interest computation in order to make a valid comparison and choose the best.

Savings Accounts

Without getting into all the many methods of interest computation that work to the banks' advantage, what you want to look at and compare when you open a savings account is day-of-deposit-to-day-of-withdrawal interest, compounded and paid (credited) daily. There is no way to squeeze more interest out of an annual percentage rate (APR) than that. By contrast, other methods of computation can yield substantially lower returns. For example a 9.75 APR as above may pay more than a 10% rate computed by other methods. Over the long haul, that one-quarter of a percentage point, compounded day after day, can add up to a big difference in financial return. Luckily for the customer, competition for savings is high and many banks offer day-of-deposit-to-day-of-withdrawal daily compounding and crediting accounts.

Loans

What about loan rates? Even more complicated, since loan officers tend deliberately to perpetuate the mystique that enshrouds borrowing for most of us. Again, without going into all the details, the best loan deal you can get (for a given interest rate) is a single-payment, simple interest note, with a provision for monthly payments.

Suppose you're shopping for a new car loan of $7,000. One bank offers it to you at 16.79 APR for 48 months on the above terms, and another bank offers you an installment loan at the same APR. On the second note, with exactly the same principal, the same term, and the same collateral, you would end up paying a total of $260 more in interest over the term of the loan.

FDIC Insurance

Many banks advertise their Federal Deposit Insurance Corporation (FDIC) insurance as providing security for depositors at no retail cost. Customers—particularly the elderly—often will deposit only in insured accounts, reasoning that the security provided in a bank as opposed to the market justifies a lower interest rate. However, since bank depositors normally receive interest rates 2% to 3% below those available on other deposit vehicles, it's fair to say that customers do pay for FDIC insurance.

From an investment standpoint, it would be better to ignore the FDIC insurance and opt for higher market rates as long as you investigate the investment carefully; substantiate corporate reserves that would be used to repay depositors/investors in the case of default. (For example, many deposit vehicles are backed by government-issue bonds.) Corporate investment opportunities frequently have better reserves than the FDIC, whose reserve to deposit ratio is a mere 1.2% on average. That inadequate figure means you pay dearly for "security" with what you lose, in interest, at your bank.

Source: Edward F. Mrkvicka Jr., founder and president of Reliance Enterprises, Inc., P.O. Box 413, Marengo, IL 60152, a financial consumer-advocacy corporation. He is the author of *Battle Your Bank—and Win!* and *Moving Up*, publisher of *Inside Financial*, a monthly newsletter, and was formerly chairman, president, and CEO of a national bank.

Tiered vs. Blended Bank Interest Rates

Ask the bank not only for the interest rate it pays but also how it calculates interest on passbook, money market, NOW or Super-NOW account balances. Tiered rates always pay more. Example: The bank pays 5.5% on balances of $1–$999, 6% on $1,000–$4,999, 6.5% on $5,000–$9,999, and 7% on $10,000 up. Tiered rates: With $10,000 on deposit, you earn 7% on the entire balance. Blended rates: With $10,000 on deposit, you earn 5.5% on the first $1,000, 6% on the next $4,000, and 6.5% on the last $5,000. *Extra earnings on a tiered account:* $80/year.

Why Not To Trust Bank Trust Departments

The horrors at bank trust departments are much worse than most people imagine. The horror stories involve people who are locked into irrevocable trusts. Many are trying to sue their way out of them. But it's virtually impossible to do that even if you can produce documents showing that the bank has been earning a compound annual average of only 3% a year for 20 years. Usually these trusts prohibit switching to any other manager.

People who are considering a trust are advised to create one that has the ability to substitute other investment managers. Have the bank act in a custodial capacity instead.

The grossest error banks make is that they just aren't good managers. It's incompetence but not malice. And it's virtually impossible to litigate incompetence successfully as long as portfolios are diversified.

One of banks' sins is that they sometimes keep ridiculously high cash balances in passbook savings accounts instead of in higher-earning money-market accounts. And instead of sweeping the accounts daily or weekly into a money-market fund, they do it monthly.

If people know how to read their bank balances, they can figure this out. But bank reports are so complex, relative to mutual funds' or brokerage firms' statements, that few people can figure them out.

A typical bank report has a principal and an income statement. Look at the income statement, find the line item marked cash balances and annualize one month's income. If the return doesn't seem the same as a money-market return, you'll know that you're being had.

Another problem associated with banks is that the typical trust officer has investment responsibilities for 200–300 time-intensive accounts. And a much too heavy load conspires against good performance.

To get better results, be a royal pain in the neck. Go to the bank and ask to see the results of all the commingled funds. Invariably the performance on those monies is better than that on trust monies. Find out who is responsible for managing those funds and then insist on having that manager for your account.

One thing that can be said about bureaucracy is that it responds to harassment. If you call and make people's lives miserable long enough, they'll eventually give in.

Or, alternatively, you can push them to put you in a bulletproof posture by continuously investing your assets in Treasury bills. You're not going to optimize your investments that way, but you can be sure they're not going to devastate you in the event that the market goes down.

The best way to protect yourself is to avoid being in a position in which you have no options. But if that sin has been committed against you by someone who set up an irrevocable trust, then conduct a well-organized campaign of terror against the bank. If it is a serious amount of money, document the sins and then hire a lawyer and a public relations firm to humiliate the bank into a posture of submission. Maybe that way you can move the money out.

Source: Michael Stolper, president, Stolper & Co., Inc., 770 B St., San Diego, CA 92101. The firm performs investment manager evaluations and helps more than 300 individual and small institutional accounts select investment managers.

Choosing Between Private and Bank Deposit Boxes

You can rent a safe-deposit box at either a bank or a private corporation that specializes in safety boxes. Weigh the advantages of both types before making a final decision. What to look for:

• Business hours: Private safe-deposit corporations have a much longer business day than banks. Some are open 365 days a year. You also can make an appointment to get into your box after business hours.

• Insurance: Some private corporations automatically insure the contents of your box for $10,000, with more insurance available at nominal prices. Banks provide a minimum amount of insurance, but the customer is free to privately insure the box with his own insurance company.

• Cost: The private safe-deposit boxes are

generally more expensive than those at banks.

• Confidentiality: Your access to a private safe-deposit box is a numbered code, not your bank account number (as with bank boxes). This insures the confidentiality of both your safe-deposit box and your bank account.

• Higher security rating: Private companies are often rated higher than banks by the Insurance Institute.

• Sealing: Bank safe-deposit boxes are automatically sealed at your death. To seal a private-company box, a court order, usually from the IRS, is necessary. And since in a private company your box is not tagged with your bank account number, it is much harder to trace—similar to a Swiss bank account.

Source: Michael Butcher, general manager, Universal Safe Deposit Corp., 115 E. 57 St., New York 10022.

All About Safe-Deposit Boxes

Can you locate all your important papers and documents quickly? Guarantee it with a safe-deposit box. Important papers will be at your fingertips and protected from fire, theft, or other casualty. Of course, you can use the box to protect your jewelry and other valuable things, too.

The fee for renting a bank safe-deposit box is surprisingly low. Only two keys are made to fit the box, and you keep both of them. The box cannot be opened without your permission unless you die or you don't pay your rental fee for a whole year. In a nonpayment situation you will receive a certified, registered letter to give you one last chance to pay up. If you don't, the contents of the box will be removed in the presence of a bank official, inventoried, verified, and then stored in a safe place until you eventually claim them.

Documents to keep in your safe-deposit box:

• Birth, marriage, and death certificates.
• Divorce or separation agreements.
• Title papers to real estate, car, etc.

- Mortgage papers.
- Contracts and legal agreements.
- Stock certificates.
- Military discharge papers.

In addition, many people keep credit cards and photographs of the inside and outside of their home in the safe-deposit box to support insurance claims.

Smart idea: Make copies of these records before you put them into the box for easy reference.

Some items should not be kept in a safe-deposit box:

- Keep your will at your attorney's office, with only a copy in the safe-deposit box. Reason: Safe-deposit boxes are sealed at death until the IRS sees what's inside. This could prevent relatives from getting into the box right away to see if a will even exists.
- Don't hide money in a safe-deposit box to prevent taxation on it. This is illegal, and your heirs might be taxed on the money at your death anyway.

Source: Rudra Nath, vault custodian, Safe Deposit Department, Marine Midland Bank, NA, 140 Broadway, New York 10015.

When Your Safe-Deposit Box Isn't Safe

It is unwise to keep anything in a safe-deposit box that may be needed quickly when the owner dies. At that time, a bank normally seals the box until legal proceedings (sometimes lengthy) take place.

Don't store:

- Original will, cemetery deeds or burial instructions. (Keep them in a safe place at home or in a vault belonging to your lawyer, executor or accountant.)
- Large amounts of cash. Money in a safe-deposit box is not working for you and suggests intent to evade income tax.
- Unregistered property (such as jewelry or bearer bonds) belonging to someone else.

Courts could presume these items to be your property, and proving otherwise might be difficult.

Store these:

- Personal papers, such as birth and marriage certificates, military service or citizenship papers, important family records.
- Jewelry, medals, rare coins, stamps, family heirlooms.
- Original signed family or business documents, such as house deeds, mortgage papers, trust agreements, contracts, leases, court decrees.
- Securities, registered or bearer.

Final check: Make sure someone knows where the safe-deposit box is and where the key is, too.

Important: Safe-deposit boxes taken out in corporate name don't get sealed upon the death of one of the principals. Might be very useful for closely held firms.

Safeguards for Safe-Deposit Boxes

Valuables stored in bank safe-deposit boxes are not automatically protected against loss through burglary, flood, or fire. To be compensated for missing valuables, depositors must initiate lawsuits against the bank. The chances of winning are very, very slim.

Safeguards: Buy insurance for the contents of the boxes even though reimbursement levels are low. And most negotiable items, such as securities, bank notes, gold, coins, and cash, are not covered.

Alternative: Store stocks and bonds at the brokerage house where they were purchased. These firms have a legal and financial responsibility to guard securities stored with them.

Another option: Open a custody account with a bank. The bank holds securities and other assets in its vault. It collects and credits all dividends, but does not manage the assets. The bank will replace any asset in the vault that is lost, stolen, or harmed. Charges are generally based on the size of the account and the composition of the holdings.

Hidden Costs of Automated Teller Machines

Hidden fees for using automated teller machines...about 40% of banks charge for withdrawals and 22% for deposits at ATMs not owned by the bank. Fees: 50¢–$1. For the bank's own ATMs, only 16% charge for withdrawals and 6% for deposits, with fees averaging 15¢. Read the fine print on the ATM agreement with your bank. If you're paying fees, shop around for a bank whose ATM use is free.

Source: Study by Sheshunott & Co., banking industry consultants, cited in *Sylvia Porter's Personal Finance.*

Beware Black-Market Foreign Exchange

Classic setup: You're in France and the official exchange rate is six francs/dollar. On the street a well-dressed gentleman offers to change your money for seven francs/dollar.

Sting: He hands you a bankroll to count— it's correct. You hand it back to get out your money. He does a quick switch, substituting a sham bankroll for the real one, hands you the roll, and disappears.

Self-defense: Exchange money only at banks and official currency exchange locations.

Another reason to use only approved exchange locations is to get a currency exchange receipt. These are often needed when you change the currency back into dol-

lars. (Receipts are proof that currency was obtained legitimately.)

Fixing Money Machine Errors

Cash-machine errors must be reported to your bank within 60 days of the date the problem appears on your statement. Under the Electronic Funds Transfer Act, the bank must investigate and report to you within 10 business days. If the bank needs more time, it can take another 45 days; but it must deposit the disputed amount into your account within 10 business days of the day it decides to extend the investigation.

Source: *Sylvia Porter's Personal Finance.*

Cashing a Letter

Letters or telegrams may serve as checks. Requirements: The letter must be addressed to a bank. And it must state that a specific amount is to be paid on demand either to the bearer of the letter or to the order of a named person. Point: If any one of these requirements is not met, the letter will not be valid as a check. Of course, the bank will make its usual effort to verify that the "check" is valid.

Source: *United Milk Prods. Co. v. Lawndale Nat'l Bank*, 392 F 2d 876, 5 UCC Rep. 143.

Checks Marked "Payment In Full"

If there's no dispute as to the amount, a check tendered for less than the amount due and marked "payment in full" (or the like) may be cashed without prejudicing the right to recover the balance.

If there's a bona fide dispute as to the amount owing, the creditor must be wary. Alternatives: Reject the check and demand full payment. Or: Accept the check but run the risk that payment will be deemed to have settled the disputed claim for the lesser amount. It's easy enough for a debtor who wants to pay less than the amount for which he's billed to create a dispute on the basis of quantitative or qualitative deficiencies in the goods or services supplied.

Stamp the check with a statement to the effect that "Check is accepted without prejudice and with full reservation of all rights under Section 1-207 of the Uniform Commercial Code." The effectiveness of this technique is untested in the courts, but it may help protect a creditor's rights and provide leverage in a settlement.

How To Deposit an Unsigned Check

Write or type the word "over" on the line where the signature would normally appear. On the back, type "lack of signature guaranteed"...and add your company's name, and your name and title. Then sign. This guarantees your bank that you'll take back the check as a charge against your account if it isn't honored. Most banks will then process the check and remit the funds. This saves you the trouble of returning the check to your customer for signature.

Source: *Credit & Financial Management*, 475 Park Ave. S., New York 10016.

How To Spot a Forged Check

• See if the check has perforations on one side. (A false check often has four smooth

sides, since the forger cuts them with a paper cutter after printing.)

• The code numbers printed on a legitimate check reflect no light. They are printed in magnetic ink, which is dull.

• About 90% of all hot checks are drawn on accounts less than one year old. The numbers in the upper right-hand corner of the check indicate the age of the account. Be suspicious of those that are numbered 101–150 or 1001–1050 (the starting numbers).

Source: Frank W. Abagnale, once a master forger and now a consultant to banks and retailers, writing in *Real Estate Today*.

How To Live on Your Float

Consumers are spending more and moving their money faster, but they're not using cash. More cash substitutes and electronic payment alternatives are available today than ever before—checks, credit cards, telephone bill-paying, and home banking services. Aside from the obvious advantages of convenience and security, cash displacement instruments and electronic payment devices have another common feature—the opportunity to create float.

Check Float

Most of us are already familiar with check float. When you pay a bill by check, for example, you know that it will take from one to three days for the check to reach its destination by mail, then another one to three days for the check to be returned to your own bank for payment and subsequent debit from your account. In the meantime, you do not need to have funds in this account to cover the check you have written. So you can cover your check by making a deposit on payday and/or keep your funds invested and earning interest. Effectively, you are using your creditor's money instead of your own during the float period.

Recommended: Pay bills close to the due

date—not when you receive them. By delaying your payment you retain use of your funds for as much as 28 days longer, it doesn't cost you anything, and you continue earning interest.

Telephone Bill-Paying

Some telephone bill-paying services can help you to control your bill paying disbursements by allowing you to specify the date on which you want the bill paid. Thus you can arrange payment immediately prior to the due date without the risk of having to estimate variable mail times and without the fear of forgetting to pay on a specific date.

Credit Cards

Credit cards are a major source of float. When paying credit card issuers, take full advantage of interest-free grace periods and payment due dates. Be aware that Visa and MasterCard payment terms are not standardized, but can vary dramatically among card-issuing banks. If you pay off your credit card bills in full every month, as do about 30% of bank card customers, most banks provide an interest-free grace period of 30 days. Some banks, however, provide less—25 days, 15 days, or even no grace period at all. Shop for the card issuer offering the longest grace period and use all of it. Know your creditors' payment policies and how they vary. American Express, for example, requires payment in full within 30 days but imposes no penalty or finance charge if the full balance is paid within 60 days.

The interest-free grace period represents only a fraction of the float created in a credit card transaction. In addition, if you pay your bills in full every month, you benefit from the time it takes for the merchant to deposit his or her sales drafts with a merchant bank; the time the merchant bank takes to process the drafts and transmit them to your bank; the time your bank takes to post the transaction to your account; and the time your bank waits to send out your bill once a month. Further, after your payment is received, you benefit from the amount of time the bank takes to process and clear your check, ranging from immediately to an additional three days. In all, you can count on an average of between 45 and 90 days of float on each credit card purchase you make—a strong incentive for using interest-free credit instead of cash.

Automated Teller Machines

Sophisticated consumers are learning to play the float game with ATMs, as well. Some ATMs are not programmed to assign float on check deposits, which means ATM users, whether for personal or small-business purposes, can get immediate use of deposited funds before the check has been processed or cleared. ATMs can provide beneficial float on cash withdrawals, as well. Most ATM networks are programmed for settlement at a specific time during the day—usually between 2 p.m. and 4 p.m. on weekdays only. Hence, if your local ATM machine settles at 2 p.m. and you make a withdrawal at 2:05 on Friday, the debit to your account might not occur until Monday. If your account is interest-bearing, you continue to accrue interest until Monday on funds you are using over the weekend.

Opportunities for generating float abound, and by understanding how they occur and developing a sensitivity to timing, you can use float advantageously in many ways. Living on borrowed money need not mean debt if you can learn to live on your creditors' float.

Source: Patricia L. McFeely, senior vice president, Littlewood Shain & Company, 175 Strafford Avenue, Wayne, PA 19087, consultants to financial institutions. As manager of the firm's Consulting Services Division, she is responsible for consulting project management, publications, and seminars. She is also the author of *Plastic Card Float* and *The Profitability of Cash Management Services* published by the Bank Administration Institute.

Float Can Work Both Ways

The textbook definition of float is "converting a negotiable instrument into cash or the transit period required to turn a contingency into an asset." This means, on the one hand, the time lapse between your deposit and the date the bank allows you to use those funds or, on the other hand, the time lapse between when you make a payment by check or other draft and the date that debit is charged to your account.

Assuming that the money in question is "working," using float is a way of "creating money." If you doubt this, be assured that while the sums involved may seem small, taking advantage of float on deposits is one of the ways commercial banks expect to make a profit. A very small ($10,000,000) bank, for example, can easily make $50,000 a year simply by instituting a policy that gives them free use of your money for as long as possible. What you stand to gain or lose from intelligent understanding and use of float will be proportionately smaller, of course, but the principle involved is equally valid: no sum is unworthy of consideration.

Perhaps the first step in dealing with float is to minimize its use *against* you. Find a bank with a reasonable "hold" policy (the delay in crediting deposits to customer accounts). The difference between a hold policy of three calendar days and 14 business days (about the most outrageous currently in use) on a NOW account with an average balance of $3,000 could be the difference between annual earnings of $165 and $0. (On a non-earning account, money is not at issue—for you—but convenience and access to your own funds are considerations.)

Once you have arranged to make your deposits work as long and hard as possible, you might give some attention to making float work to positive financial advantage. If you have a NOW account or a money-market account, by making payment by mail on the last possible day, you may keep that money earning as much as a week longer than otherwise, given mail delivery time and time for the draft to clear through the system. (A postmarked mailing is the legal equivalent of making payment in person on the same date.)

There are ways to use float in your savings program, too. There are still banks that offer an in-by-the-tenth, earn-from-the-first policy. You can routinely turn this to your advantage by the simple expedient of opening a second account in a day-of-deposit-to-day-of-withdrawal bank (we'll call it Bank 2) and playing one bank against the other: withdraw funds from Bank 2 on the tenth of the month, depositing them in Bank 1, thus earning an extra 10 days' interest on the sum every month. On the last day of the month, simply transfer funds back to Bank 2 and begin again. (Note: Some in-by-the-tenth banks offer this privilege only on a quarterly basis. Still, that's 40 days' double interest per year.)

Source: Edward F. Mrkvicka Jr., founder and president of Reliance Enterprises, Inc., P.O. Box 413, Marengo, IL 60152, a financial consumer-advocacy corporation. He is the author of *Battle Your Bank—and Win!* and *Moving Up*, publisher of *Inside Financial*, a monthly newsletter, and was formerly chairman, president, and CEO of a national bank.

Debit Cards Aren't All Bad

Debit cards designed specifically for the purpose of reducing float don't always achieve that objective. Issued for use at the point of sale, a debit card is presented by the customer in payment for a retail transaction. The card is inserted in a terminal at the store and funds are directly debited from the customer's bank account.

Because of the high cost of direct electronic interchange among merchants at the point of sale, merchant banks, intermediate data processors, card-issuer banks, and card issuers, few direct debit point-of-sale programs are fully automated at this time. Consequently, the direct debit card you use at your local gas station or supermarket (including some programs that provide cash back) can actually take longer to debit your bank account than would a check.

Source: Patricia L. McFeely, senior vice president, Littlewood Shain & Company, 175 Strafford Avenue, Wayne, PA 19087, consultants to financial institutions. As manager of the firm's Consulting Services Division, she is responsible for consulting project management, publications, and seminars. She is also the author of *Plastic Card Float* and *The Profitability of Cash Management Services* published by the Bank Administration Institute.

How Long Does It Take For a Check To Clear?

The interval between the time you deposit a check and the time your bank grants you access to the funds therein is known as a "check hold." The result of this banking practice can be a chronic delay in gaining access to your funds and significant monetary costs.

According to the Federal Reserve, since the advent of electronic clearing and funds transfer, virtually any check drawn within the US banking system will have been collected within two business days of the date of deposit. Local checks take less time.

Nonetheless, a majority of banking institutions continue to impose check holds on most accounts, varying from three to five calendar days to more than a week. A substantial number of institutions place the same holds on cashier's checks. The explanation is simple economics. As long as it has the use of your money, the bank earns interest on it at market rates.

While this makes sense for the banks from the economic point of view, there is absolutely no justification for it from your point of view—especially considering the fact that if any problem is encountered in the collection process, you can be sure you will be required to pay for it.

On the other hand, you do have alternatives. Eighteen percent of the banks surveyed in a recent study imposed no hold on local checks, and 10% grant access to out-of-state checks within two business days. So, shop for a bank with an enlightened policy. And don't overlook savings and loans and credit unions, whose policies are likely to be more liberal in this respect.

Another alternative is to either have your check deposited directly or apply for overdraft protection. Direct deposit, however, is limited to checks issued by institutions large enough to have established a direct link to the bank. Overdraft protection will free you from the inconvenience of holds, but subject you to substantial interest and/or transaction charges.

If your shopping expedition fails to uncover a better alternative, your best bet may be to try challenging your present bank. Hold policies are usually discretionary, so you are justified in complaining to the branch manager. (Most corporations and other large depositors are exempt from holds.) A bank will often remove its hold rather than risk raising the ire of an established customer.

Source: Michael G. Caudell-Feagan, executive director, National Association for Public Interest Law, 215 Pennsylvania Ave. SE, Washington, DC 20003.

What To Do If Your Check Bounces

If you have been unlucky enough to bounce a check recently, you may well have been shocked at the size of the charge ($10, $15, $25, or more) assessed to your account for this misdemeanor. Does it seem strange that with the advent of all that cost-cutting automation in the banking industry, the expense of processing an overdraft should have risen so sharply? It should. The fact is that with deregulation, many banks have decided to transform the return of customers' checks into a profitable industry by assigning purely punitive charges, totally unrelated to the real cost of processing the transaction. (The procedure involves no monetary outlay on the bank's part and the in-house paper work cost averages about 75¢ per check.) What makes matters worse, many bounced checks are created by bank policy.

Culprit Number One—The Hold

Many banks have a policy of crediting deposited checks to your account only after a specific time period, which may be as long as 10 or 14 business days, depending on certain factors. Theoretically, this is to insure that they do not allow you to draw on the funds before they have made sure the check is "good." Since, however, most checks clear within 48 hours of deposit, and since only about 1% of these will be returned for any reason, much less for insufficient funds, a hold policy of this sort is no more or less than the bank's way of securing an interest-free loan for the bulk of the hold period. If the bank can then create an overdraft by returning your check drawn on funds collected days beforehand, its profit on the deal skyrockets—unless you fight back.

What You Can Do

The basic precept to keep in mind is don't allow your bank to invade your personal finances any more than you would a thief. Most people are surprisingly passive about this trespass; they feel helpless, bound by the rules. But never forget, it's your money, not theirs, and they have enough ways of making your money work for them that you needn't put up with high-handed penalties for nonservices.

If the overdraft was the result of a bank error (losing track of a deposit, charging other customers' checks to your account, etc.), you should demand not only to have any and all charges removed, you should also see that a letter goes out from the bank to each party to whom a check of yours has been returned, explaining that the bank was at fault.

If the overdraft resulted from the bank's policy not to credit deposits to your account for the official hold period, irrespective of whether the funds have been collected, then you have reasonable grounds for a fight regardless of what the rules say.

Here are some tactics that will help you prevail:

• Above all, don't let anyone snow you with self-serving speeches about how long it takes checks to clear. Demand to know precisely when your deposits cleared.

• Be firm. Be persistent. Don't hesitate to go over people's heads. It is usually easier for a bank employee or officer to give in to your demands than have the matter come to the attention of his or her superior.

• Don't forget that you have access to small claims court, and don't be shy about making sure the bank is aware that you know this. Small claims court is a great leveler; it makes you the equal of the bank and all its lawyers and accountants. And, again, it may cost a bank considerably more to make an appear-ance in court than to give in to your point of view.

• If the threat of small claims doesn't work you might mention the possibility of legal action on a grander scale. One customer of a major Chicago bank is currently bringing a class-action suit against that institution for $10 million in punitive and actual damages equal to the bank's earnings from its check-clearing policy over a 10-year period.

Of course, if your overdraft is purely a result of your own negligence or poor arithmetic, you may well have to bear the consequences as cheerfully as you can. Meanwhile, look for a new bank, one that will not charge you for this sort of "service"—or at least keeps such charges within reason.

Source: Edward F. Mrkvicka Jr., founder and president of Reliance Enterprises, Inc., P.O. Box 413, Marengo, IL 60152, a financial consumer-advocacy corporation. He is the author of *Battle Your Bank—and Win!* and *Moving Up*, publisher of *Inside Financial*, a monthly consumer newsletter, and was formerly chairman, president, and CEO of a national bank.

When the Bank Can't Bounce a Check

The bank may have to honor a check if it takes too long to bounce it. Uniform Commercial Code requires that the bank take some action by midnight of the business day after it receives the check. But the bank gets more time if there's an emergency beyond its control, for example, computer breakdown.

Line of Credit vs. Loan Commitment

A line of credit with a bank facilitates corporate borrowing but offers less financial security than a loan commitment. The bank can cancel the line of credit at any time. Also, the bank is not required to advance the full amount of the line. A loan commitment, on the other hand, cannot be canceled during its life except under special circumstances spelled out in the loan contract. Note that the company must pay a fee for this assurance of financial availability. There is no fee for the line of credit.

Source: *Midlantic NB v. Commonwealth General,* 1980 D.C. App. (4th) 386 So. (2) 31.

If Your Statement Is Wrong and the Bank Won't Help

When you receive a checking account statement that appears to be incorrect, your first move should be to balance the account. This means making sure that all the additions and subtractions to the opening balance do in fact produce the final balance. If you have difficulty doing this, your bank should be willing to help. Almost every branch has a bookkeeper who specializes in balancing accounts. (If this takes longer than a few minutes, they will charge a fee, but it's worth it.)

This process of reconciling your records and arithmetic with those of the bank should reveal the discrepancy. Most of the possible explanations will be simple to deal with: It's either your error or theirs—a check or routine charge not recorded by you, a deposit not credited to your account, that sort of thing.

If the problem is one of those mysterious "adjustments" or "miscellaneous debits," the bank is, of course, obligated to identify and justify this to you. If they cannot do so within two or three days, insist that the disputed amount be credited to your account pending clarification.

Once you know what the bank has charged you for, you will have to pursue getting the charge dropped if you think it's unfair. For this, you will need to talk to "The Manager" (who may be hard to locate, due to the size

and organization of large banks). Discuss the dispute with him or her face to face. If you don't get satisfaction, go straight to the top—the chief executive officer. Get the CEO's name and address and write a clear letter outlining your problem. If you don't get satisfaction on this level (don't be surprised if some bank officer other than the CEO—possibly a customer relations professional—intervenes at this point), write to the nearest Federal Deposit Insurance Corporation (FDIC) office and to the local newspaper's "fix-it" column. There isn't a bank that won't respond to that combination.

Then change banks.

Source: Margaret "Marty" O. Tunnell, vice president and region manager, San Francisco Regional Corporate Center, 405 Montgomery St., San Francisco 94104.

Borrow from Several Banks

Many business advisers believe it's best to bank in one place to get more influence there. But in a tight money market, that one bank can squeeze your company—by recalling your loan or putting pressure on you to pay it off in a way you didn't anticipate. Better: Spread loans among a few banks. That way, if any one of them creates trouble for you, there's somewhere else to go immediately. This is similar to the principle of investment diversification—never put all your eggs in one basket.

Source: *Take a Chance To Be First* by the founder of Avis Rent-a-Car, Warren Avis, Macmillan, New York.

Getting a Bank Loan After You're Refused

It's unfortunate but true that banks are not only decidedly conservative in choosing whom to entrust with their money, they are also often intimidating. Banks know that a customer who is on the defensive either will be afraid to question a refusal or will be so happy to receive an approval that he won't try to negotiate a better loan rate. But it doesn't have to be this way.

Preparation

The person who goes to the loan officer armed only with some vague figures entrusted to a faulty memory is not likely to be successful (unless he or she is the bank president's golf partner, in which case it won't much matter). By the same token, any potential loan customer who clearly comprehends all the ramifications of a loan request, is on top of all the facts and figures, and has it all down on paper stands a very good chance of getting what he asks for. That kind of preparation impresses loan officers; it commands their respect.

If you are applying for a personal loan, bring an updated financial (net worth) statement. If the request is for a business loan, besides the financial statement, thorough documentation should include back tax returns for two to three years (if available), profit and loss projections for two or three years into the future, and a pro forma sheet describing clearly why you need to borrow, how you intend to use the money, and how you intend to generate enough income to pay the tariff. A competent and confident presentation accompanied by neat, clear documentation may make all the difference in your request, and will help lower the interest rate offered.

Persistence

If your banker turns you down, you can, of course, go elsewhere with your request, but the chances are that pursuing the matter further with your original bank will eventually pay the desired dividend. Most customers, in fact, don't follow up a loan denial, possibly because they're convinced that once the bank has spoken the answer is writ in stone. This is simply not the case; these decisions are often reversed "on appeal."

Your first move after receiving a turndown is to approach the loan officer and request an in-depth explanation. Having gotten the true word, ask the loan officer what it would take to elicit a positive response. Believe it or not, this simple gambit will often be enough to turn the trick!

Explanation: Sad but true, loan officers often turn down perfectly legitimate applications simply because, on some level, they can't be bothered. Yet when a customer requests that officer's assistance, this bit of flattery frequently has the effect of motivating him to take the time that should have been taken in the first instance.

Assertiveness

If the gambit does not work and the loan officer will not help, it is time to bypass him and go to his supervisor—or at least to make it clear that you intend to do so. Bankers don't like people going over their heads and will go to considerable lengths to avoid that eventuality—including granting loan requests. The same principle operates with bank officers on all levels, up to and including the CEO.

If you are not getting satisfaction within the bank organization and are convinced you are being discriminated against, you should consider filing suit under the Equal Credit Opportunity Act of 1961. But here again, the bank's awareness of your intention to pursue this course may decide the issue long before you get anywhere near a courtroom.

Other outside avenues to pursue include small claims court and lodging complaints with the comptroller of the currency in Washington, DC (if the bank is a national bank), the state banking authority (if it is not), and the Federal Deposit Insurance Corporation (if your bank is so insured). The point is not so much to actually bring these forces into play as to cause the bank to sit up and take notice. Any of these alternatives will more than likely get the bank's attention, and once your banker realizes you are serious about what you're doing, you may find your loan denial is magically turned into an approval.

Source: Edward F. Mrkvicka Jr., founder and president of Reliance Enterprises, Inc., P.O. Box 413, Marengo, IL 60152, a financial consumer-advocacy corporation. He is the author of *Battle Your Bank—and Win!* and *Moving Up,* publisher of *Inside Financial,* a monthly consumer newsletter, and was formerly chairman, president, and CEO of a national bank.

Finding the Right Loan Officer

• Shop for loan officers if you're seeking funding for your business. Key factor: Loan application approach. Before putting in your application, talk with the officer about your plans. Ask what the chances are of your loan's being granted. If the answer is something like "The committee will make that decision," try a different loan officer or another bank. Best reply: "I've been in this business 15 years and have had only three loans turned down. I don't take an application unless I expect it to be accepted."

• Bad credit need not prevent you from getting a bank loan. Key: Find a banker with clout. Junior loan officers in most banks are sternly warned never to lend to people with bad credit, no matter what explanation the applicant may offer. But a more seasoned loan officer, at the vice-president level or higher, often has the experience and authority to bend the rules.

Source: *Take a Chance To Be First* by the founder of Avis Rent-a-Car, Warren Avis, Macmillan, New York.

Tricks Banks Play with Interest Rates

Banks teach their loan officers a number of strategies to get an extra ¼% or even ½% from borrowers. Recognize some of their tricks:

• Doing the negotiating at the bank, which is familiar territory to the banker, intimidating to the borrower.

• Not mentioning rate at all, but simply filling it in on the note.

• "Since you need the money today, let's write it up at X%. Then we can talk later about changing it." The banker hopes you'll never bring it up again. He certainly won't.

• Flat statement: "The rate for this type of loan is X%." (Never true except for small consumer loans. There is always room to negotiate.)

• Postponing the rate discussion as long as possible, hoping the borrower will weaken under deadline pressure.

• Ego-building. The bank president stops by during negotiations.

• Talking constantly about how little the interest costs after taxes. And comparing it with finance company rates, secondary mortgage rates, or the cost of equity capital.

The banker looks at the company's account as a package, including loans, average balances maintained, and fees for service. Borrower options: Trade off higher average balances for a lower interest rate on borrowings, or vice versa.

The borrower is at a disadvantage because he probably negotiates a loan only once a year or less, while the banker spends full time at it. So prepare carefully for negotiations.

Good tactics for the borrower:

• Ask the interest rate question early—in your office, not his. Don't volunteer suggestions.

• Negotiate everything as a package—rate, repayment schedule, collateral, compensating balances. The banker's strategy will be to try to nail down everything else and then negotiate interest rate when the borrower has no more leverage and no room to maneuver.

• Be prepared with an expression of surprise and shock, even rehearse it before a mirror. React that way when the banker mentions the interest rate, no matter what the figure is.

Source: Lawrence T. Jilk Jr., executive vice president, National Bank of Boyertown, PA, in *The Journal of Commercial Bank Lending*.

Creative Banking . . . New Loans

Banks are getting more creative with their loan policies. And consumers can be the beneficiaries.

A bank in Connecticut, for example, has devised a painless way for families to save tens of thousands of dollars in interest on their mortgages. The method is so simple it is hard to believe: Make half the monthly payment every two weeks instead of the whole amount every month. Bonus: The mortgage is paid off much faster.

Example: A traditional $100,000 mortgage with an interest rate of 12% would have a monthly payment of $1,028.61 . . . for 30 years. The total cost of interest over that period is $270,307.85.

A $100,000 mortgage with payments of $514.31 every two weeks is paid off in 18.9 years. Total interest cost: $154,303.70.

The saving in interest is a staggering $116,004.15, and the house belongs to the family, free and clear, 11 years sooner.

There is no gimmick. It all makes sense arithmetically. The secret: The principal is paid off far more rapidly when payments are made every two weeks. That is partly because the principal is reduced every two weeks instead of every month. And the faster the principal is paid off, the less interest is paid.

The other key factor: An additional monthly payment is made each year. Twenty-six biweekly payments are equivalent to 13 monthly payments.

In 18.9 years, when the $100,000 biweekly mortgage is totally repaid, a borrower would still owe $75,749.54 in principal on a monthly basis.

Bankers like the idea as much as borrowers because it costs the bank nothing and gives it greater flexibility. It gets its principal back far more quickly, enabling it to use the funds recouped for making new loans.

The idea was introduced by City Savings Bank of Meriden, Connecticut. The bank's chairman, R.K. Montgomery, said that practically all mortgages issued by City Savings are being written on the biweekly-payment basis. He has received inquiries about the new mortgage from 275 banks in 47 states.

Other lending ideas are coming from California. There, banks are introducing car loans with small—or no—down payments and relatively low monthly payments. The plans generally are designed for people who want to buy expensive cars, although Security Pacific National Bank sets a minimum car price of only $12,000. Bank of America's plan, however, caters particularly to buyers of high-priced autos such as Cadillacs.

These loans are commonly known as "balloons" because very little principal is repaid in the monthly installments. Most of the principal comes due when the loan matures. Thus, the principal "balloons." When the loan matures, the borrower has three options: Paying off the residual value of the car and keeping it, walking away and leaving the car with the bank, or trading the car in for another, under a similar financing plan. At Security Pacific, there is a $200 charge for turning the car in.

Example: You buy a car for $13,000 and finance it over 48 months at, say, 15¼%. Security Pacific calculates that the value of the car after four years would be $5,850. That is the figure you would pay at that time to keep the car. In the meantime, if you make no down payment, you pay $280 a month on the loan. In contrast, the monthly payments on a conventional 48-month auto loan would be $363. On the balloon loan, if you put down 20%, the monthly payments are reduced to $203. There are restrictions on how many miles you can drive each year without incurring a mileage charge, and the car must be in "reasonable condition" if it is turned in at the end of the period.

Because of the low monthly payments, balloon loans enable many more people to have expensive cars. Bank of America figures that monthly payments on a $23,650 loan—at 15% interest—would be $489.97. This compares with $658 for a conventional auto loan. A similar balloon loan for $34,350 would have monthly payments of $685.02, compared with $955.96 for a conventional loan.

A Standard Bank Loan Rip-Off

Many loan customers are not even aware that they're paying credit life and disability insurance as part of their loan costs, but it is the standard policy of many banks to include this coverage in all personal loans.

A credit (or mortgage) life and disability policy is one that guarantees repayment to the bank of any unpaid portion of the debt concerned in the event of the customer's death or disability. It offers no benefits (other than possible peace of mind) to the customer or the customer's family. Now it is perfectly understandable that a bank would wish to minimize the problems that might otherwise arise in the event of such an unhappy occurrence, but asking the customer to bear the cost of this self-protection is unconscionable.

Even assuming that a loan customer is so compulsively financial-security minded as to want to cover all such eventualities, there are many more cost-effective ways to do this while securing some benefits to his or her family. A whole life policy is one such vehicle. And the chances are that such a policy, covering at least the initial debt balance, could be bought more cheaply through the family insurance agent. What makes it even more outrageous is that the coverage is generally treated as part of the loan obligation and, as such, the bank charges you interest on it! To top things off, like it or not, the bank will also be receiving a direct cash kickback of up to 40% of the premium, just for writing the policy.

Practically the only way a financially responsible adult could let such a state of affairs come about in the first place is through ignorance. Your banker will seldom if ever mention this facet of the deal he's offering you. To raise it would be to give you the opportunity to question it. (With few exceptions, no bank is allowed to make the granting of a consumer loan contingent on the customer's agreeing to pay for a credit life and disability policy; that would be grounds for a sizable lawsuit.) So, standard practice is to simply write the provision into the loan papers with nary a mention from the banker. Under these circumstances, it's easy for a customer, assuming he notices the provision at all, to assume it is a necessary condition and therefore fail to question it.

All in all, it's one of the best money-grabbing scams the commercial banking system has going for it. An informed loan customer should be alert to the policy and prepared to negotiate it out of any loan agreement he makes.

Source: Edward F. Mrkvicka Jr., founder and president of Reliance Enterprises, Inc., P.O. Box 413, Marengo, IL 60152, a financial consumer-advocacy corporation. He is the author of *Battle Your Bank—and Win!* and *Moving Up*, publisher of *Inside Financial*, a monthly consumer newsletter, and was formerly chairman, president, and CEO of a national bank.

Negotiating a Policy Exception Loan

The Federal Equal Credit Opportunity Act requires lending institutions to respond to your request for credit in a timely fashion and, if they turn you down, to tell you why. What you do depends on why you were turned down. Here are the primary policy reasons for credit refusal:

- Bad credit history.
- Excessive debt-to-income ratio.
- Inadequate collateral.

Normally, to get a loan once you've been turned down on a matter of policy, you will have to try to negotiate a "policy exception loan," best done face to face with someone you know who has the authority to make such a policy exception. If the reason was bad credit history, however, you should check this out before proceeding further.

Dealing with the Reporting Agency

The bank is required to give you the name and address of the credit reporting agency on whose records their negative decision is based. The agency, in turn, is required to furnish you with a copy of your file on request.

(Tell them you have been refused credit or you'll be charged a fee.) If the information in the file is incorrect or inaccurate, write to the agency and tell them why.

Ask the reporting agency to contact the lender who has turned you down. Also contact the company that reported you to the credit reporting agency in the first place; send them a letter and appropriate documentation, requesting an answer. Follow it up in 30 days if you don't hear from them.

Returning to the Lender

To find the person who can grant your "exceptional" loan request, start with whomever you originally dealt with and patiently work your way up the chain of command until you get to the person who answers yes to the question, "Do you have the authority to make exceptions to company policy?" This is the person on whom you must work all your powers of persuasion. Arrange a meeting and prepare to bring documents supporting your case.

If the turndown was for bad credit history, you will have to explain how the report was inaccurate or misleading (if it was), or make a strong case for why it will never happen again. You might also offer a cosigner with a clean payment record.

• If it was an excessive debt-to-income ratio, be prepared to point out additional income they didn't count or expenses they overcounted. Are there obligations you could pay off or credit lines you could close out to reduce your potential monthly outlay? (For example, the bank will consider your fully paid up $3,000 Visa credit line as $3,000 you *owe*.)

• If the problem was inadequate collateral, explore flexible alternatives. Find out how big a loan your collateral will support. If it seems appropriate to you, suggest that the difference be made up in an unsecured loan of shorter term. (More profitable to them, to cover the higher risk.)

If after fighting the good fight they turn you down again (less likely than you may think), you can always seek a lending institution with less conservative lending policies.

Source: Margaret "Marty" O. Tunnell, vice president and region manager, San Francisco Regional Corporate Center, 405 Montgomery St., San Francisco 94104.

The Myths, Half-Truths And Whole Truths about Offshore Banking

Offshore banking is not illegal, immoral or unethical, although many people think there is something unsavory about it. In fact, in recent years the popularity of offshore banking among all kinds of people—rich and poor, crooked and honest—has grown tremendously. Exact figures are difficult to come by, but Senate studies estimate that offshore banking has grown by an astonishing 30%–40% annually over the past five years.

What Is an Offshore Bank?

An offshore bank is any bank that operates outside the legal jurisdiction of the United States. That includes banks in Canada, Switzerland, the Philippines, Austria, the Cayman Islands, etc. It can also mean any branch of a bank from one country operating in another country.

Example: The branches of Barclay's of London or of Citicorp located in the Cayman Islands are subject to the laws of the Cayman Islands, not to the laws of England or the US.

Why Bank Overseas?

• Privacy. When you deposit your money in an offshore bank, your account is subject to the privacy laws and regulations of that country. The US government is powerless to investigate anybody's activities—legal or illegal—outside the US without the consent and cooperation of the country in which the investigation is taking place. And unless you are an international terrorist, a major drug dealer, or a former dictator, most governments are very reluctant to assist the US government with an investigation into your financial holdings and/or transactions.

It's even more difficult for the US government to get cooperation from countries whose laws (the tax laws in particular) differ from ours.

Example: The Bahamas and the Cayman Islands don't have an income tax. Therefore, since income tax evasion is not a crime in those countries, they are loath to help the US government investigate anyone suspected of tax evasion.

It is also next to impossible for nongovernment snoops such as private investigators, family members, business associates, etc., to find out anything about your financial affairs.

The protection of a depositor's privacy and confidentiality differs from country to country. Switzerland, the Bahamas, and the Cayman Islands are the most vigilant guarantors of privacy, while Monaco, France, and Italy offer little more privacy than does the US.

• Higher interest rates. In some countries the rates paid on typical savings and checking accounts far exceed those offered by US banks. Rule: Interest rates usually correspond to the inherent financial risk of the country. Exceptions: Countries such as Denmark and Austria pay high rates and are economically sound.

• Security of deposit. Many foreign banks offer more financial security than do US banks.

Example: Although US accounts are insured up to $100,000, many foreign banks offer unlimited insurance for the full amount of the deposit. Also, many foreign banks carry liquid reserves of up to 100% of their deposits (for every $1 of deposit, there is $1 of reserve in the bank). In the US, regulators require banks to hold only 10% liquid reserves.

Tax Status

Contrary to many people's belief, offshore banks don't provide special tax status. When you bank overseas, you are legally required to report all financial transactions and all income earned on your money in that country. Of course, in our less than perfect world many financial transactions can take place between you and an offshore bank without the IRS

every finding out. But if it does find out, the penalties are severe.

Example: You sell a valuable antique, and the buyer writes a check made payable directly to your offshore bank. When the money is deposited, there is no record of the transaction's having ever taken place except, of course, with the offshore bank. . .and it will never tell. (Note: The IRS would have to be conducting a simultaneous audit of both you and the buyer to trace the transaction.)

This is illegal. Tax evasion is a criminal offense, with a penalty of up to five years in prison and a $10,000 fine. And the IRS doesn't let violators off easily. But because the chances of getting caught are so slim, many people who receive direct compensation for their services (retailers, medical professionals, etc.) make use of offshore banks to hide a portion of their earned income.

Which Bank?

Most people find an offshore bank through friends or financial advisers. *Polk's Directory of International Banks* is an excellent source of facts and figures. It lists each country's banking laws and regulations, the banks within that country and the banks' addresses.

Opening an account is as easy as opening a money-market mutual fund in the US. Find a country and several banks within that country that suit your needs, and write a letter to the banks requesting information on opening a checking and/or savings account. Many banks accept deposits of as little as $100. And getting your money out of an offshore bank is no more difficult that dealing with a US bank. Just mail a check or a withdrawal slip.

Rules To Bank By. . .

• Avoid promoters who charge money (some as much as $1,000) to open an offshore bank account for you. There is no reason why you can't do it yourself.

• Check out the financial health of any bank you're interested in. Simply request a copy of its financial statement. Virtually all large overseas banks provide audited financial statements that are almost identical to those of US banks. They even provide English translations. (Most people think any bank other than a US bank or a Swiss bank is financially unsound. Not true. In a recent year there were 138 bank failures in the US—and fewer than 30 overseas.)

Determine what currency your deposit will be held in. Most banks will keep your account in US dollars. Advantage: You are not subject to currency risk. Some banks, however, hold deposits in the currency of their country. Risk: If the currency drops against the dollar, the value of your holdings will drop as well.

My Favorite Countries for Offshore Banking

• Austria and Denmark offer the most favorable combination of privacy, good interest rates and safety. The financial health of both countries is sound, and their privacy laws are very attractive. In Austria you can even use a password for all your transactions. Drawback in both countries: Deposits must be converted into the national currency.

• Canada offers the advantages of proximity and higher-than-average interest rates (generally a full percentage point above those in the US).

• The Cayman Islands and the Bahamas are where your favorite crooks and Wall Street inside traders love to bank. No one can find out anything about bank accounts in these countries. . .especially when the investigator happens to be the IRS.

• Switzerland is great for both safety and privacy. Interest rates on savings accounts are low but the safety of your deposit is guaranteed, and privacy is a top consideration.

• Scotland and the Isle of Man have banks that pay an unprecedented high interest on checking accounts. For long-term accounts (one to two years), the rates are even higher.

Avoid Mexico and the Philippines. Some banks in those countries are paying astronomical rates. But who wants his savings stuck in a country with a deteriorating economy?

Source: J.F. (Jim) Straw, publisher and editor of *Offshore Banking News*, 301 Plymouth Drive NE, Dalton, GA 30720.

Foreign Bank Account Loopholes

If you have more than $400 of dividend and interest income, you must answer the question about whether or not you have an account in a foreign bank. The question is on Schedule B (Interest and Dividend Income). Loopholes: Even if you do have foreign accounts, you can answer "no" if their combined value was $5,000 or less during the year. . .or if your accounts were with a US military banking facility.

Source: *Instructions to Schedule B, Form 1040.*

Swiss Bank Accounts

Swiss bank accounts are mysterious and secret. Only multimillionaires and Arab oil sheiks have them. And they're illegal. Right? Wrong—on all counts. Neither US nor Swiss law puts any restrictions on American citizens' opening Swiss bank accounts. Many Swiss banks accept modest accounts (some have no minimum). And they're no more complicated to open than an American account.

Why a Swiss Bank Account

• Privacy. Under Swiss law, it's a crime for a bank or bank employee to disclose information—even to the Swiss government. Indeed, French tax inspectors tried to obtain information on French depositors but could not. In America, many government agencies can get information. Even private investigators, such as credit bureaus, can usually find out a great deal about your financial affairs. Swiss law and tradition make leaks nearly impossible. A "numbered account," identified by code number, is the most private. The owner's name is locked in the bank vault.

• Currency restrictions. We have none now, but who knows about the future? Many governments have imposed heavy restrictions on the movement of currency in bad times.

The worse the economy, the greater the restrictions.

• Convenience. If you travel or live in Europe, or have business interests there, a Swiss account is useful for European dealings.

• Services. Swiss banks are universal banks. A single bank can perform all the services performed in America by a commercial bank, a savings bank, an investment bank, a brokerage house, and other financial institutions. Many private, unincorporated banks specialize in portfolio management and handle international investments especially well.

The Limits of Secrecy

Banks may disclose information needed to investigate or prosecute crime. During the Howard Hughes autobiography hoax, it was disclosed that an endorsement had been forged on a check deposited in a Swiss account. By treaty, the US government can get information in some cases involving organized crime. A recent treaty covers violations of Securities & Exchange Commission insider-trading regulations. The Swiss authorities make the final decision on disclosure in each case.

There can never be disclosure in cases of tax evasion, currency exchange violations or political offenses. These are not crimes under Swiss law. Disclosure may be made to courts (not the public) in bankruptcy cases and in some inheritance cases.

How To Open an Account

It's best to open an account, especially a large one, in person.

However, you can easily open an account by mail. Just write to the bank, asking for forms and information. (Type your letter. Swiss bankers complain of illegible mail from America.)

You must have your signature verified at a Swiss consulate or by a notary public. The bank will provide forms.

You should execute a power of attorney over the account (unless it's a joint account). Under Swiss law, the power of attorney remains in force even after the depositor's death. If you have qualms about a power of attorney, you don't have to deliver it to the person. Leave it with your attorney, to be delivered only in case of your death or disability.

If you take or send more than $10,000 in cash or bearer securities out of the US, you must notify the government. However, you can send checks or money orders. Bank money orders are most private.

Swiss banks offer current accounts (checking), deposit accounts (saving), and custodial accounts (the bank will hold your stock certificates, gold or other property for a fee).

As in America, there are demand deposits and time deposits. Some accounts require notice to withdraw more than a specified amount. Interest varies with the type of account. The rates are not high, however, compared with those of American banks. The appeal of Swiss banks lies in safety and the soundness of the currency.

Accounts may be in Swiss francs, American dollars or another stable currency (depending on economic conditions when the account is opened).

Taxes and Regulations

Although there are no US restrictions on Swiss bank accounts, your income tax form asks if you have any foreign bank accounts. If you answer yes, you must fill out Form 90–22.1 and file it by June 30.

Interest on foreign accounts is taxable like any other income. You can take a credit for foreign taxes paid.

If you have an account in Swiss francs, and the franc increases in value relative to the dollar, you may be liable for a capital gains tax when you withdraw money and reconvert it to dollars. Losses arising from decreases in value may not be deductible in regard to personal accounts.

Switzerland imposes a withholding tax on interest. But Americans can get most of it refunded by showing they are not Swiss residents. Your bank will send you the forms. (Note: The bank sends in the tax without disclosing depositors' names. To claim the refund, however, you must, of course, disclose your identity.)

At one time, the Swiss imposed severe restrictions on foreign accounts. Only the first 50,000 francs of an account could draw interest, and accounts above 100,000 francs were charged "negative interest" of 40%— nearly a confiscatory rate. These restrictions, or others, could conceivably be reinstated if economic conditions change.

Even when the restrictions were in force, however, they were not retroactive. They did not apply to existing accounts—only to deposits made after the rules were adopted (another reason you might want to act now).

Choosing a Swiss Bank

The Big Five among Swiss banks are the Swiss Credit Bank (Zurich), the Union Bank of Switzerland (Zurich), Bank Leu (AG) (Zurich), the Swiss Bank Corporation (Basel), and Swiss Volksbank (Berne). All are accustomed to doing business with American depositors.

Books listing the names and addresses and other pertinent information for these banks and others are in your library. Check in the card catalog under "Banking—Switzerland."

Source: Stanley C. Ruchelman, tax partner, Touche Ross & Co., 1633 Broadway, New York 10019.

If a crisis does develop, the federal government might prohibit the purchase of gold and other precious metals and would likely restore foreign currency controls. It's happened before.

Advantages of Switzerland: Financial stability with no exchange controls or rules on holding precious metals. . . government-sanctioned banking privacy. . . gold-backed currency. . . politically conservative population. Although you must disclose to the IRS ownership of foreign accounts and interest from them, other information about accounts is revealed to the US government only if it can show you have engaged in criminal activity. . .tax offenses are civil offenses—not criminal offenses—in Switzerland.

Best investment vehicle: Insurance policies, which offer tax-free interest in stable, low-inflation Swiss francs. Crisis perspective: Swiss annuities wouldn't be repatriated as other foreign investments might, even if exchange controls are imposed. Swiss banks also offer brokerage accounts (commissions are higher than in the US) for investing in other currencies and in securities and commodities anywhere in the world.

Source: Robert Kephart, consultant to Swiss financial institutions, Box 2270, Largo, FL 33540.

Why You Should Have a Swiss Bank Account

Myth: Swiss bank accounts are only for multimillionaires with tax troubles and people who need to hide ill-gotten gains. Reality: Swiss accounts and insurance policies are some of the best vehicles for protecting capital from a possible collapse of the dollar and potential future currency exchange controls.

Danger: Hyper US dollar inflation caused by a massive government bailout of defaulting debtors—Third World nations, US corporations, farms, money center banks. In an environment of low inflation and falling interest rates, the debt problem can be kept under control, but an upswing in inflation and interest rates could trigger a huge crisis.

Making Deposits and Withdrawals

Putting money in a Swiss bank and taking it out are almost as easy as making a deposit or withdrawal at your local bank. Requirement: Filing with the US Treasury Department its Form 4790 (available at any bank) whenever you deposit or withdraw more than $10,000 in cash, traveler's checks or bearer certificates. Exempt from the reporting requirement: Money transfers via bank wire, cashier's check or other instrument payable to a specific party.

Offshore Scam

Beware of offshore business trusts (contractual companies) that promise to give you financial privacy and protect your assets from the IRS. Problems: Potential for IRS litigation...high cost...extreme complexity... high profile (which defeats the purpose of a foreign trust), according to Jerry Schomp of *INVESTigate*.

Dealing with Credit Unions

You can't get rich overnight by keeping your money with a credit union. But you can find a combination of old-fashioned personal attention, modern financial services, and the lowest-cost personal financial services available.

The advantages are substantial. Credit unions commonly pay higher returns on passbook savings, certificates, and money market accounts than do other financial institutions. However, when comparing rates paid on savings accounts at credit unions, keep in mind that many still pay on the low or average monthly balance, or even on the low quarterly balance—only about one-third pay interest on the daily average balance. The effective interest rate on accounts paid on the low balance method averages about 85% of the nominal rate.

Traditionally, credit unions have offered the lowest available rates on loans for consumer purchases, such as cars, boats, and home improvements, and for student loans. Even credit life or credit disability insurance may be offered at a much lower cost than is available elsewhere. Some credit unions make loans for business purposes, generally in the form of a personal loan.

When you work for a company that has a credit union associated with it, you often can arrange to have your paycheck deposited into your transaction account for immediate access, and to have loan payments automatically deducted. If you choose, you can direct part of your pay into a savings or money-market account.

"Share drafts"—the credit union's version of NOW accounts—generally pay higher rates of interest than NOWs and most have no or very low minimum balances and service fees.

Credit cards from credit unions are also cheaper than cards from conventional financial institutions. For example, most do not charge an annual fee, and many charge substantially lower rates than other card issuers. The one drawback is that some credit unions charge interest from the date of purchase, not the statement date.

Your funds are generally as safe in a credit union as they are in a traditional bank. Nearly all credit union deposits are guaranteed up to $100,000 by either a federal agency (the National Credit Union Share Insurance Fund) or one of a number of private insurance funds. The federal insurance fund for credit unions is currently the strongest of the three federal insurers of financial institutions—credit unions capitalized the fund with close to $1 billion in 1984. Most of the private funds are also very well capitalized. As a result, serious credit union failures are rare.

Source: Jim R. Williams, president and CEO of Credit Union National Association, Inc., and CUNA Service Group, Inc., P.O. Box 431, Madison, WI 53701. He is also president of U.S. Central Credit Union. CUNA is a trade association serving over 90 % of US credit unions, while CUNA Service Group provides financial, operational, and telecommunications services to the industry.

Who Can Join a Credit Union

Credit-union membership is limited to people who have so-called common bonds—working for the same employer, living in the same neighborhood, etc. If you aren't a member of a credit union but would like to be, write to the industry's trade association for a list of credit unions you may be eligible to join.

Source: Credit Union National Association, Box 431, Madison, WI 53701.

Establishing Consumer Credit

American businesses and consumers have come a long way from the days when credit was available only to the wealthy. Recent changes in the area of consumer credit have made it possible for almost anyone with a steady job or steady income to expect some form of credit and to keep it.

What haven't changed are the basic criteria for getting credit. You still must have the financial capacity to pay your bills when they come due; and to build a strong credit history you must have a consistent record of on-time payments over an extended period.

Credit for Young People

Many credit grantors will make credit available, on a limited basis, to young people just entering the labor force. The only requirement is a steady job that assures the income necessary to meet payments. As income increases and a reliable credit history develops, credit limits will usually be increased. Also, less lenient creditors that might have rejected a young person's credit application the first time around will probably make credit available.

Advice for young people: Start small and build big. Certain credit grantors such as oil companies, large department store chains, and major credit card companies employ relatively lenient evaluation policies. Most of them solicit young people while they are still in college. If there are no service charges, accept the offer. If a credit application is denied, don't be discouraged. Changing economic times can cause credit grantors to change their evaluation policies from month to month.

Credit for Women

Federal laws and regulations make it illegal for credit to be denied on the basis of race, creed, color, or sex. The Equal Credit Opportunity Act, passed in the mid-70s, assures that women will not be discriminated against when they apply for credit because of their sex or because they have been widowed or divorced or because they plan to have children.

Advice for married women: Establish credit jointly with your husband but report to credit bureaus in your name as well as your husband's name. That way you can build up your own credit history independent of your husband's.

It is a misconception that a married woman who doesn't earn a separate income cannot obtain credit in her own name. If you would like credit entirely in your own right, simply apply in your name. Credit grantors recognize that a woman has a legal claim to half of the family's assets and income and will base their credit evaluation on that assumption.

Source: Walter R. Kurth, president and chief executive of Associated Credit Bureaus, Inc., 16211 Park 10 Place, Houston 77084, the international trade association of the credit reporting and collection services industry. He is also vice chairman of the American Society of Association Executives and a member of the board of the US Chamber of Commerce.

Which Bills To Pay First

In a cash crunch, it's important to know which bills you can't put off paying without damaging your credit rating. . .and which you can "defer." To pay immediately: Bills from credit cards issued by department stores (Sears, Macy's, etc.) and banks (Visa, MasterCard, etc.). Reason: They submit "full-file" reports (reaching back 12–24 months) on all customers every month to credit-reporting agencies. Less likely to file regular reports: Oil companies and utilities. Professionals and organizations that don't have contracts with credit-rating bureaus (most physicians and hospitals) don't file at all.

What Is in a Credit File?

The information contained in a credit file consists of computerized records on your payment history, how much you owe and to whom, indications as to whether payments have been received promptly, or late, and information regarding legal action that may have been taken as a result of your inability or unwillingness to pay bills satisfactorily. There is also a brief section on your identification, which is used to assure that the applicable information is delivered to the inquiring creditor. This section includes your name, address, Social Security number, date of birth, and other similar pieces of information regarding your identity.

Source: Thomas G. Collins Jr., director of planning for one of the five major credit reporting companies in the US, The Credit Bureau, Inc., 1600 Peachtree St. NW, Atlanta 30309. His responsibilities are business, marketing, and strategic planning for the firm.

Privacy and Credit Reports

Credit reports and credit reporting agencies are closely regulated and monitored to assure the privacy of the information in your credit file. Who has access? No individual or company may have access to the information contained in your credit report unless there is a "permissible purpose," or a bona fide business reason for inquiring into your credit history. Any creditor who inquires into a credit bureau's data base must certify a legitimate business need for the information and be a customer of the credit reporting agency. An agency may not release information to any individual or company regarding your credit history unless the information is required by that individual or company to make a decision concerning the extension of credit to you.

Source: Thomas G. Collins Jr., director of planning for one of the five major credit reporting companies in the US, The Credit Bureau, Inc., 1600 Peachtree St. NW, Atlanta 30309. His responsibilities are business, marketing, and strategic planning for the firm.

How To Find Out about Your Credit Report

The Fair Credit Reporting Act guarantees that, at any time, you can find out the contents of your credit report. How? If you were denied credit within the past 30 days, based on information in a credit report, you will be sent a notice to that effect. The creditor must provide the reason or reasons for denial as well as the name and address of the credit reporting agency providing the information. The bureau will disclose the nature and substance of the information contained in the file free of charge if notified of the denial within 30 days of receipt of the creditor's letter.

If you haven't applied for credit recently and just want to find out what is in your credit report, simply contact the credit reporting agency by letter or telephone. The agency will charge a small fee to cover any costs associated with the disclosure.

Under the Fair Credit Reporting Act, you have the right to dispute any item contained in your credit file. However, remember that credit bureaus never assign credit ratings; they only store information supplied to them by others regarding your payment history. The rating you receive when applying for credit is assigned by the credit grantor, based on your payment history.

Source: Thomas G. Collins Jr., director of planning for one of the five major credit reporting companies in the US, The Credit Bureau, Inc., 1600 Peachtree St. NW, Atlanta 30309. His responsibilities are business, marketing, and strategic planning for the firm.

Correcting a Bad Credit Report

What do you do if you are dissatisfied with a credit bureau's file and would like to contest the information contained in its credit report? Under the Fair Credit Reporting Act, you are allowed to dispute any item contained in your credit file. By law, the credit bureau is required to investigate and remove any information that is not correct.

What if you are still unhappy with the credit agency's resolution? Even if you can't change the actual information contained in the report, you always have the right to insert a statement of 100 words or less explaining why you feel the report is inaccurate.

Source: Thomas G. Collins Jr., director of planning for one of the five major credit reporting companies in the US, The Credit Bureau, Inc., 1600 Peachtree St. NW, Atlanta 30309. His responsibilities are business, marketing, and strategic planning for the firm.

Credit-Card Secrets

Credit cards are addictive. People are hooked on them—on their convenience, their power, their easy monthly payments. Most consumers don't even shop around for the best deal. They sign on with the first bank that solicits them—almost invariably an aggressive national institution.

Selective Shopping

As a matter of fact, the most favorable card rates are offered by mid-size regional banks. Any person with a decent credit history can apply for and obtain a card from one of these banks, even if out-of-state. But they won't come to you . . . you have to seek them out.

Here's how: Start by exploring the banks near you. If their rates are too high, look to banks in states that have tighter lending laws. Three leaders: Arkansas, Delaware and Oregon, where the maximum interest charged is five percentage points over the federal discount rate, but never more than 17%. To find other low-interest states, check the American Financial Services Association's *Annual Summary of State Consumer Credit Laws and Rates* (available at banks and from the Association at 1101 14 St. NW, Washington, DC 20005).

Beware: Don't assume all banks in low-interest states have low card rates. Several major banks have moved their credit-card operations to states where interest regulations are less restrictive.

Extras: In today's competitive lending mar-

ket, many of the high-fee, high-interest banks are trying to seduce applicants with credit-card enhancements. These extra services range from catalog shopping discounts to travel services to "deals" on everything from new cars to pest control. Unless you live in an isolated rural area, enhancements are rarely worthwhile. Any urbanite can get as good or better prices by shopping around.

Short billing cycles: Reject any bank that bills on a 24-day (rather than 30-day) cycle. Check statements to find the billing cycle. Besides confusing your home bookkeeping, this will cut into your "float," or grace period, during which your loan is effectively interest-free. Also avoid: Any bank that double-dips by tacking on an extra charge (beyond the annual fee) whenever you pay your balance in full.

How To Use It

After you've chosen and received your card, the challenge is to keep interest expenses as low as possible. The best strategy is to make major credit-card purchases on or just before the "cut-off" date (the average purchase requires four days for processing), so they don't show up on your next statement—but on the following one. Result: A float of up to 50 days. Check recent statements for your cut-off date. It usually falls around the same time each month.

Costliest cash: Credit cards are most costly when you use them for a cash advance. You get no float on these transactions, and an extra fee of 4% or more is tacked on to the regular interest charge. (A collateralized bank loan is far cheaper, even if it is more trouble to arrange.)

After establishing a good payment record for a year or two, many credit-card holders are invited to apply for a gold or premium card with a higher spending limit. These cards also charge higher fees.

A patient consumer need not pay that premium. While your initial credit limit may range from $800 to $1,500, it can be raised as often as once a year, either automatically or at the cardholder's request. Most standard cards can eventually be boosted to a $3,000–$5,000 limit.

Dangerous scenario: For the past year you've been consistently revolving around the top of your current limit, never paying off the full balance. Then you ask for a higher limit. In response, the bank decides you're a high risk and launches a thorough credit check. Reason: This pattern often reflects an out-of-control consumer with several cards and a bulging load of credit. If the bank's suspicions are confirmed, it may revoke further charging privileges and demand that you pay off your current debt.

Plastic Addicts

Too many plastic addicts are indeed living beyond their means.

How to tell if you're over your head: Add up all of your monthly intallment payments, including credit-card finance charges but excluding mortgage or rent. If the total is over 15% of your gross monthly income, you're using too much credit. If it reaches 20%, you're in trouble. It's time to go to the issuing bank, turn in your card, and ask them to rewrite the loan on your outstanding balance from 24 months to 36 or 48 months. The bank will accommodate you; it would rather get a smaller monthly payment than none at all.

While one credit card should be enough, most consumers would also benefit from a convenience card, such as American Express. The chief advantage isn't that many restaurants purportedly accept only convenience cards and not MasterCard or VISA. (If you call their bluff, most will take any credit card rather than no payment at all.) But convenience cards are useful for buying big-ticket items, since they have no formal spending limit. Best bet: The American Express green (or "personal") card. It's more widely accepted than Diners Club or Carte Blanche, and has the most extensive teller machine network and the lowest interest rate on long-term credit for travel tickets.

Source: Herbert Mueller, banking adviser to the American Bankers Association and president and chief executive officer of North Valley Bankcorp, 1377 South St., Redding, CA 96001.

War with Bank-Issued Credit Cards

Consumers are being taken for a ride because they are confused. In a national random survey, 60% of the people polled believed interest rates on credit cards were the same from bank to bank. And another survey found that 25% of all cardholders didn't even know what interest rate they paid on their credit cards.

To protect yourself, you must understand how bank credit cards operate and then shop for the best deal.

Contrary to popular belief, VISA and MasterCard do not issue credit cards. They sign up banks to offer their card, recruit retailers to accept their card, and then act as a liaison between the two. Each bank sets its own interest rates, rules, and fee structures. These vary considerably from bank to bank.

What To Consider When You Shop for a Bank Credit Card

• Interest rates. Beware of variable rates. Many banks issue a card at a low rate and then quietly increase their rates later.

• Annual fees. Back when VISA and Master-Card were introduced, annual membership charges didn't exist. Now they are almost universal.

• Transaction fees. These have been raised quietly. Many banks now charge 50¢ for each purchase transaction and more—up to 75¢—for each cash advance. Caution: Many banks charge higher interest on cash advances than on purchases. If you're on a trip and run out of money, it's probably less expensive to charge your purchases than to get a cash advance.

• Interest-free float. It's important to know when the meter starts ticking. Some banks charge you from the day of purchase, others from the day you are billed. Still others offer a 25-day interest-free period.

All this information is available from the bank and must be given to credit-card applicants. Trap: As many as half of the bank-card application forms say nothing about interest rates, and most people don't ask about them before applying. The bank sends this information along with the card—but at that point few people bother to read the fine print.

What To Do

Shop around. You don't have to use a credit card that's issued in your own town . . .or even in your own state. When you hear about a bank that offers a good deal, call or write for a credit-card application.

Best: A card with a low annual fee or none at all. Also desirable: A long interest-free float.

If you generally pay your entire charge at billing time, interest rates are not so important. But if you don't pay off your balance each month, a low interest rate is essential.

Beware of banks that offer very attractive interest rates and annual fees but sneak in some other unattractive features. . . like charging from the date of purchase.

Source: John C. Pollock, Ph.D., editor and publisher of the *Bank Credit Card Observer*, Kendall Park, NJ 08824. He is also president of New World Decisions, an opinion research firm.

What VISA and MasterCard Don't Tell You

One VISA card or MasterCard could be very different from another VISA card or Master-Card. What counts is the bank issuing it.

The MasterCard and VISA organizations do not issue credit cards themselves. They provide a clearing system for charges and payments on the cards and license banks to use the VISA or MasterCard name. It is the issuing bank that determines the interest rates and fees.

A bank's name on a credit card does not necessarily mean that it is the bank actually issuing the card. Issuance of credit cards is a high-risk, low-profit business. Seldom does a small bank issue its own.

Generally, a small bank will act as an agent for an issuing bank. The agent bank puts its name on the card, but it is the issuing bank that actually extends any credit.

Aside from costs, this can be important if the cardholder encounters an error. The correction might have to be agreed upon, not by a friendly local banker, but by an unknown, larger institution, perhaps in a different state.

Choosing which card to take is becoming more difficult, because some of the nation's largest banks have begun active solicitation of customers throughout the US. Individuals must be especially careful about accepting any offer that might come in the mail.

A recently discovered quirk in the federal law allows federally chartered out-of-state banks to ignore state usury laws that limit the amount of interest or fees that the issuing bank may charge on its credit cards. In Arkansas, for example, state usury laws prevent local banks from charging more than 10% interest on credit-card balances. But a federally chartered out-of-state bank, in lending to Arkansas residents, may charge whatever its home state allows. Even with individual states, the terms on credit cards can vary widely.

Aside from the actual rates and fees, individuals must carefully check the fine print of their contracts. Most banks, for example, do not charge interest on balances stemming from purchases until the customer is billed for such purposes. If the bill on which the charges first appear is paid in full by the stated due date, there is no interest charge to the holder. But some banks, those in Texas, for example, begin charging interest as soon as they receive the charge slip and make payment to the merchant. Thus, interest begins accumulating even before the cardholder receives the bill. These interest charges continue until the bank receives payment from the customer.

Source: Robert A. Bennett, banking correspondent, *The New York Times.*

Premium Card Traps

Don't be lulled into getting "premium" credit cards such as Gold MasterCard or Premier Visa. The only significant "premium" is the $20–$25 extra that you pay in the higher annual fee. Besides the fancy finish on the plastic, you get only marginally useful benefits such as travel insurance and protection on lost or stolen credit cards. Since by law you are liable for only a maximum of $50 if your regular card is stolen or lost and you report it within two business days,* the zero liability offered by premium cards is hardly worth the extra money.

Potential huge trap: Credit cards tied to home-equity lines of credit. Banks are pushing them hard. Attraction: Interest paid may qualify for a full tax deduction under tax reform, and the banks' risk is minimal with the credit line secured by the equity in your home.

Home-equity card rates are typically one to three percentage points above prime and credit lines start at $10,000 and go as high as $100,000. Cardholder risk: If you can't make the payments, you lose your house.

*If you wait longer than two days to report the missing card, your maximum penalty is $500.

Source: Consumer banking expert Robert Heady, publisher, *100 Highest Yields* and *Bank Rate Monitor*, North Palm Beach, FL.

Senior Citizen Savvy

Senior citizens may be able to get permanent no-fee cards by signing up for special package deals just for seniors. How it works: They open savings, money market and checking accounts with an institution, and it pro-

vides a no-fee card. Best: Shop around.

Source: Consumer banking expert Robert Heady, publisher, *100 Highest Yields* and *Bank Rate Monitor*, North Palm Beach, FL.

Smart Alternatives to Traveler's Checks

Credit cards are now better than traveler's checks for most trips overseas. Aside from the cards' convenience, they save as much as 6% on exchange costs. Best bet: Visa, with a conversion markup only one-quarter of 1% above the wholesale bank currency rate. Other major cards carry a 1% markup—still far better than the 3% or more you'd pay for retail markups on traveler's checks.

Exceptions: Poorer European countries such as Spain, and Third World countries, where dollar-hungry bankers often give a break on traveler's checks or cash.

Recommendation: Check expiration dates of credit cards before you leave on your trip. An unexpected expiration would be a very troublesome surprise. (Leave unnecessary cards—such as those for local department stores—at home.

Source: *Forbes*, New York.

Playing the Billing Date Game

If you play by the rules of the game, you can keep more of your funds earning interest while you spend someone else's money (at least temporarily). Credit cards provide opportunities to maximize your earnings at the expense of creditors.

Know Your Creditors' Policies

Credit-card issuers differ in the interest rates and annual fees they charge (if any). They also differ in their payment terms and finance charge calculations. The reason: most credit-card companies, such as VISA, do not set national billing procedures—the bank issuing the card establishes its own policies. Consequently, billing policies vary from bank to bank.

When do banks start charging interest? Banks use one of three options in charging interest on bank cards. The first is to begin charging on the transaction date (that is, the date the customer actually makes the purchase). The second is to charge from the posting date (the date on which your bank receives notification of your purchase). The third option is for a bank to begin charging interest on the billing date (the date on which the bank actually makes up your bill and sends it out). There can be a lapse of several days or even weeks between each of these successive dates. Recommended: Find a bank that charges interest from the billing date; then you can save interest charges that might accrue from the transaction date to the billing date—in some cases well over 30 days. Stay clear of card-issuing banks that charge interest beginning on the transaction date. You will start paying interest charges immediately, no matter how long the merchant takes to deliver your sales draft to his bank; or the merchant's bank takes to transmit the sales data to your bank; or your bank takes to post the transaction to your account and bill you. Effectively, you foot the open-ended bill for the system's inefficiencies.

Don't Pay Bills—Plan Disbursements

When paying credit-card issuers, take full advantage of interest-free grace periods and payment due dates. If you pay off your credit-card bills in full every month, most creditors provide an interest-free grace period of 30 days. Some creditors, however, provide less—25 days, 15 days, or even no grace period. Because they vary, know what your creditors' rules are in advance.

When your creditor stops charging interest (or credits your payment) can make a difference too. Although creditors are required under federal regulations to credit payments on the date of receipt, there are some notable exceptions. A few creditors credit payment receipts as of the payment postmark date, which means you can mail your payment several days later than usual and still receive timely payment credit.

Be careful of late payment charges for "nonconforming" payments. For example, bank-card issuers usually specify that payment be sent to a post office box. If that payment is received anywhere else it is considered a nonconforming payment. Further, if you pay your VISA bill at the local branch of the bank that issued your card, your bank can legally defer crediting payment for up to five days after you hand over your check. Should this occur, you could incur finance charges or late payment penalties on the entire balance in addition to losing use of your funds for those five days, even though you made payment to your card-issuer bank's branch on time.

Managing your credit-card funds means shopping for the best overall payment terms for your particular situation. If you pay off your credit-card bills in full each month, you should be indifferent to creditors' interest rates and to the timing of initiation of finance charges, but highly sensitive to annual fees and card payment terms. If, on the other hand, you incur finance charges, then interest rates and the timing of finance charge initiation would be the dominant concerns. In either case, the object of playing the billing date game is the same—to maximize your use of your creditors' money and/or minimize your payment of finance charges.

Source: Patricia L. McFeely, senior vice president, Littlewood Shain & Company, 175 Strafford Avenue, Wayne, PA 19087, consultants to financial institutions. As manager of the firm's Consulting Services Division, she is responsible for consulting project management, publications, and seminars. She is also the author of *Plastic Card Float* and *The Profitability of Cash Management Services* published by the Bank Administration Institute.

Beating the System

Credit cards have become a way of life for most Americans. However, very few people realize the unnecessary costs they incur by not utilizing their cards to their advantage or by not choosing the least expensive card to begin with.

Credit cards can be used as a bargaining chip to receive a discount from a merchant. Merchants typically pay a fee of 2%–7% of your charge when you use your credit card. With an American Express or Diners Club card, they may have to wait a while to get paid. It may be to the advantage of the merchant to go along with your suggestion of a 5% discount if you pay cash.

Another way to beat the system: Take a cash advance on your credit card and pay directly for goods and services, rather than charging them if bank-interest charges are less for cash advances. If you already are being charged interest for merchandise purchases, take a cash advance and switch the balance due to the lower rate.

If no interest charge has yet been levied, then time the cash advance to a day or two before the bill would be past due and pay off the merchandise portion of the bill. Reason for the timing maneuver: Cash advances are charged interest from the day that they are taken. Multiple credit cards come in handy if you want to go to the limit of allowable cash advances on each without having to use your card to purchase merchandise at high rates.

If you have gotten in over your head, it may be best to take out a consumer loan to pay off a number of credit-card bills. Although the consumer loan rate may not be much cheaper than the credit-card cash advance rate, it can be significantly cheaper than the card's basic interest rate on merchandise purchases. In addition, since bank credit-card payments are based on a 24-month term, one big advantage to consolidating such debt with a 36-month consumer loan is lower monthly payments.

Source: Edward Mendlowitz, a partner with Siegel, Mendlowitz & Rich, CPAs, 310 Madison Ave., New York 10017.

Special Charge-Card Trap

There are superhigh interest rates on charge accounts at a growing number of stores that offer their own cards. The biggest offenders are electronics retail chains that charge 21.6%–24% on outstanding balances. There's also a minimum of $100–$500 that must be charged the first time the card is used. Alternatives: Bank credit lines and traditional retail charge cards.

How To Sidestep Late-Payment Penalties

Late-payment penalties on credit-card accounts are becoming more common. More than one-third of the nation's banks are charging penalties of $10 or more even if payments miss the deadline by only a day or two. Some banks will waive the penalties, but the cardholder has to ask for the correction. A good payment track record and a reasonable excuse are usually sufficient grounds for having the charge lifted.

Source: *US News & World Report.*

Advantages of Credit-Card Purchases

Paying an auto mechanic by credit card is one protection against sloppy or unnecessary work. Ultimate payment can be withheld when the credit-card bill arrives. Hitches: The mechanic must be in the consumer's home state, and the bill must exceed $50. Procedure: Send letters to the credit-card company and the mechanic explaining why the repair was unsatisfactory. Propose a sum that would settle the dispute.

Source: *Credit Cards: Auto Repair Protection,* Consumer Information, Dept. 636K, Pueblo, CO 81009.

• Pay for mail-order purchases with a credit card, rather than with a personal check. Reason: If you don't receive the merchandise or it's not what you expected, you can refuse to pay (under the Fair Credit Billing Act) until the matter is resolved. But if you've paid by check and the mail-order company cashes it, you may have trouble getting a refund.
Source: *Good Housekeeping.*

• Simple expense recording. With every purchase made with your credit card, write down who and why on the slip when you sign it. This enables you to keep track of your business tax deductions and expenses in a single step.

Good Reason To Use Your Credit Card

Credit cards can protect you if a purchase turns out to be a lemon. Refuse to pay and demand that the amount be charged to the merchant. What to do: First, make an effort to settle the dispute. Then notify the credit-card company, in writing, of the transaction, the amount of money involved, the name of the merchant, and the attempts to settle. Act quickly. Once you've paid for the merchandise, your only recourse is to sue the merchant.
Source: Jean Noonan, credit-practice attorney, Federal Trade Commission, quoted in *US News & World Report.*

When Tax Status Depends on Which Credit Card You Use

The general rule is that you only get a tax deduction in the year you actually pay for a deductible expense. But there's an important exception when you pay with a credit card.

For tax purposes, payment is considered made on the date of the transaction, not on the date you pay the credit-card company. You can sign now and deduct this year but pay next year.

Many charities accept credit-card donations. You can claim a charitable contribution deduction in the year the contribution is charged. The same rule applies to payment of medical or dental expenses with a credit card.

Caution: If you charge a deductible expense on a credit card issued by the company supplying the deductible goods (or services), you can't take a deduction until the credit-card bill is paid. Example: If you have a prescription filled at a department store pharmacy and charge it on a credit card issued by the store, you can't deduct the cost of that medication until you get the bill and pay it. But if you charge the same prescription on a credit card issued by a third party, such as MasterCard or VISA, you can deduct it right away.

American Express Card Advantage

People with duplicate credit cards from a joint American Express account don't have to worry about a stop being put on both cards if one card is lost or stolen...each card has a special identifier code. This goes for the new Optima Credit Card, too. Latest information: Neither VISA nor MasterCard plans to institute such a coding system.

Credit-Card Self-Defense

Credit-card fraud hurts everybody, not just the people whose cards are stolen or used illegally. It results in higher annual fees and finance charges, fewer free services from card issuers and higher retail prices. And rather than improving, the problem's getting worse.

Common Scams and Self-Defense

• **Telemarketing rip-offs.** These ploys succeed by preying on victims' gullibility and greed and succeed surprisingly often. Scenario: A phone caller informs you that you've been selected from a market survey as one of several winners of a luxury trip, big appliance, etc. . . .free. (Callers often take numbers from the phone book at random, counting on the chance that the victim has a credit card. Or, dishonest employees at card-issuing companies sell names of new cardholders to crooks.) All you need to do to claim your prize is verify your identity by providing the number from a major credit card. What you've really won: a major hassle. You won't hear from these people again until your next credit-card bill, which is sure to be loaded with charges for merchandise you never ordered and cash advances from banks with whom you never did business. Defenses: Obviously, never give your number over the phone. Inform the card issuer immediately of any potential fraud. Liability: Up to $50 if you don't inform the card issuer before charges are made to your account.

• **Carbons.** The easiest way to fall prey, and you won't know it happened until you get your monthly bill. Scenario: you make a legitimate card purchase, sign the sales draft and take your copy. The sales clerk tosses the carbons in the trash, where patient thieves later retrieve them. Your numbers are used on counterfeit cards and to make purchases by phone. Your signature is used for tracing. Defense: Destroy all carbons yourself.

• **Stolen cards.** Whenever possible, keep credit cards separate from personal identification cards like your driver's license, Social Security card, etc. A thief who has all your ID can easily misrepresent himself as you and run up a staggering amount of charges in a single afternoon. Check your cards daily. Thieves often steal only one card, betting that you won't notice for a few days. Always inspect monthly statements for unfamiliar charges. The sooner you inform the card issuer, the less you'll have to pay.

Source: Jack Taylor, US Secret Service Special Agent.

Prevent Credit-Card Rip-Offs

Here's a simple trick: Pick a number and if possible—make sure that all your credit card charges end in that number. For example: Say you choose the number 8 and your dinner bill comes to $20.00. Instead of adding a $3.00 tip, add $3.08. When your bill comes at the end of the month, check to see if all the charges have 8 as the last digit. If they don't, compare them against your receipts and report discrepancies to the card issuer.

Credit-Card Protection

Photocopy the cards themselves to keep track of which ones you have. It's much more convenient to have all accounts on a single sheet of paper than to rely on keeping all the original agreements together. Keep one photocopy at home where it can be used to notify card issuers if a card is lost or stolen. Put another in a safe-deposit box or other safe place.

Source: Leon Gold, Phillips Gold & Co., CPAs, 1140 Ave. of the Americas, New York 10036.

Easy Way To Get Over Credit-Card Addiction

People who are in debt over their heads often blame their credit cards. Reality: Most of the problems we see are related to poor money management.

Even people who are not in trouble may want to reconsider their use of credit cards, unless they always pay the entire bill each month. Reason: Under tax reform, deductions for credit-card interest will be phased out. By 1991 none of your credit-card interest will be deductible.

It might be tempting to just cut up your

cards and go cold turkey. But we live in a credit society. It's important to learn self-discipline and good spending habits to take advantage of the convenience of credit cards.

What To Do

• Limit yourself to two or three credit cards. A bank card covers almost all purchases. Supplement this with a gas credit card and, perhaps, a card from your favorite department store. (Shop around for low-fee or no-fee bank cards. Don't get hooked into expensive "status cards.")

• Record your charges in a memo book. Because there's no written running balance as in a checkbook, it's easy to lose track of how much you're spending.

• Put a ceiling on your spending. Don't let the credit-card companies set a ceiling for you. They're only too happy to increase your limit each year because you're such a "good customer." You'll be tempted to spend that much more. Warning: Sometimes applicants for a mortgage may have difficulty obtaining the mortgage if they have a high credit-card ceiling—even if they don't use it. (They could, theoretically at least, get into that much debt overnight.)

• Spend no more than 20% of your monthly take-home income on consumer debt. (This is a general guideline. Low incomes should allow a lower percentage.) This includes car loans, credits cards, etc. If your monthly payments for debt exceed that amount, you're headed for trouble. Solution: Stop incurring debts until all your credit cards are paid off. Then follow a budget faithfully. If you are heavily in debt from credit cards or any kind of unsecured debt, find a nonprofit consumer-credit counselor, who can set up a repayment program and appeal to card companies to lower your monthly payments until the debts are paid off. (It is best to pay as much as possible as soon as possible, since interest usually continues to accrue on unpaid debt.)

• Use savings as an alternative to credit cards. Too many people are forced to use credit in an emergency because they have no savings to fall back on. Change your approach: Save to establish an emergency fund with at least six months' income. Use the money only in an emergency, and pay back that money as you would a bill.

• Know your goals and budget accordingly. Don't incur too much debt by trying to keep up with the Joneses. Know what you want out of life. Suggestion: Write down your goals, a time plan for achieving them, and the approximate costs. Then determine which goals are important, and focus your budget on the high-priority items.

Source: Cathy Pietruszewski, executive director and vice president, Consumer Credit Counselors of San Francisco and the Peninsula, 31 Geary St., San Francisco 94108.

Signs That Mean You're in Trouble

Warning signs of excessive debt: You pay more than 20% of your discretionary income (after mortgage, taxes and utilites) on debt... you fail to pay all your creditors each month... you use a cash advance from one credit card to pay the bills from another...you feel nervous about how much money you're spending.

Source: National Foundation for Consumer Credit, 8701 Georgia Ave., Silver Spring, MD 20910.

Stretching Due Dates on Bills

Due dates on bills can be stretched—but not far—without risk. Typical grace periods: Telephone companies, eight days. Gas and electric utilites, 10 days. Banks and finance companies, 10 days. Even after a late charge is imposed on an unpaid bill, your credit rating should be safe for 30 days.

Source: Terry Blaney, president of Consumer Credit Counseling Service of Houston and the Gulf Coast Area.

Credit and Divorce

If a loan to one spouse is secured by property that the court awards to the other spouse in a divorce settlement, the collateral can't be claimed by the creditor to settle the debt—he must take action against the original debtor in order to recover the loan. Even a registered lien isn't valid if it's dated after the divorce petition was filed. Exampled: A husband buys a car in his name after he and his wife petition for divorce. The wife is awarded the car as part of the settlement. The car financing company can't repossess the car if the husband stops making payments. The company's only option: Sue the husband.

Source: *Hoyt v. Amer. Traders*, SC Oregon, 9/3/86.

6 HOLDING THE LINE ON MEDICAL COSTS

How To Get The Best From Your Doctor

With medical care getting more complicated, and with the growing number of specialties and even subspecialties, the field of doctoring is becoming more of an impersonal industry. To the person with no medical problems, that's usually an academic point. But for the ill and elderly, the new situation is causing additional heavy burdens.

What used to be a simple doctor-patient relationship is now very complicated. For example, how do you . . .

• Maintain reasonable continuity of your medical records when you move from one specialist to another?

• Identify the right doctor to diagnose and treat various illnesses?

• Evaluate the medical advice you're given—and find the many alternative treatments that may be better for you than the conventional ones?

Taking an Active Role

Increasingly, patients are discovering they can no longer be passive in the doctor-patient relationship. They have to take an active interest to be sure they get not only the best care, but, in some instances, just adequate care—as the soaring number of medical malpractice suits seems to indicate.

Here is a valuable checklist of potential problems and advice for dealing with today's doctors . . .

• Checkups: The usual procedure is for a doctor to perform a physical checkup and do lab work-ups during the examination. Then, a few days later, the doctor's nurse calls and relates an oversimplified assessment of the lab results.

Instead: Arrange for a preliminary visit so that lab work can be done before the physical exam. That way, the doctor can go over the results of the tests in detail, answering any questions during the regular exam. If there is need for further lab work, it can be done later.

• Medical records: In most cases, your medical records are kept by the doctor. So if you move, decide to change doctors or subsequently see a specialist, you have to go through a long procedure to get your records.

Instead: Ask for copies of all records and keep them in your own permanent file. Especially useful: Electrocardiograms, blood tests and X-rays. The doctor might charge you a nominal fee to make copies.

• Selecting professionals: It's generally very hard to find out whether a doctor treats your particular problem or uses the procedure you need until you visit the office—a waste of your time and money, since you'll probably have to wait for the appointment and pay for the visit.

Instead: Try to get the information on the telephone. Obstacle: Most office staffs tend to overprotect doctors from such calls—even, on occasion, contrary to the doctor's inclination. Trick: Refer to yourself on the phone as "doctor." It's amazing how that can open doors with medical professionals. Not all people feel comfortable with such deception, but given the payoff, it should be considered.

• Doctor-patient relations: Doctors usually prefer to be called "Doctor." Yet they frequently call patients by their first names. That small difference helps to perpetuate the role of doctor as parent and patient as child—where the patient isn't expected to question the doctor's orders. This leaves the patient in a position of not sharing responsibility for his own health.

Instead: As a symbolic gesture, settle whether the two of you are on a first- or last-name basis.

More Ways To Win

• If the doctor always keeps you waiting, call before you leave for your appointment. Even better: Ask someone else to call and explain that your professional duties make your schedule very tight.

• If the doctor diagnoses an illness and prescribes drugs, take notes on the name of the condition and the drugs being prescribed.

• If you're overcome by the news of the illness (which isn't unusual), call the doctor after you've had some time to calm down and frame any questions about the prognosis and the method of treatment. Also, arrange to bring a relative or friend with you to emotionally charged doctor visits. That'll give you the emotional space to "collapse" or to go temporarily "deaf" to bad news, while your companion is able to listen, ask questions and interpret what the doctor says. The period right after serious illness is disclosed is hard to handle, so make arrangements to compensate for it.

Drugs

Since even the "safest" drugs usually have some side effects, it's prudent to insist that you be included in any decisions about prescriptions.

Frequently, the decision isn't only which drug to take, but whether one should be taken at all. In some cases, there are alternatives to drugs. . .changes in diet, lifestyle, or exercise. Many doctors believe, perhaps correctly, that most patients don't feel that an office visit for an illness is complete unless a pill is prescribed. Make it clear that you don't feel that way.

• Insist that the druggist include the manufacturer's fact sheet with any prescription you're given. Read it. It's technical, but with the aid of a medical dictionary you may discover things about the drug you'll want to discuss with the doctor. It's hard, if not impossible, for doctors to know current information on all drugs. You may discover that the dose is excessive or that the drug is no longer considered effective for your condition.

• If you do take a drug that has side effects (dizziness, stomach distress, etc.), start taking it during a weekend or when you're home, so you'll be in a safer and more comfortable place when they hit.

• If you or the doctor feel that the drug you're taking may not be fully effective—but is the best currently available—consider doing some of your own research.

Sources. Check medical journals that specialize in the condition you have. Also, some brokerage firms run stock analyses of leading drug companies and include comprehensive reports on new drugs.

The problem then is to find a doctor running clinical studies with the new drug. Only that doctor can legally use it if it doesn't have FDA approval. Be aware, too, that you're running a risk in using the drug. However, some new drugs have already been given full approval in other countries.

Source: Susan G. Cole, editor of *The Practical Guide to Cancer Care*, Health Improvement Research Corp., New York.

Generic Vs. Brand-Name Drugs

Generic drugs aren't always cheaper than brand-name equivalents. Though pharmacies pay less for generics, many mark them up more than they mark up brand-name drugs. Recommended: Comparison shop for each drug instead of assuming that you'll always save by picking the generic.

Source: Study by the *Journal of the American Medical Association*.

Cost-Cutting Secret

Get free drugs simply by asking for them. Doctors are constantly visited by salespeople from drug companies who leave samples. And the samples usually sit forgotten in a desk or filing cabinet. At today's prices, they're worth asking about.

Medical Test Rip-Off

Six out of 10 medical tests are unnecessary. Doctors order them because of insecurity, pressure, hospital profit, curiosity, or habit. To hold down your medical bill: Ask your doctor whether each test is really needed.

Source: Study at the University of California, reported in the *Journal of the American Medical Association*.

How To Avoid Becoming a Victim

Fully a quarter of the surgical procedures performed in the United States each year are of very limited benefit—or entirely useless. Part of the problem: In the past ten years the number of surgeons has increased, while the demand for operations has remained constant. As the opportunities per surgeon dwindle, the pressure mounts to perform surgery that is only "marginally" indicated.

Relatively few victims of unnecessary surgery come to harm, but all are burdened with needless worry and expense. Hospital stays can be lengthy, and many insurance policies pick up only 80% of the surgical cost. Worse: Operations also entail some small risk if they require general anesthesia.

Self-Defense

Unless you're a physician, you can't diagnose your own illnesses and decide by yourself whether or not you really need an operation. But you can—and should—seek a second—and third—opinion if you're considering any operative procedure. Important: Get at least one opinion, if possible, from a doctor who is not a surgeon. . .he has nothing to lose if you decide not to go under the knife.

How to get the best second opinion: Call a teaching hospital in your area, explain your problem and ask to see a specialist.

Unwarranted operations are "inspired" not only by greedy, unethical surgeons. . .but also by some patients who complain so frequently that their physicians finally recommend surgery as a way to relieve the patients' subjective complaints—if not treat their disorders. Because pain is subjective, it's hard for doctors to determine through tests alone whether the conditions are serious enough to warrant surgery. Physicians must rely on patients' reports of pain. Warning: The more you complain of pain, the more likely that your doctor may recommend surgery.

It's valuable to become familiar with the types of procedures that may be performed unnecessarily:

• Arthroscopy. A surgical technique to diagnose and repair cartilage injury in the knee. The operation is performed mostly on injured athletes. A good number of orthopedists recommend it. But for many injuries, a few months of rest and rehabilitation may be just as effective a cure. Arthroscopy doesn't necessarily prevent future knee problems or pain.

• Biopsy of the skin. The most common surgical procedure in the United States. Several million are performed each year to remove moles and lesions—many of which may be nothing to worry about. Potentially dangerous lesions: Moles that change color, darken, bleed or grow rapidly may be malignant. The procedure is simple and not high-risk, but you should definitely seek a second opinion.

• Breast biopsies. Problems: Because of the malpractice liability crisis, doctors have become fanatical about not missing any lump. . .and women also are scared that any lump means cancer. Result: Numerous unnecessary breast biopsies. These operations cost $5,000 on average (usually mostly covered by insurance), may require one to two days in the hospital and involve pain and the normal surgical risks of doctors' errors, infection, death under anesthesia, etc.

Women under 40 may be the victims of unnecessary breast biopsies. In some cases, if the doctor and patient just wait two or three months, the lump may disappear. But. . .waiting more than four months can be risky.

Recommended: If two reputable doctors tell you that you need a breast biopsy, get one. If the surgeon asks you to sign a paper allowing him to perform a lumpectomy (removal of the malignant lump) in the lymph nodes of the axilla (armpit), give your consent and have it all done at one time to avoid a second anesthesia. Breast biopsies are almost never wrong, and if cancer is found, the doctor should take care of it surgically. Caution: If the surgeon wants to perform a mastectomy (removal of the entire breast), withhold your consent until you can get second and third opinions. The need for mastectomies in some patients is controversial.

• Carotid endarterectomy. An operation to unclog neck arteries. Problems: The operation offers little relief for nearly 30% of patients. . .and the risk of complications may be great when performed on older people. Recommended: Consult a neurologist and a vascular surgeon—neurologists are likely to suggest more conservative forms of treatment.

• Coronary bypass. Very much in vogue . . .but about one-third of the 225,000 bypass operations performed each year are only marginally indicated. The major benefit—a longer life—doesn't occur in at least half of all cases. Quality of life usually improves after the operation, but there's no guarantee. Danger: This is a major operation. And the weaker the patient is from his heart condition, the more perilous it may be. Possible attractive alternatives: Angioplasty (cleaning out of arteries via a catheter) or control by medication.

• Endoscopy. About a million endoscopies are performed each year. . . but only 60%–65% are beneficial. The operation, which involves inserting a tube through the patient's mouth or anus to check the intestines for bleeding or tumors, costs $550–$650 and is very uncomfortable. Risks: Perforation of the intestine. . . or death. Recommended: When you go for second and third opinions, consult doctors of internal medicine who aren't endoscopists.

• Hysterectomy. Some unscrupulous physicians believe the mere presence of a uterus in a woman age 40 or older with gynecologic complaints indicates the need for a hysterectomy.

• Lumbar laminectomy. The removal of a disk that is pushing against the spinal cord and causing neurological impairment. Problem: Only 20% of back pain sufferers actually have a disk problem, and of these, only two-thirds benefit from this painful operation. Again, the decision to operate sometimes depends upon the patient's report of pain. Alternative: Live a healthier lifestyle. . .and lose some weight. A very, very large number of chronic back problems are caused just by excess weight and lack of exercise.

• Tonsillectomy. Many unnecessary tonsillectomies are performed at parents' insistence—they just can't stand their kids being sick all the time. Problem: If recurring sore throats are caused by a virus, they may continue even after a tonsillectomy. The operation is most commonly indicated only if a child gets more than five strep throats per year. These bacterial infections travel through the blood and can cause problems in the heart and kidneys. But if this is not the case, there may be little reason to force a child into the operating room. Consult a reputable pediatrician.

Surgery You Don't Really Need

• Most back-pain sufferers don't need surgery. Also: Three out of 10 of the most common back operations (laminectomy and spinal fusion) are failures. . .and 10% make patients worse.
Source: Dr. C. Norman Shealy, founder of the Pain Rehabilitation Center, Springfield, MO.

• Gallbladder trouble doesn't always necessitate surgery. Breakthrough: Gallstones can now be dissolved by flushing the gallbladder with a form of ether known as MTBE. Advantages: Faster recovery and minimal nausea and vomiting. The process requires one to two days of hospitalization and costs about $3,000. (Gallbladder surgery typically costs about $6,000 and necessitates a week of hospitalization.)
Source: Dr. Johnson Thistle, Mayo Clinic.

Questions To Ask a Surgeon

To protect against unnecessary surgery, ask the physician hard questions beforehand.
• What are the risks?
• How many people have you seen with similar symptoms who have chosen not to have surgery?
• How long will it take to recover?
• What is the likelihood of complications? What sort?
• Are there alternative ways to treat this condition?
• What is the mortality rate for this operation?
• How many of these operations have you done in the past year?
Always get a second opinion.

Same-Day Surgeries

You can often safely skip the cost and discomfort of an overnight hospital stay after: Hernia repair, tonsillectomy and adenoidectomy, cataract extraction, some plastic surgery, removal of a tissue lesion or cyst, dilation and curettage (D&C), tubal ligation and drainage procedures for glaucoma.
Source: *Whole Life Times*, MA.

The World of Less Expensive Health Care

There are now more than 2,000 freestanding "emergicenters" nationwide. They deal with a wide range of health crises: Respiratory illnesses, gastrointestinal problems, fractures, sprains and lacerations. Although these clinics lack the blood banks or equipment to handle major emergencies (such as a stroke or cardiac arrest), they can stabilize such patients until they reach a hospital.

In addition, there are upward of 200 "surgicenters" for minor elective operations. As surgery becomes more sophisticated and less invasive, many procedures that once required a hospital stay can now be done on an ambulatory basis, with local anesthesia. You may not be able to play golf later that afternoon, but you can go home.

These procedures range from plastic surgery to foot and skin operations, cataract laser surgery and hernia repair. In any given clinic the areas covered depend, of course, on the specialties of the participating doctors.

The most obvious advantage of the freestanding clinic (particularly to employers, who wind up paying most of the bills) lies in its economy. Comparable care typically runs at least one-third less than it would in a hospital. Examples: Treatment of a fractured arm costs on average $157 in a hospital emergency room but only $71 at a freestanding clinic. Influenza with fever: $159 at a hospital, $30 at a clinic. Arm laceration and suturing: $133 at a hospital, $75 in a clinic.

The clinics can charge less because of lower overhead. They aren't supporting expensive labs, high-tech machinery or large numbers of peripheral staff. They are usually very efficient. Although ambulatory clinics may make more extensive use of nurse-practitioners and physician assistants, they don't stint on the level of care. In fact, patients are often treated by the same doctors who work at the hospital down the block or across town—only in a different setting.

If anything, clinic patients may get more quality time and attention from the doctors. They're not competing for priority with a triple bypass on the next corridor as they might be in a hospital. Result: Operations are virtually never delayed or "bumped" for rescheduling.

The freestanding clinics also score heavily for convenience. Many are open from 7 a.m. until 11 p.m. Some stay open 24 hours a day, seven days a week. Suppose you need to have a bunion removed but don't want to lose a day of work. You could leave your office around 4 p.m., enter the surgicenter, get picked up at 10 that night, and go to work the next morning. Or you could arrange for a procedure on

Friday evening and convalesce over the weekend.

Source: Robert Williams, executive director, the Freestanding Ambulatory Surgical Association, 1040 McDowell Rd., Phoenix 85006, and Phil Wolfe, staff member, National Association of Freestanding Emergency Centers, 5151 Beltline Rd., Dallas 75240.

HMOs: Are They for You?

It is estimated that by 1990, as much as 50% of the US employed population will be enrolled in some type of managed health care system. Health maintenance organizations (HMOs), the most successful of these systems, offer a less expensive alternative to traditional fee-for-service health care.

Do HMOs really save money? Typically, HMOs charge member families a set annual fee. Thereafter, visits and treatments for the family can be obtained for nominal fees. This gives the HMO an incentive to limit patient care as a way of keeping its costs down. Most HMOs use a number of techniques to control the type and price of health care delivered to their members. Well-run HMOs can typically reduce the average health-care costs for an individual by as much as 15% to 20%. Whether such savings will be available to you depends on the local market and the benefit plans offered.

Always compare the health insurance options offered by your company. Most companies have an enrollment period once a year when you can select your insurance plan for the upcoming year. Expect to be offered a traditional indemnity program and one or more HMO programs. Compare the costs and benefits by completing a worksheet with the following information on each program:
- Monthly premium.
- Co-payments.
- Deductibles.
- Extent of coverage.
- Expected health-care needs (use last year as a proxy).

Generally, HMOs make the most sense for individuals or families who expect high health-care costs or prefer to be able to accurately budget health expenditures. Likely candidates are individuals with health conditions that require close medical attention or very young families whose children require frequent and unexpected visits to a physician. It is generally more economical for individuals or families with low expected health-care expenses to select insurance programs with significant co-payments and deductibles.

Will you get poorer medical attention from an HMO? No. Members, in general, believe they receive equal or superior care from their HMOs. A Harris poll revealed that 74% of the HMO members interviewed believed their care was at least equal to what they had previously received in a traditional health insurance program; 45% of these people were more satisfied with their HMOs. Perhaps the strongest endorsement is the fact that although HMO members are free to disenroll once a year, very few actually do.

Will you have to give up your current physician? Traditionally, people thought that joining an HMO meant giving up their existing physicians. Today, many HMO programs use a large proportion, sometimes more than half, of the private-practice physicians within a local community. These HMOs, called individual practice associations (IPAs), can give you the lower cost of an HMO and allow you to keep your present physician.

Source: Eric S. Schlesinger, manager, The Boston Consulting Group, Inc., 780 Third Ave., New York 10017. He has worked with insurers, HMOs, and hospitals to develop strategies for the evolving health-care industry.

When $$ Interferes with Medicine

Doctors in large private practices order 50% more chest X rays and electrocardiograms than those who work for health maintenance organizations (HMOs). The problem: A doctor's fee structure (fee-for-service in private practice, fixed prepayment HMOs) may deter-

mine whether or not a patient is tested.

Source: Study by Dr. Arnold M. Epstein, Harvard School of Public Health, in *The New England Journal of Medicine.*

Nonprofit Vs. For-Profit Hospitals

For-profit hospitals are much more expensive than nonprofit ones. One study shows that the average bill in profit-making hospitals is $401. That's 22% more than the bill in nonprofit institutions. The basic room cost is nearly the same at both kinds of hospitals. The cost difference comes almost entirely from ancillary services such as drugs and medical supplies.

Source: *What's Ahead in Personnel?*

Worst Times for Hospital Check-In

Avoid weekend admissions for tests or elective surgery. Chances are that you will lie in bed for two days with little or no medical care at a cost of up to $500 a day. Because most patients are discharged by the weekend, hospitals trying to fill beds will encourage weekend admissions. As a general rule insist that you be admitted right before a test or procedure is scheduled.

Also avoid admissions during major holiday seasons such as Thanksgiving or Christmas. Staffing at most hospitals is particularly low during those periods, so you may end up sitting around waiting for things to be done. Warning: If you are really sick, staff shortages may mean lower-quality care.

The worst time to be admitted to a hospital is in the month of July. Why? July is the month when residents and medical students are rotated. A major portion of day-to-day care in teaching-affiliated hospitals is performed by newly graduated resident doctors. Young residents who have just arrived or those who have just taken on greater responsibilities will not have the same level of skill and judgment as more experienced physicians.

Source: Arthur A. Levin, MPH, director, Center for Medical Consumers, 237 Thompson St., New York 10012, publishers of *HealthFacts*, a monthly newsletter that critiques medical practices.

A Good Person To Talk To

More personal attention in a hospital is available through free patient representative services. A patient representative answers your questions, acts on your concerns, and intervenes between you and your doctor or you and the nursing staff. . . if needed. A patient representative will meet you when you sign in at a small hospital. In larger hospitals, the representative's number should appear on your phone.

Source: Ruth Ravich, director, patient representative department, Mount Sinai Medical Center, New York.

Hospital Stays Can Be Hazardous to Your Health

Aside from keeping your hospital bills down, shorter hospital stays keep you healthier. Fact: The longer you stay in a hospital, the greater the risk you will end up with a problem you didn't arrive with.

Medication errors and hospital-borne infections are only two of the dangers. A research study of over 800 consecutive hospital admissions revealed that almost 40% of the individuals checked into the hospital ended up with new doctor- or hospital-caused problems.

Source: Arthur A. Levin, MPH, director, Center for Medical Consumers, 237 Thompson St., New York, 10012, publishers of *HealthFacts*, a monthly newsletter that critiques medical practices.

Most Frequent Hospital Bill Mistake

Ninety-seven percent of hospital bills are wrong, and less than 2% of those errors are in the patient's favor. Average error: $1,400. Frequent mistake: Billing for items or services never delivered. . .lab work, medication, thermometers, wheelchairs, etc., we're told by Harvey Rosenfield, head of watchdog group Bills Project. Self-defense: Insist on completely itemized bills. . .and review them carefully.

How To Protect Yourself From Hospital Billing Errors

When the mechanic hands you a bill for $500, it's unlikely that you'd pay it without a glance at the charges. But when given a hospital bill for $5,000, most people tend to do just that.

As it turns out, hospitals and doctors are far from infallible when it comes to billing. According to the New York Life Insurance Company, which has been auditing hospital bills for the past three years, the average hospital bill contains $600 worth of erroneous charges. This money comes not only out of the insurance company's pocket, but also out of yours. You can save money by knowing how the system works and how to spot billing errors.

Why Bother?

With the rising costs of health care, the current trend in the insurance industry is to have the insured employee share in the cost of health care. Under major medical plans, employees are usually responsible for a fixed dollar amount, termed out-of-pocket expenses, which includes deductibles and co-insurance. In addition, many employees pay a portion of their health-care premium, so it is to their advantage to keep health-care costs down to avoid unnecessary increases in premiums.

How it works: Let's say the out-of-pocket limit is $1,000. The insurance company usually pays 80% (and the patient 20%) of all non-room-and-board charges until the $1,000 out-of-pocket expense limit is reached. After that, insurance takes over 100%. However, most patients don't reach the out-of-pocket limit, since they'd have to run at least $5,000 worth of non-room-and-board hospital expenses or other health-care costs to do so. Therefore, while your contribution to out-of-pocket is still adding up, it clearly pays to keep costs down.

There are many billing errors for the simple reason that many hospitals have inefficient billing systems. Major problem: Hospitals are geared to making sure that patients are billed for services provided, and not toward verifying charges.

Typical mistake: Because of a clerical error, a $50 electrocardiogram is entered onto your bill at a $500 charge. Since you may not know the typical cost of an EKG, the error goes undetected.

Another example: A lab technician comes in to draw blood and finds that the patient is no longer there. However, he's still charged. Reason: Billing starts from the day the charges are entered in the book, and his charges are never canceled.

Similar mistakes occur with drug prescriptions. Example: The doctor might order 10 days of penicillin and then switch to tetracycline after seven days. If the unused three days' worth of penicillin is not returned, the patient is billed for it.

The Four Major Mistake Areas

• Respiratory therapy. Equipment such as oxygen tanks and breathing masks isn't credited when it's discontinued. Sometimes it's not even removed promptly from the room.

• Pharmacy charges. Credit isn't given for drugs that were returned, or unused drugs are not returned.

• Lab tests. Cancellations of tests aren't noted.

• Central supply items. Hospital staff or nurses may run out of something and borrow it from another patient. They intend to give credit or return the item, but often they don't get around to it.

What You can Do

• Keep track of the most basic things, such as how many times your blood was drawn. Suggestion: If you're able, jot down what happens daily. Note: If the patient is too sick to keep track of services rendered, a family member should try to keep track of the charges. Although it may be difficult to know how many routine things such as blood counts or X-rays were done, someone who visits regularly is likely to know about nonroutine services, such as barium enemas or cardiac catheterizations.

• Ask questions. Ask the doctor to be specific about tests. If he orders X-rays, ask him what type of X-rays. If he doesn't answer the question to your satisfaction, ask the nurse. Always ask. It's the most important thing a health-care consumer can do. Reassuring change: The newer generation of doctors is more willing to involve the patient in his own care.

• Insist on an itemized bill, not just a summary of charges.

• Check room and board charges. Count the days you were in the hospital and in what kind of room. Are you being charged for a private room, even though you were in a semiprivate? Some hospitals have different semiprivate rates for two-bed and four-bed rooms. Check your rate.

• Review the charges for TV rental and phone.

• Be equally careful with doctor bills. Often these bills are made out by the doctor's assistant, who may not be sure of what was done. Most common errors: Charges for services in the doctor's office, such as a chest X-ray or an injection, that weren't actually performed. Charges for routine hospital physician visits on days that the doctors was not in attendance.

Source: Interview with Janice Spillane, manager of cost containment in the group insurance department of New York Life Insurance Co., New York.

How To Prevent Medical Overcharges

Most people pay very little attention to the actual fees and expenses charged by doctors and hospitals. The lenient medical insurance policies of the past (both private and public) gave people few incentives to scrutinize their medical bills.

In the new, more competitive health care environment, there is a growing trend by medical insurers toward greater deductibles, less complete insurance coverage, and co-payment policies. The result is that Americans now have real incentives to examine their medical bills and the appropriateness of individual charges.

The first step in avoiding overcharges is always to ask, ahead of time, what a medical visit, test, or procedure will cost. Don't be shy about asking; if a doctor thinks you can pay the bill, he probably won't bother to volunteer the information. Good health practitioners should present you with a financial estimate along with any plan for major medical work.

Next, negotiate fees or charges. It is absolutely in your best interest to find out all fees and charges involved in your treatment and to negotiate those you feel are too high. Before visiting with a practitioner, find out what and how much your medical insurance plan will cover, and try to negotiate with your doctor any remaining amount. Some doctors will be satisfied with whatever reimbursement your insurance will provide.

The third step in avoiding overcharges: Shop around. It goes against the traditional notion of health care, but you can look for better rates. Fees and hospital charges vary extraordinarily from one practitioner or hospital to another.

Finally, always find out if a test or procedure can be performed on an ambulatory (outpatient) basis. Because traditional medical insurance reimbursement policies once favored it, many doctors still routinely admit patients to the hospital for tests or surgery that could be performed on an outpatient basis at a much lower cost.

Source: Arthur A. Levin, MPH, director, Center for Medical Consumers, 237 Thompson St., New York 10012, publishers of *HealthFacts*, a monthly newsletter that critiques medical practices.

What To Do if Your Doctor Overcharges

If you feel a medical bill is out of line, the first thing to do is to make an appointment to discuss it with the practitioner. Even if you feel very angry, approaching the meeting in an open and cooperative spirit paves the way for negotiation. In today's litigious climate, being too aggressive may turn a person away from a cooperative attempt to settle differences.

If you are concerned about your ability to pay the charges, be open about your finances. It is not inappropriate to discuss a payment plan as one means of settling the bill. If you have the ability to pay all the charges, but believe them to be too high or in error, you should review them with the practitioner and try to have them corrected or reduced.

If your doctor refuses to negotiate, contact your local county, regional, or state medical or dental society. Do so in writing, giving the details of your case and why you believe the charges are excessive.

Remember: There is no "official" list of acceptable charges for doctors and dentists. Most professional societies no longer conduct peer reviews of doctors' fees. Furthermore, government agencies have no blanket supervisory authority over what medical practitioners charge. Unless the charges are so excessive that they are criminal, or in cases where Medicaid or Medicare is involved, there is no sense in contacting a government agency.

Source: Arthur A. Levin, MPH, director, Center for Medical Consumers, 237 Thompson St., New York, 10012, publishers of *HealthFacts*, a monthly newsletter that critiques medical practices.

How To Beat the 7.5% Medical Deduction Limit

Medical expenses are one major category of personal expenses that you can deduct from your taxable income. How much is deductible? All of your medical expenses to the extent that they exceed 7.5% of your adjusted gross income.

Included under medical expenses are the costs of diagnosis, cure, treatment, and prevention of disease. You can deduct the cost of prescription drugs (including insulin) as well as transportation expenses to and from a doctor, dentist, hospital, or pharmacy. If you use your own car, the rate is nine cents per mile plus the cost of parking and tolls.

In addition to your own medical expenses, you can claim the medical expenses of any person who qualifies as your dependent. That includes your spouse and/or any other individual who lives with you and depends on you for his livelihood. Advantage: The definition of "dependents" for purposes of claiming medical expenses is much broader than for purposes of claiming them as tax exemptions—there is no limit on the dependent's gross income.

Timing is Critical

Time your use of the medical deduction wisely. Since medical deductions are a function of your adjusted gross income, it is best to pay for major medical expenses in years when your adjusted gross income is relatively low. For example, suppose it's close to year-end and you estimate this year's income will be $50,000 and next year's will increase to $100,000. The best time to incur major medical expenses (if you have a choice) is during the low-income year, when your 7.5% minimum only equals $3,750. If you wait until next year, you will have to incur $7,500 (7.5% of $100,000) before you can start claiming medical expenses as a deduction.

Alternatively, if you approach year-end and don't have enough medical expenses to exceed the 7.5% floor, you may want to defer as many payments as possible until next year.

You never know: You might have more medical expenses in the following year and/or your adjusted gross income (AGI) may be lower.

If your tax bracket shifts from year to year, consider taking most of your medical deductions during years when your bracket is relatively high. A $1,000 deduction at the 33% bracket saves you $330, whereas the same deduction in a year when you're in the 28% bracket will save you only $280. The years you are in a high tax bracket and can make the most of your tax deduction can, unfortunately, also be the years you have the highest adjusted gross income and are able to deduct less of your total medical expenses. This will not always be the case.

For example, assume your AGI remains the same but your taxable income drops due to larger interest expense deductions on real estate taxes (e.g., when you buy a new home). In this situation, you should pay your medical expenses in the first of the two years, when your tax bracket is higher. Many people have this situation when comparing 1987 with 1988. Even if their taxable income is relatively constant over the two years, their marginal tax rate probably decreases due to full phase-in of the new tax rates. Pay the medical expenses in the earlier years.

The Importance of Filing Status

For married couples in which one or the other spouse has large medical bills, it can be advantageous to file separate rather than joint returns. For example, assume a wife and a husband's adjusted gross incomes on separate returns are $50,000 and $350,000, respectively. If filed jointly, their total AGI would be $400,000 and only medical expenses in excess of $30,000 would be tax deductible. In this case, if the wife incurred $20,000 in medical expenses, none would be tax deductible. On a separate return, however, the wife could deduct $16,250 (the excess of $20,000 over 7.5% of her $50,000 adjusted gross income).

To see if this approach would work for you, calculate your tax liability on a separate basis, then see if the total is less than the tax would be if you filed jointly. If the total tax paid on separate returns is lower, file separately and take the medical deduction. Otherwise, file a joint return.

Source: Lawrence W. Goldstein, principal, Arthur Young & Co., 277 Park Ave., New York 10172. His specialty is individual tax and financial planning.

Getting the Most Cost-Effective Psychiatric Help

Psychiatric conditions that require professional help range from existential questions about oneself to disease entities such as schizophrenia, bulimia, and a large variety of symptoms and syndromes such as impotence, marital conflicts, alcohol abuse, and psychosomatic disorders. Many means are available for treating problems like these, but the cost-effectiveness of a particular treatment program depends almost entirely on the condition being treated.

The Correct Diagnosis

The primary rule of cost-effectiveness is to get the correct diagnosis. If you get an incorrect diagnosis in the beginning, you may become involved with a long and expensive treatment regime that does not adequately correct your condition. Once you start a particular program, it is usually difficult to end it; patients have a tendency to stay with a familiar therapist and treatment even though, by all objective criteria, the therapy is not successful.

An incorrect diagnosis may be made if you select the "wrong" clinician—one competent in only a narrowly defined area, or whose treatment philosophy is not the one best suited to dealing with your particular problem. The correct diagnosis usually requires finding an eclectic psychiatrist with the training and capacity to synthesize multiple points of view.

Referrals by friends and family are always a good place to start looking for a well-qualified psychiatrist. Most good internists are also able to make recommendations. Check therapists'

academic credentials; affiliations with academic institutions are a good sign. After you've narrowed the field, arrange to meet prospective therapists face to face. Caution: Beware of psychiatrists who talk too much, ask the same question over and over, lecture, or drop names of patients they treat.

Even if you don't intend to be treated by a psychiatrist, consult with one before deciding on a specific treatment and therapist. Psychiatrists can determine whether a psychological disorder has a biological basis—a possibility you should at least rule out before beginning therapy.

After the Diagnosis

Depending on the diagnosis, a variety of practitioners are available to provide treatment. Psychiatrists in private practice tend to be the most expensive of all mental health workers. However, major psychiatric disorders such as depression, anxiety, and thought disorders do require a psychiatrist's involvement. Since they are also MDs, psychiatrists are capable of doing comprehensive medical evaluations and can write prescriptions when pharmacological treatment is needed.

If a patient has no medical or organic problems (no symptoms that require somatic intervention), a psychologist, MSW, or other mental health worker can deliver needed psychotherapy (individual, group, family, behavioral) at lower cost.

For problems that are interpersonal in nature, group therapy can be very cost-effective. Although it is less confidential and less time is available for individual issues, it is possible to get around these problems by complementing group sessions with individual sessions regularly or on an "as needed" basis.

Couples therapy, especially when conducted in a group, can be a very cost-effective way for spouses to resolve marital difficulties. Advantages: You and your spouse become part of a support group where you can examine your relationship, be comforted that you are not alone in your struggle, learn different styles of communication, and identify with the survivors of interpersonal conflicts.

Clinics, especially those associated with medical schools, deliver good-quality, comprehensive care at a relatively low cost, even though they are largely staffed with trainees. Institutes (psychoanalytical, behavioral, etc.), also primarily staffed by trainees, specialize in more narrowly defined therapeutic approaches. However, by shopping around and choosing carefully, you can find an institute—or another of these sources—that will provide cost-effective treatment.

Source: T. Byram Karasu, MD, professor of psychiatry, Albert Einstein College of Medicine/Montefiore Medical Center, 2 E. 88 St., New York 10128. He is also chairman of the APA Commission on Psychiatric Therapies and of the APA Task Force on Treatment of Psychiatric Disorders.

Negotiate an Informal Contract with Your Therapist

Try to negotiate an informal contract with your therapist before you begin treatment. Your discussion should include the fee and optimum required frequency of visits.

What makes therapy expensive is its open-endedness and its lack of focus—or its having too many foci. This makes it worthwhile to negotiate the goal of the therapy, its focus, and the process.

Also ask your therapist to estimate the length of treatment. Many psychological problems are caused by narrowly definable conflicts that create corresponding defense mechanisms in the patient. These conflicts frequently lend themselves to short-term psychotherapies. Only lifelong characterologic problems and personality disorders may require long-term psychotherapy or analysis. Try to have your symptoms treated independently of your life and interpersonal problems. Although they are usually inextricable, it is quite possible to treat manifest symptoms with medication and to achieve behavior modifications quickly, while you work on life

problems at a slower pace.

Source: T. Byram Karasu, MD, professor of psychiatry, Albert Einstein College of Medicine/Montefiore Medical Center, 2 E. 88 St., New York 10128. He is also chairman of the APA Commission on Psychiatric Therapies and of the APA Task Force on Treatment of Psychiatric Disorders.

You Can Shorten the Length of Therapy

You can facilitate the progress of psychotherapy, shorten its duration, and save money.

1. Outside your therapy sessions, establish an internal dialog patterned on the one you have with your therapist. Continue the process of self-exploration, introspection, and honest self-confrontation.

2. Make notes on your dreams and fantasies and bring them to the sessions. They are shortcuts to the unconscious.

3. Attempt to recognize any resistance you may have to the therapy. Resistance to change is part of the process of psychotherapy and is largely unconscious; patients often spend many sessions overcoming it. Recognizing resistance and developing a therapeutic alliance with your therapist will shorten this defensive stage.

4. At regular intervals, ask your therapist to join you in an evaluation of the progress of your treatment. Lengthy impasses may require a consultation from another therapist.

Source: T. Byram Karasu, MD, professor of psychiatry, Albert Einstein College of Medicine/Montefiore Medical Center, 2 E. 88 St., New York 10128. He is also chairman of the APA Commission on Psychiatric Therapies and of the APA Task Force on Treatment of Psychiatric Disorders.

The Dollars and Sense of Being Fitted with Contact Lenses

Acquiring a pair of contact lenses is quite different from buying any other consumer product. Lenses have a critical job to do and must do it without causing irritation or injury to the wearer's eyes. Of course the physical lenses themselves are a "product," but what the contact lens wearer is actually buying is a service: An effective solution to a personal health problem.

Choosing a Practitioner

Cutting corners or making cost the deciding criterion when choosing a practitioner would obviously be foolish. Fees for a contact lens fitting can vary greatly, depending on the lens type and the complexity of your case, as well as the quality of the service rendered. But knowing up front what the charges and refund policy will be (within reasonable limits) will help you evaluate the cost-effectiveness of the care.

In addition to investigating cost, then, here are points to cover when choosing a practitioner:

• Reputation. Ask friends and acquaintances who wear contact lenses for their recommendations on practitioners.

• Competency. Inquire about the doctors' credentials and areas of expertise. Focus on practitioners who specialize in contact lenses and be sure they employ *at least* three or four various lens types from different contact lens manufacturers.

• Compatibility. A pleasant, comfortable relationship with the practitioner and staff will help insure that your needs are met. In addition, it is advantageous to work with the same doctor each time you return. This will lead to a more consistent approach in satisfying your contact lens needs.

• Convenience. A practitioner whose office is in a convenient location would be a good choice; time is money.

• Personal comfort. Pleasant surroundings are a valid consideration in selecting a practitioner, since correct fitting requires substantial amounts of time.

The Fitting Process

A proper contact lens fitting consists of four phases. Understanding the purpose of each phase will put you in a better position to make evaluations and choices along the way.

1. In the initial consultation (the cost of which you should find out beforehand), you and your practitioner will mainly exchange information. You will be asked about your health history and your requirements, goals, and expectations concerning wearing contact lenses. This visit is also your opportunity to question your practitioner on his experience, credentials, and affiliations, as well as details about the further course and cost of the fitting. It is important that you use this opportunity. It can eliminate many potential surprises down the line. At the conclusion of this consultation, it is a good idea to request a comprehensive and detailed fee schedule.

If, for any reason, you do not feel comfortable with the practitioner—or anything else about the situation—this is the time to terminate the relationship and look for another practitioner. You will, of course, have to pay for the consultation.

2. Assuming all went well at the initial consultation, you will return for a diagnostic evaluation. Your vision correction needs will be determined through careful examination of your eyes and eyelids. Based on the information collected and the goals agreed upon in the consultation and the findings of this exam, a limited selection of indicated lens types will be tried out and evaluated. Normally, this will lead to a final selection of one or more applicable lens types. If no available solution fulfills your goals, you and your practitioner must either agree on new goals or the fitting process should be terminated at this point.

3. Following a successful diagnostic, you will return for the dispensing appointment, at which the selected lenses are tried on and evaluated. Again, assuming all is well, you will be instructed in their proper use and maintenance. It is imperative that instructions pertaining to wearing, and disinfection and cleaning procedures be followed scrupulously. Failure to do so is fast becoming one of the leading causes of serious eye complications.

4. The final phase of lens fitting—every bit as important as any of the preceding ones—is follow-up care. Proper follow-up to a typical dispensing of contact lenses without complication involves approximately four visits dur-

ing the initial fitting period. Complex cases and patients who plan to wear their lenses for extended periods and/or sleep with their lenses should plan on more frequent initial appointments. Every daily-wear contact lens wearer should return once or twice a year thereafter for regular checkups, and, in the case of overnight lens wearers, as often as four times a year.

Source: Barry Farkas, O.D., F.A.A.O., doctor of optometry, 30 E. 60 St., New York 10022. He is a diplomate of the contact lens section of the American Academy of Optometry.

Health Foods: Do You Get What You Pay For?

Since the 1960s, Americans have had a love affair with health foods. Food products labeled "healthy," "natural," "additive-free," "no preservatives," and "nothing artificial" have become not only highly marketable, but highly expensive.

While health foods are usually more expensive than other food products, they are usually no better or safer. Many "natural" foods have added ingredients with little nutritional value. For example, a typical granola bar is no more nutritional than a Snickers bar and does not contain fewer calories. Furthermore, because there are many "natural" toxins in foods, the term does not even guarantee safety. It always pays to read labels carefully and be a little cynical about the claims made for any product.

A Better Value

Being healthy does not require spending extra money to eat only "health food." It is much more important to select foods that have high nutritional value and avoid those that have little. As a general rule, avoid processed food products and opt for fresh or fresh-frozen ingredients instead. This will help you minimize your intake of salts, fats, chemicals, and empty calories.

The best advice is to maximize your intake of fresh vegetables and fruits, whole grains, and sources of protein low in saturated fats. Many supermarkets are making this easier, by enlarging and improving their produce departments, and by carrying some of the grains, juices, and additive- or preservative-free products formerly obtainable only at "health food" stores—and the supermarkets are doing this at lower prices.

Source: Arthur A. Levin, MPH, director, Center for Medical Consumers, 237 Thompson St., New York 10012, publishers of *HealthFacts*, a monthly newsletter that critiques medical practices.

How To Get the Most Nutrient Value Out of the Food You Buy

• Buy whole-grain products, or at least enriched refined ones.

• Buy fresh or frozen fruits and vegetables, not canned. The best choice is freshly picked, ripe produce. Frozen produce is often more healthful than fresh, however, because it is frozen when the nutrients are largely intact.

• Low-fat dairy products should be fortified with vitamins A and D, which are fat-soluble.

• Don't soak fresh produce for long periods of time. Also, don't wash rice. This will preserve water-soluble vitamins.

• Avoid cutting and/or cooking vegetables until right before use.

• Avoid boiling vegetables. Pressure cooking and steaming preserve more nutrients.

Source: Arthur A. Levin, MPH, director, Center for Medical Consumers, 237 Thompson St., New York 10012, publishers of *HealthFacts*, a monthly newsletter that critiques medical practices.

Dial-A-Jock-Doc

Call the Sports Medicine Information Hotline* for free answers to questions on chronic sports injury problems. It handles questions on specific injuries, second opinions and possible causes, and gives you a list of two or three sports medicine specialists in your area.

*317-926-1339; in Indiana, 800-23-SPORT.

Source: Marge Albohm, certified athletic trainer, Indiana University School of Medicine, Sports Science Institute, 1815 N. Capitol, Suite 214, Indianapolis, IN 45202.

Are Vitamins Worth the Cost?

Every year $1.5 to $2 billion worth of vitamins are sold to the American consumer. To date, however, the importance of these extra doses of vitamins to our health and nutrition is largely unknown.

The controversy rages on two fronts: How helpful are moderate supplements of vitamins in maintaining maximal health; and how helpful are large (mega) doses of vitamins in either preventing or curing certain diseases and conditions? Regarding the second question, little evidence has been gathered to show conclusively that megadoses of vitamins cure or prevent serious medical conditions. The first question has proved easier to answer.

Are Moderate Supplements Necessary?

For some, definitely yes; for others, probably. For individuals who have clinically proven vitamin deficiencies, vitamins are clearly worth the cost. These people need extra vitamins because either their behavior results in a deficiency or their medical problem or treatment results in a deficiency. Examples: Heavy smokers are thought to be very deficient in vitamin C; women on birth control pills, deficient in thiamin, some B vitamins and vitamin C; those taking diuretics for high blood pressure often become deficient in B6.

Though the proof is less conclusive, most health practitioners would agree that moderate amounts of vitamins and mineral supplements are needed even by those of us who eat three square meals and don't have the clinical deficiencies described above. Exercise, stress, alcoholic beverages, dieting, and pollution all are believed to deplete the body's reserve of vitamins and minerals.

Source: Arthur A. Levin, MPH, director, Center for Medical Consumers, 237 Thompson St., New York 10012, publishers of *HealthFacts*, a monthly newsletter that critiques medical practices.

7 FRIENDS, FAMILY, & YOUR MONEY

Money Side of a Commuter Marriage

The term "jet-setter" no longer applies exclusively to the wealthy, hopping from one resort to another. Today it may more aptly describe a new generation of working couples who must travel from one home to another to maintain their two careers as well as their marriage.

Commuter marriages have increased in the past several years from approximately 700,000 to over a million. If you are faced with the possibility of entering into a commuter marriage, do not make a decision until you have given the issue careful thought and research.

A major consideration in commuting is the financial expense—it can be large, and the less obvious financial details can become very significant. Contact an accountant, who will acquaint you with the present tax laws and give you information regarding commuter marriages.

When a corporation is involved, take the time to understand the corporation's tax and legal responsibilities. You will also need to know the company's relocation procedures and schedules if you must negotiate for financial assistance.

If a home is involved, know whether your company will take responsibility if your home remains unsold: Will it absorb the cost of the sale? Will the company give rental assistance? Will it absorb the cost of your transportation from one location to another? You may need to move household goods twice in the same year; will the company pick up the tab in both cases?

A variety of options is available when it comes to arranging housing. Some couples buy homes at both ends, some rent and buy, some choose to sell their present home and buy or rent two new ones. Mobile homes and houseboats can be unique options as well.

If you decide to maintain two residences, be sure to budget realistically. Make up an initial budget for a two-residence arrangement, and for safety add 10%–15% to that figure. The major surprise to many couples is the cost of duplicating household items: Another set of dishes, spices, tools, pictures, etc. These items can add up quickly, and many of the purchases can't be deferred. Consider renting fur-

221

niture rather than buying it. In some places you can rent linens, dishes, and small appliances as a package.

There are some less obvious expenses that you must also add in when budgeting for two homes:

• Transportation costs to and from airports, train stations, or bus depots.

• The possible need for two or more cars.

• Additional insurance on rented household items.

• Additional costs for certain services, such as telephone and cable television.

• Time off from work to set up the new household and maintain your relationship.

Establishing a commuter marriage is a big step. But if it's well planned and the couple has a clear idea of the costs involved, the arrangement can be rewarding.

Source: Elaine Kay, president, Settlers Inc., 1713 Waterford Ave., Fort Collins, CO 80525, a nationwide relocation consulting firm advising corporations and real estate firms on how to better understand and assist the transferee. She has been a real estate broker for the past ten years and a relocation specialist with Settlers Inc. for the past five years.

Financing a Divorce

Fact: One out of two marriages ends in divorce. While astute businessmen usually plan out most aspects of their lives, they do very little planning for the relatively likely possibility of divorce.

Divorce courts treat men very differently than they do women. Contrary to past hopes, modern "no fault" divorce laws have not made divorce a more fair and civilized procedure, although they have eliminated some of the mudslinging of the past.

What Can You Expect?

In most states all property acquired by either spouse, including pension rights, must be divided equally between the man and the woman. Example: A 60-year-old man who divorces a 35-year-old woman after a 10-year marriage will be forced (when he is 65) to divide the portion of his pension that accumulated during the marriage, despite what the woman's wealth or need may be and no matter how destitute it may leave the man.

A man in a divorce court will lose one-half of all his other assets as well: One-half of the house, furniture, stocks, bonds, savings, life insurance, and cash. A special problem exists for the self-employed businessman and professional. He must compensate the woman for "marital goodwill" in addition to the one-half share of all the hard assets and accounts receivable.

The man also may have to pay his ex-wife alimony. The amount is often 40% of the man's gross income before personal taxes. In a short marriage of, say, less than eight years, the man will pay alimony for about four years. In a longer marriage, the man will pay until the ex-wife dies or remarries. If a man is in an upper income bracket, he may pay until his wife's death or remarriage even if the marriage was short-lived.

The man is typically ordered to pay one-half or more of the woman's attorneys' fees in addition to paying his own fees.

Planning for the Worst

Even when you are happiest, think of the worst-case situation for your marriage and plan for it.

• Use all possible means during a marriage to encourage your wife to seek a meaningful career and work outside the home. After any divorce, a man's alimony obligation will be reduced by the amount his ex-wife can earn for herself.

• Keep control of your paycheck and your use of credit. The last thing you need at the time of divorce is a heavy debt load and no savings.

• Scrupulously avoid all violence and all threats of violence. Never touch your wife in anger. Divorce judges frequently use a wife's allegations of a husband's violence as the basis for ordering the man to leave the house.

• Resist the temptation to move out of your house, at least until you have talked to an experienced divorce lawyer. If the situation is untenable, encourage your wife to move, with the children if necessary—even if the cost is substantial.

• Avoid placing a large portion of your assets in a family home. Many judges make an exception to the rule requiring equal division of marital property and allow the woman to stay in the home, delaying the sale of the house and division of the proceeds until the youngest child is 18 years old.

• Do not try to hide money or property from your wife. Legally, husband and wife are considered fiduciaries and trustees for each other. Divorce lawyers are very skilled in finding hidden assets. If they do, you can expect very little compassion from the judge.

Child Custody and Support

Rarely do men obtain full custody of their children. But you should expect liberal visitation rights. To maintain as close a parenting relationship with your children as possible, seek a visitation arrangement that allows you to have the children with you on alternate weekends from either Friday night or Saturday morning until Sunday evening; every Wednesday overnight; alternate major holidays; and one-half the vacation time when the children are out of school.

Expect to pay generous child support. This single obligation has first priority in the law and cannot be discharged in bankruptcy. Child-support obligations continue until your children reach the age of majority (18, in most states). Remember: Mothers have an obligation to support their children, too. Your child support obligation can be reduced by the amount earned by your ex-wife.

Legal Help

Always consult an excellent lawyer experienced in divorce law in the city where the divorce will take place. The policies and idiosyncracies of divorce judges vary widely from place to place, even within a state. A good lawyer will be aware of these policies and idiosyncracies.

Warning: The longer the divorce proceedings drag on, the more the divorce lawyer earns. A bad divorce lawyer can compound the pain and expense of a divorce case by stirring up trouble. Before you meet with a divorce lawyer, find out the shortest time for handling a contested divorce case in your locality. Insist that your lawyer set the case for trial and get it over with as quickly as possible.

Source: Douglas R. Page, a senior attorney at Page, Akulian, Harkins & Baker, Inc., 1000 Ygnacio Valley Rd., Walnut Creek, CA 94598. He specializes in representing only men in divorce cases. He has been divorced three times and married four times.

Veteran's Pension Is Not Marital Property

A veteran's pension and other benefits were not marital property subject to distribution on divorce, an Illinois court ruled. Federal law makes these benefits the sole property of the veteran, not subject to divorce orders. But this source of income to the veteran could be taken into account in deciding on an equitable division of other property.

Source: *In re Marriage of Hapaniewski*, Ct. App., Ill., 438 N.E. 2d 466.

Premarital Agreements

A properly drafted premarital agreement can save you time, money, and emotional stress should a second marriage end in divorce. Most Americans tend to remarry after a failed first marriage; although divorced people are willing to test the matrimonial waters a second time, they do not usually want to subject assets they acquired prior to that marriage to claims of the new spouse.

The advantage of premarital agreements is that they enable you to define your rights and those of your new spouse to assets brought into the marriage, as well as what interest you and your new spouse will have in assets acquired or money earned during your marriage. If properly drafted and prepared, premarital agreements can provide for and protect you and your spouse at the end of your marriage, whether that end is the result of divorce or of death.

Basic Precautions

For a premarital agreement to be valid and provide the protection you need, several factors must be taken into account. First and foremost, the agreement should not be written in a way that appears to encourage divorce. The agreement should cover the contingency of divorce, but not encourage either you or your spouse to that end.

Any agreement should disclose the assets you or your spouse owns and the income, if any, to be received from them. The agreement should also define what interest, if any, your new spouse will have in these assets.

The agreement should appear fair. If it does not, it is unlikely to stand up to judicial scrutiny. What is considered "fair"? A fair agreement does not result from undue influence of a spouse possessing a strong economic or other advantage. Both you and your spouse should fully discuss what you want from the agreement, and each of you should be represented by an attorney. If either you or your spouse is not represented, it is more likely that the agreement will be seen as unfair by the courts.

Effects on Inheritance

Properly drafted agreements also deal with the death of either you or your spouse. In many cases, one or both of you will have children from a former marriage. You will be concerned with protecting what you previously acquired, so that upon death your children's inheritance will remain intact.

Premarital agreements can have a significant effect on the rights granted by state law to a surviving spouse. An agreement can ensure that your spouse will be provided with financial assistance after your death and that your children will ultimately receive the underlying assets. Similarly, if you and your spouse are financial equals, an agreement can ensure that all of your estate goes directly to your children with no interest passing to your surviving spouse.

In many instances, one spouse owns a home that becomes the new family residence.

In most states, by law, a surviving spouse can reside in a home after the death of the other spouse for a period of time. If this is not desired, a premarital agreement can waive the right or set forth a specific period of time that the surviving spouse can continue to use the home as a principal residence.

Premarital agreements cannot do everything. Waiving the right to receive alimony or spousal support in the event of divorce is generally impermissible, as are provisions affecting child custody and support. Provisions that attempt to define these rights will carry no weight in court. However, by agreement your spouse can waive his or her right to receive support from your estate.

Source: Michael C. Shea, JD, partner, Shea and Ashworth, 1855 First Ave., Suite 303, San Diego, CA 92101. He is certified by the state bar of California as a specialist in family law.

Best Divorce Protection

Many of the controversies that develop between divorcing spouses could be avoided by making arrangements ahead of time. Prenuptial (or postnuptial) agreements are the easiest, most effective way for couples to vary the rights they would normally have under state laws.

Protecting Assets and Income

The best way to protect your income from divorce is to make a prenuptial agreement between you and your spouse regarding your present assets and income and future assets and income. Essential: Agreements regarding income and assets must be in writing, signed by both parties, reasonable, and not tainted by misrepresentations or duress. The validity of the agreement will be called into question if the financial means of the parties are unreasonably disproportionate.

Any agreement should list assets specifically. The only way to disallow your wife or husband's rights to a substantial marital asset is to prove that a contract addressed the asset specifically and established a fair method of disposing of the asset. If assets are acquired after the first agreement is drawn up, a new agreement should be made regarding those assets.

Personal Property and Gifts

Be sure to establish a fair means of dividing personal property in the event of divorce. Though usually of less value than other property, personal property often creates the largest problems for a divorcing couple. The effort, emotion, attorney's fees, and court time usually far exceed the actual value of the property.

Rights to pension plans and academic diplomas are, in many cases today, considered marital assets. These can represent particularly sticky areas in a divorce, so it's wise to cover them also.

Interspousal gifts usually are exempt from distribution. However, if a gift is of particular value, be sure to guarantee that the distribution remains equitable.

Gifts from parents can give rise to disagreements. Is a gift from a parent to one or both spouses? Under most wills, substantial gifts by parents to one spouse do not present a problem, because the beneficiary is specifically named. However, substantial gifts from living parents should be written into an agreement that designates for whom the gift was intended.

To protect yourself in divorce, make an agreement before the trouble begins.

Source: Carole Mehlman Gould, attorney at law, 475 Fifth Ave., New York 10017. Her practice is concentrated in family law, including problems of the elderly, wills, trusts, divorces, and child custody. She is a member of the Pro Bono Panel of the New York Council of Law Associates and of the Battered Women's Committee.

Beware of Prenuptial Agreements

A divorced woman challenged the validity of a prenuptial agreement in which she had waived her community-property rights. She had given up her interest in her husband's enormous assets.

The court held the agreement invalid. Reasoning: Though prenuptial agreements are not contrary to public policy when freely and intelligently made, the overwhelming evidence in this case demonstrated manipulation on the part of the husband. An experienced and wealthy businessman and politician, he had initiated the agreement the week before the wedding. The couple had been counseled by the husband's attorney, who neither advised the wife to seek her own legal counsel nor explained to her the practical effect of the agreement (to eliminate the accumulation of community property).

Source: *In re marriage of Matson*, 705 P.2d 817 (Wash. Ct. App. 1985).

Best Time to Negotiate a Prenuptial Agreement

Prenuptial agreements work best when negotiated well before the wedding. . . and when both parties avoid giving up too much in the name of love. Legal fees: $1,000–$10,000.

Source: Carlyn McCaffrey, a New York lawyer.

Agreement Trap

A prenuptial agreement provided that the wife would receive $200 a month for 10 years in case of divorce. When the agreement was signed, the husband was worth about $500,000. But his wealth later increased substantially—to about $8 million. When the wife filed for divorce, the court held that she was not bound by the premarital agreement, as changed circumstances had made it unconscionable. Such an agreement, the court said, must be fair not only at the time it is made but also at the time it is to be enforced.

Source: *Gross v. Gross*, Ohio SupCt, 464 NE (2d) 500.

Obstetric Alternative

Birth centers offer parents more control over how their babies are born and typically charge only half as much as a hospital for a delivery. Many insurers offer reimbursement for birth center services, and most states either already have or are drafting regulations for licensing and safety. Drawback: The centers are not as well equipped as hospitals to handle high-risk deliveries.

More Than Baby-Sitters

Trained nannies provide child care, deal with medical emergencies, even fix a blown fuse. Training: Child growth and development, health and safety, and interpersonal skills. Two hundred hours of classroom instruction and 50 hours of supervised child care are required of nannies trained at schools accredited by the American Council of Nanny Schools.

Nanny rates: $200–$400 a week, plus benefits. . .more for live-out nannies.

For schools and placement agencies in your area: Write to the American Council of Nanny Schools, Delta College, University Center, MI 48710.

How To Find the Best Day-Care Services

Day-care centers often are a must for couples who both have to work to make ends meet. Yet locating high-quality care that serves a child's individual needs can be a difficult task, particularly when it comes down to making a final selection.

First thing to do: Find out the services available in your community. Check for a child-care resource and referral service (sometimes called information & referral, I&R, or R&R). R&R services typically compile data on existing programs in your area, their vacancies, fees, ages of children served, and other infor-

mation. R&R programs are usually listed in the telephone book. If not, contact your state's child-care licensing agency (Department of Human Services, Social Services, or Health); state or national child-care advocacy groups; your employers; or ask other parents.

If no R&R service is available to you, contact the local YM/YWCA, religious groups, local colleges, vocational schools, or any of the sources listed above for information on child-care providers. In addition, local chapters of the Red Cross, the public library, and groups such as the Junior League and the League of Women Voters are good sources of information regarding programs in your community. Don't overlook newspapers and bulletin boards.

What to Expect

The most important criteria for choosing a day-care center are quality and appropriateness of care to your child's needs. The next most important are cost, location, and hours of operation.

There is a broad variety of child-care centers from which to choose. Settings range from private homes to large day-care centers or facilities located within a sponsoring institution or business. To begin the screening process, look first at licensed child-care centers. Any place that takes care of a group of three to four or more unrelated children is required to be licensed by most states. Warning: Since licensing and registration requirements vary considerably from state to state, a licensed child-care center does not necessarily mean high quality. It doesn't hurt to contact your state's child-care licensing agency to find out exactly what the licensing requirements are.

Many family day-care providers are unaware of licensing regulations and would be willing to become licensed. Parents who rule out all unlicensed care may deprive themselves of an excellent alternative. However, be cautioned that such a care giver should be willing to become licensed.

The price of day care varies substantially. Family day care usually costs from $35 to $160 per child, per week. In centers, care for infants (0–2 years) usually ranges from $60 to $150 per week, while preschool care generally costs from $50 to $120 per week. Most family day care is less expensive than center care. This in turn is usually less costly than care in the child's own home, which is covered by the minimum wage.

Unannounced Visits

Before reaching a final decision, be sure to visit the prospective child-care program. You should feel free to drop in unannounced. A good child-care center expects this of parents. What do you look for in a visit?

Staffing. Find out the extent of the care givers' training and experience. A good program has enough qualified adults to ensure that children receive individual attention. A good rule of thumb is one teacher and one assistant for the following groups of children:

- Infants—four to six children.
- One- to two-year-olds—six to eight children.
- Two- to three-year-olds—eight to 14 children.
- Four- to five-year-olds—11 to 20 children.

Group sizes should be set up to reflect these ratios, since children generally do better in small groups.

Adult/child interaction. Check to see that children are busy, happy, and absorbed in their activities. Observe the adults. Are they interested, loving, and actively involved with the children?

Cleanliness: This is a high priority for young children. Cleanliness can control the spread of infectious diseases. Check to see that teachers and other adults wash their hands frequently. Do children wash before eating and after going to the toilet? Are the rooms, toys, and equipment cleaned regularly?

Safety and emergency. Emergency plans should be clearly posted near the telephone and include telephone numbers for a doctor, ambulance, etc. Smoke detectors should be installed and fire extinguishers readily available.

Play equipment. Check to see that there is a variety of interesting play materials and equipment.

Many organizations involved with child care publish guidebooks and checklists for evaluating child care. You might want to get hold of one before you begin your visits, but good parental judgment and monitoring are the only way to ensure high-quality care.

Source: Carolyn Strnad, 603 First St., Hoboken, NJ 07030. She is the former deputy director, Child Care Action Campaign, New York, which is currently the only national agency concerned with all aspects of child day care. She has been a day-care teacher and instructor of vocational child-care classes.

Summer Jobs for Kids

Friends and relatives are the best source of help in finding summer jobs. Ask them for contacts or ideas.

Summer camps hire students for all sorts of jobs. Usual requirements: Camp experience, age 19 or older, and at least one year of college. Send applications for review by interested camp directors to: The American Camping Association, Martinsville, IN. The Association of Independent Camps, New York. Camp Consulting Services, Huntington, NY.

The National Parks Services of the Department of the Interior provides 4,500 summer jobs (and many winter jobs) annually. Applicants must be 18, high school graduates, and US citizens.

One useful approach: Advertise your services on local store and community-center bulletin boards. Two brothers kept busy painting houses (a very profitable enterprise) after putting up a note in a supermarket advertising their availability.

Many countries let foreign students work in temporary, seasonal jobs. The pay is usually low, but jobs can be interesting. Example: Working on the French grape harvest.

Work-Ethic Myth

Part-time jobs make teenagers more ambitious about education and careers. Reality:

The typical dead-end job fosters bad grades in school, more money for drugs and alcohol, and a jaded attitude toward work in general.

Source: Laurence Steinberg, professor of child and family studies, University of Wisconsin.

Parent's Guide to Corporate Training Programs

What can you do to help your child land the right job offer?

A corporate training program may be the answer, especially for liberal arts students, because it permits recent graduates to earn while they learn. Such programs give in-depth training in a specific industry while also offering a practical view of the corporate world. This hands-on training is useful in whatever field the student finally picks. Best of all, most corporate training programs pay well. Starting annual salaries for trainees range from $15,000 to more than $30,000.

Competition for corporate training programs is fierce. The applicant usually has to face a number of rejections before he's offered a job he wants.

How to prepare: There is no such thing as too much preparation for a job interview. Encourage your graduate first to learn about the industry that interests him. Then, once he understands the industry and the key players, he can zero in on particular companies. He should study their annual reports and recruitment materials, and articles written about them. (Articles can be obtained by telephoning a company's public relations department to request a press kit.)

Information interviews in advance of a job interview can also be helpful. Alumni from your son's or daughter's alma mater who are already working for that company or industry are often willing to take a few minutes—either over the phone or in person—to offer insights into what it's like to work there. Your own business contacts and friends may also be able to serve as informal career advisers.

Questions the job hunter should ask: What are the most satisfying aspects of your job? What are your priorities in an average work week? What do you wish you had known about this career field before you entered it? What about this employer?

Choice Programs

Although there are no best management training programs, there are some truly outstanding ones that have earned national reputations. (Note: All are open to liberal arts graduates as well as to more specialized degree holders.) Among them:

• R.H. Macy & Co., Inc. Macy's is considered the retail industry's top performer. Its training program has been lauded as "the Harvard of retailing" by *The Wall Street Journal*. The management training program begins with a couple of months in the classroom. During that time trainees learn everything anyone ever wanted to know about a complex organization engaged in the department store business. The sales manager's job is the first permanent placement, and sales managers often run businesses with annual sales of over $2 million.

• The May Department Stores. May offers the highest starting salaries in the retail industry (more than $25,000 to the best and brightest BAs). After a number of weeks in the classroom, trainees spend several months honing their management skills in the first permanent job assignment—department manager of group sales managers.

• Grey Advertising. New York's largest advertising agency offers a unique, flexible training program. There is constant dialogue between trainees and their supervisors. In the account management area, new hires are immediately given real work that involves considerable responsibility.

• Ogilvy & Mather. Each year this advertising agency hires a small number of assistant account executives for a comprehensive and rigorous training program. "It's a friendly place, not at all the way I envisioned Madison

228

Avenue," says an Ogilvy account executive.

• Procter & Gamble. This manufacturer and distributor of more than 300 consumer products has a reputation for promoting from within. Its reputation as a trainer is stellar. Many believe four years in brand management at P&G has more value than an MBA for those who intend to spend their career in advertising and marketing.

• SmithKline Beckman. The company's centralized training program, which consists of four assignments over the course of 18–28 months, is clearly the fast track to management careers in this health-care and high-technology company. SmithKline is particularly enjoyable because the work environment is intellectually stimulating.

• Morgan Guaranty. Formal classroom instruction lasts six months for BA hires and includes accounting, international finance and corporate finance. The bank's emphasis is on wholesale banking. Following the classroom training, hires spend three months crunching numbers in the financial analysis department, working on companies that the lending officers serve. Compensation is generous (starting salaries are $25,000+). For Morgan bankers there is a free lunch, which is served daily to promote comradeship among executives at various stages of their careers.

• First National Bank of Chicago. The First Scholar Program, the bank's most prestigious career offering, is a 30-month general management training program that combines employment at the bank with evening graduate programs at the University of Chicago or Northwestern University. First Scholars are required to take two courses per quarter. They get experience in a wide range of the bank's departments through periodic rotations.

• McKinsey & Co. There's no real training for consulting-firm research associates. From day one, hires are expected to be able to execute whatever assignments are passed their way. The associates get an insider's view of big business and complicated problem-solving—and fat paychecks (total compensation for year one on the job is upwards of $33,000). The expectation: Top BAs are hired, work for two years, and then leave the firm to return to school for an MBA or JD.

Source: Marian Salzman, author, with Deidre Sullivan, *Inside Management Training: The Career Guide to Training Programs for College Graduates*, New American Library, New York.

About the Power of Attorney

Most of us are familiar with the process of planning for death by writing a will. But how would your personal and financial affairs be handled if you were disabled by illness or accident?

The power of attorney is a written document that allows you (the principal) to appoint another person (the agent) to make your financial decisions for you if you become disabled. The document is simple to create (forms are available at most stationery stores). And, in most states, you simply insert the name of the agent you've chosen and sign the document in front of a notary public for it to become valid. Once it is created, you are in no way bound by a power of attorney; the procedure is voluntary and can be revoked at any time.

The amount of control a power of attorney hands over to an agent can be either broad (your agent has the power to do anything you could have done) or limited (your agent has only the power to sell your car). The duration of the document is equally flexible. It can remain in effect even if you lose mental capacity (called the durable power of attorney). The only limitation is that its powers end automatically upon the death of either party.

Know the Risks

The greatest risk involved with creating a power of attorney is choosing the right agent. Once a power of attorney is enacted, there is very little accountability of your agent, and he could misuse the power. For this reason, it is important that you choose an agent in whom you place the greatest trust. The best choice is usually a close family member with a good head for finance and knowledge of your personal needs. For further protection, don't give the power of attorney to the agent. Rather, tell him where it is. Without the document itself, the agent can do nothing.

There is also a risk that the power of attorney might not be accepted. Most banks will question an agent to determine if the power was revoked or if the principal has died. Some banks insist that their own power of attorney form be used; some insurance companies will not honor a power of attorney if it is more than six months old.

Latest Development

Legislation being passed in a growing number of states would enable you to appoint an agent to make medical decisions for you when you are physically unable to do so. This arrangement would be most appropriate for situations in which you might have to undergo a serious medical procedure that would leave you unable to decide the next medical step to take.

Example: Before undergoing serious exploratory surgery, a patient appoints a close relative to make necessary medical decisions. While the patient is under anesthesia, the doctor can consult with the agent about what has been discovered and the possible options.

Your risk? The agent might not make a sound decision. Pick an agent who is likely to know what decision you would make, and put your conclusions in writing so he will have guidance. Two agents can be appointed and both required to approve any decision. What is the risk of not appointing an agent? In medical situations in which there are a number of options—each with a chance of failure—lengthy, expensive legal proceedings might be necessary before the doctor or hospital is willing to act.

Special application: A great deal of public attention has been paid to situations in which medical patients not able to make decisions for themselves are kept alive by extraordinary means. Yet doctors and hospitals cannot remove life support equipment unless they have consent from someone legally appointed by the patient. Those who are older and do not have immediate family members would be

wise to create a power of attorney for this purpose.

Source: Daniel G. Fish, partner, Freedman and Fish, attorneys at law, 233 Broadway, New York 10279. He is a specialist in legal issues affecting older adults.

How To Protect Your Assets Against Catastrophic Illness

A chronic illness that requires full-time care in a nursing home (where the average annual cost runs $25,000–$50,000) can wipe out the assets of most middle-income or upper-middle-income families.

Since only limited coverage for such long-term care is available from either the federal government or from private insurance agencies, anyone who is elderly (or has elderly parents) has to consider this issue. Depending on your circumstances, you may be able to protect all or part of your family's assets.

Medicare Vs. Medicaid

Medi*care*, for which everyone over 65 is eligible, provides coverage for short-term hospitalization and a percentage of doctor bills. Medicare and most private insurance companies cover 150 days in the hospital, and many policies cover up to a full year of hospitalization (provided your condition requires acute hospital care). Coverage extends to 99.9% of all acute illnesses.

The gap arises with long-term illnesses that don't require hospitalization. Neither Medicare, supplemental policies to Medicare, nor private insurance policies cover full-time care in a nursing home or at home with a home attendant.

Who typically needs such care: The very old and frail, people who suffer from Parkinson's or Alzheimer's disease or other types of dementia, stroke, or debilitating arthritis. Because there's nothing a doctor or nurse can do, the type of care needed is classified as custodial rather than as skilled . . . and insurance covers only skilled care.

A penniless person who needs a nursing home is covered by Medi*caid*, which is only for the very poor.

The name of the game is to get the person in need of care on Medicaid. This means the prospective patient must either spend down his assets (spend everything he owns on nursing home care until he's indigent and the state takes over) or divest himself of his assets before applying for Medicaid so it will pick up the bills from the beginning. The second alternative is usually preferable.

Who Should Start Planning

People with degenerative diseases that follow a predictable course know that somewhere down the line they'll probably need a nursing home. They and people over 75, especially if they're in poor health, should have a plan.

People who have less than $20,000 or more than $300,000 don't need to do this kind of planning. (However, the upper cutoff for those who live in large metropolitan areas, where nursing homes are more expensive, is $500,000.) Poorer people will be eligible for Medicaid, and wealthier people can pay on their own. It's the people in the middle who need to prepare.

Transferring Assets

Federal law: Any money that was in the patient's name during the two years before nursing home admittance has to go toward the nursing home bill. Crucial: Advance planning. If you transfer assets the day before nursing home admission, you won't get relief until two years down the road.

It's illegal (fraud) to try to hide assets by, for example, putting them in another bank account. The government checks 1099 forms, and it will pick up anything you had in the past three years. Hiding assets carries criminal penalties. Giving assets away is more feasible.

In addition to getting on Medicaid, people should be concerned with the management of their money. Anyone with Alzheimer's or Parkinson's will eventually reach the point where he can't manage his own money. If no provi-

sion has been made, there will have to be a court proceeding to appoint a guardian. This is expensive and time consuming, and it takes away any flexibility there might have been to manage the money. Money-management options:

- Give power of attorney to someone else.
- Set up a joint account. In many states a joint account will also transfer ownership, thus making the aging person eligible for Medicaid.
- Set up a trust. Although a trust doesn't transfer ownership, it does allow someone else to manage the money.

Congress recently cracked down on the kind of grantor trusts people used to use, in which management of the trust was typically turned over to the children, while the parent earned income from the principal. Congressional rule: If the principal can be used for the grantor, it has to be considered for Medicaid eligibility. The only trust that will work is one that gives the prospective patient no access to the principal.

Homes are exempt. If your assets are in your home, or if it makes sense to put them in one, that is likely to serve as protection. Many states protect spouses, so there are often ways the spouse can keep some of the money. The third route is to transfer money to the children—which may also make sense in terms of avoiding probate and estate taxes.

Problems with transfer: There may be negative tax implications. If there is more than one child, to which one do you give the money? Children have been known to run off with a parent's assets before the parent was ready for a nursing home. Giving up financial independence is not acceptable to some people. Many people can't decide what to do because they're not sure they will wind up in a home. The state may sue the spouse or the estate after the patient's death in order to recover the nursing home fees.

Get Good Advice

In order to decide which course is best for you and your family, you'll need advice from someone who has extensive experience in geriatric law. Don't consult just any trusts and estates attorney.

To find someone good: Every county has a Legal Services for the Elderly office as part of its Department for the Aging. Although Legal Services probably won't help you directly, because it's funded to help the poor, it often knows local private attorneys who specialize in this area. The American Bar Association has a special committee on the legal problems of the elderly. Ask for attorneys on that committee's list who attend meetings and get mailings. They're not necessarily competent, but at least they're making the attempt. Clue: Does the attorney have a copy of the four-volume *Medicare and Medicaid Guide*? Only a specialist will have this.

It's not only knowing the law but knowing the system that's important. Your attorney should know, for instance, who at Medicaid decides the case and whom to contact to appeal a case. An application for Medicaid for a nursing home is equivalent to asking the state for a grant of $40,000. In most states the investigation procedures for a Medicaid hearing are far more thorough than those for a tax audit. They include personal interviews, bank-record searches and contact with the IRS. You need the most expert help you can get.

Source: Robert M. Freedman, partner, Freedman and Fish, specialists in geriatric law, 233 Broadway, New York 10279.

When Medicare Covers Home Care

Medicare will cover home health care only if all of these conditions are met: (1) The care includes part-time skilled nursing care, physical therapy, or speech therapy. (2) The patient is confined to his home. (3) A doctor determines that the patient needs home health care and sets up a home health plan for him. (4) The home health agency providing services is participating in Medicare.

Source: *Home Health Care* by Jo-Ann Friedman, consultant to the health care industry, W.W. Norton, New York.

Housing Alternatives for Aging but Able Parents

Adult children often want their aging parents nearby so they can protect and care for them. But forcing them to leave their home and community is unnecessary and unfair. Various services and housing programs throughout the US now enable the elderly to remain safely and comfortably independent.

A Parent Who Wants To Stay Home

• Community services for the elderly help those who can no longer handle all the chores of daily living. Services include daily visits by social workers, telephone check-in calls, home health care, housekeeping, home repair, meal deliveries, and emergency response systems (pocket-sized pagers alert an information center in case of emergency).

• Shared-housing programs offer companionship and the opportunity to split living costs. Two or more people occupy the home belonging to one of them. Each has private space, and the living room and kitchen are shared. Roommate matches are based on personality, interests, and needs.

• Accessory apartments created within the elderly person's own home offer him rental income, the assurance that someone is nearby, and the opportunity to exchange services. Example: The tenant may do the yard work in exchange for transportation.

• Home retrofitting* involves identifying and overcoming problems such as stairs, hard-to-turn doorknobs, and raised thresholds in doorways. Making changes such as these may enable an older person to remain at home longer.

A Parent Who Chooses To Move

• Board and care homes provide a private or semiprivate room, all meals, housekeeping, and 24-hour management, often in a family-like setting. Cost: $300–$650/month.

• Congregate housing—apartments centered around a main dining room—provides at least one meal a day, transportation and housekeeping. Cost: $500–$1,200/month.

• Continuing-care retirement communities offer apartments and nursing home facilities in one location. Residents are guaranteed complete care and services. Cost: $60,000–$250,000 entrance fee and $500–$2,000/month.

• Active retirement communities offer recreational and social activities in a campus-type setting. Residents purchase or rent a one- to three-bedroom apartment, townhouse, or home. Health care is not included. Cost: $40,000–$120,000/unit.

• An adult child's home can be an excellent option. Important: Establish the level of involvement you want in each other's lives, and stick to this plan.

Points To Remember

You and your family should take part in, but not force, decisions concerning a lifestyle change for your elderly parents. They are used to making their own decisions. Their turning 70 or 80 doesn't mean they are any less capable of or any less interested in continuing to do so.

*A free booklet on home retrofitting (including changes that can be made and how to make them) is available from AARP.

Source: Katie Sloan, senior housing specialist, American Association of Retired Persons, 1909 K St. NW, Washington, DC 20049. AARP publishes *Miles Away and Still Caring*, a free booklet, and can tell you which organizations in your area handle services for the aging.

How To Find a Good Nursing Home

Most families postpone as long as possible the decision to use a nursing home. Once the decision is reached, the process of selecting a good facility is so painful that often they move too fast. Good advice: Give your parent time to get used to the idea. Meanwhile, investigate every possible choice thoroughly.

How to begin: Get lists of not-for-profit, community-based homes from your church, fraternal order, state agency on aging, American Association of Homes for the Aging (Suite 770, 1050 17 St. NW, Washington, DC 20036), or American Health Care Association (1200 15 St. NW, Washington, DC 20005).

Costs: If your parent's resources are limited, Medicaid may provide financial support for nursing home care. Homes offering complete care in metropolitan areas usually charge $50–$80 per day (depending on the amount of care required). Some require a large advance gift or admission fee. (Health insurance sometimes covers nursing homes.) Patients paying their own way may be eligible for Medicaid assistance after their savings run out. Check the rules in your state.

Evaluating a Nursing Home

1. Accreditation, license, and certification for Medicare and Medicaid should be current and in force.

2. It's best to arrive without an appointment. Look at everything. The building and rooms should be clean, attractive and safe, and meet all fire codes. Residents should not be crowded (ask about private rooms; sometimes they're available at reasonable extra cost). Visit the dining room at mealtime. Check the kitchen, too. Visit activity rooms when in session. Talk to residents to find out how they feel about the home.

3. The staff should be professionally trained and large enough to provide adequate care for all residents.

4. If the home requires a contract, read it carefully. Show it to your lawyer before signing. Some homes reserve the right to discharge a patient whose condition has deteriorated even if a lump-sum payment was made upon admittance. Best: An agreement that allows payment by the month, or permits refunds or advance payment if plans change.

5. Find out exactly what services the home provides and which ones cost extra. Private-duty nurses are not included. Extras like shampoo or hairset can be exorbitant. (A box of tissues can cost a dollar.) Make a list of the "extras" your parent will need for a comfortable life. Try to supply some of them yourself.

Before you decide on a home, you and your parent should have a talk with the administrator and department heads. Find out who is in charge of what, and whom to speak to if problems arise.

Source: Sheldon Goldberg, American Association of Homes for the Aging.

Nursing Home Traps

Most nursing homes charge $20,000–$40,000 per year, depending on the degree of medical care provided. Even at these steep rates, private-patient waiting lists are long. Additional pressure is caused by Medicare, which often refuses to pay for hospitalization of patients awaiting nursing-home admission on the grounds that they are hospitalized inappropriately. Patients who cannot get into nursing homes are being billed by the hospital (sometimes at $300 a day or more), putting tremendous pressure on the patient's family to do whatever possible to get the patient into a nursing home quickly. Many nursing homes are quick to take advantage of this pressure.

Contracts with nursing homes are often too broad in scope. In essence, they state: You give us all your money, and we'll take care of you for the rest of your life. Some states have outlawed such agreements because of rampant abuses. A patient who paid a home $100,000 and later wanted to move when he discovered the food was dreadful could not get his money back.

Many homes demand payment of one or two years' fees in advance. This practice, too, has been outlawed in some states.

Yet another practice is sponsoring contracts to be signed with the patient's children, who guarantee that the nursing home will be paid for periods up to about two years. Often these contracts are a way to circumvent laws that forbid a home to accept more than two to three months' payment in advance.

The noninstitutionalized spouse has to pay only the first six months of nursing-home care for the institutionalized partner. Then, if the person paying refuses to pay more, the institutionalized spouse is eligible for Medicaid.

Problem: The noninstitutionalized spouse can be sued by the local agency for support. This is not always as bad as it seems, because disputes are settled in family courts, where support payments are ordered on the basis of what can be afforded, just as in child support.

One strategy: If you do not use a trust fund, transfer all assets immediately to the healthy spouse as soon as the other becomes ill.

Joint savings or checking accounts are not recommended, because they are usually considered as belonging fifty-fifty to each depositor.

Source: Charles Robert, lawyer with Robert & Schneider, Hempstead, NY.

Lending Money to Family and Friends

Loans to friends or family members can often become a sticky business. Number one rule: Use the same care—or more—in lending money to a friend as you would in lending money to an institution.

When a friend or family member approaches you about a loan, inform him that this is a business deal and will be evaluated as such. By taking this approach you help remove some of the emotional strain involved for both of you. In the long run, you will also reduce the risk of losing your money. Analyze the situation as a banker would: How good is your friend's credit? How will your friend use the money? How and when will your friend repay the loan?

Examine Alternatives

Always check to see that your friend or relative has examined the alternative sources for a loan. The most obvious include:

- Banks.
- Second mortgage on house.
- Loan on whole life insurance policy.
- Company pension, profit-sharing, or savings plan.
- Brokerage account.
- Small Business Administration, if the loan is for a new or existing business.
- Trade credit, if the loan is for a new or existing business.

The advantage of this exercise is that it casts you in the role of financial adviser, not just friend or relative. More importantly, you may help the other person pinpoint a source of funds he overlooked.

Put It in Writing

Whether a loan is to a friend or a member of your family, any agreement should be in writing. Forms of promissory notes (also known as IOUs), which are often available in stationery stores, can be used for this purpose. What should be included in the agreement? At a minimum, it should specify the amount of the loan, its terms, and the interest rate, if any.

You may want the interest on the loan to compensate you for the income forgone as a result of making the loan. For example, on a one-year loan, consider charging the going rate on one-year certificates of deposit.

Try to eliminate possibilities for future misunderstandings. If you can, address the following questions in your agreement: Will the loan be amortized? Will payment of principal and interest be made monthly or quarterly, or will only interest be payable at fixed intervals, with a balloon payment specified at the end? Will the loan have a fixed term, or be payable to you "on demand"?

The following is an example of a simple promissory note that covers these questions:

$5,000   Dated:_____
Promissory Note

FOR VALUE RECEIVED, I _____ ("Borrower") promise to pay to the order of _____ the sum of *Five Thousand* dollars ($5,000.00), payable commencing on _____ _____, 19__, and each succeeding month thereafter for ___ months in equal monthly installments of principal and ___% interest in the amount of _____ dollars ($_____).

_____ (Borrower)

The signature of the borrower is essential to making the promissory note legally enforceable. The main purpose of a written agreement is not to frighten your friend or relative into thinking you'll haul him off to court, but to emphasize that borrowing money is a serious business.

Source: Karen F. Stein, Ph.D., associate professor of consumer economics at the University of Delaware, Newark, DE 19716. Author of numerous publications on consumer affairs, she is former executive director of the American Council on Consumer Interests.

Problems With Low-Interest Loans

Be careful of low- or no-interest loans to friends or family members. The IRS now imposes both income and gift taxes on these types of loans. Prior to 1984, high-income parents could make interest-free or below-market-interest loans to their children. The children could invest the loan proceeds and be taxed on the earnings at their low (or zero) tax rate.

Now, when a lender charges an interest rate that is less than the market rate, the IRS views him as having collected the full market rate of interest and then making a gift to the borrower of the forgone interest. (Tax reform severely reduced the advantages of below-market-interest loans to minors. Parents are taxed on unearned income over $1,000 of children 14 and under.)

Exception: Loans of $10,000 or less, at little or no interest, can be made to family or friends for any purpose other than investing. The forgone interest will not be considered income to the lender. Warning: You can't beat this exception by making, for example, four loans of $3,000 each. They would count as one loan of more than $10,000 and therefore would result in tax liability for the lender.

Be careful of interest-free or below-market-interest loans to dependents. You can no longer claim the relative as a dependent if the income from the loan results in your no longer providing more than half of the dependent's support.

Source: Karen F. Stein, Ph.D., associate professor of consumer economics at the University of Delaware, Newark, DE 19716. Author of numerous publications on consumer affairs, she is former executive director of the American Council on Consumer Interests.

How To Take Your Parents as Dependents

Claim your parent as a dependent, and qualify for an additional personal tax exemption. You can also obtain the benefit of medical-expense deductions that a low-tax-bracket parent is unable to utilize.

To claim your parent as a dependent you must be able to satisfy the following list of conditions:

• A dependent must either be a member of your household or bear a family relationship to you. The IRS considers a father, mother, father-in-law, or mother-in-law an acceptable parental relationship.

• A parent claimed as a dependent must make less than $1,950 in gross income ($2,000 starting in 1989) during the year he is claimed as a dependent.

• You must supply more than one-half of your parent's support for the calendar year. The IRS includes medical expenses in its definition of support, thereby making it easier for children paying heavy medical expenses to meet the support requirement.

• If two or more children provide support for a parent and jointly meet the 50% support requirement, only one child can claim the parent as a dependent (provided the children meet a number of other IRS requirements).

• Your parent must be, for some part of the year, a US citizen, resident or national, or a resident of Canada or Mexico.

• Your parent cannot file a joint return unless it is only for the purpose of a refund or unless no tax is due.

Special note: Even if your parent provides you with the funds to pay for his medical expenses, you can still claim the expenses on your tax return. To take the deduction, the medical expenses must exceed 7.5% of your adjusted gross income, and the funds transferred by your parent cannot be specifically earmarked for medical expenses (you should have discretion to use the funds as you wish). There is a possibility of a gift tax being applied to the funds, but the annual exclusion and life-time credit for taxable transfers make this unlikely.

Source: Israel A. Press, CPA, tax partner, and Tom Spiesman, JD, tax associate, Touche Ross & Company, Financial Services Center, One World Trade Center, New York 10048. Mr. Press is the author of numerous tax articles.

Parent Supported by More Than One Child: Who Takes Deduction?

When brothers and sisters support a parent, plan things so that one of them can deduct the parent's medical expenses. Here's how:

First step: File a multiple-support declaration (form 2120). When several people contribute, this form designates the one who can take the exemption. If they pay at least 10% each, but nobody gives as much as half, any one of them can take the exemption if the others agree.

Second step: The one claiming the exemption should pay doctor bills directly and make clear (on the check) that his contribution is earmarked for medical expenses. Then he can deduct the parent's medical expenses on his tax return. Remember: Medical expenses can be deducted only for yourself, your spouse and your dependents. You can't take a deduction for medical expenses paid for somebody else unless you can properly claim the person as a dependent.

Buying Your Parents' House and Renting It Back to Them

You can create significant income and estate tax savings by buying your parents' home and renting it back to them. Sale-leasebacks, as these transactions are commonly known, enable taxpayers to sell a dwelling unit to a family member and then lease it back from the buyer. If your parents are over 55, the Tax Code will permit an exclusion of up to $125,000 profit from the sale of the dwelling.

Advantages of a Sale-Leaseback

• Future appreciation of the house is no longer included in the parents' estate.

• You can shelter income by deducting depreciation and the expenses of owning and maintaining the dwelling.

• Your parents can receive cash in exchange for the equity value of their home.

• Your parents can utilize the one-time $125,000 exclusion on the gain from the sale of their residence.

• Your parents enjoy the advantages of renting while remaining in the family home (i.e., they are no longer responsible for maintaining the property).

The most appropriate candidates for this type of arrangement are parents who have only modest savings and income but own a home with a significant amount of equity value locked up in it. A sale-leaseback is especially appropriate for parents who rely on their children for a portion of their income, since the sale's proceeds give them a steady source of additional cash.

A Valid Arrangement

For a sale-leaseback to be considered valid, the following conditions must be met:

• The home must be purchased for adequate and full consideration.

• You as the buyer must bear the risks and the benefits of fluctuations in the residential real estate market.

• Your parents must be subject to lease provisions.

• There must be no evidence of intention by your parents to repurchase the property.

• Your parents must not retain control over the property or exercise dominion and control over you.

• You must collect a "fair rent" from your parents.

Source: Israel A. Press, CPA, tax partner, and Tom Spiesman, JD, tax associate, Touche Ross & Company, Financial Services Center, One World Trade Center, New York 10048. Mr. Press is the author of numerous tax articles.

Renting Your Own House

You can get your house out of your estate by selling it to your children and then leasing it back, paying a monthly rent that equals your children's mortgage payments.

But remember, the IRS scrutinizes intrafamily arrangements closely:

• If you sell the house at a bargain price, the IRS may treat the discount as a taxable gift to your children, so sell it at close to market value.

• Mortgage interest paid by your children will be deductible by them and taxable to you.

• Rent payments received by your children will be taxable to them.

• The children will be able to depreciate the house and claim business-expense deductions for costs they incur on it (such as insurance and maintenance) if they charge you a fair rent. Such a rent may be slightly (10%–20%) below market rates because of the lower risk involved in renting to a relative.

• Make sure the paperwork is in order, and that rent and mortgage checks actually change hands each month.

• Don't peg the rent to equal monthly mortgage payments. Rather, fix the length of the mortgage so that the after-tax cost of the mortgage payments balances the fair rent you pay each month.

How To Give Your House Away

It's not uncommon for a taxpayer to give his home to his spouse or children . . . and continue to reside there. Problem: The IRS may include the value of the home in the taxpayer's estate on his death, claiming an incomplete gift. What to do: Make a formal written conveyance of the property to your spouse or children and have the deed recorded in the proper public office. File a gift-tax return and pay the tax when the gift is made. Pay the new owner a reasonable rent for your room or apartment. Do not list the property on any financial statement or loan application. And be certain that taxes, insurance policies, maintenance bills, or other documents are in the name of the new owner.

Tax Bonanza for Retired Parents and Their Children

It is legal to deduct all losses on houses rented to relatives, provided the rents are reasonable by market standards. This opens up profitable retirement loopholes. Children should buy the house their parents retire to and take the deductions for depreciation and operating expenses that would not be available if the parents owned the house. Parents can sell their old house and, if one or both are over 55, pay no tax on any profit up to $125,000. Or they can rent out their old house, take the deductions it generates, and use the income for their retirement.

Source: *Tax Loopholes* by Edward Mendlowitz, Boardroom Books, Millburn, NJ 07041.

---

8 FINANCING AN EDUCATION

Calculating the Cost of a College Education

If you're not careful, education costs can knock a huge hole in your budget. The age old message: Plan for education as early as possible.

The first and most important step is to be realistic about future costs. The following example should demonstrate a way of approaching this problem.

Suppose you have an eight-year-old son and you want him to go to a private college that now costs $12,000 a year, including living expenses.

Assuming a modest inflation rate of 5%, you calculate that your costs will run $18,616, $19,547, $20,524, and $21,550 for the four years, a whopping total of $80,237.

To cover your son's freshman year costs of $18,616, you would have to invest $9,313 for nine years at a compounded tax-free interest rate of 8%. Under the same assumptions, your son's sophomore, junior, and senior years would require investments of $9,054, $8,802, and $8,558, respectively. So the total amount that you must set aside *now* to cover your son's future college cost is $35,727.

Source: Archie M. Richards, Jr., CFP, president, Archie Richards Associates, Inc., Ten Mall Road, Burlington, MA 01803. He is on the Registry of Financial Planning Practitioners and is a member of the International Association for Financial Planning and the Institute of Certified Financial Planners. He is also a weekly newspaper columnist.

Best Ways To Save for Your Child's College Education

Inflation may be low. . .but nobody has told colleges yet. College tuitions continue to rise much faster than the general cost of living. Making matters worse: The new tax law, which undermines many tried-and-true strategies for college saving.

Paying for a child's college education has become one of the toughest financial undertakings of a lifetime.

Major blows from tax reform:

• Children under 14 are now required to pay

tax on investment income at their parents' tax rate. Under the old law, tax on this income was at the child's lower rate.

• Tax-saving Clifford trusts may no longer be set up, and the ones that already exist are much less advantageous because income is now taxed at the parents' rate if the beneficiary is under 14. Clifford trusts had been popular. Parents could temporarily shift assets to their children, letting dividends and interest accrue with little tax, and after ten years, the principal reverted to the parents.

Not All Gloom and Doom

Even if shifting assets to children doesn't save as much as it did, it still makes sense. Kids pay no tax at all on some of their earnings... and if you arrange things properly, they can pay as little as 15% tax on the rest. That's still very advantageous for most high-income families.

Key: Starting to put money aside while the child is still young—preferably at birth. Even a modest amount—$1,000 to $2,000—can grow substantially if it has 18 years in which to compound. A mother and father may each transfer up to $10,000 a year to each child without having to pay gift tax thanks to the gift tax exclusion.

Your first step should be to get your child a Social Security number, so you can open a Uniform Gift to Minors Account (UGMA). The money in this account belongs to the child, but you remain the custodian until the child turns 18. At that point, the money in the UGMA must ordinarily be turned over to the child.

Little-known: Many states actually allow custodians to specify at the outset that the child won't get full control of the money until age 21. Ask about this option at the bank, brokerage house, or mutual fund with which you set up the UGMA.

Trap: If the same person who funds a UGMA also acts as the custodian, the account is considered part of that person's taxable estate if he or she dies before the minor comes of age. Recommended: If one relative funds a UGMA, name another the custodian.

Keeping Control

If you're worried about your 18-year-old—or even your 21-year-old—blowing the whole account on a sports car rather than putting it toward a degree, consider having a lawyer draw up a formal trust. The more money you expect to accumulate on the child's behalf, the more you may feel that you need a formal trust.

Problem: Most trusts that prevent the beneficiary from gaining control of the trust funds don't qualify for the annual $10,000 gift tax exclusion. Solution: The 2503(b) trust, which substantially qualifies for the gift tax exclusion. You become the trustee, your child is the beneficiary, and you may select any age at which the child will take control of the funds in the trust.

Drawback: All interest and dividends earned by assets in a 2503(b) trust must be paid out to the beneficiary (or a UGMA for his benefit). So, if a 2503(b) trust is set up well in advance of college needs and the trust holds income-producing assets, by college time most of a child's assets will be in his UGMA—not in the trust. Solution: Emphasize growth-oriented investments, such as common stocks and real estate. All capital gains allocated to principal in a 2503(b) trust must remain in the trust until expiration.

Investment Strategies

Whether you set up a simple UGMA or a formal 2503(b) trust, remember that the new tax law treats children very differently before and after age 14.

• Before 14: The child isn't taxed at all on the first $500 of investment income and pays 15% tax on the next $500. So put enough principal in income-oriented investments to generate about $1,000 a year in taxable dividends or interest.

Possibilities: High-yielding stocks such as utilities and real estate investment trusts (REITs)...government and corporate bonds...certificates of deposit (CDs)...money-market funds...real estate partnerships...income mutual funds.

Any investment income beyond the child's first $1,000 is taxed at the parents' higher rate. So after you've reached this income limit, consider tax-advantaged investments. Attractive options:

Municipal bonds. Interest is free from federal tax and state and local tax in the state in which the bonds are issued. New twist: Zero-coupon munis, which are sold at a deep discount and redeemed at face value at maturity. Interest isn't paid out periodically, but compounds within the bonds until maturity when it is paid to the bondholder in a lump sum along with the principal. You don't have to worry about reinvesting interest yourself, but if interest rates rise, you can't reinvest interest at the higher rates.

Series EE US Savings Bonds. Tax on interest is due only when the bonds are redeemed, and even then it can be deferred still further by using it to buy Series HH US Savings Bonds. Strategy: Don't redeem bonds until after your child is 14, when the child will be paying tax at his lower rate.

• After 14: Once your child is being taxed at his own tax rate—usually 15%—your investment philosophy should change. Sell the tax-free munis, and shoot for high returns with stocks, bonds, mutual funds, etc.

Source: David Rhine, partner, Seidman & Seidman/BDO, CPAs, 15 Columbus Circle, New York 10023.

Tax-Reform-Proof Trust

To save for kids' college education: "Age-21 trust" (or minor's Section 2503(c) trust), which allows you to shift investment income to a child's lower tax bracket. Benefit: All trust income up to $5,000 a year is taxed at 15% rather than your higher rate. Catch: Assets in a 2503(c) trust belong to the child when he or she turns 21. Recommended 18-year plan: Set aside $2,000 a year, which would grow to $65,000 at only 6% interest . . . have the student receive distributions and pay college bills to avoid having trust distributions taxed to you.

Source: Larry Rabun, director of estate planning, Deloitte Haskins & Sells, Philadelphia.

Why You Shouldn't Stop Stashing Money in Your Child's Account

The first $500 of investment income earned by a child under 14 is tax free, and the next $500 is taxed at the child's own low tax rate. Thus, $1,000 of income per year is tax favored. At 1987 market interest rates, it would take an investment of about $10,000 or more to earn this much interest, so a child's account could very profitably receive gifts totaling up to about $10,000.

Also, a child's account can receive investment income exceeding $1,000 per year without increasing the tax bill by investing in tax-exempt securities (such as municipal bonds) or appreciating assets (such as growth stocks or US Series EE savings bonds). Appreciating assets can be held until after the child reaches 14, then be cashed in with the gain being subject to the child's own low tax rate.

Innovative College Financing

Nothing beats a scholarship or low-interest loan for paying tuition. But an innovative financial scheme can be nearly as effective, especially under the current tax law.

Though federal loans are still available (even to some high-income families), there's increasing pressure to eliminate them, making a personal finance plan all the more important.

The new tax law eliminated Clifford trusts as a means of deferring tax on income earmarked for children's tuition. It also took away the deduction for interest you would pay on college loans. But the law left intact both tax deferment on annuities and tax-free gifts of up to $20,000 a year.

This gives parents of college-bound children an opportunity to use annuities and gifts creatively.

Variable Annuities

With one $10,000 premium, you can buy a variable annuity that has an excellent chance of growing to $20,000 in 10 years, depending on the investment choice made. Like mutual switch funds and some new life insurance policies, variable annuities let you put your money into a wide range of investments, including stocks, bonds, and money-market instruments.

If you time your annuity right, it will be worth about $20,000 when your child approaches college age. That's when you give it to him as a gift. Under IRS rules, the gift is entirely tax free up to $20,000. The child then elects a regular monthly, semiannual or annual payout, which is only partially taxable and is taxed at the child's lower rate.

Strategy: Since $20,000 isn't likely to go far in covering four-year-college costs a decade from now, buy one $10,000 annuity per year over a four-year period, and give one annuity per year while your child is in school.

Disadvantage: As with any other kind of gift, once your child has the money, he's free to spend it in whatever way he wants.

Zero-Coupon Ploys

If your child is very young, zero-coupon, tax-free municipal bonds are a terrific way to pay for college. Reason: Unlike variable annuities and other saving devices, which depend on investment decisions, zero-coupon bonds have a guaranteed rate of return. And in the case of municipals, the return can be tax free.

Example: For $25,000 you can buy a zero-coupon municipal bond that can be redeemed for $100,000 tax free in about 18 years.

Caution: Many zero-coupon munis are callable. Look for those that aren't.

Variation on the theme: Buy a regular tax-free muni and use the payout to buy into a variable annuity. In that way you're funding the annuity with tax-free interest. And you'll still get your principal back when the bond matures.

Life Insurance Opportunities

Instead of putting money into an annuity, put the $40,000 into a single-premium life insurance policy. Its growth is tax deferred in the same way an annuity's is. But when your child is ready for college, you borrow against the policy to pay his bills instead of giving him cash.

Advantages: You can borrow at low rates. Since the money stays in your hands, there's no chance the child will squander it.

Drawback: In effect, you're paying the insurance company to let you borrow at low rates. If you don't need the life insurance in the first place, that might not make sense. Under the new tax law, interest on the loan won't be tax deductible.

Loan Opportunities

Before you start devising financing schemes, look into low-interest federal loans. Mistake: Thinking you don't qualify for state or federal education loans just because you have a comfortable income. Options:

• National Direct Student Loans are awarded by colleges on a first-come, first-served basis. It's up to the college to determine whether the applicant needs the loan.

While families with income under $30,000 usually are given preference, many students from wealthier families get these loans if the college likes their academic credentials. The loans are limited to $3,000 per year. Interest: Only 5%. Interest payments are deferred until after graduation, and the loan can be repaid over 10 years.

• Guaranteed Student Loans of up to $2,500 per year at 8% are generally made to students of families with income under $30,000.

Loophole: Families with higher income may still qualify by asking the college to calculate the need for aid with what's called the lookup table. That's federal jargon for a method of calculating how much a family can afford for college (a family with three children and $75,000 in annual income, for example, is considered able to contribute $14,160 per year to college).

If that amount is less than the cost of the student's education, including tuition, room, board, and transportation, the student is eligible for a guaranteed student loan. Since the cost of higher education is climbing at a rapid rate, more and more families are eligible.

Using the lookup table disqualifies the student from receiving a National Direct Student Loan.

Alternative: If you want to remain eligible for a Student Direct Loan as well, ask the college to calculate your need using the so-called uniform methodology instead of the lookup table. This calculates family need on the basis of income and assets.

Though this method disqualifies many families with large real estate or securities holdings, many are getting around this by taking out home equity loans, which reduce the equity value of their homes.

• Parent Loan for Undergraduate Students. Regardless of your income or net worth, you can also apply for a Parent Loan for Undergraduate Students (PLUS). They're available at most local banks at a maximum of $3,000 per year at 12% and can be repaid over 10 years.

Sources: Margaret Miller Welch, CFP, vice president, Alexandra Armstrong Advisors, Inc., 1140 Connecticut Ave. NW, Washington, DC 20036; and Anna Leider, college aid consultant and president, Octameron Press, Box 3437, Alexandria, VA 22302.

Financing Sources for College

Parents who have used up almost every available source of funds to meet their child's college tuition costs (aside from mortgaging the house and taking a part-time job) have several last-ditch alternatives to look into:

• Parent loan program, known officially as Parent Loans for Undergraduate Students (PLUS). This government-funded resource allows parents to borrow up to $3,000 a year, to a total of $15,000, for each child. The interest rate charged on the loan is below market. Repayment begins within 60 days after the funds have been released. Payments can extend for up to 10 years. Loans are made on the basis of the parents' ability to repay the loan, not on the basis of financial need.

• Unsubsidized bank loans. Many banks and credit unions offer special educational loan programs that charge interest rates generally 1%–2% below prevailing commercial rates. Financing schedules are five to 10 years longer than traditional consumer loans (specifics differ from institution to institution). As in the PLUS program, loans are made to parents rather than to students, and eligibility is based on ability to pay, not on financial need. Variation: A line of credit on which checks can be written directly to the college. Advantage: Interest is charged only when checks are written.

• Combination savings/loan plans. Many banks "leverage" or multiply the balance of a savings account as a way of providing a line of credit at prevailing market rates of interest (minimum balance amounts vary by program). Advantage: The interest on the savings offsets the interest on the loan.

• College-sponsored financing programs. Some colleges now allow parents to stretch their tuition payments over periods as long as 30 years, while charging interest and service fees similar to those of other financing arrangements. Drawback: Because of interest, insurance, and service costs, most families will spend more money than if they paid the tuition outright. Look for programs financed by the colleges themselves (as opposed to commercial banks). These frequently are offered at rates 1%–2% below prevailing market rates.

• Insured tuition plans. Some insurance companies offer a budgeting program in which parents make monthly payments to the company. Payments are based on the child's tuition. In exchange, the company pays the tuition bill each semester and guarantees that the tuition will continue to be paid in the event of a parent's death. These programs are usually accompanied by short-term low-interest loans to make up for any shortfalls the parents may encounter in making payments.

Source: Kathleen Brouder, author of *The College Cost Book, 1986–1987,* The College Board, New York.

Tuition Tactics—It Pays To Be a Resident

Becoming a resident: Students who attend a state college or university outside their home state pay much higher tuition than do residents of that state. In addition, nonresidents do not have access to statewide scholarship and student aid programs.

However, the Supreme Court has ruled that although state colleges and universities can charge nonresidents higher tuition, those students must be allowed to earn residency status during the period of their enrollment.

Public institutions are subsidized by the tax dollars of the citizens of the state. Substantial tuition income is lost when out-of-state students become entitled to lower resident tuition. Therefore, the process is strictly regulated—and requirements are becoming more stringent. For instance, the University of California added to its simple requirement of a year's residence in the state the stipulation that a student also must prove financial independence.

Although requirements for residency vary from state to state, most follow similar patterns. All states, for example, require continuous residence for a period of time immediately preceding application—usually one year, but as little as six months in a few states.

Some states require evidence that the student intends to become a permanent resident of the state. However, the emphasis placed on this factor varies greatly. In some states, such as New York, no such requirement exists. In others, the application forms are designed to elicit such information indirectly.

When a nonresident student enrolls, the institution assumes that he is there for educational purposes rather than for a permanent change of residence. Therefore, the burden of proof is on the student to prove desire to become a bona fide resident.

Basic questions a residency applicant is asked:

• Have you filed an income tax return in the state?

• Are you dependent on your parents for support, or are you financially independent?

• Have you registered and voted in the state?

• Do you have a driver's license or car registration in the state?

• Do you have a record of employment in the state? (Students who are seeking financial aid are expected to earn some money through summer and part-time employment.)

College-Aid Update

Five federal programs pay billions of dollars in aid to qualified students. All students must demonstrate financial need as dependents (under 24 years of age) or independents (self-supporting and/or 24 years or older). Graduate or professional students are automatically considered independents. The programs:

• Pell Grants provide up to $2,100 per year to undergraduates, based on financial need.

• Supplemental Educational Opportunity Grants, also limited to undergraduates, pay up to $4,000 per year, but normally colleges don't pay more than $2,000 per year to each student. (Since each school gets a limited amount of SEOG money, it's important to meet the college's deadline.)

• College Work-Study provides part-time jobs (either on campus or for a nonprofit organization) for needy undergraduate and graduate students.

• Perkims Loans (formerly National Direct Student Loans) charges only 5% interest, with payment beginning six months after the student is no longer attending at least as a half-time student. Undergraduates can borrow up to a total of $4,500 for the first two years and $9,000 for the remainder of undergraduate school (not to exceed $3,500). Graduate and professional students can borrow up to $18,000 (including money borrowed for undergraduate studies).

• Guaranteed Student Loans are made by

private lenders and insured by the government. Interest rates are 8% for new borrowers. Ceilings: For undergraduates $2,625 per year for the first two years of study and $4,000 per year for the remainder. Maximum for undergraduates: $17,250. For graduate students the ceiling is $7,500 per year, and the maximum $54,750.

Source: Dr. Herm Davis, National College Services, Ltd., 16220 S. Frederick Rd. Suite 210, Gaithersburg, MD 20877.

How To Send Children to College Without Sending Yourself to the Poorhouse

The cost of a college education in 2004 for a child born in 1986 will range from $100,000 at a state school to more than $240,000 at an elite private college.

To help families cope with the projected annual increase in college costs, many schools now have programs that enable parents to start paying while future students are still infants. Others have loan and aid plans to make education possible for those who otherwise couldn't attend.

The newest development on the college financing scene is the tuition future. How it works: For a child born this year who'll attend college in 18 years, parents make a one-time investment with a school in the expectation that when the child is 18, that's where he'll go to school. That one-time investment, compounded over time, pays for all four years of college. The younger the child's age when you make the investment, the less you'll have to pay.

Traps: No one has examined the tax implications. . .How will the investment—and earnings on the investment—be taxed?. . .Who's liable for taxes, the donor or the college?. . . What happens if, 18 years after the investment is made, the child decides not to attend that

school?. . .What if the child wants to attend but doesn't meet the school's academic requirements?. . .And from the college's point of view, does accepting the investment mean that the student's been accepted "sight unseen."

Other innovations: Private colleges that make up the difference between the costs of attending the private college and the cost of a state school (Bard College, Annandale-on-Hudson, NY, makes the offer to applicants in the top 10% of their high school class). . .Tuition prepayment, where freshmen lock in prices by paying for their second, third, and fourth years at the beginning of freshman year.

Source: R. Jerold Gibson, president, and Gayle Speck, vice president, Pacesetter, an educational financial planning service, 73 Trapelo Rd., Box 78, Belmont, MA 02178. In addition to his work in fiscal services at Harvard, Mr. Gibson has also served as financial aid consultant to the US Department of Education.

Uncle Sam Helps Pay the Way

The IRS shares part of your tuition bill by allowing you to take tax deductions for certain payments. . .

Expenses for money borrowed to pay your child's tuition. Because of the new tax law, interest paid on educational loans is only partially deductible in 1987 and will not be deductible at all after 1990.

What to do: Consider restructuring your loans. Instead of taking out a student loan, you could remortgage your residence and use the proceeds to pay for the education. This converts the soon-to-be-nondeductible interest into fully deductible mortgage interest. Reason: Interest on a mortgage secured by your personal residence plus one second home will remain fully deductible under new tax laws.

Fine points: You cannot remortgage the house for an amount greater than its present fair market value. With that overall limitation, you are allowed to deduct interest expense for a mortgage of an amount up to:

- The original cost of your home, plus
- The cost of any improvements you've made over the years, plus
- The amount used for medical and educational expenses within a reasonable time before or after you receive the loan proceeds.

Housing expenses for college students. Instead of paying for housing for your child at college, purchase an off-campus house or apartment. There are two different ways to treat the house for tax purposes:

- Treat the house as a second home. Under the new tax law, you can deduct interest paid on a mortgage on your principal home plus one second home. Advantages: Your child will get a free place to live. You'll get mortgage and property-tax deductions against your regular income. By the time your child finishes school, the house may well have appreciated in value, and you will gain on the sale.
- Treat the house as rental property. The rules here are very complex. You must charge your child and your child's housemates a fair market rent, and you must actively manage the house yourself. Advantages: You can deduct maintenance, utilities, depreciation, property taxes, etc., from the rental income. If you end up with a net loss, you can use it to offset your salary, dividend, interest, and capital-gain income. Limit: You can deduct up to $25,000 of loss if your adjusted gross income (AGI) is $100,000 or less. The $25,000 maximum deduction is phased out if your AGI is between $100,001 and $150,000.

Expenses for nursery-school tuition and day care. The child-care credit is available when both spouses work and the children go to nursery school or day care or are cared for at home by household help. In some special cases a married couple can take the credit when only one spouse works:

- The nonworking spouse is a full-time student for five months of the year.
- The nonworking spouse is physically or mentally unable to care for himself or herself.

Generally, the higher your AGI, the lower your child-care credit. The calculations are based on your qualifying expenses plus AGI.

Tax-free dependent care. Up to $5,000 paid by your employer for care of your dependents while you work needn't be included in income. Your employer must have a qualified dependent-care-assistance program.

Expenses for special schooling. Expenses of sending a physically or mentally handicapped child to a special school that has the resources to ameliorate the handicap can qualify as medical-expense deductions. Deductible items: Tuition, related expenses such as transportation to and from the school, and meals and lodging if the child lives there.

Combined child-care plus special-school expenses. Sometimes the same expenses for special schooling qualify for both a medical expense and the child-care credit. You can't use the same expenses to take both. However, if you use only part of your expenses to get the maximum child-care credit, you can apply the unused expenses to your medical deduction. Or you may apply the whole expense toward your medical deduction. Generally, if you have low medical expenses, you will get the lowest tax bill by applying the expenses to your child-care credit first. Recommended: Figure out your taxes both ways to see which is more beneficial for you.

Adult education expenses. You can deduct tuition, books, supplies, and fees when you take courses to maintain or improve your present job skills or because they are required by your employer to keep your job. Transportation expenses, including parking and tolls, are deductible if you commute to school directly after work.

Important tax reform limit: These expenses are categorized as miscellaneous itemized deductions by the new tax law. Your total miscellaneous expenses are deductible only to the extent that they exceed 2% of your AGI.

Tax-free education. Up to $5,250 of expenses paid by your employer for educational expenses needn't be included in your taxable income. Your employer must have a qualified educational-assistance program. Of course, if your employer pays your tuition bill, you may not deduct the same items on your tax return.

Source: Pamela J. Pecarich, partner, and Jeffrey S. Hillier and Steven M. Woolf, tax managers, Coopers & Lybrand National Tax Services, 1800 M St. NW, Washington, DC 20036.

Tax Trap for Scholarship Winners

Under tax reform, scholarships are tax free only to the extent they're used for tuition, fees, books, course materials, supplies, and other items directly connected to their education. Any amounts given for room, board, and personal expenses are taxable. For students who aren't candidates for college degrees, all scholarships and fellowships are fully taxable.

Record keeping: Students should keep records and receipts for all money spent on tuition, university fees, books, school supplies, and the like. It's up to the student to prove how much of the scholarship went for these purposes and how much, if any, for personal living expenses.

Another trap: If the student is required to perform any services (teaching—for instance) as a condition of receiving the scholarship, some or all of the grant is regarded as taxable compensation.

Source: Richard Shapiro, National Director of Taxes, Oppenheim, Appel, Dixon & Co., CPAs, 1 New York Plaza, New York 10004.

Obvious... and Less Obvious Ways To Get Money for College

Most parents overlook the largest—and least-used—source of college money: Their own employers and companies that operate where they live. In 1986, almost $8 billion in college scholarships and low-cost loans was available to employees and their children. And...75% of it wasn't claimed.

Other Sources

• Athletic scholarships are an enormously overlooked source of funds. You don't have to be a potential Big Ten halfback to be eligible. For example, 900 schools offer women's tennis scholarships, and about 5,000 students will reap the benefits. You needn't be a top player, either. Just be a good player who's academically qualified to attend a particular school. There are also about 5,000 women's volleyball scholarships available.

Helpful: Scholarships in these and less-popular sports—badminton, crew, fencing, riflery, skiing, squash, and water polo—exist because of the law that requires schools with football scholarships to offer scholarships in other sports...with equal amounts of money going to both men and women.

If no one applies for a scholarship in a less popular sport, colleges can claim the unused funds for their football programs.

• Private foundations can be rich sources of college funds, but they hate to give money to people who haven't "done their homework" on the foundation, and they are known to reject applicants for what appear to be petty reasons.

• Parents and students can trade their creative or entrepreneurial skills for college money.

Possibilities: If you're in advertising, try donating ideas for an ad campaign that would attract more students to the school... in exchange for tuition. Or work as an unpaid recruiter or interviewer.

Public relations people may be able to write press releases for the school's alumni association that would make alumni reach for their checkbooks. One golf pro sends his son to college by coaching the school's golf team.

Keys to using this strategy: Make your offer to trade your services for tuition as palatable as possible to the school. Keep in mind that schools hate for their willingness to barter to become public information. If you manage to strike a deal, keep quiet about it.

• Armed forces. Money is available to veterans, those who haven't yet served, and those currently in the uniformed services. But you must give the military something in return—a commitment to serve full- or part-time for a specified period of time. Check for specific details with military academies, service academies, ROTC programs, the National Guard, and Reserves.

The military also offers special programs for

247

health science specialists—doctors, nurses, medics, and technicians. Army and Navy ROTC also have college money available for people enrolled in affiliated nursing schools.

For civilians with military relatives, several programs have been developed to help pay college costs . . . without requiring a term of service.

- Big business. Several companies offer money to people other than employees. Examples: Avon, Food Fair Stores, Gannett, Gemco.

As a Last Resort

Be outrageous. There are plenty of super-rich people out there. Most are well insulated from financial requests, but every once in a while one slips through. Whether because of the creativity of the approach or the worthiness of the need, purse strings have been known to be loosened. Cost to you: Time, energy, a little money. . .and perhaps some ego damage. Resource: The 400 richest people in America, whose names are published yearly by *Forbes* magazine.

Source: John Bear, PhD, author of *Finding Money for College,* Ten Speed Press, Berkeley, CA. He has spent more than 10 years reviewing virtually every source of scholarships and grants available in the US.

Quirky Scholarship Qualifications

Special scholarships have been endowed for an amazing variety of student interests and circumstances. Here are just a few samples of special grants. (Some have never been claimed, and amounts of money vary.)

- Children of glassblowers.
- Students interested in the study of fungi, speleology (cave-related research), horticulture, funeral direction, or wine-making.
- Rhode Island students studying Italian.
- Female helicopter pilots.
- Texas students who want to study and live in Sweden.
- Children of Jewish war veterans.

- Students who have roped calves in a rodeo.
- Former golf caddies in New Jersey.
- Students involved in dog breeding and shows.
- Indiana high school seniors dedicated to the ideals of Dwight D. Eisenhower.
- Harvard students whose last name is Anderson, Baxendale, Borden, Bright, Downer, Haven, Murphy, or Pennoyer.
- Eventual students at the Rochester Institute of Technology who were born on June 17, 1979 (its 150th anniversary).

Special Scholarship Opportunities for Being Special

If your child is a left-hander planning to attend Juniata College in Pennsylvania, or a bagpiper headed toward Hamilton College in New York, a scholarship may be just an inquiry away.

Grants for students with quirky talents or particular names are numerous. They make up a sizable portion of the $15 billion in grant money logged in by scholarship search services, ranging from a flat $500 gift to full tuition payments for four years. Funded by both private and college sources, they may or may not be limited to a particular campus.

Exciting as they may sound, these scholarships should not be a student's first priority in the search for college financing. The primary resource for any student should be the financial aid office of his or her school. College financial aid officers have a responsibility to help students locate and qualify for government and college loans and grants, including scholarships that might apply to that particular school. Many colleges have athletic scholarships, for example, and some have reinstituted merit scholarships. . .though in a small way. Point: Don't limit your child's choice of colleges simply because of cost. Scholarship money is available to a wide range of students with varying talents and incomes. Some private colleges have larger endowments with which to aid students than most of the public universities can offer.

After the family has studied the college's financial aid package, it might want to try tracking down additional help through special scholarships. Your local community can be helpful. A parent's employer or social organization often sponsors scholarships, and more and more grant dollars are being awarded through high schools to college-bound seniors.

It's important to do your homework in the search for scholarships. Look at the financial aid section of college catalogs in your local library. Also check the library's scholarship listings (a collection of notices, pamphlets, and other materials) and how-to-find-financial-aid manuals. High school guidance counselors also should be able to provide materials.

Another useful tool is a scholarship search service. Most require a detailed application. Going on the information you provide, they send you a relevant listing of which scholarships you may qualify for. Scholarship listings are constantly updated, and the good services provide counseling and suggestions for applying. Fees run $35–$50. The best services do your research for you, but they make no guarantees of success. The worst ones can be just a waste of your money. The two that are by far the biggest, most trusted, and best-known are the National Scholarship Research Service and the Scholarship Search Service.

Since the massive federal cutbacks in aid for higher education, the trend in federal money has shifted toward loans and away from true grants. The private and business sectors are becoming the best sources of untapped scholarship aid. With diligence and research, almost any college freshman can get some private-sector scholarship help.

Sources: Mary Armbruster, director of financial aid, Sarah Lawrence College, Bronxville, NY 10708; Joseph D. Gargiulo, National Scholarship Research Service, Box 2516, San Rafael, CA 94912; and Mary Ann Maxin, Scholarship Search Service, 407 State St., Santa Barbara, CA 93101.

Best Way To Find a Scholarship

Computer search services claim they match qualified students to available scholarships. Problem: The data provided by these services (at $20–$50) are usually outdated, overly general, or inadequate, according to the National College Board. Better: A visit to a competent high school counselor or a college financial-aid office.

Where To Look for Money

Basic services:
• College Student Financial Aid Services, Shady Grove Rd. and Route 355, 16220 S. Frederick Rd., Suite 208, Gaithersburg, MD 20877, 301-258-0717.
• College Selection Service, c/o Peterson's Guides, Box 2123, Princeton, NJ 08540, 609-924-5338.
• College Scholarship Service, College Entrance Examination Board, 45 Columbus Ave., New York 10023-6917.
• National Scholarship Research Service, 122 Alto St., San Raphael, CA 94901, 415-456-1577.

Each of these services charges a price ($35–$50) for reports or printouts that attempt to match you with useful funding sources.

Family of military:
• Army Emergency Relief Assistance Program. Loans and scholarships for needy, unmarried dependent children of current or former members of the Army. Department of the Army, 200 Stovall St., Alexandria, VA 22332.
• Air Force Aid Society. Low-interest loans to children of Air Force personnel. General Arnold Student Loan Program, 1735 N. Lynn, Rm. 202, Arlington, VA 22209.
• The Navy Relief Society. Loans for unmarried, dependent children of present or former

Navy or Marine personnel. 801 N. Randolph St., Suite 1228, Arlington, VA 22203.

• Retired Officers Association, for children and wards of present or former officers in any of the uniformed services. Funds are awarded only after the applicant has shown that all other sources have been investigated. 201 N. Washington St., Alexandria, VA 22314.

Low-Cost High-Performance Colleges

Having smart children has never been more expensive. Cutbacks in federal financial aid add to the problem . . . now few families earning over $30,000 a year are eligible for grants. Although many of the best schools devise combinations of loans and grants that make it possible for everyone they accept to attend, the payback hardships are considerable. Students may be distracted by jobs while in school, and they often graduate with debts that will burden them for years.

Solution: Inexpensive colleges with high standards. They have the prestige to attract an excellent student body, they are highly regarded by employers and their alumni turn up in *Who's Who in America* with the same frequency as graduates of more expensive schools. Best:

• Cooper Union for the Advancement of Science and Art, New York. An extraordinary private school of art, engineering, and architecture. Its engineering programs match those of MIT and Caltech in quality of instruction and students, and because of its endowment it charges no tuition. Extremely competitive, it accepts only 10% of applicants in art and architecture and 25% in engineering.

• Georgia Institute of Technology, Atlanta. One of the best state-sponsored engineering schools in the country. Academic standards are very high.

• University of California, Berkeley. One of the toughest public universities to get into. Its social prestige ranks with that of Stanford. Of accepted applicants, 87% are in the top fifth of their high school class. Undergraduate classes are large, but the faculty is world-class, especially in business management, ethnic studies, and cinema. Unusual majors include Dutch studies and Southeast Asian studies.

• University of Colorado, Boulder. Unique in that it draws students almost equally from the East Coast and the West Coast. It's strong in liberal arts and sciences . . . and unbeatable in parks and recreation and in other outdoor subjects. Of accepted applicants, 95% are in the top half of their high school class. The setting is astonishingly beautiful, and then, of course, there's the skiing.

• University of Illinois, Urbana-Champaign. Very big and very good. The library is the third-largest on the continent, and a mind-boggling variety of majors is available. Instruction is excellent in engineering, sciences, and other professional subjects.

• University of Michigan, Ann Arbor. It retains old ties to the Eastern elite (its football team used to play in the Ivy League, and the faculty maintains strong Ivy connections) but is supported by the state. UM offers more than 150 majors, most of them very strong, and some of them (such as creative writing) superb.

• University of North Carolina, Chapel Hill. A great old state university in a region that until recently has been overlooked by college applicants. Especially strong: Liberal arts and social sciences. Twelve and a half percent of nonresident applicants and 55% of resident applicants are admitted.

• University of New Hampshire, Durham, NH. A beautiful small-town campus in the heart of New England, UNH is a comprehensive university, offering majors in more than 95 fields. It far outranks neighboring Bennington in terms of alumni achievement.

• University of Texas, Austin. One of the biggest institutions of higher learning in the country . . . and certainly the one with the biggest budget. If it's possible to buy academic quality, UT has done it. The facilities are lavish, and the faculty has been improved significantly in recent years, thanks to the huge endowment. Academic emphasis is prevocational.

• University of Virginia, Charlottesville. Stunning grounds with historic buildings designed by Thomas Jefferson, a comprehensive range of excellent academic programs and prestige that trails only those of Harvard, Yale, Princeton, and the University of Pennsylvania . . . at less than half the cost. For all practical purposes, UVA is the peer of any school in the country. It rejects 75% of all applicants . . . a higher percentage from out of state.

Source: Gene Hawes, author of *The College Board Guide to Going to College while Working,* College Entrance Examination Board, New York.

Nontraditional College Degrees

Although a college degree is a valuable commodity, it does not come cheap. Additional problem: The years of full-time study that a person in mid-career generally can't afford.

Alternative: Nontraditional-degree programs earned entirely off campus, at your own pace—and at less than half the cost of traditional degrees.

Many of these programs are offered by major accredited universities. Many others are unaccredited (and even cheaper) but perfectly legitimate. They are accepted by hundreds of companies as credentials for hiring, promotions, or raises.

To make sure you're not dealing with a diploma mill, you can investigate an unaccredited program with the state's education department. It's unlikely that a completely phony school will have a state license. Request a list of alumni in your area, and check on their experiences. Obtain a detailed list of faculty—if most or all of them received their doctorates from the unaccredited school in question, it's a bad sign. Don't depend on unofficial reference books—one major publi-

cation listed an Arkansas "university" whose proprietor was in prison for selling fake medical degrees.

Bottom line: If it looks too good to be true (it promises a doctorate next week for $400), it probably is.

Routes to a Nontraditional Bachelor's Degree

• Earning credit by exam . . . through the College Level Examination Program (CLEP) or the Proficiency Examination Program (PEP). Many of these are one-hour, multiple-choice tests in a wide variety of fields. You can't fail, as such. Your score (from 200 to 800) earns so many credits, depending on a given college's standards. Many people have taken five of these tests in one day and earned 30 credits—the equivalent of one year in school. You could conceivably get a bachelor's degree in one month. Cost: $50–$70 per exam, with heavy discounting if you take more than one the same day.

• Credit for life experience. Literally thousands of skills people may take for granted are worth credit, from fluency in French to Army jeep repair.

• Credit for business experience. Here you need to demonstrate mastery of skills ranging from finance, marketing, and employee relations to typing and computer skills. Many corporate programs (from one-day seminars on up) earn automatic credit on the directory of the American Council on Education. If you developed these skills less formally, however, you may be able to get credit through a life-experience portfolio. Aside from the standard resume, this will include detailed letters from co-workers or internal reports that confirm your mastery.

• Credit through interview. Let's say your area of expertise is marketing in the Middle East. The school invites you in for two to three hours of discussion with two professors in the field. These experts will then decide how much your knowledge is worth (usually from five to 75 credits). Cost: $400–$500 per interview.

• Traditional correspondence classes. These are worth two to six credits each. In some cases

251

you can get full credit merely by passing the final exam. Cost: About $25 per credit.

You can mix credits from several sources to earn your degree. Two particularly flexible schools are the University of the State of New York (based in Albany) and Edison State College (Trenton, NJ). They have no campus, faculty, or classes. But they evaluate work done elsewhere, administer exams and interviews, and award fully accredited degrees. Cost: About $200 for the paperwork.

Graduate Work

Advanced degrees aren't much more difficult to obtain. Major difference: You must demonstrate the ability to do original work in your field. But this need not be a traditional academic thesis, and some schools allow submission of previously completed projects. One businessman earned his MBA with a 150-page report on whether his company should build a factory in South America. An author could submit a novel . . . a psychologist, some case histories.

Some schools require a limited residency. At Syracuse University, MBA students attend three eight-day summer seminars a year apart to plan and monitor their programs. Other outstanding nonresidential master's programs: Beacon College (Washington, DC), Empire State College (NY), and California State University. Cost: $5,000–$7,000 for an accredited degree and $2,500–$3,000 for an unaccredited degree. (Recommendation: Make sure a degree from an unaccredited school is acceptable to your company before you enroll.)

If you're aiming for a nonresidential PhD, it's often possible to skip the master's or to obtain a combined degree. The requirements are similar, although some schools demand an internship—about 50 hours of real-life experience in a business or agency unrelated to your own.

The best nontraditional PhD programs: Union Graduate School (Cincinnati, OH) and Nova University (Fort Lauderdale, FL). Foreign schools that enroll Americans: The University of London and the University of South Africa–Pretoria. Cost: $8,000–$11,000 for an ac-

credited doctorate and half that for an unaccredited degree.

Source: John Bear, author of *Bear's Guide to Nontraditional College Degrees* (new edition), Ten Speed Press, Berkeley, CA.

Better Than Summer Jobs . . . Summer Businesses

With college costs rising and the summer job market tightening, many students turn to their own resources to earn a buck. In the process, a number of the traditional avenues for self-employment—baby-sitting, tutoring, teaching a sport or a musical instrument, triming shrubs, mowing lawns—are widening into much more imaginative and lucrative small enterprises.

Samples of Summer Projects That Pay

• Two enterprising young men came up with a unique way to market clams to vacationing families. Instead of just digging clams and selling them by the bucketful, they offered to deliver cleaned, opened clams with a dish of cocktail sauce at the exact time the buyers wanted to serve them.

• Two young women stuck in the city for the summer came up with an inexpensive gourmet lunch to sell from street carts to busy office workers and tourists who wanted an al fresco break. They worked out recipes for three cold soups that could be sold with breadsticks for $1.50 a serving. They did the shopping and cooking themselves, rented three carts and hired other students to man the carts for 30% of what they sold.

• A student who had worked as a ticket seller for the Martha's Vineyard ferry noticed that newcomers to the island had a real problem figuring out where they wanted to go. He started a package bus-tour service to both Martha's Vineyard and Nantucket that attracted 5,000 people the first summer.

How To Get an Enterprise Started

• Think about services that are missing in your community. The first step is to consider what people in your town need. Students have been very successful with catering hors d'oeuvres and supplying bartenders and clean-up crews for parties in many areas. Organizing interesting field trips for young children to local museums, parks, or historic landmarks is a more lucrative variation on baby-sitting. Putting together food, games, and entertainment for children's birthday parties is a similar project that succeeds in some towns. Student cleaning services that include washing windows and scrubbing floors and student house-painting teams are often profitable with a minimum of investment. Shopping services can work in a community with a large population of older people without cars.

• Get professional help. Some communities have an executive volunteer corps manned by retired businesspeople who can help youngsters work out proper business plans and accounting procedures.

• Work from strengths. A stereo nut with good equipment and a thorough knowledge of the latest music can hire himself out as a disc jockey for parties, tailoring the music to the hosts' preferences. Youngsters who are particularly good with animals could organize a pet-care service for vacationers or a dog-training service for working couples.

Student summer entrepreneurs often find hidden talents for business that can help them make money during the school year. Or they may discover some talents or personality traits that will help in career choices. A successful summer enterprise earns a student special self-confidence as well as money.

9 RETIREMENT PLANNING

Arithmetic To Do Before You Retire

How to size up your financial situation:

1. List your assets. Include income-producing assets (stocks, bonds, annuity-generating insurance policies, real estate, company profit-sharing plans), plus non-income-producing assets (paid-up life insurance, furniture, and household goods), and assets that require expenditures for maintenance (houses, cars, etc.). Estimate total dollar value, factoring in appreciation.

2. Figure out postretirement income. Add up income from assets, pensions, and Social Security.

3. Calculate postretirement expenses, then deduct costs stemming from work (commuting, clothes). Next add on the cost of benefits (health insurance) that will no longer be covered by an employer. Estimate an annual dollar figure. Factor in inflation rate.

4. If postretirement expenses outstrip postretirement income, develop a plan for liquidating assets. Rule of thumb: The percentage of total capital that a retired person may spend annually begins at 5% at age 65, and increases by 1% every five years. At age 80, it is 10%.

Bottom line: Only those whose postretirement expenses still outstrip total income at this point will have to cut back. Generally, retired people need 75% of their preretirement, after-tax income to maintain their present standard of living.

Formulas To Use in Retirement Planning

One of the great tragedies in America today is most people's lack of adequate retirement planning. Out of every 100 people who retire, three are financially independent, 27 must continue to work to maintain their standard of living, and 70 remain dependent on family and social welfare to exist. In addition, the Social Security system reports that 85% of all

Americans reaching age 65 do not have as much as $250 in personal savings.

The main reason for this problem is simple—lack of planning. People often forget that their prime earning years, between 30 and 60, should be spent not only earning enough income to support themselves and their families, but also accumulating enough funds to live from age 60 to 90. My first and most important piece of advice: Don't wait until you're 65 to start thinking about what you will realistically need for retirement.

The first planning step is to determine the three major factors for your future retirement —present resources, income needs at retirement, and income resources from investment assets and other sources when you have retired. The goal of any retirement plan is to accumulate as large a fund of investment dollars as possible, with the ultimate goal of reallocating those funds into a mix of assets that will provide you with a steady income and some growth potential. In all scenarios, inflation will be your worst enemy. (At 7% inflation, prices double every 10 years.) To protect yourself against inflation, invest a portion of your retirement funds in growth assets. The majority of your funds, however, should be invested in secure income assets to provide a reliable income base. Expect your retirement needs to be approximately 85% of your present working gross income.

The following formulas and example illustrate how to determine what you should set aside each year to maintain a satisfactory lifestyle during retirement.

Retirement Worksheet

Note: You will need access to a business or scientific calculator, a personal computer, or present value of annuity tables in order to complete this worksheet.

Assumptions:
You will retire in ___10___ years from now.

You will require $*100,000* per year for *22* years after retirement.

You now earn $*200,000* gross pretax income.

Step 1
Gather all financial data. Establish balance sheet, cash flow needs, and rough tax analysis (for the current year).

Step 2
Determine assets available:
  a) Cash/cash equivalents $*50,000*

    Invested assets at fair market value
    Certificates of deposit $*60,000*
    Treasury notes $*20,000*
    Stocks $*70,000*
    Real estate $*300,000*
    Total (a) $*500,000*

  b) Investment debt $___*0*___
    Bequests $*200,000*
    Other $___*0*___
    Total (b) $*200,000*

  c) Total available assets
    (2a – 2b) $*300,000*

Step 3
Determine the future value of available assets: (What your assets will be worth at retirement)

  a) Total from Step 2(c) $*300,000*

  b) Future value (FV) calculation
    Number (n) periods (years)
    until retirement *10*
    Rate of return (i) after tax *6* %
    Future value factor $(1+i\%/100)^{n}$
        $(1+.06)^{10} = 1.791$

  c) Multiply 3(a) by future value factor to determine value of available assets at retirement
    Future value of assets at retirement
    FV: ($*300,000 \times 1.791*$) = $*537,300*

Step 4
Estimate retirement income fund:
  a) Annual income needs during
    retirement $*100,000*

  b) Expected Social Security and other retirement
    benefits and income from
    other resources $*60,000*
  c) Net income needs during

retirement—subtract 4(b)
from 4(a) $40,000

d) Income adjustment for
inflation
Number (n) periods (years)
until retirement _10_
Rate of inflation (r) _5_ %
Future value factor $(1+r\%/100)^n$

$$(1.05)^{10} = 1.629$$

Multiply 4(c) by future value
factor to determine annual
income needs during retirement adjusted for inflation

$$(40,000 \times 1.629) = \quad \$65,160$$

e) Retirement fund needed
Number (n) of periods (years)
of retirement assumed _22_
Rate of return (i) after tax _6_ %
Rate of inflation (r) _5_ %
Annual income after retire-
ment—Payment (PMT) $65,160
Calculate the lump sum
needed at retirement to
provide PMT over n years:
Adjusted interest factor—
$[\frac{(1 + i\%/100)}{(1 + r\%/100)} - 1] = f$

$$\left[\frac{1.06}{1.05} - 1\right] \qquad f = 0.00952$$

Lump sum $= PMT \times (1+f) \times [\frac{1-(1+f)^{-n}}{f}]$
Lump sum =

$$65,160 \times (1.00952) \times \left[\frac{1-(1.00952)^{-22}}{.00952}\right]$$
$$= \$1,300,100$$
(rounded)

Step 5
Amount needed for emergency fund at
retirement
a) Emergency fund needed in
today's dollars $20,000
b) Future value calculation
Number (n) of periods (years)
until retirement _10_
Rate of inflation (r) _5_ %
Future value factor $(1+r\%/100)^n$

$$(1.05)^{10} = 1.629$$

Multiply 5(a) by future value
factor to determine future

value of emergency fund
needed at date of retirement
Future value of emergency fund
FV: $(20,000 \times 1.629) = \$32,580$

Step 6
Determine additional savings at retirement:
a) Resources needed
  From Step 4(e) $1,300,100
  From Step 5(b) $32,580
  Total resources needed $1,332,680
b) Resources available
  From Step 3(c) $537,300
c) Subtract 6(b) from 6(a) total
Additional savings needed at
retirement $795,380
d) Deflation calculations
Number (n) of periods
(years) to retirement _10_
Rate of inflation (r) _5_ %

Present value factor $\frac{1}{(1 + \frac{r\%}{100})^n}$

$$\frac{1}{1.05^{10}} = 0.614$$

Multiply additional savings
needed at retirement by present value factor to determine
the savings needed at retirement in today's dollars
Present value of additional
savings needed at retirement

$$(795,380 \times 0.614) = \$488,360$$

Step 7
Determine the amount of money (after tax)
that needs to be saved annually:
a) Savings (S) needed at
retirement from Step 6(d) $488,360
b) Serial savings calculations
Number (n) of periods
(years) to retirement _10_
Rate of return (i) after tax _6_ %
Rate of inflation (r) _5_ %
Calculate the first serial payment to be invested at the
end of the current year:
Adjusted interest factor—
$[\frac{(1 + i\%/100)}{(1 + r\%/100)} - 1] = f$

$$\left[\frac{1.06}{1.05} - 1\right] \qquad f = 0.00952$$

First serial payment—

$$PMT = \frac{S}{\left[\frac{(1+f)^n-1}{f}\right]}$$

$$\frac{488,360}{\frac{(1+0.00952)^{10}-1}{0.00952}}$$ $\underline{\$\,46,780}$

c) Inflation adjustment
   Annual savings required
   from Step 7(b) $\underline{\$\,46,780}$
   Rate of inflation (r) __5__ %
   Multiply annual savings by
   inflation rate (written as
   1 + r%/100)
   Adjusted serial payment
   $\underline{(46,780 \times 1.05)}$ = $\underline{\$\,49,120}$

d) Percent of income needed to be saved
   Annual adjusted savings $\underline{\$\,49,120}$
   Gross income (pretax) $\underline{\$\,200,000}$
   Divide annual adjusted
   savings by gross income
   to determine percent of
   income to be saved
   $\underline{(49,120 \div 200,000)}$= $\underline{24.6\%}$

Source: Paul E. Ferraresi, president of Founders Group, 11 Greenway Plaza, Suite 3030, Houston 77046. Mr. Ferraresi advises individuals and corporations on investment, tax, and estate planning. He is also an instructor and lecturer, as well as the publisher of a national newsletter, *Personal Money Management.*

A Threat to Retirement

Baby boomers have to secure their retirement future now, or they'll be forced to continue working "forever." Companies are offering decreasingly generous pension plans; many people no longer stay at one job long enough to accumulate significant pension benefits; Social Security—burdened by the growing elderly population—is being pared down; Medicare benefits are likely to be trimmed back. Self-defense: Establish a savings and investment plan now to meet current and future needs.

Source: Anna Rappaport of financial consultants William M. Mercer-Meidinger Hansen, Inc., Chicago.

More Social Security Income for Wives

Becoming a partner in her husband's business could boost a woman's ultimate Social Security retirement benefits. As a partner, the woman will have self-employment income. When she reaches retirement, her benefits will be based on that income. This could far exceed the 37½% to 50% of her husband's retirement benefits that she would get if she had no earnings of her own on which to compute her Social Security entitlement.

Source: Dr. Robert S. Holzman, professor emeritus of taxation at New York University and author of *The Encyclopedia of Estate Planning*, published by Boardroom Books.

Checking Up on the SSA

The Social Security payments you receive monthly upon retirement will depend on both the age at which you retire and the dollar amount of earnings credited to your account by the Social Security Administration. Problem: The SSA's records may reflect less than your earnings.

Social Security records should be checked every two years to ensure that the right amounts have been credited. The SSA won't correct errors that are more than three years, three months and 15 days old. Because it takes the SSA about a year to update its records, there's often very little time to check for errors before the deadline passes.

How to do it: Call a Social Security office and ask for a postcard Form 7004 (request for statement of savings). A report of your account will be sent to you about two months after you mail the form.

The service is free. Don't be taken in by companies that offer to obtain your savings records for a fee.

Source: Social Security Administration, 6401 Security Blvd., Baltimore 21207.

Break on IRA Withdrawals

At age 70½, you must begin making withdrawals from your Individual Retirement Accounts. In the past you had to make at least a minimum withdrawal (figured from IRS life expectancy tables) from each of your IRA accounts. Now you can figure the total required withdrawal and take it out of any account or any combination of accounts. (This helps, for example, if you have CDs, some of which may be subject to early-withdrawal penalties.)

Retirement Update: Maximizing Future Wealth

Before tax reform, most people could rely on IRAs and 401(k) plans to supplement their pensions. Now, to build wealth for the retirement years, you must also use other types of safe, income-producing investments.

What's New

Tax reform put big limitations on the amount you can put into tax-sheltered retirement accounts and made it less advantageous to withdraw pension benefits.

Trap: Some people believe that there's no reason to continue contributing to IRAs because they have lost the tax deduction. Fact: The $2,250 contribution that employees with nonworking spouses can make ($2,000 each for two-income couples) can still earn compounded income tax-free until it's withdrawn. That's still a big plus for retirement planning. Recommended:

• If you don't currently have an IRA and don't anticipate needing the money before you're 59 years old, start an IRA now. If you do have one, keep putting the maximum allowable amount in each year.

• Keep accurate records of all contributions you make to your IRA. Because that money no longer is tax-deductible, you'll end up paying taxes on it a second time when you withdraw your IRA funds if you don't show the IRS that you made the contributions after 1986.

401(k) plans: Though the maximum contribution is $7,000, down from $30,000 under the old law, these plans are still a great way to build up tax-deferred savings. If your company offers one, contribute to it. Since 401(k)s are really a type of deferred compensation plan, you get a double bonus by contributing.

How it works: The contributions you make reduce your salary. If you earn $50,000 and contribute $5,000 to a 401(k) plan, you report a salary of $45,000 on your taxes.

Pension Plan Changes

Under the new tax law, unless you turned 50 before January 1, 1986, you're not entitled to use the old law's 10-year income-averaging method of calculating taxes on lump-sum pension payouts. Instead, you're required to use five-year income averaging, which increases the tax bite from withdrawals.

Moreover, if you don't take your pension money in a lump sum upon retirement, but you do take more than $150,000 per year, you're subject to a 15% excise tax on the amount over $150,000 that you withdraw.

Recommended strategy: If you can live comfortably in retirement without your pension money, you'll benefit by keeping the pension funds untouched until age 70½. At that point you're required to start withdrawing your pension. But the longer you leave the funds invested, the more tax-deferred earnings they'll accumulate.

If you do need to draw on your pension fund, consider either taking part of it in a lump sum and rolling over the remainder into your IRA, or taking regular monthly annuity payments from your pension. Either way, you pay taxes only on the amount withdrawn. With the new lower individual tax rates, retirees who take pension withdrawals are better off than they were under the old tax law.

Tax reform also dealt a big blow to high-income individuals who participate in a com-

259

pany's defined-benefit plan. Under the old law you could make tax-deductible contributions to the defined-benefit plan that would give you annual distributions of up to $90,000 per year after age 59½. Now, however, the amount must be actuarially reduced for employees who retire under the plan before reaching age 65.

Shrewd Investments

If your projected retirement income was based on making annual 401(k) contributions of more than $47,000 plus the higher pre-tax-reform income from your pension, now's the time to set aside a portion of take-home pay to make up for the shortfall. Recommendations:

• Real estate. A good way to invest in real estate is to buy rental property. Reasons: Mortgage interest, maintenance expenses, and depreciation are deductible and therefore shelter most of the rental income. If you're planning to retire in a home you haven't bought yet, consider buying it now and renting it out until you're ready to occupy it.

Or look for a multiple-family building in a growing neighborhood. By the time you retire, the sale price of the property may give a profit that makes up a big portion of reduced retirement savings. Income-oriented limited partnerships also may be attractive.

• Variable rate annuities. Fortunately, tax reform hasn't tarnished the beauty of these savings vehicles. You buy an annuity from an insurance company (for as little as $5,000) and specify how you want the money invested. Usually the choices include stock mutual funds. The earnings on your money fluctuate with market conditions. At age 59½ you can start taking money out in regular monthly payments and pay taxes only on the amount withdrawn. (If you take money out before age 59½, the IRS will apply a 10% penalty on the amount withdrawn.)

• Municipal bond mutual funds. Tax reform made these funds ideal for retirement savings. Reason: Tax-exempt municipal bonds are among the few remaining legitimate tax shelters and demand for them is expected to soar.

What not to put retirement money into: Commodity futures, precious metals, and hotel properties. In the past, some investors have made a lot of money from these ventures. But now they're a gamble, with far too much risk to anyone's retirement.

Source: Alexandra Armstrong, president, Alexandra Armstrong Advisors, Inc., financial planners, 1140 Connecticut Ave. NW, Washington, DC 20036.

Investment Alternatives That Deserve a Second Look

Tax-favored retirement investments that are worth considering now:

Commercial annuities and other life insurance company products look more attractive as retirement investments than they did before tax reform.

Advantages:

• You don't pay tax on the income your money earns in an annuity until you begin receiving payments. Part of each payment will be treated as a return of your initial investment, and not taxable, and part will be taxable earnings.

• Unlike IRAs, annuities do not have to be aggregated for withdrawal tax purposes. If you put $2,000 into an annuity contract tomorrow and took the money out the day after, none of it would be taxable since you didn't earn anything on it. (Of course you wouldn't get the full $2,000 back because of fees and penalties, but the full withdrawal would be treated as a return of your own already-taxed investment.)

• An annuity provides a level of retirement security, since the insurance company is guaranteeing to pay you retirement checks— for instance, $X a month for life starting when you're age 65.

Drawbacks to life insurance-type products:

• The insurance company charges a fee. (You don't pay any fees if you put your money in a bank.)

• You'll pay a penalty if you cash in the contract before the annuity payments start.

260

• You may be subject to a tax penalty if you cash in the contract before you reach age 59½.

Single premium life insurance is another of the few remaining investments to provide tax-free accumulation. It comes in several varieties, but basically involves the payment of a single premium up front—usually $5,000. The money is invested and the value of the policy builds up tax-free. Upon the death of the insured, the money goes to the beneficiary free of any income tax. (It may be subject to estate tax.)

Tax-exempt municipal bonds offer an investment opportunity with well-known tax advantages—the income is tax-free, except on certain bonds that are subject to state taxes and/or the alternative minimum tax. Depending on how much risk you want to take, you can get a low or high return on your money.

Zero-coupon bonds: The big advantage of bonds as a retirement investment is that they lock in a fixed, known rate of return. The bonds are issued at a deep discount and redeemed for face value at maturity. You get no interest until the bonds mature (although you have to accrue the interest each year and pay tax on it).

Since you don't actually receive the interest until the bonds mature, you don't have to worry about where to invest the annual earnings, as you would if you bought bonds that paid interest each year.

Risk: If interest rates rise, the market value of zero-coupon bonds falls more than that of ordinary bonds—a problem if you sell the bonds before their maturity.

US Series EE savings bonds earn a minimum of 6% or 85% of the rate paid on five-year Treasury securities—whichever is greater.

Tax benefits:

• Savings bonds are exempt from state and local taxes.

• You can defer paying federal tax on interest until the bonds mature.

• You can defer tax beyond maturity by rolling over matured Series EE bonds into Series HH bonds. Tax on the Series EE interest isn't payable until you redeem the Series HH bonds.

Source: Peter I. Elinsky and Deborah Walker, partners, Peat Marwick Main & Co., 1990 K St. NW, Washington, DC 20006.

How Safe Is Your Pension?

How to check on the safety of your retirement income:

For employees of public companies: Basic information is included in the firm's annual report. Usually the size of a firm's unfunded pension liability and the size of its past service liability are disclosed in footnotes. More detailed information is available in the financial section of the firm's 10K report, filed with the Securities & Exchange Commission.

For employees of private companies: Everyone who is in a qualified plan (one approved by the IRS under the Code) has the right to obtain information about his pension from the trustees of the plan. They may be either internal or external trustees. The average person may not be able to decipher the information. If you can't, then take it to a pension expert, actuary, lawyer, or accountant for an analysis. Cost: $500–$800. Whether you are examining pension information of public or of private firms, you are seeking the same sort of basic information.

Principle: The size of a company's liability for retirement payouts is not as important as the assumptions about funding these liabilities. Like a mortgage, these obligations don't exist 100% in the present. Concern yourself with how the company expects to fund its liabilities.

Types of Liabilities

Unfunded pension liabilities. The amount a firm expects to need over the next 20–30 years to supply vested workers with promised pension benefits. These figures are derived from various actuarial assumptions.

Past service liabilities. Created when a company raises its pension compensation. For instance, a company may have been planning to provide 40% of compensation as a pension. One year it may raise that to 45% and treat it retroactively.

Trouble Signs

A poor record on investing. Compare the market value of the assets in the pension with their book value. If book value is more than market value, the trustees have not been investing wisely. If the fund had to sell those assets today, there would be a loss. You might also get a bit nervous if the fund is still holding some obscure bonds or other fixed-income obligations issued at low rates years ago.

Funding assumptions are overstated. Actuaries have myriad estimates on how long it takes to fund pension plans and what rate of return a company will get. What to look at:

• Time frame: This should not be long. If the firm is funding over 40 years, you will want to know why and how, since 10–20 years is more customary. The investment world will be different in as little as 10 years from now; assumptions made on 40 years may not hold up at all.

• Rate of return: If a company assumes a conservative 6%–7% or less right now, you can be comfortable. If the assumed rate is 10% or more, you will want to know how it is going to meet that expectation for the entire fund over the long run.

• Salary and wage scales: The company should be assuming an increase in compensation over years. Most plans have such provisions. They must start funding now for future salary increases.

• Assumptions about the employee turnover rate: These should be consistent with the historically documented turnover of the company. If a firm has a very low turnover rate and assumes a 4% turnover, the plan will be underfunded at some time. Estimates should be conservative.

To assess your own status in a corporate pension plan, see how many years you have been vested. Many people have the illusion that they are fully vested for maximum pensions after only five years or so. In truth, companies couldn't afford to fully vest people with such short service. They may offer some token pension for such service, but most people are not fully vested until they have worked for the firm for 10 or even 20 years. Even then, they might be vested only to the extent of their accrued pension to date, not the full pension expected at normal retirement. With so much job-hopping in the past two decades, an individual's pension-fund status may be much less than imagined.

Employees of troubled or even bankrupt companies need not panic. Trustees of the plan have an obligation to the vested employees. The assets of the plan are segregated, and no creditor can reach them. In fact, as a creditor, the corporate pension plan can grab some corporate assets under certain circumstances. And if there has been gross mismanagement of pension funds, stockholders of a closely held company can be held personally liable.

Source: James E. Conway, president of Ayco Corporation, a consulting firm specializing in executive finances, 1 Wall St., Albany, NY 12205.

Why 401(k) Plans Are Better Than IRAs

If your employer has a 401(k) plan, take full advantage of it, even if participating in the plan makes you ineligible for deductible IRA contributions. 401(k) plans are better than IRAs. Here's why:

• You can put in more money. The limit is $7,000/year (indexed for inflation). For an IRA, the limit is $2,000 a year or 100% of your pay, whichever is lower.

• Many employers make matching contributions to the plans, the most common being one dollar for every two from the employee up to a prescribed level.

• The plans are managed by professionals, saving you the trouble of handling your own account.

- Contributions to the plan are by payroll deduction, a nearly painless way of saving.
- You can borrow from your account tax-free, if the plan permits. By contrast, borrowing from an IRA is considered a withdrawal, subject to tax.
- You can withdraw money from 401(k) plans for heavy medical expenses, and some of that withdrawal will not be subject to the 10% penalty that is generally imposed on pre-age 59½ withdrawals. This isn't permitted with IRAs.
- You can terminate employment at age 55 and withdraw your 401(k) money without penalty. With an IRA, you have to wait until age 59½ unless you take the money in the form of a life annuity.
- When you finally withdraw your account, if you take it in a lump sum, you may qualify for five-or 10-year averaging, a big tax break not available to IRAs.
- Contributions to a 401(k) plan reduce your adjusted gross income (AGI). This can result in bigger medical, casualty, and miscellaneous deductions, all of which are based on a percentage of your AGI. More: If your AGI is reduced below $40,000 (joint filers) or $25,000 (single), you could participate in the 401(k) and also make deductible IRA contributions.

Source: Frederick W. Rumack, director of tax and legal consulting, Buck Consultants, Inc., a leading pension and employee benefits consulting firm, Two Pennsylvania Plaza, New York 10121.

Keogh Plans: Still Winners

Keogh plans—retirement plans for people with self-employment income—were almost untouched by tax reform. You may still make yearly tax-deductible contributions of up to 20% of self-employment income or $30,000 (whichever is less) to certain defined-contribution plans.

If you're nearing retirement age, you may be able to contribute even more using a defined-benefit plan, which basically allows you to contribute as much as necessary—even if it is virtually all of your self-employment income—to ensure a set income from the plan in retirement. (Check with your tax adviser.)

Complication: If you set up a Keogh plan for yourself, you must also set up one for your employees. Tax reform accelerated the vesting schedules for company retirement plans, including Keoghs. Your employees either must be 100% vested after five years or must gradually vest over seven years, starting after the third year, at 20% annually.

You don't have to be a full-time business owner to qualify for a Keogh. You may contribute up to the deductible limit if you have any self-employment income, including revenue from sideline businesses and freelance and consulting work—just about any income that you report on Schedule C.

Source: Peter J. Elinsky and Deborah Walker, partners, Peat Marwick Main & Co., 1990 K St. NW, Washington, DC 20006.

What to Expect from Your IRA

For years, everyone has been aware of the tax advantages of reducing current income by investing pretax dollars in IRAs and allowing those funds to accumulate, tax-deferred, until retirement. However, not everyone appreciates the vast impact of compounding, a factor that makes these retirement accounts safe vehicles for accumulating wealth.

If tax reform has eliminated your deduction for IRA contributions, investments in an IRA will be made with after-tax dollars, but the effects of compounding will be just as impressive. Of course, if your employer doesn't have a pension plan, you may still fund your IRA with pretax dollars (subject to the annual limits of $2,000 for an individual and $2,250 for a couple that includes a nonworking spouse).

The following charts illustrate the dramatic effect of compounding on IRAs.

Full Annual Contribution: $2,000

Number of years	Rate of return			
	8%	10%	12%	14%
5	$ 11,733	$ 12,210	$ 12,705	$ 13,220
10	28,973	31,874	35,097	38,675
15	54,304	63,544	74,599	87,685
20	91,524	114,550	144,104	182,050
25	146,212	196,694	266,667	363,742
30	226,566	328,988	482,665	713,574

Full Annual Contribution: $2,250

Number of years	Rate of return			
	8%	10%	12%	14%
5	$ 13,201	$ 13,736	$ 14,294	$ 14,873
10	32,596	35,858	39,485	43,508
15	61,092	71,487	83,880	98,645
20	102,965	128,869	162,117	204,806
25	164,489	221,281	299,999	409,208
30	254,887	370,112	542,997	802,766

Source: Geraldine Parrott, a certified financial manager for Stifel, Nicolaus & Co., 615 E. Michigan Ave., Suite 400, Milwaukee, WI 53202.

When Are Contributions Deductible?

Who can make fully deductible contributions:
- All taxpayers not covered by a company pension plan at any time during the year.
- Single taxpayers who are covered by a company pension plan but whose AGI is less than $25,000.
- Married taxpayers who are covered by a company pension plan but whose combined AGI is less than $40,000.

Who can make partially deductible contributions:
- Single taxpayers who are covered by a company pension plan but whose AGI is $25,000–$35,000.
- Married taxpayers who are covered by a company pension plan but whose combined AGI is $40,000–$50,000.

Note: The minimum allowable IRA contribution is $200 per year.

Who can't make any deductible contributions:
- Single taxpayers who are covered by a company pension plan and whose AGI is over $35,000.
- Married couples whose AGI exceeds $50,000, if either spouse is covered by a company pension.

Deductibility Loophole

Say you are covered by a company profit-sharing plan, but the company won't make any contribution to the plan this year because it won't make a profit. Can you make a deductible IRA contribution?

Yes. An individual is not deemed a participant in a profit-sharing plan during a year in which no employer contributions or forfeitures are credited to the individual's account. Thus, if you are not a participant in any other qualified plan, you will be able to make a deductible IRA contribution this year, regardless of the restrictions imposed under tax reform rules.

Correcting a Big Mistake

If you claim an IRA contribution as a deduction on your tax return, then realize that you forgot to actually make the contribution to your IRA, what should you do? File an amended tax return, Form 1040X, for the applicable year, correcting the mistake by omitting the deduction and paying the tax due on the contribution.

You should do this right away, not only to cut off the interest that's running on the underpayment, but also to minimize the risk of incurring tax penalties. If you report the mistake yourself, you will be more likely to avoid penalties for negligence (or fraud) than you will be if the IRS discovers the error on its own. And it probably will discover the mistake eventually, since IRA contributions are reported to the IRS via computer tape by the institutions that receive them.

IRA Strategies after Tax Reform

Under tax reform, you are no longer allowed to make deductible IRA contributions if your adjusted gross income is more than $50,000 ($35,000 if you're single)—and either you or your spouse is covered by a company pension plan or a Keogh plan.

If your AGI is between $40,000 and $50,000 (between $25,000 and $35,000 for single taxpayers), you may make partially deductible contributions. If your income is less or if you and your spouse aren't covered by any retirement plan, you may make fully deductible contributions as before.

Nondeductible Contributions

Even if you are no longer permitted to make deductible contributions, you still may make nondeductible contributions, which grow tax-deferred until withdrawal. The contributions themselves may be withdrawn tax-free, but all earnings taken out are taxed.

Caution: You can't just designate a withdrawal as being made from nondeductible contributions. The new law provides a formula for determining which portion of a withdrawal is taxable and which part is nontaxable:

$$\text{Nontaxable percentage of a withdrawal} = \frac{\text{Total nondeductible contributions}}{\text{Total value of all your IRAs}}$$

Example: Your IRAs are worth $48,000. You make a nondeductible contribution of $2,000. Suppose you then decide to withdraw $1,000. The nontaxable percentage of the withdrawal will be $2,000/$50,000 or only 4%. The remaining 96% will be taxable.

Whether to Contribute

If you're still eligible to make mostly or fully deductible contributions, they're as good an investment as ever. But if you may make only nondeductible contributions, the only advantage of an IRA is tax-deferred growth. The decision to contribute will depend on your complete financial picture and retirement plan, so it's wise to consult with your financial adviser. Two points to take into account:

For younger taxpayers: Nondeductible IRA contributions can be a good investment, because the money will have many years to grow free from taxation. Be cautious, though, if you expect to need cash in the near future—to buy a home, pay for children's education, etc. Taxable IRA withdrawals made before age 59½ are penalized 10%. Because early withdrawals are taxed according to the same formula as regular withdrawals, if accumulated earnings and deductible contributions are substantial, an early withdrawal can be expensive.

For taxpayers closer to retirement: Tax-deferred growth is less valuable. If you already have a sizable IRA, the taxable percentage of any withdrawals will be high. Other investments may be more suitable for retirement funds than nondeductible IRAs.

New IRA Investments

Certain investments that previously were unappealing or illegal for IRAs are now worth considering, thanks to the tax law.

Growth stocks. Long-term capital gains used to qualify for favorable tax treatment not available to IRAs, so most taxpayers would buy growth stocks outside their IRAs and put income-producing securities into their IRAs.

Now, however, tax advantages for long-term capital gains have been repealed, so IRAs have become one of the best ways to shelter long-term gains from growth stocks. If a stock is sold at a profit within an IRA, no tax is incurred on the gain, all of which can be reinvested. (Of course, all gains are eventually taxed at withdrawal.)

Gold and silver. IRAs used to be prohibited from investing in precious metals or collectibles. But the law now permits investment in certain US-issued gold and silver coins. Taxpayers interested in hedging against inflation may want to consider this option.

Source: Deborah Walker, partner, Peat Marwick Main & Co., 1990 K St. NW, Washington, DC 20006.

The Best Ways To Make Your IRA Grow

Don't worry about the taxability of the earnings in your IRA. All growth inside your IRA is tax-deferred, whether or not your original IRA contribution was deductible when you made it. Many people put taxable investments inside their IRAs and keep tax-exempt investments outside their IRAs. Better idea: Choose investments that have the best solid long-term growth, regardless of their tax status.

Decide how much risk you want to take. Choose investments that are very safe or at most have only modest risk. Not recommended: High-risk investments of any kind.

The Best Investment Choices

Mutual funds. These are set up by managers who pool many investors' contributions and invest in 50–150 different stocks or bonds. You share proportionately in the income and gains or losses.

Advantages: You reduce the risk of taking a large loss that could result from putting your entire contribution into one stock or only a few different types of stock. You can invest in a mutual fund that has a higher risk/higher growth potential or in one that invests in conservative common stocks with less fluctuation and risk potential. Or you can choose a combination of the two.

Length of investment: Plan on leaving your IRA in a common-stock mutual fund for at least four years to get the advantage of the long-term growth trend and to reduce the effect of short-term market fluctuations. What to expect: On the average, common-stock investments have grown at a rate 6% better

than the rate of inflation, when measured over a period of many years.

• Self-directed IRAs. With a self-directed IRA you manage your own investments rather than pooling with others and relying on a professional manager.

Caution: Self-directed IRAs are appropriate only for very experienced and knowledgeable investors. Don't even consider a self-directed IRA unless you know how to choose investments or know how to work with a broker—and you or your broker has had a successful track record over a long period of time. However, if you fit into this category and believe in risk taking, the growth potential may be worth it.

• Bank money-market accounts and money-market funds. These are the safest kinds of investments for an IRA and are best for people who don't want to take risks—or shouldn't take risks—because they are near retirement. You earn interest on the money, and your principal is completely protected.

Bank certificates of deposit are longer-term and usually give you a higher interest rate. However, if interest rates go higher than the rate you are earning, and you take the money out of the certificate, you will probably be penalized.

IRAs After Tax Reform

Even if you can't deduct your IRA contribution, you should still make one. Contrary to most people's belief, the benefit of the tax-free compounding in the plan is even more important than getting the tax deduction in the beginning.

Example: A one-time contribution of $2,000 invested at 10% for 20 years outside an IRA with a 28% tax rate will leave $8,034 in your pocket after taxes. Inside an IRA, the same one-time contribution of $2,000 will leave $10,248 after taxes. The figures are even more impressive if you invest for a longer period of time at a better growth rate. If you invest $2,000 outside an IRA at 15% for 30 years, it will yield $43,400. The same money invested inside an IRA will yield $95,900—more than twice as much as the same investment outside an IRA—because of the tax-free compounding.

Source: Arnold Corrigan, vice president, Neuberger & Berman Management, 342 Madison Ave., New York 10173. He is the coauthor (with Phyllis C. Kaufman) of *The No-Nonsense Financial Guide to Understanding IRAs*, published by Longmeadow Press, and author of *How Your IRA Can Make You a Millionaire*, published by Harmony Books.

Picking the Right Stocks for a Retirement Account

Most IRA investors can make the best use of their retirement funds by putting them into stocks, particularly a family of non-load mutual funds. But the volatility of the stock market means that there still are times when an IRA owner should get out of the market to reduce risk.

How do you determine those times? There is a technique for keeping your eye on only two simple indicators—both of which have to be positive to enter or remain in the stock market.

Follow the Prime Rate

The market's major direction depends in large part on the trend in interest rates and in Federal Reserve Board policy.

The prime rate is especially convenient to use as an indicator because it generally doesn't change frequently (less than once a month, on average). And changes in the prime are hard to miss because they always make headline news.

When to take action: If the prime is below 8%, a sell signal occurs on the second of two increases in the prime or on an advance of a full percentage point in the rate.

Tracking the prime in the future:

• If the prime has been climbing but hasn't yet reached 8%, move into stocks at the first drop in the rate.

• If the prime is climbing and is 8% or higher, move into stocks only after two consecutive drops in the rate or a full percentage point drop.

• If the prime is dropping but is still 8% or higher, move out of stocks whenever the rate starts to rise again.

Pay Attention to Price Trends
Guidelines:

• Keep a record of each weekly close of the *Value Line Composite Index*. You'll usually find the figure in the weekend financial pages of most major newspapers and in *Barron's*.

• Check to see if the index climbs 4%. A 4% change, not simply a four percentage point change, on a weekly closing basis, indicates a move to stocks.

• Maintain that position as long as the weekly index doesn't drop 4% or more.

The price trend indicator is right only about half the time, but stock profits made from the times that it's right are substantial. If you prefer to switch investments less often than this indicator might provoke, simply increase the "4% rule" to 5% or 6%.

These indicators can be used by the most conservative IRA investors to minimize risk. How to do it: Wait until both the prime rate indicator and the price trend indicator signal "buy," choosing stocks over money-market instruments.

This conservative system will occasionally miss an up market, but you'll be able to sleep at night, and you'll be playing the stock market only when the odds are greatly in your favor.

Source: Martin Zweig, chairman of the Zweig Fund ($370 million under management) and author of *Martin Zweig's Winning With New IRAs*, published by Warner Books.

IRA Setup and Transfer Fees in Mutual Funds

Most mutual funds charge an annual fee for custodial duties as well as a fee for setting up an individual retirement account. The custodial fee is a pass-along because of charges by the bank's trust department, which provides the accounting services required by the IRS.

Frequently the largest expense for IRA investors is the transfer fee incurred if they wish to change their IRA from one brokerage or fund to another, from a broker to a mutual fund, etc. The problem: This entails a change in trusteeship (the bank providing the custodial service). And that can be costly as well as time-consuming. Believe it or not, it often takes three to six months. Reason: Those trusteeships were set up with the belief that the accounts would be held there until retirement. The trustees never expected to give up the accounts quickly. To discourage transfers they require all kinds of information and material from the investor, and they charge heavily for making the transfer.

Better transfer method: Roll over your IRA account instead of transferring it directly. In a rollover, you close your account and take personal possession of your IRA money for up to 60 days. You are allowed one rollover per year. All funds, brokers, and trustees are set up to do this easily. Rollovers are faster than transfers, and at most firms they are less expensive.

Another way to avoid transfer fees: Use a no-load family of mutual funds. Then, when you are unhappy with the stock market, you can switch into another type of investment fund free of charge, and switch, and switch.

Banking alternative: Banks don't charge fees for setting up IRAs, since they are trustees for themselves. There is, however, a hidden fee. Banks give a lower rate of return on your money. The differential between what an investor can expect to earn in bank certificates of deposit and a growth-stock mutual fund over a 10- to 20-year period is very large. Estimate: Banks will average 10%, while growth-stock mutual funds can average 20%.

Source: William E. Donoghue, chairman of The Donoghue Organization and publisher of *Donoghue's Money Letter* and *Donoghue's Mutual Fund Almanac.*

How Inflation Can Ravage an IRA

When looking for an investment vehicle for your retirement funds, always remember the disastrous effect inflation can have on those funds. Even low levels of inflation can easily negate the benefits of compounding. For example, an average inflation rate of just 5% over 35 years will reduce the purchasing power of $1,387,145 to the paltry sum of $344,634. The farther away you are from retirement—or the longer your retirement—the greater the impact.

To avoid this consequence, keep an eye toward growth. Consider using mutual funds as the vehicle for your IRA investment. Recommendation: Split your $2,000 annual contribution into two parts, with one half invested in a high-quality bond fund and the other half invested in a growth mutual fund. In alternate years, substitute one of your investments with an investment in a real estate income program. Your returns should still be relatively high, your risk minimal, and your investment will be hedged against the possible onset of high inflation.

As you approach retirement, begin reducing the amount devoted to the growth portion of your funds—but don't do away with it altogether. Even retired people need protection from the danger of inflation.

Source: Geraldine Parrott, certified financial manager for Stifel, Nicolaus & Co., 615 E. Michigan Ave., Suite 400, Milwaukee, WI 53202.

Borrowing from Your IRA

Borrow from an IRA legally by making a short-term loan. Generally, IRA borrowings are prohibited. But it is possible to move funds from one IRA to another, as long as the transfer is completed in a 60-day period. Benefit: You have use of the funds for 59 days. Warning: The exact amount you take out of the first IRA must be placed in the second one within the 60 days. And you can use this device only once in a 12-month period.

Tax Penalties Can Be Avoided

The 10% penalty tax on early withdrawals from IRAs applies to all qualified retirement plans, thanks to tax reform. ("Early" means before age 59½.) But the penalty does not apply if:
- You become permanently disabled.
- You withdraw the money as an annuity.
- You have reached age 55 and take distributions under an early retirement provision of the plan.
- You withdraw an amount for medical care—to the extent that it doesn't exceed your allowable medical deduction under the tax law. (Note: This exception does not apply to IRAs.)
- Distributions are made under a domestic relations order (alimony, child support, etc.).
- You take certain types of distributions from an employee stock ownership plan (ESOP).

Caution: Tax reform also created a 15% penalty tax on "excess distributions" from all IRAs and other qualified plans. "Excess" generally means a total amount from all plans of more than $150,000 in any one year, or a lump-sum distribution of more than $750,000.

This penalty applies to taxpayers of any age as well as to the estates of deceased taxpayers. If there's any chance you could run afoul of this provision, consult your tax adviser.

All about Rollovers

Sometimes the best thing to do with a lump-sum distribution from a qualified pension, profit-sharing, or Keogh plan is to roll it over into an IRA, where the funds can grow tax-deferred until they are withdrawn. (Like a contributory IRA, funds distributed from a lump-sum rollover are treated as ordinary income.) You have 60 days from the time of the distribution to shelter the money in an IRA rollover. After that, the lump sum is subject to tax as ordinary income (although a five- or 10-year forward averaging option may be available) and the chance for tax-deferred growth is forfeited.

You can begin withdrawing from your IRA at age 59½ and are required to begin distribution by age 70½. Your payout will be calculated on the basis of your life expectancy and can be recalculated each year. The advantage of this system is that you can draw out money over a longer period of time and have the opportunity to leave a substantial amount of your IRA rollover to your heirs.

Your age, financial requirements, and tax status are important considerations when deciding whether to roll over a lump-sum distribution into an IRA. If you are uncertain of your future financial situation, you may want to roll over only a portion of the funds. As long as you receive at least 50% of the entire credit balance of a distribution plan and the amount is paid to you within one year, you are eligible for the rollover option. You determine how much of the distribution to place in an IRA.

Unless you specify otherwise, your employer is required to withhold tax on lump-sum distributions. If you elect not to have taxes withheld on your payment, you can roll over the full distribution into an IRA. If tax is withheld, you still have two options. First, you can roll over only the cash you receive, but this means you will have to pay ordinary income tax on the amount withheld. Your second option is to roll over the full lump-sum distribution by making up the amount of the withholding tax from other assets. The withheld tax is not lost: It can be either credited against taxes you owe, or claimed as a refund on your next income tax return.

Source: Nancy Weinberg, assistant vice president of E. F. Hutton & Company, Inc., 31 W. 54 St., New York 10004.

Creditors and Retirement Accounts

A pension-plan account may be safe from creditors, but money in an individual retirement account is not. When Jack Innis declared personal bankruptcy, the court ruled that his creditors could press claims against the money in his IRA. Key: IRA rules allow the owner of an IRA account to withdraw from it at any time (subject to a 10% penalty if the owner is under age 59½). And since the owner can take money out of the IRA, creditors can too.

Source: *Jack Innis*, Bankr. SD CA., No. 86-01837-LM7

Double-Rollover Loophole

A woman rolled over a pension distribution into an IRA. Then she withdrew part of this IRA and rolled it over into another IRA. IRS ruling: She did not violate the rule against more than one rollover in a year. The once-a-year rule applies only to rollovers from one IRA to another. It does not apply to rollovers of pension distributions. So the taxpayer had made only one rollover subject to the rule. IRS Letter Ruling 8651085.

IRS Rulings on Inheritances and IRAs

• The tax choices when an IRA owner dies. A surviving spouse who is the beneficiary of the deceased's IRA can continue deferring distribution and taxes from the IRA. How: Roll the IRA into the surviving beneficiary's name. Distributions won't begin until the survivor reaches 70½. Alternate: Leave the IRA in the decedent's name. Distributions won't begin until the decedent would have reached 70½. IRS Letter Ruling 8635043.

• Tax-free transfer. A man died without naming a beneficiary for his pension plan, so the money went to his estate. His wife inherited the plan's proceeds. IRS ruling: She can transfer the money, less his contributions to the plan, to her IRA without incurring any tax on the transfer. IRS Letter Ruling 8649037.

• Switching IRAs after death. A woman was the beneficiary of her parent's IRA. Her parent died before any distributions were made to her parent from the account. IRS ruling: She is allowed to transfer the IRA to a new trustee, as long as the new trustee maintains the IRA in her parent's name. She is also allowed to receive annual distributions from that account for 16.9 years, the life expectancy of her parent. IRS Letter Ruling 8716058.

Winning Retirement Spots

Many of us hope that snow shovels, galoshes, and earmuffs will be things of the past when we reach our "golden" years. And unless you're one of those hearty individuals who can't wait for the first nip of frost, a white Christmas, and delicious, sweet sap running from the maples, you're probably dreaming that your magic retirement address will be somewhere in the Sun Belt. But instead of following the crowd, you may be hoping to find a more private haven.

Using a combination of standards—including cost of living, crime rate, temperature and humidity, air quality, housing, medical facilities, and cultural and recreational activities—we arrived at the leading candidates.

North Carolina

Tryon: This little city, population 4,000, is called Shangri-La by some of its residents. It's in the western end of the state, in the Appalachian Highlands. But don't assume it's in the sticks, just because it's off the beaten track. About half its residents are retired, sophisticated people from all parts of the US and the world, representing both business and the arts. Its Fine Arts Center is home to theater, art, music, and films.

One feature that attracts people to Tryon is its weather. It's in a thermal belt that makes its weather uniquely comfortable year-round. With mountains to the north and east, it's sheltered from the cold. But since it's exposed to the south, warm air swaddles the area in a temperature inversion that keeps the temperature relatively stable from summer to winter. Sun is plentiful, making it a gardener's delight, with the growing season lasting about 200 days. That creates an abundance of fresh farm and orchard produce.

Sports facilities are abundant, too: Well-lighted tennis courts, a year-round swim club, two golf courses, horseback riding, hiking, and even special "enrichment centers" that provide game and craft activities for retired residents.

Housing is more than adequate. Medical facilities are also good, and comparatively inexpensive.

Some drawbacks: Until recently, North Carolina prohibited selling hard liquor in bars and restaurants, except for "private clubs." The state has approved a local-option measure, and liquor is becoming more available. Also, since public transportation is poor, you must have a car.

Georgia

Jekyll Island: This community is one of the three so-called Golden Isles off the Georgia coast. State-owned Jekyll Island has only about 1,200 residents. It used to be a retreat where the Rockefellers, Morgans, Goulds, and Vanderbilts built "cottages." Although the island has been converted into a public park, private homes are available under an unusual arrangement: You can buy a house, but the land upon which it sits must be rented (on a 99-year lease) from the state.

The weather is moderate. And although the island occasionally has snow, it's not unusual to eat Christmas dinner outdoors in shirt sleeves.

Medical facilities in Brunswick are superior. Living costs are moderate. If you fish for your supper, which many do, and frequent the local farm stands, grocery bills will be even lower.

Florida

Mount Dora: This community of 6,200 lies right in the so-called Retirement Belt, near Orlando (which is close to Disney World and the Space Center). Yet it's thousands of miles away in other respects. Mount Dora is the New England of the South, nestled among hills and lakes on a 1,844-foot bluff overlooking Lake Dora. It boasts huge oak trees and lantern lamp-posts (one reason that it's also called the Antique Center of central Florida).

The weather is splendid, averaging 61°F in the winter, 70° in April and October, and 82° in July. Health care facilities are excellent.

Housing is attractive and not expensive. Rentals are modest.

Culture is not ignored. There are regular theater and musical programs, and sports activities are varied.

The population is about 50% retired, many coming from New England and the Midwest.

Alabama

Fairhope: This town of 9,000 is on the Gulf coast, built on high bluffs overlooking Mobile Bay. It's noted for its magnificent waterfront, breathtaking views, and thriving artists' colony. Although the weather is mild, Fairhope is one of the southernmost points in the US that still has four distinct seasons (July's temperature average is only 82°, while January's is 54°). Because it's a coastal town, humidity is high (average, 70%) but refreshing winds travel up from the Gulf of Mexico. As a result, it is a gardener's paradise.

Living costs are low. Housing is abundant and modest. Some of the building lots can be rented (with a 99-year lease), which keeps building costs down.

Fairhope is a cultural center. It has a well-stocked library, a summer theater, and an active art association where art classes are conducted.

Medical facilities are exceptional. About 15 doctors live in town.

Louisiana

Covington: This lovely town (population 8,000) is only a half-hour ride from New Orleans and right in the middle of the so-called Ozone Belt (a pine-covered section north of Lake Pontchartrain, considered by many to be one of the world's most healthful regions). The land is above sea level and remains cooler than New Orleans in the summer. Although winters are mild, there are occasional cold snaps with snow. The mean temperature in January is 55º, in July, 80º. Autumn days have the crispness of New England, and the leaves turn orange and gold.

Home prices range widely.

Medical facilities here are exceptionally good.

The area has a well-rounded cultural program, independent of nearby New Orleans.

Texas

Kerrville: With a population of 19,000, Kerrville is in the Texas hill country, site of the late President Johnson's LBJ Ranch. The area is high (elevation, 1,650 feet) and surrounded by cedar and oak. The weather is on the cool side, averaging 63º in the summer and 47º in the winter.

One-third of the residents are retired, and they initiate most of the area's cultural activities.

The medical facilities are modern.

The nearest big city is San Antonio, which, despite the presence of skyscrapers, has a small-town atmosphere.

New Mexico

Roswell: In the middle of the state's retirement center, Roswell has a population of 50,000. Summer temperatures average 77º, with low humidity (30% in the midafternoon). Nighttime temperatures often drop to freezing, but since the sun shines 70% of the time, the days warm up quickly. In this wide-open country you can drive for hours without seeing a house. Roswell is the largest town in the area, an urban oasis in the desert.

Although the town has the best medical facilities in the area, they are not quite as good as those of the other areas mentioned in this article.

Housing is inexpensive.

Cultural activities include a symphony orchestra and a little theater.

Arizona

Prescott: In the middle of the state—about an hour's drive from metropolitan Phoenix—Prescott is in excellent skiing country. Many wealthy people have "cabins" in the area, which has a population of 23,000.

A major attraction of the city is its healthful air. With an elevation of 5,354 feet, Prescott is a haven for people with respiratory problems. But beware: Living in an area a mile high takes some getting used to, even if you're young. A couple of beers can leave you feeling pretty tipsy because of the altitude.

The weather is about perfect. Summers average about 70º, with a high of 87º. At night it dips to the 50s. In winter, the temperature swings from nearly 60º to freezing. Humidity hovers near 50%, so cold or hot, Prescott is comfortable.

Prescott has a reputation as a health center, since its medical facilities are unusually good.

Living costs in general are not cheap, because nearly everything must be shipped from Phoenix. A state income tax runs about 10% of the federal tax.

Housing is abundant, with most people living in cabin-type homes in the woods. Some rentals are available.

About 25% of the area residents are retired. The sports facilities are varied and abundant because the climate is so invigorating. The area is big on arts and crafts, and a junior college offers extension courses.

California

Hemet: Midway between Los Angeles and San Diego (about a 90-minute drive to either), it's distant enough to avoid the smog and the congestion of LA, yet close enough for a day trip. With year-round sun, it specializes in growing avocados (you can raise them in your backyard) and in housing retirees escaping the big-city life. Population is 30,000. Because it's warm and dry, many people with rheumatism and respiratory ailments come to Hemet. Summers are warm, with an average high of 95°, but the low humidity makes it comfortable. April, the coldest month, posts an average high of 65°.

Living costs are low compared with other areas in Southern California. Local foods sell at roadside stands for a fraction of supermarket prices.

Medical facilities are quite adequate.

The well-planned town has many civic boosters. As a result, despite its recent growth, there's no congestion or serious suburban problems. Because the area is flat, it's perfect for bicycling. Although Hemet is not a high-culture center, adult education is big.

The Overview

Large metropolitan areas with the best retirement ratings are in Southern California—the Anaheim-Santa Ana-Garden Grove and San Diego areas. For medium-sized metropolitan areas there are Austin (TX) and Santa Barbara (CA). For small metropolitan areas, two Texas towns, Midland and Tyler, get excellent ratings.

That's not to say other areas should be avoided. But generally they contain one or more drawbacks that keep them out of the top groupings—and out of the mainstream of those hurrying to find a retirement home. Still, some people's blemishes are other people's beauty spots. Not everybody agrees that Southern California and Texas are the Edens of Retirementville.

Source: Peter A. Dickinson, author of *Sunbelt Retirement*, a survey of the best cities in the Sun Belt to consider for retirement. He is also the author of two related books, *Travel and Retirement Edens Abroad* and *Retirement Edens Outside the Sunbelt*. All three can be ordered directly from him at 47 Chestnut Ave., Larchmont, NY 10538.

Safeguards When Retiring Abroad

• Protect your dollar assets. Maintain assets in US institutions and forward the funds as needed. High inflation, even in comparatively cheap countries, can destroy a nest egg with horrible speed.

• Wills can be especially tricky for overseas retirees. Best move: Have two wills—one for US assets, the other for foreign assets. This strategy will avoid the possibility of international cross claims that could complicate disposal of the estate.

• Plan for health insurance. Blue Cross and Blue Shield protect travelers but not expatriates. However, there are several types of international health insurance policies, and many countries have local insurance plans similar to those of Blue Cross and Blue Shield.

• Medicaid and Medicare don't extend coverage beyond the US.

• Many countries let foreign residents take advantage of their government-run health plans, which offer medical care at little or no cost. (Countries with first-class medical care: Australia, Barbados, Canada, Costa Rica, Israel, and most European countries.)

Working after Retirement

Many retirees would like to keep working after retirement, at least part-time. But those who want to work for financial reasons should be aware of these drawbacks:

• You can work and still collect full Social Security benefits, but for every $2 earned above a government-determined ceiling you lose $1 in benefits. When you add your commuting costs, job-related expenses, and payroll deductions, you may find part-time work doesn't pay off.

• If you continue working part-time for the same company, you may not be eligible to collect your pension. One way around this, if the company will go along, is to retire as an employee and return as a consultant or free-lancer. Since you're now self-employed, your pension won't be affected.

• Although most employees can't legally be compelled to retire before age 70, companies still set up retirement ages of 65 or under. You can work past that age, but you won't earn further pension credits. And you lose Social Security and pension benefits while you continue to work.

A very attractive alternative to working part-time is to start your own business. Professionals such as lawyers can often set up a practice, setting their own hours. Or you might turn a hobby into a business.

Source: William W. Parrott, a chartered financial consultant at Merrill Lynch, Pierce, Fenner & Smith, Inc., 1185 Ave. of the Americas, New York 10036.

The Benefits of Early Retirement

Collecting Social Security early can pay off. Even though benefits are reduced, they'll usually add up to more in the long run. Example: If full benefits are $750 per month for retiring at age 65, you can get reduced benefits of $600 a month by retiring at age 62. You'd have to collect full benefits for 12 years

to make up the $21,600 you'd receive during the three years of early payments.
Source: *Changing Times*, Washington, DC.

You Can Get More Out of Medicare

It's possible to get more Medicare coverage than is automatically granted to protect you from catastrophic medical bills, but you have to act. Overlooked: Plan B, an optional, premium-carrying policy (premiums are deducted from your Social Security check) that you must request within three months of your 65th birthday.

How it works: At age 65, you automatically become a recipient of Medicare's Plan A in-hospital insurance coverage, at no charge. About four months prior to your 65th birthday, Medicare will inform you of the Plan B option. You have until three months after your birthday to respond. Miss that deadline and you have to wait for the yearly general enrollment period—January 1 to March 31. Traps: 10% increase in the Plan B premium for late filers; if you become sick or injured while waiting for the enrollment period, you're not covered.

Plan B coverage: Doctor's fees, tests, and other out-of-hospital services, such as nursing or home health care. Plan B carries a deductible and covers 80% of expenses. Drawback: No coverage for prescription drugs.

10 INSURANCE TACTICS & STRATEGIES

How To Pick an Insurance Company

Your number one consideration as you're selecting an insurance company should be its financial strength. Buying insurance (especially life and health insurance) is—we all hope—a long-term proposition. You want to be sure that the company you are buying it from will be healthy for many years.

Nevertheless, most people fail to verify the strength and stability of the company they are choosing. It has taken the failure of several firms to drive home the point that not all insurance companies are created equal. But analyzing a company on your own is virtually impossible. Their statements are inscrutable, even to accountants without special training. Leave the analysis up to the professionals.

Helpful Guidance

The main source of financial information about insurance companies is *Best's Insurance Reports,* published since 1905 by A.M. Best Co., Oldwick, NJ. The Life/Health volume rates over half of the companies it lists. Companies are given a rating of A+, A, B+, B, C+, or C. The report costs more than $200, but is available in many libraries.

What To Look For

It's wise to deal only with companies rated A+. To be even safer, check back further. Reason: Before 1976, Best Co. used a more rigorous system ("recommending" companies instead of assigning a letter rating). In 1975, 119 companies received the strongest recommendation. The next year, 203 firms got an A+.

The most conservative customers should choose a company that, in addition to having rated A+ since 1975, also received the strongest recommendation in 1975.*

In order to read Best's 1975 recommendations, however, you have to know its code— the qualifying adjectives and adverbs. The strongest companies are described as having "most substantial margins for contingencies" and "most favorable operating results." The word very substituted for most indicates a weaker company. And if the qualifier is omitted, the company is even weaker.

Quality of Service

The best way to gauge the service of an insurance company is to find out how satisfied its current customers are. Unfortunately, there is no comprehensive nationwide ranking.

The best alternative: A few state insurance commissions publish "complaint ratios" for companies licensed to operate within their borders. These give consumers some indication of the kind of service a company will provide.

Example: Each year, the Illinois Department of Insurance issues pamphlets that compare the number of complaints made against each insurance company with the dollar value of the premiums the company has written in the state. Each figure is listed separately. The companies are then ranked, from the best to the worst, in terms of complaint ratios.

The Illinois Department of Insurance offers four complaint-ratio pamphlets: Automobile, Homeowner's, Life, and Accident & Health. They are available from the Illinois Department of Insurance, 320 W. Washington St., Springfield, IL 62767.

If you do not live in a state that publishes complaint ratios, you can use another state's listing as a guide. A company that offers poor service in one state is unlikely to do much better in another.

*For a list of the companies, contact *The Insurance Forum,* Box 245E, Ellettsville, IN 47429.

Source: Joseph M. Belth, publisher of *The Insurance Forum,* a newsletter for the insurance industry. He is professor of insurance at Indiana University and author of *Life Insurance: A Consumer's Handbook,* published by Indiana University Press.

Protection from Tricky Salespeople and Their Companies

With tax reform in place, cash-value life insurance remains one of the few investments whose earnings can build up tax-free and that can protect your family from the financial consequences of your untimely death.

But be wary. In the scramble to persuade you to buy their products, many life insurance companies and their agents are using misleading sales techniques and aggressive investment practices that have turned once boring (but usually safe) policies into high-risk gambles. Some agents will do almost anything to make their policies appear attractive. Common deceptions:

Using "unguaranteed" rates of return that are higher than current market rates. The government bond market may be paying only 7½%, but the insurance salesperson shows you an illustration using an unguaranteed rate of 10%–11%. Or the agent uses illustrations based on "past experience," for example, choosing interest rates in effect years ago, when rates were much higher.

Protection: Find out if the company pays a guaranteed rate and, if so, what it is. Ask the salesperson to rework the illustration using current market rates.

Illustrating nonguaranteed results for unreasonable lengths of time. Salespeople who guess at future interest rates may compound the deception by extending the illustration to periods as long as 40 years. Result: Expected interest rates will be greatly exaggerated. The difference between 7% and 10% annual rates of return compounded over 40 years can be enormous.

Protection: Ask for demonstrations using realistic rates for shorter periods of time—say, 10 years and 15 years.

Offering high first-year interest rates. Some companies entice buyers by inflating the first year's interest rate and reducing the rate in following years. However, because of high expenses in the first year, during that time there is usually little cash in the policy to earn that tantalizing interest.

Protection: Find out exactly how much of your first-year premium will be eaten up by expenses and commissions, how much will be left to earn interest, and what will happen to rates in future years.

Dangerous Investment Strategies

With competition so intense, some companies are wooing buyers by offering high rates of return on even their most conservative fixed-rate products. *Danger:* They may have turned to increasingly risky investment practices to sustain these rates:

Investing in low-quality, high-yield bonds.

Some insurance companies have devoted as much as 50% of their portfolios to risky "junk" bonds. In the old days, insurance companies invested only in the most conservative government and top-rated corporate securities.

Protection: Request a copy of the insurance company's investment portfolio to see what percentage is devoted to bonds rated BB or lower. There is reason for caution if junk bonds comprise over 10%–15% of the company's portfolio.

Investing in longer-term securities—such as 30-year bonds. Better: Less volatile short-term securities, such as five- to 10-year bonds. Although long-term bonds pay higher rates than short-term bonds, the value of a long-term bond declines much more rapidly than the value of a short-term bond if interest rates increase, causing returns to diminish. If they fall significantly, dissatisfied policyholders might surrender their policies to take advantage of higher rates elsewhere. Likely consequence: The insurance company would be forced to raise cash quickly by selling its investments at depressed prices—which would further reduce its returns and threaten its financial security.

Protection: Find out the average maturity of the company's investment portfolio. Anything longer than seven to 10 years is cause for concern.

Source: Charles Rohm, senior vice president, The Principal Financial Group, Des Moines, IA. The firm provides a wide range of financial services, including insurance for individuals and corporations, pensions, 401(k) plans, and residential mortgages.

The Best Insurance Buys

We spend a lot of money for insurance. The industry, directly or indirectly, takes in about $3,600 a year from every four-person household in America. Each family could save hundreds of dollars a year by simply learning some rules of the game.

A savvy consumer must personally cut through the sales pitches (there are currently 250,000 agents selling just life insurance in the United States) and find the best protection for the least cost. Here are some practical guides through the maze.

Life Insurance

Almost all adults—if they need life insurance—should buy renewable term insurance and do their saving and investing elsewhere. It stretches your dollars farther. Also, you can comparison shop and find the best price; there is no practical way that a bright consumer can make an intelligent choice among other types of life insurance.

In certain situations—a business partnership, for example—there may be some tax advantages to other types of insurance. But don't deal with an insurance agent until after your tax expert has helped you define exactly the policy that you need.

If you are still hanging onto an old whole life policy, you should borrow against it up to the limit you are allowed at the advantageous guaranteed rate (some are as low as 5%). Invest the money in safe, long-term Treasury bonds or some such investment and get the higher return the policy will never pay. Or consider dropping the policy, taking out the cash value, and starting over again with term insurance and a separate investment fund. (Make sure the new policy is in effect before you cancel the old one.)

Health Insurance

If you qualify for a group plan, that is the best deal. Just be sure the maximum benefit keeps up with inflation ($25,000 is not really enough any more). In buying supplementary insurance, avoid duplication of coverage.

If you are not part of a group, Blue Cross/Blue Shield generally offers the best coverage. Major medical plans sold by life insurance companies do allow you to save by taking higher deductibles, however, and many offer low rates to the young and healthy. Shop around.

If you leave a group plan with an option to convert to an individual policy, you can get the new policy without a physical, a good option if you have medical problems.

Auto Insurance

Compare prices. For example, one company in California (20th Century Insurance) limits its coverage to good risks. If you qualify, you can save up to 50%. Rather than going through an independent agent, you should at least consider saving money by dealing with the direct writers like State Farm, Wausau Insurance, and Geico.

Choose the highest deductible you can afford. Bonus: Unreimbursed casualty losses over $100 are income tax deductions. For old cars with little book value, don't buy collision or comprehensive coverage.

Homeowners Insurance

Shop around and take high deductibles. Put the difference in premium costs for high deductibles in a savings account for covering small losses. Chances are you will be well ahead very soon. However, there is no saving in underinsuring your home. In the case of a partial loss, your insurer will not pay you fully unless your house is covered for at least 80% of its replacement cost. Don't skimp on liability coverage.

Disability Insurance

Unless you are covered by an employer, you should have enough coverage to supplement Social Security payments. The only way to save on costs is to take a six-month or full-year waiting period before the benefits begin to pay out.

Source: Andrew Tobias, author of *The Invisible Bankers: Everything the Insurance Industry Never Wanted You to Know,* published by The Linden Press.

interest rates over the past decade may have lowered premiums more than your increasing age may have raised them.

Source: Christopher Collins, CLU Solomon, Collins & Associates, Lincoln, NE.

Insurance You May Not Know You Own

- A homeowners policy usually covers stolen purses and wallets, lost luggage, and property taken in a car break-in. It also may cover many offbeat accidents, such as damage to a power mower borrowed from a neighbor; trees, shrubs, fences, or tombstones; damages by vandals or motor vehicles; and property lost or damaged while moving.
- $25,000 in travel life insurance is provided if a ticket is bought on an American Express, Diners Club, or Carte Blanche card.
- American Automobile Association (AAA) members have automatic hospital and death benefits if hurt in a car accident.
- Many clubs and fraternal organizations have life and health benefits.
- It's possible to collect twice on car accident injuries, once through health insurance and again through the medical payments provision of auto insurance.
- Family health policies usually cover children away at college. Check before buying separate policies for them.

A New Policy May Be Better Than an Old One

Buying a new policy may be cheaper than reinstating a lapsed one, if you're considerably older now. Age is only one factor in setting premiums. Of equal or greater importance are fluctuations in the interest rate. The higher the rate, the lower the premium. Generally higher

Insurance You Shouldn't Waste Your Money On

Americans spend about 12% of their disposable income on insurance. And too much of that is money spent unwisely.

Rule of thumb: Buy only comprehensive insurance coverage against catastrophic economic losses. If you buy a policy that covers just one type of illness (such as TV-advertised cancer insurance) or that provides only limited reimbursement (such as "we pay $100 per day" medical insurance), you'll still need coverage for the more common illnesses (such as heart disease) and coverage for the true cost of a hospital stay.

Also, piecemeal policies leave gaps in coverage. After years of paying premiums, you get absolutely nothing if your accident or illness falls between the policies' provisions. In addition, piecemeal coverage is always more expensive than comprehensive coverage.

What you do need:
• Life insurance (only if you have dependents).
• Health insurance.
• Auto insurance.
• Homeowners insurance.
• Disability insurance.

A "rider" or "floater" attached to a standard insurance policy should cover any other exceptional needs. (A rider or floater is an amendment to a policy that extends, broadens, or restricts the contract.) For instance, a valuable painting or necklace can be covered with a floater on a regular homeowners insurance policy.

What To Avoid

Insurance policies against being beaned by a UFO or audited by the IRS are some of the exotic contracts you're better off without. Other "bad bets":

• Rental car insurance. Before you rent a car, check the auto insurance policies for the cars you own—about 60% cover any damage you may do to a rental car.

If you don't own a car or your policy doesn't cover rental car damage, you might consider buying the "collision damage waiver" (CDW) insurance that counter personnel at rental car agencies hard-sell ($6–$9/day premium). Its price is exorbitant, but the protection may be worth it if you have no other coverage and only rent a car a few times a year.

Rental car companies have upped the ante. Renters used to be liable for only up to $500–$1,000 worth of damage to a rental car if they didn't buy CDW insurance, but now most companies make renters liable for $2,000–$3,000 (the amount covers the deductible that the rental company must pay). Some companies stick renters with the total bill if they wreck a rental car and they're not covered.

If you rent cars often, consider switching your auto insurance policy to one that covers rental cars. And if you often rent a car for business, check your company's rules. Some companies prefer to absorb the costs of infrequent collisions rather than pay a daily CDW charge for each employee's rental car.

• Automobile medical insurance. Your comprehensive health plan will cover your medical expenses, while auto liability coverage will take care of your passengers.

• Mortgage or credit insurance. To protect your family against the economic consequences of your death, buy adequate annual renewable term (ART) life insurance instead. ART serves the same purpose as, and is much less expensive than, mortgage or credit insurance.

• Air travel insurance. A typical policy offers $150,000 in coverage for a $5/flight premium. Your family collects only if you die in a plane crash—if you die of a midflight heart attack or in a car crash on the way to the airport, your family gets nothing. Better: Adequate regular life insurance, which covers your family however you may die accidentally. And if you die in a plane crash, your family can even sue the airline (and probably win more than $150,000). The only "bargain" in air travel insurance is the free coverage some credit card companies offer when tickets are charged on their cards.

• Accident life insurance. Will your survivors need more money if you die in an accident rather than from natural causes?

• Pet medical insurance. Annual premiums of $50–$110 (plus a deductible) make it highly unlikely that you'll break even unless you have a chronically sick animal.

• Cancer insurance. Another example of piecemeal coverage you don't need if you have good major medical coverage.

• Children's life insurance. Unless your

child is the major breadwinner in your family, the loss would be emotional, not financial.

• Mugging insurance. Still another type of overpriced insurance designed to play on your fears.

• Moving insurance. Premiums vary widely according to the worth of your belongings. Coverage provided by moving companies often requires that company employees pack and unpack every item—while you pay them standard hourly wages. Best bet: Pack your belongings yourself, and move precious items in your own car or rented truck. Homeowners or renters policies usually don't cover belongings in transit, because they're defined by the bounds of the residence. Even if the moving van winds up at the bottom of a lake, you can always sue the moving company.

• Contact lens insurance. The premiums can range from about 35% to more than 100% of the cost of replacement lenses per year. Since losing a contact lens is not a catastrophe, you can afford to take your chances.

• Vacation rain insurance. These policies pay back your vacation expenses if it rains more than a certain number of days in your vacation spot. Typical premium: $150 to cover a $5,000–$10,000 vacation. These insurers use weather statistics to gauge the chances of rainy days (the number depends on where you're vacationing), and it's extremely unlikely you'll ever collect.

• $100-a-day hospital insurance. The cost of a hospital stay is usually closer to $300/day, and a good major medical plan should cover 100% of the costs.

Source: J. Robert Hunter, president, National Insurance Consumer Organization, 121 N. Payne St., Alexandria, VA 22314.

The Secrets of Avoiding—or Fighting— Bad Ratings

The discovery that an insurance company is charging you extra for an individual health,

life, or disability insurance policy can be infuriating—especially when you're not told why. Almost 10% of all health, life, and disability insurance applicants are hit with extra charges (ratings, in insurance jargon) for medical or moral reasons.

What They Can Pin on You

Health problems, such as high blood pressure or obesity—which you may have had years ago and since resolved.

Drug or alcohol abuse. Occasional use is easily exaggerated by malicious colleagues or neighbors.

Psychiatric conditions. Even light therapy may make extracautious underwriters nervous about your mental stability.

Criminal associations. If a relative or close friend is a known member of organized crime, you're considered a greater risk.

Homosexuality. Not just because of AIDS, but merely for moral reasons.

In-Depth Investigation

When you sign an insurance application, you give an insurance company permission to undertake a thorough investigation of your medical, social, and financial history. When they delve into your past, insurance companies look for consistency—a straight story. They ask the same questions of several sources and ask each source the same question three or four times from different angles. The more inconsistency they find, the more they dig. Sources:

You. When filling out applications or answering questions at medical examinations, keep it simple. Make yourself as small a target as possible. Important: If you hide a condition that later forces you to make a claim within the so-called contestability period—usually two years—an insurance company will cancel your policy because you have misrepresented yourself to them. For example, if you hide a known heart condition and die of cardiac arrest six months later, your life insurance policy will be canceled and your family will collect only a half year of returned premiums.

Your doctor. Ask your physician to examine your medical file to see if it conveys an accurate picture of your current physical condition. If an item could be misconstrued, ask the doctor to attach an explanatory note.

References. Insurance companies usually ask for an accountant, a friend, and a business associate. Pick carefully. Warn your references about any topics that they might know about that you prefer they avoid, like the one time you tried race-car driving.

Your agent must file a report on you, but is unlikely to be a problem since an agent is always interested in making the sale.

Information-gathering services investigate you, looking for both medical and moral problems. (Most companies now use Equifax.)

The Medical Information Bureau (MIB) compiles information on previous insurance applications and claims in search of special health situations.

Knowing You're Rated

All your careful efforts notwithstanding, you've been rated if:

• You are rejected outright for coverage.

• The premium charged is higher—or the benefits less—than your agent originally quoted. With disability insurance, terms may be less favorable.

• Your policy arrives with the words *rating* or *modified benefit* printed on the page where your name appears.

• You are required to sign a rider or amendment.

Fighting Back

You must refute the existing underwriting records. An insurance company's information may be completely mistaken or, more likely, out of perspective—old, exaggerated, or misinterpreted. Unfortunately, the nature of the negative information will not always be volunteered. The law requires, however, that an insurance company surrender the reason for a rating to you—or your doctor, if medically oriented—upon written request.

A good agent can make your case to the company. Advantage: If they are respected, agents' arguments will carry more weight.

Medical situations. Generally, you or your agent will have to present a letter and test results from a doctor to the company's medical director. Suppose you had high blood pressure when you first applied for insurance, but that was because of stress on your old job. If a physician can show that you no longer have this condition, the company may reconsider.

Trap: The insurance company may have received information from your physician with a request that it be kept from you. You won't get that information from the insurance company. You will be told, however, that the rating is based on confidential information from your doctor.

Moral ratings. These are even harder to fight. Often, you will not be told the exact source of a bad reference. You will just get a very general statement. Such sources may be vindictive or mentally unbalanced.

While you won't have an opportunity to answer these charges directly, the Fair Credit Reporting Act does give you the right to make the insurance company and its sources recheck their facts. This shouldn't take more than two or three weeks.

If the charge is proven wrong, the insurance company will probably correct its files. If the charges are based on opinion rather than fact, have your own response placed along with the allegations in your file. Ask the company to talk with other sources. Give the company personal references.

Battling an insurance company requires patience and dedication. However, if you make enough noise, and with good reason, your chances of erasing a costly insurance rating are very good.

Source: Leonard B. Stern, president, Leonard B. Stern & Co., an insurance and consulting firm, 305 Madison Ave., New York 10165.

You Can Avoid a Physical Exam

Insurance medical exams are being abandoned by some insurance companies, even for $100,000–$200,000 term insurance sales, according to a major insurance broker. The reasons are the high cost of the exams and the poor reliability of the information given by those seeking insurance. Even the best exams, say the insurers, protect them for only about six months anyway. They often rely on a medical history taken by the insurance broker. They may also request an electrocardiogram and a chest X-ray.

Finding a Lost Insurance Policy

Hundreds of life insurance policyholders die each year and their named beneficiaries either don't know they are beneficiaries or can't find the policies. If you suspect that you are the beneficiary of a lost policy, don't expect a life insurance company to volunteer the information. The search is up to you.

Check the obvious places first: The box with the tax records, the desk with the cubbyholes full of papers, and the safe-deposit box. Talking to family lawyers and insurance agents helps, too. If you don't find what you're looking for, try these other sources of leads:

Checkbooks. Check stubs often tell the tale. Keep alert for checks made out not only to insurance companies, but also to trusts, trade associations, alumni organizations, and individual agents.

Employers. Company personnel offices can provide information on benefit plans, including voluntary programs, life insurance, and severance benefits. Their computers or files can quickly determine who the employee chose as a beneficiary if they know of a policy.

Supplemental life insurance agents. These may have had contact with your loved one in or out of the workplace. They usually remember their prospective clients well.

Money orders. Try the company credit union, the local bank, or even the drugstore to find out if a money order was purchased to pay for an insurance policy.

Insurance agents. Anyone in the insurance business—friends, acquaintances from religious organizations, relatives, or neighbors of the deceased—can be a source of facts.

Old policy applications. These are always a good place to look because they contain a list of previously owned insurance.

Veterans Administration. Check for National Service Life Insurance.

Relatives. Older members of the family may recall a policy taken out as a present.

Loan documentation. Frequently, this will reveal insurance policies used as collateral.

Possible former beneficiaries. These can include a former spouse or lover or anyone else who may have been a beneficiary at one time.

The funeral register. Former insurance agents, unknown associates, and acquaintances may have the information you're looking for.

The Medical Information Bureau. This clearinghouse for medical and lifestyle information has computerized facts about many who have applied for insurance, but does not readily provide information; you may have to hire a lawyer or go to court to find out anything. The address is Box 105, Essex Street Station, Boston, MA 02112.

If you uncover a company name through this search, the next step is to write to ask about policies that might have been in effect when your loved one died. Provide the company with the deceased's full name, any other names the person might have used, date and place of birth, and Social Security number. If you still haven't come up with a company name, you can contact all insurance companies in states where the deceased lived. The names of these companies are available at state insurance departments, although the lists won't include companies no longer in business or mail-order companies.

If all else fails, there is the American Council of Life Insurance. This trade organization will forward your inquiry to about 100 member companies. Their address is 1850 K St. NW, Washington, DC 10006. Attention: Policy

Search Department.

Source: Benjamin Lipson, president, Benjamin Lipson Associates Insurance Agency, Inc., 7 Bulfinch Pl., Boston 02114. Mr. Lipson is an independent insurance broker specializing in insurance for people with medical problems. He is also the author of *How to Collect More on Your Insurance Claims* and writes a weekly newspaper column.

Mistakes in Filing Property Claims

Failure to accurately calculate losses. It's hard to believe, but many people can't accurately determine their losses—whether by damage or theft. They fail to maintain effective accounting and record-retention procedures to document the losses. It's not uncommon to hear of a situation where a theft loss amounted to $250,000, but the claimant could only substantiate $100,000 of the loss. It's important to plan ahead with your accountant to determine the best procedures for demonstrating what you own, should you have to make a claim.

Overstating the loss. This is a subtle problem. If a claimant purposely overstates the loss to the point where the insurance company could question his integrity, the company will take a hard line. Generally, if the claimant takes a fair position, the insurer will still bargain over the loss claim but will be more reasonable.

Underestimating the loss. This sounds like a contradiction of the above, but it's not. Immediately after losses are claimed, an adjuster will ask the claimant for an estimate of the damage, not an accurate, justified number. The insurer requires such a rough estimate, but be wary of providing a number before taking time to get a reliable estimate. If the adjuster reports a number that's too low and then must go back later to the insurer and restate it much higher, his credibility and yours are hurt, making future loss negotiations tricky. So tell the adjuster about any problems in coming up with a number.

A Canceled Check Is Not Enough

Fire and casualty policies should be in hand (on file) before the full premium is paid. One firm, after finding its plant burned to the ground, didn't have the policy it had paid for. Though it produced the canceled check to the broker, its claim was disallowed. The wise course is to buy insurance as you would an automobile: Give the broker a small deposit, but don't pay up until the policy is delivered.

Trouble with a Claim?

Before a Claim

Before you have a claim, it is a good idea to read your insurance policy closely. Write a letter to the company informing them what you think the policy covers. If you are right, they will tell you. If you are wrong, they should say so; you can then ask the company to change the situation or choose to go to another company.

If there is ultimately a problem with a claim, the courts should hold any ambiguous language in the policy in your favor, since the insurance company wrote it and you were stuck with the language. Further, the courts look to the "reasonable expectation" of the insured when a claim occurs. State your expectations in writing up front when you first purchase coverage, and they will more than likely be binding later.

Also, know what you are insuring before a claim: Keep detailed records of what you own and its condition. For example, make records of the condition in which you keep your car. Then, if an accident occurs, you will be able to prove that the car was in excellent shape. Make an inventory of your home. It's surprising how many important items people are not able to recall after a fire. Document ownership with photos, to give the claims adjuster sufficient evidence. All valuables should also be documented with sales slips or periodic appraisals. Be sure to keep these records in a safe-deposit box or at work—records are not much good if they're destroyed along with the contents of your home.

After a Claim

Do not sign any insurance company releases without careful consideration. Document everything that happens first: When did the insured event occur? What were the circumstances? Who are the witnesses? When did you inform the agent or company? Who did you talk to? What did that person tell you?

Keep a complete record of each contact with the insurance company. Your ability to have a claim paid will be directly proportional to the quality of your recordkeeping. If the company tries to delay or reduce the size of the claim, you will be able to document what is happening and will have the evidence you need to appeal higher up in the company or to the state insurance department or, if need be, to court. If you go to a lawyer, you not only will have a better chance in court with good evidence, but if the insurance company gives you an abusive runaround, you may also be entitled to sue for punitive damages in some states.

Complaints should be directed first to the company (write to the president). Be reasonable, but don't believe everything the insurance company tells you. If that avenue of relief fails, appeal to the state insurance department. Be brief and factual. Clearly state the relief you want. If you do not get a satisfactory response from the state and the money is significant, you may have to be prepared to go to an attorney.

Source: J. Robert Hunter, president, National Insurance Consumer Organization, 121 N. Payne St., Alexandria, VA 22314, the first nonprofit national organization established to promote the interests of insurance buyers. He is also a former Federal Insurance Administrator and is a Fellow of the Casualty Actuarial Society.

When a Lawful Claim Is Refused

When you buy an insurance policy, you are purchasing protection for yourself, your family, and your possessions. If your car is totaled or you're disabled by a fall or your home is burglarized, you submit your claim and wait a reasonable time for your check. It's a simple enough transaction in theory.

But now, in too many cases, the check never gets there. The insurance company balks and refuses your claim or it offers a sum far lower than your actual loss.

What do you do then? In nine of 10 cases, people do nothing. They figure there is no use in fighting this $200 billion industry. And that's a shame, because policyholders have strong legal rights under both statute law and case law. You can take on an insurance company and win. The right tactics:

Never inflate your claim. This will annoy the claims adjuster and make payment more difficult. At worst, it can make you vulnerable to a criminal charge of fraud. An honest claim lays the foundation for further action, should the company refuse to settle.

Request a written explanation of why your claim was denied. An explanation is required by law in most states. If the explanation cites some technicality, such as failure to file on time, the company is probably out of line. Even if you are months late in filing, your claim is still valid unless the company can show that its investigation was harmed by the delay.

Keep in mind that the company's interpretation is not gospel. Insurance firms are no friendlier than other corporations. The fewer claims they pay, the larger their profit. They can be highly subjective—and sometimes ridiculous—in interpreting a policy's language.

Example: One company refused to pay a medical claim for a patient on a respirator in an intensive-care ward. The company insisted the patient had received "custodial" care, which was excluded in the policy.

Even in an honest disagreement, courts have repeatedly ruled for the policyholder whenever a policy's language was deemed unclear. Bottom line: If you think your interpretation is reasonable, stick to your guns.

Don't be bullied by the fine print. If your claim was denied because of a fine-print "exclusion," take heart. Most courts have ruled that the company must prove that such exclusions were phrased clearly, plainly, and conspicuously.

Ask for a breakdown of medical expenses, lost earnings, and pain and suffering when the company offers a personal injury award. Then it may make sense to apply the "rule of three," which is often a good test of whether you're getting a fair shake.

Example: You've had $5,000 in medical bills and have lost a month's salary of $4,000. Add those figures together ($9,000). Then multiply $9,000 by three to calculate the value of your pain and suffering ($27,000). Your total settlement ($9,000 plus $27,000) would be $36,000. If the company offers much less, push it.

Ask your agent to go to bat for you. Insurance agents want to see valid claims paid, if only to keep their customers happy. A nudge to the home office may help grease the wheels. On the other hand, the most honest agent in the world may have little influence over some distant adjuster.

If you're still not satisfied, take your case to higher-echelon people in the insurance company—first by telephone, then by mail. The company may decide to pay your claim after hearing your side of the story. But if it fails to respond to two letters, write a third letter that says you will commence legal action within 30 days. Given the size of some recent court awards, this can work wonders. While you wait, keep a log and a copy of all communications.

Contact your state's department of insurance. In some states these departments are helpful consumer advocates. In others, they are understaffed or are heavily influenced by insurance-industry interests. Even at best, however, a state agency does not have the authority to force a company to settle.

Take the company to small claims court. You can represent yourself, and you will get quick results. One major drawback: Most of these courts have a jurisdiction limit of $1,500 or less.

If all else fails, see a lawyer. To find someone experienced in this particular area of the law, contact your state or local trial lawyers association or consumer advocate group. Many attorneys will take insurance claims cases on a contingency basis. If you win your case, the lawyer keeps a portion of the award, usually one-third. However, if you lose, you pay nothing.

About 95% of insurance suits are eventually settled out of court. But extreme cases—in which a policyholder's attorney can demonstrate "bad faith" by the insurance company—can result in huge punitive awards.

Source: William M. Shernoff, an attorney who pioneered "bad faith" litigation against insurance companies, 600 S. Indian Hill, Claremont, CA 91711. He is the author of *Payment Refused*, published by Richardson & Steirman.

The Most Common Mistakes in Buying Life Insurance

In addition to offering protection for your family, life insurance can be a good investment. But life insurance policies are complicated, and without facts and comparisons it's easy to spend a lot of money for the wrong coverage. Here's a list of the most common mistakes to avoid and recommendations on what you should buy.

Mistake: To buy life insurance when you have no dependents. Agents tend to create needs where none really exists in order to sell policies. If you are single, you don't need life insurance.

Mistake: To buy mail-order insurance. It's a bad bargain for most people.

Mistake: To buy life insurance for your children. Unless there's some extraordinary reason, there are better ways to save money.

Mistake: To put money into a cash-value life insurance policy, unless you have an IRA for yourself and your spouse. (Cash-value policies are whole life, universal life, variable life, or any form of life insurance that contains a saving element.) Stay away from variable life. It has very high built-in expenses. If you want a cash-value policy, buy universal or whole life—provided you know how to choose the right policy and company and intend to keep the policy at least 10 years. Otherwise you'd be much better off with term insurance.

Mistake: To buy a cash-value policy from a high-pressure salesperson. Keep in mind that agents make five to 10 times as much commission selling you a $100,000 cash-value policy as they would on a term policy for the same amount. So you should always be alert to the hard sell for such policies.

Mistake: To buy life insurance and not disability insurance. People may automatically buy life insurance without realizing that a long-term disability can be an even worse financial event for their families than dying. If you're disabled, you not only lose your income, but you are still around incurring expenses. You don't have to buy disability insurance if you're covered at work. However, only 30% of workers have such coverage. Everyone is covered by Social Security disability, but it's very restrictive, especially for white-collar workers.

Mistake: To buy riders on your policy, such as the accidental death benefit or the additional-purchase option. These should be treated like options on a car—high-profit items that are best avoided. Example: Double indemnity; contrary to popular belief, you're not worth more dead in an accident than dead otherwise. Controversial rider: The waiver of premiums in case of disability. You don't need it if you're covered for disability. If you become disabled, you'll have enough money to keep up your life insurance premium.

Smart Buying

The safest and best insurance protection is the purchase of annual, renewable term insurance. For a family with one wage earner, five times annual income is the rule of thumb for determining the amount of coverage to buy. Premiums are low compared to those for other types of policies.

Compare any cash-value or term policy you're thinking of buying with the policies sold by USAA Life of San Antonio, TX (phone 800-531-8000). Salaried representatives at its home office sell by phone. It has the best values on whole life, universal life, and term insurance. Also check with the rate-of-return service run by the nonprofit National Insurance Consumer Organization (NICO), 344 Commerce St., Alexandria, VA 22314 (phone 202-549-8050). Some policies are so complicated that it's impossible to figure out exactly what you're getting without a special computer program.

Example: If a universal life policy says it pays 11%, that may be figured on whatever is left after a lot of expenses. You have to compare it with what you would have earned if you had bought term and invested the difference. Assuming you hold the policy 20 years, 11% may turn out to be more like 9½%.

Reevaluate your older policies. If your old policy is a term policy, you should assume you can replace it with a lower-priced policy, at least if you're a nonsmoker. If your old cash-value policy doesn't pay dividends, it probably should be replaced. If it does pay dividends, you'll be better off keeping it, especially if it has a low policy-loan interest rate that allows you to borrow on it and reinvest elsewhere.

Source: James H. Hunt, director of National Insurance Consumer Organization, a life insurance actuary and former commissioner of banking and insurance for the state of Vermont.

How Much Life Insurance Do You Really Need?

The function of life insurance is to replace the economic value of a family member and to provide liquidity to meet the surviving family's cash needs as the estate is settled. Thus the amount of insurance you *need* is not necessarily the amount you can *afford*. Before you visit with a life insurance agent, take a few minutes to understand the logic involved in determining your life insurance needs.

Talk with your spouse or "significant other." What would he or she do if you were not around? The answer dramatically affects the amount of life insurance you need. He or she could decide to stay at home and care for the family or return to work. Returning to work may require paying for some additional education. Alternatively, relocating the family may reduce the amount of income needed to maintain a similar lifestyle.

Determine your family's income needs. Most people underestimate the amount of money it takes to live from month to month without a change in lifestyle. Try working from a cash-flow page to estimate what costs would change if you were no longer in the picture. Cash flows will differ as the family ages: (1) while children live at home; (2) after the children leave home; (3) while your spouse is in retirement.

Determine what will generate the required amount of income. Remember that funds can be invested a number of ways, each of which will generate a different amount of income. Also keep in mind the effects of taxes and inflation on your family's income stream.

Evaluate your liabilities. Some liabilities should be paid off immediately at your death. Others, like a 7% home mortgage, may not be difficult for your surviving spouse to meet.

Estimate a college education fund. Determine the amount of money that you would have to invest today to meet the expense of college for your children when they turn 18.

Estimate readjustment emergency funds. Most people go through a period of grieving when it may be impossible to earn income and start a new life simultaneously. Funds will be needed for ordinary and unanticipated expenses during this time.

Calculate last expenses. In addition to funeral costs, there is the expense of getting your estate passed to your heirs. Assume 7%–9% of the total value of your estate will be needed for administrative expenses.

List your assets. Know what is already available to your survivors.

Once you've done some thinking, make the following calculations to determine your insurance needs. And don't forget that your family's circumstances can change—these calculations should be reevaluated at least once a year.

Add

Lump sum necessary to provide income
    while children are at home   _____
    after children leave home   _____
    for spouse in retirement   _____
Debts that should be paid off   _____

College education fund   _____
Readjustment/emergency funds   _____
Last expenses   _____
    Amount of estate required   _____
Subtract
Available assets   _____
Existing insurance payable
    to survivors   _____
    Amount of insurance needed   _____

Source: Karen P. Schaeffer, president, Schaeffer Financial, 7855 Walker Dr., Greenbelt, MD 20770, a financial-planning firm affiliated with Hibbard Brown & Co. She is a frequent speaker, has appeared on syndicated television, and is an adjunct faculty member at the College for Financial Planning.

A Quick Way To Estimate Coverage

The multiples-of-salary chart was developed to permit a breadwinner to estimate life insurance requirements in the event of premature death. While many factors besides these multiples should be accounted for when arriving at a final figure, the chart will give you an idea of what to expect.

The calculation is based on your current income and on the assumption that your family will receive Social Security benefits in addition to insurance proceeds; it also accounts for your spouse's age. For example, if your gross income is $30,000, your spouse is 45 years old, and your goal is 75% net income replacement, you will need a policy worth 8.5 times your gross income, or $255,000.

Multiples-of-Salary Chart

Your present gross earnings	25 years 75%	25 years 60%	35 years 75%	35 years 60%	45 years 75%	45 years 60%	50 years 75%	50 years 60%
$15,000	4.5	3.0	6.5	4.5	8.0	6.0	7.0	5.5
23,500	6.5	4.5	8.0	5.5	8.5	6.5	7.5	5.5
30,000	7.5	5.0	8.0	6.0	8.5	6.5	7.0	5.5
40,000	7.5	5.0	8.0	6.0	8.0	6.0	7.0	5.5
65,000	7.5	5.5	7.5	6.0	7.5	6.0	6.5	5.0

Source: Morton Tolchin, a chartered life underwriter with HL Financial Services of New York, Inc., 780 Third Ave., New York 10017, and a member of the American Society of Chartered Life Underwriters and the Association for Advanced Life Underwriting.

Meeting the Insurance Needs of Women with Families

When purchasing insurance, many families underestimate the wives' and mothers' economic contributions to their households. As a result, women's insurance needs are inadequately covered. Insurance should be purchased to meet all of the following:

• Final expenses. Dying costs have increased greatly in recent years; a conservative estimate of final expenses is $10,000 for medical, funeral director, and cemetery costs.

• Cost of services. If a woman is a homemaker, either full or part time, insurance will be needed to pay someone to perform some or all of the work she does: Child care, cooking, washing, cleaning, shopping, sewing, chauffeuring, etc.

• Earnings. In the event of the wife or mother's death, insurance will be required to replace the value of her earnings, to maintain the family's lifestyle.

Source: Morton Tolchin, a chartered life underwriter with HL Financial Services of New York, Inc., 780 Third Ave., New York 10017, and a member of the American Society of Chartered Life Underwriters and the Association for Advanced Life Underwriting.

Should You Insure Your Children?

After other life insurance needs are satisfied, many parents and grandparents buy life insurance for their children—not because they expect them to die, but because they expect them to live. The best reasons for insuring children:

• They will probably need life insurance at some time in their lives.

• Coverage is available at bargain rates.

• Insurance is a gift that grows in value.

• The children will be protected against the possibility of being uninsurable at some future date.

• Insurance provides a future source of ready credit for the children.

Example: For a one-year-old child, a rapid pay (or vanishing premium) life insurance contract with a face value of $100,000 and assumed interest of 10% would cost $360 a year in premiums for only five years. When the policyholder reached age 60, the cash value of the policy would be $202,297 and the death benefit, $381,391. At age 70, the cash value would be $434,744 and the death benefit, $664,402.

Source: Morton Tolchin, a chartered life underwriter with HL Financial Services of New York, Inc., 780 Third Ave., New York 10017, and a member of the American Society of Chartered Life Underwriters and the Association for Advanced Life Underwriting.

Alternatives to Whole Life Policies

If you're interested in permanent life insurance, what kind should you buy? Here's a primer on some alternatives to whole life, illustrating their strong and weak points.

Economatic Policies

If you need more permanent protection than you can immediately afford with whole life, you may be interested in an "economatic" product. This type of policy combines whole life and term insurance, with dividends used over time to convert the term to permanent protection. The major advantage of this type of policy is that you can buy permanent protection at a cost lower than that of ordinary whole life. The policy builds a cash value, and you can borrow from it at any time.

A limited number of life insurance companies now offer a new type of flexible life insurance that extends the limits of earlier economatic products. The new product is a flexible combination of the three basic life insurance types—whole life, term, and paid-up insurance. Generally, the insurance is backed by a company's entire investment portfolio, which softens the impact of dramatically changing interest rates.

This type of policy allows you to custom design your insurance at time of issue. You decide the premium you can afford and, depending on the protection you need, direct the proportion of your premium into permanent insurance, term insurance, and paid-up additions. You can also use a lump sum—a single premium—at issue and buy a chunk of single-premium insurance to obtain tax advantages and to increase cash-value buildup.

Universal Life

In the late 1970s, in response to high interest rates, some insurance companies began offering universal life insurance—a flexible premium insurance plan that combines term insurance with a separate investment fund often tied to short-term interest rates. A prime feature of universal policies is that premium payments are optional. Like whole life policies, earnings on the cash reserve portion of a policy are tax-deferred until withdrawal.

Though policy owners may find the flexibility of universal life insurance convenient, this flexibility can cause problems. The ability to reduce or even stop premiums may be too tempting and may override your commitment to your insurance program's future. Another potential problem is that the short-term investments that back many universal life products make them vulnerable to major investment or interest rate changes.

Some universal life policy owners have received notices from their insurance companies stating that their "permanent" insurance will not last as long as expected, unless they increase their premiums. And the notices have announced that death benefits and cash values, as projected just a few years or even months earlier, also will drop unless premiums are increased.

How do you compare whole life, economatic, and universal life products? The flexibility available with an economatic policy may make it more attractive than whole life insurance. Because of its emphasis on long-term investments, the economatic policy also may be a better choice than universal life. However,

for careful policy owners, universal life may be preferable because it permits skipping a premium or paying a lower premium than originally planned.

Variable Life

For policy owners who want to control how their cash values are invested, a number of companies now offer variable life insurance. Like traditional whole life, variable life has a fixed annual premium, and you can borrow against a policy.

The unique feature of variable life is that part of your premium is invested in an investment pool of your choice. The investment pool can be a money-market fund, a stock fund, a bond fund, or—with some companies—a managed combination of the three. Some companies will let you invest part of your premium in each, and you can even switch among funds. If your investment pool fares well, the cash value and pure insurance value of your policy will increase. If your investments don't fare well, however, neither will your cash value, although your insurance benefit will never drop below its initial value.

Source: Mark J. Lucius, advertising and corporate information specialist for Northwestern Mutual Life Insurance Company, 720 E. Wisconsin Ave., Milwaukee, WI 53202. Mr. Lucius is responsible for national publicity for the "Quiet Company's" activities and products.

Understanding Term Insurance

Term insurance is usually the least expensive form of insurance to get for a maximum of five years. The choices:

Yearly renewable term. The rates start low and rise annually as your age (which increases the risk) goes up. Choose this policy if you're in a short-term venture (for example, a construction project or a short-term contract).

Five- and 10-year term insurance. Appropriate for a person starting a high-risk or highly leveraged business when the bank may insist that the entrepreneur's life be covered by a large policy for a specified period of time. The premium is averaged out on an annual basis over the life of the policy.

Yearly renewable term policy with a reversion to lower premiums on evidence of insurability. This is a recent development. At a specified time (usually after four or five years), if you pass a medical exam, the premiums can be reduced by perhaps 35% of what they might have been. Example: If your insurance premium starts at $1,000 a year and climbs $200 annually, you must pass an exam during the fifth year to get the premium lowered to $1,200. Potential problem: Bad health at the time of the examination will negate the possibility of lowering the premium.

Avoid term insurance even for the short haul if you are almost 70 years old. Since the risk at that age is so high, the point at which the term and straight-premium rates would cross would be attained within five years. At that point, a permanent (or straight) life policy is best.

If you need life insurance for more than five years, permanent insurance is usually best. The reason for this is that the total acquisition price usually evens out over a period of 10 years. If you are relatively young, say in your 30s, the cash value of the policy may increase at a greater rate than the premium after the third year. The straight-life policyholder may borrow on the cash value at a low rate of interest.

Alternative: Some creative insurance agents combine the two types of insurance coverage, thus lowering premium costs and ensuring cash value at a specific time.

Source: Leon Sicular, president, Leon H. Sicular Associates, New York.

Are You Special?

People with chronic physical ailments or who enjoy risky hobbies must take special measures to obtain adequate life insurance coverage. Insurance companies make their money by selling insurance to the "right" people—people in good health who lead "low-

risk" lives. Special-risk people—such as those who suffer from cancer, diabetes, nervous disorders, alcohol problems, or hypertension, those who have had bypass surgery, are older, or are scuba divers or pilots—are not the kind of clients insurance companies favor.

If you have any reason to believe that you are a person with special risks, don't be afraid to "sell" yourself to the insurance company. It's legal and moral, and you owe it to yourself and your family to be properly protected.

Passing the Physical

• Go early. People who take physicals early in the morning are most likely to pass. Your weight is lower in the morning, you are usually under less stress, and you haven't eaten, so you are prepared for a blood test.

• Control your vices. Don't eat, smoke, or drink before your physical. Alcohol, salt, and coffee can produce an undesirable effect on your blood pressure or blood analysis.

• Try to provide a urine specimen before your blood pressure is taken. Urination reduces blood pressure. If you jog or exercise heavily, be sure to tell the doctor. Oftentimes, heavy exercise will cause urine specimens to turn up "abnormal."

• Don't withhold information about your smoking habits. If you smoke, admit it. Chances are the physician will find out anyway, and you could be rejected for withholding information.

• Consult your own doctor *before* the insurance physical. The doctor should know precisely what your condition is in order to help answer possible questions by the insurance company. Be sure to ask about stress and/or other special tests you might be given. Some of these may not be safe for you, and your own doctor can recommend suitable equivalents.

• Don't change your medical routine just before the insurance examination. Your system may react badly or unusually. Always provide a record of any medication you're currently taking.

• Preparation counts. Try to find out what questions you'll be asked. Plan your answers and obtain records to back up your statements. Try not to forget anything; if the insurance company thinks you're withholding information, you can be rejected.

• If you've just gotten over a cold or are feeling tired, you won't test well, so it's smart to reschedule the exam. Once you've been turned down for a medical reason, an insurance company will rarely reconsider.

Beyond the Physical

Apart from passing the insurance physical, there are other things you can do to get coverage. Undergo regular physicals and keep records of the results. Underwriters can be swayed by evidence that you've controlled a chronic condition such as hypertension or diabetes.

Shop around. High-risk insurance candidates frequently fail to shop enough.

If you've already been rated and assigned to an expensive, high-risk premium category, don't give up. Ratings can be reversed. For example, three years after a cancer operation, you could legitimately receive a removal of a rating that imposes a surcharge of $15 per $1,000 of coverage. New information, actuarial studies, and correcting simple errors may make it possible to reduce your premiums over time.

Remember, if you face special risks, don't apply for insurance in the usual manner. Know what your options are, keep records, be patient, and never take no for an answer.

Source: Benjamin Lipson, president of Benjamin Lipson Associates Insurance Agency, Inc., 7 Bulfinch Pl., Boston 02114. Mr. Lipson is an independent insurance broker specializing in insurance for people with medical problems. He is also the author of *How to Collect More on Your Insurance Claims* and writes a weekly newspaper column.

What You Should Know about Life Insurance Replacement

People who hold old cash-value life insurance policies (most of which carry interest rates as low as 5%) are being urged to replace them with new policies with higher returns.

Although such substitutions make financial sense in some situations, in other cases the client stands to lose.

Best-case scenario: The client who changes saves up to 25% on premium costs. Drawback: Since he's buying a new policy, he has to pay the acquisition cost—which often amounts to as much as one year's premium.

People buy cash-value life insurance for two reasons (one of them usually takes precedence):

• Permanent insurance protection. If this is your primary reason for owning a policy, you may come out ahead by switching. Even though you're buying insurance at an older age (which carries a higher premium base), new actuarial tables could lower your actual premium layout. (Note: People who need short-term protection for, say, five years are often best off with term insurance. Generally speaking, cash-value life insurance is best for people who want long-term—even lifetime—protection.)

• Accumulation of capital. If this is your primary reason for owning coverage, you may lose in a replacement. Usually you do better by negotiating a conversion of your existing policy to a higher rate of return than by paying a second set of acquisition costs. Example: Most insurers will raise your interest to the current T-bill rate if you agree to pay them the market rate for loans.

Important: Your math must be correct, and so must your reason for buying the insurance.

What To Do

Without a detailed financial and actuarial analysis, it's impossible to predict whether a specific replacement is prudent. There's no rule of thumb, since insurance companies have reacted to the rash of replacements with incentives (such as higher dividends on old policies, premium discounts on new insurance, and even free insurance for up to 10 years) for customers who keep their original policies and agree to pay the market rate on loans.

Consumer laws forbid insurance brokers to make a replacement without first conducting a full analysis, submitting substantiating evidence to the insurance company, and having the client sign a statement verifying that he saw all the data before he made his decision. This regulation has been difficult to enforce, however.

If, without making an analysis, your broker categorically tells you a replacement is good for you, he is acting in his best interest— not yours. On the other hand, if your broker suggests doing the analysis to find out whether you can gain, he's acting on your behalf.

Source: Arthur Schechner, chairman, Schechner Lifson Ackerman & Chodorcoff, insurance agents and brokers, Millburn, NJ.

Borrowing from Your Life Insurance Policy

Is your life insurance policy a good source of readily available funds? When should you borrow from it?

The rate at which you can borrow from your life insurance policy depends primarily on when you bought it. If your policy is more than 10 years old, you may be able to borrow at 5% or 6%. Policies less than 10 years old generally have 8% loan provisions. If you've purchased a policy since 1982, your policy probably has either an 8% loan provision or what is known as a "variable loan rate." The latter means that the rate at which you can borrow varies and is pegged to an index such as Moody's Corporate Bond Index.

One certainty is that, regardless of the rate at which you can borrow, policy loans are somewhat more expensive than they used to be. The Tax Reform Act of 1986 treats the deductibility of policy loan interest the same as other consumer interest deductions. Deduction of policy loan interest is being phased out over a five-year period.

Despite this revision, borrowing from a life insurance policy is still less complicated than most other borrowing. You can borrow from your policy without delay—and without the approval of a bank officer.

However, because the cash accumulation inside a life insurance policy is tax-deferred, and depending on your tax bracket, you may find that you are better off borrowing from a bank than borrowing from your policy, particularly when interest rates are low. Borrowing from a life insurance policy at 8% is convenient, but may prove more costly in the long run.

Why? You may find that borrowing from your policy affects the dividends you receive from your life insurance company. If you have a "participating" life insurance policy—one that pays dividends—talk to your agent or life insurance company before borrowing. If dividends are calculated by a technique called "direct recognition," you may get higher dividends and greater tax-deferred cash accumulation if you don't borrow from your policy.

Source: Mark J. Lucius, advertising and corporate information specialist for Northwestern Mutual Life Insurance Company, 720 E. Wisconsin Ave., Milwaukee, WI 53202. Mr. Lucius is responsible for national publicity for the "Quiet Company's" activities and products.

The Darlings of Tax Reform

With tax reform now in the picture, the insurance industry's deferred annuities are becoming one of the most attractive investment products around.

Deferred annuities can serve as an alternative for individuals whose incentive to continue to make IRA contributions was greatly weakened by tax reform. Although contributions to a deferred annuity are not tax deductible, earnings do accumulate tax deferred. Advantage over an IRA: There is no limit to the amount of money you can invest in an annuity.

The new variable annuity can serve as the ideal replacement for investments that used to receive the benefit of favorable long-term capital gains treatment. Long-term gains from investments in stocks can be sheltered in a variable annuity. That income is not taxed until you withdraw your money.

How Annuities Work

An individual buys an annuity from an insurance company, paying a lump sum or a series of payments over time. In return, the insurance company guarantees that the funds will grow at a certain tax-free rate. Then, beginning on a specified date, the individual receives regular income payments for life.

Payments depend on the amount of money contributed to the account, the length of time the funds are left in it, and the rate of return earned on the funds. Also a factor in determining the size of the payments is whether you include your spouse and other heirs as beneficiaries. Different options enable you to have payments continue to your spouse, or to your children, or for a minimum of, say, 20 years, regardless of who is there to receive them after you die.

Deferred annuities therefore can be considered part insurance and part investment. If you are willing to part with at least $5,000 (the minimum amount can differ from company to company) for five years or longer, you can be guaranteed a competitive, tax-free return on your funds. Because the earned income is not taxed until you begin withdrawing the money (presumably at a lower tax rate), your funds accumulate much faster than they would if they were taxed. The insurance component, of course, is guaranteed regular monthly income payments for the rest of your life—taking the worry and risk out of budgeting for your retirement income. Also, should you die before you begin receiving payments, your heirs are guaranteed to receive the full amount of your original principal.

Fixed Rate Versus Variable

There are two basic types of deferred annuity—fixed and variable.

Fixed annuity: The insurance company guarantees that your funds will grow at a specified rate for a specified period of time. Most companies guarantee a specific rate of return for at least the first year. Thereafter, the rate usually fluctuates at least once a year, according to the then-prevailing interest rates. Although the rates of return for fixed annuities may vary, your principal always remains intact.

Variable annuity: The rate of return is determined by the performance of investments you select from a broad range of mutual funds offered by the insurance company. Investing in a variable annuity is almost identical to investing in a family of mutual funds. You have the same exchange privileges and the choice of putting all your money into one fund or a blend of different funds, or even of dividing your money between a fixed annuity and a variable annuity. You can earn a much larger return than you might with a fixed annuity. However, if your investments perform poorly, your original principal may diminish.

The minimum investment for a deferred annuity is generally $5,000, although some single premium annuities can require a one-time lump-sum investment of as little as $2,500. A flexible premium annuity, paid over time, may have an initial minimum as low as $1,000 and require small monthly payments.

Most companies levy an annual management charge of 0.5%–1.5% of total assets. If you invest in a variable annuity, you will also pay a percentage of your total assets to cover management costs for the mutual fund.

Insurance companies typically charge a declining surrender fee of 5%–6% (which usually falls to zero after five or six years) if you liquidate the principal of your annuity. And if you withdraw your money before age 59½, the IRS will charge you a penalty.

Source: Alexandra Armstrong, Alexandra Armstrong Advisors, Inc., 1140 Connecticut Ave. NW, Washington, DC 20036.

Good News: Single Premium Life Insurance

Don't let the name fool you. The purpose of single premium life insurance is to accumulate money tax-free with no investment risk. It has little to do with traditional insurance.

Single premium life insurance policies

(SPLs) are investments that can be compared to municipal bonds, but they're better. They offer comparable yields, but guarantee your principal. Yields, which are adjusted annually and guaranteed for a year, mirror closely those on long-term AA-rated municipals.

How It Works

The investor pays a single premium for a life insurance policy that provides the minimum amount of life insurance allowed by law to qualify it as a life insurance product. That premium is then invested by the insurance company (mostly in corporate bonds and short-term mortgages). Minimum premium: $5,000. As long as it isn't withdrawn from the policy, the interest accruing on those investments is tax free.

The principal in SPLs is guaranteed. No matter how high interest rates soar, your investment remains safe and, the higher they go, the greater your yield. In a period of climbing interest rates, SPLs are far superior to municipal bonds. (Of course, the reverse is true when rates are dropping.)

Drawback: There is no way to add money to the policy once you've paid the initial premium. To invest new funds, you must purchase a new SPL.

Long-Term Only

Don't buy an SPL if you think you might want to cash it in within the next eight years or so. Surrender penalties start at 7% the first year and decline slowly over an eight-year period to zero. Worse: If you cash in a policy, you must pay tax on accrued interest.

Unfortunately, you may not deduct interest payments on loans against principal or accrued interest. You are allowed to write off payments on loans against multipremium policies for which you have paid at least four of the first seven premiums, but they aren't investment-advantaged, with their hefty commissions and high rates for life insurance.

If you're not in good health, you may have trouble getting a policy in which you are the insured. You can, however, make any family member or business associate the insured and still remain the owner of a policy. The death

benefit can be 50%–600% of the value of your premium, depending on the insured's age. The coverage is paid for out of the difference between what the insurance company actually makes investing your premium and the return it pays you—about two percentage points.

Selecting a Policy

Stockbrokers, financial planners, and insurance agents all sell SPLs, but beware of these advisers. Stockbrokers will likely have to offer the product their company tells them to sell you, most financial planners lack the insurance expertise to choose wisely, and many insurance agents just don't know enough about investing.

Of the companies offering SPLs, three are outstanding organizations with exceptional products: The Equitable, Confederation Life, and Life of Virginia. They've each been in business for at least 100 years (as Will Rogers put it, "It's not the return on my money, but the return *of* my money, I'm interested in"). Each has at least $1 billion in assets; all are rated A+ by A.M. Best, the insurance company rating service. Each pays for your life insurance protection out of the investment spread, none charge a front-end load (sales commission), all offer zero-net-cost loans for accessing interest and charge no more than three percentage points over the yield on loans against principal. Finally, all of them guarantee not to lower the yield for current policyholders below that offered to new clients.

Source: Andrew D. Westhem, chairman, Western Capital Financial Services, Los Angeles.

Profit From Life Insurance

It's possible to come out ahead by donating a paid-up life insurance policy to charity. *Key:* Your contribution will not be valued at the policy's cash value, but rather at its *replacement* value, which may be much *greater* than its cash value. You can then obtain additional coverage for yourself by buying inexpensive term insurance.

Source: *Joseph T. Ryerson,* 312 US 260.

Single Premium Variable Life Policies

With tax reform having done away with most traditional tax shelters, single premium variable life insurance (SPVL) is more attractive than ever. With SPVL, you pay a single premium to buy a life insurance policy, and your money is invested by the insurance company in selected mutual funds managed by an investment firm. Your earnings—as well as the stability of your principal—depend upon the performance of the funds chosen and are therefore variable. You can select the markets to invest in or you can choose to have a professional manage your account for you.

Major advantages: You pay no taxes on earnings unless you cash in the policy. With no taxes subtracted, earnings compound faster in your account. And when the insured dies, the cash value of the policy (the original premium, plus additional premiums and earnings) and the term insurance pass to the policy's beneficiary outside probate and free of income tax.

You buy SPVL as an investment—never for the life insurance. But the insurance is a nice extra. The amount of insurance that you get varies with the age and sex of the person you decide to insure.

Great Flexibility

Depending on the insurance company, SPVL accounts offer five to 10 different mutual funds to choose from and let you divide your investment among as many as five funds at a time. Options:

- Aggressive growth stocks.
- Blue-chip stocks.
- High-grade corporate bonds.
- High-yield junk bonds.

- Money-market instruments.
- US government bonds.
- Zero-coupon bonds.

Like many mutual fund families, several insurance companies allow you to switch money from fund to fund by simply calling a toll-free number. Free switches: 4–12 a year.

Edge over ordinary mutual fund switching: If by switching you incur a capital gain, you pay no tax on it. However, if you have a loss, you may not deduct it.

Fully managed accounts adopt multiple strategies, including investing in foreign stock. A professional portfolio manager makes all switching decisions for you.

Taking Money Out

If you remove money from the policy, you must pay income tax on any earnings, but you may borrow up to the equivalent of 75%–90% of a policy's cash value from the insurance company at a very low net interest cost (0.5%–1%). The policy's cash value acts as collateral.

The net interest cost to you of the loan is the difference between the interest rate that the insurance company charges for the loan and the rate that is earned by the funds that have been put aside as collateral for the loan. Most insurance companies offer a guaranteed maximum rate.

High Maximum Investment

Drawback: Relatively high minimum investment—$5,000–$10,000. Most mutual funds have $500–$2,000 minimums. However, for investors interested in a fully managed account who are comparing the SPVL minimum with those of professional investment counsels ($200,000 and up), the SPVL minimum is actually low.

Most SPVL accounts invest 100% of your money, deducting no sales charge (or load) from your premium. Earnings on your entire investment begin to compound immediately. Catch: The charges are withdrawn from your account periodically.

This is why annual costs are relatively high—2%–2.5%—compared with those of mutual funds (0.75%–1.5%) and professionally managed accounts (1%–2%). Costs include the deferred sales charge, administrative charges, state and local premium taxes, the cost of insurance, and fund management fees.

Right for You?

SPVL offers substantial benefits to high-tax-bracket individuals who expect to make significant investment returns in the future. But SPVL isn't for all high-bracket investors.

Problem 1: Early surrender charges are steep—7%–8% in the first year, declining gradually to 0% by the eighth year. So you must be sure that you won't need the money that you invest for several years.

Problem 2: If you cash in a policy, income taxes must be paid on all earnings.

The risk/reward ratio on an SPVL policy is much greater than that on a whole life policy, which guarantees your principal and sets a fixed rate of return annually. With SPVL, you can make much more money if the markets you have invested in go up, but your principal isn't guaranteed in the event of a downturn.

If you invest in an investor-directed account, be sure that you have the time to follow the markets. Helpful: Newsletters that track SPVL mutual funds, such as *Mutual Fund Investing* (7811 Montrose Rd., Potomac, MD 20854, 301-340-2100) and *Telephone Switch Newsletter* (Box 2538, Huntington Beach, CA 92647, 714-898-2588). If you don't have the time to supervise your account, seriously consider a fully managed account.

Selection Criteria

• A policy should offer telephone switching for self-directed accounts. If it doesn't, you lose valuable time in responding to market changes.

• Funds should be managed by a top-notch investment firm. Most insurance companies use money managers at major New York investment banks to manage their funds. Key: The money managers' strength—not the insurance company's.

• Loans should be available by phone. And there should be minimal follow-up paper work.

• The guaranteed maximum net cost of borrowing should be 1% or less.

• Total annual charges should be no more than 2.5%. And there should be no up-front sales charge.

Source: Andrew D. Westhem, chairman, Western Capital Financial Services, Los Angeles.

Single Premium Insurance Vs. Annuities

Single premium whole life insurance may be better than annuities for your financial circumstances. Single premium life gives you a fully paid-up life insurance policy, and death benefits are payable to your heirs tax free. Annuities are simply tax-deferred investment accounts with no insurance benefits.

Source: *Donoghue's Moneyletter*, Holliston, MA.

Keeping Insurance Proceeds Out Of the Wrong Hands

The settlement from a life insurance policy can end up in the wrong hands, unless these rules are followed:

• Specify full name, nature of relationship, and date of birth of beneficiaries. If a policyholder's mother and ex-wife are both named Jane Smith, both can claim the settlement.

• Name primary, secondary, and tertiary beneficiaries. If a policyholder and the sole beneficiary die at the same time, the settlement goes into the estate of the policy owner. Name several beneficiaries in order of preference to establish a clear line of succession.

• Update the policy to reflect life's changes.

A person who has remarried might want the settlement to go to the second spouse. But if the policy is never updated, the second spouse will have no legal claim to the money. Or, if the policy says "Mrs. Jones," both wives may claim it. Alternatively, a remarried policyholder may want the money to go to children from a prior marriage.

Source: Leonard B. Stern, president of Leonard B. Stern & Co., estate planning and financial services, 305 Madison Ave., New York 10165.

Guarding Your Life Insurance from the IRS

The cash surrender value of a life insurance policy is subject to an IRS lien for unpaid taxes. Even if you have given the policy away, it's vulnerable if you have retained any right in it whatsoever (e.g., the right to borrow against the policy or to change the beneficiary).

To protect the beneficiary fully, it's necessary to write to the insurance company and renounce totally any and all rights in the policy. Another way: Buy only term insurance, which has no cash surrender value for the IRS to levy against.

Health Insurance: An Overview

With medical costs rising at two and three times the rate of inflation and the cost of even a moderate stay in the hospital approaching six figures, the lack of adequate medical or health insurance is tantamount to playing financial Russian roulette. To get properly insured, however, can require that you wade through a vast array of insurance products, application costs analysis, etc. For example,

product classification alone can be broken down by method of underwriting (group or individual), peril (accident or illness), contract (commercial, industrial, special), type of loss (medical expense, income), or size of benefit (first dollar, catastrophic).

Three Types of Coverage

For those just starting the process, the two most important categories to consider are medical care and loss of income. The main types of coverage include (1) basic hospital, surgical, and regular medical coverage; (2) major medical coverage; and (3) disability insurance.

Basic medical coverage pays for part of your hospital expenses, your room, some lab expenses, specified surgery, and certain non-surgical doctor's fees. Payments typically start early with relatively low deductibles. Most basic plans cover nearly all routine hospital expenses from the onset of illness or injury up to an aggregate expense cap of, say, $25,000. The only drawback is that once you reach your expense limit, you're on your own.

Major medical or catastrophic insurance coverage, on the other hand, is not intended to cover every visit to the doctor, or even the cost of some minor surgeries. Coverage is instead based on the premise that most individuals can absorb the small medical expenses, but need insurance against catastrophically large medical expenses, such as those incurred in a life-threatening illness or accident.

To keep costs down, a typical major medical policy contains a relatively high deductible amount: As high as $2,500 for individuals, and as much as $200,000 for a large group policy. Once the deductible amount is reached, all expenses are covered up to a total that usually ranges between $500,000 and $1 million.

The main distinctions between major medical and basic medical coverage are that the former (1) generally has much higher maximum limits, (2) has more extensive (blanket) coverage, (3) has much higher deductibles, and (4) usually requires additional coinsurance. As a rule, the coinsurance clause demands some participation by the insured even after the deductible amount is met. For example, the insured may be required to pay 100% of the first $2,000 (deductible) and 20% of the next $3,000 (coinsurance amount), with the carrier paying 100% of the amount beyond $5,000 up to the policy limits.

The third type of health insurance available, disability coverage, does not pay for any medical expenses. Instead, it replaces a portion of lost income and wages that may result from the insured's inability to perform the normal duties of his occupation due to illness or injury. It is particularly important protection in the event of a long-term disability.

Source: Karen P. Schaeffer, president, Schaeffer Financial, 7855 Walker Dr., Greenbelt, MD 20770, a financial-planning firm affiliated with Hibbard Brown & Co.

The Best Buys in Health Insurance

Finding the absolutely best deal in health insurance would probably require a company-by-company and policy-by-policy search. To avoid spending most of your free time for the next several months doing that kind of research, try following a few general rules to help keep costs down without sacrificing coverage.

The first rule: You can usually obtain the most cost-effective insurance by purchasing major medical instead of basic health coverage. This allows you to assume the small risks of everyday bumps and scratches and to pay for routine medical care, while insuring yourself against the risk of potentially devastating major illnesses and injuries.

The second way to contain costs is through group insurance. Most employers offer some form of group insurance at a cost that may be 20%–40% less than individual coverage. You usually don't have to take a physical and coverage stays in force until you leave the company.

The number of employees in the group will determine the most inexpensive type of coverage. If more than 100 employees are

involved, self-insuring may provide substantial savings. The one problem with this type approach is the risk of a large claim during the first few years of the plan, before a sufficient reserve has accumulated. However, the company may be willing to assume this risk or to obtain regular group coverage during the accumulation period.

Group underwriting offers another way of cost cutting through shared funding. The employer, employee, and the insurance company share in the losses up to a predetermined limit, say $10,000 per individual. After the limit is reached, the insurance company assumes full responsibility up to the limits of the policy. The split among the three parties is determined on an actuarial basis, according to the group census.

Under either a self-insurance plan or shared-funding plan, you must calculate in advance whether there are true cash-flow gains or whether the payments have simply been deferred to the end of the contract year.

Another cost-containment strategy for group health plans is precertification. Under a precertification contract, employees must obtain authorization for prospective hospital coverage or operations in order to be reimbursed. Prior to any operation, the employee submits a detailed plan from the doctor to the company outlining the procedures to be undertaken and the estimated costs. Any expenses incurred without approval, except emergency room visits, are not covered by the policy.

Some insurance companies seek to reduce costs and lower premiums by requiring second opinions before any surgical procedures. Although the second doctor's appointment increases the up-front costs, over time the reduction in unnecessary surgery more than offsets it. These savings may be available in the form of reduced premiums for individual as well as group plans.

A final trend toward lower costs in group health insurance is restricted access for employee dependents. Many companies are offering insurance only to their employees, requiring substantial if not total contribution for any benefits to the employees' families.

The result is a reduction in premiums for the company, but the plan may not be the best one for you, depending upon your family's needs.

Source: Karen P. Schaeffer, president, Schaeffer Financial, 7855 Walker Dr., Greenbelt, MD 20770, a financial-planning firm affiliated with Hibbard Brown & Co.

Collecting More on Your Company Health Policy

Health insurance policies are not etched in stone. There are contractual provisions in the insurance policy that are negotiable.

Most companies give health insurance to engender goodwill among employees. Many problems in collecting the maximum due you are a result of incompetence or of negligence on the part of the administrators in your company who handle insurance benefits. They may be too busy or unaware of how to get more for you. Three ways to improve your ability to collect:

• Know the insurance contract and all its provisions. Be aware that everything is negotiable. Example: Home health care by someone other than a registered nurse or practical nurse is not covered in the policy. Contractually nothing needs to be said, but administratively an alternate source of home health care could be covered. It is really a question of negotiation.

• Have the company's insurance broker help negotiate with the insurer. He is the one who is making the money from selling your company the policy. He also has more leverage than you do with the insurance company. If he is unwilling to help, encourage your company to switch to a more cooperative broker.

• Set up a liaison. The individual in your company in charge of claims should have a good working relationship with the insurance company. If a settlement is too low or doesn't fully cover your needs, the claims person at your firm can make a better settlement. After all, the insurance company is selling policies.

If your claims person is uncertain whether you can get more compensation for an ailment or treatment, ask for permission to contact the broker. The broker should know the terms of your contract and be familiar with the people at the insurance company. He should have an idea of how to get the claim paid, especially if it's a legitimate claim but a trifle unusual.

Coverage for Couples

Take advantage of situations where both spouses are covered at their jobs by group insurance policies to increase your benefits.

Example: You both have Blue Cross to cover hospitalization and, in addition, you both have major medical. Typically, the major medical has a $100 deductible. The insurance company will pick up 80% of the next $2,000 and 100% thereafter. However, if both spouses coordinate their policies, you could wind up using the other's policy to pay that remaining 20% of the $2,000.

Don't expect to make a profit by having several insurance policies. Years ago many health insurance policies were not coordinated and it was possible to get duplicate payments. Today all plans are coordinated so you can't get duplicate payments.

Unallowable Treatments

Trying to make specifically unallowable treatments allowable: This is between the doctor and you. For instance, if you want to claim cosmetic surgery necessary for health reasons, consult your doctor. If he won't go along with it, you are not going to get anywhere with the insurance broker, the personnel at your office, or the insurance company.

If you're stuck with a flawed company policy and have huge deductibles and other uncovered expenses, take out a personal policy that coordinates with the company's.

Source: Leonard Stern, president, Leonard B. Stern & Co., an insurance consulting and brokerage firm, 65 E. 55 St., Suite 303, New York 10022.

Health Insurance Traps and Pitfalls

Nothing is more vexing than submitting a substantial medical bill to an insurance carrier only to have it returned, riddled with partially rejected claims or, worse yet, turned down completely. In most cases, the problem arises out of ignorance of a policy's details—available coverage, the limits of coverage, or the compliance or administrative requirements. Usually, the simplest answer is self-education. On certain occasions, the answer is a new insurance company.

Know What To Expect

When it comes to insurance policies, there is no substitute for reading the fine print. This is especially true for basic insurance coverage, where policies set forth which procedures are covered, partially covered (and the extent to which they are covered), and totally excluded.

Always take note of the areas not covered by a policy—these can be the greatest source of confusion. The most commonly excluded items are cosmetic surgery or certain other "voluntary" operations, such as reverse sterilization; certain prescription drugs, such as birth control pills; and vitamins.

Some policies put ceilings on the amounts payable for very serious areas of medical expense. For example, there may be a limit on the total payable amount for stays in an intensive-care unit. The limit can be in the form of a cap on either total days or total expenses. Some policies limit intensive-care-unit payments to 1½ or 2 times the semiprivate room rate. Given the astronomically high cost of intensive-care-unit treatment, a limit such as this is entirely inadequate and a signal to look for a new insurer.

In the same vein, some older policies restrict total payment for hospital stays. For instance, a policy providing the average semiprivate room rates or $120 per day, "whichever is less," is unrealistic in today's health care environment.

Pay close attention to a policy's treatment of "preexisting conditions." Almost all policies exclude preexisting medical conditions from coverage by attaching exclusionary riders. If you fail to disclose a preexisting condition in your application, you leave yourself open to the total rejection of your policy, at the company's discretion, at any time during the first two years of ownership.

Problems with Group Coverage

Group health insurance can cause even more headaches. Many employees may not have ready access to the master policy in order to review the details of coverage. Yet it is critical to insist on full information to forestall problems.

Restrictions may apply to employees hired after the group policy is in force; for example, a newly hired employee with a preexisting condition, which may have been assumed under the original policy, may be eligible for only limited coverage, if any, under the same plan. Failure to comply with precertification or preauthorization requirements can result in the complete rejection of an employee claim. Since much of the cost of group insurance is being shifted to employees, copayments, deductibles, and limits also can present unpleasant surprises to the uninformed.

The most general problem of group plans is their lack of transferability. Although a new law requires your employer to keep you on the group plan for 18 months (36 months in some cases), the premium becomes your responsibility once you quit or are fired. In addition to the financial burden, you may have a serious problem in the case of chronic illnesses that develop and are treated under a current plan. When you apply for new coverage, the ailment in question may not be included in the policy. In the worst case, the ailment may be so severe that coverage is denied completely. As a result, unless you have private health insurance, your employment options may become subject to your insurance needs.

Source: Karen P. Schaeffer, president, Schaeffer Financial, 7855 Walker Dr., Greenbelt, MD 20770, a financial-planning firm affiliated with Hibbard Brown & Co.

Health Insurance if You Are Not in a Group Plan

Most people have their health insurance needs taken care of by their employers. For those not covered by an employer, the task of obtaining adequate medical coverage can be difficult as well as expensive. Good coverage can cost between $750 and $1,750 a year for an individual and from $1,500 to $3,500 a year for a family; even then, the policy may have large deductibles that require you to pay some portion (often 20%) of remaining expenses. Policies that cost much less than these amounts probably don't offer good coverage.

If you must buy health insurance on your own, consider a health maintenance organization (HMO). For a set fee, you will receive all of the coverage you need but without deductibles and coinsurance. This goes for people on Medicare as well. If you cannot find anyone in your area qualified to provide information on HMOs, contact the Group Health Association of America, 629 9 St. NW, Washington, DC 20001.

If you decide not to join an HMO, then Blue Cross/Blue Shield is probably your next best buy. These policies usually return 85%–90% of the premiums paid in claims, although in some instances people have had difficulty getting their claims paid.

Major medical policies from life insurance companies return about $.60 per $1.00 in premiums. For younger people and those willing to take a fairly large deductible, these policies may be the best choice.

If you are under 65 and have a health impairment, there may not be a suitable program for you. Some individuals may be able to get coverage from Blue Cross/Blue Shield (although most plans can reject you for health reasons); a few people may be able to obtain coverage through the use of riders or extra premiums.

If you are thinking about leaving a job that covers you with a group policy, take the time to learn about the policy's privileges regarding conversion into an individual policy after you leave. Oftentimes, conversion privileges provide for an expensive individual policy with only limited coverage.

If you can't afford any of these alternatives, you may qualify for Medicaid. Check with the local social services agency in your state. For those 65 or over, Parts A and B of Medicare should be purchased. Your local Social Security office can provide you with information.

Source: J. Robert Hunter, president, National Insurance Consumer Organization, 121 N. Payne St., Alexandria, VA 22314, the first nonprofit national organization established to promote the interests of insurance buyers.

Something To Tide You Over

Temporary health insurance is available for periods when you're between jobs, starting a new business, etc. Policies are sold for specific periods of 30 to 180 days and are generally renewable only once. Most don't cover pregnancy or preexisting disabilities. Rates are low.

Medicare: What It Doesn't Cover

Don't fool yourself that all your old-age medical needs will be taken care of by Medicare. This program is riddled with coverage gaps. Be aware of what not to expect from Medicare.

What Is Medicare?
Medicare must be distinguished from Medicaid, which is the federal program providing medical coverage for the indigent of all ages. Most elderly people wind up on Medicaid when their assets are exhausted paying for what Medicare doesn't cover. This can be a tragedy for people who had hoped to leave something to their children.

Medicare is an insurance program for people over 65. It is subsidized by the federal government through the Social Security Administration. Each month, elderly people pay premiums to private insurance companies (Blue Cross/Blue Shield or companies like them), which act as fiscal intermediaries for Medicare. The program is overseen by a watchdog agency, a Professional Standards Review Organization (PSRO), which makes sure hospitals are not used improperly. Drawbacks: Private insurance companies, acting in their own best interests, tend to deny benefits whenever possible. PSROs interpret Medicare regulations restrictively, since they must save government money.

Major problems with Medicare:

• Congress passed much of the Medicare legislation with the intention of helping the elderly by keeping them out of institutions. However, the local agencies administer Medicare restrictively in a misguided attempt to save money. Actually, money is being wasted by forcing the elderly into nursing homes unnecessarily. Result: Benefits we thought would go to the elderly don't materialize.

• Medicare does not deal with the problem of custodial care. It is geared toward rehabilitation, which is hardly realistic for the population it serves.

• Medicare is part of an overall supply-and-demand problem. There are simply more and more old people every year, as modern medicine enables us to live longer. While the over-65 population expands, nursing homes are filled to capacity and have long waiting lists, and Social Security benefits and services to the elderly are being cut back.

• Hospital cutoffs are the biggest problem with Medicare today. Example: An elderly woman goes into the hospital with a broken hip. After surgery, she cannot go home because she can't take care of herself. She needs nursing home rehabilitation or an around-the-clock companion at home. Because of the shortage of these long-term-care alternatives, she has to remain in the hospital, though everyone agrees she is ready to leave. But Medicare cuts off hospitalization benefits, claiming that she no longer needs hospitalization. The family gets a threatening letter from the hospital—if she isn't out in 24 hours, the family will have to pay privately. At the present rates for a hospital bed, the family's assets will be wiped out very quickly.

The Appeal Process

The only way to deal with such unfair (and inhumane) bureaucratic decisions is to appeal them aggressively. Chances on appeal: Very good. At the highest level, federal court, the reversal rate on Medicare cases is extremely high.

There are four levels of appeal:

• Reconsideration is a paper review by a bureaucrat. You can request this when Medicare is first denied. Some 95% of reconsiderations confirm the original denial of benefits.

• An administrative law judge will review the case after the reconsideration is denied. You present evidence at this hearing, and a lawyer is recommended. Some of these judges are competent and sympathetic. However, many judges fail to understand the issue.

• The Appeals Council in Washington is the next step. They will usually rubber-stamp the decision of the administrative law judge.

• Federal court is your final crack. You do stand a good chance of winning here, because judges at the federal level are not employees of the Social Security Administration. They tend to be less sympathetic to the agency's viewpoint.

At this level a lawyer is necessary. Important: No new evidence can be presented in federal court, so be sure all your facts are presented to the administrative law judge.

Medicare and Nursing Homes

Under the law, up to 100 days of skilled nursing care in a nursing home are to be paid for by Medicare. In fact, Medicare pays for an average of only five days, claiming that nursing homes do not provide skilled care. This is another patently unfair decision that must be appealed on an individual basis.

Beyond 100 days, you're on your own as far as nursing-home care is concerned. Medicaid will take over only after your assets are totally exhausted. At an average cost of $30,000 per year, few families can afford long-term nursing-home care. Important: Plan ahead for this possibility well before a nursing home becomes necessary. Transfer your assets to your children, or set up a trust fund that the government can't invade. Be aware: You may be liable for payment if your assets have been transferred within less than an average of two years before entering a home, depending on the state.

Recommended: Consultation with a specialist in geriatric law. Ask your lawyer or a social worker in a local hospital or nursing home to recommend one.

Home Care

The home care situation under Medicare is also dismal. Medicare will pay for a skilled person to come into the home occasionally on a doctor's orders to perform tasks such as giving injections or physical therapy. There is virtually no coverage for the kind of help most elderly people need—a housekeeper/companion to help with personal and household tasks. Many senior citizens groups are currently lobbying for this type of home custodial care to be provided by Medicare.

Assignment Rate

As far as general health is concerned, Medicare supposedly pays 80% of the "reasonable rate" for medical care as determined by a board of doctors in the community. In reality, the "reasonable rate" is usually set so low that most doctors will not accept it. So instead of paying 20% of their doctor bills, the elderly frequently wind up paying 50% or even more.

Suggestions

Don't drop your major medical insurance when you retire. If you keep it up, it will cover the gaps in your Medicare insurance. It is extremely difficult to buy such coverage after you reach 65.

• Be wary of insurance company policies that supplement Medicare. You must be extremely careful when you buy one. Be sure it complements rather than duplicates Medicare coverage.

• Get together with other senior citizens to create consumer leverage. If a group of 50 seniors goes to a doctor and all promise to patronize him providing he accepts the Medicare assigned rate, it might be worth his while.

Source: Charles Robert, an attorney specializing in geriatric law, Hempstead, NY.

Supplemental Health Insurance if You Are on Medicare

Although Medicare provides national health insurance for the elderly, the program actually covers less than half of health expenses. The gaps in coverage are difficult to understand and constantly changing; as a result, many elderly people end up buying supplementary insurance that is inadequate.

Those whose coverage at work is not extended upon retirement to supplement Medicare should consider the best Blue Cross/Blue Shield Medicare supplement policy available and the Prudential policies offered through the American Association of Retired Persons. In some states, anyone 65 or over can become a subscriber to Blue Cross/Blue Shield, without evidence of insurability, during the annual "open enrollment" periods.

Buying more than one supplemental policy will not necessarily increase your coverage. Most policies have provisions that require claims payments to be coordinated with other policies so that one policy won't pay if another does, or both policies will pay only half. Medicare supplemental policies almost never cover nursing homes or extended care. Some insurers have begun to offer such coverage, but a congressional study has criticized many of these policies.

Source: J. Robert Hunter, president, National Insurance Consumer Organization, 121 N. Payne St., Alexandria, VA 22314, the first nonprofit national organization established to promote the interests of insurance buyers.

Before Choosing a Nursing Home Policy

What to consider before choosing a nursing home policy: Cost of nursing homes in your locale; whether the policy requires hospitalization before entering a home; the amount of the deductible; coverage for custodial care as well as for skilled care; the duration of coverage; whether mental illnesses are included or excluded. A policy that excludes mental illness only if there is no organic cause still protects you in the event of Alzheimer's disease. The younger the insured, the lower the premiums.

Policies now available (although not in all states): CNA's Continental Casualty, Amex Life, Transport Life, and Travelers. The American Association of Retired Persons is testing a policy for its members through Prudential.

Source: *Business Week*, New York.

Disability Insurance: What You Need, What To Look For

Too many people overestimate their ability to withstand the financial impact of a disability lasting more than 90 days. Their most common misconceptions:

• Their employers "will take care of them" either through a formal income replacement program or by simply keeping them on the payroll.

• Their family's standard of living can be lowered to accommodate the loss of income.

• A spouse who has not worked outside of the home for a number of years can attain a relatively high-paying job in a short period of time.

• A growing net worth, which may be invested in illiquid assets or assets that could only be sold at a substantial discount, can cover their loss of income.

Don't underestimate your needs for ade-

quate disability protection. If you aren't in a position to readily self-insure against the risk of a disabling accident or illness, you need some form of insurance to help fill the gap.

Maximizing Value

Whether you are seeking employer-provided or individually purchased coverage, the objectives and criteria for selection are essentially the same. The key in both cases is to maximize the value of the premium dollar by budgeting for smaller losses and insuring against the catastrophic occurrences that could ruin your personal financial plan.

A major point to consider when choosing a plan is the need to keep your "waiting or elimination period" (the period during a disability when the insurer is not responsible for paying you benefits) between three and six months. These are usually financially acceptable waiting periods. Purchasing the traditional 30-day elimination period can be as much as 40% more expensive and often provides unnecessary coverage.

The "benefit period"—the length of time you can expect to receive disability income—should extend to at least age 65 for each separate incident of disability. For extra safety and where the family unit is relatively young, pay a higher premium in exchange for a lifetime benefit period.

As you get older, you can reduce your coverage and save money by increasing your policy's elimination period and/or reducing the benefit amount. In most cases, a family's financial burdens decline over the years and its ability to meet those burdens improves. As children move out and investment assets are accumulated, the necessity for maintaining disability insurance declines, although it may not be eliminated. However, you should generally avoid cutting costs by reducing your benefit period. If you were struck by a catastrophic disability, you would want benefits for as long a period as possible.

Another major concern is the manner in which the condition of disability is defined in an insurance contract. Some policies use the "pure residual" approach, with the reduction in the level of earnings as the sole criterion.

Since this approach is relatively objective, such contracts are frequently less expensive than those using the alternative approach: Evaluating your ability to perform the duties of an occupation or profession. This approach has many variations, ranging from "ability to perform any duties of any occupation or profession" to "ability to perform the material duties of your profession until age 65." Since the approach is more subjective, premium rates are generally higher.

Normally, the policy with the broadest definition of disability is best, unless you can claim true "specialist" status and justify the added cost. Therefore, the residual approach is suitable for occupations offering the flexibility of reduced hours and duties, while the "ability to perform" approach is best for professions that lack that flexibility—for example, the medical profession. Some policies do feature characteristics of both approaches.

Source: Andrew E. Gross, treasurer and shareholder of Dennis M. Gurtz and Associates, Inc., 4910 Massachusetts Ave. NW, Suite 112, Washington, DC 20016, a financial-planning and consulting firm. The author has an extensive academic and professional background in accounting, risk management, and other financial-planning matters.

More about Disability Insurance

Most people shy away from buying disability insurance because they think they'll never become disabled. Statistics show, however, that at age 37, you're three and a half times more likely to become disabled than to die, and that disability remains more likely than death until you're 68. Many people suffer injury or illness severe enough to make them unable to work, but insufficiently serious to kill them.

Disability policies are among the most confusing to decipher. Look for:

• Noncancelable by the company—only by you.

• Guaranteed continuable until age 65–70 (75 is even better).

• Restrictive riders shouldn't be added by the company when the policy is issued. Look for the broadest coverage you can find.

• Premium cost should be guaranteed not to rise before you reach 65. Trade-off: Your coverage will remain flat, regardless of inflation. You can pay extra for a cost-of-living adjustment rider to pick up the slack.

• Prompt processing of claims—within 10 business days, unless the claim is complicated. (One otherwise good company processes claims through its zone managers. If a manager has a bad quarter with a lot of claims, your claim might be held back and not processed until the following quarter.)

How Disability Is Defined

A useful definition of disability is "your inability to perform the material and substantial duties of your occupation." Under this definition, for example, an anesthesiologist who contracted hepatitis and could no longer practice had to change his profession to hospital administrator, and he was covered. He received $4,000 a month from the insurance company in addition to his regular salary.

Bad definition: One that deals with your inability to work—period. A policy like this won't protect you at all. (The definition used by Social Security is the inability to perform any occupation.)

Injury versus sickness. Insurance companies handle injury claims differently than claims due to illness. Illness-related claims almost always pay fewer benefits than accident claims. Sometimes the company will simply change the classification to its own advantage.

Example: In a policy, the wording "After a stated period of time after your accident, we'll pay you as though you were sick" will reduce both the amount of money you'll receive and the length of time that you'll receive it—sometimes from a lifetime (the longest possible length of payments for an accident claim) down to as little as five years. Much better: That payments for injuries due to an accident remain in the injury-claim classification, regardless of how much time elapses.

Disability insurers also use tricky language to define exactly when you get sick. Since getting a claim approved hinges on when you became ill, using the wording "when the illness first manifests itself" permits the company to deny the claim on the grounds that the illness predated the policy but wasn't diagnosed until after the policy was signed.

Typical: An insurer denies a claim for cancer because the policyholder had the disease for years before the problem became apparent.

Occupational classes. Disability benefits are highly dependent on your occupation at the time of the accident or illness. How long you'll receive benefits depends on the complexity of your training for your current job and the ease with which you might be trained for a new one. Examples: Surgeons are covered for life; managers, 10 years; salespeople, five years; barbers, two years. Good insurance agents help find the company with the most favorable length of occupational coverage and will help you get into the best category.

Specialties within a profession. Some insurance companies don't recognize specialties, and, for example, lump together all their insured lawyers. Avoid these companies. Look for an insurer that differentiates between a litigator and a patent attorney and differentiates in payments for, say, a broken leg, which obviously incapacitates the litigator much more than the patent attorney.

Residual (partial) disability. This desirable rider—available at extra cost—will pay you if, after an illness, you can work only one or two days a week. Usually, if you lose 20% or more of your earned income, you are considered to be residually disabled.

Exclusionary Period

You can choose from exclusionary periods (also known as elimination or deductible periods) of 7, 14, 30, 60, 90, and 180 days—the number of days after the onset of illness or injury it will take for payments to begin. The longer the period, the lower the cost of the policy. Your choice should depend on what other insurance benefits you have. Recommended: 60–90 days.

Amount of coverage. Most companies won't insure you for more than 50%–60% of your earned income. Payments are tax free if you—not your employer—have paid for the policy. You often can end up with as much as 85% of your after-tax income.

Best package. If your funds to buy insurance are limited and you're a professional or executive, buy lifetime accident coverage, sickness to 65 (lifetime, if you can afford it), and residual disability, with a 60- or 90-day exclusionary period. Cost-of-living adjustment riders can be added or dropped each year.

Traps

There are some serious drawbacks to group disability plans—even though group plans often seem attractive—that can leave you high and dry in the event of an accident or illness:

• The issuer can cancel the policy.

• Premiums aren't guaranteed—the issuer can raise them dramatically.

• Coverage and claims practices favor the company, not the insured.

Source: Leonard B. Stern, president, Leonard B. Stern & Co., a financial services and consulting firm, 305 Madison Ave., New York 10165.

How Much Disability Insurance Is Enough?

Before buying disability insurance, assess what resources you already have that would enable you and your family to manage in the event of an accident or illness. Compare these resources with your expenditures. Then, make up any gap with disability insurance. Key questions:

• Would you get partial pay from your employer? How much? For how long?

• Do you have a benevolent family member you could count on to keep you going or at least to help?

• What assets do you have that could be converted quickly?

• Are you already covered by disability insurance policies? (Don't forget to check what's provided by credit cards and association memberships.)

• What could you expect from Social Security?

Reassess your disability coverage whenever:

• Income changes. Almost everyone increases lifestyle and financial needs when income increases.

• Financial responsibilities increase. Examples: You have a new child, a new mortgage, or build a new house.

There is a Social Security trap to watch out for in planning your insurance needs. To get disability payments from Social Security, you must have paid into the system for 40 quarters. But there are errors in the Social Security records, and you may find out too late that records are wrong and you're not covered.

Safeguard: Write to the Social Security Administration, 6401 Security Blvd., Baltimore, MD 21235, every three years for a copy of your account. If there's a mistake, correct it immediately—there's a three-year limit on making changes.

Homeowners or Renters Insurance

Homeowners insurance provides protection for risks such as fire, lightning, wind, hail, and theft. It does not cover some catastrophic events such as flood, earthquake, and nuclear accident. Policies also include liability coverage in case someone sues you for an accident other than an auto claim, such as a dog bite or a fall on your property.

Renters insurance, which is usually inexpensive, covers your own personal property (furniture, etc.) and most liabilities you may incur when renting a property. Similar coverage is available for owners of condominiums, cooperatives, or mobile homes.

Buying Suggestions

To decide how much homeowners cover-age you need, deduct the value of the land and foundation from your property's market value to calculate the maximum policy limit. If you live in an old house whose replacement cost is greater than its market value, then base your policy limit on the estimated replacement cost.

In order to receive reimbursement for partial losses on a replacement basis, rather than a depreciated basis, buy a policy limit equal to at least 80% of the replacement cost of the house (not the land and the foundation). For example, if it would cost $50,000 to replace your house, purchase a policy with a limit of $40,000. Don't let your insurance agent or company convince you to cover your home for a higher amount, because premiums are proportional to policy limits. For instance, premiums on a $120,000 policy cost about 20% more than those on a $100,000 policy, even though the extra risk for the company is far less than 20% (since most claims are small). Also, consider increasing your deductible to lower your premiums, depending on what you feel comfortable with.

Note: If you qualify, the federal government will sell you flood insurance (call 800-638-6620). The government does this because private insurers are unable to provide protection for this risk. Also, if you have trouble obtaining fire insurance, about half of the states have a plan (the Fair Access to Insurance Requirements Plan, or FAIR Plan) that guarantees coverage for your property if you can pay the premium and your home meets building code requirements.

When shopping for a homeowners policy, keep in mind that you can usually save money by buying from a direct-writing insurer (one that doesn't use so-called independent agents). And, according to *Consumer Reports* readers and state complaint statistics, consumers get better service from these lower-priced insurers.

Source: J. Robert Hunter, president, National Insurance Consumer Organization, 121 N. Payne St., Alexandria, VA 22314, the first nonprofit national organization established to promote the interests of insurance buyers.

Better Home Insurance Buying

Many people spend far too much money for home insurance and then end up with the wrong coverage. Key: Don't waste money protecting yourself against small losses. What you should look for:

Home replacement coverage: Protect yourself against the total destruction of your house. Urban and suburban homeowners may need to buy coverage for only 80% of the replacement value of a home because local fire services in the city are quicker to respond than those in rural areas. If your insurance is for a dollar amount, check annually to see if it will still pay for a replacement home.

High deductibles: A $1,000 deductible can cut insurance premiums by more than one-third. The savings will normally more than make up for the cost of repairing minor damage such as a broken window.

Extra coverage of high-value items: Most policies limit payment for certain valuable items. Typical: Jewelry losses can't exceed $500, silverware, $1,000. To insure these for their true value, purchase a personal articles floater that spells out how much the company will pay in the event of a loss.

Adequate liability protection: Most policies provide only $100,000 for personal liability. That's not enough coverage if you have above-average income and assets. Better: An umbrella policy that picks up where your homeowner and automobile insurance policies leave off. (A particularly good idea for pool owners, for example.)

Source: *Rodale's Practical Homeowner,* Emmaus, PA.

Easily Overlooked Discounts

Homeowners policy discounts are offered by many insurers for sprinkler and alarm systems (up to 15%); burglar alarms and fire department inspections (up to 9%); deadbolt locks and smoke alarms (up to 4%). Other discount possibilities: No smokers in the household. Homeowners who are 55 or older.

Source: *Medical Economics,* Oradell, NJ.

Coverage for College Students

A college student's valuables may be best insured by personal articles "floaters." These extend standard homeowner policies. Most reasonable rates: Stereos, cameras, and musical instruments. Bonus: Floaters provide coverage for loss or accidental damage as well as for theft.

Source: *Sylvia Porter's Personal Finance,* New York.

Homeowners Insurance Pitfalls and Ways To Avoid Them

Most people buy their homeowners insurance from the company that gives them the best price. And for many buyers, that's the smart way to go. But if the insureds' property—home and belongings—is valued at more than $200,000, or if they also have a vacation house and some jewelry, silver, and fine art, they may be inadequately covered or may be wasting money on overlapping coverage.

Insurance companies usually aim for one segment of the marketplace. Most go after the big middle market—homes valued at under $200,000 and owners who have few or no valuables such as fine art, jewelry, furs, or silver. And for those people, the homeowners policies issued by these firms are indeed adequate. In fact, the cost of that type of coverage is usually quite competitive because so many firms are fighting for a share of that large pie.

But when the value of property starts to climb, the owner should look at insurance in a fundamentally different way: Are the changing values of possessions being tracked? Prices for fine art and jewelry don't remain static. They may rise or fall, depending on market conditions. Some fine art posts dramatic swings, especially the moderns.

With mass-market insurance policies, upper dollar limits are usually built into the coverage of some items. These limits vary for different parts of the country.

Of course, you can consider buying additional coverage for items that exceed the upper dollar limit. This extra coverage is called a personal articles floater (known as a PAF in the trade). However, in order to get higher-value PAF coverage, you will have to prove the value of those items, either by providing a bill of sale or by getting an appraisal from an expert in the field.

Insurance firms that aim for the middle market may discourage such special coverage for valuable items because they don't really have a ready-made policy to offer. Their prices for special items are usually not competitive. And, before offering coverage, they may require an appraisal (inconvenient and not that inexpensive) on an item valued as low as $1,000.

Some people who started out adequately covered by the midrange homeowners policy when they were young find after several years that they are starting to grow beyond the protection of their coverage.

What To Do

Just as some insurance firms specialize in the middle market and thus offer the best prices for that one, other insurance firms specialize in the narrower, higher-bracket markets. Once the value of your home and belongings exceeds $200,000, you should investigate what coverage is available from these firms. They may offer not only a better price, but also policies that are tailored to your special needs.

If your current agent represents only middle-market firms, ask him to recommend an agent or broker that can service you. Other routes: Contact your local insurance association, or call the National Association of Casualty and Surety Agents at 301-986-4166.

Second Home

If you own a vacation house in addition to your main residence, be aware of the gap trap or the overlap trap. Often a vacation-home owner buys coverage from a broker or agent in the vicinity of the dwelling on the theory that if anything should happen, the representative is there. That is logical—up to a point. Problem: The agent at the vacation spot may assume that, say, a small boat is covered by the insured's main policy. So he omits it from the vacation-home coverage. Or the insured may have the boat covered under both policies. With two uncoordinated policies, the insured may be paying for too much liability coverage.

There is no discount for coverage on two houses, as there is for coverage on two or more cars.

Other Considerations

Important basic: What formula does the homeowners policy use to settle claims? Many midrange policies guarantee to pay actual cash value (known as ACV in the trade). That certainly sounds good—until you discover (perhaps belatedly) that the insurance company subtracts from the actual cash value the damaged article's depreciation.

To see how ACV works, let's use as an example a damaged sofa that cost $5,000 new and has a useful life of 10 years. It has depreciated by $500 a year. If the sofa is eight years old when damaged, the owner will wind up with a settlement check of $1,000 (minus, probably, a $250 deductible).

Some policies have a four-times ACV clause for settlement, which means the owner of the sofa will get a check for $4,000 (minus the deductible). And still other policies call for payment of full replacement cost of the damaged item. Considering inflation, that could put the settlement check at something like $7,500.

A conscientious agent or broker will point out these and other policy differences that could have a substantial impact on the settlement you receive as a result of a loss.

Source: Robert Fergusson, assistant vice president and personal client services marketing manager, Marsh & McLennan Companies, Inc., New York.

You're Covered— Or Are You?

An "all-risk" homeowners policy isn't necessarily what its name implies. Some policies may not give you protection against heavy damage caused by a flood, hurricane, or other natural disaster.

For adequate protection, insure your house for at least 80% of replacement value—the cost of rebuilding it with the same materials, at today's labor rates. Also, pay the added premium for a "replacement cost endorsement" on your home's contents. Otherwise, the insurer will pay you only a depreciated amount on items that suffer wear and tear.

Source: Benjamin Lipson, Benjamin Lipson Associates Insurance Agency, author of *How to Collect More on Your Insurance Claims*, published by Simon & Schuster.

While You Were Gone...

Homeowners insurance trap: Letting friends use your home when you're not in residence may invalidate your insurance. Insurance companies assume that the owner will take better precautions to protect the property than a renter will. If you rent out your vacation home, for example, purchase either "all-risk" or "special multiperil" insurance. These policies cost more, but they'll cover both theft and liability losses.

Source: *Profit Building Strategies for Business Owners*, Scarsdale, NY.

Protection for Renters

Only one renter in five has property or liability insurance. Problem: The landlord's policy covers only the building, not tenants' possessions. Guidelines:

• For adequate property protection, buy a policy with full replacement coverage. This will cost 15%–40% more than the same policy at actual-cash-value coverage (replacement less depreciation), but is well worth it.

• The standard policy sets a liability limit of $25,000, inadequate for most people. For $10 or so extra, you can raise the limit to $100,000.

• Expensive jewelry, watches, and furs are best protected by a personal articles floater, a policy amendment that insures each item individually.

• You can save 10% by raising your deductible from $100 to $250, and another 10% by increasing it to $500.

• Don't overlook discount insurers such as USAA, Colonial Penn, and Geico.

Source: *Money*, New York.

How To Save on Auto Insurance

There are four major areas of coverage in a typical auto insurance policy:

• Bodily injury liability (including personal injury protection in "no-fault" states), in case you injure someone.

• Property damage liability, in case you damage someone else's property.

• Collision, in case you damage your own car.

• Comprehensive, in case your car is stolen, vandalized, or otherwise damaged.

Each of these areas is subject to cost cutting.

Don't buy unnecessary coverage. As a rule, every $1.00 of auto insurance premiums returns approximately $.60 in claims—the rest is overhead. By self-insuring for the small risks you can afford, you can save up to 40%.

Avoid collision insurance on older cars. Collision insurance is generally expensive relative to other types of coverage and is not economical if your car is not very valuable. Comprehensive insurance is a less expensive alternative and, given the chance of total loss due to theft, should probably be purchased anyway.

Increase your deductibles. You can save approximately 20% in premiums on collision insurance for a newer car by increasing your deductible from $100 to $250. Better yet, a $500 deductible will save you about 35%. The trade-off is that you are required to pay for more small claims. Over time the savings in premiums should, however, more than pay for your claims if you are an average or better driver. And because small claims increase your premiums, filing fewer claims will reduce the chance that your premiums will rise in the future.

Avoid incidental coverages. Buy good medical insurance and skip auto medical payments. (In no-fault states, use medical insurance in lieu of personal injury protection if you are able to legally.) Avoid coverage for substitute transportation, which pays for rental cars when your car is being repaired, for towing coverage, and for memberships in insurance company auto clubs, which are not good values.

Shop around. Some companies charge two or three times what others charge for identical coverage. Compare the rate of your present company to State Farm Insurance, which has competitive rates. Use these prices as a guide when you shop.

Trouble Finding Coverage?

Six states (Hawaii, Massachusetts, Michigan, North Carolina, New Hampshire, and South Carolina) guarantee motorists with good driving records the right to buy coverage from any company they choose. In many states, however, claims or other items such as where you live, how you look, or how you live, or even the whim of the insurance company, may cause inexpensive insurers to reject your application. As a result, you may be forced to seek insurance from high-rate companies that specialize in selling insurance to people who have difficulty finding coverage. In some cases, you may be better off going to the state-guaranteed assigned-risk plan than paying the rates of some of these high-risk insurers. These state-required mechanisms must sell auto insurance to licensed drivers who have the money to pay their premiums.

Source: J. Robert Hunter, president, National Insurance Consumer Organization, 121 Payne St., Alexandria, VA 22314, the first nonprofit national organization established to promote the interests of insurance buyers.

Children's Car Insurance Costs

You can cut car insurance costs when children who still live with you start driving.

• List them as occasional drivers, not principal drivers. That alone will cut the premium by up to one-third for boys and by one-fourth for girls.

• Allow your child to drive only one of your cars (if you have more than one), preferably the least expensive one. If more than one child has a driver's license, cover girls for driving the more expensive car.

• Make sure the youngsters take driver education. Insurance discounts of 10% are available for those who pass.

• Look into "good student" discounts. For the minimum discount, your child must maintain at least a B average; maintaining a higher average increases the size of the discount. Good student discounts commonly cut the premium by one-fourth.

• If your child is going to a college more than 100 miles from home and does not have a car on campus, try to get a college student discount of 10% to 15%.

• If your child has a car, have it put on your policy. Multicar discounts can be anywhere from 10% to 25% depending on the insurance company.

Guarding Against the Uninsured

An accident with an uninsured or underinsured motorist can be financially ruinous. As part of your own policy, underinsured (in some states) and uninsured motorists coverage is obtainable to deal with such accidents.

Uninsured Coverage

Most states have statutory requirements that automobile liability insurance policies include uninsured motorists coverage.

• Financial responsibility limits. The law requires that uninsured motorists coverage be provided in an amount mandated by the state. These financial responsibility limits vary.

• Getting more coverage. Usually you can buy coverage up to your liability limits. Example: If you carry $300,000 in liability, you can get the same amount in uninsured coverage.

• Proof of fault. Under uninsured coverage, your company has to pay you only what the other party is legally liable for. So, the other party must be proved at fault.

• Comparative negligence provisions. In some states, if the other driver is proved somewhat at fault, you can recover proportional damages from your own insurance company.

• Making a claim. You are placed in an adversary position with your own insurance company. You must prove the extent of the injury, establish its value, and negotiate with your own carrier to settle. If you can't reach a settlement, most claims will go to arbitration, not to court.

• Limits. Most mandatory uninsured motorists protection covers only bodily injury. Property damage is covered under your collision insurance, after the deductible. (As with any collision claim, your rates may go up after filing.)

Underinsured Coverage

This type of coverage is becoming more and more popular. Some states require that underinsured coverage be offered. In others, it is optional. With underinsured coverage:

• You must first recover the maximum amount from the other party's liability policy before you can collect on your own policy.

• As with uninsured coverage, you are in an adversary position with your carrier and must prove that the value of your injury has exceeded the liability limits of the other party's policy.

Important: Uninsured motorists coverage will not pay you if the other driver has any insurance at all, no matter how inadequate.

Pedestrian Accidents

You will be covered by your uninsured motorists coverage just as if you were in a car at the time. If you don't own a car, you might be able to get coverage under the policy of a family member in your immediate household who does own one. If neither you nor anyone in your family has coverage, you can apply to a fund that some states maintain to cover such accidents, or pursue a court action directly against the responsible party.

Source: Richard P. Oatman, assistant claim counsel for Aetna Life & Casualty, Hartford, CT.

A Big Gap in Car Insurance

In most cases your own automobile insurance policy protects you when you're driving a rented car, even if you cause an accident. But most policies don't cover damage to a rented car when it's parked and struck by a hit-and-run driver or an uninsured motorist causes an accident. To make sure you won't have to pay the deductible for damage to a rental, purchase a collision damage waiver from the renting company.

Hold Onto Your Title Insurance

Keep your title insurance policy even if you sell your home. The insurance is permanent protection for you. Example: If an unknown claim against the house you sell surfaces, even if it was against a previous owner, your buyer can sue you to recover the cost of settling the claim. The title insurance company will pay for any loss you suffer, if you still have the policy.

Insurance for Wiring: A Bad Bet

Telephone-wiring insurance—sold for a monthly fee by local phone companies—is not a wise buy. Inside phone wiring rarely needs repairs. Handy owners or electricians can fix it themselves. Apartment dwellers often will be protecting only a few inches of wire.

Behind the insurance: Since the AT&T divestiture, homeowners are responsible for their inside wiring. Bell decided to charge for repairs.

Bond Insurance: Not What It Seems To Be

More and more municipal bond investors are trying to limit their risk exposure by purchasing insurance to cover potential losses due to default. But they may be buying less security than they think and more than they need.

Bond insurance merely transfers risk from the bond issuer to the insurer; it doesn't eliminate the risk. Recommended: If you feel

that you must buy insured bonds, at least diversify. Don't buy issues all backed by the same insurer. If an insurer's financial position deteriorates, its rating will fall, dragging down the ratings—and prices—of all the bonds it insures.

Also keep in mind that bond insurance is expensive. For example, an uninsured A-rated bond will generally yield 0.75% more than an insured AAA-rated one.

Source: Barnet Sherman, municipal bond analyst, Smith Barney, Harris Upham & Co., New York.

Insuring Artwork

If you have art holdings valued at over $5,000, you should insure them separately, since the standard homeowners policy does not list artworks individually, and valuation isn't made until after the object has been lost, making it difficult to settle a claim. Also, standard policies do not take into account the tendency of art to appreciate rather than depreciate in value.

Recommended: A fine-art floater as an extension of your regular policy. This will list each object at its appraised value, providing all-risk coverage that includes all loss and damage. Standard exclusions in art policies are damages from wear and tear or stemming from restoration, moths, normal deterioration, war, and nuclear disaster. Important: Have your art collection reappraised every two or three years, then change the policy accordingly.

If you plan to lend a work, get "wall-to-wall" coverage, which insures the work from the moment it leaves your custody until its return.

Source: *Investor's Guide to the Art Market.*

313

11 ESTATE PLANNING

What Gets Taxed and How the Tax Is Calculated

To achieve your estate planning goals, the first step you should take is to understand the size of your estate and the manner in which it (not your beneficiaries) will be taxed. The following guidelines should enable you to make estimates for federal tax purposes.

The Gross Estate

The gross estate includes all property you own, some property you may not realize you own, and property you no longer own. Property you own includes cash, stocks and bonds, real estate (including your home), and other personal property—car, furniture, jewelry, etc.

Property you may not realize you own often comprises the largest assets in an estate. Among these are life insurance proceeds that are either payable to your estate or payable to others (if you own the policy). Pension and profit-sharing plans, once eligible for certain exclusions, are now also fully included.

Other property you may overlook includes joint tenancy property. Only half the value of joint tenancy property held by a husband and a wife is included in the gross estate of the spouse who dies first—regardless of who actually provided the funds for its purchase. Other joint tenancy property, however, is fully included in the gross estate unless the estate can show that some or all of the funds used to purchase it came from another joint tenant.

Property you no longer own that is included in your gross estate is generally property you've transferred to others, but over which you still retain certain rights. For example, if you made a gift of stock to your children but retained the right to the dividends, the entire value of that stock would be included in your gross estate. Another example would be a condominium you gave to your children but that you continue to use throughout the year.

Deductions From the Gross Estate

The gross estate is reduced by deductions for debts (including home mortgages), funeral expenses, expenses of administering the estate, amounts transferred to charity and, perhaps most significantly, amounts passing to your surviving spouse.

Oftentimes, the primary objective of estate planning is to give as much property to the

315

spouse as possible without paying taxes. The "marital" deduction is available for property passing outright and for amounts left in trust, assuming you meet certain conditions. Of course, an estate tax will ultimately be payable by your spouse's estate.

Calculating the Tax

After reducing your gross estate by allowable deductions, the remaining amount is your taxable estate. Normally, this is the figure on which the tax is based, although there is a further adjustment for gifts made after 1976 in excess of an annual $10,000 per donee ($20,000, if you are married). For every taxpayer, the federal government grants a credit against the estate tax, computed so that estates of $600,000 or less are not subject to the tax. In excess of this amount estates pay tax at a minimum rate of 37% and at a maximum rate of 50%.

Source: Gary Hart, president of Gary Hart & Associates, Ltd., 333 West Wacker Drive, Suite 700, Chicago, 60606, a certified public accounting firm providing tax, financial planning, and accounting services to individuals and closely held businesses. He is also a frequent speaker on personal financial planning and estate planning.

Tough-Minded Estate Planning

It may seem callous to even think about taxes when a loved one faces a life-threatening illness. But if tax planning is ignored at that point, assets carefully accumulated over a lifetime may be squandered unnecessarily. For many facing a final illness, dealing with these matters provides a life-oriented focus that helps them combat depression and achieve a sense of completion in seeing that their affairs are well ordered. Some things to consider:

• Gifts by the patient. In many cases, estate taxes can be saved by making gifts to family members and other intended beneficiaries. An unlimited amount may be transferred gift-tax-free provided no one person receives more than $10,000. The maximum tax-free gift per

recipient can increase to $20,000 if the patient's spouse is still alive and consents to treat each gift as having been jointly made.

Under the old law, gifts made within three years of death were figured back into the taxable estate. The 1981 tax act repealed this "contemplation-of-death" rule in most cases. One major exception: The old rule still applies to gifts of life insurance.

• Gifts to the patient. This tactic may seem useful when the patient doesn't have enough property to take full advantage of the estate tax exemption ($600,000). Reason: Property that passes through the decedent's estate gets what's known as a stepped-up basis. That is, the person who inherits it is treated for income tax purposes as though he bought it and paid what it is worth on the date of death. (Or what it was worth six months after the date of death if the executor chooses this alternative date to set the value of the taxable estate.)

Example: Mr. Jones, a cancer patient, has $150,000 worth of assets. His wife has a large estate, including $75,000 worth of stock that has a tax basis of $10,000. That means there's $65,000 worth of taxable gain built into the stock. She gives the stock to her husband. (There's no tax on gifts between spouses.) Mr. Jones leaves the stock to the children. The children inherit the stock with the basis stepped up to $75,000. So if they turn right around and sell it for $75,000, there's no taxable gain. With these shares, Mr. Jones's estate is still only $225,000—under the exempt amount. So the stepped-up basis is achieved without paying estate tax. And the property is taken out of Mrs. Jones's estate, where it might be taxed.

In most cases, it doesn't pay to use this tactic with property that will be bequeathed back to a spouse who gave it to the patient. Reason: Unless the gift was made more than a year before the date of death, stepped-up basis will be denied. But when the patient is expected to survive for substantially more than a year, this tactic can be quite useful.

Example: Mr. Smith owns a $150,000 rental property with a $25,000 tax basis. Mrs. Smith has a disease that will be fatal within two to five years. She has few assets of her own. So Mr. Smith gives her the building and inherits it back from her a few years later with the basis stepped up to $150,000. This substantially increases his depreciation deductions if he keeps the building and eliminates any taxable gain if he sells it.

• Loss property. In general there is a tax disadvantage in inheriting property that is worth less than its original cost. Reason: Its tax basis is stepped-down to its date-of-death value and the potential loss deduction is forfeited. If the patient has substantial income, it might pay to sell the property and deduct the losses. But it doesn't pay to generate losses that are more than $3,000 in excess of the patient's capital gains. Reason: These excess losses can't be deducted currently, and there's likely to be no future years' income on which to deduct them. Alternative: Sell the loss property at its current value to a close family member. Result: The patient's loss on the sale is nondeductible, because the purchaser is a family member. But any future gains the family member realizes will be nontaxable to the extent of the previously disallowed loss.

• Charitable gifts. In some cases, bequests to charitable organizations should be made before death. Benefit: Current income tax deductions. But it's important not to give too much away. This tactic may generate more deductions than the patient can use.

• Flower bonds. Certain series of US Treasury bonds can be purchased on the open market for substantially less than their full face value, because they pay very low interest. But if a decedent owns these so-called flower bonds on the date of death, they can be credited against the estate tax at their full face value.

Timing: Flower bonds should be bought when death is clearly imminent. There's little point in holding them for substantial periods before death because they yield very little income. On the other hand, it does no good for the estate to purchase them after death because they won't be applied against the estate tax. In some cases, flower bonds have

been bought on behalf of a patient in a coma by a relative or trustee who holds a power of attorney. The IRS has attacked these purchases. But the courts have, so far, sided with the taxpayer.

A power of attorney should be prepared early on. If it's properly drafted, it can cover flower bond purchases and authority for a variety of other actions that can preserve the patient's assets and allow for flexible planning.

Income Tax Planning

A number of income tax moves should be considered:

• Income timing. If the patient is in a low tax bracket, it may pay to accelerate income. The key here is to compare the patient's tax bracket with the bracket his estate is likely to be in. In some cases it will pay to accelerate income to make full use of deductions that would otherwise yield little or no tax benefit. Medical deductions, in particular, may be very high.

• Choosing gift property. In making gifts to save estate taxes, it does not pay from an income tax standpoint to give away property that has gone up in value. Reason: The tax basis of gift property is not stepped up. So the recipient will have a potential income tax liability built into the gift. This potential is eliminated if the property is kept in the estate and passes by inheritance. For similar reasons, the patient should not give away business property that has been subject to depreciation. (There's a built-in tax liability for recapture of the depreciation deductions. This is eliminated if the property passes through the estate.)

• Other moves. For owners of stock in an S corporation, it may pay to accelerate distribution of income, particularly if the ill shareholder has previously taxed income that wasn't distributed.

Where death is expected, but not clearly imminent, a private annuity may be a useful way of disposing of property. Reason: IRS regulations will key the required annuity payments to a healthy person's life expectancy.

An experienced estate planner can help you

explore all aspects of these moves and other possibilities.

Source: G. William Clapp, partner, Bessemer Trust Co., N.A., New York City.

Flower Bond Rewards

It's still possible to cut estate taxes with flower bonds. These bonds were issued by the US Treasury before March 4, 1971. Their yields are very low, so they sell at a discount. But they can be used at their full face value to pay estate taxes. One case: Bonds purchased for $293,000 were used only two years later to pay off more than $400,000 in estate taxes.

Source: Wachovia Bank & Trust Co., 499 F. Supp. 615.

Avoiding Probate by Becoming Your Own Beneficiary

Three good reasons for keeping your property out of probate court if you can possibly do so:

• Cost: Probate involves fees to the court, executors, attorneys and possibly others (such as appraisers and accountants).

• Time: It can take years to settle an estate. Meanwhile, the heirs can't get their inheritance.

• Publicity: Probate proceedings are public records, open to inspection.

Some assets automatically go to the beneficiaries without probate when the owner dies. Insurance proceeds are paid to the named beneficiaries, as are many pensions, annuities, and company benefits. Jointly held property goes directly to the survivor, bypassing probate. Almost everything else, however, must be probated—and it makes no difference whether there's a will or not.

Create a Living Trust

An individual can avoid probate by putting property into one or more revocable trusts, naming himself the income beneficiary for life. Upon death, either the trust assets can be paid out to designated beneficiaries or the trust can continue. A common provision: After the taxpayer's death, income goes to his spouse for life. The remaining assets then go to the children on the spouse's death.

A single trust or separate trusts can be created for different types of property or different beneficiaries.

It's a good idea to make the trust the beneficiary of insurance policies, pensions, annuities, company death benefits, Individual Retirement Accounts, Keogh Plans or any other payments to be made upon death.

Since the trust is revocable, it can be added to, property can be taken out, the beneficiaries can be changed or the trust can be ended altogether. In short, the person who sets up the trust retains complete control, but the property escapes the probate court.

Estate-tax impact: Avoiding probate doesn't mean avoiding estate tax. The only way to do that is to give everything away before death—but then a gift tax must be paid, unless the gift is to your spouse.

Setting Up the Trust

Appoint yourself as trustee and appoint a co-trustee. One advantage in naming a bank or financial institution as co-trustee is that, unlike an individual, an institution can't die or become incapacitated.

If an individual co-trustee is appointed, be sure to name one or more alternatives to serve in case the first named is unable to do the job. It is possible to give the co-trustee the power to appoint others. Trap to avoid: If a sole trustee dies or becomes incapacitated, court proceedings will be required to administer the trust.

If the trust is not intended to continue after death, the designated beneficiary of the trust can be named trustee with the sole duty of transferring the property to himself after your death.

Transferring property to the trust: It's not enough just to draw up a trust agreement. There must be an actual transfer of property to the trust. Stocks and bonds must be sent to the transfer agents to be put in the trust's name. Bank accounts must be transferred and placed in the trust's name. Real estate must be deeded to the trust and the deeds properly recorded. Cover everything.

Trusts Vs. Joint Property

Probate can also be avoided by placing property in joint ownership with a beneficiary. But this means loss of control over the property. Joint ownership is not revocable. If the original sole owner changes his mind, there's nothing he can do about it—except ask the beneficiary to give the property back. Note: If the transfer into joint names is to anyone but a spouse, there may be a gift tax to pay.

Tax advantage to trusts: If the property increases in value, there's an advantage to a trust. When the person who created the trust dies, the tax basis of the trust property is stepped up (increased) to its fair market value on the date of his death. If the property is later sold, the profit is figured on the stepped-up value, not the lower original cost. For joint property, the step-up applies only to the decedent's half. Example.

A trust owns property purchased for $100,000 but now worth $300,000. At the taxpayer's death, the basis of the property becomes $300,000. If it is then sold for that figure, there is no taxable gain.

Now, suppose the same property is owned jointly by the taxpayer and his spouse. After the taxpayer's death, the basis is only $200,000. (The taxpayer's half goes from $50,000 to $150,000, but the spouse's half remains at $50,000.) If the property is then sold for $300,000, the surviving spouse will face a taxable capital gain of $100,000.

Source: Isaac W. Zisselman, partner with the law firm of Young, Kaplan, Ziegler & Zisselman, New York.

Sprinkling Trusts

With trusts commonly lasting 10 years or more, it's difficult for a settlor to predict what long-term tax and management benefits his beneficiaries will need. Many trusts in which income is always uniformly distributed are too inflexible to adapt to beneficiaries' changing circumstances.

Classic problem: Income from a trust is equally distributed among beneficiaries in different tax brackets. The result is that income is eaten up by the taxes of the wealthy beneficiary, while too little income is directed to the beneficiary in a more favorable tax situation.

The flexibility to solve this problem can be built into a trust with an income "sprinkling" (or "spray") clause. This arrangement gives the trustee discretionary power to disburse or accumulate income and principal during the life of the trust.

Income sprinkling trusts can create two types of tax benefits. First, by favoring lower-tax-bracket beneficiaries, a sprinkling feature can produce family income tax savings. Second, a sprinkling trust can yield estate tax savings by restricting the disposition of unnecessary income to wealthy beneficiaries, thus avoiding buildup of their estates.

Here are factors to consider when establishing a sprinkling trust.

1. You must provide detailed and comprehensive guidelines for the trustee regarding the purpose and priorities of the trust.

2. Try to create a trust in which sprinkling is established between a beneficiary and his descendants, rather than among beneficiaries. By doing this you may eliminate potential conflicts over unequal distribution of trust income.

3. If the beneficiary is to be your surviving spouse, he or she should be provided with a set minimum amount of income that is excluded from the discretionary powers of the sprinkling clause.

4. If you retain benefits from or control over a sprinkling trust, you will be taxed on the trust's income.

5. Careful consideration must be given to the trustee of a sprinkling trust. If one of your beneficiaries serves as sole trustee, income will be taxable to the beneficiary. If you give him sprinkling power over the trust, the trust's property will, for tax purposes, be included in his estate. This is also true even if the beneficiary is only a co-trustee. To provide the fullest tax advantages, it is best not to have a beneficiary serve in this capacity.

Source: Israel A. Press, CPA, tax partner and Tom Spiesman, J.D., tax associate with Touche Ross & Company, Financial Services Center, One World Trade Center, New York 10048. Mr. Press is the author of numerous tax articles.

Be Careful of Leaving Everything to Your Spouse

Husbands and wives often leave everything to their spouses to escape death taxes. Transfers in any amount between spouses, during life or at death, are not taxable, but you should nevertheless avoid making such transfers to excess.

If you and your spouse don't take full advantage of your lifetime transfer credits, the survivor's estate could pay more tax than necessary. The credit allows every estate to leave $600,000 tax free.

Example: A husband dies before his wife and leaves an estate valued at $1,200,000 to her. Because of the marital deduction, no tax is payable from his estate. However, the husband forfeits his lifetime transfer credit by overusing the marital deduction. The spouse has only one $600,000 lifetime exemption to offset estate taxes, meaning that the remaining $600,000 will be taxed heavily.

A better alternative: Instead of leaving the entire $1,200,000 to his wife, the husband should leave her only $600,000 and put the balance in a trust for her benefit. The trust preserves the use of the credit in his estate and prevents the property from being taxed in

hers. Both estates utilize their $600,000 lifetime exemptions; neither one pays transfer taxes, and the entire $1,200,000, although benefiting the wife for her lifetime, passes to the children tax-free.

Source: Archie M. Richards, Jr., CFP, president, Archie Richards Associates, Inc., 10 Mall Road, Burlington, MA 01803. He has been admitted to the Registry of Financial Practitioners and is a member of the International Association for Financial Planning and the Institute of Certified Financial Planners. He is also a weekly newspaper columnist.

Q-TIP Trusts: Estate Planning Opportunity

There is an unlimited marital deduction for federal estate tax purposes. No matter how big your estate is, if you're married and you leave everything to your surviving spouse, not a penny of federal estate tax will have to be paid on your death. Tax will be postponed until your spouse's death.

Planning Problems?

One way to take advantage of the marital deduction is to leave property outright to your spouse, with no strings attached. But that creates problems.

Problem one: When you leave assets to your spouse outright, you relinquish the right to control who gets the remainder of the estate after your spouse's death. The widow (assuming the husband has the assets and dies first) can do whatever she wants with the property she inherits. She could remarry and leave everything to her second husband leaving nothing to the first husband's children.

Problem two: An estate left outright to a spouse who has no knowledge of the money market or investments can easily be frittered away.

The Q-TIP Solution

You can solve these estate planning problems by putting some of your estate into a

Qualified Terminable Interest Property Trust, or Q-TIP trust.

A Q-TIP lets you provide for your spouse for her lifetime, get an estate tax marital deduction and control how the property is disposed of when your spouse dies. To qualify as Q-TIP property:

• All the income from the trust assets must go to your spouse, payable at least annually, for life.

• Your executor must elect to have the property qualify for the marital deduction in your estate.

• There can be no restrictions whatsoever on the spouse's right to receive income. For example, she must continue to get income even if she remarries.

Angle: None of the money in the Q-TIP can be paid out directly to other family members while your widow is alive. For example, you can't have the trust pay for your children's college education. However, money for this purpose can be distributed to your spouse from principal at the discretion of the trustee, and she can spend it on the tuition.

Taxes and Q-TIPS

The Q-TIP property will be taxed when your spouse dies. When setting up the trust, you must consider the taxes your spouse's estate will have to pay.

Trap: Putting too much of your estate into the Q-TIP. This could cause taxes on the combined estates of you and your spouse to be higher than they would be if only a limited amount had gone into the trust.

Put into the Q-TIP only an amount that exceeds your exemption equivalent—$600,000. This is the amount that can be left to your heirs tax-free, apart from amounts that qualify for the marital deduction.

If you have an estate of $1,000,000 (and "plan" to die this year), $400,000 can go into the Q-TIP ($1,000,000 less your $600,000 exemption equivalent).

The balance: It can be put into a "nonmarital trust." This is a trust that will not qualify for the marital deduction and will not be taxed in your estate as long as the value is below your exemption equivalent.

Example of a nonmarital trust: Income to widow and/or children as trustees see fit. Balance on her death or remarriage, or at stated intervals, to children.

Another reason for not putting the whole estate into the Q-TIP: If your widow lives to be 100, your children could be 75 or so before they inherit. That may be too long for them to wait.

Source: Edward Mendlowitz, a partner in Siegel, Mendlowitz & Rich, CPAs, 310 Madison Ave., New York 10017.

Smarter Than Leaving Everything to Spouse

New York attorney Marvin W. Weinstein, who specializes in taxes and estate planning, suggests using dual trusts in some cases, with one qualified and the other not qualified for the marital deduction. Important when the objective is to provide liberally for the surviving spouse, but reduce estate taxes on transfers to the next generation.

A marital trust is eligible for the marital deduction from the estate tax, but it has the disadvantage that the assets will be taxed in the wife's estate when she dies.

By contrast, a nonmarital trust isn't eligible for the marital deduction from the estate tax. The assets are moved to the next generation without being taxed in the widow's estate when she dies. A typical non-marital trust would be one in which the widow gets all of the income as long as she lives, but on the death the principal passes to the children.

The two types of trust differ in the degree of control of the assets that the widow has. And there are legal/technical requirements that a good trust lawyer should handle.

These procedures are unnecessary if the estate is less than $600,000, because there's no estate tax below that.

Avoid Tax on Debts

Suppose your son owes you $10,000. Your will provides for cancellation of that debt upon your death. Tax result: Even though your estate does not collect it, the value of that debt is considered an asset of the estate that is subject to federal estate tax.

Better way: When the debt is first established, spell out that the payment obligation will cease at your death. Result: When you die, there is no repayment right for your estate to succeed to and there is no asset to be taxed.*

Caution: The transaction establishing the debt should reflect the cancellation feature. Example: Your son is buying some stock from you. The stock is worth $100,000. If he gives you a note with a cancellation-at-death clause, the purchase price should probably be higher than $100,000. Otherwise, the IRS can argue that your son got more than he paid for and treat the transaction as partly a sale as well as partly a taxable gift.

Estate of Moss, 74 T.C. No. 91.

Tax-Free Gifts To Family Save Estate Tax and Income Tax

Annual gifts up to $10,000 a year per recipient are not subject to gift tax. Married couples can give twice as much. Every year for the rest of your life, you and your spouse can jointly give $20,000 tax-free to each heir and reduce your taxable estate by the same amount.

Tax savings are impressive even if you're widowed or divorced. An individual with four married children and ten grandchildren can give the children, their spouses and their grandchildren $180,000 a year with no tax.

Avoiding tax on gifts over $10,000: Give a part interest each year. Or transfer property through an installment sale, taking back notes that are payable at annual intervals. You can cancel these notes as they fall due.

Gifts to reduce family's total income tax: Transfer income-producing assets to low-bracket members. Children under age 14 can receive up to $1,000 of income from the asset before the parent has to pay income tax in his higher tax bracket. (No gift tax if $10,000 limit is observed.)

Reducing heir's income tax: Give assets to minor child by putting them into a trust that accumulates up to $1,000 per year in income. Income can be paid to a custodian or can be taxable to trust so as not to propel heir into higher bracket.

Divided Ownership— A New Way To Avoid Estate Tax

How it works. Two persons of widely different ages buy income-producing property. (Usually, the parties are related—parent and child—but they don't have to be.) By agreement, the senior owner gets a "life estate"... meaning he gets the income from the property for life. The younger owner gets a "remainder" interest...meaning he gets the property when the senior owner dies. Each party pays the actuarial value of his interest, based on tables provided by the IRS.

Advantages. The income yield to the senior owner is improved, as the senior gets the full income from the property for life, even though he paid only part of the purchase price. And the property passes to the younger owner free of estate tax, because the senior owner had only a lifetime interest, so there's nothing to be included in his estate.

Example. Father (age 65) and daughter buy property for $200,000. Father takes the life estate—daughter takes the remainder interest. Using the IRS tables (which show how much a life estate is worth at any given age), father pays about $136,000, daughter the remaining $64,000. Essential: Daughter must put up her own money. If father pays the entire $200,000, the property will be included in his estate.

Assume the property has a yield of 7.5%. On a $200,000 investment, that's $15,000 a year. But father paid only $136,000, so he's really getting 11% on his money. And daughter benefits by getting the property free of estate tax...even if it has greatly increased in value.

Note: If daughter dies before father, her interest in the property goes to her heirs or the person named in her will. It does not automatically go to father.

Source: Robert A. Garber, vice president of a major investment-banking house.

The Role of Lifetime Giving in Financial Planning

Gifts made during your lifetime should satisfy two primary objectives: The personal needs and desires of you and your beneficiaries and your tax saving needs. Personally, you will want to provide as much financial support to both children and adult beneficiaries. As for tax savings, there are two basic motivations. The first: To achieve income tax savings through transfer of income producing property to lower tax bracket recipients. Another way of thinking about it is that if you have to provide financial support to members of your family anyway, gift giving enables you to save tax dollars while in the process. The second tax motivation: To transfer your wealth and its potential for future appreciation at the lowest possible transfer tax (gift and estate) cost.

To successfully accomplish these goals requires a sound understanding of the available gift tax exclusions and exemption, gift and estate tax rates as well as income tax rates for you and your beneficiaries. Ideally the property you transfer should satisfy the dual objective of being able to generate current income that is available to your beneficiary

(and removed from your tax bracket) as well as removing any potential appreciation in the property's value from your estate. The form of the transfer will be equally critical. You have the choice of outright transfer or a custodianship or trust arrangement that allows for more management and control over the transferred property.

Tax Considerations

Any property over a certain amount that is transferred during your lifetime is subject to gift tax. Transfers that occur at death are subject to estate tax. Since the US transfer system is "unified," estate and gift tax rates are the same, and the amount of taxable gifts an individual makes during his lifetime is included in the final computation of his or her estate tax. In essence, then, gift tax is nothing more than a prepayment of estate taxes. However, it should be noted that gift taxes paid are removed from the transfer tax system and are never subject to gift or estate tax.

Most important tax-free gifts: The annual exclusion allows a tax-free transfer of $10,000 per year to each donee on the condition that the transferred property is available currently for use by that donee—the donee receives the current income or has current enjoyment from the property. If your spouse joins in the taxable gift or the property is jointly owned or owned in community title, then the annual exclusion can be doubled to $20,000 per donee. Over a long-term period this transfer technique can result in a substantial overall tax savings. For example, a husband and wife with three children can give $60,000 to their children every year tax-free. Benefit: Gifts that are excluded from tax under the annual exclusion also are not counted in computing estate taxes.

A problem with using the annual gift exclusion is that you must give up entire control over the property to your beneficiaries to qualify for the tax exclusion. In theory, an individual could avoid all estate taxes by planning to give all his property to children throughout his lifetime. However, in the case of children, this usually is not desirable; and you will probably want to exercise care in giving up too much financial independence too soon.

Tax benefits: All *income* tax on gift property that is transferred outright or in a trust (with the income being distributed to the beneficiaries) is based on the donee's tax bracket, not on your income tax bracket provided the donee (recipient), if a child, is over age 13. Otherwise, if a minor child under 14 receives the income under Tax Reform Act 1986, it is taxed at the parent's top bracket. Trickier situation: For property that is transferred through a trust but where the income is not currently distributable to the beneficiary, the trust itself is subject to income tax. (In these cases, the income from the trust is taxed upon distribution to the donee under a complex "throwback" rule, that looks upon the distribution as being made in the year in which the income was accumulated.) Also, it is subject to a compressed, i.e., higher, tax bracket than if distributed in many cases.

For all gifts to be considered a tax-free transfer it is esential that you relinquish all rights of control over the transferred property.

Taxpayers should be cautioned about making gifts to family members more than one generation younger than the donor (i.e., grandchildren). These gifts are subject to a generation skipping transfer tax of 50% in addition to gift tax. There are broad exemptions, so this tax applies only to large gifts. Since this tax, when added to gift taxes is confiscatory in nature, individuals planning gifts to younger generations should be careful to meet one of the exemption rules.

Source: Byrle M. Abbin, managing director, Office of Federal Tax Services, Arthur Andersen & Co., 1666 K St. NW, Washington, DC 20006.

What Types of Property Should Be Transferred in Trust

The major objective of most major gift giving is to transfer income to other family members and thereby lower the taxes paid on the income. Since you want to shift income and potential future appreciation you must choose property that produces the desired amount of income and is likely to generate significant appreciation. In most cases, you will have to make a compromise between the two objectives. For instance, a transfer of cash invested in high-yield bonds would shift income for income tax purposes but perhaps only result in a moderate ability to shift any appreciation. On the other hand, assets with high-appreciation are not likely candidates for transfer because they throw off little or no current income and produce minimal income tax advantages for the family overall.

Special situation for business owners: Stock interest in a closely held family business is frequently used as lifetime gifts even though there are little or no current earnings to be derived. In these cases, the goal of removing future appreciation from the donor's estate outweighs income tax planning motivation. Word of warning: If there is too much control by the donor, it is possible for income from the transferred property to be reallocated to the donor regardless of the legal transfer of title. The IRS may also attempt to include the property in the donor's estate.

Avoid making gifts of property that have depreciated significantly. Reason: The depreciable "basis" of the property the donee receives will be equal to the lesser of fair market value at the date of the gift, or donor's "basis." A better approach would be to sell property with a current value less than your "basis" so that you may claim the benefit of the loss. The proceeds of the sale then should be given to the donee.

Of course, a better gift would be property that has appreciated in value. Result: Any gift taxes that have to be paid on the property will increase its "basis." Also, the gain on the sale will be taxed in the donee's lower tax bracket.

Long-term trusts: For individuals with significant assets who want to exercise more control over their distribution, a longer term trust can provide for a term of 20, 30, or 40 or more years with distributions tailored to the desire of the donor. To qualify for the $10,000 annual exclusion, income from the trust must be distributed as it is generated, or the donee must be given the privilege of taking distributions from the trust ("drawing down").

All of these types of transfer are irrevocable. Once the gift is made, it cannot be modified without eliminating the tax benefits of the trust.

For the sophisticated "giver" there are a number of deferred gift techniques that allow you as the donor to retain income interests (or an annuity) for a set period of time or your life. Effect: To reduce the gift tax value of the remainder interest since the benefit of ownership to the donee is delayed.

For the charitably minded, a charitable lead trust provides income to charity for a period of time, after which the property goes to designated family members (outright or in trust). This form of delayed family gift also reduces the gift tax value.

Source: Byrle M. Abbin, managing director, Office of Federal Tax Services, Arthur Andersen & Co., 1666 K St. NW, Washington, DC 20006.

Gifts to Minor Children

For adults, an outright gift of property is usually the most efficient and practical way for you to distribute assets to your beneficiaries —the title is simply transferred from you to the beneficiary. This is not usually the case with young children. You may want to make a gift for tax purposes or other personal reasons but do not want to give up complete control of the property to your children.

The simplest solution is to establish a custodianship under the Uniform Gift to Minors Act (UGMA). The UGMA enables you to transfer ownership of property to a custodian who has broad management powers over the property until the child reaches a specific age, generally 18 or 21, when ownership reverts fully to the child. While the property is in custodianship the income and property may be used only for the benefit of the minor for whom the UGMA account is established. In this case, you as the donor should not be the custodian, otherwise the assets will not be removed from your estate. The only drawback with UGMAs is that there are limits on the type of assets that may be placed in the account.

Common mistake: A strategy sometimes used, but improperly, is one in which assets are transferred to a joint or trusteed bank account for a minor's benefit. Problem: In most of these cases the income from the property is at least partially taxable to the donor and the property may be included in the donor's estate at death.

The 2503 or "Children's" trust gives control of the assets to a third party until the minor donee becomes an adult. Income and/or principal of the trust may be withheld until the child reaches the age of majority. Because of the special rules pertaining to trusts of this type, gifts to the trust will qualify for the $10,000 per donee annual gift exclusion, even though the donee cannot have immediate access to the property. To qualify for the full set of tax benefits of the trust, it is preferable for a nonparent to be the custodian or trustee to hold title of the property.

Short-term trusts used to be attractive for individuals with high current income who wanted to reduce their current taxable income but who wanted the principal assets of their gift to revert to them at a later date, perhaps at retirement. Income paid to the beneficiary was taxed at the beneficiary's lower tax rate; accumulated income was taxed to the trust. Tax Reform Act 1986 prohibits establishing new, or adding to old 10-year trusts, if the property reverts to the donor or his spouse. Income shifting will be prohibited and taxed to the donor. Pre March, 1986 trusts will continue to be effective as long as the beneficiary is not an under 14-year-old minor.

Source: Byrle M. Abbin, managing director, Office of Federal Tax Services, Arthur Andersen & Co., 1666 K St. NW, Washington, DC 20006.

Protecting a Valuable Collection

If breaking up your collection would greatly reduce its value, consider forming a corporation to inherit the collection under your will. It can then be sold as an entirety and the proceeds distributed to your heirs and beneficiaries (to whom you would will specified numbers of shares in the corporation). If the collection is willed to various individuals, it may make the sale more difficult and less lucrative.

Head Off Trouble

If you own a tax shelter, or any investment that might involve you in a dispute with the IRS, think twice before leaving it to your spouse or children unless they share your financial sophistication—and your willingness to battle the government. Alternative: Leave it to someone with a lot of financial savvy, or put it in trust and appoint a smart trustee.

Estate Planning Mistakes

Without an executor, even the best estate plans can't be put into effect. But, incredibly, many otherwise smart businesspeople bungle the process of naming an executor.

Problem: Family members can usually be trusted as executors, but they're not always capable, especially if they're distraught after a death. Lawyers are usually capable, but may not be privy to important details—such as location of assets, records, or debts that are owed to the estate.

Solution: Name coexecutors—a family member to administer the estate and a professional to handle the paperwork. Essential: State in your will who is responsible for which functions. . . .and say who will have the deciding vote in case of a disagreement.

It's also important to list backup executors in your will. If only one executor is named and that person dies or declines the responsibility, the courts will appoint an administrator as though an executor were never named. If you choose a banker or a lawyer, it makes sense to name the firm, not the individual. That way, if something happens to the person chosen, another member of the company can step in.

Other Frequent Mistakes

• Out-of-date will. Whenever tax laws change, you should go over your will to ensure it's consistent with the law. This is especially important when your estate passes the federal tax-free level of $600,000. Even if tax laws don't change, it pays to review your will carefully every five years.

• Not informing the person you've named as executor. If you haven't talked with the executor ahead of time, there's a chance that the person will refuse to do the job.

• Not writing a new will when you move to another state. States have different laws on what is required for a will to be valid. Virginia, for example, requires that one of the executors of a will be a state resident. And only two witnesses are necessary in most states, but in New Hampshire, South Carolina, and Vermont, three are required. If your will fails to meet all of your new state's requirements, it might end up being tossed out by the courts.

• Listing bequests in dollars. If the size of the estate is reduced after a will is written, it's possible that specific dollar amounts will deplete all assets before all inheritors are provided for. Better: Make bequests as a percentage of the entire estate.

• Storing your will in your own safe-deposit box. In many states, boxes are sealed upon the death of the owner. It can sometimes take months to have it opened. Better: Leave the will with your attorney or have your spouse keep it in a separate safe-deposit box.

• Listing assets in the will. A will isn't rewritten often enough to keep up with frequent changes in assets. Instead, write a letter of instruction that notes your assets and their locations, and file it separately. Do the same with your burial instructions.

• Keeping old wills. When you write a new will, destroy the old one. That way there's no chance it will be used to contest the most recent one.

Source: Alexandra Armstrong, president, Alexandra Armstrong Advisors, financial planners, 1140 Connecticut Ave. NW, Washington, DC 20036.

Writing a Will that Works

• Include a simultaneous-death clause that dictates how property will be disposed of in the event both you and your spouse die simultaneously in a common disaster. This prevents acrimony among the beneficiaries as well as potential litigation.

• Consider a no-contest clause to prevent a disappointed beneficiary from suing to have your will overturned. Such a clause says that any beneficiary who challenges the will must forfeit his share under the will.

• Tailor bequests to the beneficiary. Leave property to each beneficiary in the form he can best handle it. This may mean outright transfers. But depending on the beneficiary's age, experience, financial sophistication, and personal inclinations, a trust or a custodianship, or some other form of management may be more appropriate.

• Avoid giving complicated or risky investments, such as tax shelters, to financially unsophisticated beneficiaries who may not have your desire to fight the IRS.

• Don't leave property in joint ownership when one of the co-owners is likely to be dominated by the other.

• Don't give undivided fractional interests in property to beneficiaries who have very different ideas about the management or selling price of the property. Instead, transfer the property to a corporation and give the beneficiaries voting shares.

• Consider percentage bequests to favored

beneficiaries, rather than absolute dollar amounts. In inflationary times, an estate can turn out to be worth far more than anticipated. A bequest of a dollar amount, no matter how generous it seemed at the time you made it, may be embarrassingly small in relation to the size of the inflated estate.

Source: Dr. Robert S. Holzman, professor emeritus of taxation at New York University and author of *Estate Planning: The New Golden Opportunities,* Boardroom Books, Millburn, NJ.

Why You Need a Common Disaster Clause in Your Will

Include a "common disaster clause" in your will to cover the possibility that you and your spouse (or other beneficiary) may die together in an accident. Otherwise, your state's "simultaneous death statute" will govern all questions of inheritance, taxation, the marital deduction, the disposition of jointly held property, who gets insurance proceeds and all other questions of who gets your property. The provisions of the law may not be to your liking. Even if they are, your circumstances may change or the law may be amended. The only way to be sure your wishes are carried out is to put a provision in your will.

Do-It-Yourself Wills

Writing your own will is very dangerous. The requirements that must be met for a will to be valid vary in almost every state.

Example: A will written in New York may be unacceptable in Vermont because there weren't enough witnesses.

If the courts rule a will to be invalid, the estate will be divided up according to state law, which may be very different from the way that you want it done.

Source: Alexandra Armstrong, president, Alexandra Armstrong Advisors, Financial Planners, 1140 Connecticut Ave. NW, Washington, DC 20036.

Keeping Peace Among Your Beneficiaries

A man's will provided that his daughter could choose "any three items in my estate," with the remainder distributed to others. His estate included 19 thoroughbred horses, and the daughter selected all 19 as a single item. The other beneficiaries sued—one horse, one item, they claimed. The judge disagreed; all 19 counted as one.

Though extreme, this example demonstrates the family discord that can arise over vaguely worded instructions regarding the disposition of property. The market value—not to mention the high emotional value—of furniture, jewelry, and other tangible property makes it imperative to avoid carelessly planned dispositions that ultimately may have to be handled in court.

The Problem of Equal Shares

Suppose you own securities, tangibles of moderate value, and a magnificent $300,000 desk. Everything is to go to your children in equal shares. With the desk indivisible, how can your children apportion all the tangibles and still maintain equality? The solution: Add a codicil to your will which allows for the disproportionate allocation of your securities to adjust for inequality in the tangibles.

Avoid catchall phrases in your will. References such as "the contents of my safe deposit box" simply invite conflict. Allow for moderate inequality by permitting the tangibles to be divided in *substantially* equal shares. Making gifts during your lifetime also helps reduce friction when you are no longer around.

You don't have to amend your will every time the plans for your tangibles are changed; the will can refer to a nonbinding memorandum to be rewritten by you from time to time. However, if the executor of the will is empowered to make allocations, make sure he is not one of the beneficiaries.

Placing tangible property intended for one family member temporarily in the hands of another can also result in inequalities. A mother left a painting to her minor daughter. The father was allowed to take temporary possession of the painting, which he later sold. The daughter had legal recourse, but decided not to sue her own father. The mother could have avoided this by providing that the painting be left in storage to await her daughter's possession.

Be wary of the impact of estate taxes. If an estate contains shares of stock, for example, a number of them may be sold to provide tax money. The same cannot be done with a valuable chair—chipping off a leg to raise taxes is impossible. Conflict is guaranteed if one beneficiary receives the chair and another pays the taxes derived from it.

Source: Archie M. Richards, Jr., CFP, president, Archie Richards Associates, Inc., Ten Mall Road, Burlington, MA 01803. He has been admitted to the Registry of Financial Planning Practitioners and is a member of the International Association for Financial Planning and the Institute of Certified Financial Planners. He is also a weekly newspaper columnist.

Why A Wife Needs A Will

Wives need wills as much as husbands to protect the surviving spouse. If a man has converted assets into gifts for his wife for tax purposes, they could pass to her relatives if she dies without a will. And after a husband's estate passes to his widow, her will could protect his children of a former marriage.

Source: *Life Insurance Selling,* 408 Olive St., St. Louis 63102.

Use of Mutual Wills Can Forfeit Marital Deduction

A husband might want to leave a big chunk of property to his wife when he dies, but he may fear that she will make no provision to bequeath any of this property to his relatives or friends. She may feel the same way about leaving property to him. One solution to this dilemma is to have the spouses make mutual wills, in which each party agrees to leave inherited property to the survivor, who after death will leave specified property to designated relatives or friends of both parties.

Problem: The solution may create tax problems involving marital deductions on the estate tax return. If the wife, for example, was contractually bound by a mutual will to bequeath whatever remains of her late husband's property to, say, the children, his property has not passed on to her without strings. This deduction only applies if the property passes outright.

State law is important here to determine whether the property passing to her under her husband's will was really contractually subject to a condition. In one decision on this frequent issue, the court held that under New York law, a state resident is bound by such a restriction and hence the property earmarked for the children upon the death didn't qualify for the marital deduction because she didn't receive this property outright and without strings.

Indicated action: Check with tax counsel for the precedent in your state.

Source: *David A. Siegel Estate*, 67 T.C., No. 50.

Old Will Traps

"My mother recently passed away. She left a will, but it was 30 years old and all the witnesses have died. Can I still submit the will or can I file intestate? And how will it affect the tax bill?"

If your mother left a legally drawn up will, you have no choice. You must submit it. It makes no difference that the witnesses have died.

The $600,000 estate-tax exclusion applies whether the estate passes through the will or not. Even if the estate is larger than that, the will should make little estate-tax difference, unless it contains tax-planning provisions or other provisions affected by the tax code.

Of course, the tax law has changed a great deal in the last 30 years, so any tax-planning provisions contained in the will are likely to be obsolete. This is the reason why wills and estate plans should be reviewed periodically, while the planner is still alive.

Who Gets Your Money if You Don't Leave a Valid Will

Most Americans don't have a will. And they probably have no clear idea what will happen to their property when they die.

State laws vary, but the provisions of most are very similar when someone dies without leaving a will.

• Surviving spouse: A surviving spouse is always entitled to a substantial part of the estate, sometimes all of it. If there are also surviving children, the spouse's share is usually one half or one third, depending on state law and on the number of children.

If there are no children or grandchildren, the spouse often takes the entire estate. Some states, however, give a share to parents or brothers and sisters. The spouse usually takes a specified amount plus a fraction of the balance.

It doesn't matter if the parties have been separated. Only a legal dissolution of the marriage (by divorce or annulment) will cut off the spouse's right to inherit.

• Descendants: Subject to the rights of the spouse, descendents usually have first claim on the estate. Each child takes an equal share, and the children of deceased children take the share their parent would have received. If all children are deceased, the grandchildren inherit. If great-grandchildren enter the picture, the same rules apply.

The rules on adopted children vary from state to state. The trend is to treat them exactly the same as non-adopted children. Illegitimate children inherit from their mother. But the laws on inheriting from the father vary widely.

• Ancestors: In practice, this means parents. In rare cases, a grandparent may survive though both parents are dead. If the deceased left any descendants, parents generally take nothing. If a spouse survives, but no descendants, parents take a share in some states. If there are no surviving descendants or spouse, the surviving parents or parent usually takes the entire estate. Some states divide it among parents, brothers and sisters.

• Collateral relatives: If there is no surviving spouse, descendant or ancestor, the estate goes to those with the closest degree of blood relationship to the deceased. Some states bar remote relatives by limiting inheritance to a specified degree of relationship.

If there is no relative who can inherit and no will, the property goes to the state.

One misconception: Lack of a will won't keep your estate out of the courts. Even holding property jointly won't necessarily do that. Most assets such as stocks, bonds, and savings accounts above a certain amount cannot be transferred without court administration.

• Administration: The court will appoint an administrator, usually one of the heirs. The administrator normally has to post bond, with the cost paid by the estate. If there's more than one heir, any unreasonable disputes among them (including who is to be administrator) must be settled by the court. Such family quarrels can be highly destructive, especially if the estate includes a going business or any other assets that require management.

Once appointed, the duties of an administrator are the same as those of an executor: To collect and manage the assets and distribute them to the proper persons.

• Minor children: If any of the heirs are minors, the court must appoint a guardian or trustee of the property. The trustee's job is to conserve the inheritance until the minor grows up. Income from the property can be used for the child's benefit or saved, but the principal can't be touched without a court order. This can mean a great deal of trouble and expense if money is needed to cover items such as educational costs or medical bills for the minor.

Here's how to avoid problems:

A simple will (without trusts) drawn up by a competent attorney should cost no more than $150, depending on local custom. It can avoid many of the possible costs and problems of administration as well as making sure that your estate goes to persons you really want to have it.

Source: Edward D. Moldover, senior partner, Moldover, Hertz, Presnick, & Gidaly, New York.

Naming the Right Executor

It's a touching gesture to name a spouse or grown child an executor. And they'll also get to keep the estate's administration fee (which can run to 4% or more of the gross estate). The fee would otherwise go to an outsider.

True, the relative (most often the widow) may not have any specialized knowledge of estate administration matters, but so what? An experienced lawyer and accountant can be hired to see things through. You might even supply a few recommended professionals to help when the time comes.

Life—and death—aren't that simple, however. Point: The executor is personally responsible for estate-tax liabilities and late filings, as well as for making sure that the estate is distributed in accord with the will. He is not relieved of this responsibility by delegating to a lawyer the task of "doing whatever is necessary."

Exception: In a very few cases, courts have waived personal penalties when an executor with no business or tax experience, and with scant formal education, had relied upon a seasoned lawyer to take care of the matter. Warning: The great weight of court authority is to the contrary.

An executor also may have to pick up the bill personally if he distributes estate assets to beneficiaries so that there isn't enough left to pay federal taxes. That would happen if there was any reason to suspect that the IRS would still be owed money.

Example: An IRS agent warns the executor that the value of shares in a closely held corporation as shown on the federal estate tax return probably will be jacked up.

The executor may also be held personally responsible for unpaid taxes if the IRS had not put him on notice that more taxes might be payable.

One case: An executor spoke to an officer of the bank where the decedent hadn't paid any federal tax on his considerable earnings for years. This should have alerted her to the fact that estate assets couldn't all be distributed to heirs without leaving enough for what Uncle Sam would demand. The IRS was paid out of her own funds.

Another liability: An heir can hold the executor personally responsible for the amount the heir may have lost through mismanagement of the estate's assets.

Other problems for a spouse: A spouse, in particular, may be too emotionally upset to do a competent job as executor. That has happened even when the spouse was an attorney with vast estate-tax experience.

A spouse or other really close relative is also at a disadvantage in gathering all of the estate assets as required by law. Relatives and friends may insist that money or property which the decedent had lent to them really had been intended as gifts, with an alleged "understanding" that the advance would be forgotten when the decedent died. A widow would have the unpleasant task of trying to collect

from her husband's relatives—or of having to sue them. A common occurrence in such cases: The widow instead fails to report assets of that type on the estate tax return, then gets caught by the IRS.

Another danger: An executor might regard her husband's will and its property dispositions as sacrosanct, to be honored at all costs—including the cost to herself.

Example: State laws generally allow a widow a certain percentage of her husband's estate, such as 35%, as dower rights. If he leaves her a lesser amount, she can "take against the will" and get this 35% at the expense of other beneficiaries. But, to preserve family sensitivities, the executor might refuse to tamper with her husband's instructions and hence would be shortchanging herself.

The saving on administrative fees is not large enough to make that the basis for selecting a family member. An individual is not subject to federal tax on what he or she inherits. But if the widow is executor, the IRS may claim that part of what she inherited actually had been intended to be payment for administering the estate, and she will be assessed income tax on it.

The other side: Consider the potential expense and other consequences of being an executor. That should help to shape your response if a relative or friend flatters you by inviting you to serve as his executor. Even if they offer you a fee, it may not be worth it.

What Your Executor Needs to Know

You choose your executor with great care and expect him to do a good job. But he can't be effective unless you provide him with some essential information. Questions:

• How can an executor collect all of the estate's assets if he doesn't know precisely what or where they are or the extent of your interest in them?

• How can he prevent co-owners of bank or brokerage accounts from drawing out funds if he doesn't know that the accounts exist? How can he put a stop payment on the accounts? How can he prevent safe deposit boxes from being invaded by co-owners and those in possession of keys or combination numbers?

Solution: Write your executor a letter listing all the facts he must have in order to effectively administer your estate. Include:

• A complete list of what you own and where it is, plus any identifying serial numbers (such as those on stock certificates, bank accounts and insurance policies). If there are co-owners or persons holding power of attorney over any of your property, supply the details.

• The location of all documents the executor will need immediately—your most recent will, cemetery plot deed or number, marriage license, divorce decree.

• A description of the rights you have, or may have, under the retirement plans of all employers you have ever worked for. You may have vested rights under the plan of a company you worked for many years ago. If you were in the armed forces or with a government agency, identify which one and give your serial number. Are you a member of a fraternal organization or lodge that may provide death benefits or survivor rights?

• The name of the person who prepared your federal income tax returns, at least for the past three years. Who has the work papers? Who understands them?

• The names of your insurance broker and stockbrokers Where are brokers' confirmation slips of all purchases you have made anytime?

• A list of all money, jewelry or other property you've lent. Are you the co-owner of any property that may not be in your possession? Does anyone, including the IRS, owe you money?

• A list of all your debts, including insurance policy loans and tax assessments.

• The whereabouts of copies of all the federal gift tax returns you ever filed. Your executor may need these returns to prove that gifted property isn't part of your estate. Similarly, where are the deeds of gift or transfer of other property that might be erroneously included in your taxable estate?

• A list of all documents that could establish the value of property you own or the price that your executor could get for it. Include: Financial statements of closely held corporations in which you own stock, partnership agreements, buy-sell agreements between a corporation and its shareholders or between the shareholders themselves, real estate or jewelry appraisals, special markets where estate assets such as collectibles might be sold at a good price.

Put the letter in a well-sealed envelope with your executor's name on it. Attach the envelope to your will or put it in your safe deposit box.

Source: Dr. Robert S. Holzman is professor emeritus of taxation at New York University and the author of *Estate Planning: The New Golden Opportunities*, Boardroom Books, Millburn, NJ.

Scariest Tax Audit Is the One Right After You Die

It is standard operating procedure for the Internal Revenue Service to examine the federal income tax returns of a decedent for the three years prior to his death.

Unless clear and well-documented work papers can be shown and explained to the IRS by a knowledgeable person familiar with the facts, there are apt to be disallowances because of lack of substantiation.

Can your returns be explained satisfactorily by someone else when you are not available?

Information as to where records are located should not be in the will. Rather, include it in a separate communication to the executor in advance, or leave it among personal possessions.

Source: *Estate Planning: The New Golden Opportunities* by Robert S. Holzman, Boardroom Books, Millburn, NJ.

Cash Found in Decedent's Safe Deposit Box

What was the source of any cash in a safe deposit box or in your home or office? In the absence of proof to the contrary, the Internal Revenue Service will consider any unexplained cash to represent previously untaxed income. This presumption can be refuted if there is credible evidence. For example, there may be a letter to your executor stating that Social Security checks or horse track winnings (reported) will be converted into cash, to be kept in the box as an emergency fund. Correspondence can identify cash as having been found money, which had been turned over to the police department and given back to the finder when no claimant appeared.

Source: *Encyclopedia of Estate Planning* by Robert S. Holzman, Boardroom Books, Millburn, NJ.

• Don't stash cash . . .without a note explaining its source. A man died, and when his safe-deposit box was opened in the presence of tax officials, a large amount of cash was found. There was no evidence showing where this money had come from. The IRS wanted the money allocated as unreported income for the years that he rented the box. And the Tax Court agreed.

Source: *Aggie L. Mizell,* TC Memo, 1984–254.

How To Choose a Guardian for Your Children

Whom do you want to take care of your children in the event you and your spouse die in the same accident?

This important estate-planning question exasperates most parents. But if you don't appoint a guardian, a probate judge will. And you are likely to make a better choice than the judge. To do the job right, follow these guidelines:

• Prepare a list of possible guardians. Rate each individual or couple according to their degree of responsibility, accessibility, lifestyle, moral tenets, opinions on child raising, and personal compatibility with your children. Other factors: The candidates' ages, whether they have children and their children's ages.

• Have meetings with the candidates. From these meetings you should learn each individual's willingness to become your children's guardian, the individual's short- and long-range plans, and his or her viewpoints on issues that are crucial to you as parents.

• Select only individuals who satisfy all your criteria. And remember to provide for a succession of guardians. Choose alternates in case your first choices become unable or unwilling to carry out their duties of caring for your children.

• Keep in touch with the guardians you have appointed. Meet with them from time to time to fill them in on the current needs and plans for your children. These meetings will also give the guardians a chance to voice changes in their own lifestyles that might have a dramatic impact on your children. You may decide to change guardians because of impressions you pick up. You might also use these sessions to let your children and their guardians get to know each other.

• Prepare a memorandum of instructions for the guardians, and keep it up to date. Include a list of things important to your children's well being, such as their allergies, medical requirements, family medical history, personality traits and behavior responses. State your personal opinions about allowances, dating, schooling, driving, drinking and other areas of parental discretion.

• Provide direction about spending funds to achieve short-range and long-range goals. Indicate which goals have priority. For instance, are short-range goals such as a car or a vacation in Europe more important than long-range goals such as college or a nest egg for going into business?

• Set a minimum monthly allowance to be paid to the guardians for the children's day-today spending needs. This monthly amount should be reviewed from time to time for reasonableness. Give your trustee the power to increase the allowance to meet your specified spending goals or to adjust for inflation.

• Project your estate's future cash flow. How much will be available after taxes are paid on the income earned? You need this figure to set a realistic monthly allowance. What will the earning power be after money is spent on a long-range goal, such as a college education for one of the children? Much care must be used in projecting both future cash flow and future budget requirements.

Source: Alan Gold, CPA, senior tax associate with Siegel, Mendlowitz & Rich, CPAs, 310 Madison Ave., New York, 10017.

Personal Risk Protection

If you're well-off and travel a lot, have health problems or engage in a high-risk business, consider providing a trusted friend or adviser with an evergreen power of attorney over your financial affairs. Unlike ordinary powers, evergreen powers remain effective even if you're in a coma or are otherwise unable to act. By giving the holder the legal right to manage your affairs, evergreen powers insure that your estate won't become paralyzed should you be disabled or detained in a foreign land. Of course, you can revoke an evergreen power of attorney at any time.

Source: Robert Beshar is an attorney practicing at 100 Maiden Ln., New York, 10038.

Prepaid Funeral Plans

Trap: Consumers who buy them may lose out if the company selling the plan misappropriates the money or if the funeral home goes out of business. Before investing in a prepaid plan, call your state attorney general's office and/or the Better Business Bureau to see

if there are any problems with the company. . .then, check out its track record, and review the contract with an attorney. Safer alternatives: Set up your own trust fund or savings account, or add to your insurance policy to cover funeral expenses.

Pay-before-you-go funeral programs allow you to make all arrangements in advance, sparing your family difficult decisions. Payment can be made in installments through an insurance plan that covers all costs even if you die before all the premiums are paid.

Who Pays the Legal Fees When a Will Is Contested

Helen Safran's will was contested by her relatives. The contest dragged on for several years. When it was settled, the estate tried to deduct more than $100,000 in legal fees that it had run up as an administration expense. Court: Too late. More than three years had passed since the estate had filed its tax return, so the statute of limitations had run out. No refund was possible. Better way: The estate could have made a protective refund claim when the contest started. That would have kept a deduction available for expenses incurred in the future.

Source: *Joseph I. Swietlik*, CA-7, No. 85-1887.

Unexpected Liability for Estate Taxes

If an executor distributes an estate without leaving enough to pay the federal estate tax, the government can assert transferee liability against any or all beneficiaries to the extent of the property each has received.

Moreover, the government doesn't have to apportion the tax among the beneficiaries; it can collect the entire amount from any one of them, if that person has received enough from the estate to cover it. The beneficiary can then try to recover a proportion of the tax from the executor or the other beneficiaries, but that means a great deal of trouble at the least, and possibly a protracted law suit.

What to do: If you're the beneficiary of an estate, check to make sure all taxes are being paid. If you're naming an executor in your own will, be sure to pick someone who understands the duties of the position and knows how to carry them out.

Estate Borrowing Trap

A person borrowed against his real estate shortly before he died. The loan terms did not allow early repayment. After the borrower died, the estate tried to deduct the interest payments that is still owed. IRS ruling: No deduction. An estate cannot deduct interest payments owed on borrowings, unless the borrowings were essential for the administration of the estate.

Source: *IRS Letter Ruling 8444003.*

Estate Tax Loophole

A person died while jointly owning bank accounts and savings certificates with his wife and children. Within nine months of his death, his children filed valid disclaimers of their interest in accounts and certificats. IRS ruling: The money now all goes to the wife. Tax benefit: Property that passes to a spouse is protected by he marital deduction, so it escapes estate tax. If the money had gone to the children, it would have been subject to tax.

Source: IRS Letter Ruling 8625001.

If You Own a Family Business

Harry Lee owned 100% of the stock of a family business, and transferred it to his son, Robert. Harry continued to receive a large amount of income from the corporation under an oral agreement with Robert. Then Harry died. Court: The stock was taxable to Harry's estate because he had really kept an interest in the stock after nominally giving it away to his son. That was the only way to construe the continuing payments. Better way: Harry could have gotten the stock out of his estate and kept a healthy income by entering into a formal agreement with the company that would have provided him with compensation payments independent of stock ownership.

Source: *Robert A. Lee,* WD Ky., No. C 84-0139-L(B).

Homeowners Exclusion By Executor

Taxpayers who are at least 55 years old can elect to exclude from tax up to $125,000 of profits on the sale of their principal residence. Question: Can a deceased taxpayer's executor exercise this taxfree election for him? IRS ruling: Where a taxpayer made a binding contract to sell his house before he died, leaving only technical details to be completed, his executor could elect to exclude $125,000 of the gain from the sale on the taxpayer's final income tax return.

Source: Revenue Ruling 82-1.

12 INVESTING TO WIN

Setting Your Investment Objectives

In setting investment objectives, few investors effectively unify their understanding of their personal financial circumstances, risk preference, and knowledge of the financial markets. Instead, a close inspection of most investors' objectives indicates a foundation of wishful thinking.

This lack of perspective and realism is exemplified in the financial press all of the time: Relatively safe returns of 9% are put down in favor of highly risky "opportunities" for 20+% returns. It may be true that 20+% returns would multiply an investment almost a hundred fold in 25 years—but how many people have enjoyed that kind of success? Remember, too, that 9% is close to the long-term average return to common-stock investors, who have accepted considerable risk to achieve it. Identifying resources, including future earnings, carefully calibrating future needs, understanding personal risk tolerance, and allowing low-risk investment returns to compound have worked magic for many investors.

Failure to diversify is another product of many investors' wishful thinking. Putting all of your eggs into one high-flying basket can be exciting and, if you are right, ultimately can lead to the greatest potential returns. But if you have a lot to lose (such as your life savings), then disaster may be waiting just around the corner if you don't diversify. On the other side of the coin, hedging every potential development is probably only appropriate for the extremely wealthy. If you fall somewhere in the middle, always employ reasonable diversification, both in terms of types of investments and within the selected types. This will temper the risk and opportunity reflected in your investment objectives.

Source: M. David Testa, vice president and director, T. Rowe Price Associates, Inc., 100 East Pratt St., Baltimore 21202. As chief investment officer, he manages $20 billion in mutual funds and separate accounts; in addition, he is president and portfolio manager of the $1 billion T. Rowe Price Growth Stock Fund.

Before You Invest

Before investing in stocks and bonds, you should set aside at least three months' income

337

in liquid savings (money-market or passbook savings accounts). Other prerequisites: Adequate life, health and disability insurance coverage. . .a willingness to assume risks.

Source: *The Bank Book* by Naphtali Hoffman, Harcourt Brace, New York.

Investment Strategies for High-Net-Worth Individuals

While only an in-depth analysis of an individual's risk tolerance and financial condition will produce an intelligent investment strategy, general strategies can be devised for the high-net-worth individual based on assumptions of changes in risk tolerance and in earning power that reflect the investor's age. Four such strategies follow.

Earning power	Age	Investments
High	30–40	30% high-quality growth stocks
		30% aggressive growth stock
		40% real estate (investments, not personal residences)
High	40–50	25% high-quality growth stocks
		25% municipal bonds
		25% income stocks
		25% real estate
High	50–60	50% high-quality bonds
		25% income stocks
		25% high-quality growth stocks
None	Retirement	75% high-quality bonds
		25% income stocks

Source: Jeffrey J. Miller, CFA, executive vice president, Provident Investment Counsel, 225 South Lake Ave., Pasadena, CA 91101. Mr. Miller's responsibilities include portfolio management of over $400 million in assets, research, and marketing. He serves on the board of directors of the Association of Investment Management Sales Executives and the board of governors of the Investment Counsel Association of America.

Portfolio Strategies

• Conservative: Invest 27% in domestic and 8% in international growth funds and 65% in cash equivalents.

• Venturesome: Invest 45% in domestic and 15% in international growth funds, 5% in international bond funds and 35% in cash equivalents.

Source: William E. Donoghue, chairman, The Donoghue Organization, publisher of *Donoghue's Moneyletter.*

The Real Impact of High- Risk Investments

Some investors go for the quick kill. They select investments, not for reliable growth, but to attain riches they don't feel they can acquire through their own earnings. Some do this by investing in speculative stocks on margin; some purchase futures or puts and calls.

Success with high-leverage, high-risk investments requires tremendous attention and skill. It usually requires buying when most others are selling and selling when others are buying. Investing against the grain is no easy task.

The danger of high-flying investment strategies is that when you lose, you usually lose big. And, when you suffer an investment loss, your funds must work extra hard to make up for the loss.

For example, if you invest $100 in the stock market, suffer a 10% loss in the first year and realize a 10% increase the next year, your investment is worth $99, not $100. Even worse, if your $100 investment declines by 50% in the first year and increases by 50% in the second, it is worth only $75—far short of the original amount, despite a spectacular turnaround.

When an investment incurs a loss in the initial stages, it must work much harder thereafter to attain the initial objectives. Let's say you expect an investment to appreciate at 10% a year for five years. But in the first year, its value drops by 10% instead. Your investment must now compound at a rate of 15.7% annually to catch up with your initial five-year expectations; such a high rate is usually attained only by buying common stocks at the depth of a recession and holding for a market recovery.

Source: Archie M. Richards, Jr., CFP, president, Archie Richards Associates, Inc., Ten Mall Road, Burlington, MA 01803. Mr. Richards is a member of the Institute of Certified Financial Planners and has been admitted to the Registry of Financial Planning Practitioners. He is also a weekly newspaper columnist.

Inflation Hedges

The primary types of investments to avoid when inflation hits are those that produce fixed incomes and are interest-rate sensitive. These investments do well during flat markets and recessions, but their traditionally "safe" value is eaten away by inflation and rising interest rates.

During inflationary periods it's much better to stick to short-term, liquid investments like Treasury bills or money-market funds if you need safe income. It's a good idea to keep at least a six-month liquid cash reserve at all times.

The Virtues of Real Estate

For income and capital gains, a favorite investment is rental real estate. Even during bad times, rental real estate, ranging from single-family homes to large apartment buildings, offers income, equity buildup, tax shelter, and appreciation. If you want to avoid the headaches of individual ownership-property selection, management, and maintenance—the best alternatives are carefully selected real estate partnerships and investment trusts sold through brokers and financial planners. In an increasingly uncertain world, income-producing real estate comes as close to certainty as you can get.

Reliable Stocks

If you want to invest in the stock market, focus on areas that are traditionally relied upon during inflationary periods—hard assets, natural resources, and commodities.

For growth and income, gold stocks and the integrated international oils are safe bets. South African gold stocks offer terrific yields, especially the large mines with long lives and low production costs. Good advice: Wait until the political situation settles down in South Africa before you invest in the country's stocks. Until that time, it would be a better idea to stay close to home by investing in premiere North American mines. The yields are not as good as from South African stocks, but the risk is considerably less. The capital gains should be comparable.

If you've got a gambler's streak, take a chance with some of the North American penny (low-priced) mining stocks traded over-the-counter or on the Spokane, Vancouver, Toronto, or Denver exchange. The risks and volatility are high, but the capital gains can be spectacular.

For the Integrated International Oil Companies, higher inflation means higher earnings and dividends, in addition to significant price appreciation in the stocks. Despite weaknesses in oil prices, oil stocks can maintain consistently high values. Some stocks, like Exxon, also offer terrific dividends.

Precious Metals and Currencies

If you are interested primarily in capital gains, consider the precious metals—platinum, silver, and gold—in that order. Aside from traditional bullion and bullion coins, you can find great potential for appreciation in rare coins, and precious metal certificate programs. Dealers who handle these include Rulfco, Deak-Perera, Mocatta Metals, and Merrill Lynch.

Speculating in currency can be a fairly simple way to play off increasing inflation. Inflation is a monetary phenomenon—the loss of purchasing power caused by the oversupply of money. As the dollar's purchasing power declines, the value of many other currencies rise. Opportunities in foreign currencies abound, particularly in the British pound, the Swiss franc, the Japanese yen, and the German deutschemark. The simplest way to invest in foreign currencies is to purchase traveler's checks denominated in the currency of your choice. Traveler's checks pay no interest, but their values fluctuate along with the currency's.

Another way to bet on changes in currency

values is to buy foreign-currency certificates of deposit (CDs). They pay a nominal interest rate, but offer capital gains as well. Reputable dealers can arrange the purchase of 3-, 6-, 9-, or 12-month CDs issued by foreign or domestic banks. The minimum investment can be as low as $3,000.

Options

Options give you the ability to speculate on traditional inflation hedges without actually having to own the hedges themselves. Options are available on gold stocks, precious metals, stock market indexes, and foreign currencies. Options provide terrific leverage, but unlike futures, you won't get a margin call if you wind up on the wrong side of the market. Your risk is limited to the amount you initially invest, while your profit potential is virtually unlimited. You should only buy options when you are certain a trend is firmly in place, and when you can afford to lose whatever money you put into the market.

Source: Howard J. Ruff, editor of *Ruff Times*, Target Publishers, Pleasanton, CA 94566. Author of several books, including *How to Prosper During the Coming Bad Years, Survive & Win in the Inflationary 80's,* and *Making Money;* he is widely known through his television and radio shows.

An Investment Strategy for All Seasons

There is no investment for all seasons, but there is a season for each investment. The primary factor determining that season is inflation. During periods of decelerating or stable inflation financial assets—stocks and bonds—are the superstars. During periods of accelerating inflation, real assets—real estate, precious metals, and commodities—are winners.

The problem for investors is trying to determine whether inflation is going to remain stable, accelerate, or decelerate. Inflation is primarily caused by government monetary and fiscal policy, so the most important economic indicator for investors to keep track of is what government policy makers are actually doing (as opposed to what they *say* they are doing).

The following guidelines should help you determine when inflation is beginning to speed up and when the best time is to change the character of your portfolio to take advantage of changes in the inflation rate.

Changes in Money Supply

The main ingredient for accelerating inflation is excessive growth in the country's money supply. If the percentage change in the money supply, measured on a year-to-year basis, begins to rise sharply, you can reasonably expect an increase in the inflation rate. The lag between an acceleration in the money supply and an acceleration in the inflation rate is approximately two years. That gives the astute investor ample time to restructure his or her investment portfolio accordingly. On the other side of the coin, when the monetary growth rate begins to decline as measured by the year-to-year percentage change in the money supply, it is probable that inflation will also decline in approximately two years.

Acceleration

When the monetary growth rate accelerates for more than six months and rises by more than three percentage points from its low, it's time to prepare yourself for an acceleration in the inflation rate. Since the trend may change slowly, it's best to first liquidate only half of your long-term financial assets. Sell the remainder of your assets when bond and stock prices fall below their respective 39-week moving averages. Recommendation: Initially invest the funds generated by the sales in short-term financial instruments such as certificates of deposit and/or Treasury bills or money-market funds.

Investments in inflation hedges should be made only after the monetary growth rate has accelerated for more than six months and the year-to-year monetary growth rate is more than three percentage points from its recent low. Additionally, the economy should be expanding and an index of inflation-sensitive commodity prices should be above its 20-week moving average. The best equity investments in an inflationary environment can typically be made in mutual funds containing stocks of gold and silver mining companies. Holding a portfolio of short-term money-market instruments is a conservative way to keep pace with inflation, since short-term interest rates rise sharply once inflation takes hold. Also, when inflation is accelerating in the United States, the dollar usually declines in value. To take advantage of a weakening in the dollar, try investing in foreign stocks or mutual funds with portfolios of foreign stocks.

Deceleration

Use a similar process to anticipate decelerating inflation. Wait for the monetary growth rate to decline for at least six months and to fall at least three percentage points from its recent high. The economy should show signs of weakness and an index of inflation-sensitive commodity prices should decline below its 20-week moving average. At that point, liquidate inflation hedge investments and invest the proceeds in money-market instruments or money-market mutual funds.

Source: Roger Klein, president, The Interest Rate Futures Research Corporation, 55 Princeton-Hightstown Rd., Princeton Junction, NJ 08550, money manager and consultant to financial institutions. Dr. Klein is editor of *The Klein-Wolman Investment Letter* and coauthor, with William Wolman, of *The Beat Inflation Strategy*.

Securities and Commodities Fraud

To reduce chances of becoming a victim of an investment swindler, send for the free pamphlet *15 Questions to Turn Off an Investment Swindler*, National Futures Association, 200 W. Madison St., Chicago 60606.

All About Hiring an Investment Counselor

The trick in hiring an investment counselor is to demystify the position. Put it in a realistic context . . . you are hiring an employee who works outside of your home or office. The longer he has been doing the job effectively, the more likely it is that he will continue to do so.

Until the early 1970s, the services of investment counselors were available only to the very, very rich. Computers have made it easier and more profitable for counselors to take on smaller accounts. Today, individuals with $200,000 to invest can find counselors willing to manage their accounts. (Until you have accumulated that kind of capital, your best bet is mutual funds.)

Three groups to avoid:

• One-man firms. These are limited to the ideas of the founder, and the accounts can't be supervised when he or she is out of the office.

• Bank trust departments. They are generally disadvantaged by low salary levels and too many committees. Talented money managers cannot afford to stay at most banks.

• Brokerage firms. Their money managers are often limited to using research generated inside the firm. They also channel most of their clients' investments through their own firm.

Myths Debunked

Several misconceptions surround the investment management business:

• You will have a custom-designed portfolio. Reality: At almost all firms, all accounts are managed essentially the same way.

• You will receive personal attention. Reality: Good portfolio managers do not have time to speak with their clients often. Most will talk to you once a quarter and meet you face to face annually.

• Your existing portfolio will be scrutinized closely. Reality: When you turn your portfolio over to the firm, the manager will scan the list to see if he actively follows any of the stocks. If not, he will sell them. If you do not want the stock to be sold, you should not have the issue managed.

What to Look For

Ask to see the performance record for the entire time the firm has been in business. Beware of 20-year-old companies that show you only five-year results. . .what happened in the previous 15 years?

Compare performance for each quarter of the last eight years with the Standard & Poor's 500 Index. The company should have outperformed the index, especially in down markets.

Look for a firm that is registered as an investment adviser with the Securities & Exchange Commission. And ask the firm for its disclosure form ADV-II to make sure that the people responsible for whatever success the firm has had still work there.

Meet the portfolio manager who will handle your account. Find out how the firm is organized, so you know who will make your investment decisions.

Get client references that go back through periods of stock market adversity such as 1973–74, 1977 and 1981–82.

What It Costs

Annual fees usually range from .5% to 3% of the amount of the account. Accounts over $1 million are able to negotiate fees at a number of good firms.

It is, of course, important to monitor your investment counselor. A reasonable rate of return on your money over several years is 1.2 times the 90-day Treasury bill rate. A 12%–15% compounded rate or a rate that beats inflation is a very good performance. If after a full market cycle (usually three to five years) the account has a gross return of less than 25%, you should look for a new investment counselor.

Source: Michael Stolper, president, Stolper & Co., a consulting and performance-measurement firm, 525 B St., San Diego, CA 92101.

How To Evaluate a Money Manager

Selecting a money manager takes more than just looking at recent performance numbers and picking the firm that ranks at the top. If it were that simple, you could pick a money manager using a computer. The four basic criteria to be considered before you place your money in someone else's hands are: (1) philosophy, (2) process, (3) personnel, and (4) performance.

Philosophy

A prospective money manager's philosophy is his beliefs about how to successfully make money in the market and do better than the major stock averages. Does the manager focus on growth stocks or high-yield stocks? Or is he or she a contrarian, always investing in out-of-favor stocks? Investment philosophy can also include a manager's belief about his or her market-timing ability, that is, being 100% invested in equities in an anticipated bull market and then moving to cash-equivalent securities when the market is expected to be bearish.

Your main objective in determining a manager's investment philosophy or style is to see if the manager has been consistent over time, and whether his style goes along with your basic investment instincts. If a prospective manager's style has been continually changing, be cautious—a successful style should be able to stand the test of time. Also, knowing a manager's style helps you to evaluate performance. For example, a high-yield manager should do well when interest rates are falling, but might not be at the top of the pack when interest rates are rising.

Process

Be familiar with the way a manager chooses specific securities for his portfolios. One typical process is the "top-down" approach, whereby the investor begins with projections for the economy followed by a determination of the industries that should do well in the forecasted economic environment. Within the favored industries, specific stocks are selected that should benefit most from the industries' growth. Another process is the "bottom-up" approach, in which stocks are picked on their own individual merits and only secondarily on the basis of their industry and its relationship to the economy. Make it your objective to find a manager whose process makes sense to you.

Personnel

What is the manager's experience in the business and what kind of backup support does he have? How long has the individual been in the business? Has he been through the good and bad times? Is the manager a Chartered Financial Analyst? Who manages the portfolios while he is out of the office? Are there other individuals who will be familiar enough with your account to handle it when the manager is on vacation?

Performance

The last consideration should be performance. What kind of long-term track record does the manager have? These figures may be difficult to get from the manager, but it's worth pushing a little to find out. When reviewing a prospective manager's track record, be sure to compare performance to the market (Standard & Poor's 500) or to a universe of professional money managers (this information is available from various consulting services). The minimum time period to consider is one market cycle, which will show how a manager performed in both up and down markets. If he hasn't done better than the market or the average manager, it's probably a good idea to consider someone else.

Source: David C. O'Donovan, vice president, SEI Corporation, Funds Evaluation Services, 2 N. Riverside Plaza, Chicago 60606.

Finding the Right Stockbroker

The risky and expensive way to find the right stockbroker is by experimentation—switching from one account to another. Instead, minimize the cost of your search for the right broker by considering the following points.

• A broker's livelihood depends solely on commissions generated by transactions. The pressures of the securities industry can cause some brokers to unnecessarily buy and sell securities in an account for the sake of generating commissions ("churning"). To resolve this issue, ask a prospective broker what his philosophy is regarding holding periods for stocks. If the broker is a short-term trader—one who typically holds stocks for a year or less—look elsewhere unless this matches your investment philosophy. You may be in for heavy commissions.

• How well do you communicate with the broker? Will he be readily available? Does the broker answer your questions directly, or evade issues? The question of communication is most important for accounts in which you do not plan to give the broker discretionary power over buying and selling. Does the broker try to find out about your investment objectives and risk tolerance? How will the broker communicate with you on a regular basis—by newsletter, research reports, monthly calls, quarterly meetings? What will your responsibilities be as a client? Will you be expected to monitor your own account, or wait for the broker to make recommendations? It is essential that you clarify each person's responsibilities at the outset.

• What is the average rate of return you should expect as a client? Is the response you receive to this question realistic? Does the broker promise guaranteed returns? Beware if he claims to have a surefire way to beat the market.

• Does the broker invest his own money in the market? If the broker does not, why is he recommending that you do so? Ask to see the broker's own account record for the past several years. This will tell you what his past results were and the types of securities the broker buys and sells. Remember, however, that brokers sometimes buy riskier stocks for their own acounts.

• Find out about the broker's clients, to determine if they are similar to you. What is the average client like? Older? Younger? High-income? Are they high-risk investors? Are they more interested in investment vehicles such as limited partnerships, load mutual funds, and insurance products? Be sure to ask the broker for references—and call them. Since you will only be referred to the broker's most satisfied clients, always ask the clients how long they have been with the broker. This will tell you whether they have gone through several market cycles with the broker.

- What is the broker's experience? How long has he been in the industry? Be wary of new brokers; in general, they rely on others to tell them what to recommend. This can be a problem if the firm is pushing its brokers to sell certain stocks, such as new issues. New brokers also have not had the invaluable chance to learn from their mistakes.

- How does the broker pick stocks? Does he have a system? If so, does it make sense? What does the broker read and who does he listen to for advice? Does the broker talk directly to corporate officers and analysts?

- What is the broker's firm like? Are the rates charged in line with the services provided? Has there been a major change in the account executives recently? If so, are there problems at the branch office?

- Once you've signed on with a broker, review the broker's performance regularly. Is he really making money for you—after you deduct commissions? Set regular periods for review of your account results with your broker. If the broker consistently reduces the value of your account in both up and down markets, it's time to apply these search ideas to the next candidate.

Source: Laura Waller, president, Laura Waller Advisors, Inc., 201 East Kennedy Boulevard, Suite 1109, Tampa, FL 33602. She is a certified financial planner, a registered principal of NASD, a registered representative of Investment Management & Research, Inc., and a licensed insurance agent. Southern regional director on the national board of the Institute of Certified Financial Planners, Ms. Waller is a frequent speaker and has been quoted in many financial publications.

How To Choose a Full-Service Broker

In today's increasingly complex financial world, it is almost mandatory for the busy individual to have a full-service broker at his or her disposal. And that doesn't just mean a stock picker. In fact, the term broker itself is no longer appropriate. The title financial consultant much more accurately describes the position. A full-service broker must belong to a firm that can provide superior investment advice, tax planning, estate planning, and a menu of investment vehicles such as money-market funds, checking and borrowing capabilities, zero-coupon bonds, certificates of deposit, municipal bonds, commodities, and options.

Referrals from friends are a good way to start. But remember, your investment style might not be the same as your friends'. Find a broker who meets your needs, not someone else's.

If you have to start the search cold, it's a good idea to pick several large brokerage houses in your area that you think will be in business in the future. Be sure that the brokerage firms are members of all major stock exchanges and that you are able to select from a wide variety of investment vehicles in addition to stocks and straight debt securities. Find out if the brokerage firms are properly insured. Also determine whether they have the necessary communications and computer equipment to execute transactions quickly and effectively.

When you've narrowed down your prospects to one brokerage house, go to the firm's main or largest office in your area. Speak directly to the senior manager of the office. (The trick is to start at the top and work your way down.) Carefully review with the senior manager your investment objectives as well as the kind of investments that appeal to you. Also discuss the type of broker you are looking for. Finally, arrange a face-to-face interview with several prospective brokers recommended by the manager.

Questions to ask a prospective broker:

- How long have you been a broker?

- How long have you been in the securities industry?

- How long have you been associated with this firm?

- What type of clients do you have? Are

they income, speculative, or tax shelter-oriented?

- Do you specialize in any one area?

- What is your attitude toward risk?

- Do you advise any of the senior officers of this firm?

- Do you have any clients that I could speak to regarding your performance?

The last question is certainly the most important. Referrals are the best test of a broker's quality; don't be afraid to ask for them. Equally important as a broker's performance record, is his or her ability to communicate. Make sure you understand one another. Good rapport with your broker is critical.

Source: Stanley P. Heilbronn, vice president Merrill Lynch, Pierce, Fenner & Smith Inc., 717 Fifth Avenue, New York 10022. Mr. Heilbronn advises clients—including individuals in the fields of entertainment and medicine—on their investments. In addition, he is a contributor to *Medical Economics* magazine.

What To Expect of a Full-Service Broker

If you like to map out your own investment strategy, do your own research, and closely monitor all of your stock transactions, then you probably won't want a full-service broker. Why pay full commission when you won't utilize a broker's advice and services? However, if you're like many people and don't have the time to devote to watching over your stock portfolio, then a full-service broker can be well worth the extra money you will pay in heftier commissions.

What You Pay For

The process of choosing a full-time broker should be handled with care, since the quality of his or her advice will largely determine how well you do with your investments. The following list will tell you what you should expect from a good full-service broker.

- Advice. A full-service broker is full of investment ideas. If he is good, those ideas will be tailored to fit your financial requirements and investing style. If the broker is very good, he will help develop your financial plans in the same way an accountant might handle your taxes or a lawyer might draw up your estate. But remember: a stockbroker only makes money when a you make a trade. You must ask yourself if that type of incentive system bothers you.

- Monitor your stocks. A good broker can watch over your stocks and help you trade more effectively. An experienced broker will know trading techniques that might not be familiar to the average investor. You can decide the extent to which a broker monitors your portfolio—whether the broker calls you before each transaction or takes full control.

- Research products. Large brokerage houses spend millions of dollars each year on providing research products. Reports published by these firms can be of great value to the investor who wants to stay up-to-date on industries, specific companies, the overall stock market, and new investment areas. Check to see that your broker's firm offers a high-quality research product. It should be meaningful, comprehensive, and timely. (Each year, Institutional Investor ranks Wall Street's research departments according to their ability to provide the soundest investment advice.)

- Other investment products. A full-service broker also will provide you with a wide range of alternative investment vehicles, including municipal bonds, zero coupon bonds, tax shelters, mutual funds, real estate investments, and insurance. Other extras include free checking, money market accounts, and borrowing facilities. Alternative investment products can become increasingly important during changing economic times, when you have entered a new stage in life, or when you have simply changed your investment strategy.

Choosing a Broker

Contrary to conventional wisdom, referrals from friends are not the best way to make your selection. A broker may have performed exceptionally well for your neighbor, for instance, but because of a different style or different financial profile, he or she may not be appropriate for you and your needs.

Before choosing a broker, always try to accurately establish your investment goals: are you looking for safety, or are you primarily a speculator? Do you have need of immediate income, or will you need income in the future? How much risk are you willing to assume? What rate of return would adequately compensate you for assuming that amount of risk?

When you've decided what your investment goals are, take the time to meet and interview all prospective registered "reps." The primary trait to look for in a broker is compatibility. You want your broker's investment style and trading technique to be suited to your investment goals. For example, if you are looking for long-term capital gains, then stay away from brokers who are more interested in making short-term gains in the options market.

Always test a broker for personal professionalism, and examine his or her firm, noting the level of seriousness you find there. Is it a noisy office, with loud talk about sports, movies, etc.? A lack of adequate secretarial help is also a dangerous sign. (A firm building a relationship with the public relies on clerical help.) Are the employees doing their work? Remember, the seriousness of any investment company may be measured in inverse proportion to the level of "horsing around" prevalent in its branch offices.

If a broker meets the compatibility test and the professionalism test, then it's time to ask for at least two references. Make sure that you ask for references from people whose goals are similar to your own. If their recommendations are strong, open an account and watch it carefully to check on the quality of your decision.

Source: Louis Ehrenkrantz, full-service broker, serving as a Director of Ehrenkrantz and King, 50 Broadway, New York 10004. He is the publisher of *The Ehrenkrantz Letter.* Mr. Ehrenkrantz has 26 years of experience in the investment field, and is a contributor to dozens of magazines nationwide. He writes the weekly Market Beat column in *The NY Post* every Wednesday.

When To Use a Discount Broker

If you are an independent thinker and like to make your own investment decisions, then a discount broker is probably for you.

Discount brokerage firms (independent or bank-affiliated) offer no advice, a limited number of products and services, salaried brokers to take your orders and much lower commissions. Generally, commission rates for discount brokers are 50%–70% lower than the published rates of full-service brokers. Of course, if you are a substantial investor you can usually bargain for a discount from your full-service broker, but, the commissions still won't be as low as a discounter's. (A substantial investor can always bargain with a discount broker as well.)

Discount brokers don't make sense when you invest infrequently and/or when your transactions are $2,000 or less. That's because most discounters charge minimum commissions of $30-$45. So, if you are only going to save $5 once in a while, you might as well use a full-service broker. At least then you'll get research reports and other services.

Discount brokers do offer some services. Some will give you copies of Standard & Poor's or Value Line research reports, sell you mutual funds or unit investment trusts, and pay interest on your cash balance. Discounters affiliated with a bank will automatically switch your funds between your brokerage and bank accounts.

If you are nervous about relying solely on a discount broker, consider using both a discounter and a full-service broker. Many substantial investors have two or more brokers: a full-service broker for ideas research and for watching certain investments, and a discount broker when the investor knows what he or she wants or when commissions cut too deeply into profit margins.

Source: J. Bud Feuchtwanger, president, Feuchtwanger Group, 161 E. 91 St., New York 10128. He is a consultant to commercial banks, savings and loans, insurance companies, and securities firms on marketing, product development, and distribution.

How To Make a Deal with Your Broker

Many companies charge a range of prices for the same goods and services. This means some people are paying less than you for the identical item . . . a hotel room, car rental . . . anything that can't be warehoused and sold later. That's why, although they'll never brag about it, most sellers actually need to negotiate.

So-called standard rates are almost always negotiable. Suppose you like your stockbroker but want to pay lower commissions and interest rates. Check the ads in *Barron's* or call a couple of discount brokers for their rate structures. Once you have the facts, visit your broker and explain that other brokers charge much less than he does, and that you'd like to discuss a new, fairer arrangement.

Show your proof (ads or notes you took while calling discounters). Expect the usual responses about excellent service, discounts that depend on volume, your account is too small, etc. Your response: "My account doesn't require much servicing, I don't use your research or other expensive facilities and I'm not asking for the moon. I just don't think it's fair that I have to pay the top rate."

If the broker says that he can't help you, ask him who can. Inside information: The broker probably has more discretion than he's willing to disclose. He should be able to arrange a 20%–30% discount off the top rate.

That accomplished, ask for one last favor: You're paying the firm's highest interest rate on your debit balance, and you'd like a one-percentage-point discount. Since brokers usually charge one-half to two percentage points above prime, a one-point reduction off the high end of this gravy isn't unreasonable. . .even for a small account. If you're told that rates are based on the size of the debit balance, explain that you know rates are negotiable, that others pay less and that you'd like the same treatment as those paying less.

Later: Negotiate for your share of free stock guides and charts, access to the broker's financial library and occasional shares of "hot" issues.

You have a right to these, but you won't be handed them on a silver platter. You have to ask for them.

Source: Ralph Charell, former CEO of his own Wall Street securities firm, 242 E. 72 St., New York 10021.

When Not To Listen To Your Broker

The few words the average investor finds hardest to say to his broker are, "Thanks for calling, but no thanks." There are times when it is in your own best interest to be able to reject the broker's blandishments.

• When the broker's hot tip (or your barber's or tennis partner's) is that a certain stock is supposed to go up because of impending good news. Ask yourself: If the "news" is so superspecial, how come you (and/or your broker) have been able to learn about it in the nick of time? Chances are by the time you hear the story, plenty of other people have, too. Often you can spot this because the stock has already been moving. That means that insiders have been buying long before you got the hot tip. After you buy, when the news does become "public," who'll be left to buy?

• When the market is sliding. When your broker asks, "How much lower can they go?" the temptation can be very great to try to snag a bargain. But before you do, consider: If the stock, at that price, is such a bargain, wouldn't some big mutual funds or pension funds be trying to buy up all they could? If that's the case, how come the stock has been going down? It's wildly speculative to buy a stock because it looks as if it has fallen "far enough." Don't try to guess the bottom. After all, the market is actually saying that the stock is weak. That is the fact, the knowable item.

• Don't fall for the notion that a stock is "averaging down." It's a mistake for the broker (or investor) to calculate that if he buys more "way down there," he can get out even. The flaws are obvious. The person who averages down is busy thinking of buying more just when he should be selling. And if a little rally does come along, he waits for his target price "to get out even"—so if the rally fades, he's stuck with his mathematical target.

Stock market professionals average up, not down. They buy stocks that are proving themselves strong, not ones that are clearly weak.

If Your Broker Goes Broke

Your money may be tied up for months if your brokerage house fails. Although brokerages are insured by the Securities Investor Protection Corp., assets are frozen during the bankruptcy period. You will receive any gains, but market losses are not covered. Alternative: Ask your broker to send your stock and bond certificates to you for keeping in your safe-deposit box.

Source: *Sylvia Porter's Personal Finance,* New York.

How To Bypass Brokers

Buy stock directly from companies if you want to save all brokerage fees. Many utility companies and certain major corporations, including W. R. Grace (1144 Ave. of the Americas, New York 10036) and Control Data (8100 34 Ave. S., Bloomington, MN 55420), allow you to buy their shares directly. To find out whether a company in which you're interested will sell you its stock directly, write the firm's shareholder relations department.

Source: *How to Invest $50–$5,000* by financial analyst Nancy Dunnan, Harper & Row, New York.

What To Watch Besides the Dow

Too many investors rely exclusively on the

Dow Jones Industrial Average for a quick view of what the market is doing. But the Dow reflects only stock price changes of 30 large, mature companies. Their performance does not necessarily reflect the market as a whole. The Dow should be supplemented with these indexes:

• The Over-the-Counter Composite Index gauges the cumulative performance of over-the-counter issues. It points to a bull market when it outpaces the Dow Jones Industrial Average and to a bear market when it is weaker.

• TRIN, an acronym for the trading index, measures the relative volume of rising and declining issues. The market is bullish when the TRIN falls from a reading of above 1.20 to below .70 during one day of trading. It is bearish when the TRIN goes from below .70 to 1.20. A reading of 1.00 shows an even relationship between advancing and declining stocks.

• The Quotron change, named for the company that developed it, measures the daily percentage change for all issues on the New York Stock Exchange (the QCHA index) and the American Stock Exchange (QACH). It gives an excellent picture of what the market is doing in broad terms. Mutual funds track more closely with the Quotron change than the Dow Jones Industrial Average.

• The Dow Jones Transportation Average is a generally reliable lead indicator of intermediate trends. The Dow Jones Utilities Average reflects income- and interest-sensitive stocks. It's a good long-term lead indicator.

• In a bull market, the total number of shares traded expands on days when advances outpace declines. The opposite occurs in a bear market. A sign of market reversal is a high-volume day when the market moves in one direction all morning, then turns around.

Guide to Stock Market Indicators

• Speculation index: Divide the weekly trading volume on the American Stock

348

Exchange (in thousands) by the number of issues traded. Calculate the same ratio for New York Stock Exchange trading. Divide the AMEX ratio by the NYSE ratio to calculate the speculation index.

To read the index: Strategists believe the market is bearish when the index is more than .38 (and especially so if it rises to .38 and then falls back). Less than .20 is bullish.

• Member short selling: Divide the number of shares NYSE members sell short each week by total NYSE short selling.

To read the index: It is bearish when readings of .87 are reached. A reading below .75 is very bullish, particularly if it lasts several weeks.

• New highs–new lows: The market is usually approaching an intermediate bottom when the number of new lows reaches 600. The probable sign of an intermediate top is 600 new highs in one week, followed by a decline in number the next week.

• NYSE short interest ratio: The total number of outstanding shares sold short each month divided by the average daily trading volume for that month. A strong rally generally comes after the ratio reaches 1.75.

• Ten-week moving NYSE average: Compute the average NYSE index for the previous 10 weeks. Then measure the difference between last week's close and the average.

• How to read it: When the gap between the last weekly close and the 10-week average remains at 4.00 or below for two to three weeks, investors can expect an intermediate advance. Market tops are usually near when the last week's index is 4.00 or more above the previous 10-week average.

• Reading the indicators together: Only once or twice a year will as many as four of the five indicators signal an intermediate bottom, but when four do, it is highly reliable. The same is true for intermediate tops.

Source: All indicators available weekly in *Barron's*. The Speculation Index was developed by *Indicator Digest*.

To Find Out Which Way the Market's Going

A quick, easy technique to determine the market's general direction: The outlook is bullish if the discount rate is greater than the three-month Treasury bill rate. . . the federal funds rate is lower than a year ago. . .the three-month T-bill rate is below 7% and lower than a year ago. . .and rates on seven-year Treasury notes and 30-year Treasury bonds are lower than a year ago but higher than rates on three- and six-month T-bills. The outlook is bearish if the opposite is true for all of the above. (All rates are listed in your daily newspaper.)

Source: Elaine Garzarelli, chief quantitative analyst, Shearson Lehman Brothers.

How To Recognize a Stock Market Rally Before It Gets Going

Stock market rallies don't begin without some kind of warning. In most cases, market advances and rallies have been signaled long before their arrival. Most of the data required to track these indicators are available weekly in newspapers that provide extensive financial coverage. Here are some especially accurate indicators that can help you predict when the market is likely to stage a major advance or rally.

• Declining member short sales ratio. Members of the New York Stock Exchange (NYSE) are usually very astute traders. When they cut back their short selling, it's likely that the stock market is ready for an advance. The "member short sales ratio" is the amount of members' short sales as a percentage of the total short sales on the NYSE each week. Look for ratios of 78% and below as signs of optimism on the part of the sophisticated members.

• Favorable Federal Reserve action. The market loves to watch the Federal Reserve for indications of changes in monetary policy. Falling interest rates are usually very bullish for the stock market. A really strong signal is a drop in the discount rate (the rate the Fed charges for loans to banks) two times in succession without an intervening rise. This action implies a bull market that could last for months rather than weeks or days.

• NYSE "new lows" reach a high level and then turn down. Long market declines are usually concluded when the number of weekly new lows rises over 300 and then declines to under 150. Major bull markets often follow this signal.

• The advance/decline line shows strength after an intermediate low point. Expect a sharp market advance if the following conditions are met: (1) the NYSE Index falls to a four- to five-week low, then (2) the market stages a strong daily rally—850 more stocks advance than decline. Odds are good that the market advance will be strengthened if volume increases sharply.

• Nonmember or "public" short sales go up. When the general public is most bearish, expect a market upturn. To measure the public's bearish sentiments, divide the amount of shares sold short by the public (nonmembers) in a week by the total trading volume on the NYSE for that week. Look for public short selling in excess of 1.75% of total trading volume. In this case, stocks are likely to advance over the coming weeks. Also, odd-lot (transactions of less than 100 shares) short selling tends to peak just prior to important market rallies. Odd-lot short sales, which can be found listed in *The Wall Street Journal,* are often placed by small traders, who tend to be less than accurate in their day-to-day market timing. Ten thousand odd-lot shares or more indicate an imminent market advance; 15,000 shares or more are an extremely bullish sign.

• Newspapers and magazines become overly bearish. The public media always follow rather than lead the investment markets. You can tell a bear market has bottomed out when front-page articles recall the crash of 1929 and unfavorable articles are written about major corporations such as IBM or General Motors. You can usually invest safely when such articles become commonplace.

• Brokerage stocks start to show strength. Brokerage stocks, such as Merrill Lynch, often lead the list in a bull market rally and can be very reliable in calling market turns.

Source: Gerald Appel, president, Signalert Corporation, 150 Great Neck Road, Great Neck, NY 11021. In addition to being an investment adviser, he is the author of several books, a regular contributor to investment periodicals, and a frequent lecturer.

Bullish Indicator

Stock mutual fund liquidity. Historically, mutual funds' holding a big portion of their assets in cash is a sign of an imminent stock market rally. Reason: Cash represents buying power, and once it's poured back into the stock market, a new spurt in prices is fueled.

Source: Norman G. Fosback's *Market Logic,* Fort Lauderdale, FL.

Bull Market Trap

When the market is in an up cycle, prices of many stocks with a weak earnings potential are pushed up by the market's overall momentum. Inevitably these issues will drop in value before the market as a whole declines. Safeguard: If insider sellers greatly outnumber buyers, it's a clear signal to stay away.

Source: *The Insiders,* Fort Lauderdale, FL.

Downturn Warning

Investors must watch market signs closely and react quickly when indicators change.

A key indicator that the market is about to turn bearish is a shortening of money-market fund maturities.

Traditional average: 30–45 days. Once these maturities drop down to 37–38 days, it's time to reassess your entire stock position—individual issues *and* mutual funds. When money-fund maturities shorten significantly, a stock market downturn will follow almost immediately.

Source: William E. Donoghue, chairman, The Donoghue Organization, publisher of *Donoghue's Moneyletter.* He's also author of *William E. Donoghue's Lifetime Financial Planner,* Harper & Row, New York.

When To Get Out of the Stock Market

Be ready to sell stocks as soon as a major market top starts to form. Definition of a major top: The beginning of a market decline that lasts from six months to several years. A typical long-term stock market cycle is about four years—from one major bottom to the next.

To spot a top: You must follow two different kinds of market barometers.

• Fundamental indicators, which warn when stocks are getting overpriced.

• Technical indicators, which provide early clues to market behavior.

When To Sell

• Scenario I. The blue-chip stock averages keep hitting new highs, but the indexes of smaller, secondary stocks (the NASDAQ Composite and Value Line) stall. The rally won't have long to go.

Check the newspaper each week for the number of stocks making new 12-month highs on the New York Stock Exchange. If that number is falling while the Dow Jones Industrial Average (DJIA) is rising, a major market correction will probably hit within a few months—at the latest.

• Scenario II. The DJIA stops rising, and market action begins to focus on the secondary stocks and stocks concentrated in a few select groups. Trap: A speculative binge would be underway. . .and the smart money would

have already begun to leave the table.

Whether the action starts to narrow in blue-chip stocks or in secondary issues, any sign that fewer investment sectors are participating in the rally should prompt defensive action.

Readying Your Defenses

• Lighten holdings as soon as a major top starts forming. You probably have two to eight months to act, so don't panic. . .but pay off any margin debts and accumulate cash.

• Identify stocks you own that have stopped rising. Either sell them or place protective stop-orders* with your broker. If a market slide begins, those stocks will be sold automatically at the price you've specified.

• Get out of any mutual fund whose net asset value suddenly drops 5% or more. Be very cautious with aggressive growth funds.

• Buy only cash equivalents (money market funds and Treasury bills) unless you're a very nimble seller.

If you have a lot of cash and a recession comes along, you'll be in a position to buy up assets cheaply at the next market bottom.

*A stop-order is an order given to a broker to sell a security at a specific price below the current market price, if the security falls to that price.

Source: Gerald Appel, president, Signalert Corp., money managers, 150 Great Neck Rd., Great Neck, NY 11021.

How To Tell When Stocks Will Tumble

It is unfortunately the case that the American public usually enters the stock market after prices have risen, rather than before. The obvious result is that the market soon reverses itself, and investors get caught in the downswing.

This doesn't have to be the case. The stock market tips its hand, so to speak, often far in advance of a general decline. Here are some guideposts to alert you to a coming downturn.

• Heavy NYSE member short-selling. Members of the New York Stock Exchange (NYSE) have had an excellent record of calling market tops as well as bottoms. The market is probably ready for a fall when NYSE members increase their short-selling activity. Track the number of shares sold short by NYSE members as a percentage of all short sales on the NYSE during the week (member short sales/total short sales). The warning sign is flashed when member short sales exceed 87% of all short sales within a given week, or exceed 85% of all short sales over a four-week period. This will give you about one to three weeks to act before the stock market actually peaks. Information regarding short sales is available in *Barron's, The Wall Street Journal,* and many advisory letters.

• The Federal Reserve increases interest rates. Stocks are extremely sensitive to actions taken by the Federal Reserve, especially with regard to interest rates. The market usually declines when it appears that the Fed is going to pursue a restrictive policy (*i.e.,* increase interest rates). The time to be cautious is when the Fed has raised the discount rate (the rate charged by the Fed for loans to banks) three times in a row with no intervening reductions.

• Heavy stock churning. Market peaks are often marked by churning—volume is heavy, but prices go nowhere. The way to recognize churning is to check the number of issues advancing on the NYSE and the number declining. Expect a market downturn when advancing and declining issues remain in relative balance over a period of five weeks. A second method is to compare the number of the week's issues that reach 52-week highs versus the number that reach 52-week lows. The outlook is very bearish if 150 issues reach new highs *and* 150 or more reach new lows during the same week.

• A bearish presidential election phase. Stocks usually rise in price during the two years preceding a presidential election and fall during the year or two following. 1984 was an exception, but the pattern held true for the 1968, 1972, 1976, and 1980 elections. This is probably because presidents do whatever possible to support the economy prior to election; the bad news comes the year after.

• Excessively bullish sentiment. When speculation is at its highest, the market is usually overpriced. That's the time to get ready for a correction. In other words, when everyone has fallen in love with the stock market, it's time to get out. Look for the following signs.

Frequent newspaper and magazine articles that feature discussions of a rising stock market.

A plethora of bullish investment advisory advertisements.

Sharp price rises in speculative stocks.

A flood of "hot" new issues.

A high level of secondary stock offerings.

Friends on the golf course boasting about profits they've made in the stock market.

• Secondary markets fail to keep pace with the major market averages. Be cautious when gains in the stock market are limited to blue-chip issues. Check the percentage gain each week in the NASDAQ Composite Index. Be prepared to sell if, after several weeks, these gains do not match gains in the Dow Jones Industrial Average.

Source: Gerald Appel, president, Signalert Corporation, 150 Great Neck Road, Great Neck, NY 11021. In addition to being an investment adviser, he is the author of several books, a regular contributor to investment periodicals, and a frequent lecturer.

How Bear Market Rallies Can Fool You

Bear market rallies are often sharp. They're fueled, in part, by short sellers rushing to cover shares. However, advances in issues sold short often lack durability once short covering is completed. Details:

• Bear market rallies tend to last for no more than five or six weeks.

• Bear market advances often end rapidly—with relatively little advance warning. If you are trading during a bear market, you must be ready to sell at the first sign of weakness.

• The first strong advance during a bear

market frequently lulls many analysts into a false sense of security, leading them to conclude that a new bull market is underway. The majority of the bear markets don't end until pessimism is widespread and until the vast majority is convinced that prices are going to continue to decline indefinitely.

• Although the stock market can remain "overbought" for considerable periods of time during bull markets, bear market rallies generally end fairly rapidly, as the market enters into "overbought" conditions. An "overbought" condition occurs when prices advance for a short time at a rate that can't be sustained.

One way to predict a decline—using the advance-decline line as a guide: Each day, compute the net difference between the number of issues that rise on the Big Board and the number that decline. A 10-day total of the daily nets is then maintained. During bear markets, be careful when the 10-day net differential rises to +2,500 or more, and be ready to sell immediately once this figure is reached and starts to decline. The decline will usually indicate that the advance is beginning to weaken.

Sources of Information On Stocks

You don't have time to read every newspaper and financial publication or listen to all the investment advice available. Still, take your investment homework seriously. Informed investors—those who base investment decisions on careful analysis of a stock, the company's industry, and general stock market conditions—are more likely to be successful investors.

A vast array of investment vehicles merit your attention: stocks, bonds, Treasury bills, money-market funds, mutual funds, commodities, etc. Similar resources provide important investment information regarding each of these vehicles.

• Daily newspapers, financial publications. Tracking stocks on a daily, weekly, or even month-to-month basis can help you get a clear picture of what is happening to a company or an entire industry. *The Wall Street Journal* and the business section of *The New York Times* provide extensive daily coverage of markets, industries, and individual companies. You can expect that most pertinent business news will be printed in one or both of these publications.

• Market guides and newsletters. An exceedingly broad variety of publications provide detailed reports on individual stocks, industry trends, where pension and mutual-fund managers are investing, and emerging growth companies. The list of subjects for market guides and newsletters is virtually endless. You can find publications devoted to one particular industry, a specific region of the world, leveraged buyouts, insider trading, specific investment vehicles, such as options or futures, or just plain old technical market analysis. The range in the quality of these publications is equally broad. Many have been very successful in forecasting trends in the economy or particular stocks, while others have not called a market turn in the history of their existence.

Though often worth the investment, subscription costs of market guides and newsletters can be high—up to $300 a year and more. Before you subscribe, visit a local library or call a stockbroker. Check the accuracy of the newsletter's past predictions. Make sure the newsletter bases its advice on substantial research. It helps if the publication employs a variety of market analysis techniques. Many investment firms will provide certain guides and newsletters to clients at little or no cost. In today's high-tech home environment, you can even gain access to research services on your home computer screen via data base services.

• Corporate publications. If you have been tracking a stock in the press and had your optimism reinforced by a market advisory report, the corporation is the next place to turn. Public corporations are required by the Securities & Exchange Commission to publish documents describing almost every aspect of their current and historical operations. Annual and quarterly reports, proxy statements, and certain financial filings are available to potential investors either through stockbrokers or directly from the corporation. Note: No matter what a stockbroker or a friend may tell you about a "hot tip," always look at the company's financial statements before investing in it.

• **Personal knowledge.** Investors, and in particular novice investors, often overlook personal knowledge of a company or industry when making investment decisions. Some of the most successful investments may be sitting in your own backyard. If a local company has just concluded favorable labor negotiations, applied for a patent on a revolutionary new design, made a major sale to an international client, or recently signed a long-term contract, take a closer look at the company. Think about the products you and your friends use. Try to avoid investing in companies and industries you know nothing about, have not carefully researched, and whose business does not interest you.

Outside Help

You don't have to wade through this ocean of research by yourself. Your stockbroker can help, although you should make it your business to develop at least a general understanding of how to pick and follow an investment.

Large investment firms employ full-time staffs devoted to studying individual investments and market trends. In fact, the advice your stockbroker gives is largely based on the opinions of these experts—industry specialists, technical analysts who track and study market data, experts in particular types of investments, and economic research teams who follow the health of the overall economy and certain segments of it.

Any securities analyst's job is to use the available resources to determine which stocks are most valuable. He or she then makes buy, sell, or hold recommendations accordingly. To analyze your own investments, do your homework; evaluate what you've learned and consider all the alternatives. Then, take advantage

of your investment firm's research services. If their advice matches your own opinions, you can invest with added confidence. If there is a mismatch, find out why—you may want to rethink your choice to insure that your final decision is one you feel comfortable with.

Source: Stanley P. Heilbronn, vice president, Merrill Lynch, Pierce, Fenner & Smith Inc., 717 Fifth Avenue, New York 10022. Mr. Heilbronn advises clients—including individuals in the fields of entertainment and medicine—on their investments. In addition, he is a contributor to *Medical Economics* magazine.

Investing with the Investment Newsletters

Investment advisory newsletters are there to help you choose individual stocks and bonds, put together investment portfolios, and even time your moves in and out of the markets.

Some are highly focused, providing advice exclusively on small over-the-counter stocks, or on mutual funds, or on more esoteric investments such as options and commodities. Others inform you of investment opportunities in a wide variety of markets.

With hundreds of newsletters to choose from, at subscription rates of up to $300 a year, it is important to pick the right one and, more important, to steer clear of the bad ones.

Look Twice At . . .

• Newsletters that make near-impossible claims. Virtually all investment newsletters are bought through the mail. To attract subscribers, many of them display outlandish quotes such as "I made 1,000% in one year with no risk." Be very cautious. Take the time to determine whether the claims are truly within the realm of possibility. Preferable: A newsletter that claims it made 20% a year during the last 10 years over one that claims 500% in just one year. Twenty percent annually over 10 years is a very respectable return. At least it doesn't insult your intelligence.

• Newsletters that quote performance results out of context. Since *Hulbert Finan-*

cial Digest is the only publication that ranks the performance of newsletters, many stretch the truth to advertise that they were listed among the best. Problem: They may have been ranked in the top 10 for one month. . .but their overall performance may be horrible. Look for newsletters with consistent performance through good and bad markets over at least two to three years.

• Unfamiliar newsletters that don't offer a trial subscription. Most newsletters offer an inexpensive trial subscription for two weeks to three months. Such offers are an ideal way for you to study the newsletter's style, methodology and performance. . .and to see if it is truthful about its record.

Once You've Subscribed, Be Wary Of. . .

• Newsletters that quote selectively from previous issues. Many newsletters provide both the bearish case and the bullish case. Then, two months later, they quote whichever case most closely corresponds to actual market events.

• Newsletters whose recommended issues disappear or fall through the cracks when their performance turns out to be poor. A bad newsletter makes lots of recommendations and then neglects to report on their later performance—especially when the performance turns out to be bad.

• Newsletters that cover up or make excuses for their mistakes. A newsletter that admits its mistakes and is objective about the future is preferable to one that spends most of its time making excuses and explaining why the market didn't do what it was supposed to do. A newsletter is supposed to predict the turn of events—not explain why the market didn't move in its favor.

• Newsletters that do not make specific recommendations. Some offer strict portfolio recommendations, telling you exactly what and when to buy and sell. Others are general and vague. If you're going to pay $150–$300 a year for a subscription, you should get concrete, worthwhile suggestions. You don't want to have to read between the lines, as you are forced to do with the more general newslet-

ters. Remember, you don't have to follow advice just because it *is* specific.

• Highly aggressive newsletters (unless the potential returns are large enough to justify the risk). Many newsletters take incredible risks in an attempt to win a high-performance ranking to use in their advertising. The safest newsletters have been the buy-and-hold newsletters, which recommend a stock and then stick with it. The riskiest have been those that employ a market-timing strategy that requires investors to move in and out of different stocks, industry groups and markets on a monthly, sometimes weekly, basis. Irony: In recent years the more conservative newsletters have actually performed better than the most aggressive newsletters on a risk-adjusted basis.

Source: Mark Hulbert, editor of *Hulbert Financial Digest*, Washington, DC. It ranks 100 of the best-known investment newsletters on a monthly basis.

Computer Services for Individual Investors

Until the 1960s, the ticker tape was the only way the outside world could keep track of the activity of the New York Stock Exchange. Then the ticker tape gave way to the electronic quotation terminal, marking the first major change in information availability and market access. Next came the development of the electronic market and automated trading. By the mid-1970s, paper was virtually eliminated as a means of conducting securities transactions, and regional stock exchanges were electronically integrated into a national market system.

These changes reflected the successful application of technology to securities transactions, but the beneficiaries were institutional investors and their brokers. Individuals were at a disadvantage—they saw the news too late, heard of price changes after the close, received statements weeks after the close of the period, and were subject to slow, poor-quality trade executions.

Access to market quotations improved for individual investors with the development of time-sharing services and professional-level quote machines. The benefit of quote machines was that they offered unlimited use, but at a high monthly fixed cost. Time-sharing services have an insignificant monthly cost, but large costs for "connect time"—the amount of time a service was actually used.

Today, individual investors are finally receiving the full benefits of the technological changes of the past two decades. Dramatic developments in home computers, software, and services provide fingertip access to investment information; instantaneous trade executions are possible; up-to-the-second portfolio records can be displayed; and the analytical power of the microcomputer can be applied to the investment process.

Time-sharing services from Dow Jones, CompuServe, and *Readers Digest* (whose service is called The Source) provide varying packages of research, news, quotations, and access to personal portfolios and to the market, with discounted commissions. Such services can be accessed by any kind of personal computer or terminal through the local telephone number of one of several networks that facilitate communications between computers Users are charged for each minute they are connected to a service. Investors who want quotes throughout the day without high fixed costs or connect-line charges can turn to products like *Signal* and *PC Quote*, which provide unlimited quotes for a monthly charge below that of professional-level quotation terminals.

A growing number of investors are supplementing services with software designed to operate on the personal computer. The software often utilizes prices "downloaded," from time-sharing services and can be employed to create charts, sort data, and evaluate portfolios. Smith Micro Software, Summa Technologies, Telescan, and Iceberg Financial Systems, Inc., are just a few examples of companies making these tools available to individual

investors who want the advantages formerly monopolized by the pros.

Source: Charles M. Spear, chairman and CEO, Spear Securities, Inc., and chairman of its parent, Spear Financial Services, Inc. Spear Securities, 510 West 6th St., Suite 525, Los Angeles 90014, provides on-line investment services to individual investors; these services are available through The Source.

How Computers Help You Invest

Computer programs can't make your investment decisions, but they can save huge amounts of time in analyzing stocks.

How Investment Software Works
Programs can store and digest financial information so you have instant access to data such as a stock's latest price, debt-to-equity history, and price/earnings ratios for the last several years.

Some software will also help you screen promising stocks.

Example: You can ask the computer to list all pharmaceutical industry stocks with sales over $50 million a year. Then you can ask it to select companies from that group with price/earnings ratios of 10 or less.

The advantage is speed. An investor would have to spend many hours a day analyzing data that a computer can handle in seconds.

Recommended: An IBM desktop computer or an IBM-compatible model. Reason: The best investment programs run on IBMs or IBM clones.

Up-to-the-Minute Quotes
One of the computer's most valuable assets is its ability to store the latest stock prices. That helps with buy and sell decisions, especially for a stock with big daily price fluctuations.

Once you put the software in the computer, you must also feed financial information into the program. Special FM radio stations and cable TV channels supply price quotes and other current stock market data. Fundamental information about specific companies can be bought on floppy disks.

Most cable TV companies supply stock data for about $20 a month. Or subscribe to one of the two main FM radio stock services that cover most major cities:

• Radio Exchange, from Telemet America, 325 First St., Alexandria, VA 22314.

• Signal, from Lotus Information Network Corp., 1900 S. Norfolk St., San Mateo, CA 94403.

Best programs for screening stocks:

• *Fundamental Investor,* from Savant Corp., Box 440278, Houston 77244. Cost: $395 for the program plus $23 per disk for up to 12 disks containing complete financial data on 10,000 companies. Updated disks are available monthly for the same price.

• *Stockpak II,* from Standard & Poor's Corp., 25 Broadway, New York 10004. Cost: $30 initial setup charge and $245 per year per 12-disk subscription to monthly data on 1,500 companies from the New York Stock Exchange, American Stock Exchange and over-the-counter market, or 1,500 NYSE stocks or 800 AMEX stocks. . .$490 for all 2,200 OTC issues.

• *Value/Screen Plus,* from Value Line, Inc., 711 Third Ave., New York 10017. Cost: $348/yr. for monthly data on 1,650 companies.

Deeper Analysis

For even more thorough computer investing there are programs that estimate how well an investment in a stock will do over the next several months.

Recommended: *Compustock,* from A.S. Gibson & Sons, Inc., 1412 Vineyard Dr., Bountiful, UT 84010. Price: $69 plus $199/yr. for the monthly database of 1,100 or more stocks.

Once you've whittled down your list of prospective buys, *Compustock* analyzes each one in terms of:

• Its latest price. Is it high or low in comparison to the company's rate of earnings growth?

• Serious financial problems. Are there any in the company, based on its latest balance sheet and income statements?

• The company's price/earnings ratio compared with the industry average.

• Its projected earnings and dividend rate based on past performance and forecasts of future economic growth and inflation.

By the time you run each of your stock prospects through these tests, you'll have a reliable estimate of how well an investment in each issue will do over the next few years.

Source: Michael C. Gianturco, president, High Technology Investments, an advisory firm, 5925 Kirby St., Houston 77005. He's the author of *The Stock Market Investor's Computer Guide,* McGraw-Hill, New York.

How To Analyze Corporate Earnings

There are ways that a dedicated investor who's willing to do some serious work can get an edge on the market. That's by looking for significant data in the financial reports that managements issue each quarter. Many professionals overlook the early warning signs that are revealed in corporate shareholder reports.

Start with a company's annual report. Read the *Letter to Shareholders* that's usually the first thing in the report. Compare what management is saying now with what it said last year. Was it right? Is it glossing over bad news? The purpose of this review: To assess the integrity of management. That's an important fact in company performance that most security analysts and money managers ignore.

A double check on management: Ask the company (as a stockholder or potential investor) to be put on the list to receive the company's 10K report that's filed with the Securities & Exchange Commission (the company's annual report to the SEC) and also the 10Q report (quarterly report to the SEC). Compare what the company reports to the SEC with what it reports to the shareholders. What you can learn from focusing on the differences:

• The Rolm Corp. 10Q reported that the company was being impacted severely by price competition, whereas this information was not disclosed in the company's quarterly shareholder report. That was a real red flag.

357

Shortly afterward, Wall Street was "surprised" by bad news from Rolm, but any investor who had looked carefully at the 10Q would have been forewarned to act.

• Baldwin United had tremendous differences between its public and its SEC reports long before the company's problems surfaced. For instance, in its quarterly reports, Baldwin was reporting after-tax earnings to the shareholders. But the more detailed 10Q revealed that the company was running pretax losses that were covered by tax credits.

Significance of these differences: If management cuts corners in its reports to its shareholders, what is it doing in company operations and in the accounting department to dress up earnings?

Secrets on taxes: Look, too, at the item called Deferred Taxes on the company's year-end financial sheet. The more aggressive a company is in its accounting, the greater the difference is likely to be between its shareholder books (its regular profit and loss statement) and the way it reports income to the IRS. Companies can legally report income and expenses differently to the public and to the tax authorities. *Example:* Capital purchases can be depreciated more slowly in the shareholder's report (enhancing earnings) than in the report to the IRS (where accelerated depreciation decreases earnings and taxes).

Lesson: You can rely more on the earnings reports and the projections made by managements that are conservative in their accounting. For example, two of the best-run companies, IBM and General Electric, use accelerated depreciation for both their tax and shareholder accounts.

Tax rates are important to look at, too. Here the important thing to observe is a change in the tax rate from year to year. If the company's tax rate (usually noted in the P&L review) goes down suddenly in the fourth quarter—say, from 34% to 25%—earnings for the quarter may look very good. An investor probably can't count on that boost in earnings turning up again. This can mean that future earnings may be disappointing, and Wall Street may be caught with another earnings "surprise" on the downside.

The signs are often not what they seem. A big drop in the cost of goods sold, general and administration expenses, or research and development as a percent of overall revenues may not be all good news either. The decline may be nonrecurring. Then what does the company do for an encore in comparative reporting?

Sharp investors keep a keen eye on inventory figures. If inventories are rising faster than sales—especially for a retailer—there's trouble ahead. Get out of any stock where the inventory turns* are steadily declining. That was an early warning sign for W.T. Grant—long before it filed for bankruptcy. Declining retailer inventory turns in many cases are caused by a buildup of slow-moving goods that should have been pushed out the door rather than kept in inventory.

Another trick that works like a charm for firms—especially high-tech firms—but is very rarely used by the so-called experts on Wall Street: A big increase in finished goods in inventory, but work-in-process inventories that don't go up nearly as much, and raw materials inventories that actually drop. What that means: Management is bearish regarding its near-term prospects and so has slowed down buying raw materials. The reverse, of course, is positive: A bigger increase in raw materials inventories than in finished goods means that management is filling the production pipeline because incoming orders are excellent. (Be careful that the increase isn't due to some major price increase in raw materials for the industry.) Probability: This inventory indicator works about 80% of the time. The fundamentals to check in every earnings report:

• A bulge in accounts payable. The company may be short of cash and stretching out bill payments. Watch out!

• Short-term debt. Look carefully at this because many companies are covering up short-term liabilities (such as commercial paper) and calling it longer-term debt since it's covered by a bank's line of credit. Short-term debt is a burden on a company, making it vulnerable to interest rate increases. Also, the company's bankers may force the company to amend loan covenants, curtailing the operating flexibility of the company in a way that can be detrimental to the long-term interest of all the present shareholders.

• Dividend payout. Too many managements are unwilling to cut dividends during tough strikes or other sharp reverses. When a company's resources are drained to pay a dividend, start worrying about the quality of management. It takes tough managers to cut a dividend. And, in the long run, tough managers are usually very good to shareholders.

One of the most bullish signs in an earnings report is a big bath—a big writeoff, often associated with a long overdue restructuring of operations, including the sale of losing or low-margined businesses. Among the classic examples: Beatrice Foods, Gulf & Western, and Ralston Purina. Chances are good, with a big bath, for a real turnaround in earnings. Wall Street may be disappointed at first, but it usually reads a big bath positively and increases the price/earnings multiple on the stock.

*A few companies report their inventory turns in their financial reports. But if this information isn't there, divide the cost of the goods sold by the company's average inventory for the year.

Source: Ted O'glove, author of *The Quality of Earnings Report,* published by Reporting Research Corp., Englewood Cliffs, NJ.

Hidden Balance Sheet Values

Most top Wall Street research analysts base their stock recommendations on a set of sophisticated earnings estimates. It's difficult for amateurs to develop comparable estimates because they lack professional investors' combination of experience, access to information sources, and ties to industry. But there is a way for amateurs to beat the pros: by looking for hidden value in a company's balance sheet.

The best tools for finding value are the annual report and the company's 10K. Both can be acquired from the company itself or the Securities & Exchange Commission (SEC).

Read the Fine Print

Begin your search with the footnotes. If taken seriously, a reading of the footnotes can reveal an abundance of information that many investors are simply too lazy to track down. The following list will point you on your way.

• Company pension fund. Until the 1980s, the pension obligations of American industry were dramatically underfunded. Since then, pension assets have built up more rapidly than obligations. The result has been a vast net overfunding. Thus, what appears to be a liability—a pension obligation—is often a net asset that can be easily tapped by management as a source of ready cash. Exceptions to this overfunded situation are primarily companies in industries characterized by years of strong union domination.

• Inventories. A company that uses what is referred to as the LIFO (last-in first-out) system of accounting for inventories may have a huge cushion of extra value hidden in its inventory account. That's because the LIFO values method values inventory at historic costs rather than at the cost of the inventory if a company had to purchase it today.

To gauge hidden value, the investor must distinguish between raw materials and finished products. The closer inventory is to the raw materials stage, the more likely it is that the LIFO values in inventories can be ultimately realized.

• Natural resources. These assets may be well above their carrying value in the balance sheet. Thus the investor has to distinguish between raw materials that have declined in value in recent years and those that have risen. For example, even with the price of petroleum far below its peak levels, oil reserves are often carried at conservative valuations if their discovery cost was low. As a crosscheck use the calculation required by the SEC of the present value of its oil reserves.

• Business segments. Probably the most

important way to locate hidden value is through a careful analysis of a company's different business segments. The footnotes in a 10K and annual report provide fairly detailed information regarding a company's lines of business, separating them in terms of investment, capital spending, earnings, and other important variables.

What investors should look for is a company's "crown jewel"—a highly profitable or potentially profitable segment—which may be masked by poor financial results in the company's other operations. The stock market's overall appraisal of the company may not reflect the potential of the profitable division. The payoff comes if you can find a diversified company with a top-performing division that may become the target for a potential acquisition. Acquirers of diversified businesses often look for one profitable segment, calculating that they will be able to dispose of the losers.

• Company property. The value of the company's property could be grossly understated. The 10K normally indicates how much square footage the company leases and owns. Most important is office and commercial space. Unless you are familiar with the particular real estate market in which the company's property is located, it may be difficult to estimate the property's value. However, by examining the company's plant account, with a close eye to location, you may find a clue to the value of company owned real estate. Similarly, even though they are labeled as liabilities on the balance sheet, assignable leaseholds at below-market rates can be enormous assets.

• Intangible assets. Large hidden assets that have no place on the balance sheet include brand recognition, technology, distribution and marketing networks, franchises, etc. Intangibles such as these may have taken years to build up and could very well be a company's most important assets. They are usually of enormous value to potential acquirers.

Note: Beware of capitalized expenses for R&D costs. These expenses are treated as assets on the balance sheet. If the product to which the R&D is devoted does pay off, there may be an eventual write-off. Also beware of deferred marketing expenses.

Source: Michael Metz, market strategist and senior vice president, Oppenheimer & Co., Inc., Oppenheimer Tower, World Financial Center, New York 10281.

Spotting the Traps in Earnings Figures

Figures on company earnings are deceptive. They are useful guides only to investors who interpret them correctly.

• Retained earnings for some American companies can be overstated by significant amounts. Example: $1 in after-tax profit shrinks to just 60¢ after 40% is subtracted to adjust for the effect of inflation on depreciation and costs. Another 40% might then be deducted in order to pay out a dividend.

• The real corporate tax rate is elusive. Reason: Inflation boosts costs, resulting in inventory profits and underdepreciation of plant and equipment. Advice: Have more confidence in the earnings reports of companies that use last-in, first-out (LIFO) inventory accounting methods that make adjustments for inflation.

• Return on equity is often one-fourth of the reported percentage. Reason: Profits are nearly halved by inflation. But the book value might be almost doubled when current prices are used to calculate.

In most cases, it is not worth trying to make a quick trade based on a quarterly report. Reason: There is almost always a correction that brings the stock price back to where it was before the report. When to trade: After the price settles back.

What to focus on:
• Deviation in the long-term trend of a company's earnings.
• Changes in net margin. If sales move ahead but income is level, watch for a trend toward lower profits. And vice versa.
• Underlying changes, such as currency fluctuations, tax rate, and number of shares outstanding. They all affect earnings per share.

Translating the earnings figures into the price/earnings ratio is even trickier because the price of a stock is based on anticipated earnings, but the ratio is calculated on earnings in the previous 12 months.

Brokers are quite shameless about recommending one stock to a client as a good value (because the p/e ratio is low) and another as an excellent growth stock (because company prospects are so exciting that the p/e ratio is meaningless).

Rationale for buying low-multiple stocks: There is less downside risk in a declining market. And they have higher upgrade potential in an advancing market.

Rationale for buying high-multiple stocks: If the company really grows by 40% a year for the next 10 years, paying 40 times earnings is acceptable. Current earnings of $1 compounded for 10 years at a 40% rate amounts to nearly $30 of earnings 10 years from now. Even if the p/e ratio falls to 10 by then, the stock will have gone up more than seven times in value (from 40 to 290).

Bottom line: Keep a clear head when earnings, earnings forecasts, and p/e ratios are being loosely presented as reasons to buy now.

Source: Peter De Haas, portfolio strategist, L.F. Rothschild, Unterberg, Towbin, New York.

Truth About Stock Buybacks

Offers by companies to buy back shares at premium prices usually are worth accepting. In fact, these buyback offers are often 10% or more above market levels. If you hold your shares, chances are they won't go up more than 2%–3% in the months following the buyback because the market will already have discounted the impact of the offer. Added risk: Buybacks divert large amounts of company cash from other productive investments, lowering the potential for future share price increases.

Source: *Changing Times.*

Dividend Reinvestment

Dividend reinvestment plans permit shareholders to buy additional stock by automatically reinvesting dividends. A list of more than 700 firms offering reinvestment plans is available for $2 from Standard and Poor's Corp., 25 Broadway, New York 10004.

Source: *How to Invest $50–$5,000* by financial analyst Nancy Dunnan, Harper & Row, New York.

Making Profits on a Stock Split

When a stock splits, the average profit to an investor is 20%. But the greatest profits are generally made in the three to six months before the split is announced. The general pattern is that the price stays high for two days after the split announcement and then declines. To spot a candidate for a split, look for:

• A company that needs to attract more stockholders, diversify or attract additional financing.

• A takeover candidate (heavy in cash and liquid assets) whose management holds only a small percentage of the outstanding shares. (Companies with concentrated ownership rarely split stock unless there are problems with taxes, acquisitions or diversification.)

• A stock priced above $75. A split moves it into the more attractive $25–$50 range.

• A stock that was split previously and price has climbed steadily since then.

• Earnings prospects so strong that the company will be able to increase dividends after the split.

Likely prospects are over-the-counter companies with current earnings of $2.5 million, at least $2 million annually in preceding years and less than 1 million shares outstanding (or under 2,000 shareholders). A stock split is necessary if management wants to list on a major exchange.

Source: C. Colburn Hardy, *Dun & Bradstreet's Guide to Investments,* Thomas Y. Crowell Co., New York.

Wisdom from a Wise Source

Smart investors avoid the following big mistakes:

• Assuming that a stock that's moving in a certain direction will continue to move in that direction forever. When a stock is heading for the moon, take profits. . .and when a stock is headed for zero, be a buyer. Veteran's insight: Very few stocks get to zero, and none reach the moon.

• Worrying about whether the stock market is too high. The stock market isn't a single entity. . .it's a universe of individual stocks. Smart investor's goal: To buy value whenever it's reasonably priced. Even when the market as a whole is too high, there are always a few undervalued stocks around.

• Believing every stock story you hear. Wise rules: Never follow the crowd. . .avoid fads . . . investigate thoroughly every story that seems plausible.

• Buying stocks for dividends. This has recently become popular thanks to tax reform's lower tax rates and the elimination of tax-favored treatment of capital gains. Dividend income has become more attractive relative to capital appreciation. Risk: Common stock dividends *aren't* guaranteed. If the going gets rough, many companies will cut their dividends.

Only source of guaranteed income: Top-quality bonds. . .but even these aren't risk-free. If interest rates rise, the market value of bonds falls. And if you have to sell the bonds before maturity, that can be a problem.

• Paying too much attention to market gurus. No one person has ever been able to predict consistently what's going to happen in the stock market. Problem: Unpredictable events that affect the overall market, such as wars, assassinations, OPEC decisions, etc. Safer: Predicting that an individual stock will rise if the company's earnings are growing 20% a year and it's a leader in its industry. Whether or not somebody shoots the President, its value will continue to go up.

• Not being patient enough. Patience is the key to making money in stocks. Unfortunately, 90% of investors—including institutions—lack it. Everybody thinks short term . . . and the "short term" is even shorter now that the new tax law has eliminated the distinction between short-term and long-term gains. To beat the market: Keep your eyes fixed on the long-term horizon. Do your homework, and then give your stock selections time to perform. Often it takes years for an investment scenario to play itself out.

• Acting too quickly. There's always time to buy a stock. If it's now at $22 a share and it's rising to $50, does it really matter if you pay $22 or $24½?

Never take action until you understand why a stock is moving. When to suspend judgment: Triple Witching Hour—the third Friday in March, June, September and December—when stock index futures, stock index options and individual stock options all expire and the market often makes wild swings up or down. Wait at least a day to confirm the trend.

With the increasing sophistication of computerized program trading, this extreme volatility has started to pop up on other days, too. Whatever happens, don't be panicked into making a move that you might regret later.

Source: Louis Ehrenkrantz, director, Ehrenkrantz & King, money managers, 50 Broadway, New York 10004, and publisher, *The Ehrenkrantz Letter.*

Those Great Old Investment Theories

Ever since the stock market's inception, investors have been searching for theories and rules of thumb to help them decide whether, how and when to invest in a particular stock. The theories that have evolved range from the very complex (detailed calculations of risk, economics and financial analysis) to the very simple (tracking newspaper headlines or even gauging the strength of the tides).

Here is an analysis of today's most popular investment theories:

Theories That Work

• **Small-firm theory.** This is probably the most tested, well-documented investment theory on Wall Street. How it works: Small stocks (issued by companies with a market capitalization between $20 million and $100 million) have provided consistently higher returns over time than large stocks . . . even when adjusted for risk. Probable reason: The large institutions avoid many small yet high-quality stocks, leaving opportunities for individual investors. If the stock continues to do well, the institutions eventually jump in, bidding up the price of the stock significantly. Results: Since the Depression, small stocks have provided returns that, on average, are annually 3%–4% higher than returns from large stocks. Over time that kind of spread can significantly boost the total return of a portfolio. Risk: Small stocks are much more volatile than large stocks . . . when the market goes up, small stocks increase in value very rapidly, but when the market goes down, they fall fast too.

• **Contrarian-investing theory.** Stocks that are out of favor (neglected by the big institutions, research analysts and the press) have provided higher returns than stocks considered "hot." Best ways to identify out-of-favor stocks:

Low price/earnings multiples. (The size of the stocks that you compare must be constant.)

High dividend yield.

Low institutional ownership. If more than 10 to 12 institutions own a stock, it is probably too popular. Monthly institutional ownership figures can be found in the *Standard & Poor's Stock Guide.*

Strategy: When the market heats up, find the stocks investors are ignoring. Then do a thorough job of fundamental research to determine whether there is a strong chance for future gains.

• **Calendar-effect theory.** Although this one defies all logic, certain days do provide consistently higher returns than other days. Best: Don't trade solely on the basis of calendar effects. But keep these points in mind . . .

Fridays tend to be up, Mondays tend to be down. If you plan to buy stocks late in the week, do so before early Friday, or wait until late Monday. If you plan to sell, wait until late Friday or early Monday.

The first half of the month usually outperforms the second half. The difference between these two periods is significant . . .as much as 1% for the first half of the month. Over a year, that can really add up.

Preholiday trading days are very positive. The day immediately preceding a major holiday tends to be bullish. The biggest preholiday day is December 31.

January is the best month of the year . . . especially for small stocks. This period includes the last trading days of December to the last days of January.

• **Dollar-cost-averaging theory.** This is one of the most profitable ways to invest and to minimize risk. How it works: Invest a set amount of money in one particular stock at regular intervals over an extended period of time (usually one full market cycle)—regardless of whether the stock is up or down. Rationale: If you invest the same amount each time, you end up buying less of the stock when the price is high and more when it is down. Over time, the strategy irons out the wrinkles of a volatile market.

• **Insider-trading-activity theory.** What corporate insiders do with their company's stock is a very accurate indication of how a stock will perform over the long run. Warning: Since corporate insiders buy and sell on the basis of their long-term views, you shouldn't expect immediate results. The Securities & Exchange Commission prohibits trading by corporate insiders on the basis of material nonpublic information.

• **High-relative-price theory.** A stock selling for a price that's high relative to its average historical price tends to do better than other stocks. You may not believe in technical analysis, but this simple stock-picker's rule has turned out to be a notable exception.

Theories That Don't Work

• Market-timing theory. Trying to move in and out of the market on the basis of short-term movements has never worked as well as buying and holding a stock for an extended time. The attraction: Some investors can call market twists and turns for short periods. But no one can keep this up indefinitely. Risk: If you lose with this strategy, chances are that you'll lose big. Also, the more trading oriented your investment strategy becomes, the greater your transaction costs.

• Penny-stocks theory. "Small is beautiful" goes only so far. Although a high-quality small stock can do very well over time, an extremely cheap stock (issued by a company with market capitalization of less than $20 million) can be highly risky. Many investors think that a low-priced stock, such as a 50-cent stock, will offer a huge upside potential and little downside risk. Wrong. Studies have shown that portfolios of very low-priced stocks have performed far worse over the years than other portfolios.

• Low-price/book-value theory. Because industries' accounting practices differ so greatly, it is exceedingly difficult to assess accurately the value of a company's underlying assets and then determine its true book value/share. Leave this calculation to the accountants. It is not an accurate indication of a stock's potential for appreciation.

• Technical-analysis theory. Except for the high-relative-price theory mentioned above, virtually all forms of technical analysis—stock-price runs, charting, moving average and so forth—have proved almost worthless as investment strategies.

Source: John Markese, Ph.D., vice president and director of research, American Association of Individual Investors, 612 N. Michigan Ave., Chicago 60611.

Trading Stocks by the Clock and Calendar

Investors can increase their odds of successful stock trading by planning purchases and sales around certain times and dates. The following observations should be of help.

Best Times of the Day
• Stocks usually reach low points each day at around 10:45 a.m., 1:25 p.m., and again at around 2:50 p.m. If you plan to take a position in a rising market, try to purchase around these times.

• Keep track of market action between 3 p.m. and 4 p.m. (closing); pay special attention to activity during the final few minutes of the day. A strong final hour and/or a strong final five minutes usually means a strong opening the next day. If the market closes with a very powerful burst of trading, the odds are high that the next day's opening will be strong, but that stocks will sell off later that day.

• High points during market rallies tend to occur at 10:30 a.m., 2:30 p.m., and, if it is a strong day, at the close.

Best Days of the Week
• Mondays tend to be weak days for the stock market, especially in the morning. If prices show little change for Monday, but edge up near the close, expect Tuesday, a stronger day of the week, to show a gain.

• Fridays tend to be favorable days for stocks, especially right at the close. Most Fridays show price gains in the final few minutes of trading.

Best Days of the Month
• The market is usually strongest the final trading day of one month and the first four trading days of the next month. This is a well-documented pattern; traders make extensive use of it. Price gains during these five-day periods often exceed gains shown in all the rest of the two months' trading days combined.

Best Months of the Year
• Stock market lows frequently develop in late June and during October and November.

These are excellent months to accumulate stocks. March is usually another good month. It is riskiest to purchase in May and late in September, because the subsequent months are weak. Strength in January has tended to carry through for the rest of the year.

Holiday Buying

• The stock market tends to be strong one or two days before a holiday. A really good time is a preholiday period that coincides with turn-of-the-month strength.

• Expect excellent performance during the period prior to July 4 and between Christmas and New Years.

The Political Cycle

• Stocks tend to rise during the two years prior to a presidential election, and have historically been weaker during the two years following an election.

• Bear market bottoms tend to be spaced approximately four years apart (1966, 1970, 1974, 1982).

A Special Coincidence

• For no explainable reason, years ending in "5" have proven to be extremely strong for the stock market.

Source: Gerald Appel, president, Signalert Corporation, 150 Great Neck Road, Great Neck, NY 11021. In addition to being an investment adviser, he is the author of several books, a regular contributor to investment periodicals, and a frequent lecturer.

When Experts Trade

Popularly traded issues show distinct tendencies during the course of the day. Reason: Traders tend to buy and sell at certain hours. Astute investors can take advantage of these patterns:

• Day traders often buy early in the morning or on evidence of overall stock market strength that day. If the market is weak, traders will sell short at the earliest opportunity. Positions on the New York Stock Exchange are normally equalized between 3:30 and 3:45 p.m. there.

• On stronger days, expect temporary weaknesses in the issue at about 3:30 when most traders close out their long positions. Buyers should try to place orders during this period. Sellers should wait until just near the close when prices often recover. (Another point of market weakness is between noon and 1 p.m.)

• On weaker days, short sellers should expect some price recovery at about 3:30 p.m. when some traders are covering their shorts.

How Stan Weinstein Beats the Stock Cycles

By tracking the price cycles of stocks, investors have a good chance of timing investments for maximum appreciation.

To plot the cycles chart the 30-week moving average for stocks that you hold or may want to trade. The chart can be plotted from the closing Friday prices available in financial journals or most daily papers. Then compare this moving average with the latest price in the daily papers.

From the chart, you'll be able to recognize the four stages of each cycle:

• Stage 1: The base. The first sign of this stage is that daily prices start to nudge above the 30-week average. This typically occurs immediately following a major price decline. At first glance, it might appear that this is the time to buy. . .but don't buy stock at this stage. It's impossible to tell how long the price will remain flat, and you could have your money tied up for a long time with no movement.

• Stage 2: The advance. As this phase begins, prices surge ahead of the 30-week average. This is the ideal time to buy the stock—the major advance is first getting under way.

• Stage 3: The top. The surest sign of a top is that daily prices are no longer consistently above the 30-week average. Instead, they move within a narrow range above and below the average. At the same time, trading volume steadily increases. This is the time to consider selling the stock.

• Stage 4: The decline. Now the stock trades increasingly below its moving average. Stay away from the stock throughout this period.

Source: Stan Weinstein, founder, *The Professional Tape Reader*, Hollywood, FL.

Chart Patterns To Help You Time the Purchase And Sale of Stocks

Graphic representations of stock market trends are readily available to all investors. Each day, newspapers such as *The Wall Street Journal* and *The New York Times* print charts of the movement of the stock market for recent time intervals. Other financial newspapers and investment newsletters provide longer-term, sometimes weekly or monthly, charts of the same movements. Investors with home computers can even purchase moderately priced software that receives data and generates stock and stock market charts.

By themselves, charts cannot guarantee successful stock market trading. However, they can serve as useful tools for general market timing. The following tips should help you know when movements in the market are going to take place.

Congestion areas. A congestion area is a price area in which a large amount of trading takes place without much price movement. *Example:* The Dow Jones Industrial Average trades for several weeks between 1280 and 1320. The 1280–1320 range is considered a congestion area.

Prices tend to stall just under previously developed congestion areas (areas of resistance). The market is bullish if prices penetrate and rise above a previously formed congestion area. Conversely, price declines tend to stop just above previously formed congestion areas (areas of support). The market is bearish if prices penetrate downward through such an area.

Uptrends and downtrends. Uptrends in price may be considered intact as long as prices continue to reach new high levels on each upswing and continue to find support at progressively higher levels. Downtrends may be considered intact as long as each decline carries the market lower and each rally fails to reach the highs of the previous rally. Remain in the market during uptrends; stay out during downtrends.

Double bottom formation. A double bottom occurs when the stock market declines to a certain level, rises, declines back to the area of the first low, and then starts back up again. The entire formation looks like a "W" on a chart. When the "W" is complete, the market usually continues to advance. Patterns that take only a few trading sessions to develop indicate short-term rallies. Patterns developing over a period of several weeks suggest longer advances.

The reverse pattern appears as an "M" on a chart. It indicates a future market decline.

Volume patterns. Most charts carry volume data in addition to price movement data. The following are bullish volume patterns.

• Stock prices rise broadly off a low, on sharply increasing volume. It is especially bullish if prices rise on strong volume at the same time a "W" formation is completed.

• Prices pull back after a few days of a strong advance on sharply reduced volume. Pullbacks during strong uptrends usually last for a week to 10 days. Expect prices to retrace about 40% of the gains recorded on the previous advance. This is a good time to accumulate positions if you missed the initial leg up.

• It is usually bullish for the intermediate trend (lasting for several weeks to a few months), if the Dow Transportation Average performs at least as well as the Dow Industrial Average. It is bullish for the major trend (lasting for months to years) if the Dow Utility Average performs at least as well as the Dow Industrial Average.

Time cycles and stock purchases. Chart patterns often reveal time cycles that underlie stock price movements. Low points for stocks tend to occur at fairly regular intervals. Once you recognize those intervals, you can often anticipate when low points are likely to develop, sometimes weeks in advance. The following are regularly repeating cycles for the stock market.

• Stocks tend to reach their bottom in a minor price swing at 13- to 15-day intervals. Market lows tend to be spaced about three weeks apart.

• A more important market cycle is the six- to eight-week market cycle. Low points tend to occur at intervals of approximately seven weeks. Once the market turns up at the seven-week low point, expect the advances to last for about two to three weeks.

• Important low points tend to be spaced at approximate intervals of between 16 and 18 weeks. This very important cycle provides the most significant intermediate market movement.

• It is very bullish when a 16- to 18-week low point coincides with a seven-week low point. The nesting of these two cycles indicates a strong market advance for the future.

• Very few market swings—upward or downward—last for longer than five to six weeks before a price reversal takes place. If the market has already risen for five to six weeks, wait to buy; you usually will be able to get a better price later. If, on the other hand, the market has been falling for five to six weeks without an intervening rally, then your gains are likely to be greater if you wait to sell.

Source: Gerald Appel, president, Signalert Corporation, 150 Great Neck Road, Great Neck, NY 11021. In addition to being an investment adviser, he is the author of several books, a regular contributor to investment periodicals, and a frequent lecturer.

The Lessons of Technical Analysis

The last speculative push that ended the long bull market in 1929 was concentrated primarily in about 50 blue-chip stocks. The rest of the market had been spelling out approaching trouble for many months. The only investors to recognize the trouble in time were technical analysts—not bankers, economists, college professors, or government officials. If more investors had understood then what we know now about technical analysis,

disaster might have been averted.

Jesse Livermore, a flamboyant trader of the 1920s who sold out before the crash, knew the importance of two things other traders didn't—the new high/new low indicator and the advance/decline line. For several months preceding the crash, both indicators demonstrated that a dangerous loss of upside momentum was occurring in the market. Fewer and fewer stocks were participating in the market's advance and eventually the market just gave out.

The study of market momentum indicators is the best technique for detecting the right times to buy and sell stocks. All the great turning points in the stock market are signaled by a loss of upside momentum at new highs in the Dow Jones Industrial Average and loss of downside momentum at new lows in the Dow.

The next most important indicator is volume. Volume—not price—accurately measures the supply and demand for a stock. "On-balance volume" is a sophisticated means used by technical analysts for determining whether a stock is under accumulation or distribution. For example, suppose a stock closes an eighth of a point higher on a volume of 5,000 shares and the next day falls an eighth of a point on 3,000 shares. Following only price, it would appear that the stock was doing nothing. However, by adding total volume on upside days and subtracting total volume on downside days (+5,000 – 3,000 = +2,000), you can see that something is different. At the end of two days, the on-balance volume of +2,000 shares shows that the stock is stronger: more accumulation occurred at the higher price than at the lower. As long as on-balance volume is in an upward trend, the price of the stock can be expected to rise. Conversely, a declining trend in on-balance volume denotes price trouble in the future.

Source: Joseph E. Granville, publisher of *The Granville Market Letter*, Kansas City, MO. Mr. Granville is best known for his stock market books, including *Granville's New Strategy of Daily Stock Market Timing for Maximum Profit* and *The Warning*, and for his autobiography, *The Book of Granville, Reflections of a Stock Market Prophet*.

The Best Ways for Making Money in an Up And Down Market

One common rule has never been broken . . .Stock market leadership goes to the companies with the best relative earnings and strongest potential for growth. It's a simple rule—but many people are forgetting it in today's crazy market.

Stock-Picking Strategy

You should insist on:

• Good earnings momentum. Look back 12 months to find stocks whose earnings are increasing at a rate faster than the Standard & Poor's 500. Then look ahead 12 months to see whether the estimated earnings of those stocks will also exceed the estimated earnings of the S&P 500. Check quarterly earnings very carefully to make sure that there has been no earnings disappointment in the interim period.

• Relatively low price/earnings (p/e) multiples. The goal is always to buy the most earnings growth for the lowest p/e multiple. That's the best way to minimize the downside risk and increase your chances for bigger-than-average returns. Calculation: Divide the company's last 12 months' p/e ratio by its projected earnings growth rate for the next five years. This gives the p/e ratio as a percentage of the company's growth rate. Calculate the same percentage for the S&P 500 and compare the two. You want companies with much lower percentages than the S&P 500. Example: If the S&P 500 sells at a multiple of 12 and its growth rate is estimated at 9%, then the S&P 500 is selling for 133% of its growth rate. Your aim is to buy companies selling for less than 133% of their growth rate. Another test: Find relatively low p/e stocks that are trading at the bottom half of their last 12 months' p/e multiples.

Source: Robert Chesek, president of the Phoenix Series Funds and manager of the Phoenix Growth, Stock and Balanced Funds, Phoenix Mutual Life Insurance Co., 1 American Row, Hartford, CT 06115.

How To Make Money on Insider* Trading

Watching the trades of corporate insiders can give investors valuable information about the direction of a stock's price. When corporate insiders buy or sell, you should follow their lead. Reason: They have solid information about their company's future. And since their lives, careers and personal wealth are usually tied to their investments, they're very cautious and are not often wrong.

Corporate insiders were bullish in 1982 (before the market began to take off) and massive sellers in 1983 (just before the market fell). They became even more bullish in 1984, before the big rally. Investors who use insider traders as a bellwether have beaten the market 11 years out of the last 13.

When three or more insiders are buying, it's a buy signal. It doesn't matter if it's the treasurer buying 100 shares or the chairman buying 10,000. What's important is the action, reflecting the insider's belief that the company's stock is going to rise.

Caution: Insiders buy for the long term. Sometimes their buying begins long before the stock turns around.

Example: Cullinet insiders began buying the company's stock when it was at 17. The stock finally bottomed out in October 1986 at 6¼. The insiders' buy signal was too early.

*Corporate insiders (not to be confused with people who trade securities based on *illegally* obtained inside information) are officers, directors and beneficial holders of the company's stock. Their transactions are reported to the government and become public information.

Source: J. Michael Reid, editor/publisher of *Insider Indicator*, Portland, OR.

Insider Buying Vs. Insider Selling

Insider selling is less meaningful than insider buying as an indicator of a company's prospects. Since sales may be made for a variety of reasons (diversification, shortage of cash, etc.), sales by two insiders in a company should be accorded roughly the same importance as one purchase by an insider.

Source: Norman Fosback, editor, *The Insiders*, Institute for Econometric Research, Fort Lauderdale.

Signal That a Large Block of Stock Is About To Be Dumped on the Market

Very frequently, knowledge that a large block of shares of a particular stock is up for sale can influence the decision on whether to buy or to sell those securities. For example, you might postpone or permanently avoid purchasing shares about to come under institutional liquidation. Or you might choose to sell before a competing large sell order becomes operative.

While mutual funds and other institutions don't "advertise" that they plan a liquidation prior to actual sale, such information, not infrequently, manages to "leak out," and this often puts a sizable dent in the stock's price. There usually are hints available to the alert investor that a liquidation of the block is imminent.

The major indication that a block is coming up for sale lies in a sudden shrinkage of the trading range of the issue in question. For example, a stock might usually demonstrate an average trading range of perhaps a full point or point and one-half between its daily high and low in a typical trading day. If, for two or three days, this trading range shrinks to, say, one-tenth to three-eighths of a point, you might anticipate a block is coming up for sale at near current market levels or below.

The shrinkage probably represents awareness on the part of knowledgeable floor and other traders that a large sell order exists and an unwillingness to bid up for the stock until the overhead supply, which is immediately forthcoming, is fully liquidated.

How To Find Tempting Takeover Targets

Short of consulting a crystal ball, the best way to tell if a company's a possible takeover target is by watching the buying patterns of investors with top track records. You can do this by tracking SEC 13D filings.

They're required within 10 days of a purchase that brings an investor's holdings to 5% or more of a company's outstanding stock.*

That's not to say you should blindly follow. You must also analyze the company's balance sheet and market position.

When calculating a company's book value to compare it with its market value, research its adjusted book value—including assets that don't show up on the balance sheet (find them in annual report footnotes)...most commonly, an overfunded pension plan or Last In-First Out (LIFO) inventory reserves. Reasons: Spectacular rises in the stock and bond markets boost dramatically the funds held in pension plans...and if a company uses LIFO accounting procedures, its inventory is usually worth more than stated on the books.

Valuable insight can also be gleaned from an examination of the company's securities portfolio, also listed in annual report footnotes. Question: Is the portfolio's market value higher than its stated book value? When the Dow Jones averages are as high, almost any company with a securities portfolio has these high off-balance-sheet assets.

It's also important to take a look at the market value of a company's real estate holdings. Where to find them: The company's Form 10K, filed annually with the SEC and available from the company's investor relations department.

You'll have to research land values in the area...and will usually discover that the value of the property is higher than stated on the company's books. Finally, find out from its annual report whether the company has a tax-loss carryforward that might benefit another party.

In addition to hidden balance-sheet assets,

you need to know how the company is faring within its own industry. How: By comparing its price/earnings ratio with p/e's in the rest of the industry and with the general market. That gives an idea of whether it's fairly, over- or undervalued. Best: Undervalued.

Next area to investigate: The company's market share or penetration in its industry. Is it a major player or an also-ran? Always go for the major players.

*How to get 13D's: They're available from the SEC in Washington on the day they're filed and in Chicago, Los Angeles and New York one or two days later. Other sources: *SEC Today* and *Street Smart Investing*. In addition, Bechtel Information Services (800-231-3282, 212-425-5210) and Disclosure, Inc. (800-638-8241) will put a "watch" on a company and send filings upon release. Cost: 20¢–30¢/page.

Source: William Wood, senior vice president, Street Smart Inc., publisher of *Street Smart Investing*, and *13D Opportunities Report*, Yorktown Heights, NY.

About Mergers and Acquisitions

Mergers and acquisitions generate some of the largest and quickest profits on Wall Street. W.T. Grimm reports that the 1985 average one-week premium paid over market was 37.1%. Moreover, because cancelled transactions represent less than 10% of net M&A announcements, the price volatility relating to mergers has a definite positive bias.

The small investor tends to be at a disadvantage in trying to make profits from takeovers. Leaks of insider information would normally reach the institutional community before the small investor. Moreover, high commission costs on low-volume trades make arbitrage profits more difficult to come by for the small investor.

Identifying Possible Merger Targets

Clearly, there is no set formula for identifying merger targets, and most of the odds of a successful merger are probably reflected in the target's price.

Generally, those companies that are under-valued on a fundamental basis are most likely to be desirable merger targets, because acquirors tend to have a longer time horizon than the average investor. Thus companies with low prices relative to their future cash flows are probably the most likely merger candidates. Because acquisitions may require debt issuance, companies with strong cash positions and low debt levels are perceived as more attractive targets. Companies with strong brand names (*i.e.*, Revlon, General Foods), franchises (ABC), or assets that are similarly difficult or expensive to replace or develop are attractive merger targets. Concepts from technical analysis are generally not useful for the identification of merger targets although upward price momentum may hasten a buyer to announce an offer.

Arbitrage

Significant profits (and losses) are generated by arbitrageurs (especially institutional), who try to make profits on small price spreads. For example if Firm A was trading at \$23/share, and Firm B makes a tender offer for Firm A at \$30/share, and the price of the stock rises to \$29, an arbitrageur may buy the stock of Firm A in order to gain the \$1, while assuming the risk of the offer falling through and of the stock falling back to \$23.

The small investor is at a disadvantage in arbitrage situations, because relatively high commission costs for small volume trades may significantly lessen the spread. Moreover, professional arbitrageurs use resources not at the disposal of the individual investor, including teams of lawyers and analysts.

Furthermore, the increasing supply of arbitrage funds makes competition for those profits difficult. Some argue, however, that because the dollar values of today's largest mergers (*i.e.*, greater than \$5 billion) exceed the level of arbitrage funds (\$3–\$4 billion), there are still opportunities for profits, especially when more than one billion-dollar deal is occurring simultaneously.

Risks

The risks in mergers run from being negligible to being quite significant. An investment in a company that is not currently rumored as a target has no merger-related downside risk if no merger surfaces. The stock of a company that is widely rumored to be an imminent target may slide a few points if those rumors are not confirmed. Finally, the collapse of a publicly announced deal might cause significant losses as the price returns to trading on fundamentals.

While the potential for profits is great, the announcement of a merger immediately brings attention to a stock. Accordingly, merger targets should be among the most efficiently valued securities, leaving little room for successful bargain hunting.

Source: Bruce H. Monrad, analyst, mergers/acquisitions & leveraged buyout department, Prudential-Bache Securities, Inc., Prudential-Bache Building, One Seaport Plaza, New York 10292.

How To Make a Killing in The Penny Stock Market

Penny stocks or venture capital stocks are the stocks of small start-up companies that go public at prices between 1 cent and $5. They offer investors the opportunity to make low-cost investments that could rack up potentially huge returns.

To make a killing in penny stocks, invest in high-quality new issues underwritten by brokerage firms that support their deals in the aftermarket. Of course, this is never quite as easy as it sounds. It takes an experienced eye to recognize quality in penny stocks and diligence to monitor the ups and downs of the 30 or so penny stock underwriters. Here are some tips on how to possibly double or triple your money while limiting the risk of losing all or part of your investment.

• Find out about the newest issues. A variety of newsletters concentrate solely on stocks that sell for $5 a share and under. Let the newsletters do your groundwork, then concentrate only on the most promising underwritings. Some of the newsletters also rank penny stock underwriters by past performance; use them to pick out the underwriters who successfully support their new issues after they begin trading.

• Do your research. If a new company sparks your interest, find out everything you can about the organization and its background. To begin with, get a copy of the prospectus from the underwriter and read it from cover to cover. Look for a strong operating history and a management with good relevant experience. Stick to companies that offer both. Check to see where the funds from the offering will be spent; beware of a company that will use the funds to pay off existing debt or to line the pockets of the company's principals.

Investigate the underwriter, too. Find out how the underwriter's last three offerings performed: What were the prices of the offerings? How high (or low) did the stocks go? What prices are they trading at today?

• Getting in on the action. It's difficult to get stock in the hottest new penny stock issue, because it usually goes to the underwriter's best customers. Don't get frustrated. Until you are in the underwriter's inner circle, choose seven or eight of the most appealing new issues. The more you try, the better your chances are of getting at least a part of what you want.

• Limit your purchases to $500 for any one issue. Also spread out your risk by purchasing several stocks.

• Getting out at a profit. Take your profits when you can. A winner today may be a loser tomorrow. Penny stocks are notorious for their volatility, so keep your greed in check. Take your profits when the opportunity arises, rather than holding on for large gains that may never come.

Source: Gail Snyder, editor of *Speculators Magazine*, 55 E. Afton Ave., Yardley, PA 19067.

Surviving the Over-the-Counter Stock Market

Over-the-counter stocks, being small and often not well followed by many brokers, are especially susceptible to rumors and false reports. Stockbrokers and underwriters flourish on heavy trading and are usually themselves the source of misleading reports. Basic wisdom: When a company sounds too good —its product will replace toothpaste—watch out!

• Rule of thumb: If you don't know why you own a stock—or why you're buying—or why you're selling—then you're in someone else's hands. This makes you more vulnerable to the caprices of the market.

• OTC stocks, particularly new issues, are usually short-term plays. One should never buy without having a sell target in mind.

• If the selling price is reached, even within a week of buying, stick to the sell decision unless there is some major mitigating factor you hadn't considered before.

• About 80% of all new issues will be selling below their issue price within 18 months. Reason: Most new issues are overpriced in relation to existing companies. But they are all destined to become just another existing company within a year.

• In evaluating a new issue, find out who the people involved are. If the underwriter is or has been the target of the Securities & Exchange Commission's investigations, this is often mentioned in the prospectus. The SEC prints a manual of all past violators. Avoid underwriters that have had lots of SEC problems. The strong companies rarely use them to go public.

• Check out the auditors of a new-issue company. (They will be named in the prospectus.) If the auditor is not well-known or is in trouble with the SEC, question the numbers in the financial reports.

• A danger in over-the-counter stocks is a key market maker who crosses buy and sell orders among its own brokerage customers so that the market price is artificial. If such a broker collapses, so will its main stocks. This illustrates the danger of buying a stock dependent on only a single market maker. To avoid such a problem, invest in stocks quoted on NASDAQ, where by definition there are at least two strong market makers, and hopefully a lot more.

• Spot companies just before they decide to go onto NASDAQ. When they do, their price inevitably rises because of the increased attention. Very often the managements will simply tell you if they have NASDAQ plans or not. Tip-off: If they've just hired a new financial man, it's often a sign of a move to NASDAQ.

Source: Robert J. Flaherty, editor of *The OTC Review*, Oreland, PA.

Techniques for Evaluating Over-the-Counter Stocks

• Growth potential is the single most important consideration. Earnings increases should average 10% over the past six years when acquisitions and divestitures are factored out.

• Cash, investments, accounts receivable, materials, and inventories should be twice the size of financial claims due within the next year.

• Working capital per share should be greater than the market value of the stock (an $8 stock should be backed by $10 per share in working capital).

• Long-term debt should be covered by working capital, cash, or one year's income.

• The balance sheet should show no deferred operating expenses and no unreceived income.

The criteria for final selections include:

• Ownership by at least 10 institutions reported in *Standard & Poor's Stock Guide*.

• Public ownership of between 500,000 and one million shares, with no more than

10% controlled by a single institution.

- Continued price increases after a dividend or split.

- Strong likelihood of moving up to a major exchange. (A good sign is strong broker and institutional support.)

Avoid companies that are expanding into unrelated fields, where they lack the required management experience and depth, and have stock selling at prices far below recent highs. This sign of loss of investor support can take months to overcome.

Source: C. Colburn Hardy, *Physician's Management.*

About New Issues

Investors will always have a hard time solving the two big problems of initial public offerings (IPOs):

- How to choose companies that haven't been analyzed extensively by professional investors.

- Where to find a broker who will sell the newly issued stock, which is often grabbed up by a few of the underwriter's favorite clients.

Profits and Safety

Conducting a shrewd analysis of companies that go public is the only way to minimize the enormous risk of investing in IPOs. As a group IPOs have risen in price an average 64% in the first year of being publicly traded. Some of them double in value after even minutes of being traded. The downside: About 40% of all IPOs lose half their value in the first year, and a substantial number go bankrupt.

The document to ask your broker for is the final prospectus of the IPO. What to look for:

- How money raised from the initial stock sale will be used. Proceeds from the offering should be used to improve or expand what the company is currently doing. Examples: Increase production or pay for a major marketing plan. Be wary when: Proceeds of an IPO go toward retiring debt or entering new fields.

- What the IPO's past performance has been. Even if the company has been operating for only a short time (less than three years), there's usually evidence in the prospectus of management's ability to find a market niche and make a profit. It there's no track record of this ability, avoid the stock.

- How the original owners profit from the IPO. When a company goes public, owners occasionally take out big cash profits for themselves. That's bad because big profits at an early IPO stage mean the owners are more interested in making quick profits than in keeping an equity stake while they run the company.

Evidence of this shows up in the prospectus under the heading Beneficial Ownership After Offering. It's usual for an officer to take a small profit, but the prospectus also lists the number of each owner's shares that are being converted into cash. Be cautious about an IPO if all the officers as a group are selling more than 15% of their shares.

- Who the underwriter is. Brokerage houses have cycles of success and failure in taking companies public. For that reason it's usually safe to buy an IPO whose underwriter has had a good track record for the previous six months to a year. But don't expect an underwriter that had great success two years ago necessarily to maintain its pace today. (The success/failure record of underwriters is regularly reported in publications that specialize in new offerings and occasionally in the general financial journals.)

- If warrants were issued to the underwriters. Check the final prospectus to see whether the underwriter is receiving part of its fee in warrants that give it the right to buy the stock at a fixed price in the future. Willingness to accept warrants means the underwriter has more than average confidence in the IPO. Historically, these stocks have a better chance of appreciating in value than others.

- Who the venture-capital investors are. It's also a sign of confidence when prominent venture-capital firms are listed as shareholders, or if they put up capital earlier when the company started up. Participation of these firms is

373

also assurance that new management talent can be brought in if the existing team falters. (Most brokers can tell you if a venture-capital firm has a good track record of backing start-up companies.)

Finding the Impossible

If demand for a new issue is high, it's usually impossible for any but the broker's favored clients to get shares at the initial price.

The first step is to get advance information on which IPOs are coming up. Best sources: SEC filings (available at the commission's regional offices) and publications that specialize in new issues.

Next, tell your broker as far in advance as possible which upcoming offering you're interested in. Because prices of new issues aren't decided until the last minute, give your broker a top limit on what you're willing to pay for the stock. Caution: If your limit is $16 per share, for example, and the price is set at $18, you can cancel the deal. But don't expect your broker to put out an extra effort the next time around.

Even if the broker's own firm is participating in the underwriting, he may have trouble getting shares when demand is high. In that case only clients with large trading accounts can expect access to shares.

If your broker can't promise you the shares, it often pays to try one of the smaller, regional brokers that are participating in the underwriting.

If that fails, it frequently pays to open an account with the brokerage firm that's managing the underwriting. The managing underwriter is usually allotted more shares than the others and may be willing to arrange a sale, especially for someone opening an account.

Don't take no for an answer, even if this ploy fails. As a last-ditch maneuver, call one of the directors of the new company directly. The director may be willing to ask the underwriters to reserve shares for you. This is especially likely if it's a local firm interested in signing up local investors.

If it's impossible to get shares in the initial offering, consider buying them in the first trading session after the initial offering. Usually the price won't have climbed too high, and some investors are quick to sell and take an immediate profit. Profits may be smaller by buying in this secondary market, but they can still be substantial.

Example: Home Shopping Network shares sold in the initial offering for $18. Within minutes after trading began, shares were going for $38. Three months later, each of these shares was worth more than $130.

In fact, if there's little demand for the IPO, it may make sense to wait to buy it until trading begins. Reason: There's sometimes a 10%–20% decline from the IPO's price in early sales.

Besides screening new issues carefully, the best protection is to diversify your IPO investments into different companies and industry groups. When the market as a whole is high, there won't be many long-term values in IPOs because their prices will be high too. These shares may be more attractive for short-term profits though, because prices may double or triple during the first few months.

If the market is generally weak and there's not much speculative excitement, it's time to look for long-term returns from IPOs. What to look for: As with other types of investments, look for young growth companies that can be bought for well below their value.

Source: Norman G. Fosback, editor, *Income & Safety*, 3471 N. Federal Highway, Fort Lauderdale, FL 33306.

Big Opportunities in Small Company Stocks

Though investing in less-well-known businesses can lead to big payoffs, investors must be prepared to do more homework to find them than they'd do if they wanted to invest in better-known companies. Some data can be found in annual reports and filings with the Securities & Exchange Commission. Look for:

• A 15% annual revenue growth. If a company's increase in sales is below that level, high dividends and stock appreciation are unlikely. Also look for companies in industry segments that are growing.

• Large market share. This is especially important because small companies are very vulnerable to economic slowdowns. Market share is about the only cushion that can carry them through rough times. The safest businesses for investors are those with at least a 20% share of their market. Caution: Avoid investing in small companies that are competing against giants. They may do well in good times but be squeezed if the economy falters.

• Good management. This factor is the toughest to judge. Solid management is much more important to the success of a small company than to that of a big one, whose momentum can drive it for years. Look through the company's annual reports of several years… then look at its current 10K and 10Q SEC filings to see whether performance has lived up to management expectations. (These filings are available from local SEC offices.) The 8K also reveals extraordinary changes in a company's situation, such as key management moves and litigation. If possible, talk with the company's executives, customers and suppliers. And, of course, obtain copies of research reports by the major brokerages.

• Good value. The most attractive stocks will have a price that's no more than 10–12 times earnings.

Useful guideline: Invest in companies that have a price/earnings ratio well below the company's expected annual growth rate. A company with a price/earnings ratio of 12 and annual sales growth of 18%, for instance, is one that you would usually move into.

Also watch the relationship between the company's capitalization (total value of outstanding shares) and its sales. We look for companies whose market capitalization is less than their revenues. Avoid stocks of companies whose sales are three times or more greater than their capitalization.

Avoiding the Pitfalls

Prices of secondary stocks are very volatile. And, there's danger that the company will issue new shares, which lowers the value of shares that are already in investors' hands. If there are rumors of a new issue, wait until all the new shares have been absorbed in the market. Then the price will almost certainly be depressed.

Probably the biggest mistake investors make is buying stock in industries they're not familiar with.

Source: Richard F. Aster, president, Aster Investment Management Co., which manages the Meridian Fund, a no-load mutual fund specializing in secondary growth stocks, 60 E. Sir Francis Drake Blvd., Larkspur, CA 94939.

How To Recognize Undervalued Industrial Stocks

A favorite investment approach is to look at unpopular stocks of good companies, particularly companies with small market capitalizations. Disregard the big names and the Wall Street "whiz stocks." They've already been touted and bid up—way too far.

There are many small to medium-sized companies that merit your attention because of their potential long-term appreciation. Sifting through them can seem like an overwhelming task, but there are two good techniques any investor can use for finding undervalued companies.

Price/Sales Ratio (PSR)

The PSR is computed by dividing the total market value of a company by the company's total sales. PSRs provide a useful valuation technique for comparing large numbers of potential investment candidates.

Oftentimes, good companies will have reduced earnings and temporary losses, but their sales will remain stable. Because of the decline in their earnings, Wall Street assigns a lower value to the stocks. However, since sales have remained the same, there is a good chance that earnings will return to prior levels and that the stock prices will rise along with earnings.

Debt Adjustment Factor (DAF)

Using the PSR you can sift out a large number of potentially strong, undervalued companies. The next step is to find the companies with strong balance sheets by using the DAF to determine whether a company has too much debt on its books.

To perform this calculation, divide the current assets by the current liabilities. This will give you the current ratio. Divide the current ratio by 4. Then divide shareholders' equity by total assets. Add the equity/assets and the current ratio/4. If the total is 1.00 or greater, the balance sheet is strong. If the total is less than 0.80, the company has too much debt.

Using only PSRs and DAFs, you can consistently pick stocks that outperform market expectations. You can further improve your chances of picking an undervalued stock by utilizing other tools of fundamental analysis (evaluating the quality of management and competition, insider trading, etc.), but the key to winning with undervalued stocks is to buy unpopular stocks of good companies and to hold them long enough for their quality to be reflected in the stock prices.

Source: Kenneth L. Fisher, chief executive of Fisher Investments, 301 Henrik Road, Woodside, CA 94062, an investment management firm. Mr. Fisher is the author of a regular column in *Forbes* and of a book, *Super Stocks*.

How To Recognize an Overvalued Stock

How many times has your broker sent you a glowing report about a great company whose stock price is bound to skyrocket? How many times has he or she been right? Probably few or none. Investors need to take the upper hand and be able to identify quickly whether a company is overvalued in the stock market.

One of the best tools for determining whether a stock is overvalued is the price/sales ratio (PSR): The price per share/sales per share. If the PSR is greater than 0.75, the stock is too expensive—investors are paying a premium for future growth, so the upside potential in the stock's price is dwarfed.

Example: IBM reported revenues per share of $74.98 for its 1984 fiscal year. At the time, the price of the stock was $127.50. IBM's PSR was equal to $127.50 divided by $74.98, or 1.70. This was too high. While IBM is a great company with a strong potential for future sales growth, investors had already incorporated their expectations for growth in the current stock price. If you had bought the stock in 1983 at a price of $123.75, held it for a year, and then sold it for $127.50, your total annual gain would have been only 3%. You would have been better off with an almost risk-free money-market fund.

It's important to know that initial public offerings (IPOs) are generally overvalued stocks. The purpose of a stock offering is to raise cash for a company, whether it's to open a new plant, pay off old debt, or accomplish some other business purpose. Unless it is desperate, company management will wait to make the deal until it can receive the maximum amount of cash possible. As a result, the offering price of the stock will be at or near the highest price level to be expected—there is a very strong chance that the price of the stock will decline when it starts trading in the open market. How can you profit from this? Let the stock price drop after the offering, then buy the stock when the PSR is at a more reasonable level. (Of course, do not buy the stock from any offering without first checking the PSR.)

Insider selling is another good indicator of overvalued stocks. If management does not want to own its own company's stock, then why should you? Vicker's Stock Research of New Jersey publishes the *Weekly Insider Report*, which allows investors to see exactly who is selling how much of what stock. Often, insiders sell stock of companies with high PSRs.

High PSR stocks are frequently high price/book value stocks as well. Book value is the company's assets minus *all* liabilities. In other words, it is the company's net worth on the books. You have a much better chance of making money with stocks selling at less than book value than those selling for more than book value.

Example: 53 companies with high PSRs were featured in the *PSR Stockwatch* investment newsletter. During one year, 37 stock prices tumbled, compared to gains in only 16 companies. Many of the values were halved or worse, because the stocks had been too popular. If you don't beat everyone else to the investment, you can't hope to beat them to the profits.

Source: Margaret Brill, a former stockbroker at L.F. Rothschild, Unterberg, Towbin, in San Francisco, is now editor of a newsletter on undervalued stocks, *PSR Prophet* (previously, *PSR Stockwatch*), 1001 Bridgeway, Suite 244, Sausalito, CA 94965.

Contrarian Investment Strategies

A contrarian investment strategy involves buying financial instruments that are "out of favor," that are in industries that are shunned as boring, or whose prices have fallen sharply. Contrarians invest "against the grain" of conventional thought. A contrarian assumes that the market frequently overreacts to both good and bad news, and invests counter to the consensus.

The history of the market is full of examples of low expectation stocks whose results have exceeded those expectations. At the start of World War II, John Templeton instructed his broker to purchase 100 shares of every stock on the New York and American Exchanges with a price below $1. Importantly, Templeton did not exclude those with the worst possible expected future: A third of the companies were in bankruptcy proceedings. Four years later his portfolio had quadrupled, significantly outperforming the market.

Conversely, there are also numerous examples of the demise of so-called glamour stocks whose future seemed particularly bright. Xerox, once dominant in duplicating office equipment, sold as high as $170/share in 1972 with earnings of only $3.16. In 1985, earnings per share were only $3.46, and the stock sold at about $60.

Some Techniques Used by Contrarians

Contrarians look at many signals of overly low or overly high market expectations. These would include:

• Low p/e investment strategies. The classic contrarian investment strategy may be buying low p/e stocks. Given an earnings level, low p/e stocks tend to be stocks whose prices are depressed or at least are not lofty. Frequently, low p/e stocks have low expected earnings or are simply perceived as stodgy investments. The key to the strategy is this: If the low expectations pan out, there will be no negative surprises to cause selling of the stock. If, however, earnings exceed expectations, the surprise is positive and the stock will rise.

• New highs, new lows. Stocks that approach new highs are presumably more vulnerable to price drops on bad news. Stocks that reach new lows are more likely to have most or all of the bad news reflected in the low price.

• Market newsletters/research reports. A uniformly bearish consensus of market newsletters and brokerage house research reports is perceived as a bullish sign for the market. It is thought by some that investors who follow the advice of these newsletters would have sold all their stock in the face of bearish recommendations, making further selling pressure unlikely. As the opinions of the reports change to a bullish tone, these investors will buy back in, raising stock prices. Conversely, a bullish consensus is considered a bearish sign for the market: Market tops occur when all the bulls are fully invested, and market bottoms occur when all the bears have sold.

• Institutional cash positions. This is a frequently used measure of market sentiment. If institutions are fully invested, *i.e.,* cash positions are low, new buying of stocks will be unlikely. On the other hand, high institutional cash positions (greater than 15%, for example) suggest untapped buying power.

• Cash flow analysis. Inasmuch as a primary tool for valuation is a p/e ratio, investors often focus on reported earnings. However, substantial depreciation and amortization (non-cash) charges to reported earnings may mask a company's operating stability. For example, in 1985, Chevron generated funds from operations of $6,521 million. However, net income was only $1,547 million. Depreciation depletion and amortization charges (well in excess of capital expenditures) accounted for the bulk of the difference, but required no cash outlay. Accordingly, the cash flow (earnings plus non-cash charges) measure of profitability reflects a much more stable and healthy operating picture.

While some allowance must be made for future capital expenditures and working capital needs, it is useful to look at cash flow. Often, companies with weak earnings figures may have relatively stable cash flows. Accordingly, a contrarian may see greater than perceived stability and value in a company with negative earnings but positive cash flow.

• Asset values. Companies that sell at a discount to asset value may be undervalued. A contrarian may buy companies with temporarily depressed earnings and stock prices if the assets of the company are perceived to be worth more than the current market price. Obviously, determining so-called asset value is an imprecise task. If these assets are worth more to another company, a takeover could yield significant profits to investors. Such would be the case of significant tax-loss carry-forwards. Assets may also have a liquidation value in excess of current market prices (which may reflect only short-term earnings potential). While book value is not synonymous with asset value, companies with prices below book value are more likely to fall in this category.

Contrarian investment strategies often require patience because success requires a change in the market sentiment that initially created an overvalued or undervalued security. Moreover, contrarian investing is a more difficult investment strategy to follow because it involves investing against the tide of conventional wisdom. However, investors who bet against the prevailing short-term market sentiment may realize significant profits.

Source: Bruce H. Monrad, analyst, mergers/acquisitions & leveraged buyout department, Prudential-Bache Securities, Inc., Prudential-Bache Building, One Seaport Plaza, New York 10292.

Why Buy the Stock of a Bankrupt Company?

The stocks of bankrupt companies are high-risk investments—but like all high-risk investments, the potential for great returns is significant. For example, in December 1984, the stock of bankrupt Charter Corporation sold for $1.00 a share. By February of 1985, the stock had risen to $4.00 a share, a 400% rise in just two months. Other companies like Penn Central, Miller-Wohl, Toys "R" Us, Saxon Industries, and Wicks have made large fortunes for investors patient enough to hold onto their stocks even during the bad times.

There are two rules to follow when making this type of investment. The first is to wait until a company actually goes into bankruptcy. Before that time, the company's stock price goes nowhere but down. Second, after a company has publicly declared bankruptcy, you must find ways to reduce your risk.

As with any other investment, you should try to dilute risk through diversification. Don't buy just one bankrupt company—buy several.

Also, plan your investments on the basis of how the stock of a bankrupt company trades. Normally, the stock free-falls for a few months prior to bankruptcy. After the bankruptcy announcement, the stock price plummets another 30% to 50%, then hibernates. As investors take year-end losses in the stock, the price may drift slowly downward. If the company is going to go under, the stock will continue its descent; if the company is going to survive, the stock may hover until there is some kind of positive news about the company's recovery. The key, again, is patience. Bankruptcies can drag on for months, sometimes years.

Another strategy for reducing risk is to buy companies that have been in Chapter 11 proceedings for a while. Newly bankrupt companies are usually unpredictable—they fire key personnel, write off losses, dump liquid assets, and avoid communication with the outside. It can take 12 to 18 months before a bankrupt company's fate becomes clearer.

Pay close attention to a bankrupt company's cash flow and the potential for stock dilution. If there is enough cash flow to pay back creditors, even slowly and at a discount, odds are the stock will recover and new shares won't have to be created. If a company's creditors think they can get 50 cents on the dollar in the future, rather than 10 cents on the dollar now, they probably will be patient and let management repair the damage.

Profitable divisions reduce risk. Diverse companies are better than single-product or single-service companies in bankruptcy. It is easier to resurrect a business if it has at least a few profitable divisions, since losing divisions can be closed to allow management to concentrate resources on divisions that make money.

You can also reduce your risk by investing in preferred stock or convertible bonds. In the event of liquidation, these instruments are paid off before common stock. But remember, because preferred stock and convertible bonds reduce risk, the potential for high returns is also reduced. For example, while Charter Corporation's stock quadrupled, its bonds only doubled in value.

Source: Kenneth L. Fisher, chief executive of Fisher Investments, 301 Henrik Road, Woodside, CA 94062, an investment management firm. Mr. Fisher is the author of a regular column in *Forbes* and of a book, *Super Stocks*.

Turnaround Stocks

- They're too risky.
- The companies may never recover.
- Their earnings will go nowhere.
- You could lose all your money.

That's what most investment experts will tell you about investing in the stocks of bankrupt or distressed companies. Where were these experts when Chrysler's stock went from $3/share in 1982 (when the company declared bankruptcy) to $47/share four years later—a 2,250% gain? Or when Toys "R" Us went from 75¢/share in 1978 to over $34/share in 1986?

When a company declares bankruptcy and goes into Chapter 11, most investors are sure it has reached the end. Their immediate response: To sell their stock and stay far away. Institutional investors don't want to get caught with a bankrupt or troubled stock in their portfolio. And individual investors sell because everyone else is selling. Result: The stock price plummets. . .and stays there.

Reality: Far from being the end of the road, Chapter 11 offers a unique opportunity for a company to reorganize and restructure its business. Under the protection of a bankruptcy court, companies in Chapter 11 can sell off unprofitable businesses, close down factories and stores, restructure their financial obligations, and renegotiate labor contracts.

Bottom line: Chapter 11 gives companies the opportunity to take action that would not be possible for profitable companies. Another plus: Tax-loss carry-forwards from money-losing years can be used to offset taxes when the company's earnings do turn around.

Finding the Right Stocks

The key to making money in turnaround stocks lies in the selection process. Many distressed companies are on the skids for good reason. No matter what their opportunities to reorganize, their basic business is so bad that they'll never stage a comeback. You want to find bankrupt companies that will succeed in turning around.

Since traditional analytical yardsticks such as earnings per share, price/book value and earnings growth are not very useful with distressed companies, different criteria are necessary. Here's what to look for:

- Solid core business. For a turnaround to succeed, the company needs a business that can provide adequate cash flow and serve as a source for future growth. (Bonus: Side businesses that can be sold to raise cash.) The solid core business needn't be the company's largest or best-known business. It could be a successful or potentially successful side business that the company can rebuild itself around.

Example: Itel, a lessor of IBM computer hardware, was sent into Chapter 11 in 1981, after IBM changed its product line and the computer market softened. In bankruptcy, the company shed its high-tech leasing business and became a lessor of railroad equipment and shipping containers—a side business that originally accounted for only a fraction of the company's sales. Itel successfully emerged from bankruptcy in 1983, and its stock rose from virtually nothing to $18/share.

• Opportunities to improve cash flow. Most distressed companies get into trouble because their cash flow is insufficient to meet their financial obligations. The best turnaround candidates can generate cash quickly through their core business, sell off assets or restructure their debt. Positive signs: Plants that can be closed, stores that can be sold, businesses that can be spun off, creditors that are willing to exchange debt for company stock or to extend debt payments. Most important: Positive cash flow from at least one of the company's businesses.

• A change in management. A troubled company needs a fresh perspective. Old management is usually responsible for having got the company in trouble in the first place. Best sign: A new management team with experience in turnaround situations.

• Concentrated stock ownership. Management that owns a large share of stock has a strong incentive to make the company profitable again. Also, major shareholders outside the company—an individual or another company—can help support the stock's price during the transition period.

Obstacle: Finding information about bankrupt companies can be difficult. Companies in Chapter 11 sometimes stop filing financial reports with the Securities & Exchange Commission. Good sources of information are *The Wall Street Journal* and the various industry magazines.

Many attractive turnaround opportunities may exist in your own area, making it easy to do some detective work. Is the company hiring more people? Is its chain of stores looking better? Has a new CEO moved into town?

Expect to hold an attractive turnaround candidate at least a year, maybe two, before you begin to see concrete results. Bankruptcy stocks typically decline dramatically in value after the first round of bad news is released. They hover at that low price for six months to a year, until their efforts to restructure are publicized.

The key to reducing risk is diversification. Buy at least four stocks. One or two of these should increase dramatically in price—zooming far above the market averages. One stock may keep pace with the market. The fourth will go nowhere, or even decline.

Source: George Putnam, editor of *The Turnaround Letter,* Philadelphia.

Spotting Low-Priced Stocks Ready To Bounce Back

The key to success in the stock market is knowing how to recognize value, and value has little to do with a good company versus a bad company. A top-quality large company selling at a high price/earnings multiple is less attractive than a lesser-quality company selling at a depressed price in terms of its past and future earning power, working capital, book value, and historical prices.

Here is where analysts look for value:

Stocks that have just made a new low for the last 12 months.

Companies that are likely to be liquidated. In the process of liquidation, shareholders may get paid considerably more than the stock is selling for now.

Unsuccessful merger candidates. If one

buyer thinks a company's stock is a good value, it's possible that others may also come to the same conclusion.

Companies that have just reduced or eliminated their dividends. The stock is usually hit with a selling wave, which often creates a good buying opportunity.

Financially troubled companies in which another major company has a sizable ownership position. If the financial stake is large enough, you can be sure that the major company will do everything it can to turn the earnings around and get the stock price up so that its investment will work out.

Opportunities, also, in stocks that are totally washed out—that is, situations where all the bad news is out. The stock usually has nowhere to go but up. How to be sure a stock is truly washed out:

Trading volume slows to practically nothing. If over-the-counter, few if any dealers making a market.

No Wall Street research analysts are following the company anymore.

No financial journalists, stock market newsletters, or advisory services discuss the company.

Selling of the stock by company's management and directors has stopped.

Signs of turnabout:

The company plans to get rid of a losing division or business. If so, be sure to learn whether the company will be able to report a big jump in earnings once the losing operation is sold.

The company is selling off assets to improve its financial situation and/or reduce debt.

A new management comes on board with an established track record of success with turnaround situations.

Management begins buying the company's stock in the open market.

Also, be sure to follow 13D statements filed with the Securities & Exchange Commission (SEC). A company or individual owning 5% or more of a public company must report such holdings to the SEC. If any substantial company is acquiring a major position in a company, it's possible a tender offer at a much higher price is in the wind.

Source: Robert Ravitz, director of research, David J. Greene & Co., an investment management firm, 30 Wall St., New York 10005.

Rules for Picking Common Stocks

• Try to buy the industry leader or, at the very least, a company that has an important position in its industry.

• Look for an industry with a limited amount of competition.

• Avoid an industry that is an essential part of the Gross National Product or the Consumer Price Index, such as autos or steel. Reason: Highly visible companies are easy targets for government pressure.

• Stick to stocks that have price/earnings ratios lower than that of the Standard & Poor's 500 Index.

• The stock should yield at least 4½% to 5%.

• The company should have a record of significant dividend increases.

• The market price of the stock should be close to book value per share.

• Both the industry and the company should have growth rates higher than the median of American business. One rule of thumb: Sales and earnings ought to have doubled over the past decade. If they haven't, you probably won't be able to keep ahead of inflation in the years ahead.

• Stay away from companies that are too heavily in debt, especially in relation to industry-wide standards.

• Look for companies where managers are owners, too. Nepotism can be a danger in such situations. More often, though, owner-management is a big plus. Owner-managers have a real incentive to keep the company growing as well as to boost the stock's value.

While you may not find a stock with all these characteristics, insist on at least these two: It should be in a growth industry with owner-management.

Source: Roy Papp, investment counselor, 5631 Echo Canyon Circle, Phoenix, AZ 85018.

How To Make Big Money In Good Markets and Bad

Have strict rules about when to buy stocks and when to sell them, and never deviate from these rules. They give structure to philosophy: Earnings are the central influence on a common stock's price.

The Ideal Company

• Dominates its marketplace as an "unregulated monopoly."

Example: Paychecks Corp. is similar to Automatic Data Processing, which handles payrolls for firms with 100 or more employees. Paychecks' payroll companies have fewer than 100 employees. It now has an unregulated monopoly in that segment of the market and is thriving.

• Grows more than 20% per year in both earnings and sales.

• Has a high return on equity. Avoid off-the-wall companies, start-up companies and new issues. Buy only companies with $300–$500 million in sales and a track record of at least five years.

Rules for Buying and Selling

In addition to the above criteria, buy only:

• Stocks that are undervalued. How to measure: A company that has grown 35% per year over the past five years and has a price/earnings multiple of less than half that rate (17) is attractive. Low p/e multiples are important. It's easier to expand the multiple from 10 to 18 than from 20 to 30.

• Stocks that you think will meet a specific price objective. For each stock you buy set a goal based on its price over the past years. If it reaches your goal, take a hard look to determine whether you should stay with the company.

Automatically unload stocks that report a decline in earnings. This decline is for a single quarter, compared with the same quarter the previous year. Never violate this rule. Reason: If you find enough good companies you don't have to risk keeping one in decline. When something bad happens to a company (a down quarter is a strong indication of trouble), it usually takes time for it to turn around.

Source: Eugene G. Martin, executive vice president and portfolio manager, National Investment Service, 815 E. Mason St., Milwaukee, WI 53202.

One Way To Spot A Good Investment

Big cash reserves usually mean companies are strong investment prospects. Reason: They can use cash to repurchase stock, fund expansion, and invest in securities that bolster profitability. Result: The stock market favors firms with cash amounting to 15% or more of the market value of their shares, and so share prices perform comparatively well in market downturns.

Source: *Merrill Lynch Market Letter,* New York.

Investing in Blue Chips

Conservative or blue-chip stocks (the stocks of very stable companies such as IBM, Exxon, General Motors, etc.) usually pay high dividends and can be owned with very little risk to the investor. They are, as most analysts call them, low beta stocks, because their prices fluctuate relatively little.

The great advantage of conservative stocks is that when the economy goes into a recession and the market takes a turn for the worse, conservative stocks normally are the least affected. For this reason, blue chips can act as a cushion for the rest of your portfolio, even taking the place of bonds or other cash instruments. The goal is usually to have about 30% or 40% of your portfolio invested in conservative stocks.

Selling the Successes and Failures

The best way to make money with blue chips is through constant turnover. Since you are not going to double or triple your investment with one stock, you have to be willing to sell your successes and reinvest in other blue chips immediately.

Say you have a portfolio of 100 blue chips, if one of your stocks rises by 20% or 30%, check the stock's fundamentals to see whether something really good is happening. If it is, you may want to add to that stock, but normally the best strategy is to sell it and add to another stock in your portfolio that has a chance of earning 30% for you. If you can make 30% returns six times in a year, you will quadruple your money.

A common problem is that investors in conservative stocks may make 30% on a stock, but instead of selling it immediately, hold onto it for three more years. The result is that a 30% gain turns into a 7% or 8% gain.

In addition to selling your successes, sell a blue chip whenever the fundamentals go wrong—for instance, when the industry or the product is about to deteriorate. Use the gains from all of your sales to invest in other companies with sound fundamentals whose stocks haven't appreciated.

Source: Peter Lynch, executive vice president and managing director, Fidelity Investments, Fidelity Management & Research Company, 82 Devonshire St., Boston 02109.

Selecting Superstocks

Everyone dreams of finding another IBM or Xerox or Hewlett Packard—a "superstock" that appreciates many times in value. The problem faced by all investors is that out of the thousands of stocks available for investment today only a small fraction of them will turn into the "superstocks" of tomorrow. In most markets, careful examination of the superstock successes has revealed each to have the following eight characteristics.

1. Small to Medium Size

Small to mid-sized firms with annual sales of $25 million to $100 million usually are neglected in Wall Street, either because they are hard to analyze or, more importantly, because they do not represent enough liquidity (that is, they do not have enough tradeable shares of stock) to interest institutions. Yet smaller firms usually represent outstanding value in terms of growth in earnings per share and assets.

Look for companies with innovative managements that find a niche and fill it with a new product or service. Such managements usually have a dedication to quality rather than price and tend not to diversify. They also avoid building bureaucracies (no overstaffing or private planes).

The most attractive prospects are smaller companies on the threshold of growth. Companies with $25 million–$500 million in sales usually combine management that is reasonably well-seasoned with a sales volume large enough to be generating a meaningful cash flow. The firm (or the market it serves) is generally not quite large enough to attract major competition and is eager to grow.

The bad news is that the smaller company is more vulnerable to industry downturns due to less diversification, is more in need of costly debt financing, and has less staying power in a recession. These are the trade-offs investors must consider when attempting to reap the potentially higher rewards.

2. Rising Unit Sales Volume

Rising sales are essential to any growth company. How fast should sales be rising? As a general rule, growth should not be less than an annual rate of 12%–15% during a strong economic year. The prospects of at least 15%–20% annual growth should not be out of reach.

It is important for investors to realize that a rising sales trend does not necessarily mean a company is enjoying greater prosperity. Sales may be going up, but the cost of producing products or services may be rising even faster. It's possible for a company to survive this squeeze temporarily by cutting expenses or producing more with the same or less labor and equipment, but without sales growth, a company is ultimately doomed as an investment prospect.

A good signal for investors is a three-year total sales increase (in percent) that is higher than the total increase in the Consumer Price Index over the same period. If sales growth is equal to or lower than that index, the company just isn't growing.

3. Rising Pretax Profit Margin

A company's profit margin can be defined as the relationship of income (profit) before or after taxes to net sales. The best measure: The pretax margin reflects the efficiency of a company in extracting a profit from each dollar of sales. Also, more than any other ratio or percentage, the pretax margin indicates just how profitable and effective a company has been within its industry. Most experts favor pretax profit margins as an analytical tool, since the profitability of different companies can be compared without having to account for variations in tax rates.

4. Above-Average and Improving Return on Equity

The profit earned on the stockholders' investment is the indicator of management's efficiency in using the stockholders' funds remaining in the company. In other words, management's productivity of capital. Return on stockholders' equity tells you how successful management has been with the stockholders' money. This profit, or the percentage return on stockholders' equity, is found by dividing net profit after taxes by stockholders' equity.

What constitutes an above-average return? There is no single answer, but in a superstock search, look for a company whose return is (1) better than the competition's; (2) above the aggregate rates of return of the companies in broad market averages such as Standard & Poor's and the Dow Industrial; and (3) above

the prevailing level of interest rates. Any return on equity below 15% is unsatisfactory. Moreover, like pretax margins, the trend is important. As the company matures, its productivity improves and its assets are used to greater advantage.

Above-average returns are essential to growth. If a company earns 20% on stockholders' equity and pays out half in dividends, the remaining 50% will be plowed back into the business to produce a future growth rate of roughly 10% ($0.20 \times 0.50 = 0.10$); if the company pays out only 15% of earnings as dividends, the remaining 85% will sustain a growth rate of about 17% ($0.20 \times 0.85 = 0.17$).

5. Low, But Rising Dividends

Dividend statistics are an important indicator of a company's value in the marketplace and its future growth. Two dividend ratios can be used: (1) the dividend yield is expressed as a percentage calculated by dividing the current annual dividend by the market price of the stock; (2) the dividend payout ratio is the percentage of the company's earnings paid out in dividends to the stockholders.

Dividends cut two ways. On one hand, the payment of at least a modest dividend helps stocks gain acceptance in the marketplace among institutional investors, setting the stage for eventual price appreciation. On the other hand, the higher the dividend payout, the less of a company's earnings remain for reinvestment in operations. Plowback of earnings increases the company's future earning power and, eventually, the price of the stock.

6. Low Debt Ratio

How much debt is too much? The answer depends on the industry and stability of earning power, the company's profitability, and, of course, the level of interest rates. For utilities, where the markets are monopolistic (only one company in the area), a debt level of 50% to 60% of total capitalization is acceptable. For cyclical companies such as those in the steel, aluminum, and copper industries, debt above 25% of total capitalization is dangerous. As a general rule, for growth companies, debt should not exceed 35% of total capitalization;

when interest rates are high, debt should be even lower.

7. Institutional Holdings

Look for growth stocks that are relatively unknown, but not completely obscure. Since institutional research is intensive and thorough, buying stocks with some ownership by institutions vindicates your own research process and investment decision. The information on institutional ownership is available for most companies from services such as Moody's or Standard & Poor's.

Look for stocks with institutional ownership of less than 10%. When institutions own 20% or more of a stock, the growth company has been "discovered." The probable result is that your stock will become fully priced; no one will be left to bid up its price.

8. Increasing Price/Earnings Ratio

The price/earnings (p/e) ratio indicates investors' attitudes toward a company's earnings and growth potential. The ratio's significance stems from the fact that price appreciation in a growth stock is achieved not only by steadily increasing earnings per share, but also by the amount, or p/e multiple, the market is willing to pay for each dollar of those earnings.

To use the p/e ratios first compare the ratios of companies within the same industry. Next, compare the ratio of your prospective growth company with the ratios of the overall market. (The Dow Jones Industrial Average and Standard & Poor's are commonly used indexes.) Also examine trends in p/e ratios to discern how attitudes have changed over time.

Generally, investors pay higher p/e ratios in bull markets than in bear markets, and when interest rates are low. Speculative or "hot" stocks usually carry high ratios. Look at "undiscovered" growth stocks whose p/es are rising rather than falling. If the earnings potential of two companies is the same, buy the company with the lower p/e (considering the other seven superstock characteristics, of course). The company with the lower p/e will

be cheaper—the market might not know what it's missing.

Source: Frank A. Cappiello, president of the investment counselling firm McCullough, Andrews & Cappiello, Inc., 502 Washington Ave., Suite 240, Baltimore 21204. Mr. Cappiello is also chairman of The Carnegie-Cappiello Growth Fund, Carnegie-Cappiello Total Return Fund and Director of a number of publicly owned financial and industrial companies. He is widely known for his regular appearances on "Wall \$treet Week with Louis Rukeyser."

How To Win With High-Tech Stocks

Over any 5- or 10-year period, high-tech stocks have outperformed the broad market averages by three to six times. Why? Most high-tech companies grow much faster than the rest of the economy. And, because of the major impact electronics and computer technology has on our economy, this superior performance should continue into the foreseeable future.

The danger with high-tech stocks in the short run is that they are more volatile and, therefore, riskier than most other stocks. Investments in high-tech stocks should be made with long-term investment funds; you must be willing to ride out large price fluctuations if you want to reap large rewards.

You don't have to be an engineer or computer scientist to make money in high-tech stocks. In most instances, common sense and sound investment principles will lead to success. Ask yourself two questions before you invest: Is this a company I would invest my capital in, at any price? If so, at what price should I buy the stock?

The First Question

To answer the first question, look at three factors: Management, market, and product. Product is last on the list, because technology always changes. In the long run, it is most important to invest in a company with excellent management operating in a large market that can develop products needed for the future.

The best way to assess management is to review several years of annual reports and compare the president's letters with the subsequent years' results. Did the company accomplish what it set out to? Can management execute their strategy? Or do they make excuses for poor performance?

Next, look for large, fast-growing markets. Magazines such as *High Technology,* trade papers such as *Electronic News,* high-tech investment advisory newsletters, and brokerage firms' reports give you statistics on size, growth, and market structure. Use common sense when evaluating market size. Do the market forecasts seem rational? If they don't—walk away.

The best way to check out a company's product is by reading reviews and *asking users.* You would be surprised how few Wall Street analysts actually ask users how they like and use a product, yet users' opinions are some of the best indicators of a company's potential for strong growth. Remember, high-tech products evolve rapidly; whole technologies can change in just a few years. However, if a company's products are number one or number two in a rapidly growing industry and the company devotes enough of its resources to R&D (6%–10% of revenues), good management can keep up.

The Second Question

If a company meets this first set of criteria—good management, large markets, and sensible products—then you are ready to ask the second question: At what price should I buy the stock? Three rules are used for determining the best price to pay.

• Price/Sales Ratio. Divide the total market value of the common stock (number of shares outstanding times today's stock price) by the total revenues of the company. This is the ratio of market value to revenues, or the price/sales ratio. A fairly priced industrial company will usually sell at a ratio of 1.0, *i.e.,* total market value usually equals revenues. A faster-growing high-tech company will usually sell for higher ratios. Look for ratios less than

3.0—those are reasonable. Ratios between 3.0 and 5.0 are cause for concern; you would probably pay too much for the company's future earnings. In the bull market of 1983, some new issues came to market at ratios around 10.0. Within two years, virtually all of these stocks declined 80%–90% in value.

• Book value per share. Pay no more than 1.5 times book value per share. Few technology investors look at book value because high-tech companies are usually too young to have accumulated much stockholders' equity (the basis of book value). However, book value is vital if you are looking at long-term rates of return on an investment. For example, an exciting high-tech company may earn a sensational return on book value (earnings/book value per share)—say, 36% per year. However, if you buy the stock at 4.0 times book value, you may be paying too much despite the high returns; if you divide 36% by 4.0, your long-term return is only 9%.

• Price/Earnings Ratio. Pay a price/earnings ratio that is no more than ⅓ of the company's growth rate. For example, if a company is growing at 27% per year, pay no more than 9 times earnings for the stock. For 50% growth, pay no more than 17 times earnings for the stock. Only professional investors should ever pay more than 20 times earnings. Growth rates are calculated by looking at how fast you expect the market and the company's revenues to grow over the next five years. For earnings, always use the most recent four quarters of data (trailing 12 months).

It's very likely that no stock will meet all three of these strict rules. However, if, for a particular stock, you calculate a hypothetical price for each rule and then average the three prices, you will have a good estimate of the downside risk in the stock. Try not to pay more than 20% above the downside-risk average estimate. This will help you to limit your potential losses and to invest in well-managed, fast-growing companies at attractive prices.

Source: Michael Murphy, CFA, is founding editor of *California Technology Stock Letter,* 155 Montgomery St., Suite 1401, San Francisco 94104. He has been following high-tech stocks for more than 15 years.

How To Win With Small Pharmaceuticals and Biotech Stocks

Small pharmaceuticals and biotech companies comprise the most rapidly growing portion of the health care industry. These high-growth companies, many with speculative figures, are worthwhile investments if their stocks are purchased on the basis of what the companies can earn three to five years down the road, not in the next six months.

Your criteria for investment in these companies should be the same as for other high-growth stocks—high-quality management, a strong product line, solid financial performance, and reliable customer support. Also, small pharmaceutical and biotech stocks are uniquely affected by government regulations, namely, the Food and Drug Administration (FDA) approval process. (The FDA determines when new pharmaceutical products are introduced or marketed to the public.) A company's reputation with the FDA, though difficult to measure, can be critical to the success of its operations. What to look at:

- The history of product approvals (how many approvals over how many years).
- Product recalls (Any? How many?).
- Time periods from original application to approval.

What Investors Should Look For

- Above-average growth rates in sales (especially unit volumes) and earnings. Any company growing in excess of 15% compounded over the past five years is a good initial candidate. Beware of companies with 50+% growth rates. Such growth puts great strain on an organization and cannot be maintained for long without problems.
- Proprietary products or services. These include a drug that captures high market share, a biotech diagnostic kit or machine that does the same. Find out who buys the product. Are they blue-chip customers or average customers? Why do they keep buying the product?

- Experienced management. Look closely at the background of the company's officers (found in the 10K and proxy statement). Are they from older, established drug companies or research houses? Have they had experience with the FDA and the medical end-user community? Are they well respected in the medical community? Is their strategy for the company clear and achievable? Do you feel comfortable entrusting your money to these entrepreneurs? Go to the annual meeting, if you can, to see the officers and meet them. (At least get transcripts of the president's recent speeches.) Also note the flow of key people into and out of the organization, as well as whether employees are exercising their stock options.

- Cash, cash flow, and a strong balance sheet. Superior products generally produce above-average margins (pretax income/sales and net income/sales). High margins mean high reinvestment rates and usually low debt-to-equity ratios. Compare a company's balance sheet with its competitors. Watch out for high levels of debt or low levels of cash. What is the historical trend in the company's pretax income margin? Look for pretax margins of 15%–25%. Return on capital (net income/all debt plus stockholders' equity) should be 10% or better. The rate of spending on R&D should be 10% of sales or better.

Purchase Price and Timing

When you're ready to make an investment, review the price/earnings multiple. If a company has a 30% compounded growth rate and is expected to grow at 20%–30% per year for the next three to five years, expect to pay 20 to 30 times the trailing 12-month earnings. Example: Company *A* earned $1 per share in its January 1986 fiscal year. $20–$30 per share is a reasonable price, if Company *A* is expected to experience a 20%–30% compounded growth rate through the 1989–91 period. Beware of paying more than 35–40 times earnings.

Also look at the timing of your purchase. Buy stock at two or three different times, investing the same dollar amount in each purchase. This will smooth out acquisition costs and the price/earnings ratio.

A portfolio of 20 carefully selected high-growth companies should include three to five health-care companies. If you are in the medical profession, you may want to lean more heavily toward health-care companies, to reflect your personal interest and knowledge. Expect 25%–30% of your high-growth companies to experience problems, delays, crises, etc.; the best 60% of your holdings should be able to carry your portfolio.

Source: Samuel S. Talbot, founder and president of Growth Stock Services, Inc., 68 Beacon Street, Boston 02108, a contract research provider. He manages a recommended securities list, which is a personal portfolio; the list and a monthly newsletter are published for institutional fund managers.

How To Win With Home Furnishing Stocks

Home furnishing stocks were once considered dull, conservative investments. Not anymore. In recent years, excellent price performance in these stocks has forced professional money managers to take a fresh look at the home furnishings industry.

Industry Cycles

The best way to make money with home furnishing stocks is to closely follow the industry's cycles. Furniture and carpeting are postponable purchases. When consumer confidence is low, unemployment high, and housing activity sluggish, consumers tend to limit their buying of these items.

The best barometer of future furnishings sales is housing activity (the sale and exchange of new and existing homes—not just housing starts). Interest rates, in turn, are usually the best indicator of future housing activity. So, understanding trends in interest rates allows you to foretell the intermediate outlook for the housing industry and the home furnishings industry. A good point to remember is

that manufacturers who target the lower end of the market are more affected by economic cycles than those who target their products to the middle and high end of the market.

In addition to cycles in the economy, home furnishings manufacturers are affected by cycles in style and products. The manufacturer that enjoys great product success one year may not be able to repeat or continue that success once the style or product acceptance has leveled off.

Investors caught at the wrong part of the business cycle needn't despair, however. As the "baby boom" population continues to age, the underlying demand for home furnishings will generally continue to rise—at least to the mid-1990s. With these stocks, patience will usually reward an investor with an upturn.

Price Movements and Float

Recently, major home furnishing manufacturers have traded between a 30% discount to the Standard & Poor's 500 p/e ratio to a 30% premium. A useful investment strategy is to examine the price moves of several attractive home furnishing stocks to determine their potential appreciation. Find the stock whose performance has been poor. If the underlying fundamentals are sound (*i.e.,* strong financials, good management, etc.), this stock will offer the best chance for appreciation. Stocks that have recently had superior price movements or are trading at high premiums, will not appreciate as quickly.

Float is the percentage of a company's total stock outstanding that is actively traded in the open market. Major home furnishing stocks, especially over-the-counter stocks, have traditionally had small floats, causing the prices of these stocks to move strongly, up or down, on relatively small trades. For this reason, do not make large purchases or sales all at once; make them over an extended period of time. Otherwise, the price will go up when you try to buy or decline when you try to sell.

Source: Budd Bugatch, security analyst for Baker, Watts & Company, 100 Light Street, Baltimore 21202. He is responsible for coverage of the furniture industry.

How To Win in Insurance Stocks

If you're looking for a sound investment don't neglect the insurance industry—it's one of the longest-running growth shows in town. The insurance business is unique because it is populated both by 100-year-old companies that continue to grow and by fast-growing newcomers whose first-generation management is still in control.

Diversity and Opportunity

Insurance companies differ in size, operating characteristics, profitability, and stock market price action. This diversity can represent a potential headache for some but an opportunity for those who take their investment homework seriously.

The three broad categories of insurance companies are life insurance, property/casualty, and multiline companies. Today, there are very few "pure" life or "pure" property/casualty companies. Most firms specialize in one or the other area, but have subsidiaries involved in a variety of other lines of the business.

Until recently, life insurance companies were considered relatively predictable investments. Any life insurer with good products, solid marketing, and adequate expense control could be counted on to show healthy, stable returns over both the short and long run. Property/casualty insurers were usually more cyclical than pure life insurers—their earnings tied to competitive conditions and catastrophe experience—but over the long haul, property/casualty companies also produced healthy rates of return.

During the last few years, the life insurance industry has gone through a product revolution in response to high and volatile interest rates. The introduction of new interest-sensitive and investment-type policies has caused problems for many traditional companies serving the upscale market, and created exciting opportunities for aggressive competitors. Some companies have suffered substantial earnings declines for the first time in their operating histories while others have grown faster than most people believed life insurers could.

Property/casualty insurers, meanwhile, have continued their cyclical way with a vengeance. This time around, excessive competition for commercial business from 1979 to 1984 severely curtailed earning power for the best of companies and crippled others that lacked the necessary financial and management resources. Since then, pricing and terms have improved dramatically so that earnings for well-positioned underwriters are moving up strongly.

On the investment side of their business, insurance companies are receiving lower yields on new funds being generated by operations, but the decline in interest rates has increased the value of their older portfolio holdings resulting in substantial realized and unrealized capital gains. While this illustrates the fact that lower interest rates are really a mixed blessing to insurance companies as investors, there is little doubt that the shares of these growth stocks benefit from a low inflation and interest rate environment.

Guidelines for Investment

• Look beyond the big names. Size does not necessarily go hand in hand with growth, profitability, or quality. The problem with the strategy of most investors, including a large number of professionals, is that they limit their participation in the insurance industry to the biggest, best-known insurers, usually because it's too much trouble to investigate and follow the lesser-known names. That's a mistake. The bigger the insurance company, the more efficiently priced its stock will be and the less chance you will have of making large price gains.

• Emphasize the differences. The insurance industry's diversity means that economic and other events can have equally diverse effects. In any typical year, apparently similar firms may experience opposite market price actions and valuations, particularly if they operate in limited geographical areas or specialized market niches. It pays to know the companies—

how or why they are unlike their competitors—before you invest, in order to take advantage of low prices resulting from market inefficiencies.

• Examine management. The most important investment task is to recognize differences in managements and identify those best equipped for the particular demands of their business. While this is difficult to accomplish without personal contact, much can be learned from annual reports and the trade press. Is management motivated by the same goals as shareholders (*i.e.,* long-term growth in earnings, dividends, and market price)? Is management consistent—does it stick to areas that make sense in light of its resources and abilities? Is management willing to change when conditions point to potential problems? Beware, however, of companies that plan to move aggressively into a new or untested area of business. If the market is already filled with a large number of competitors, chances are that a new player will have little chance of making money.

• Be an investor, not a trader. A successful insurance operation takes time to develop; when you find a good one, stick with it. Overtrading, trying to catch popularity swings or profit cycles, can produce very poor results. By the same token, don't be afraid to change your mind if your ongoing research suggests a faulty initial premise or an adverse change in long-term conditions.

• Diversify to reduce risk. In an industry with hundreds of companies to choose from, it makes sense to invest in more than one or two issues unless you are certain that those are the best to own without any question. If your basic selection process is sound, diversification reduces the risk that an occasional loss will ruin your entire investment program.

• Average your cost per share. Since it's virtually impossible to predict the market's short-term direction, investing all of your available funds at one time is bad strategy. The safer alternative is to buy equal dollar amounts at intervals, buying more shares when prices are low, fewer shares when prices rise. The results are a lower average cost for your total holdings

as well as an increased number of opportunities to reevaluate the soundness of your investment program.

Source: William W. Dyer, trustee, Century Shares Trust, One Liberty Square, Boston 02109, a mutual fund worth more than $150 million concentrated in insurance company stocks. In addition to being an insurance stock analyst for more than 20 years, he has written articles in a variety of financial journals.

Make Money With Communications Stocks

The communications industry has undergone great changes over the last two decades as a result of the combined effects of new technology and a national trend toward competition in place of regulation. The divestiture of AT&T's local telephone operations into seven regional holding companies has set the stage for accelerated growth and new opportunities for communications companies and investors alike. The future growth of telecommunications stocks will be driven by more cost-effective pricing of services, a broader range of product offerings, and more aggressive marketing.

Evaluating communications companies in this changing environment requires a very different set of measures than was previously used by investors. Here are some of the more important indicators used to analyze these investments.

• Return on equity is still the most important measure of a telephone company's performance. All local telephone companies—and, for the present, AT&T—are regulated on a rate-of-return basis. The best non-Bell companies earn more than 15%. The stocks with the greatest chance for appreciation will be from companies whose earnings are less than 15%, but who have the prospect of earning more in the future.

• Dividend increases tend to raise stock prices. Look for companies with lower-than-average dividend payout ratios. They are more likely to increase their dividends, and thereby increase the price of their stock so as to maintain a constant yield level.

• Growth in telephone company earnings is generated from three primary sources: rate increases, growth in customer base, and expense reduction. Almost all telephone companies are engaged in reducing their operations staff levels and upgrading their plant efficiency, so it will be difficult to distinguish companies on the basis of cost cutting. More importantly, companies located in higher-growth areas, such as the Sun Belt and California, will probably show larger growth in their core businesses.

• Local regulators still have considerable influence over the financial health of telephone companies. Look for responsive commissions that can strengthen a company's ability to earn more attractive returns and compete more effectively against potential competitors.

• Check a company's accomplishments in new businesses, such as cellular mobile radios, premise equipment sales, consulting and tenant services. These new areas are all capable of contributing significantly to earnings and thereby have a strong impact on a company's overall growth rate.

• Competition in major markets is increasing rapidly. The result may be that new growth will not be channeled through the local operating companies. To retain the high-profit business segment of the market, companies are being forced to lower prices. The effect has been that local operating companies may retain customers, but significantly reduce overall profit margins.

• New technology provides significant benefits to the companies that utilize it. For example, digital switching offers lower purchase and operating costs and allows the delivery of an expanded, more flexible array of services.

• Local telephone company dividend yields are closely tied to bond yields. As with bonds, if yields increase, prices will tend to drop. Therefore, telephone company stocks will perform best when there is a declining interest-rate outlook.

Companies To Consider

In the interexchange, or long-distance, market, AT&T's competitors have a unique opportunity to gain market share and additional revenues. Who are the likely challengers? Companies equipped with efficient networks of their own, such as MCI Communications and U.S. Sprint.

In the local exchange business, the Bell regional companies are still finding their way after the AT&T breakup. So far, they have exhibited impressive financial results. Bell regional companies are less diversified than non-Bell companies such as GTE Corporation, Contel Corporation, or United Telecom. As a result, they bear less risk of new venture losses. These factors make the regional Bell companies a good focus for investor attention.

Source: Neil D. Yelsey, telecommunications services analyst for Salomon Brothers, Inc., One New York Plaza, New York 10004. The areas he covers include Bell regional companies, non-Bell telephone companies, and long-distance carriers.

Investing in Entertainment

For most people, the entertainment business has an aura of glamour and excitement that make other investments pale in comparison. But don't be blinded by the glitter; the business is far more complicated than it first appears and the chances of making money in it are not always good. For example, out of 10 feature films, an average of seven may be unprofitable to the producer, one will break even, and two will make money. The first rule to remember when investing in entertainment is that in order to really come out ahead, your few winners must more than make up for many losers.

There are basically two entertainment investment options: Direct purchases of the equity and debt securities of publicly traded companies that produce and distribute feature films and television programs; and purchases of shares in a limited partnership that may provide some tax advantages.

Limited Partnerships

Prior to 1986 tax code revisions, many large brokerage firms offered some form of entertainment limited partnership. These partnerships provided investors with a tax write-off of their investment and a reasonable chance of making a long-term profit. For example, one popular partnership cushioned risk through depreciation write-offs against ordinary income. In addition, initial cash investments were returned before the film studio and/or distributor took a full distribution fee (which would normally be 30% of gross receipts). Under the new rules, however, master limited partnerships will likely be structured along the lines of an interest-free loan, perhaps with an equity kicker. The investor receives a guarantee for the return of the original capital over, say, a five-year period. Post-1986, tax advantages will be minimal.

Stock and Bonds

The major publicly held entertainment companies are involved primarily in the production and distribution of feature films and television programs. Securities are available for the large studio/distributors such as Warner Communications, Disney, and MCA. There is also Coca-Cola, which owns Columbia Pictures, and Gulf & Western, which owns Paramount. The large studios finance feature films, handle the distribution of movies made by independents, and also own extensive libraries of films used in the pay cable, home video, and syndicated television markets. In these large companies, the impact of a hit film or series is diluted over many shares, whereas the positive effects of a hit are more clearly felt if the originating company is smaller.

Smaller production companies principally engaged in the production of feature films include the Cannon Group, Orion Pictures, New World Pictures, and a slew of others. Small, independent film-makers cushion their risk by preselling exhibition rights to various ancillary markets. However, such strategies also often put a lid on upside earnings potential.

Emerging investment sectors encompass independent video publishers/distributors of feature films and other programming materials. These companies, including Vestron, Inc., Prism, and Commtron, for example, service special niches.

Specialty television programming companies focus on the production and/or distribution of television series either to networks for the evening prime-time viewing periods or to the syndication market, which is comprised of television stations. Syndicated programs (for example, game shows) are either first-run (produced for the first showing) or derived from a series or program that has completed its network run.

Major companies in the television market include Lorimar-Telepictures, King World, Reeves Communications, Fries Entertainment, and several others (including the large feature-film studios). These have real money-making potential, since television stations are paying higher and higher prices for syndicated programs. The result is that the television distribution and programming business has become very profitable, although changes in the Federal Communications Commission's financial interest and syndication rules (which expire in 1990) could have a significant impact on these earnings over the next several years.

Source: Harold L. Vogel, vice president of Merrill Lynch Capital Markets, World Financial Center, North Tower, New York 10281, as well as the author of *Entertainment Industry Economics*, Cambridge University Press.

How To Pick Leisure Stocks

The great advantage of leisure companies—manufacturers of recreational products such as golf clubs, boats, running shoes, etc.—is that you don't need a Wall Street analyst or industry expert to tell you how a product works and/or how successful it might be. With most leisure stocks, your own judgment is good enough to pick out the potential winners from the losers.

For this reason, leisure stocks are perfect for

the investor with an eye for changes in the public mood. Trends in sports or exercise, such as the jogging craze, or new developments in old products create opportunities for growth almost overnight. For example, a few years ago, there was a strong demand for a boat specifically designed for sports fishermen, one of the largest groups of boat buyers in the country. Several small, innovative companies recognized this need and produced what is now known as the "bass boat." The result was instant success for the companies involved and sizable stock price appreciation for the companies' stockholders.

The second advantage of leisure stocks is that they tend to be much less cyclical than industrial or high-tech stocks. It doesn't seem to matter whether the economy is good or bad, once Americans take an activity to heart, money is no object in acquiring the equipment to pursue it.

Remember, however, that identifying emerging trends in the leisure market or potentially hot new products is only half the battle. You still have to make sure the company fulfills the rest of your investment criteria—strong growth rates, solid, innovative management, a strong balance sheet, etc.

Also, with any industry governed by popular taste, you have to be careful of investing in companies that rely on one particular trend for most of their earnings. If the trend is short-lived or brings with it a great number of competitors, as was the case with running shoes, you may see your company's profits squeezed from all sides.

Source: Scott Miles, president, Miles & West Insurance Agency, Inc., 12221 Merit Dr., Suite 940, Dallas 75251. He is responsible for marketing and finance at the agency.

Selling Is the Toughest Decision

Numerous investors, who pick the right stock and watch the price increase dramatically, see most or all of their gains eliminated because they don't have the discipline or foresight to get out of their investments when the going is good. This is what is called the "selling trap."

If an investment goes up in price, the trapped investor doesn't want to sell because the investment may continue to appreciate and/or a stiff tax will have to be paid on the gain. In the case of an investment that declines in value, the investor doesn't want to sell because he or she doesn't want a loss or because there is always the chance the investment will return to its former price level.

To avoid the selling trap, clearly define the criteria for the sale of your investment at or before the time of the investment. Once you've set up your criteria, you must have the discipline to stick to them.

Avoidance Tactics

• Set defined limits on price movements to reduce your losses. This can be done on a percentage basis (15% on the downside and 50% on the upside). Communicate these limits to your broker.

• If the investment moves up in price, sell half of the position to lock in the gain. Keep the remainder for potential future gains.

• Hedge your investments. If there are listed options traded on an investment, use them. Purchase a "put" (the right to sell a security at a certain price in the future) against the position. These options reduce the downside risk and produce extra income.

• If a stock goes up in value, don't risk your profits. If you buy a stock at 30, for example, and it moves to 42 and you feel it is going to move higher, try one of these maneuvers:

1. Put a stop-loss order in to sell the stock at 39 or 39½.

2. If there are listed options, buy a 40 put.

3. Sell the stock short against the box—this will protect a profit and defer recognizing a gain.

• If you purchase a security in anticipation of a certain event (*i.e.,* speculation of a buyout or the success of a new product) and the event does not become a reality, reevaluate the security and ask the question, "Would I buy it now at today's price?" If the answer is no, sell the investment and switch to one that makes sense.

• If you're holding a security for which a tender offer has been made, sell the security in the marketplace rather than run the risk of the deal falling through. Holding and tendering to get the last 10% can be costly.

• When an investment begins to sour, don't wait to figure out what to do with the funds before divesting. The sale decision should be made on its own merits. Short-term money market instruments can be your interim investment vehicles.

• Finally, distinguish between tax and investment considerations. With the tax changes in the Tax Reform Act of 1986, many people made changes in their portfolios just to realize profits at a lower capital gains rate in 1986 than would be in effect in 1987 and later years.

While taxes are an important consideration, more important are what one considers the outlook for the basic investment. Do you want to hold it for a short period of time (one to two years) or for many more years; what you think you can earn with what is left after paying taxes even at a lower rate; and the overall balance/imbalance of the portfolio. It is more desirable to pay some taxes and realize a profit than to hold on and have an investment decline to the point where there is no profit to tax.

Source: Derick L. Driemeyer, CFA, senior investment strategist and corporate vice president of A.G. Edwards & Sons, Inc., One North Jefferson St., St. Louis, MO 63103, has been with that firm in various research capacities for 17 years. In addition, he authors *Investment Strategy,* a monthly report on investment, which comments on market trends.

Stock Sales Caution

When you sell part of your stock in a company, the IRS assumes that you're selling the first ones purchased. This can be costly if early purchases were much cheaper than sub-

sequent blocks you bought. Example: You purchase 100 shares of a company for $5,000. Six months later you buy another block of 100 shares for $8,000. When the price of the stock drops to $7 per share, you sell 100 shares. Trap: The IRS will assume there's a capital gain of $2,000 and tax it accordingly, unless you direct your broker in writing to sell the second block. In that case, there's a $1,000 loss with no tax due.

Source: Leon Gold, Phillips Gold & Co., CPAs, 1140 Ave. of the Americas, New York 10036.

How To Make Money in The Stock Market in Tough Times

Short selling is easier than you think . . . but it's risky. Short selling involves borrowing common stock from another investor and then selling it in the hope that the stock's price will fall and you'll be able to replace it at a lower price. Instead of going down, however, the stock's price could go up . . . and there's no limit to how high it could go . . . losses can be staggeringly large.

Classic example: In 1901 Northern Pacific Railroad's stock shot up from under $150/share to $1,000 in just a few days—wiping out all short-sellers. Such a big move in a stock's price rarely occurs, but a swing of just 10–20 points can also be devastating to a short-seller. Lesson: Never stay short when the market turns against you—buy the stock back quickly . . . and get out.

Psychological Factors

Short selling is unpopular, and especially unpopular in bull markets, when people think that stocks will go up forever. Of course, no market goes up forever. Signs of an overvalued market ripe for decline:

• Everyone talking about his or her market gains.

• Magazine covers emblazoned with a rampaging bull.

• No one urging caution.

Even when investors think that the market may be headed for trouble, most either just refrain from buying stock or move to cash. These are solid protective steps. But they don't enable investors to make money in a downturn—as short selling does.

Underrecognized: Investors can actually make money much faster by selling stocks short than by buying them as investments. Reason: Stocks go down much more rapidly than they go up. Typically, if it takes a stock a year to go from $20/share to $30, it can fall back from $30 to $20 in as little as two or three days in a bear market.

There's a place for short selling in any kind of market. Investors who have a substantial portfolio ($50,000 or more) should hedge by putting 5%–10% of capital into short sales.

Selecting Shorts

Companies are always eager to talk about good news that they expect, but in order to find out about possible earnings declines or dividend cuts, short-sellers must do their own homework. Signs that a sector is overvalued:

• A sharp run-up in stock prices in that sector.

• Stock sector analysts rationalizing the run-up and claiming that the stocks are still undervalued.

• Extensive media coverage.

Signs that a stock is overvalued:

• A rapid price increase on the promise of a concept that's caught people's imagination but hasn't yet been developed into a marketable product.

• The company finally coming out with a new product that was extensively promoted but doesn't measure up to its promise.

• The stock hitting a new low in volume after a long increase.

In general, when a sector weakens it's best to short the companies that have been laggards. They will decline first and furthest.

Source: Louis Ehrenkrantz, director, Ehrenkrantz & King, money managers, 50 Broadway, New York 10004. Mr. Ehrenkrantz also manages the Ehrenkrantz Fund (an open-end mutual fund) and is publisher of *The Ehrenkrantz Letter.*

Protection from Short-Selling Risks

Although short selling is frequently used, the risks are great. To protect yourself: Leave a buy-stop order with your broker, limiting possible losses. . . avoid shorting stocks at new highs, since they often continue to climb. . . don't short thinly traded stocks that you may be forced to replace in the event of a "short squeeze."

Source: Stan Weinstein, publisher, *The Professional Tape Reader,* quoted in *Fortune.*

Selling Short in a Bull Market

Short selling opportunities develop even during bull markets. Most such markets are interrupted at least once by a severe decline.

Suggestions for profitable short selling:

• Sell only heavily capitalized issues with a low outstanding short interest. They are less likely to be subject to a short squeeze (sharp rallies caused by many short sellers rushing to cover and too few shares available).

• Cover short sales during moments of market weakness. Take advantage of market declines that are stimulated by bad news to cover into periods of weakness. Warning: Do not wait for a rally to cover shorts. What the pros do: Cover short sales just before weekends in case favorable news triggers sharp Monday rallies.

• As an alternative to selling short, consider the purchase of puts (selling an option contract at a stated price on or before a fixed expiration date).

• A stock that is sold short can decline by only so much, but there's no limit on how much it can rise. Result: Short selling bucks the odds because the ultimate risk is always greater than the potential reward. Place stop loss orders to cover when the short sale goes against you by more than 10%–15%.

• Sell short stocks that show definite signs of overhead resistance (areas of heavy trading in that stock just above your short selling level) on their charts. Such areas tend to impede upside progress.

• Do not sell those short issues that have just made new highs. Wait for definite signs of weakness before selling short.

Source: *Personal Finance,* Kephart Communications, Alexandria, VA.

What To Do When A Company You Have Invested in Goes Bankrupt

You basically have two choices when a company you've invested in goes bankrupt: Sell the stock and take a loss; or hold the stock and hope the company and its stock recover.

A bankrupt company will do one of two things. It may reorganize under Chapter 11, in which case it is maintained as a viable public entity and given the chance to reverse its losses and pay back its creditors. Or, the company may be dissolved as a public entity under Chapter 7 or 13, with its assets liquidated to pay back the creditors. Both outcomes are decided by a bankruptcy court on the basis of creditors' needs and the ability of the company to repay its debts.

The worst case for the owner of common stock occurs when the company files under Chapter 7 or 13. After the firm's liquidation, taxes, wages, and court costs receive top priority. Debt holders and preferred stockholders are next—common stockholders are last in line. Most often, liquidation barely raises enough cash for the company's debt holders.

The best scenario for stockholders occurs when the company is allowed to reorganize under Chapter 11, is made profitable in a relatively short period of time (a few years), and its creditors are paid back. Then the stock may recover a portion of its value or even return to its original price.

There are several questions you must ask yourself, when deciding what to do with your stock. First and foremost, how likely is it that the company will be allowed to reorganize under Chapter 11? If you think the firm will be liquidated, it's probably better to sell the stock when you can still get a fraction of its original value. However, if the company is allowed to reorganize, what are the chances of the stock recovering even part of what you paid for it? What are the opportunity costs of holding it—that is, what could you do with the money if you sold the stock? What value is the tax loss to you this year? Can you handle the emotional stress involved in holding a bankrupt company?

One of the decision-making problems you face is that you can't know how long bankruptcy proceedings will last: They may end in a couple of months or drag on for years without a satisfactory resolution. Another problem is that the company may come out of reorganization, not make a profit, and fizzle back into Chapter 11 later. Your biggest risk is that after the company goes into Chapter 11, it may run into hard times and be liquidated under Chapter 7 or 13.

Risk Reduction Tactics

The best way to minimize your risk is to remain well informed at all times. Try determining what the bankruptcy court will decide before its decision is announced. Unfortunately, once a company goes into bankruptcy proceedings, information becomes scarce, but you can look for indications that the company can pay back even a portion of its debt.

The single most important indicator to look for is available cash flow. If the company has sufficient cash flow to pay down debts slowly at some modest discount from full value, it's likely the court will allow the company to exist. But beware of dilution. The company may try to issue new shares as a way of raising additional capital. While stock issues are a good sign that the investment community has faith in the company's future, they also mean that the value of your shares will decline.

Profitable divisions of the company can help your chances of recovering your equity.

In many cases, bankruptcies are due to one or two unprofitable divisions of a diversified company. If a large part of the company is still profitable, there's a good chance the unprofitable divisions can be sold or shut down.

A strong equity holders' committee can help, too. These committees are established after bankruptcy is announced and serve as the only means for stockholders to influence the outcome of the legal proceedings.

If you are a large stockholder in the company or just want to play an active role in the proceedings, you have a good shot at becoming a member of the equity holders' committee. This will give you access to a great deal of information. The only drawback is that you will be considered an insider by the Securities & Exchange Commission and severely restricted in your buying and/or selling of the company's stock.

Source: Kenneth L. Fisher, chief executive of Fisher Investments, 301 Henrik Road, Woodside, CA 94062, an investment management firm. Mr. Fisher is the author of a regular column in *Forbes* and of a book, *Super Stocks.*

Before Investing in a Foreign Company

If you're unsure about a foreign company being all it claims to be, check to see if it has been put on the Securities & Exchange Commission's "Foreign Restricted List." Call the SEC at 202-272-2309.

Foreign Investing Risks

(1) If you buy stock in a country whose currency falls against the dollar, gains in the share price are reduced by the currency loss. (2) Information about most foreign companies is less detailed than that of US companies. That adds to the risk of buying the shares. (3) Most foreign stock markets are so small that a single large share transaction can swing the entire market.

Source: John Rutledge, writing in his *Main Street Journal,* Claremont, CA.

Good Way To Buy Foreign Stocks

Foreign stocks need not always be bought on exchanges abroad. Easier: Buying shares of a foreign company through American Depository Receipts (ADRs). These instruments are available for some foreign stocks. They trade on US exchanges and are treated just like US securities. They generally are available in units that represent one to 10 shares of a foreign company's stock. They certify that the shares have been bought and are being held by a custodian outside the United States. Advantages: Lower brokerage commissions than on trades of actual foreign shares . . . dividends paid in US dollars.

Source: Joseph Velli, ADR business manager at the Bank of New York in New York City.

A Safe Way To Invest in Foreign Stocks

Foreign stock investments should be hedged against fluctuations in their countries' currency. Each position in a country's stock should be paired with an opposite forward position in the country's currency. This will eliminate changes in stock value due to changes in currency value and result in a portfolio that can be compared with US equity portfolios.

Source: Michael Adler, professor, Columbia University, Graduate School of Business.

Convertible Bonds

Convertible bonds are hybrid securities that carry a fixed interest rate like a bond, but may be exchanged for a specified amount of the issuing company's common stock. (Usually the issuer will spell out several limitations regarding when and how conversion can take place.) Convertibles' dual character produces dual advantages. The bonds provide you with interest income that is usually higher than what you would receive from a common stock dividend, but lower than the income from a straight debt security. At the same time, the bonds' convertibility feature gives you the chance to play the stock market.

Convertibles act as a compromise investment for times when you are uncertain about the future of the bond market and uncertain about the future of the stock market. When stock prices climb, convertibles rise. When they fall, convertibles don't fall quite as quickly, and still pay you reasonable current income. As a result, convertibles allow you to smooth out the effects of a volatile stock market.

What To Watch For

Keep an eye on the market for rare opportunities. There are situations in which the market for convertible bonds and the market for the bonds' underlying stocks are not well coordinated. The result is inefficient pricing. In these situations, it is possible that (1) a bond's underlying common stock actually provides a higher yield than the convertible, and/or (2) the convertible bond is selling at or below its conversion value. Both situations would allow you to purchase the underlying common stock at a discount.

Convertibles are fairly complex instruments to understand. The pricing can get tricky and most individual investors end up paying a fairly large premium for the opportunity to play both the bond and stock markets. Also, by trying to have the best of both worlds, you can severely limit your potential gain from either one. Remember, too, if both the bond and the stock markets drop, the price of a convertible could decline substantially.

Special notes on buying and selling:

• Before buying a convertible bond, check its "call" provisions—the right of the issuer to redeem your security. Call provisions can sometimes have a very substantial effect on the price of a bond over time.

• When you decide to convert a bond into its common stock equivalent, wait until after the next interest payout. Interest on convertibles is paid semiannually and does not accrue.

• Unless you are a large investor, consider using no-load mutual funds, which specialize in convertible bonds.

Source: Jay Goldinger, an investment broker specializing in tax-advantaged investments and fixed income securities with Cantor, Fitzgerald and Company, Inc., 232 North Canon Drive, Beverly Hills, CA 90210.

A Sleep-Easy Bond Investment System

Consistency can be the best policy for investors who want to conserve their capital. A good number of affluent investors deliberately ignore the hoopla of the stock market and follow an almost humdrum technique of bond investing that allows them to sleep well at night. It's a technique that could be adopted right now by investors who want to realize their gains from the equity market but haven't been sure about what's the best place to put the money.

The simple idea is to *ladder* the maturities in a portfolio of bonds that come due over the next 10 years. That means putting 10% of the allocated funds into a bond that matures in 10 years, 10% into one that matures in nine years, 10% into one that matures in eight years, etc. The key: Stay in intermediate issues, going no further out than 10 years. Laddering smooths out risk because:

• The average maturity in the portfolio is about five years, at which point the investor will realize 100¢ on the dollar—no matter what happens to interest rates in the meantime.

• Intermediate bonds are not likely to

decline more than 20% below face value, even in a severely depressed bond market. (Long-term bonds, however, are much more volatile and can lose 40% on their value.)

• Each year at least 10% of the capital can be renewed at current interest rates. That provides an opportunity to raise the yield on the entire portfolio if interest rates go up, and it keeps the overall yield fairly high even when rates start to drop.

Comfortable Returns

Investors who have stuck with this technique in recent years are very likely now enjoying top-quality bond portfolios that yield about 10% or top-grade municipal portfolios that yield about 8%–8½%.

The chief value of this approach, however, is that it produces returns stable enough that bond investors are not so tempted to panic at the wrong moment if interest rates go up and the value of their bonds declines. Many individual investors dumped their long-term bonds in 1981 after seeing 40% of their value evaporate and—just at the wrong time—went into short-term Treasuries.

Investment Strategy

Construct a ladder with Treasuries and government agency bonds (such as Federal Home Loan Bank or Student Loan Marketing Association issues). Corporate bonds might be used in the five-, six- or seven-year steps of the ladder to increase the overall yield. They're rarely issued for the shorter terms. But investors on their own should not accept ratings below AA in building their laddered bond portfolios. In selecting a bond fund, look for one that doesn't dip below A ratings for its selections.

Of course, issuers call in bonds and pay them off at face value if they have the opportunity to do so when interest rates decline. For the investor using a laddered technique, counting on the yield over time, calls are a disruption. But the callability problem is negligible in a ladder of intermediates. Most municipals with a term of 10 years or less are not callable. Treasuries and agency issues are usually not callable at all.

Conservative laddering such as this can get

way out of sync with current market yields if interest rates go up sharply and relentlessly over a three- or four-year period. But rates rarely do that. Even in the steep climb of the 1970s, rates bobbed around on an upward trend line. Bond investors who used this laddering technique fared far better than those who were fully exposed in long-term issues.

To build a laddered municipal portfolio most effectively, an investor needs about $1 million, because the round-lot purchase is around $100,000. However, it can be done relatively effectively with about $250,000, putting $25,000 at each step of the ladder. With any sum less than that, most investors would be safer with the diversification of a municipal bond fund that uses a similar investment strategy.

Source: David Lindsay, senior vice president, David L. Babson & Co., Inc., 1 Boston Place, Boston 02108. Mr. Lindsay manages the Babson Bond Trust, the Babson Tax-Free Income Fund (which has one portfolio run by the laddered technique described in this article) and the Babson Money Market Fund.

Deep-Discount Bonds

Investing in deep-discount corporate and government bonds near their maturity dates is a low-risk way to generate profits and offset capital losses. Many of the bonds in today's secondary bond market are high-grade corporate bonds issued in the 1950s and 1960s when coupon rates were as low as 3%–5%. Because these yields are much lower than what many recently issued high-grade corporates are paying, these older bonds sell at a substantial discount from their face value. But, when deep-discount bonds reach maturity, they appreciate significantly because they can be redeemed at full face value. And, because they are purchased near maturity, the bonds do not fluctuate in price but steadily increase until they reach 100, or par.

Holders of deep-discount bonds, therefore, receive the same total income as they would from a regular bond, even though most of it comes only when the bond matures. Besides the appreciation, holders collect the coupon income.

But the real appeal of deep-discount bonds is that the appreciation offsets capital losses on a dollar-for-dollar basis. Normally, only $3,000 worth of capital losses can be written off in a single year. However, if an investor had lost, say, $7,000 in the stock market, he could buy deep-discount bonds to generate $7,000 in profits, cancel out the losses on a dollar-for-dollar basis, and have no tax liability whatsoever on those profits.

Source: Jay Goldinger, an investment broker specializing in tax-advantaged investments and fixed income securities with Cantor, Fitzgerald and Company, Inc., 232 North Canon Drive, Beverly Hills, CA 90210.

Investing in Junk Bonds

A few years ago, nobody talked about junk bonds as a viable investment. Today, they're in the news all of the time. Close to 40 mutual funds are active in the junk-bond market, with collective assets of $11 billion.

Technically, junk bonds are bonds that have been assigned a "less than investment grade" rating by either of the bond rating agencies (below a BBB rating from Standard & Poor's or below a Baa rating from Moody's Investor Service). The companies that have junk bonds outstanding fall into two groups: (1) those in need of growth capital, but too small and/or too young to qualify for an investment-grade rating; and (2) larger, usually older companies whose earnings and, more importantly, whose cash flows are too inconsistent to guarantee adequate servicing of their debt obligations. The latter companies have commonly been referred to as "fallen angels."

What makes junk bonds so attractive—especially in a time of declining interest rates—is the large interest rate spread they offer over yields on long-term government bonds. This spread can amount to anywhere from 2.5% to about 5% over US Treasury bonds and all other issues that are keyed to long-term Treasury yields. In other words, the yields on junk bonds can be up to 40% higher. Junk-bond issuers offer such high interest rate spreads as a way of compensating the investor for the extra risk incurred.

How much riskier are junk bonds? Several studies have shown that the additional risk is more than made up for by the higher income the bonds offer. The most famous, the Hickman Study, demonstrated that the lowest-rated corporate bonds, as a group, produced the highest return in spite of a higher default rate; the overall rate was 0.8%. Other studies have shown that junk bonds default at a slightly higher rate—about 1.5%. The methodology of these studies differed in terms of which bonds were included, but all illustrate the importance of a highly diversified portfolio.

Picking the Winners

A number of investment strategies work well with junk bonds. Here are a few:

• Solid companies with a franchise. Buy junk bonds from companies with solid market positions and good products that won't become obsolete. Both Turner Broadcasting and MCI got their expansion financing from the junk-bond market.

• Convertible preferred stock selling on a yield basis. Oftentimes the yields on these hybrid, bondlike securities can be as high or higher than a company's comparable debt security.

• Turnaround situations. Look for industries that are coming out of troubled times. Because of their poor earnings history, any debt security they issue will receive a low rating. But if you're astute, you can pick companies in the industry that are turning around and therefore able to service their debts.

• Troubled industries. A few notorious failures can lower the ratings in an entire industry. While this will affect price, it does not mean that you can't find healthy companies within the industry that offer impressive returns. Savings and loans are a good example of this phenomenon.

Of course, if you're still uneasy about buying single junk bonds and don't have the investment capital to purchase a diversified portfolio, consider the mutual fund route.

Because mutual funds can diversify their portfolios across a broad cross section of the economy, they can offer greater safety while providing high current yields.

Source: Warren K. Greene, president, D.H. Blair Advisors, Inc., Box 2500, Greenwich, CT 06836.

Junk-Bond Myth

Insider trading scandals have jeopardized the smooth functioning of junk-bond markets, thereby increasing the risk for investors. Reality: Even if the scandals lead to federal restrictions, the market for such issues will remain strong. Reasons: There are plenty of competing investment houses eager to enter the market, and bond traders have already discounted the potential impact of scandals.

Source: Glen Parker, publisher, *Income & Safety,* Fort Lauderdale.

Buy Zero-Coupon Bonds Better

Zero-coupon bonds are a powerful but often misunderstood investment tool. How they work: The bond pays no cash interest to its owner. Rather, it's bought at a price far below its face value and is held for appreciation. For example, a 12% 20-year bond that will be worth $100,000 on maturity might be bought for only $10,000 today.

The big benefit derived from these bonds is the compound interest factor. In effect, your return on the bond is automatically reinvested in it at the same interest rate.

Example: The 20-year bond mentioned above provides about $90,000 of appreciation earned at a rate of 12% annually. By contrast, a conventional $10,000 bond earning 12% will pay only $24,000 in cash interest over the same 20 years. It's up to you to find a way to reinvest this cash. If you can't do so at a rate of at least 12%, you'll lose out.

But there are drawbacks to zero-coupon bonds as well:

• The bond's annual appreciation is taxable income to its owner, even though the bond generates no cash with which to pay the tax. Advice: Avoid this tax trap by buying bonds through your IRA or Keogh account, which is tax exempt. Or place a bond in trust for a child who's in a low (or zero) tax bracket.

• The compound interest factor can work against you if interest rates go up after you purchase the bond. When higher interest rates are available from other investments, the market value of your bond might well go down.

• Because of this interest-rate risk, zero-coupon bonds are not good liquid investments. You should plan on holding the bond until it matures.

Zero-coupon bonds can be bought with maturities ranging from six months to 30 years. Bonds may be backed by both federal and local governments, as well as by corporations and banks. Ask your broker for details.

Source: Glen Miller, director of tax, Arthur Young & Co., 1 IBM Plaza, Chicago 60611.

Zero-Coupon Bonds

Zero-coupon bonds, considered one of Wall Street's most appealing "new products," are simply ordinary US government bonds stripped of their coupon yields and sold at a deep discount from their face value. Like US savings bonds or Treasury bills, they pay no current interest to the investor. Instead, the bonds increase in value until they mature, when they can be redeemed at full face value. Interest that normally would have been paid out to the investor over the life of the bond is used to increase the value of the bond.

For example, buy $5,000 worth of zero-coupon bonds due in the year 2006 and appreciating at a compounded rate of 11%, and they are worth $50,000 when they mature.

401

Return, Tax, and Cost Advantages

Zero-coupon bonds offer some of the highest overall returns to be found among US government-backed securities. In addition, they provide a fixed rate of return for the reinvestment of your interest income. The problem with most bonds is that you have to reinvest your interest income. Zero-coupon bonds eliminate the burden of reinvestment, because interest income is reinvested at the rate initially guaranteed to you when you bought the bond.

Zero-coupon bonds are ideal fundings for tax-free or tax-deferred investment vehicles. Their most popular uses are in qualified pension/profit sharing retirement plans, IRAs, Keoghs, or financing a college education. However, be careful how you fund the latter. If the zero bonds are purchased for a custodial account by a parent for a youngster under 14, the unearned income in excess of $1,000 per year accruing inside the zeros is taxable at the parent's tax rate. If the child is over 14, the income is taxable at his rate.

Think twice, also, about investing in zero-coupon bonds if you're not using a tax-advantaged investment vehicle. Even though you don't receive interest payments on a zero-coupon bond, the IRS requires that you pay the annual income tax on interest you would have received. The only exception to this are zero-coupon municipal bonds.

Source: Jay Goldinger, an investment broker specializing in tax-advantaged investments and fixed income securities with Cantor, Fitzgerald and Company, Inc., 232 North Canon Drive, Beverly Hills, CA 90210.

Zero-Bond Trap

• When zero-coupon bonds are called and you miss notification of the call, unredeemed bonds stop earning interest. The longer the bonds go unredeemed, the greater the loss. Investors who move frequently are most vulnerable since many zero-coupon-bond issuers send notice of calls through the mail. Safeguards: (1) Ask the broker who sold you the bonds to check at least twice a year on whether they've been called. (2) If you move, notify the paying agent bank (listed on the bond certificate).

Source: Ben Weberman, senior editor, *Forbes.*

• When zero-coupon bonds are called early, the issuer may have no way of notifying the holders other than through an ad in the financial pages. If you don't see the ad, your money will remain with the issuer at zero interest. Some investors have lost years' worth of earnings.

Source: *Kiplinger Washington Letter.*

New Traps & New Opportunities in Municipal Bonds

There's no such thing as a bad bond. . .at the right price. Tricky: Determining the right price. Though touted by brokerage firms as easy, investing in municipal bonds is anything but straightforward.

Because many municipals offer relatively high tax-exempt yields, they have a legitimate place in the average investor's portfolio. But they're much riskier than money market investments and, of course, less safe than US government securities. Risks:

• If interest rates rise, the market value of the bonds falls.

• Defaults are uncommon but do occur, especially in nonrated revenue bonds.

• If there were a bond market crisis,* issues that trade inactively in small markets usually would be difficult to sell at a fair price.

Trap: Trying to navigate through this market with the help of the average registered representative. . . most lack the expertise required.

Better: Take your municipal bond business to a firm that specializes in municipals. Alternative: Deal with your bank's or brokerage firm's municipal bond department. Often individual investors must push hard to get to speak with a municipal bond analyst, but it's worth the trouble.

Unit Investment Trusts

Diversification is, of course, the best way to reduce the risk in any single type of investment. One simple way of diversifying in municipals is to buy through a unit investment trust (UIT), which is a diversified, unmanaged portfolio of bonds. Investors buy shares in it called "units." The composition of the portfolio remains fixed, and all bonds are held until maturity.

Drawbacks: Most UITs carry a sales commission of 4.5% or more. . .and also charge you .25%–.50% a year in various fees and administrative costs. You could save money by simply buying individual top-quality bonds.

Another disadvantage of UITs is that the market to buy and sell units is essentially set up by the firm that acts as the sponsor. Risk: If a sponsor is acquired or merged into another firm, investors have no assurance that the new sponsor will run the units market as well as the original sponsor. If your circumstances make it necessary to sell units back to the new sponsor, you may not get a fair price.

Mutual Funds

Mutual funds are managed portfolios of bonds. Many carry loads (sales commissions)—usually 5%–8.5%—but some are no-load. Since all studies have shown that there is no difference in performance between load and no-load funds, always buy no-load.

In general, mutual funds make the most sense for people investing in higher-yield, lower-quality issues. Reason: Constant monitoring of changing market conditions is a must. If, however, you invest in top-grade, lower-yield municipals, you may be better off buying and holding UIT units or individual bonds.

Individual Issues

If you buy individual bonds, a key concern is call protection. Read and fully understand the fine print that specifies when an issuer may call in a bond—that is, cancel its debt obligation to bondholders and return their principal.

Issuers tend to call in bonds when interest rates have fallen and they can refinance their debt at lower rates. Problem: Investors with returned principal are then stuck reinvesting it at the lower rates. Recommended: In general, look for 10-year call protection.

Zero-Coupon Bonds

Zero-coupon bonds are purchased at a deep discount and pay off at face value at maturity. Because the imputed interest is automatically reinvested at a given rate (rather than paid out), prices of zeros swing much more widely than those of ordinary bonds as interest rates fluctuate.

Added risk: They are usually more vulnerable to early calls. Especially vulnerable: Housing bonds issued prior to September 1, 1982. These were issued in bearer form, which means that the trustee has no record of where individual bonds are. Danger: When a bondholder goes to collect at what he thinks is maturity, he may find that his bond was called years earlier. . .and that he's earned nothing since then. Protection: If you own zero-coupon bonds that are not registered, have your broker keep a close watch on called bond numbers.

Junk Bonds

In the municipal sector, junk bonds are bonds issued by cities that have financial problems (Cleveland, Detroit, New York). . . bonds of big public power projects that either have been unsuccessful or have a cloud over them. . .pollution-control bonds for companies whose corporate debt is considered junk grade. . . bonds of nursing homes, life-care facilities and hospitals that either are heavily in debt or are in distressed areas.

There are a number of well-managed junk (or high-yield) municipal bond mutual funds. They offer diversification, and their managers work hard to follow the financial health of lower-grade issues. . . but theirs may be an impossible task. Danger: The municipal junk-bond market has never been tested in a general market down cycle. . . no one knows what might happen if in a crisis the big funds tried to unload substantial portions of their portfolios all at the same time.

Safest Plays

Longer-term, escrowed issues offer safety and respectable yields. The money needed to pay off the principal and interest on these bonds has been placed in escrow accounts and invested in US Treasury securities.

But don't lock up all your money in long-term issues. A portion of your tax-exempt portfolio should be in short-term bonds, which allow you to get a look at your money every few years without incurring transaction costs. . . and reinvest it elsewhere if that's appropriate.

*A crisis might occur if the economy fell into a recession. Issuer's revenues would be lower than expected, and some might default on payments.

Source: Paul J. Isaac, partner in charge of municipal bonds, Mabon Nugent & Co., securities broker/dealer, 115 Broadway, New York 10004.

Small-Town Vs. Big-City Municipals

Small-town bonds pay better returns than their big-city counterparts. Reason: Because these municipal-bond issues are small—usually less than $10 million—rating companies don't bother to evaluate them. In most cases the issues are just as safe as rated bonds. But because they're unrated, the yield is higher. Safest: Invest in municipal-bond funds that spread their money around many small issues.

Put Bonds

Scary: You purchase municipal bonds, expecting interest rates to fall or stabilize. But rates rise—and the value of your bonds plummets.

To avoid this risk you can buy "put bonds"—medium- and long-term municipal bonds you can sell back to the issuer before maturity at face value, regardless of market value. Three kinds:

• Fixed-rate put bonds have guaranteed coupons and can be redeemed at face value periodically (every six months, every three years, etc.). Advantage: The bonds hold their value even in the face of rising interest rates. Yields, which are usually lower than those on comparable long-term bonds, are closer to those on shorter-term bonds. For example, a 20-year put bond with one year until its next put date usually has the same yield as an otherwise comparable one-year bond.

• Adjustable-rate put bonds are similar to the fixed-rate, but they change their coupons at each put date to keep pace with market interest rates. Apparent advantage: If interest rates rise, so does your return. Danger: Issuers often reserve the right to switch the bonds to fixed-rates whenever they want. . .likely to be desirable (for them) if rates are climbing fast.

• Put option program bonds (POPs, also called TOPs—tender option program bonds) are imaginative *and* advantageous. Unprofitable institutions with portfolios of old low-yield tax-exempt bonds they no longer need sell them to investors with two- or three-year put options at discounts that guarantee a yield to maturity higher than that on comparable two- and three-year bonds. The institutions get cash to invest in higher-yielding short-term taxable securities, while investors get higher short-term tax-exempt yields. Important: Unless interest rates plummet, investors must not miss the put date. . .on these bonds, there's usually only one. Otherwise they're stuck with long-term bonds that have below-market yields. As of this writing the IRS has yet to rule on the tax-exempt status of these bonds, but no problem is foreseen for current issues.

Most put bonds are revenue bonds, not general obligation bonds, which means the issuer can't simply raise taxes to cover a large redemption. Recommended: Before buying a bond, find out if the issuer has secured a letter of credit from a bank to cover large puts.

Source: Howard D. Sitzer, vice president and director of municipal bond research, Thomson McKinnon Securities, 1 New York Plaza, New York 10004.

Tax Reform Bonus—New Tax-Free Bond

One positive result of tax reform is the introduction of a new tax-free bond—a stripped zero-coupon municipal bond. Not only is it tax free, it is guaranteed.

It could be the ideal investment to meet future financial needs such as:

- Your child's college education.
- Large mortgage payments coming due.
- Retirement.

Zero-coupon bonds are issued at a deep discount and redeemed for face value at maturity. Zero-coupon, tax-free municipals have been available for a few years, but suffer from a major disadvantage. . . they can be called in before maturity. Most were high-yield housing bonds. The housing authorities that issued them were required to call them in when funds were available. An investor who thought he had locked in a 9% yield for 10 years suddenly discovered that part or all of his investment had been called in.

Not so with the new bonds—because they are stripped of their coupons, as permitted by the new tax law. The stripped bonds are then repackaged and sold under such names as Salomon Brothers' M-CATS (Municipal Certificates of Accrual on Tax-Exempt Securities) and Goldman, Sachs' MRs (Municipal Receipts). The names aren't important: All stripped, zero-coupon municipal bonds are virtually the same.

Guarantee: The stripped bonds are "pre-refunded." This means they are backed by US Treasury bonds which have been bought specifically as a guarantee. If the municipality goes bankrupt, or is slow in paying, you are guaranteed payment of both principal and interest on time. That guarantee gives these new bonds a Triple A rating, which makes them worry free assuming the investor holds them to maturity.

- Education: If you expect to need money for your children's education, say in 10 years, you can plan for it by buying M-CATS or MRs that will mature when they enter college. Bonus: You won't have to worry about reinvesting periodic interest payments (possibly at a lower rate), as you would with a conventional bond.
- Retirement: Taxpayers who can no longer make deductible IRA contributions may find stripped zero-coupon municipals a better way to provide for retirement. Their income is entirely tax free. IRA income is only tax deferred.
- Selling the bond before it matures: There is a market trading in these bonds if you need to sell before the bond matures. Obviously if interest rates move up, the price of the bond will decline and an investor may suffer a loss.

Source: Marilyn Cohen, an investment broker specializing in tax-advantaged strategies, with Cantor, Fitzgerald and Company, Inc., 232 North Canon Drive, Beverly Hills, CA 90210.

All About Stripped Municipals

Stripped municipal bonds are attractive investments for people who know exactly when they will want to use their money and are in a high tax bracket. Unlike zero-coupon municipals, most of which have maturities far greater than 10 years, stripped municipals offer maturities of less than one year to 30 years, making them ideal for investors with short-term goals.

Also, stripped municipals are never callable.

Like zero-coupon Treasuries, stripped municipals don't pay interest. They are sold at a deep discount to their face value. Instead of current interest payments, investors receive the full face value of the bond when it matures. The gain comes from the difference between the discount price of the bond and its face value.

Example: A stripped 10-year municipal bond with a face value of $5,000 and paying 6% now sells for $2,768.

Because stripped municipal bonds are tax exempt, investors who hold them until maturity do not pay any tax on their investment.

Risks

Stripped municipal bonds (like all zero-coupon bonds) are not readily marketable. Investors should be prepared to hold them until maturity.

If, for whatever reason, you must sell before maturity, it's important to know that stripped municipals are more volatile than traditional municipal bonds. Reason: They don't have the cushion of regular coupon payments.

The Making of a Stripped Municipal

In concept, stripped municipals are the same as zero-coupon Treasury bonds. Issuers (major brokerage houses and investment banks) buy a large block of municipal bonds. Instead of selling these bonds to investors, they hold them, and market stripped municipals with varying maturities. The issuer then uses the payments coming from the original bonds to pay off different maturities of stripped municipals as they come due.

Example: The earliest interest and principal payments received by the issuer are used to pay off the stripped municipals with the earliest maturities.

A stripped municipal therefore represents a part interest in a large block of municipal bonds. Advantage: Since the issuer receives a stream of interest and principal payments over an extended period, it is able to create stripped municipals in maturities ranging from only several months up to as long as 30 years.

Types To Choose From

• Stripped municipals backed by "prefunded bonds." The underlying bonds are collateralized by the purchase of US Treasury securities. This is the closest a stripped municipal gets to having government backing. In general, the longest maturity these bonds carry is 10 years.

• Stripped municipals backed by high-quality triple A general-obligation bonds. These securities offer the widest range of maturities (one year to 30 years). Investors have great flexibility in picking a target date on which to reclaim their money.

• Insured stripped municipals. These are attractive for investors who want the added protection of an insurance policy on the coupon payment. They are insured by various bond insurance consortiums, such as MBIA (Municipal Bond Insurance Agency) and FGIC (Federal Guaranty Insurance Corporation).

Source: Robert S. Dow, partner, Lord, Abbett & Co., 63 Wall St., New York 10005. He is portfolio manager for the six Lord, Abbett bond funds, which have more than $2 billion in assets.

A Best Buy

Low-risk government bonds: Those with two- to five-year effective maturities, we hear from bond portfolio manager Theresa Havell of Neuberger & Berman. Reason: Intermediate-term bonds offer 88%–95% of the yield provided by 30-year bonds . . . yet the risk to principal if interest rates rise is only 25%–30% of that carried by long-term bonds.

Today's US Savings Bonds

US savings bonds were once considered the ugly duckling of personal investments. They paid below-market interest rates and had lengthy maturities, making them uneconomical for most investors. The only time you bought them was when you felt particularly patriotic or when you couldn't think of a better birthday or Christmas present.

That's not true anymore. Today, you can buy EE US savings bonds for any amount between $25 and $15,000, with the purchase price equal to half the bond's face value. You pay no commission charge (one reason you won't hear about these bonds), they are virtually risk-free, and they are extremely liquid.

Interest and principal on the EE savings bond are paid in a lump sum at the bond's maturity, making it, in effect, a zero-coupon bond. If held for five years or longer, EE savings bonds offer a variable interest rate compounded semiannually, with a guaranteed minimum rate of 6%. The floating rate is set every May and November at 85% of the average market yield on five-year Treasury notes and bonds sold during the previous six months.

What is the advantage of a variable interest rate? The bond offers unlimited upside interest with a fixed downside. This enables you to stay in step with inflation, while being protected from a decline in interest rates.

The best feature: EEs are not only exempt from state and local taxes, but with EE savings bonds you can defer the federal income tax liability until redemption. In effect, then, you are buying a zero-coupon bond with none of the obligations to pay taxes on interest you don't receive until the bonds' maturity. Remember also, as US savings bonds, EEs are virtually risk-free. And because they have a variable interest rate, your principal is always secure. Disadvantages: None, except the maximum that an individual can invest in EEs is $15,000 per year under one name and Social Security Number.

Source: Lawrence A. Krause, chairman of the board of Lawrence A. Krause & Associates, Inc., 500 Washington Street, Suite 750, San Francisco 94111, a financial planning firm with a nationwide clientele. He is a Certified Financial Planner and on the Registry of Financial Planning Practitioners. Mr. Krause also writes a monthly column in *California Business.*

How To Guard Against Losses in the Options and Futures Markets

Most amateur investors lose money with high leverage investments because they carelessly put most of their trading capital at risk in the hope of making large, quick profits—they invest on the basis of emotions rather than a disciplined trading strategy.

Contrary to popular belief, disciplined trading is the real way to make consistent profits over the long term in either the options or futures markets. The key to successful, disciplined trading is managing your capital, controlling your risks, and watching the markets.

Managing Your Capital
Don't commit funds to leveraged investments that you can't afford to lose. Since you only make big profits in futures and options markets when you assume a correspondingly high level of risk, always limit the capital you commit to an amount you feel comfortable about losing completely. As a general rule, if you can't handle large losses over a short period of time, you probably shouldn't be trading in options or futures.

Once you've determined the amount of capital you can devote to trading, always keep a large portion of capital in reserve. Never risk all or most of it on a single trade, regardless of how successful you've been in the past or how attractive the next trade appears. Remember: there will always be losing trades. By compounding your capital after a few profitable trades, you can only expose yourself to potentially dangerous losses. This strategy will give you the staying power to ride out losses and, ultimately, to make a profit.

Controlling Your Risk
Diversify your positions. The old rule still applies: Never have all your investment eggs in one futures or options basket.

For futures trading, maintain a minimum of two position in different futures complexes. (The major futures complexes consist of stock indexes, metals, financial instruments, meats, and agricultural commodities.) A long position in gold and a long position in silver does not constitute diversification. Don't just trade on the long side (buying with the hope that prices will rise). Since markets rise and fall, you must learn to trade on the short side as well (profiting from a decline in prices).

For options trading, maintain at least two positions in different underlying instruments. Also try to invest in puts as well as in calls.

Protect against major losses by using "stop-loss" orders. Diversification will help protect you against adverse moves in a particular market, but protective stop-loss orders will close out losing positions before they deteriorate into huge losses. Determine your stop-loss points in advance and stick to them, 50%

maximum loss on your original investment is appropriate for most trades.

Watching the Markets

Many futures and options traders are short-term-oriented, and their approach tends to be technical in nature. This means that they analyze past trends in price and volume to predict future market direction. It is also possible to look at markets in terms of fundamentals, such as interest rates, inflation, production, and demand. However, although these will ultimately dictate price movements, it is very difficult to translate them into profitable short-term trading programs.

Closely follow the markets that most interest you. It's the only way to gain a feeling for a market's underlying direction. Don't be afraid to utilize the advice and recommendations of outside advisory and information services. Most good traders rely on a number of excellent information sources beyond just the daily financial press to help determine market movements. Sources include investment advisory services, brokerage reports devoted to futures and options, chart services, and computer data bases.

Source: Bernard G. Schaeffer, executive director, Investment Research Institute, Inc., 110 Boggs Lane, Suite 365, Cincinnati 45246. He is coeditor of *THE OPTION ADVISOR®* and several other newsletters on short-term trading, as well as coauthor of *The Options Handbook* and *The Trader's Handbook*.

How To Profit With Options: The Basics

The sad truth about options is that most people who invest in them end up losing money. That is primarily because few investors take the time to learn exactly how options work or, more importantly, how to use them up to make money. Good advice: Always learn the basics well, then proceed with caution.

For serious investors, options can serve three basic functions:

- High-risk speculation on the direction of the market.

- Supplementing current dividend and interest income from a portfolio.

- Hedging against portfolio risk.

But, again, options only provide these advantages to investors who know what they're doing.

The Basics of Options

An option is nothing more than a contract that gives you the right to buy or sell a security at a set price by a specified date in the future. There are two types of options: a call, the right to *buy* a security at a set price in the future; and a put, the right to *sell* a security at a set price in the future.

Example: Company *X*'s stock sells for $30 a share. You buy a call, which expires in three months, at $35 a share. This means that within three months, you have the right to purchase the stock of Company *X* for $35 a share no matter how high the share price has risen.

The price of the option, better known as the premium, is 50 cents. This represents, essentially, the time value of the option. It is based on the length of time before the option expires and the likelihood of the stock actually reaching the option's exercise price. If investors think there is only a small chance that Company *X*'s stock will reach $35 in three months, then the premium will be low. If, on the other hand, investors think there is a large chance that the stock will reach $35, then the price of the option will be higher. At 50 cents, investors probably think there is relatively little chance of the stock reaching $35.

A month later, the price of the stock jumps to $40. The value of the option is now $5, because you could exercise the option, buy the stock at $35, and then sell it for $40 in the open market. Your 50 cent investment is therefore worth 10 times its original value. If the stock did not reach the exercise price of $35, however, the option would expire worthless.

A put operates in the reverse fashion. If you think a stock will go down in price, you buy a put or the right to sell the stock at a set price in the future.

Example: Company *X* is selling for $35 a share. This time, you think the price will go down, so you buy a put to sell the stock for $35. The premium you pay for the option is $1. One month later, the company experiences problems and the price of the stock drops to $30. You can now buy the stock for $30 in the open market and, by exercising your put sell the stock for $35. Your profit is $4 or a 400% gain on your original investment.

Huge Returns—And Risks

With options, a very small investment can rack up huge returns in a very short period of time. To otherwise achieve the same results in the stock market would take massive amounts of capital and a great deal of patience.

The risk is that most options expire worthless. Unlike the stocks themselves, if an option's underlying stock or index does not perform according to your expectations, the options contract expires with no value at all—you lose your entire investment. Also, options are typically short-term investment vehicles; they usually involve a great deal of buying and selling. As a result, total commission costs can be very high.

Source: Carl A. Futia, investment consultant, 16 Colles Ave., Morristown, NJ 07960.

Options Investing Strategies

Professional investors have devised a large and impressive array of investing strategies utilizing the options market. Some of these strategies are exceedingly complex, and because of the large amounts of capital involved, are not recommended for use by individual investors. However, a number of basic options strategies can expand your investing capabilities significantly.

Selling Options on a Stock Portfolio

Selling options on a stock portfolio, better known as "writing covered calls," allows you to generate current income over and above the income received by dividends. Instead of buying call options, you actually "write" or

sell them on your own portfolio. In return for selling the call option, you receive a premium from the investor who purchases the call. This strategy is used when you don't expect your stocks to move much either up or down.

Example: You own 200 shares of Company X at $40 a share. Company X pays a regular quarterly dividend of $1 or an annual yield of 10%. This is a respectable dividend, but you want more current income. You believe that the stock of Company X is going to remain relatively stable for the near future, so you decide to write a covered call on your stock of Company X at an exercise price of $45. The investor who buys the call pays you a premium of $1.

As a result of this transaction, you have doubled your quarterly income in no time at all. The risk, though, is that your outlook for Company X is not correct and the stock's price will actually rise above $45. Then, your stock can be called away any time before the option expires. If this happens, you will not participate in the stock's gains beyond $45. And, if it is called away from you before a quarterly dividend date, you won't receive your dividend, either.

Sale of a Naked Call

This is a much riskier version of writing covered calls. The main difference between the two is that when you sell naked calls, you receive a premium without actually owning the underlying securities. Who should use this strategy? Investors who are willing to take on large and sometimes unlimited amounts of risk. Why are naked calls so risky? If you sell a naked call for $45 and the stock rises above that exercise price, you are responsible for purchasing the stock in the open market at the current market price.

Example: If the naked call is exercisable at $45 a share and the price of Company X's stock rises to $50, you will have to buy the stock at $50 in the open market and sell it to the owner of the call for $45. Your loss will equal $5. In theory, your loss is potentially limitless.

Straddles

Use a "straddle" when you think a stock will move dramatically up or down, but you're not sure which direction it will take. This situation might arise when a company's future earnings will be severely affected, positively or negatively, by a specific event—for instance, a court ruling on a series of new products, the movement of interest rates, or cutoff of supply of natural resources.

Example: Company *X*'s stock trades for $40 a share. An FDA ruling on a new product will dramatically affect Company *X*'s potential for future earnings. You're not sure which way the stock will move, so you buy a $40 call and a $40 put. The cost of each option is $5—your investment is $10. Now, if Company *X* stock goes above $50 or below $30 before the put and call expire, you will make a profit.

Hedging a Broad Stock Portfolio

Options on market indexes can be used to hedge against a portfolio's inherent market risk. Use this strategy when you own a broad portfolio of stocks and are uncertain about the future movement of the stock market as a whole and, hence, of your portfolio. If this is the case, buy a put option on the most comparable market index (Standard & Poor's 500, Value Line, etc.). If the market and presumably your portfolio do in fact decline in value, you will make a profit on your put. If your prediction does not come true, then the rise in the value of your portfolio can offset the premium you paid for the option. Index options (unlike stock options) are settled with cash.

The advantages of hedging a portfolio, rather than liquidating it outright, are that you save a significant amount of money in brokerage commissions, and you are able to hold onto stocks you believe are fundamentally sound long-term investments. However, there are also risks. If your portfolio is not well correlated with a specific market index, you will not be fully protected. You can potentially lose money on your hedge and your portfolio. If the stock market goes up, you do not get the full benefit from the increase in the value of your portfolio.

Limiting Your Losses

Most first-time options investors lose. So, be careful: Don't let your losses amount to more than 50% of your initial investment. Options investors are notorious for waiting out a downturn in the market in the hope that their position will become profitable by expiration time. When your loss amounts to 50%, admit you were wrong and liquidate the position to insure that the option won't turn into a 100% loss by expiration day.

Source: Carl A. Futia, investment consultant, 16 Colles Ave., Morristown, NJ 07960.

How To Make Money With Futures

Futures trading is a high-risk business that offers potentially huge returns for relatively small initial investments. Most of the people who invest in the futures markets have one common trait—they have a great deal of money to put at risk and an emergency cash reserve to cover losses that go beyond their original investments.

Futures trading is nothing more than the buying or selling of goods at prices agreed upon today, but with actual delivery in the future. Futures contracts are sold for everything from orange juice and soybeans to gold and Treasury bills. For each futures market, there are two parties involved: hedgers and speculators. Hedgers are people like farmers who must transfer risk to protect themselves against a movement in the price they will receive for a commodity such as corn or pork bellies. Speculators, on the other hand, buy and sell futures contracts in anticipation of future price movements.

Speculation

If a speculator believes the price of a commodity or financial instrument will rise, he or she buys a futures contract for delivery of the commodity at today's price. If the price rises, the speculator buys the commodity for the price of the futures contract and sells it at the current market price. In the majority of futures trades, the positions are closed out before expiration of the contracts and the physical commodities are rarely delivered or received.

Why are futures so attractive to investors? Futures prices are usually highly volatile: Large swings in price can come and go rapidly. Investors who understand (or think they understand) the future movement of a commodity's price can make large returns in a very short time. Futures also offer tremendous leverage. Like stocks, futures trade on margin. The key difference is that the minimum margin account for futures can be as low as 5% or 10% of a contract's value.

Example: Product *X* trades at $5 a pound for delivery of 10,000 pounds in six months. The value of this futures contract is $50,000. Because you can purchase the contract on margin, it only costs you 5% of the contract, or $2,500. Now, assume the price of Product *X* rises by 5% and the value of the contract increases by $2,500. The result: You have made 100% on your initial investment. The risk: You can potentially lose much more than your initial investment. If the price of Product *X falls* by 5%, then you will lose $2,500— your initial investment is wiped out. If the price falls by 10%, you will owe $2,500 to cover your losses. You can see the potential for disaster.

Hedging With Futures

In addition to high-leveraged speculation, interest rate futures and stock index futures allow you to hedge a stock or bond portfolio against market risk. The stock indexes are composite prices of large groups of stocks. Delivery on stock index futures is made on a cash-settlement basis, instead of turning over the stocks themselves. The indexes differ in the type of stocks they contain and how they are calculated, but all serve to transfer risk.

If you believe your stock portfolio will eventually go up in value, but the market looks as if it will turn downward temporarily, rather than sell the stocks in your portfolio, sell stock index futures contracts. If the market does decline you will obtain a profit from the sale of the stock index futures, which can be used to offset any loss on your portfolio. This risk is that your portfolio might not be well correlated with the index on which you sold the futures contracts. As a result, your portfolio would not be adequately protected. If you see the market ready to go back up, you can buy back the futures with a profit and still own all of your original stocks.

Hedging a bond portfolio is accomplished in the same manner as hedging a stock portfolio. Interest rate futures are sold for a wide variety of financial instruments, including T-bills, long-term Treasury notes, Ginnie Maes, and others. Each type of financial future reflects a different maturity and yield. Decide what combination of financial futures best reflects your bond portfolio and sell the appropriate amount.

Source: Kevin Simmons, market analyst and trader, REFCO, Inc., 111 W. Jackson Blvd., Chicago 60604.

Trading Commodities

The fundamental fact about commodities that all players must reckon with: Incredible volatility. The fluctuation per day averages about 1%. Multiplied by a leverage factor of 20, the trader can anticipate at least a 20% profit or loss per day. It's hard to have the stomach to cope with these losses or gains in a businesslike fashion. But anyone who actively trades tangibles (gold, diamonds, paintings, or antiques) is probably a good candidate for commodities.

In the stock market, you can lose money in bits and pieces. You don't realize a loss until you sell out your position. Capital invested in the commodities market is all at risk. You don't have to place a buy or sell order to win or lose. Money is credited to your account if your position is right. If it's wrong, the broker tells you how much you owe.

For Beginners

Brokerage houses will let you put up as little as $50,000 for an individual commodities trading account. There are also managed group accounts for people who are ready to put at risk only $10,000–$20,000. Caution: A few of these groups have good records, but most are only a couple of years old. Results are not sufficient to evaluate them.

Making an emotional move is the most common way speculators get hurt. The market is so volatile and moves so fast that an investor is, in effect, constantly making a buy or sell decision. And the leverage is so great that a move of a few cents means a few thousand dollars.

Investors must: 1. Expect to make wrong decisions that could cost a great deal of money. 2. Set a time horizon once a decision is made, and stick to it.

General rule: With leverage so high, you may expect to win or lose 25% of capital on any day. Problem: When you are making and losing such large sums you forget one of the basic principles of running a business—recognizing the real costs.

The average holding in commodities is only four or five days. A $60 commission every time you make a move can mean thousands of dollars in commissions a year and that can wipe out a good part of your gain.

The difference between the bid and asked prices for a commodity can run three times the commission cost. Result: When you get to a commodity you are frequently already down to 20%.

Human frailties are likely to emerge in commodities trading. Reason: People get excited about making a lot of money, due to the volatility. Professionals recognize that the chief effect of volatility is to relieve the public of the maximum amount of money in the minimum amount of time.

The Psychology of Trading

• Movements during the day play on the emotions. If you are wrong, you have to adopt a very unemotional attitude toward the loss. The worst thing to do: Keep calling your broker all day.

• Have the moral fiber to stay with your conviction. The average trader must increase the time horizon for holding a contract 15-fold before getting the chance to make a profit. Example: Instead of trading every three or four days, hold on to the contract for 50 days. That gives you a saving on commissions and the bid/asked penalties.

• Worst mistake of all: Doubling up after a gain or loss. When you do this just a small loss will wipe you out.

• Looking for bargains is a mistake in the commodities market. When prices drop, don't buy. It is better to short when things start to look cheap.

Strategy For Outsiders

Don't convince yourself that you can read the daily financial pages and get sufficient insight into commodities. You are trading against experts who know the number of freight-car loadings in Peru and the hourly temperatures in Russia. Whatever insight you have probably won't be superior to theirs.

Exception: If you are in a business where you are sensitive to certain trends (like the impact of a fall in sugar prices on the candy business), your understanding may be of value in a long-term time frame.

Personal knowledge gives you a realistic outlook that helps you invest in commodities. If this is the case: Consider at least a six-month horizon in which you want to move. Don't put up a minimum margin. Put up 15% instead of the required 5%. Plan on maintaining your position.

Fundamental impact of interest rates on commodities: When rates are high, everything else goes down. Investors lose sight of this, because when rates are high everything is usually booming. They forget that a disaster could just be around the corner. If you are long when interest rates are high, you will get wiped-out.

Rule: Go against short-term trends and with long-term trends. Example: If soybeans have gone down 15% in a month and up 3% the last week, don't buy. Sell short!

Source: Victor Niederhoffer, chairman, Niederhoffer, Cross & Zeckhauser, Inc., a merger and acquisitions firm that specializes in selling companies in the $2 million to $25 million range, 49 W. 57 St., New York 10019.

A Simple Case for Mutual Funds

There are at least 100 variables that may influence the future values of any security. How can the amateur investor balance those variables and decide how each will affect an investment? By following a simplified step-by-step decision-making process that seldom requires dealing with more than two variables at a time.

• Stocks or bonds? Historically, the Standard & Poor's 500 Index has outperformed bonds almost three to one. If you are confident you can invest in stocks successfully, this decision is not difficult—go with stocks.

• Do it yourself or delegate? Although many investors think they can beat the system, it's smart to delegate stock investment decisions to professionals. Historical results indicate that professionals have the advantage.

• Stockbroker or portfolio manager? It's best to delegate the decision-making process to fee-based portfolio managers. Stockbrokers graduate to fee-based management only if they are successful; when you choose a portfolio manager, you have a better chance of getting someone with a proven record.

• Private or public portfolio managers? Most successful portfolio managers have minimum account sizes of $100,000 to $5,000,000. If you are a smaller investor, you have the option of joining forces with other investors, retaining some of the best portfolio managers, and investing in publicly owned mutual funds. These funds offer diversification to protect you from stock risk. Also, most funds are members of a family of funds, each with a different investment objective. Once you have invested in a family of funds, switching back and forth between funds usually can be accomplished without a commission or fee.

• What kind of fund is right for you? If you are young and have many years to retirement, you may be best served by a growth-oriented mutual fund. If you are nearing retirement, a more conservative growth and income fund may be appropriate. At retirement, many investors seek the extreme safety of bond or income funds.

• Load or no-load funds? No-load funds make the most sense. Load funds charge up-front commissions or expensive liquidation fees. No-load funds have no commission at the time of purchase and can be liquidated without penalty. To date, no-load funds have performed as well as load funds, so there is no reason to accept the extra burden of a load fund.

• Buy and hold or use market timing? If you make the decision to buy and hold a mutual fund, you are relying on the abilities of a portfolio manager to diversify your investment among stocks that will generally go up in bull markets and not go down in bear markets. Yet diversification will not protect a portfolio from the 25%–50% declines suffered in a major bear market.

The goal of market timing is to be in equity funds during market advances and safely moving to money market funds during market declines. Market timing of no-load funds can cut the risk of investing by approximately 50%. Most market timers are in equity funds about half of the time, during which they are exposed to whatever risk or volatility factor each fund carries. The other half of the time the funds are in near-zero-risk money-market funds.

• Do it yourself or professional market timing? This decision depends on whether you have the ability, time, and desire to manage your investments on a daily basis. Although there can be no guarantees of profitability, hiring a professional market timer relieves you of this obligation and allows you to concentrate on evaluating only his or her performance.

• Newsletter or private management? The key to market timing is the signal that instructs you either to be in equity funds or safely in money-market funds. Market timing signals can be purchased from services that contact you through the mail or by telephone. Or, for those who do not want the responsibility of tracking a newsletter or contacting mutual funds, there are a handful of managers who will perform the switching function without client involvement. A few private management services provide timing for accounts as small as $2,000, but most have minimum account sizes of $25,000 to $100,000.

Source: Paul A. Merriman is a Registered Investment Adviser and president of Paul A. Merriman & Associates, 1200 Westlake Ave. N., Suite 507, Seattle 98109. The firm market times over $28 million of no-load mutual funds on a private management basis. Mr. Merriman is publisher and editor of *The Fund Exchange* and the author of *Market Timing With No-Load Mutual Funds.*

Selecting the Right Mutual Funds for Your Portfolio

Selecting the mutual fund that's best for you hinges on five basic rules:

1. Diversify.
2. Analyze performance over a long period of time.
3. Seek funds with continuity of investment style.
4. Use your money fund wisely.
5. Recognize mistakes.

Diversify

Even with mutual funds, it pays to diversify your portfolio. Select at least three basic types of mutual funds as your foundation. Choose among the broad groups of ''growth'' and ''growth and income'' funds for your portfolio's anchor. To satisfy your opportunistic side, add a ''sector'' fund (which invests exclusively in a particular area, such as technology, health care, finance, or energy) or a ''small company growth'' fund. Maintain a money-market fund as your reserve.

Consider a ''fixed-income'' fund if you are building your portfolio in a tax-sheltered retirement plan; the high yield will compound your tax-deferred income. You may be able to capitalize on volatility of interest rates or make this fund the longer-term reserve element of your portfolio. But, don't remain in long-term fixed-income investments if inflation begins to reemerge.

Analyze Performance

Evaluate a fund's performance over a long period of time in order to analyze how a fund performs under varying market conditions. Does it rise faster than the general market, but fall faster too? Does it climb steadily and hold its ground well? How do these characteristics mesh with your strategy?

Go to the rating services to evaluate a fund or group of funds. Rating services generally can be grouped into two types: quantitative and qualitative. The quantitative services measure performance results, using total return as their indicator. The other services provide advice on market timing and reveal general attitudes toward funds, particular groups of funds, and/or fund managements.

Seek Continuity of Style

Carefully read the fund's annual and interim reports, the proxy statement and statement of additional information. Call the president or the vice president of marketing of the fund for answers to these questions: Have there been important shifts in strategy? If so, when? How has this affected the fund's tactics? Did it help results? Have there been changes in personnel? Why? Who is the portfolio manager? For how long? If there have been any significant changes in style, strategy, or personnel, it will be difficult to evaluate the past as a guide to future success. Be cautious.

Use Your Money Fund Wisely

Separate your cash-management money from your investment reserves. Emphasize convenience and service when selecting a money market fund. The quality of the assets held in the portfolio is more important than the small difference in yield among money-market mutual funds. Also look for ability to exchange with other funds in a family of funds.

Recognize Mistakes

As with any other investment, cut your losses. Monitor your funds' strategies and their results. Most well-selected mutual funds will remain appropriate as investments for a long time. However, opportunistic funds are more vulnerable to changes in the economy; monitor these funds very closely.

Source: A. Michael Lipper, CFA, president, Lipper Analytical Securities, Inc., 74 Trinity Place, New York 10006, publisher of performance reports on the mutual fund industry. Maureen J. Busby, CFA, president of Lipper Advisory Services, Inc., 322 East Michigan Street, Milwaukee 53202, a registered investment adviser.

For Conservative Investors

Equity/income mutual funds have portfolios consisting of common or preferred shares (equity) of established companies that pay high dividends and high-rated bonds for steady earnings (income). Advantages: Low risk with strong earnings and excellent chances for capital gains if interest rates decline, thereby boosting bond prices. If rates rise, the fund's bond portfolio suffers, but losses are partially offset by stock dividend payments. And when rates plateau, the fund again becomes an attractive investment prospect.

Source: William E. Donoghue, publisher, *Donoghue's Moneyletter.*

Mutual-Fund Selection Secrets

It's most important in picking mutual funds first to define your investment objective. Usually, investors either are interested mostly in preserving capital they already have (and invest for income)...or they want primarily to increase their capital (growth). Few people shoot for 100% income or 100% growth, but you should choose a fund that emphasizes either one or the other.

• Identify several top-performing no-load funds that pursue your objective. Helpful: *Donoghue's Mutual Funds Almanac, Dow*

Jones-Irwin Mutual Fund Yearbook, Handbook for No-Load Fund Investors, and *Wiesenberger Investment Company Service.* All are available in public libraries.

• Analyze performance in depth. Don't just glance at overall five- or 10-year returns. For stock funds, look for 10 years of annual gains that have consistently beaten the Standard & Poor's 500 stock index in up *and* down years. If a stock fund did badly in 1973, 1974, 1977, 1981 and the first half of 1982, it will probably perform poorly when the next bear market hits. For bond funds, compare performance to the Salomon Brothers Bond Index.

• Opt for consistency. If two funds have similar returns but one's share price swings widely while the other's is relatively stable, go for the least volatile. Reason: If you suddenly have to sell your shares, there's less risk they'll be significantly depressed.

• Investigate the current portfolio manager. Is he the same one responsible for the fabulous gains of the past 10 years? Or has the star-performer moved on to manage another fund?

Little-known: Many of the top-gun investment advisers who require a prohibitively large personal portfolio ($1 million or more) before they'll accept your business also manage mutual funds. You may be able to tap their brainpower with a tiny fraction of that amount.

• Think small. Mutual funds with more than $1 billion in assets have a harder time producing superior results because they must invest in larger, more lethargic companies. Dangerous pattern: A fund becomes a hot performer and suddenly receives a tidal wave of cash...the manager is forced from small stocks into big ones... and the exciting returns evaporate.

• Don't invest in new funds. They don't have a track record.

• Don't accept biased advice. Brokers and financial planners who recommend funds usually receive a commission when you buy in. Taking their advice is okay only if you make sure the funds they suggest meet the criteria outlined above.

• Don't jump in and out of funds. Professional investment advisers know that for growth, they must be in the market at all times. . .though the percentage of their portfolios kept in the market may vary depending on the outlook. For most people, market timing is a risky business and highly impractical.

Source: Kurt Brouwer, director, Brouwer & Janachowski, investment advisers associated with Birr, Wilson & Co., Inc., investment bankers and brokers, 155 Sansome St., San Francisco 94104. The firm advises pension plans and corporate executives on the selection of no-load mutual funds.

How To See Through Murky Advertising of Mutual Funds

Mutual-fund advertising often confuses investors. . .whether or not funds intend to do so. Mutual-fund advertising is actually more heavily regulated than advertising in banking, but most consumers are more familiar with personal banking than fund investing and are easily led astray.

Mutual funds and bank accounts are completely different animals. While a bank can promise you a federally insured account with a fixed yield, the stability of principal and rate of return in a mutual fund depend on market factors and can't be guaranteed. All numbers that appear in mutual-fund ads describe only past performance.

Potentially Misleading

• Track records. Every fund tells the best story that it has. . .but all the stories are different. Example: One fund claims, "We're up 200% in the last four years," while another says, "We're up 250% in the last five years." Both claims are true, but they can't be compared meaningfully. To make a significant comparison: You have to compare funds' performance data for the same periods (available in the prospectuses or by phone from the funds).

• "Current" yields. The numbers in magazine ads are often two to five weeks old. Trap: Using old yields to compare bond funds.

• Load (sales charge) status. Unfortunately, funds aren't simply "load" (with a sales charge) or "no-load." Some are pure no-load funds and have no initial or deferred sales charge and no redemption fee. . .but many others carry one or more of the above. Initial sales charges run as high as 8.5%, but are usually 4%–6%.

Deceptive: Funds advertised as "no-load" that charge you a fee when you sell your shares. This can be done through a contingent deferred sales charge, which runs as high as 6% if you sell shares within the first year of ownership (it usually declines by one percentage point each year thereafter). The charge is generally explained only in the fine print of the prospectus.

The other back-end charge: A fixed redemption fee—usually 1% to 2%—which applies no matter how long shares are held.

• 12b-1 plans. The Securities & Exchange Commission allows funds to charge an annual fee to pay for advertising and distribution costs. . .as high as .25%. Self-defense: Compare performance *after* the fee has been taken into account.

• "100% insured" and "government guaranteed." Many bond funds purchase issues whose principal and interest are guaranteed by a private insurer or federal, state or local governments, but bond funds themselves—unlike bank accounts—are never insured or government-backed. Risk: If interest rates go up, the shares of all bond funds—even those of US Treasury bonds—will fall in value.

• Phantom income. Under tax reform, because of the way in which mutual funds are structured, they have to report to the IRS more taxable income than they pay to shareholders. Sample result: If you earn 8%, you may have to pay taxes on 8.5%. The fund retains half a percentage point for its expenses. . .which the IRS considers taxable income paid to you.

Funds aren't required to disclose in ads the percentage of phantom income reported, but this number must appear in the prospectus.

• Switching costs. Some fund families charge $5 every time you move money from one fund to another. Others offer a limited number of free switches per year and charge per switch beyond that limit.

IRA trap: Many fund families charge IRA accounts a $10 annual fee for each fund in which the IRA has invested during the year. So just three switches could cost $40 in IRA fees.

And if your money isn't in a tax-deferred account, remember that when you switch out of a fund in which you have made a capital gain, you must pay income tax on that gain (up to 28%).

Source: William Donoghue, publisher, *Donoghue's Moneyletter* and *Donoghue's Mutual Funds Almanac.*

How to Read a Mutual-Fund Prospectus

Once you've narrowed down the vast number of mutual funds available to a few top performers, send for the prospectus and annual report prepared by each. The prospectus is required to disclose any information that would be needed to make an informed decision regarding investment in the fund. The annual report must contain the financial reports on the fund, but may include other information as well. A fund's "statement of additional information," which you can also request, provides detailed information on the fund and its practices.

Use these reports to determine how well each fund you have tentatively selected compares to your particular investment goals and preferences. The following checklist will guide you in covering a fund's most important characteristics.

• Date of inception. A fund that has existed less than one year is difficult to judge since, technically, it doesn't have a performance record. At times, it may be possible to rely on the record of the new fund's manager to gauge performance, but older funds are obviously going to give you more to go on.

• Investment adviser's performance history. The big question here is whose performance record is being relied on for the period being measured? Traditionally, a record belongs to the person or persons who are responsible for

buying and selling securities during a particular period of time. Occasionally a fund will have an excellent long-term record in spite of changing advisers. In this case, the record may be credited to the person(s) selecting the advisers.

Information on registered investment advisers is a matter of public record. Each adviser must file a form ADV with the Securities & Exchange Commission. A fund may be willing to provide this information if requested.

• External advisers. Since advisory fees tend to be among the largest of a fund's expenses, any fund that hires outside advisers tends to have a higher expense ratio than those depending on in-house staff. However, if performance indicates that the fund has benefited from external advisers, the expense may be justified.

• Expense ratio. The average mutual fund expense ratio will be 1% or less. If the ratio is greater than 1%, try to determine the cause in order to make a judgment about whether the expense results in any added value. A good place to check for the cause is the management or advisory fee, since this generally is a mutual fund's largest expense.

• Turnover ratio. This figure indicates the level of trading in a fund's security holdings. If the ratio is greater than 75% to 100%, the fund's expense ratio and, ultimately, shareholder's return may be adversely affected by high transaction expenses.

A high turnover ratio may be acceptable in one situation—specifically, a change in advisers. A new adviser will often sell many of the securities purchased before his appointment. This may be beneficial to a fund particularly if poor performance was the reason for the change in advisers.

• Fund's portfolio. The prospectus will reveal what kinds of securities are being invested in and how diversified the portfolio is. Diversification usually reduces risk. So a sector fund, investing in securities in a single industry, will be riskier than a general stock fund.

• Total assets under management. Large fund groups can take advantage of certain economies of scale by spreading their costs over a larger asset base. On the other side of the coin, smaller funds—with about $100 million in total assets—often find it easier to locate and purchase high-quality investments. Smaller funds can also change direction more quickly than the large funds if circumstances warrant it.

• Other fees. Many funds charge fees for processing certain kinds of shareholder transactions. This is especially true for IRAs. All charges should be explained in the fund's prospectus.

• Shareholder services. These vary considerably among funds. Some funds, particularly those that are part of a large fund group, offer almost every conceivable service from check writing to telephone transactions. Other funds are strictly invest-by-mail organizations.

Source: Elizabeth A. Watson, assistant to the chairman and assistant treasurer, the Ivy Fund, 40 Industrial Park Road, Hingham, MA 02043. Ms. Watson is also director of shareholder services for the firm's 35,000 shareholders and its marketing program.

No-Load Mutual Funds

For much the same reasons that discount brokers flourished in the late 70s, no-load mutual funds are flourishing now. No-load mutual funds, which are sold without any commissions, are among the most cost-effective means of acquiring professional portfolio management for investments in almost every kind of security—from money-market instruments and municipal bonds to Government National Mortgage Association certificates and US government bonds, from zero-coupon bonds and international stocks to index options and equity in specific industry sectors.

One advantage is clear. By not charging any initial front-end fees for investing, no-load funds significantly lower the cost of a mutual-fund investment. The traditional load fund carries an 8½ % front-end sales charge. That means, of a $10,000 investment in a load mutual fund, only $9,150 would actually go

into your account—$850 would be used to pay brokers' commissions. The same $10,000 invested in a no-load fund would go directly into your account.

The impact of this difference in cost on your overall return increases substantially the longer you hold your investment. For this reason, no-load funds are especially attractive for IRAs and other long-term investment plans. Thirty years' worth of $2,000 annual IRA contributions into a no-load fund with an annual average return of 10% would grow to $397,784. The same investment made in an 8½ % load fund with the same average annual return would grow to $363,973—$33,811 less, although only $5,100 had been paid in commissions.

Consider also the examples in the accompanying table, which illustrate the differences in value between no-load and load fund investments over periods of 15 to 30 years. The figures are based on an identical average return of 10% for each fund, compounded monthly, with annual $2,000 investments. The same general principle applies to investments made in Keogh accounts, 401(k) plans, or any other long-term investment programs, tax-qualified or otherwise.

Compounded Differences in Funds

Number of years	No-load fund	8½ % load fund	Difference
15	$ 72,906	$ 66,709	$ 6,197
20	132,569	122,216	11,353
25	233,434	213,592	19,842
30	397,784	363,973	33,811

When no-load funds first appeared, investors were concerned that returns would not be as high as those achieved by load funds. Yet overall, funds that charge a fee for their services have not performed any better. No-load funds are consistently among the top-performing mutual funds in every major category—over the long term or just over the latest quarter.

Source: Laura J. Berger, executive director, No-Load Mutual Fund Association, 11 Penn Plaza, Suite 2204, New York 10001, the association of 94 management companies for 454 no-load and low-load mutual funds.

Mutual-Fund Sales Charges

Beware of funds that charge redemption fees. They're not the same as deferred sales charges. Reason: A redemption fee is a percentage of the value of your investment at the time of redemption. A deferred sales charge is a percentage of the initial investment but paid upon redemption. Result: Funds that charge deferred sales fees leave you with more money. Example: A $10,000 investment that doubles in value will be redeemed at $19,400 if the fund charges a 3% redemption fee (3% of $20,000 = $600). But a fund that has a 3% deferred sales charge will reduce the value of the $20,000 investment by only $300 upon redemption.

Source: Norman Fosback, publisher, *Mutual Fund Forecaster,* Fort Lauderdale.

How to Buy a Money Fund

Money funds offer instant liquidity, full market rates of interest, check writing, and a high degree of safety. Nevertheless, there are differences among money funds, and investors need to know those differences before buying.

Yield

Money funds are mutual funds that invest their shareholders' assets in high-quality government and corporate securities, and in bank deposits. Their operating expenses are relatively low; all it takes to run a money fund is a portfolio manager, a computer, and a staff of telephone operators. As a result, money funds are usually able to pass through to shareholders upwards of 99% of their gross investment income.

Money funds can have the upper hand over banks. Banks have hefty overhead expenses, capital construction costs for buildings, and stockholders who demand profits. Larger, efficient money funds therefore can afford superior managers, attract more shareholders, and offer yields consistently superior to yields on consumer money-market accounts at banks and thrifts.

Most newspapers report money-fund yields on a weekly basis, but be careful when judging the results: Various funds compute their yields differently. Merrill Lynch, for example, uses a computation method that results in volatile yields that can be extremely high one week and very low the next. The best policy is to ask money funds for their average yields over the last several months.

If you're a high-tax-bracket investor, put your money in a fund that specializes in short-term municipal securities. The returns are fully exempt from federal taxation.

Unlike money-market accounts in a major bank, money mutual funds are not entirely risk-free. Still, the money fund industry's record for safety has been relatively solid. In the late 1970s a few large funds such as First Multifund for Daily Income and Dreyfus Liquid Assets took a bath and investors in the former took a loss. To avoid disaster, pay close attention to the phases of the economic cycle and to the following three factors.

• The quality of a fund's portfolio. Some funds own exclusively US Treasury bills, the safest investment. Most other funds buy high-quality bank deposits and corporate securities. The highest-risk funds attempt to boost their yields buy purchasing low-quality securities, such as low-grade or unrated commercial paper and certificates of deposit of small banks. Pay careful attention to the percentage of a fund's assets made up of these high-risk investments.

• Average portfolio maturity. The maturity of investments in a typical taxable money fund is between 25 and 60 days. The average maturity of tax-free money fund investments is normally about twice that. Watch out for funds that extend their portfolio maturity significantly beyond the industry average. These funds are probably trying to lock in higher yields from longer-maturing investments. If interest rates rise sharply, the value of longer-maturing securities can decline, resulting in losses to money fund investors.

• Portfolio disclosure. Money funds are required to publish details of their portfolios only twice a year. Since typical fund investments mature in just a couple of months, much can happen in a six-month period that goes unreported. Before buying any money fund, ask for a current or very recent portfolio. Avoid funds that refuse to comply.

Service

Money funds offer a broad range of shareholder services. Be sure to check them thoroughly before investing. Minimum initial investments are usually quite low, typically about $1,000. Most funds offer nearly unlimited and free check-writing privileges, subject only to a minimum check amount of $250 or $500. Some funds don't have any minimum at all. Most funds can also establish special accounts for IRAs, Keoghs, and other retirement plans.

Liquidity is the greatest service. Investors can get their money back from a fund at any time without penalty. Interest is fully credited to accounts right up to the day of withdrawal.

It is actually easier to open a money fund account than it is to open a bank account. Investors can call most money funds from their home or office on toll-free telephone numbers to obtain an account form, a prospectus, and a current portfolio. Many money funds are also set up to handle wire transfers.

For investors who like to play the market, most money funds have relationships with other mutual funds that invest in stocks, bonds, and other securities. A phone call can usually switch an investment from a money fund to another type of fund or vice versa.

Source: Norman G. Fosback, editor of a consumer guide to high yields, *Income & Safety,* 3471 North Federal Highway, Fort Lauderdale 33306.

Money-Market Funds

A complete free list for individual investors (there are more than 300 funds) is available from The Investment Company Institute, 1600 M St. NW, Washington, DC 20036. And the Money Fund Safety Ratings* publishes a free pamphlet, *A Beginner's Guide to Money Funds*, with basic information on all such funds.
*Money Fund Safety Ratings, 3471 N. Federal Hwy., Fort Lauderdale 33306.

Bond-Fund Traps

Check mutual funds' performance over a period of years, including both up and down markets. Be wary of bond funds' figures. Since there's no standard method of calculating yields, each fund uses whatever system makes it look best. Also be wary of government-securities-fund advertising, which suggests the government "guarantees" the fund's yield. Bonds themselves may be guaranteed, but prices fluctuate with the interest rate.
Source: *US News & World Report.*

What the Experts Say About Some Funds

• Junk-bond funds may not be much safer than a single junk bond. Problem: Junk-bond funds are relatively new and have not been tested in a rough economic environment, warns Lou Ehrenkrantz of Ehrenkrantz & King.

• Municipal-bond funds are a great way to play falling interest rates for investors in the over-33% marginal tax bracket, says Norman Fosback of the Institute for Econometric Research.

• Tax-reform funds. Caution: So-called new mutual funds designed to benefit from tax reform are merely repackaged old goods. They concentrate on short-term gains with the aggressive use of leveraging, short selling, options and futures...all not very new...from Bill Donoghue.

- Tax-free money funds offer the highest after-tax yields for investors in 31% or higher tax brackets, calculates Norman Fosback.

- Low-risk stock funds. Growth & income funds, which invest in seasoned growth companies. Benefits: Regular dividends. . .growth of principal. . . stability. Bonus: Dividend-paying stocks should do well under the new tax law. . .from Carl Sargent of United Business Service Co.

- Public futures funds. Beware: Commodity futures funds are poor investments. Drawbacks: Low returns. . . inconsistent performance. . .high risk due to huge leverage. . . exorbitant fees. Warnings from Drs. Edwin Elton and Martin Gruber of New York University's Graduate School of Business Administration.

A Very Risky Kind Of Fund

Commodity-pool investments organized by brokerage firms are two to three times riskier than most stock and bond funds. . .and offer lower returns in exchange for the additional risk. In three of six 12-month periods studied, the average return on commodity funds was negative, compared with positive returns on most stock and bond funds. Other findings: The large front-end costs and management and transaction fees drag earnings down further. And the funds do not act as inflation hedges (as they are supposed to do).
Source: Study by New York University's Edwin Elton.

Investment Clubs

The average investment club doubles the value of its portfolio every five years. Few mutual funds can claim such a record.

The little clubs beat out big mutual funds for several reasons:

- Funds have to pay their managers.

- Clubs can invest in small, fast-growing stocks while the funds, because they are so large, must favor large companies.

- Quarterly reporting requirements force funds to do a lot of costly trading.

- When the market is low and stocks are cheap, funds are constrained by their unsophisticated individual investors who tend to pull their money out just when it's time to buy.

Club Investing
Philosophy: Invest small amounts (on average $20–$25/month per member) on a regular basis. . .in up and down markets. Doing this reduces the average price paid per share of stock.

Example: When a stock is trading at $4/share, $24 buys six shares. . .but if the stock rises to $6, the same sum will buy only four shares. You purchase more shares when a stock is cheaper—fewer when it's more expensive.

Clubs usually reinvest all dividends and select only stocks that they think have a good chance of doubling in value within five years. They also try to diversify their holdings, maintaining a portfolio of 12–20 different issues.

No matter how thorough a club's research, not all its picks will double. . .a few will even go down. But in most clubs' experience, there are always several big winners that pull up overall results.

Tried and true: If stocks are researched and selected carefully and a club invests on a regular basis, it will make money—often a lot—over the long term.

Trap: Going into an investment club to get rich quick—it won't happen. But within three to five years most clubs begin to realize a handsome payoff on their investment.

Forming a Club
The best way to get into an investment club is to form one yourself. Clubs have prearranged member limits, so unless you have a friend in a club, chances of getting in are slim. Optimal number of members: 10–15. . .a group that can meet at members' homes.

Look for prospective members in social or

business groups that you belong to. Ask each interested person to bring a friend. Try to assemble a group that's not too homogeneous . . . in which each member contributes something different.

Example: One member may be a computer whiz. . .another, someone with good intuition about trends . . . another, a very sharp stock picker . . . etc.

Schedule monthly meetings on the same night each month—for example, the third Monday—so that everyone can plan ahead.

Big mistake: Starting out with substantial lump-sum investments of, say, $500 or $1,000. If the market happens to be topping when this first investment is made, losses and disappointment will ensue. Better: Set a regular sum of $25–$30—more if everyone is willing—and start investing those small amounts regularly. Later, members will be able to increase their participation, if desired.

Investment decisions should be made by vote at each meeting. If some members have invested more money than others, votes should be weighted proportionately.

Structure a Partnership

A partnership is a more favorable structure than a corporation because, unlike shareholders, partners don't pay tax on profits twice. Corporations pay corporate income tax, and then individual shareholders are liable for tax on dividends. But in a partnership untaxed earnings flow through to the partners directly and are taxed only once at the individual's level. Extra tax benefit: Potential losses are also passed through to partners, who can use them to offset gains for tax purposes.

In most states partnerships are exempt from the onerous registration requirements and regulations that govern corporations. But even as a partnership, a club must register its name with the county clerk and pay a small fee. Recommended: Check your state's registration requirements with an attorney.

You'll also need a lawyer to draw up a partnership agreement. This spells out the purpose of the club, its organizational structure, how accounts and bookkeeping will be han-

dled, and what happens if a member dies or wishes to withdraw funds. It should be signed by every member of the club.

Because money is involved, the agreement should also state what partners may *not* do. Examples: Obligate the partnership to any extent whatever . . . or use the partnership's name or property without proper authority.

At the first meeting the club members should elect a presiding partner to run meetings . . . a recording partner to keep minutes . . . and a financial partner to keep records of receipts and disbursements, place buy- and sell-orders with the club's broker and prepare a statement of the liquidating value of the club's portfolio before each meeting is held.

The Broker

When the club's funds are still small, you may have trouble finding a broker willing to take your account. Helpful: Explain that you will add to the club's portfolio monthly. To facilitate relations, call your broker early or late in the day and keep the conversation short. It's least confusing to have only one member deal with the broker.

Before each meeting, check with the broker for any comments on your holdings and any new ideas or recommendations on the two or three stocks that the club will be discussing that evening. Encourage your broker to provide annual and quarterly reports—and analysts' research.

The relationship with the broker should be governed by a signed document in which both sides agree to their responsibilities. Securities can be kept in a "street name" with the broker, in the club's name or in the name of one or more nominated members. Easiest: Keeping stocks in a "street name" at the broker's office.

But some clubs prefer to actually hold the stock certificates and receive dividend checks directly. If stocks are in the name of the club or club members, company mailings such as quarterly reports and proxies also will arrive directly. Caution: If stock certificates are held by the club or members, keep them in a very safe place. It's very difficult and expensive to replace lost certificates.

It's impossible for a broker to attend every meeting, but invite him or her at least once a year.

Broadening Horizons

The main function of membership is to learn about investments and how the economy works. Best training: Researching an individual company. Great resource: The broker's office, where you will find abundant research information that's available to the firm's customers.

Some clubs name one member their "economist." Duties: To follow economic indicators that could affect the club's holdings and report to the group on a regular basis.

To learn more about investing and the stock market, you can also plan joint meetings with other clubs, dinner meetings with speakers or field trips to local stock exchanges.

Source: Thomas E. O'Hara, chairman, National Association of Investment Clubs (NAIC), 1515 E. Eleven Mile Rd., Royal Oak, MI 48067.

Safer Than Banks

Investors suffering from high anxiety are turning more and more to the safest investment there is: US Treasury securities.

Treasury bills (maturing within one year), notes (maturing in two to 10 years) and bonds (maturing after 10 years) are actually safer than government-insured bank accounts. Trap: There's only 1¢ in government insurance for every dollar of insured bank accounts. Even worse: Some of the insurance funds aren't in cash, but in illiquid receivables accepted from troubled banks.

By contrast, every penny of a T-bill is guaranteed by the full faith and credit of the federal government. And the government has *never* failed to pay its obligations.

Bonus: Liquidity, especially if they're purchased through a mutual fund that offers check-writing privileges. Special tax status: T-bills, notes and bonds bought by individuals

aren't subject to state income taxes. When these securities are purchased through a mutual fund, 25 of the 40 income tax states levy a tax.

Source: James M. Benham, chairman, Benham Capital Management Group, 755 Page Mill Rd., Palo Alto, CA 94304.

About Bank CDs

Bank certificates of deposit are worth a second look. There are still penalties for early withdrawal, but these CDs have virtually no risk. They're advised for investors willing to go out six, 12 or 18 months.

Safeguards: Deal only with institutions insured by the Federal Deposit Insurance Corporation or the Federal Savings & Loan Insurance Corporation. Put no more than $100,000, including the interest that will be earned, in any one bank account.

If you follow these recommendations, it's safe to put deposits into even small banks that have to pay the high rates to attract funds. They're listed weekly in *Barron's* under the heading "Top Savings Deposit Yields."

Get answers to these questions:

• Is the bank federally insured?

• Is the rate quoted in this week's *Barron's* still in effect?

• If my deposit reaches the bank tomorrow, will I still get that rate?

Not every bank will do it, but ask if the bank will designate a preassigned account number for you. Then you can make out your check to the institution, but mark it *For Deposit Only* into that account number. When the canceled check is returned, you'll have a record of the transaction.

It's also a good idea to send checks by Federal Express or Express Mail to ensure that the money arrives the next day.

Many investors don't realize that they can also buy bank CDs through Merrill Lynch and other brokers. Benefit: Merrill Lynch maintains a market in CDs, so it's possible to sell them back before maturity.

Source: William E. Donoghue, chairman, The Donoghue Organization, and publisher of *Donoghue's Moneyletter.*

CD Savvy

• Customers who deposit more than $50,000 into a certificate of deposit (CD) can usually negotiate their own maturity date and when and how interest will be paid. Not negotiable: Minimum penalty for early withdrawal. That is mandated by federal law.

• Buy several CDs in small denominations instead of one large one. Reason: If you need only part of the money, you won't have to withdraw it all and pay an early withdrawal penalty on the full amount.

Source: Bill Donoghue, chairman, The Donoghue Organization in Holliston, MA and publisher of *Donoghue's Moneyletter.*

Investing in Mortgage-Backed Securities

Pass-through securities based on pools of mortgages are attracting investors interested in higher yields than those from comparable fixed-maturity securities. The size of the yields is the trade-off for variable cash flows and maturities and for the accounting problems associated with holding these securities.

Mortgage-backed securities reflect the underlying cash flows of their respective pools of mortgages. The mortgages produce monthly payments of principal and interest, but monthly prepayments can vary. This unknown factor is largely a product of fluctuations in interest rates.

When interest rates are declining, mortgage holders generally speed up prepayments, effectively shortening the maturity of the pass-through security. For the investor, this means

reinvesting the capital sooner—at the current lower rate. Conversely, as interest rates increase, prepayments decrease. The maturity of the security is lengthened just at the time the investor wants to shorten it to protect his capital.

The accounting problems attached to mortgage-backed securities stem from the need to keep track of monthly cash flows. For example, the investor must reduce his cost basis by the return of principal, calculate whether there is a profit or loss and whether it is short term or long term. Also, the amount of the monthly interest—as opposed to principal—payment must be accurately recorded. Nevertheless, the yield spread on these pass-throughs makes them very attractive.

Government-Sponsored Securities

While any institution may pool mortgages and sell interests in those pools, the three best-known sources of mortgage-backed pass-throughs are the Government National Mortgage Association, also known as GNMA or Ginnie Mae; the Federal Home Loan Mortgage Corporation, FHLMC or Freddie Mac; and the Federal National Mortgage Association, FNMA or Fannie Mae.

As an agency of the US government, Ginnie Mae guarantees the timely payment of principal and interest for FHA and VA mortgages submitted to it by mortgage originators. The mortgages are pooled by Ginnie Mae and sold to investors. Freddie Mac, a corporation owned by the Federal Home Loan banks, provides its guarantee to those mortgages submitted to it for pooling. Fannie Mae is a federally sponsored, publicly owned corporation that also guarantees the cash flow of the mortgages behind its pass-through securities. Thus, while all of the mortgage pools are guaranteed by each entity, only Ginnie Mae is backed by the full faith and credit of the US government.

The three government-sponsored securities provide investors several advantages: mortgage quality is standardized; there is geographic distribution within pools; and the size of origination is conducive to an active and liquid secondary market in mortgage-backed securities.

Mutual Funds

Mutual funds of mortgage-backed pass-throughs have made it possible for more investors to enjoy the benefits of these securities. The $25,000 minimum investments for government-sponsored securities close the primary market to the small investor, but also prevent even the large investor from plowing back cash flows as they are received, thus reducing total return. Mutual funds have lower minimums for both initial and subsequent investments. They also simplify the accounting process, provide professional management, offer diversification, and, by pooling the funds of many investors, reduce the markups entailed in buying and selling the securities. For a fee, the mutual funds turn a complicated investment into a relatively simple—and profitable—one for all types of investors.

Source: Jack H. Lemein, vice president and portfolio manager, Franklin Resources, Inc., Box 5994, San Mateo, CA 94402.

Ginnie Maes vs. Treasury Bonds

When interest rates are likely to drop you're better off investing in Treasury securities than in higher-coupon Ginnie Mae bonds. Reason: As rates move down, the mortgages backing the Ginnie Mae bonds will be paid off, thereby reducing the return to Ginnie Mae investors. But Treasury bonds can't be paid off early, so buying bonds will produce capital appreciation as lower rates make bonds more valuable.

Source: John Rutledge, chairman, Claremont Economics Institute, writing in his *Main Street Journal*.

Gold Vs. Inflation–Gold Vs. Deflation

Gold is an investor's best insurance against the changing value of money. It's common knowledge that gold tends to appreciate in value during inflationary periods, just like other tangibles such as collectibles, precious gems and real estate. Little-known: The price of gold also rises in deflationary times.

Deflation usually occurs when people get themselves so deeply in debt that they must produce and sell increasing quantities of goods and services to raise the money to meet their interest payments. As more and more goods and services get dumped on the market, their prices fall and the real value of cash rises.

At first glance, it would seem that in this scenario the price of gold would go down. Reasoning: People with gold would sell it to raise cash to make interest payments. But this logic doesn't take into account the complexity of the financial system. The price of gold would actually rise.

How this would happen: In a severe deflation, widespread default on bank debt would cause a rapid erosion of confidence in the bank system. Panicked investors would convert cash into gold, boosting the price of the metal. This buying would counter the selling of gold to raise cash to pay down debt.

To restore confidence in the financial system, as a last resort, central banks would have to raise the price of gold to such a high level that gold holders would finally be willing to sell it in exchange for paper money.

This occurred in the deflation of the 1930s, when the government had to boost the price of gold by about 70%—to $35 an ounce—to stabilize the financial system.

How to Buy Gold

• Gold coins are the most convenient way for most people to buy gold. Best: The Mexican Gold Peso and Austrian Gold Crown, whose prices closely reflect their gold content. Collectors' coins, such as the American Eagle, carry a significant numismatic premium.

• Gold-mining stock mutual funds.

• Gold-mining stocks. On the surface, the best value are the blue-chip South African shares. But given South Africa's political troubles, they're high-risk.

Source: John Hathaway, principal, Hudson Capital Advisors, 3 E. 54 St., New York 10022. The firm advises wealthy individuals and corporate pension funds.

Jeff Nichols's Gold Investing Strategy

Since the price of gold often moves in the opposite direction of bonds and inflation-sensitive stocks, gold is a good hedge against a downturn on Wall Street.

The only golden rule about gold is that there are no golden rules.

But there is a useful guideline: Put 10%–20% of your investment portfolio into gold-related assets. If you hold a large number of interest-sensitive stocks such as banks and utilities, invest toward the higher percentage.

If you already own many stocks that tend to move up with inflation (real estate and natural resources, for example), use the lower percentage for gold.

Nichols's Strategy

• Coins. Stick to the one-ounce Canadian Maple Leaf and the one-ounce American Eagle. They're widely traded, and dealer quotes are available in most daily papers. Avoid: Coins where premiums are high and markets thin.

• Certificates and storage programs. Banks and large brokerage houses sell gold by issuing certificates, passbooks or periodic account statements. Physically, the gold stays in the possession of the issuing institutions.

Advantages: Investors don't have to worry about storing the bullion. These are highly liquid because the issuers will repurchase your gold at any time.

Price: Commissions vary substantially. It pays to shop around! Moreover, issuers usually charge an annual storage and insurance fee. Typical: 1% per year.

• Stocks. For investors who want gold mining stock, North American companies are strongly recommended.

Reasons: Production costs are low, often $150–$225 an ounce. When they're far below current bullion prices it means profits can rise even if gold's prices stay flat. Many North American gold mining companies are well managed.

• Mutual funds. Like other mutual funds,

the gold-oriented ones can take some of the risk out of investing in individual companies. That's especially useful for gold mining, where investors often lack the expertise to evaluate these companies.

Source: Jeffrey Nichols, president, American Precious Metals Advisors, 45 E. 25 St., New York 10010. He's author of *The Complete Book of Gold Investing*, Dow Jones-Irwin.

Investing in Diamonds

There is no question that in the 1970s, diamonds outperformed most investments. For instance, a $5,000 purchase in 1970 would have netted $25,000 in 1975. A $5,000 purchase in 1975 would have netted $60,000 in 1980. However, a $5,000 purchase in 1980 would have netted $2,500 or less in 1985, depending on diamond size and grade. Why did the price fall, and what does this signify for investors?

The prices of diamond "rough" (before the diamond is cut and finished) steadily increase over the years, but not necessarily every year or in predictable amounts. There were four price increases in 1973 that amounted to a 38.2% return overall, no price increase in 1974 or 1975, major price increases in 1977 and 1978, and few changes for several years after that. In the early 1980s, when investors switched from diamonds to high-yielding money-market funds, many cutters were forced to liquidate their inventories; the result was a downward price trend. Since a prerequisite of sound investment is to buy when prices are low, these fluctuations mean opportunities for substantial gains.

Rising Prices

Four elements contribute most directly to increases in diamond prices.

• World prosperity. If the global economic situation is strong, demand usually rises.

• A weakening dollar. Since diamonds are

priced in US dollars, the weaker the dollar, the higher the price.

• Chaotic conditions. Diamonds are the most portable concentrated form of wealth that is internationally marketable. Millions of dollars of wealth can be taken out of a country privately and undetected. With increases in political turmoil in certain parts of the world, diamonds and other gems play an increasingly important role.

• Inflation. Diamonds have traditionally increased in value over inflation. The price of diamond rough increased an average of 16% per year from 1966 through 1979. When high inflation returns, it may be a major factor in increasing diamond prices.

Purchases and Liquidation

When buying diamonds, always deal with a reputable firm, preferably one that has been in business at least 15 years. All too often, people buy diamonds from a company only to find, several months later, that the company has gone out of business. Also, when you buy, ask for a 30-day refund policy in case you change your mind. You should have a clear understanding at time of purchase of the liquidation policy of your diamond source.

Know what you are buying. Have your purchase accompanied by a trade laboratory report issued by the Gemological Institute of America (GIA). GIA is the most respected gem laboratory and its reports are recognized throughout the world. Three gemologists judge a stone's color, cut, clarity, and weight, and provide comments. (Having a GIA report also is of great benefit during liquidation.) Price lists accompany diamonds with GIA reports. These are excellent guides for price comparisons, to make sure you aren't overpaying as well as to check the current value of your diamonds.

Source: Will Hurwitz, president of Colonial Jewelers, 9 West Patrick Street, Frederick, MD 21701 and of Colonial Diamond Brokers, 2000 Broadway, New York 10023. He is an associate member of the American Society of Appraisers and past chairman of the Jewelers Liaison Committee to the International Investment Gemstone Council.

Why Rubies, Emeralds, And Sapphires Are a Safer Investment Than Diamonds

When prices of investment-grade diamonds plunged as much as 30%, colored gemstones magically held on to heady price gains. Reason: Scarcity. Only some $200 million in rubies, emeralds, and sapphires were sold in the US in a recent year, a fraction of the amount of diamonds sold.

The areas where the finest stones come from: Cambodia, Thailand, Sri Lanka, Burma and parts of Africa. Scarcity factor: These areas are politically unstable and, therefore, are not reliable sources.

• Grading. Although techniques in grading colored stones are less advanced than those for diamonds, tests under microscopes and refractometers allow gemologists to distinguish synthetic stones from real ones. They can often tell you the origin of the stone. Certain countries of origin command higher prices. Example: Burma rubies.

• Flaws. Although all stones have flaws, gross flaws ruin the stone.

• Setting. Determine whether the setting does justice to the stone. Does it overwhelm the stone?

• Color. It is the most important determinant of price once the stone is adjudged authentic. Never view a single stone. Compare it with several others. Why: The clarity of the redness of a ruby, and the absence of orange, pink, purple or brown, is what makes it most valuable. The variation is best seen by looking at several stones.

A family-owned jewelry retailer with an excellent reputation is the best place to buy. They are willing to risk their own money investing in fine gems from around the world. Larger chains of jewelers can't afford to invest. They custom-order.

In small towns without direct access to a large selection of colored gemstones, go to reputable jewelers and commission them to find the kind of stone you like and can afford.

Many fine jewelers have connections with the American Gem Society, which will send them a selection of stones for conditional purchase. The jewelers receive a commission for their advice and service.

The best gems to buy are stones over one carat that are free of externally visible flaws. Buy one that will look good mounted in jewelry. That way, if the investment does not gain in value, at least you will have a remarkable piece of jewelry, not just a stone in a glass case.

Expect to keep a colored gem for at least five years, when buying for investment. Then evaluate what the stone would go for on the dealers' (wholesale) market. Alternative: Put stones up for auction at Sotheby's or Christie's. Although you cannot be sure of a definite sales price, you can put a minimum price on your item.

Should You Invest in Art?

Art should be purchased because it provides pleasure, not because it may appreciate. Historically, the art market has been unstable and, generally, unpredictable. It progresses in cycles: What is desirable today may be undesirable tomorrow. Due to the number of variables involved in these cycles, it is best not to classify art as a sound financial investment.

Investment-Quality Art
For any work of art to become a good investment, it must be able to stand the test of time. The value of an item rarely appreciates overnight. Instead its value develops over a period of time, often after decades have elapsed.

Art that does appreciate is usually an outstanding example of a specific type of art. It becomes investment-quality because of its uniqueness and because it exemplifies the artist's style and period.

Trying to find these examples on today's art market is difficult. When they do appear, they are generally sought by museums, major institutions, and established collectors. Most contemporary art available for purchase has not met the tests of time or uniqueness.

Be especially careful of purchasing prints as an investment. In general, contemporary art that is mass-produced does not appreciate. Most prints, whether they are designated lithographs, serigraphs, etchings, mezzotints, or something else, are simply prints on pieces of paper containing an artist's signature. There may be thousands of these prints available from a given work. Only a minute percentage of them will ever appreciate. Remember that an original is always more valuable than a mass-produced duplicate.

The Best Reasons for Acquisition
Art is an expression of a given artist. It is something that conveys a message, a thought, or a feeling. If you are interested in acquiring a work of art that may appreciate, ask yourself not only whether it has stood the test of time and is unique, but also whether it conveys anything to you.

Do not allow your judgment to be clouded because an item appears to be increasing in value. Disregard advice that says it is a good investment. Some dealers will tell you, "This is a great investment." Do not let them persuade you. If it is such a great investment, why is it still on the market, or why hasn't the dealer added it to his or her private collection?

Buy a work of art because it appeals to you and you feel that it will bring you pleasure. These should be your primary reasons for acquisition.

Source: Richard Friedman, president, auctioneer, and appraiser, Chicago Art Galleries, Inc., 20 West Hubbard Street, Chicago, IL 60610. He is a member of the National Auctioneers Association, Appraisers Association of America, International Society of Appraisers, the Illinois State Auctioneers Association, and the American Arbitration Association, Panel of Arbitrators.

Nineteenth and Twentieth Century Oil Paintings

The art market—like any other market—runs in cycles: There are periods when certain types of paintings are more desired than others. Recently, there has been a marked increase in the popularity of quality paintings from the nineteenth and early twentieth centuries. Those most likely to appreciate in value are storytelling paintings of the Victorian era and the turn of the century.

European Art

There has been a tremendous increase in popularity in "Orientalist" paintings. These were done chiefly by late nineteenth century European artists such as Rudolf Ernst, Abraham Cooper, Horace Vernet, Eugene Delacroix, John Frederick Lewis, Adolf Schreyer, and others. The subjects are mainly Middle Eastern scenes: Bedouins on camels or horses in battle, Arab warriors, rug merchants, and harem girls. Some are fantasies. Others are depictions of Far Eastern cultures.

Prices of Orientalist paintings on the auction market are soaring. A painting that sold for $10,000 just 10 years ago now brings a price in the area of $100,000. Eventually, the demand for these types of paintings will level off, but this will probably not occur in the near future.

European oil paintings of the Modern, Impressionist and Post-Impressionist periods have also seen tremendous leaps in value. Works by Renoir, Gauguin, Van Gogh, and others now fetch well into seven figures.

American Art

Paintings by American artists of the late nineteenth and early twentieth centuries, such as Guy Wiggins, J.G. Brown, Alfred Thompson Bricher, Thomas Moran, and Mary Cassatt, are surging upward in value. Record prices have recently also been received for American Impressionists, some of whom had been relatively unknown.

American artists of the first half of the twentieth century deserve special attention. A thoughtful collector would be wise to start a good collection of late nineteenth and early-to-middle twentieth century paintings by American artists such as Emil Carlsen, William Chadwick, Charles Curran, Ray Sloan Bredin, Wilson Irvine, Alson Clark, Henry Ward

Ranger, James Carroll Beckwith, Chauncey Rycer, and others. Their value is unquestionably increasing.

Source: Richard Friedman, president, auctioneer, and appraiser, Chicago Art Galleries, Inc., 20 West Hubbard Street, Chicago, IL 60610. He is a member of the National Auctioneers Association, Appraisers Association of America, International Society of Appraisers, the Illinois State Auctioneers Association, and the American Arbitration Association, Panel of Arbitrators.

Bronze and Marble Sculpture

If you plan to buy a bronze sculpture strictly for decoration or sentiment, don't hesitate. If you plan to buy it as an investment—think twice. The bronze market is flooded with reproductions and prices have begun to fall, because the reproductions are so good that they are almost indistinguishable from the originals.

On the other hand, if you plan to buy a bronze sculpture because you wish to own an original by a famous artist or artisan, make certain that you go to a reputable dealer or auction house. If you are not knowledgeable, always seek expert advice.

Old and New Bronze

An original will be accompanied by a history or provenance. It will have been authenticated as an original work of the artist. Be prepared: Since old original bronze castings have all but disappeared from art market inventories, an original will probably also have a high price.

Because of the flood of reproductions into the marketplace, many serious collectors have turned away from the eighteenth, nineteenth, and early twentieth century masters. They are now more interested in modern and contemporary masters. As a result, these works are bringing record auction prices.

To acquire the work of a modern master, watch the auction market carefully for artists' works that rise in value. Good sources of information are magazines such as *Art & Auc-*

tion and *Art & Antiques. Leonard's Art Auction Index* and Mayer's *International Auction Records* are also valuable sources.

Marble and Alabaster

Unlike bronze sculptures, marble and alabaster sculptures are difficult to reproduce and relatively few copies have been made. Consequently, sculptures in these materials that appear on the market have increased in value. Some marble and alabaster pieces of fine quality are available at less than exorbitant prices. Many late nineteenth and early twentieth century works—good examples of the work of French, German, American, and Italian artisans—can be obtained in estate sales.

Source: Richard Friedman, president, auctioneer, and appraiser, Chicago Art Galleries, Inc., 20 West Hubbard Street, Chicago, IL 60610. He is a member of the National Auctioneers Association, Appraisers Association of America, International Society of Appraisers, the Illinois State Auctioneers Association, and the American Arbitration Association, Panel of Arbitrators.

Finding Good Sources And Honest Dealers for Collectibles

How do you locate the best dealer or source for collectibles? Whether you are interested in paintings, sculpture, silver, or antique furniture, most major cities have a range of sources, including auction houses, dealers specializing in particular items, art galleries, and wholesale/retail stores. To find out which of these are good sources and honest dealers:

• Make inquiries of persons who have dealt with businesses in your area of interest.
• Ask opinions of dealers in the trade.
• Check with the local Better Business Bureau for information about local business practices.
• Study publications such as *Dun & Bradstreet,* which provide specific information on corporate conditions and credit ratings of individual firms.

Buying at Auction

Auction houses are excellent sources for collectibles, antiques, and works of art. They usually have their own experts who can answer questions and advise you. Their auction catalogs give valuable information on the history, provenance, and condition of the items that are for sale. *Note:* The conditions of sale will be published in the catalog. Read them carefully; each auction house has its own set of conditions.

Trust officers of banks can be one of the best sources of information on the reliability of auction houses. Why? They are often called upon to liquidate estates through auction. Also, a variety of magazines and newspapers publish information on auctions. Among the more widely read magazines are *Art & Auction, Art & Antiques, Connoisseur,* and *Antique Monthly.* Some newspapers that publish information about auctions are *The New York Times, The Boston Globe, The San Francisco Examiner, The Washington Post, The Chicago Tribune, Antique Week Tri-State Trader.*

Buying from a Dealer

If you don't have connections with the art world, magazines and newspapers are a good place to start when searching for a reputable dealer. The more prestigious magazines are selective in their choice of advertisers. You can expect that the dealers who are accepted as advertisers have been checked out and are generally reliable. Still, it is prudent to investigate them. Make inquiries from publishers, editors, and critics of these publications.

Seek the opinions of those in the trade. Ask dealers their opinions about the reliability of other dealers. Look for dealers with connections to public and private institutions such as museums and banking establishments. Ask the curators of these institutions who they use for the acquisition of works of art for collections.

In addition to helping you locate the item you want, a reputable dealer will always try to answer questions. If an answer is not readily available, he or she will assist you in finding it.

Dealers sometimes allow you to purchase

an item on approval. If, within a designated period of time, the item is not what you want, you may return it at no charge. Reputable dealers usually issue a certificate of authenticity for an item they sell. Some dealers also offer guarantees; others offer exchange privileges that hold for a particular period of time. Find out about the dealer's policy in these areas before making a purchase.

Source: Richard Friedman, president, auctioneer, and appraiser, Chicago Art Galleries, Inc., 20 West Hubbard Street, Chicago, IL 60610. He is a member of the National Auctioneers Association, Appraisers Association of America, International Society of Appraisers, the Illinois State Auctioneers Association, and the American Arbitration Association, Panel of Arbitrators.

How an Insider Buys at An Auction

Here's how you can bid like an insider at an auction.

• Obtain an auction catalog. Read the descriptions of the items for sale, noting their estimated selling prices (prices may not be included in the catalog). Also read the conditions of sale printed in the front of the catalog; these vary from auction house to auction house.

• Research the terminology that will be used in the auction. A glossary is usually part of the catalog.

• Attend the pre-auction exhibition to scrutinize the items that most interest you. Leave no unsettled questions. (Once they are sold, items are the responsibility of the purchaser.)

• Ask for estimates if you do not know them. Decide what you are willing to spend and set your limits.

• Arrive at the auction early and select a location accessible to the vision and hearing of the auctioneer. Dealers generally sit or stand at the rear of the audience to gain an overview of the proceedings. They are interested in seeing who is bidding and how the bidding is progressing.

• Take note of your competition. Insiders, particularly dealers, are customarily discreet in their bidding. Occasionally, they will use a prearranged signal to alert the auctioneer. Most bidding is indicated by a wave of a hand, a catalog, or a paddle.

• To minimize the chance of error, verbalize your bid if it varies from the increment established by the auctioneer.

• Do not exceed your preset limit unless the item is rare and may not come on the market again. Do not be carried away by emotion. Only novices do that.

• You may bid against a known dealer. If you bid after a dealer has stopped bidding, realize that you may buy the item and will probably pay far less for it than you would in the dealer's shop.

Intangibles Are Important

Act with assurance by appearing to know more than those around you, even if you do not. Assume command of a situation when it is to your advantage and remain silent when it is not. Address people by their first names, especially the auctioneer. If you can, chat with the auctioneer before, during, or after the auction. Conversely, you may choose to remain inconspicuous, sitting quietly, waiting for what you came to bid upon.

Insiders are astute and concise. They know when, where, how, and how much to bid. Most importantly, they know when to stop bidding.

Source: Richard Friedman, president, auctioneer, and appraiser, Chicago Art Galleries, Inc., 20 West Hubbard Street, Chicago, IL 60610. He is a member of the National Auctioneers Association, Appraisers Association of America, International Society of Appraisers, the Illinois State Auctioneers Association, and the American Arbitration Association, Panel of Arbitrators.

Choosing an Appraiser

The qualifications of an appraiser are critically important to an appraisal's value. When you choose one, seek a professional rather than a local antique dealer who may have just opened last week and hung a sign in the window professing to be an appraiser.

Recommendations from people familiar with an appraiser's work are invaluable; attorneys, accountants, and bank officers frequently utilize the services of appraisers. The local Chamber of Commerce and the local Better Business Bureau also may provide information regarding the business practices of appraisers. In certain instances, the opinions of other appraisers can be helpful as well.

Since the appraisal industry is not regulated, it is important that an appraiser belong to a recognized appraisal organization. These have developed strict requirements for membership and insure that anyone carrying their credentials will know what he is doing. Some of the more highly esteemed organizations are the American Society of Appraisers, the Appraisers Association of America, and the International Society of Appraisers. Most qualified appraisers belong to one of these organizations, and some belong to two or more.

Experience is important, too. An appraiser's years of experience give some indication of his knowledge and expertise. Do not expect to find an appraiser who knows everything. As in other professions, appraisers specialize in specific areas. Ask if the appraiser is qualified to appraise the items you have. Find out his areas of specialty.

Finally, check on the appraiser's fee in advance. It is a fairly accepted practice among appraisers to base their fees on the time they spend executing the appraisal, rather than on a percentage of the value of the appraisal.

Source: Richard Friedman, president, auctioneer, and appraiser, Chicago Art Galleries, Inc., 20 West Hubbard Street, Chicago, IL 60610. He is a member of the National Auctioneers Association, Appraisers Association of America, International Society of Appraisers, the Illinois State Auctioneers Association, and the American Arbitration Association, Panel of Arbitrators.

What You Should Know About Appraisals

When you need an appraisal for any type of collectible, certain information should always be included: The qualifications of the appraiser, the purpose(s) of the appraisal, a description of the object being appraised, its history or the provenance, the economic factors at the time of the appraisal, the date, and the appraiser's signature. Sometimes a photograph of the object is included.

The qualifications of the appraiser are of primary importance and should always be stated on the appraisal. They should encompass the appraiser's professional affiliations, his or her particular area of expertise, and the length of time he or she has been appraising.

Appraisals may be done for several reasons: For insurance purposes (retail replacement value), tax purposes, donation purposes, and "fair market value" purposes.

Note: Appraisals for tax purposes should be executed by members of recognized appraisal organizations. To be accepted by the Internal Revenue Service, the appraisal must fulfill the requirements outlined in IRS regulation number 20.2031–6, paragraph 6407.25. Most appraisal societies have established criteria for doing appraisals similar to those of the IRS.

The description of the object should be well detailed. It should state what the object is, the material of which it is composed, its size, color, clarity, subject, rarity, age, uniqueness, and any other information the appraiser feels is important.

The item's history or provenance tells where the item originated, which galleries or dealers have sold it and for what prices, and gives an evaluation of its quality relative to others of its kind.

Since the art market fluctuates continually, the appraisal should state the pertinent economic factors prevailing at the time of the appraisal. What is important today may not be important tomorrow. For example, a silver spoon currently valued at $50 may be valued at $6 tomorrow because of a drop in the price of raw silver.

Source: Richard Friedman, president, auctioneer, and appraiser, Chicago Art Galleries, Inc., 20 West Hubbard Street, Chicago, IL 60610. He is a member of the National Auctioneers Association, Appraisers Association of America, International Society of Appraisers, the Illinois State Auctioneers Association, and the American Arbitration Association, Panel of Arbitrators.

13 MAKING MONEY WITH REAL ESTATE

Property Ownership That's Right for You

Property can be held in a variety of forms—as an individual, a corporation, a partnership, a trust, or a syndicate, pool, or joint venture. Within each general category there are further variations that affect your tax treatment and legal liability. The primary factors to consider when choosing among the different forms of ownership are the degree of economic protection and the tax incidence. Use the following list of general guidelines when deciding on the most appropriate form of ownership for you.

• Individual ownership. This is the simplest form of ownership: The economic profits and tax benefits of property flow directly to you. Yet it does have disadvantages. It exposes you to the greatest risk—your liability is unlimited. This form of ownership should therefore only be undertaken if the property in question does not unduly expose you to potentially excessive losses or legal claims from third par-

ties. Also, for taxpayers in a high personal tax bracket, property held in this form that starts to produce operating profits may result in needlessly high taxation. Finally, individually owned property often becomes the center of disagreement during marital discord and divorce. (A spouse usually does have rights in such property.)

• Corporate ownership. To limit your liability and gain the ability to effectively transfer ownership interests without triggering local real estate transfer taxes, consider corporate ownership. The two kinds of corporations are the so-called "C corporation" (whose income and losses are generally taxed separately from those of its shareholders) and the "S corporation" (whose income and losses are generally passed through and taxed to its shareholders proportionately).

C corporations insulate owners from the profits and losses of the property (both economically and taxwise). However, profits are subject to double taxation—first when earned by the corporation and again when dividends are distributed. A solution to this problem is to extract the profits from the corporation through tax-deductible owner-employee compensation arrangements. However, C corporations also subject the latent gain in corporate assets to double taxation—when such assets are sold and/or the corporation is liquidated. And this double-taxation of gain may generally only be avoided by electing "S corporation" status considerably in advance of sale.

S corporations allow profits to pass through and be taxed (only once) to the shareholders at their normal personal tax rates. Shareholders' deductions for losses generally are limited to the extent of their loans and capital contributions made directly to the corporation. Under the new tax law, these corporations are compelled to utilize the calendar year as their tax year.

Use great care when employing the S corporation. The tax laws regarding its operation can be tricky.

S corporations may have no more than 35 qualifying shareholders (a husband and wife are treated as one). Generally, only individuals, estates, and special trusts can qualify.

There can only be one class of corporate stock, but voting differences are permitted.

Election of S corporation tax status requires the consent of all the shareholders. Election must have been made during the preceding tax year of the corporation or by the fifteenth day of the third month of its current year.

Different rules apply to the taxation of an S corporation's passive income (for example, rents, dividends, interest) and long-term capital gains. Tax treatment will depend on whether the corporation was an S corporation from inception or operated previously as a C corporation.

• Partnership ownership. Most frequently used for multiparty ownership, a partnership is not treated as a separate taxable entity; it merely acts as a conduit for gains and losses to pass to its members. A partnership facilitates the maximum use of tax-shelter deductions. As a partner, you can personally deduct losses to the extent of your capital contributions and loans to the partnership. In the case of real estate, you also can deduct losses to the extent of third-party nonrecourse loans to the partnership. A limited partnership, which has both general and limited partners, provides limited liability for the limited partners, while exposing the general partners to the greatest legal and economic risk.

• Trust ownership. Several states allow the creation of a "land trust," which operates solely as a title holding vehicle—the trustee has no actual power over the property. Trust ownership of this type is not treated as a taxable entity, but merely as a conduit to the owners. It is important that the trustee not have "real" powers over the trust, or it will be considered a "business trust." In this event, unless very carefully structured and operated, the trust will be taxed as a corporation.

Real estate investment trusts (REITs) are a special kind of trust whose treatment under the tax law is similar to that of mutual funds. To qualify as a REIT, the trust must meet strict ownership, income, and asset tests and must actually distribute 95% of its taxable income (excluding net capital gains). This kind of distributed income is taxed to the beneficiaries upon receipt rather than to the trust, and the remaining 5% is taxed to the trust at regular corporate rates. Because REITs can only be effectively utilized for large, specialized ventures with numerous participants, this form of ownership has limited application.

• Syndicate, pool, or joint venture. These are business labels for a group of individuals, partnerships, trusts, or corporations that have joined together to acquire, hold, and/or develop an interest in property. The distinction among the terms is not well defined, although, for tax purposes, each is generally treated as a partnership. Broadly defined, "joint venture" denotes a team effort on a single transaction; "syndicate" denotes the sharing of financial responsibilities; and "pool" emphasizes the joining of the participants' financial and management resources.

Source: Richard J. Flaster, Esq., president, Flaster, Greenberg, Mann & Wallenstein, PC, 5 Greentree Centre, Suite 200, Marlton, NJ 08053. In addition to working as a tax attorney, he has written several books and lectured widely on a range of tax subjects, including real estate taxation, divorce taxation, and personal tax planning.

How To Win The Real Estate Game

First low inflation. . .and then tax reform. For a while the combination looked like a one-two punch to knock out real estate as an investment. But that was a snap judgment. The reality is that real estate is still a very good investment.

But there is a change. Real estate investors must stop thinking about quick profits that occurred when inflation was high. Today they must get used to having money tied up longer—six to seven years, on average.

Examples: Property that produces rental income or that has a good chance of appreciating in value.

Economic appreciation is especially important now since capital gains are now taxed for individuals at the same rate as any other income. (Formerly, 60% of long-term capital gain was tax-free.)

Today's Best Investments

• Buying rental property has become about the best way for an individual to invest in real estate. Look for: Rental income that's high enough to cover operating costs. This is particularly important for people with adjusted gross incomes of more than $150,000, because they can no longer deduct real estate losses from their personal income taxes.

Best: Multiple-family buildings with up to 10 units that are located in the same town as the owner. They're small enough to be managed by the owner. Look for a building in a stable or improving neighborhood. Caution: Investigate local rent laws carefully before buying—rent control and noneviction rules can cut profits drastically.

• Limited partnerships are coming back into favor, particularly newer offerings with investment units priced as low as $1,000 each, compared with the typical $50,000 and up for traditional syndicates. By investing in a limited partnership, the individual avoids the problems of finding the right property to invest in and managing it once the deal is closed.

Look for properties that are already in the black. Important: That limited partners take priority over the general partners when it comes to distributing profits. Rule of thumb: If a property can't produce at least an 8% annual return to limited partners, it's probably not a good investment. Bonus: Cash received from these partnerships is usually sheltered at the partnership level, so it's not taxable as income when it's distributed.

Best properties: Those already occupied by profitable businesses and that have a high value to boot.

Example: Nurseries are especially attractive. Because demand for plants and shrubs is steady throughout the year, they net a more regular profit than food crops do. In most cases, nurseries are located near major cities and suburbs, so the land itself increases in value as the cities grow.

Other Investments

• Real estate investment trusts have traditionally invested in profit-making properties, so they aren't seriously affected by tax reform.

How they work: Investors buy shares for $5,000–$10,000 each. The money is then invested by the trust managers in a variety of income-producing properties. Investors receive regular income based on their participation. When the properties are sold, investors receive special dividends based on the appreciation of each property. Added safety: Because REIT shares earn income, they're far more liquid than interest in tax shelters. In some cases REIT shares can be sold back to the trust manager.

• Mortgage loan partnerships are the fastest-growing type of real estate investment and also one of the safest. As a rule, they invest in properties that have significantly higher values than the mortgage amounts and high returns because a portion of rent increases is passed on to the investors.

How they work: For as little as $1,000 investors can buy a share in a partnership that purchases mortgages on commercial properties. These mortgages are written, however, so that

435

the management company will get a portion of the rent increases on the property.

Example: The partnership may mortgage a property for 10%, but if rents rise above an amount stated in the contract, mortgage payments rise by several percentage points. The additional income is passed on to investors. For safety, virtually all mortgage loan partnerships put up less money than a particular property is worth. Investors should look for partnerships that offer 12%–14% annual returns over the life of the deal, typically 10–20 years.

Caution: Because mortgage loan partnerships are relatively new (the first gained SEC approval in 1979), often there isn't a secondary market for the securities. That means investors may find their money locked up for the duration of the mortgage.

What to avoid:

New construction in depressed markets. Even though building owners and banks are now offering strong incentives for investors to buy new buildings that were put up during the past 10 years—typically in the Sun Belt—it's unlikely that they can become profitable for years.

Raw land. Incredible profits can be made by buying cheaply land that's in the path of major urban and suburban developments. But the odds are tremendously against accurately forecasting where, when, and if the growth will occur. If you're willing to take this type of risk, make sure the general partner is very close to local planning commissions.

Source: Craig B. Haber, tax manager, Touche Ross Financial Services Center, 1 World Trade Center, New York 10048.

Best Investment for a Retirement Plan

Properly structured real estate securities are, by far, the favorite alternative for retirement plans. Investors have found that these securities have the potential to deliver the best features of both equity and debt instruments.

The securities being chosen are real estate limited partnerships—specifically, partnerships that invest in a pool of shared-appreciation mortgages or a pool of all-cash purchases of income-producing properties or a combination of the two. Real estate investment programs such as these provide tax-exempt investors with the broadest range of benefits in exchange for the smallest degree of risk.

Shared-appreciation real estate mortgages lock in an attractive contractual return and offer an additional return based on a share in increases in rental income and sale proceeds. Much less common, but also available, are investments in the all-cash purchase of income-producing property. These can provide the same types of benefits as participation mortgages when they are structured to ensure the safety and certainty of income. The requirements are economically sound properties, leased to financially responsible tenants, on leases with escalating base rents.

Either type of real estate limited partnership can satisfy all eight of the criteria commonly agreed upon as the most important in any retirement plan. Here's how:

• Safety—invested capital is preserved and has very little chance of being eroded.

• Income—attractive returns are locked in and can compound tax free.

• Growth—both the underlying asset and the income stream can grow, and the investor shares in that growth.

• Inflation hedge—tax-free compounding and the potential for growth protect the retirement plan from erosion by inflation.

• Liquidity—certain real estate securities are structured to provide more liquidity than would be available if real estate were owned directly.

• Ease of administration—once the decision to invest in a specific partnership has been made, the investor is relieved of most decision-making responsibilities.

• Professional management—real estate securities provide not only an income-producing asset, but also professional management of the asset.

• ERISA compliance—partnerships specifically structured for retirement plans involve individuals who are responsible for ensuring that the investments are in full compliance with ERISA's requirements.

Source: Barry L. Shulman, one of the nation's leading analysts of real estate limited partnerships. He is the president of Shulman & Co., Inc., an independent securities firm, 1200 112 Ave. NE, Suite 250, Bellevue, WA 98009. He is editor-in-chief and publisher of *The Shulman View,* a monthly real estate subscription newsletter.

How To Use Real Estate Shelters Profitably

Although tax reform changed the tax benefits from ownership of real estate, there are still significant tax advantages that continue to make these shelters smart investments.

Real Estate Strategies

• Invest in income-producing shelters if tax shelters you own from previous years are still generating tax losses. This will balance out shelter losses that you otherwise wouldn't be able to deduct because of the passive-loss rules. The income from the income-producing property will be tax free because it's offset by the losses.

Example: You own real estate that has been generating tax losses. To offset them, you buy property that yields a 10% return. Since the losses from the one property will balance out the income from the other, you will get the 10% tax free.

To find the income-producing shelters, look at . . .

Interest expenses. A shelter purchased mainly with borrowed funds will have a very high interest expense and therefore lower income. Look for a shelter with less debt.

Depreciation schedules. Real estate placed in service after December 31, 1986, must be depreciated over 27.5 years if it's residential property and over 31.5 years if it's commercial.

Since real estate was depreciated over no more than 19 years before tax reform, the depreciation expense is much greater for shelters created on or before December 31, 1986. When buying an income-generating tax shelter, choose one created after tax reform, so the depreciation expense will be lower.

• Take advantage of the phase-in of the passive-loss rules. Up until 1991 you will be allowed to use a percentage of your net passive losses to offset your active income if you invested in the tax shelter before November 22, 1986. How it works: Let's say that after netting passive losses and passive gains you have a net passive loss. During 1987 you can use 65% of that loss to offset your active income. In 1988 you can use 40%—and 20% in 1989, 10% in 1990 and none in 1991.

• Aggregate your losses from all tax shelters, not just those from real estate tax shelters. Losses from a real estate passive activity can offset income from any other type of passive activity and vice versa. Be sure to look at all your passive shelters, including equipment-leasing deals, research and development shelters, cattle-feeding shelters, etc.

• Invest in real estate for the pure economics of the deal rather than for the tax savings—especially when you believe it's a good bargain. You'll eventually make considerable money when the property appreciates in value. Bonus: The appreciation on the property is tax free until you decide to sell.

Source: Arthur I. Gordon, tax partner, Ernst & Whinney, 787 Seventh Ave., New York 10019.

Passive-Loss Rules

All rental real estate activity (with one exception noted below) has been categorized by tax reform as a "passive" activity. General rule: Losses from passive activities can be used to offset passive-activity income only. They can't be used to offset portfolio income (interest, dividends, capital gains, etc.) or other income (salary and wages).

A passive activity is one that the investors

don't materially participate in managing. Someone else takes care of the day-to-day business decisions, supervision, and operations for the investors. The investors' main contribution to the business is cash.

Special exception: Taxpayers can offset some rental real estate losses against their salary and portfolio income. Taxpayers who actively manage rental real estate and whose adjusted gross income is under $100,000 are allowed to offset up to $25,000 a year in losses against their nonpassive income. This deduction is gradually phased out for taxpayers whose AGI is $100,000–$150,000. The deduction is unavailable to those whose AGI exceeds $150,000.

Source: Arthur I. Gordon, tax partner, Ernst & Whinney, 787 Seventh Ave., New York 10019.

For the Income-Oriented Investor

Unleveraged equity investment programs and participating mortgage loan funds can produce real rates of return regardless of an inflationary environment. Programs such as these are appealing to income-oriented investors because they feature low risk, high current return, and capital growth potential.

Equity Programs
Unleveraged equity programs (usually executed through limited partnerships) purchase properties with cash and assume all operating risk associated with the properties. Many sellers will negotiate a significantly discounted price for a property in exchange for an all-cash payment. As a result, buyers are able to acquire high-quality, debt-free real estate at very attractive terms. The discounted price creates a "built-in" level of appreciation that pays off in later years when the property is sold.

The major benefit of equity programs to the investor is that income from the real estate operations flows directly to the partnership and then to the limited partners. Since there is no debt service, the bulk of the cash flow can be distributed in a steady and predictable income stream. For rental properties, it is possible to maintain a positive cash flow even in times of low occupancy, and there is little risk of losing the properties.

Results of equity programs depend for the most part on the income-producing potential of the underlying real estate. Other factors are the sponsor's ability to acquire quality properties at the best price, manage them efficiently, and sell them at the right time.

In general, all-cash purchases are a very conservative way to invest in real estate. They offer investors greater income potential and stability—and hence, less risk—than most other traditional investments.

Participating Mortgage Loans
Mortgage loan funds lend investors' capital to other real estate investors. In return, investors in participating mortgage loans earn a fixed rate of interest plus a share of any future increase in cash flow and property appreciation. The mortgage terms secure both types of payments and each mortgage is secured by the property it is financing.

The major benefit to investors comes from participation in the increases in current income and appreciation. As tenant leases in a property expire, new leases are written. Typically, new leases call for a rent increase, which in turn produces a growing stream of revenue to the property's owner. In a participating mortgage, the lender begins to share in the increased revenue once a prenegotiated level is reached. Increased revenue from the property also produces appreciation of the property's value. The investor shares in this growth at the time of sale or refinancing.

Investment results depend largely on the expertise of the mortgage loan fund's sponsor or general partner to finance properties with high income potential. His ability to negotiate the highest percentage participation and loan interest rate for the investor relative to the amount financed is also an important consideration.

In deflationary periods, when interest rates are likely to drop, the fixed-income component of a mortgage loan provides a high current return. In the reverse scenario—an inflationary period with rising interest rates—investors benefit through participation in rent and equity increases.

Source: Arthur H. Goldberg, president and chief operating officer, Integrated Resources, Inc., 666 Third Ave., New York 10017, a diversified financial services company offering a variety of limited partnerships, mutual funds, as well as insurance products and annuities to individual, corporate, and institutional clients.

Traps and Opportunities in Limited Partnerships

Limited partnerships are legal entities created by state law that enable individuals to invest in a project with the benefits of the investment passing through to them. The investors/limited partners are not responsible for managing the venture and do not share in the legal liability of the project. Responsibility for operating the partnership is given to a general partner (GP). In exchange for their investment, limited partners generally receive cash distributions and sale proceeds, as well as a share of the tax benefits from the investments. Their liability will be limited to the amount of their investment under the new tax law.

In most limited partnerships, the GP is also the partnership's sponsor. Although it benefits the GP to have a program succeed (so investors will be interested in the GP's future syndications), the main purpose of the syndication is too often for the GP to make money; the benefit to the investor is secondary. For this reason, it is necessary to approach all limited partnership investments with a high degree of suspicion.

We review over 200 limited partnership offering memorandums and prospectuses each year and like about 15 of them. We find that over 90% of the prospectuses we review cannot satisfactorily answer the most basic questions one should have regarding an investment. In most cases, the deal does not make enough economic sense, there are too few benefits for the investor, the front-end costs are excessive, the GP has too little experience, or the risks are simply too great.

Here are the basic questions you should have answered before even considering an investment in a limited partnership:

• What type of program is it and what benefits can I realistically expect from it?

• What is the size of the investment unit being sold? What is the payment schedule? Can I afford those payments?

• Who is the GP? What is his record in both good and bad markets? Does the GP have a substantial net worth that would enable him to infuse cash into the program if there were problems?

• How is the money raised by the GP being spent? How much is actually going into the program? How is the GP compensated? How much does the GP's compensation depend on the success of the program?

• Do the potential rewards of the investment warrant the risks? Before making an investment, be sure to answer these questions satisfactorily. In my experience, less than 10% of the people who invest in limited partnerships take the time to find the answers. Yet most of the answers should be contained in the offering memorandum, which by law must be given to potential investors before they invest. If the information isn't there, call the GP directly for answers.

In spite of the traps involved, limited partnership investments can be very successful: At least 5% of these investments have real value. By investigating prospective investments thoroughly, you can help ensure that you invest in that 5%.

Source: Malcolm H. Gissen, owner of the financial planning and investment advisory services firm, Malcolm H. Gissen & Associates, 1 California St., San Francisco 94111. He is an attorney, a Certified Financial Planner, and a Registered Investment Advisor. A frequent speaker, he has talked to legal, accounting, and financial planning groups around the country about investments and financial planning.

Real Estate Partnerships for Economic Returns

Real estate partnership investments should be made on the basis of true economic potential, which generally translates to a competitive cash-on-cash return. The following is a "back to basics" approach for analyzing the economic potential of a real estate syndication.

Carefully review the underlying properties of the investment. In most cases you will be looking at improved real estate, such as an apartment complex. For substantial investments, use someone with expertise to personally inspect the property and the community for you. Many factors affect the value of a property:

• Acquisition cost of the property, including land and buildings, on a square-foot basis and capitalization-rate basis. Compare the cost to recent transactions on similar properties.

• Type and quality of construction—wood frame, brick, etc.; amenities—pool, fireplaces, landscaping; and the quality of heating, air conditioning, plumbing, electrical, and insulation.

• Age—quality of the structure.

• Occupancy (present and projected).

• Projected cost for proposed improvements to the property, whether for maintenance, upgrade, or rehabilitation.

• Financing—avoid short-term balloon payments (less than 10 years in most cases). Except in isolated instances, assume that you will hold a property for at least 10 years. Carefully examine interest rates and amortization periods, and conflicts, such as loans and fees payable to the general partner or related parties.

• Take into account all expenses, i.e., fees, commissions, and participations in sale and income proceeds.

Learn as much as you can about the sponsor. A partnership's sponsor can make or break the investment. The first thing to look for: Depth of real estate management and experience with the type of property and in the area of your investment. You want a good, well-financed manager as general partner. If the investment is substantial, arrange to meet the general partner and key staff members in person. Look for hands-on long-term real estate acquisitions and in-house property management experience.

• Carefully analyze the sponsor's track record. Remember, because of high appreciation rates, real estate investments covering the period of the late 1970s almost always look good, regardless of the sponsor's ability.

• Find out if the sponsor plans to invest cash. If so, is it really his or her own? Cash invested by the sponsor that has been taken out of the up-front fees charged by the sponsor is not a signal of good faith in the partnership.

Study estimated returns and objectives. Accurate projections are crucial to the success of a real estate investment. Therefore, make sure that the assumptions used in the sponsor's projections are conservative. Look closely at assumptions regarding rent increases, operating budgets, refinancing terms and interest rates, inflation projections, sale price and terms, and any other factors that affect the projected return. The projected increases in expenses should go up at the same rate as projected increases in rents. Don't be afraid to ask the sponsor to provide you more conservative projections if you don't agree with them.

Look closely at the effect on you of projected tax losses (income), credits, tax preference items, investment interest expense, and cash flow as a percentage of investment to date. Make sure you can use projected tax losses in light of current tax laws.

Compute the payback period (the time it takes to get your investment back through all projected benefits). Carefully consider the number of years in absolute dollars and the number of years in discounted present value dollars.

Examine major tax-deductible items you can claim over the pay-in period. Items to consider:

• "At risk" issues.

• Valuation issues. (Is there any appraisal to support the valuation?)

- Unusual tax structures.
- Accrual issues.
- Allocation issues.

Find out whether a respected tax firm states unequivocally in its tax opinion that the tax treatments to be claimed by the partnership are correct. Also make sure a reputable CPA firm is associated with the estimates of future operations and investor benefits.

Source: Arnold G. Rudoff, J.D., CPA, director, partnership analysis, national, Price Waterhouse, 555 California St., San Francisco 94104. He assists clients in analyzing, structuring, and financing real estate partnerships and direct investments.

The Newest Tax-Favored Investment: REMICs

The Tax Reform Act of 1986 created a brand new type of investment called a REMIC—a Real Estate Mortgage Investment Conduit. A REMIC can issue various classes of securities backed by pools of mortgages on commercial and residential real estate.

High return for investors. Mortgage pools that qualify as REMICs will be free from federal income tax, enabling them to pay investors more. . . just as a corporation could pay higher dividends if it were free from corporate income tax.

Types of REMICs

REMIC securities come in two varieties: Regular interests (similar to bonds) and residual interests (similar to partnership interests).

- Regular interests are closely akin to bonds, though they may be called by other names. They're issued for specified dollar amounts ($1,000, $2,000, etc.) and pay a fixed rate of interest. (Variable or floating rates may also be allowed, depending on Treasury Department regulations.) The income is considered portfolio income, not passive income.

REMICs can issue different classes of regular interests with different maturity dates, different interest rates, etc., enabling them to appeal to investors with different purposes—for example, safety, yield, long- or short-term investments.

Example: A REMIC creates a Class A interest paying 8% and a Class B interest paying 10%. Holders of Class A must be paid in full before payment can be made to Class B members. A third class might be paid an even higher rate, but only after Class A and B holders are paid.

- Residual interests are similar to common stock or partnership interests. After payment is made to the holders of regular interests, all profits (or losses) of the REMIC belong to the residual-interest holders and are taxed to them directly. The REMIC itself pays no income tax. They are higher yield and higher risk than regular interests. These interests may be freely bought and sold—unlike pre-REMIC mortgage pool securities whose salability was severely restricted by IRS rules.

Only one class of residual interest is permitted to a REMIC. All residual-interest holders must be treated alike and paid in proportion to the value of their holdings.

Income (or loss) from residual interests appears to be a flow through of portfolio income (or loss).

Where To Buy a REMIC

REMICs are relatively new, but regular interests will be available soon from banks and brokerage houses. Many may just be awaiting fuller Treasury regulations, but some temporary regulations have already been issued. Minimum investment: May be as low as $1,000.

Most residual interests will be privately placed at first, but may become available to the general public later.

Expect to see mutual funds offering REMIC funds before long. Participation in mortgages on commercial properties will yield more than on residential and will be of high quality. If Treasury regulations permit, you may see such features as coupon stripping, adjustable and variable rate REMICs, and other innovative forms of REMIC securities. If you're interested, check with your bank or brokerage house.

Source: Robert A. Garber, vice president of a major investment-banking house.

Investing in REITs

In 1960, the US Treasury laws were amended, allowing the average person to invest in the shares of real estate investment trusts (REITs) in the same manner that he or she could invest in mutual funds. Throughout the middle and late 60s and early 70s, REITs—especially those engaged in making short-term land development or construction loans—were some of the hottest securities on Wall Street.

When the recession occurred in 1974, real estate values were the first to suffer, causing most REITs to experience substantial losses. Since the beginning of the 80s, however, the REIT industry has recovered strongly and the REIT index has outperformed other stock market indexes. This record of success has allowed the industry to raise several billion dollars in the public marketplace.

The questions that face today's investor are whether to invest in real estate generally, and, if so, whether it is preferable to invest in REITs or to invest in real estate directly. Most investors don't have the time, experience, and required money to invest in substantial real estate properties directly. Hence, REITs are their best choice. In addition, a prime advantage of investing in REITs that are listed on a public stock exchange (and most REITs are) is liquidity. Direct investments in real estate are not easy to dispose of quickly, especially in deteriorating real estate markets. A publicly listed security, on the other hand, can be traded almost on a moment's notice and converted into cash.

Currently, there are three general categories of REITs: (1) equity, which invest in property ownership; (2) mortgage, which engage in lending; and (3) hybrid, which are mixtures of the first two. Some REITs restrict their investments to specific geographic areas; others concentrate on certain types of properties; still others have mixed portfolios. Many REITs utilize the services of outside advisors.

Not all REITs are equal. The best have a proven track record demonstrating an ability in both important areas of real estate investing—acquisition and management. Also, look closely at any REIT's cash flow history, as distinguished from net taxable income. Normally, there will not be much of a differential between the two in a mortgage REIT (although there are many mortgage REITs that have consistently increased their earnings and dividends, with resultant increase in share values). An equity REIT, however, has the opportunity to achieve a cash flow substantially in excess of net taxable income and to build up a reserve.

Source: Sylvan M. Cohen, founder, president, and trustee, Pennsylvania Real Estate Investment Trust, Cedarbrook Hill III, Mezzanine 26, Wyncote, PA 19095, as well as chairman of the law firm of Cohen, Shapiro, Polisher, Shiekman and Cohen. He is the author of numerous articles and a frequent lecturer on real estate and real estate law.

Profit Opportunities in Today's Tricky Real Estate Market

The newspapers claim that the country is "overbuilt." Although that's true for certain types of real estate, it makes no sense as a blanket statement. There's still money to be made in real estate.

Shopping centers and industrial properties aren't in oversupply, and many office buildings are attractive long-term values. Closest to a bottom: The battered real estate markets of the Southwest.

But don't sink everything into real estate. Risk: When interest rates continue to move up, many properties can be hit hard. (Because most real estate is bought with borrowed money, if interest rates rise, fewer people can afford it.)

The average investor should have 5%–20% of his or her investment portfolio in real estate. Historically, real property has been a great hedge against inflation, and well-selected properties invariably appreciate over the long run.

Commercial real estate holdings are similar to utility stocks in that they pay generous dividends and generate long-term capital appreciation. But whereas utilities are heavily regulated, real estate is almost totally unregulated. Edge: There are no government officials deciding how much profit investors should be allowed.

Equity-Oriented REITs

REITs are entities that buy properties and/or mortgages and pay out 95% of their income to shareholders. Unlike corporations, they don't pay taxes on earnings...which are taxed only after they've been passed on to shareholders as dividends.

Equity-oriented REITs hold mostly (or only) properties rather than mortgages. The investor should look for seasoned equity-oriented REITs with exceptional growth records—10% to 20% annual compounded total return over the past 10 years. Avoid upstarts. And concentrate on REITs that specialize in shopping centers.

Participating Mortgage REITs

Some REITs hold mortgages that also offer some degree of equity participation in the properties financed. Participating mortgage REITs may receive, in addition to normal mortgage payments, a percentage of the rental income from the properties financed or the right to convert their interest in the properties into partial ownership. So they collect current income but their shares may also appreciate in value.

Caution: Some overly optimistic borrowers are using participating mortgages to cover up negative property cash flow. Not being able to afford to make normal interest payments, they offer lenders equity participation instead. Before you invest in a participating mortgage REIT, find out what the occupancy rate of the properties backing the mortgages is.

Best: REITs with at least 9% yield—and a steady income stream.

Source: Kenneth Campbell, president, Audit Investments, Inc., 136 Summit Ave., Montvale, NJ 07645, an independent real estate investment manager. He is also publisher of *Realty Stock Review.*

Five Simple and One Sophisticated Way To Analyze Rental Real Estate Investments

Even with the shrewdest real estate and tax experts at your side, it's essential to understand the basic economics of a rental real estate investment. While the combination of variables involved often makes it difficult for investors to compare the merits of different properties, there are five fairly simple formulas that can give you some help.

The first step is to draw up an annual pro forma operating statement demonstrating the annual income, expenses, and tax benefits expected from a proposed investment. Next, these figures and further information about the price of the property, type of financing, appreciation rates, etc., are evaluated according to several different criteria. The following definitions and explanations cover five of these criteria, along with the advantages and disadvantages of each, to help buyers make better investment decisions (and help sellers better assess a property's worth).

1. Gross Rent Multiplier (GRM)

GRM = Sale Price/Gross Annual Rent.

The GRM (also known as the Gross Income Multiplier) tells you the number of years of rent you would have to receive to equal the sale price of the property. The lower the GRM, the better.

Ideal for comparing a variety of separate, yet similar properties, GRMs can vary widely depending upon the age, location, type of tenant, and state of repair of the structures. The GRMs for very old buildings in poor repair with high tenant turnover may be quite low (sometimes less than 5); for new homes they may be above 12.

The GRM is simple to calculate, but does not make allowances for differences in investor objectives, financial terms, operating costs, changes in the annual income stream, tax considerations, appreciation, or the time value of money. It can be misleading.

2. Debt Coverage Ratio (DCR)

DCR = Net Operating Income/(Annual Mortgage Principal + Interest Payments).

The DCR indicates the ability of a project to service its debt obligation without recourse to outside resources. Its most popular use is in comparing the merits of various financing arrangements rather than evaluating a project's profitability. The higher the ratio, the less risk there is of the project not being able to make its mortgage payments.

Lenders generally like a DCR to be at least 1.25. This means that net operating income will be at least 25% larger than the principal and interest payments. A ratio of less than 1.0 means that funds from outside the project will be required to meet annual mortgage payments.

The DCR is easy to use and a very meaningful indication of an investment's cash flow characteristics. However, it does not incorporate estimates of a property's potential for appreciation, the time value of money, or the tax ramifications of the investment.

3. Overall Return on Total Capital (OAR)

OAR = Net Operating Income/Total Investment.

The OAR measures the productivity of an investment. It is more reliable than the GRM because it accounts for operating expenses, vacancies, and bad debts by using net rather than gross income. Generally, the higher the rate, the better. What is an acceptable minimum rate really depends on your particular investment needs and alternatives.

OAR is a straightforward way of comparing the returns from various rental properties. It does not, however, account for differing financial terms (most importantly, the degree of leverage involved in the investment), tax factors, and the time value of money.

4. Cash-on-Cash Return (COC)

COC = Cash Flow Before Taxes/Initial Investment.

Many investors use the COC ratio as an indication of how productive their equity would be in a given project. Ratios a few percentage points above rates available on savings accounts at local banks and thrifts are frequently considered acceptable.

The COC ratio is suitable for investors who are primarily concerned about the cash flow of a project. The ratio assumes that all the benefits derived from an investment are in the form of cash flow—tax considerations and appreciation potential are ignored, as is the time value of money.

The COC is often negative, because many projects in today's market have a negative cash flow before taxes for the first few years. Thus a negative ratio can misrepresent the merits of a property; the investment may be very sound if tax advantages and appreciation factors are considered.

5. Equity Dividend After Taxes (EDAT)

EDAT = Cash Flow After Taxes/Equity Investment.

The EDAT ratio shows how productive your investment would be on an after-tax basis, in contrast to the before-tax analysis of the COC. It is reasonable to expect the EDAT on real estate investments to be in excess of 15%.

Most investors insist on a return that is at least equal to what they could earn on their best alternative investment, plus additional allowances for risk and the lack of liquidity associated with real estate. Although the EDAT will give you some idea of what the return would be, it fails to consider the time value of money.

6. Present Value (PV) Technique

The present value concept is a sophisticated technique for evaluating alternative investments in rental real estate. It has two major advantages over the more simple methods discussed above. First, it provides dollar value for a specific property. This is in contrast to other criteria that help an investor choose among projects, but do not indicate the precise dollar worth of any particular project. Second, the PV recognizes all of the critical investment considerations, since it is based on the time value of money.

The time value of money is critical because a dollar received a year from now is worth less than a dollar received today even ignoring inflation. The dollar in hand can be invested to earn interest for you; the dollar you haven't received yet obviously can't. Hence you can only determine that future dollar's value by discounting it to reflect the interest you have foregone.

In real estate, the present value is defined as the current worth of a property's anticipated future costs and benefits, after those costs and benefits are discounted at a specific rate of return (or discount). The size of the discount depends on what rate the investor could have earned if the equity had been put to another use.

Example of PVs: The present value of a dollar to be earned in the future depends on both the discount rate and the length of time until that dollar is actually received. Thus the PV of a dollar to be received one year from today with a 6% discount is approximately 94¢: $1.00/$1.06 (what it would be worth in a year if it could be invested now at 6% simple interest) = $0.9434. If that dollar is not to be received until two years from now, the PV drops to roughly 89¢ ($1.00/$1.12 = $0.8929). If the discount rate were 10%, the PV of a dollar to be received in one year would be about 91¢ ($1.00/$1.10 = $0.91).

The basic technique in calculating the PV of an investment property is to add the following three figures:

1. The present value of the property's cash flow after taxes for each of the years of the holding period.

2. The present value of the net equity reversion (i.e., the selling price at the end of the holding period minus all the selling expenses and mortgage retirements).

3. The initial amount of the mortgage balance.

The total is the maximum amount an investor can pay for a property and still earn the specified rate of return on the cash investment. (The rate specified will depend on the investor's objectives and constraints.) Of course, the PV estimate will rise if the investor is willing to accept a lower rate of return on the equity (i.e., a lower discount rate).

This technique is far more comprehensive and accurate than other methods of evaluating rental real estate investments. The only limitation is that it requires reliable estimates of future revenues and expenses; the results are only as valid as the assumptions used.

Source: Dr. Arthur L. Wright, economist in the Real Estate Center, Texas A&M University, College Station, TX 77843, as well as founder and CEO of Wright Properties. He is the author of more than 100 publications on various aspects of real estate and economics and has been active in both the local and the National Apartment Association.

Key Requirements for Real Estate Investments

Most people believe that the three key words in real estate are location, location, location. Wrong. In today's real estate market, the three key words are research, research, research. Only thorough research will enable you to determine if a property meets your economic requirements in the following key areas, whether you are looking at income-producing real estate or a primary residence.

• Positive economic environment. The most important factors to evaluate here include the area's unemployment rate versus the national rate; the level of bank deposits compared to the national average; retail sales per capita; and migration and demographic patterns.

• Location. Location is the specific site you choose within a generally defined area. Ingredients that determine a good location include proximity to shopping and employment; convenient access to the property; availability of cultural activities; and minimum levels of noise and distraction.

• Structural integrity. In addition to being attractive, a building must be structurally sound. Before purchasing, make sure you have prospective real estate properties inspected by a qualified, unaffiliated structural engineer. Remember, the replacement cost for one roof could wipe out your cash flow for an entire year.

• Amenities. The features that are unique to the property, such as recreational facilities, meeting rooms, parking spaces, and architecture, should match your personal or tenant profile. In the case of income-producing property, for example, if 90% of your tenants are married and over 65, a weight-lifting room may not be as attractive as a cardroom.

• Capitalization ratio. Your capitalization ratio—net operating income (operating revenues minus operating expenses) divided by the purchase price—is the purest form of analysis of your potential cash return from a real estate investment. Tax benefits and the availability of mortgage money are excluded from the analysis, giving you a better understanding of the actual amount of cash that will be generated by a project.

• Mortgage. Determining your capitalization ratio will enable you to design the most appropriate debt service schedule for your needs. (All too often, investors do this in reverse—they figure out their mortgage first.) The most important issues when considering a mortgage are the term of the mortgage and the interest charged.

• Leverage. Leverage is the crucial link in a profitable real estate program. When used with discretion, borrowing can significantly expand your purchasing power.

Source: Allen Cymrot, president and CEO, Woodmont Realty Advisors, 1050 Ralston Ave., Belmont, CA 94002.

How Real Estate Investors Get Tricked

The urge to invest in real estate, which is still strong in most parts of the country, exposes buyers to sharp practices by sellers.

The most common distortion is a claim of high-paying tenants. If the rent roll of a commercial building shows that nine tenants pay $6–$8 per square foot and three pay $12, find out who the high-paying tenants are. One may be the building owner, and the other may be affiliated with the seller.

Any fudging of current and future income can cost an investor tens of thousands of dollars. In a small building, where the seller

reports that 10 tenants pay $400 a month ($48,000 a year), if buildings in the area sell for six times gross, the market price would be $288,000. But suppose the owner had prepared to sell the building by raising the rents from $350 to $400 a month. That increase in the rent roll cost the buyer $36,000 (the difference between six times $48,000 in annual rents and six times $42,000).

Even worse would be the impact on future rent increases. If the rents in the building were close to market before the increase, the owner may well have offered tenants a free month's rent or a delayed increase. A delayed increase means that the buyer will not realize as much income as forecast. A free month's rent means that the actual increase in rents was only $17 an apartment, not $50. If the new owner tries to jump rents well above that, tenants may move.

Other Seller Claims To Investigate

• Low operating expenses. Sellers may be operating the building themselves to avoid a management fee. If buyers cannot take care of the building personally, this fee must be added to real operating expenses. And if sellers do not factor it in, the bank will when it calculates the maximum supportable mortgage.

• Reasonable property tax. If the building has not been assessed for several years, the buyer may have a substantial tax bite on the next reassessment. Also the seller may have made an addition to the building that has not yet been recorded with the tax assessor. As a precaution, ask the local assessment office for a tax card or listing sheet. It will show the building's assessment and when it was assessed. If it was assessed a year and a half ago and there has been no significant addition to the building, reassessment may not hurt the buyer. But if it has not been assessed for eight years, there could be a significant tax boost.

While checking the tax card or listing sheet, check the owner's property description against the one listed. If the owner says that 20,000 square feet are being sold but the tax card says 15,000 square feet, there has been some addition to the structure that has not been recorded, and therefore, has not been assessed. Or there may be an assessment error that, when corrected, will raise costs.

• Low insurance premiums. Is coverage in line with the structure's current value? What does the policy cover? Ask to see the policy. Ask an insurance adviser if coverage is insufficient, how much more will proper coverage cost?

• Energy efficient. Verify the owner's claim with the local utility to determine actual energy costs. Also check with regulatory commissions to see whether utility companies are scheduled to increase their tariffs.

• A real buy. Check the income statement with those of comparable buildings in the area. Consult the annual income and expense analysis by geographical area and building type with the Institute of Real Estate Management (430 N. Michigan Ave., Chicago 60611).

Source: Thomas L. O'Dea, O'Dea & Co., Inc., 2150 Country Club Rd., Winston-Salem, NC 27103.

How To Successfully Manage Rental Housing

Do you really have the time and/or dedication to manage a rental property, maintain its physical structure, and provide good service to your tenants? The problem with rental real estate as an investment is that once you own a property, you have to figure out a way to manage it. For owners of single homes or properties consisting of only a few units, the solution is usually easy—perform all the management activities by themselves. For owners of larger units, however, delegating some or all of the manager's responsibilities to others is a much more practical solution.

Whether you manage a property yourself or turn over the responsibility to someone else, learn the essential elements of good rental property management.

• Marketing. Renting apartments requires you to match the services of a unit (i.e., location, lifestyle, amenities, and cost) to the needs of your prospective tenants. The first step is to develop and maintain a current rate schedule for the property by keeping abreast of market conditions for comparable rental units. Additionally, pay attention to the number of vacant units and concessions being granted by your competition.

The purpose of the market survey is to estimate the demand for particular types of rental units. Beyond knowing what your competition is up to, sound estimates of rental demand allow you to project the number of units that could be rented and the number left vacant at each of a series of different rental rates.

• The value of vacancies. Remember that "vacancy" is not a bad word. Apartments are like any other commodity—there are trade-offs between increasing rental rates and decreasing the occupancy rate. To achieve the greatest economic returns may mean less than 100% occupancy. Any property manager with 100% occupancy is probably charging too little for the apartments.

Rent reviews should coincide with changes in your area's economic activity and housing conditions. For example, to maximize profits in a rapidly growing economy with a shortage of housing, you should shorten the period between rent reviews. On the other hand, when supply and demand for housing change relatively infrequently, 12 months or more may be a sufficient interval between reviews.

• Advertising. You may want to maintain a certain degree of similarity among tenants in your rental units, e.g., single adults, young couples with children, retired couples, white-collar workers, or students. The best advertising is usually geared to the individual traits of the group you've targeted. The three best forms of advertising are classified newspaper ads, word-of-mouth referrals, and a sign in front of the property. As a general rule, if you have trouble renting a unit to at least one out of five eligible prospects, there is probably something wrong with the rental rate, advertising technique, or condition of the property.

• Leasing. A successful marketing and advertising program will usually attract several prospective tenants. The next step is carefully screening each applicant by using a lease application form and a required deposit.

447

These have a double advantage: You should be able to screen out most of the nonserious prospects, and you will have additional information with which to evaluate your prospective tenant.

The four major criteria to use in evaluating a tenant:

Income level. (The household's monthly income should be approximately three times as large as the rent.)

Employment record. (Indicates a tenant's employment stability, responsibility, and willingness to cooperate with other people.)

Credit references.

References of the tenant's previous landlords.

On the lease, directly state the attributes required of tenants living in the property. Be careful: As an owner you must guard against any violation of a tenant's civil rights. It is fair to evaluate tenants on the basis of income level and household size. It's illegal to judge on the basis of race, color, religion, national origin, or sex. There are also some state and/or local laws relating to facts such as age, handicap, or sexual preference.

Don't try renting an apartment without a written lease. Comprehensive leases address issues not specifically covered by the general body of law. The most important of these issues are delinquent rents, eviction procedures, property damage and repairs, or abandoned personal property.

• Repair and collection policies. To protect your property against damages, use a "Move-in, Move-out Condition Form." New tenants should use this form to note all the major defects in an apartment (such as damaged or broken mirrors, appliances, carpets, or walls) when they first move in. Use the same form, when the tenant moves out, to assess the condition of the unit and to determine who should bear the cost of repair. As an owner, expect to bear the cost of normal wear and tear; your tenants are liable for damages in excess of that amount.

A fair but firm collection policy reduces payment problems. For late rent payments, you may want to institute a progressive "late fee" for each delinquent day. Talk to the tenant immediately, send statements of overdue rent two days after the rental due date, and follow the statement by a "final" notice shortly thereafter. If you don't get satisfactory payment, then begin eviction proceedings after more than two weeks.

• Tenant relations. Sound tenant relations are crucial to the successful operation of a rental property. Poor communication between tenants and management can result in false expectations, misunderstandings, and conflict.

One study found that more than 70% of the lawsuits initiated by management were related to delinquent or nonpayment of rents; 14% were due to destruction of property; and 11% were due to tenants moving out before the leases expired. Of tenant-initiated lawsuits, 62% concerned security deposit refunds; 33% were due to conflicts over maintenance and repair problems; and 5% involved charges of discrimination.

• Personnel/Management. If you have a large operation you can't manage by yourself, hire employees who have adequate technical skills and, almost as important, an ability to get along with you and the tenants. Before you hire, make sure that employees clearly understand their assigned duties and responsibilities, conditions of employment, working hours, vacation days, and sick leave.

• Physical care of the property. Taking proper care of the premises prolongs its economic life and provides tenants with clean and secure facilities. The manager's responsibility is to authorize the appropriate amount, timing, and type of operating and repair expenditures.

The best maintenance and repair arrangements will depend on the size of your operation. For large complexes, an on-site maintenance person is preferred. If there are fewer than 80 to 100 units, agreements with repair and maintenance firms should suffice.

• Recordkeeping. Any good record-keeping system includes a detailed account of all operating income and expenses relating to each property, as well as maintenance and repair records, employee activities, and tenant information. Most small rental operations (fewer than 15 to 20 units) can use a simple journal of receipts and expenditures. Beyond that size, a simple-entry "pegboard" system works well. Computerized systems usually are not economically feasible until several dozen units are under management.

Source: Dr. Arthur L. Wright, economist in the Real Estate Center, Texas A&M University, College Station, TX 77843, as well as founder and CEO of Wright Properties. He is the author of more than 100 publications on various aspects of real estate and economics and has been active in both the local and the National Apartment Association.

How To Protect Yourself From Your Broker

People who invest in real estate directly will find that a good relationship with a broker is probably the most important link to a potentially rewarding investment. For most busy investors, an experienced broker will serve as the primary source of leads and insights into a particular real estate market.

Here are a few general guidelines to follow to insure a successful relationship with your broker.

• Make sure that the communication with the broker goes both ways. He should have a clear picture of your needs and objectives.

• Be straight about your financial situation—a good broker will always keep it in confidence. If a broker is misled about your investment ability, he will probably not be as willing to work for you.

• Always be ready to inspect a property at a moment's notice. In real estate, timing is often everything. Failure to investigate an opportunity when it presents itself can mean lost income for you and lead a broker to think you aren't serious about investing.

• After you inspect a property, communicate your reaction clearly—both positives and negatives. By the second inspection, everyone concerned with the buying decision should have seen the property and voiced their opinions.

• Don't be afraid to rely on the broker to guide you when making an offer. An initial offer that is too low can give owners a bad picture of your intentions and may cause them to dismiss you as a potential buyer. It's always wise to have a second offer ready, should the first one be rejected. Remember: Try to keep the negotiations from stalling. Alternatively, if your price is accepted, be ready to move quickly to consummate the deal.

A knowledgeable broker will keep you up to date on market conditions and suggest the best times to sell a property for the greatest gain. He can also put you in touch with other investors who might be interested in structuring a partnership. Brokers should be able to help you get financing for additional purchases and provide guidance in such areas as tax considerations, property maintenance, and zoning restrictions or variances.

How To Spot a Bad Broker

Tip-offs that indicate you're dealing with a bad broker:

• When a broker does not reveal major defects or impediments of a property.

• When a broker does not bring to your attention changes in price or terms.

• When a broker is slow in conveying a seller's response to your offer. (You may lose the sale in the meantime.)

• When a broker wastes your time by calling about properties he should know you have no interest in or are out of your price range.

• When a broker misleads you by indicating there are other offers for a property—in effect pressuring you to make an offer when he knows there is really no other immediate interest.

Source: Austin K. Haldenstein, consultant to Douglas Elliman-Haldenstein, 2112 Broadway, Suite 509, New York 10023, a division of Douglas Elliman Gibbons & Ives, one of Manhattan's oldest and largest residential real estate firms. The division specializes in the sale of brownstones, co-ops and condominiums, and investment properties. He is also adjunct professor of real estate at the New York University Real Estate Institute, where he offers a bi-annual seminar on purchasing small investment properties.

Real Estate Appraisers: Making the Right Choice

Today's prudent real estate owner can no longer rely on information from traditional sources such as friends or neighbors to determine the value of a piece of property. Brokers, while helpful, are still concerned with the marketing of real estate (finding buyers), rather than tracking the sale of every single property in every single marketplace.

The best way to determine the value of a property is by using a professional appraiser. For a flat fee that ranges widely, depending on the type of real estate being appraised, an appraiser will compute the "fair market value" of a piece of property. Fees can range from $150 for a single-family home, condominium, or townhouse to as much as $10,000 for commercial or industrial properties. Most appraisers rely on a study of comparable transactions in your particular geographic region to arrive at that value.

Finding an Appraiser

Financial institutions are a good place to start your search for an appraiser, since most standard real estate loan applications require a property's appraisal. This category of institutions includes commercial banks, savings and loans, and mortgage brokers. Attorneys and real estate brokers are also excellent sources.

Like other service occupations, the range in expertise among appraisers varies enormously. Be careful in your selection; thousands of dollars can hinge on an appraiser's opinion of value. The following should aid you in your choice:

• The type of property being appraised. The first questions you ask a prospective appraiser should regard his experience, expertise, and reputation for appraising the type of property you are interested in. To check an appraiser's experience, begin with references. Don't be satisfied with a list of names: Call the references, find out the types of property appraised and the ultimate accuracy of the appraisals.

• The appraiser's credentials. Appraisers with the Member of the Appraisal Institute or MAI designation generally have a very high level of training that includes economics, product knowledge, financial matters, and demographics. Another prestigious designation is the SRA, from the Society of Residential Appraisers. Ask the appraiser what he had to do to earn these designations.

• The appraiser's data base. When interviewing an appraiser, find out about methodology: Where does he get sales information regarding comparable property? How does the appraiser make use of information regarding comparable transactions? What are the dates of the sales? What was the market climate during the time the comparable properties were available? What are the current trends in your particular marketplace? Is it a buyer's or a seller's market?

In today's real estate market the difference between making a killing and taking a bath can depend on knowing what your real estate property is actually worth at the time you buy it and at the time you sell. Getting the right appraiser will help insure that you don't make an expensive mistake.

Source: Sheldon F. Good, president, and Steven L. Good, vice president/general counsel, Sheldon F. Good & Company, 333 W. Wacker Dr., Chicago 60606. One of Chicago's largest commercial, industrial, and investment real estate brokerage firms, the company and its subsidiaries in Houston and Boca Raton have sold more than 8,000 properties in 26 states over a three-year period.

Read This 2X in Real Estate Contracts

• "Mother Hubbard" clause. It is important to have a true description of the property being conveyed. Sometimes there is more than one description of the property because it consists of several tracts of land. There may also be rights to travel over and use adjoining property. To cover the situation a clause may be added to the effect that the seller is conveying any and all property rights owned at a particular location.

• Certificate of occupancy. The buyer may

ask for a current certificate of occupancy to be sure the buildings are in compliance with local laws.

• Flood areas. If there is any doubt have the seller warrant that the property is not located in a flood-prone area. (If it is a flood-prone area, don't buy it.)

• Brokerage fees. It is not cast in stone that either party to a sale must pay the cost of brokerage. This sum can be a wide-open topic for negotiation, and the contract can specify any division of responsibility for payment.

• Inspection clause. The purchaser may obtain the right to inspect the property at specified times. Often, the purchaser will negotiate the right to inspect 48 or fewer hours before closing, to be sure all is in proper order as indicated in the contract of sale.

• Condition precedent. The purchaser or seller may want a specific event to occur before the obligation becomes fixed. For example, a purchaser may want the town to approve a building of a new road before the contract binds him to the purchase. Likewise, a seller may require that before the purchaser's rights become fixed there must be a third-party guarantee of the purchaser's payments under the contract.

• Authorization. If the purchaser is a corporation, partnership, or a representative, the seller may want proof of his authority to close the transaction. The form of such a proof should be determined by counsel.

• Survey. An accurate survey can be very expensive and either party can be forced to absorb this expense. It is a point of negotiation.

• Building permits. The seller may be asked to make the sale conditional on the purchaser obtaining necessary building permits within a specified period of time. The buyer may also pay a set sum to have the seller put the sale at risk during that period.

• Guarantee. The seller may desire the purchaser to obtain a guarantee of payment by a financially sound and acceptable third party.

• Risk of loss. Damage to the property after signing of the contract but prior to the closing can be borne by either party. The seller can be obligated to restore the property or may be able to subtract its loss of value from the purchase price.

• Title report. Who pays for the title report is another item that is open for negotiation. The name of the title company that performs the work is also a matter for discussion.

• Assignment. A buyer may want the contract of sale to be assignable. The seller will have to agree that such a substitution can be made.

• "As is" clause. The seller may allow the purchaser ample time to inspect the property to determine whether it meets his investment needs. At that point, the seller may wish an "as is" clause, stating that he is not making any representations or warranties of any kind.

• Zoning. The seller may be asked to warrant the zoning applicable to the property. Proof of zoning may be in the form of a letter from the local zoning board showing the present zoning classification.

• Encumbrances. The title report will examine all the encumbrances on the property, such as mortgages, leases, easements, and restrictions of use. How these items affect value is a matter for negotiation.

• Title insurance. The cost of title insurance is often a major cash expense at closing. Who pays for this insurance is an appropriate item to bargain for.

• Time of essence. Unless the contract states that time is of the essence, delays of the closing date by the buyer or the seller may be excused. This clause removes all doubt that the closing must be held on a specified date.

• Purchaser or seller action. Where either party allows the contract to be contingent on something the seller or purchaser must perform, there should be a clause to assure compliance. Such a clause appears where zoning must be changed, plans must be drawn, tests must be made, inspections must be done, or some other matter affecting the property needs to be taken care of before both parties are satisfied. Sometimes such actions can be on a "best efforts" basis.

• Mortgage assumption. If the purchaser is assuming an assignable mortgage on the property, the specifics should be detailed. The seller may want more money because the purchaser is obtaining financing below the rates currently available in the marketplace.

Source: *How to Make Money in Real Estate,* Steven James Lee, Boardroom Books, Millburn, NJ.

Figures To Check at a Real Estate Closing

- Monthly payments.
- Per diem figures for utilities, taxes, and/or interest.
- The broker's commission.
- The rent, security deposits, and/or interest on deposits that have not as yet been transferred.
- A charge for utility bills already paid.
- A charge for loan fees already paid.
- A contractor, attorney, appraiser, or some other party to the contract who has not been paid.

Reducing Real Estate Tax by Challenging Assessments

Effective real estate tax is tax rate multiplied by assessed value. There is not much an individual can do about tax rate, but assessment can often be challenged successfully. Requirements: Owner must show either that property is overvalued or that assessment is higher than on comparable property in the same area.

When to ask for reduction:

- Just before making necessary repairs of damages or deterioration that has lowered the value of property.

- Local tax records err in description by overstating size or income.

- Net income drops due to factors beyond owner's control.

- When price paid for building in arms-length transaction is lower than the assessed value.

What to do:

- Determine the ratio of the assessed value to the present market value. Compare against average ratios of similar properties recently sold in the same area. Sources: Ratios available to public in tax districts. Real estate brokers, professional assessors can also be consulted.

- Check tax records for description of property, income.

- Consult lawyer on strength of case, whether it can be handled by informal talk with assessor, how much it will cost if formal proceeding or appeal are necessary.

14

BUYING & SELLING A HOUSE, CONDO, OR CO-OP

Tax Benefits and Disadvantages of Owning a Home

In a low-inflation environment, buying or building a home for investment purposes is not nearly as attractive. But the tax advantages of home ownership still remain. Here are the pros and cons, from a tax standpoint, of owning a home.

Points

If you finance your new home via a mortgage, you're likely to pay "points" to the lender. (One point is equivalent to 1% of the amount borrowed; if you borrow $50,000 and pay two points, you will pay $1,000.) If these points are a charge "for the use of money," you can probably itemize them as a deduction on your tax return. The IRS will allow you to take the deduction if (1) the loan is secured by your principal residence; (2) the charging of points is an established business practice in your area; and (3) the points charged do not exceed the points generally charged in your area. Avoid financing the points through the mortgage, or you won't be entitled to the deduction. Rather, obtain the full amount of the loan, and pay the points to the lender by a separate check.

Interest and Property Taxes

Mortgage interest and real estate tax payments are both deductible on your federal tax return. This important deduction results in significant tax savings and effectively lowers the rate of borrowing. Example: If you have a 12% mortgage and are in a 28% marginal tax bracket, the effective rate of your loan is about 8.6%. Note: Mortgage interest is deductible on your principal residence and other residences to the extent the mortgage does not exceed $1 million in acquisition debt (to buy, build, or improve the residence) plus $100,000 in home equity debt (for any purpose). Note: The dollar limits don't apply to mortgages taken out before October 14, 1987. However, under any circumstances, the loan can't exceed the fair market value of the residence.

Refinancing

Many homeowners buy a home, make all the payments over a period of years, and never tap the potential cash value, or equity, a home has built up. Yet as a large asset, a home can serve as a substantial borrowing base.

453

By refinancing your mortgage, you can realize the cash value of your home without selling it and paying capital gains tax. Example: You built a home for $85,000 in 1970. Your present mortgage balance is $22,000 and your home is worth $195,000. Your borrowing base is approximately 80% of your $173,000 in equity, or $138,400.

There are several reasons for refinancing: Payment for college education, starting a new business, major improvements to your home, or an investment that might yield more than the interest expense associated with the loan. However, there is also a disadvantage: Steeper loan payments. In addition, points paid to the bank on refinancing aren't deductible in the year they're paid, but must be spread over the life of the loan.

Home Improvements

Once you own your home, any permanent improvements are added to the original cost, with the result that they help lower your future taxable gain. Only improvements can be counted, not maintenance and repair costs. (Remodeling your kitchen is a permanent improvement; fixing a leaky pipe in the kitchen is not.) Remember to keep adequate records of all improvements you make, including canceled checks and invoices. If you sell your home, you may be asked to furnish them to the IRS.

Tax Deferral

As long as you use the proceeds from the sale of your house to buy a new, more expensive home, you are not required to pay capital gains tax on the profit. However, if you don't buy another one with the proceeds or you buy a less expensive home, you will be required to pay the tax. You must buy or build and occupy a new home within two years before or after the sale of the old one to qualify for this deferral.

Remember, however, this is a tax deferral, not an elimination of your capital gains tax. Example: You sell a house for $150,000 that cost you $90,000 to buy and improve. If you buy a new house for $150,000 or more, you don't pay any taxes on your $60,000 gain. However, if you sell the second home and don't buy another home with the proceeds, your taxable gain on the transaction will be increased by $60,000. Of course, if you sell your home at a loss, you do not receive any tax benefit.

One-Time Exclusion

If you are 55 or older, you can exclude up to $125,000 of capital gains from the sale of your home. The only requirements are that you, or your spouse if a joint owner, must be at least age 55 and have lived in the house for three of the last five years.

Use this exclusion carefully—you only get it once. There are situations in which it is wiser to hold on to the exclusion. Example: You make a $50,000 profit on a home you sell for $200,000. Then you buy a new home for $185,000, using your tax break to exclude the $50,000 gain. Later, you sell the second home for $230,000, and your $45,000 gain is fully taxable. A better alternative would be to pay the tax on the $15,000 gain at the time of the first sale ($200,000 – $185,000) and defer the $35,000 balance. Your gain on the second home would then be $80,000 ($45,000 + $35,000), but it would be fully excluded from tax.

As a general rule, if you plan to buy and sell a home more than once, it's best to keep deferring your capital gains tax until you reach the $125,000 exclusion limit. People over 55 who want to sell their home but have used up their exclusion can consider renting it out. By keeping the house you'll avoid paying any capital gains tax, and when you die your heirs will receive the property.

Source: Author William J. Roll, CPA, partner in the CPA firm Herring & Roll, PC, 41 South Fifth Street, Sunbury, PA 17801. He is the author of several tax articles.

How Much House Can You Afford?

When buying a house, the critical question always is: How much can you afford? Many people answer this question using simple rules, such as 25% of your income should be spent on housing, but these rules can be con-

Worksheet for Mortgage Loan Qualifications

Name _____

Cost of property $ *125,000*

Down payment *25,000*   Down payment is ___*20*___%   Loan/Value ___*80*___%

Mortgage loan *100,000*   Interest rate *10.5* %   for ___*360*___ months

1. Monthly housing expense to income ratio (Maximum is 25%)

Income	Per month	Housing expense	Per month	Ratio
Gross normal	$ *3,600*	Principal & int.	$ *914.74*	Housing expense
Co-borrower	*1,450*	Mortgage insurance	*N/A*	÷
Dividends		Real estate tax	*208.33*	Income
Interest		Hazard insurance	*30.80*	
Rental (net)		Association fee	*N/A*	*1,153.87* = ⎛*22.8%*⎞
Other		Total housing expense		*5,050.00* ⎝*(Ratio)*⎠
Total	$ *5,050*	(Ratio purpose)	$ *1,153.87*	*QUALIFIES*

2. Monthly debt repayment to income ratio (Maximum is 33%)

Installment debts (6 months or longer)	Per month		
Revolving accounts	$ *60.00*	Total housing expense + total monthly debt	
First Nat'l Bank	*150.00*	Total monthly gross income	
Auto Loan	*165.00*	*1,153.87* + *375.00* = *30.3%*	
Total	$ *375.00*	*5,050.00* *QUALIFIES*	

3. Cash required for settlement

Liquid assets		Cash needs	
Sales contract present house	$_____	Contract sales price	$ *125,000*
Less _____% commission	_____	Estimated settlement charges	+ *3,400*
Less mortgage & liens	_____	R.E. tax escrow & adjustment	+ *2,500*
Less payoff of debts	_____	Partial association fee	+ *N/A*
Plus savings	*30,000*	Less deposit	– *5,000*
Plus other	_____	Less this mortgage loan	– *100,000*
Total liquid assets	$ *30,000*	Total cash needs	$ *25,900*
Net surplus/deficit	$ *4,100*	*QUALIFIES*	

fusing and are not applicable to all situations. If you overestimate your ability to pay back a mortgage, you may find yourself living a substantially lower lifestyle than you expected.

Ultimately, the amount of house you can afford will depend on your personal needs, desires, and financial capabilities. The best

approach to take when determining actual amounts is to write up a household budget for the first five years of home ownership. This should give you an honest picture of how much you will have available for housing expenses.

The accompanying budget worksheet

Housing and Household Budget Worksheet

	1st Yr.	2nd Yr.	3rd Yr.	4th Yr.	5th Yr.
I. Income					
Wages & salaries					
Self					
Spouse					
Savings & investments					
Other (bonuses, etc.)					
Total before taxes					
II. Nonhousing Expenditures					
Consumption					
Food at home					
Food away from home					
Apparel & service					
Transportation					
Vehicle payments					
Gasoline					
Maintenance					
Public transport					
Household furnishing & equipment					
Health care					
Entertainment					
Personal care services					
Education					
Telephone					
Cash contributions					
Miscellaneous					
Life & other personal insurance					
Taxes					
Personal income					

	1st Yr.	2nd Yr.	3rd Yr.	4th Yr.	5th Yr.
Federal					
State					
Local					
Personal property					
Social Security					
Other					
Pensions					
Total nonhousing expenditures					
III. Income Minus Expenditures (amount available for housing and savings)					
IV. Housing Expenditures					
Principal & interest for mortgage					
Mortgage insurance					
Real estate taxes					
Property insurance					
Condominium fees					
Maintenance & repairs					
Utilities					
Electric					
Gas					
Water					
Sewer					
Total housing expenditures					
V. Savings (remainder after IV is subtracted from III)					

should help you make the appropriate calculations. Include a determination of the savings you will have available for a down payment and closing costs. Also, be sure to use a reasonable projection for inflation and to make reasonable allowances for purchases of major consumer durables (automobiles, home furnishings, appliances) and for education—especially if you will have children entering college. If you use consumer credit for some purchases, include an estimated monthly payment in your budget.

If you do not currently own a home or are moving to a new area, get help estimating your housing expenses. Most realtors and homebuilders can provide you with appropriate estimates, particularly for real estate taxes and utilities. Allowances for property maintenance and repairs should be 1% to 2% of the purchase price of the home, unless you intend to purchase an older unit needing sub-stantial work. To determine your estimated principal and interest payments, you will have to get at least an initial estimate of mortgage amounts. Most personal computers have built-in amortization tables that can help you in this process. If you don't have a computer, there is always the almanac.

Write up your personal budget in conjunction with a mortgage loan qualification form. (See the accompanying mortgage worksheet for an example.) A realtor or builder can provide you with estimates of closing fees, such as settlement charges and tax escrow, to complete the form.

Source: Robert J. Sheehan, vice president and a partner of the management and economics consulting firm, Regis J. Sheehan and Associates, 1606 Wrightson Drive, McLean, VA 22101. He is also the author of *How to Acquire Land*, a contributor to professional journals and a management/economics newsletter, and is widely quoted in the media.

Way To Pay for Your Dream House

Renting out a room or apartment in your expensive house offsets monthly payments and provides tax breaks for maintenance/repairs and depreciation. Result: More money available for more house.

Source: Jay G. Baris, New York City attorney.

Home Ownership as an Investment

If you are buying a home now, you will want to get every bit of appreciation you can from your investment. This certainly won't be as easy as it was in the days when average home inflation hovered between 15% and 20%, but there are some basic points you can cover to insure that your home gives you the highest possible return over the long run.

• Economic outlook. The prospects for the local economy should be strong. Rising employment and income are good signs, since employment gains usually precede increases in land values.

• Home prices. Make sure average home prices in the area are not excessively high. If prices have escalated too much, future appreciation gains will be limited.

• Structure. Buy the type of structure most favored in the area. For instance, a six-bedroom house in a three-bedroom community is out of place and can be difficult to sell. As a second example, some areas have a high concentration of ranch homes, while others favor colonials.

• Turnover. Areas with a high turnover of homes are better than those with a lower turnover. Realtors are more comfortable showing these homes and current market prices are easier to estimate.

• ARM mortgages. Consider an adjustable rate mortgage (ARM). ARMs are about 150

Buying & Selling a House, Condo, or Co-op

basis points (1½ points) less than fixed mortgages, and are usually much better for families who think they will be moving in the near term or for young families who can benefit from initially lower mortgage payments.

• Renegotiate. If you prefer a fixed rate mortgage, don't hesitate to renegotiate if market rates decline 250 basis points. This is an especially good idea for retirees, who usually find fixed rate instruments more appropriate for their fixed incomes.

• Existing homes. Existing homes located near higher-priced new developments of similar structures usually offer quick appreciation. Most older units do not have the price premiums of new homes.

• Length of mortgage. Carefully consider the choice between 15- and 30-year mortgages. The total interest savings that comes from shorter maturity is considerable, but carries the cost of lost investment opportunities. However, if you are a disciplined saver/investor, use a long-term mortgage and make alternative investments. (Remember, you can always make additional payments to reduce your mortgage balance.) If you have trouble saving, the shorter-term mortgage may be the better choice.

• School system. Look for areas with good school systems, even if you don't have young children. When it comes time to sell, your home will be more attractive to high-income households.

• Bond issues. Avoid townships that are undergoing rapid growth in school-aged children. Taxes will rise where there is a need for large bond issues for schools or other services.

• Home equity. Learn how to use your home as a source for short-term credit or long-term cash needs. Financial institutions have established loan programs that allow qualified individuals to borrow against the equity established in their homes. Another recent development is using the asset base of a house to provide retirement benefits.

Source: Richard E. Mount, senior economist, Merrill Lynch Economics, World Financial Center, New York 10281. He manages research for housing and construction.

Best Time To Go House Hunting

Save your house hunting for the off-season. During an August heat wave or a snowy winter weekend, you may be the only prospect out there. Result: An anxious owner may offer a better deal.

Avoid Vacation Time-Sharing Traps

Some owners of time-shares in beach and ski-area condominiums are becoming disenchanted. They find that committing themselves to the same dates at the same resort every year is too restricting, or they find they overpaid. To avoid problems:

• Locate one of the companies that act as brokers for swapping time-shares for owners of resort properties in different areas.

• Don't pay more than 10 times the going rate for a good hotel or apartment rental in the same area at the same time of year.

• Get in early on a new complex. Builders usually sell the first few apartments for less.

• Choose a one- or two-bedroom unit. Smaller or larger ones are harder to swap or sell.

• Deal with experienced developers who have already worked out maintenance and management problems.

• Pick a time in the peak season. It will be more negotiable.

• Look for properties that are protected by zoning or geography. Vail, Colorado, for example, has a moratorium on further time-share development.

• Beware of resorts that are hard to reach or are too far off the beaten track. Your time-share will be harder to rent, swap, or sell.

What To Ask a Seller

• Is the house built on a landfill? If it is, it may be settling and may continue to sink, causing cracks in the plaster and more serious, recurrent structural problems.

• Is the foundation's exterior surface waterproofed?

• What's the R factor (the ability to resist heat flow) of the insulation? Good ratings: R 22 for ceilings, R 13 for exterior walls. For colder climates: R 38 and R 19.

• Are windows insulated or double-glazed?

• Has the house been protected against termites? Look for written proof from a pest-control firm.

• What is under the wall-to-wall carpeting?

• Is the waste system hooked up to a city sewer?

• What is the inside diameter of the water pipes? Acceptable: ½ inch for feeders, ¾ inch for main runs.

• Are major appliances and heating and cooling units on separate electrical circuits?

Inspection Checklist Before Buying a House

Most home-shoppers know that it's a good idea to have an engineer check out a house for major defects before buying. But the buyer should precheck the structure so that he can direct the engineer to report on specific details.

Start in the basement, where defects are the most obvious. Check walls for inward bulge, cracks or crumbling mortar, fresh patches, and high-water marks. Check floor for signs of leaks, seepage, or damp odor. Look for a hidden sump pump, indicating frequent flooding.

Use a pocketknife to probe for termites or decay. If knife goes in easily, the wood is rotten. Other danger signs on joists: Marks of water seepage from kitchen or bathroom above. Pulling away from supporting masonry.

Notches more than one-third into the joist for pipes. If joists are propped up, find out why.

Check basement pipes for corrosion. Hot-water pipes should be copper, preferably insulated. Cold-water lines should be copper or plastic.

Check fuse box for power adequacy (16 to 20 circuits with circuit breakers needed for an 8- to 12-room house).

Study house from outside for sag, alignment of walls, missing mortar, broken bricks, cracks in walls. One tipoff to trouble: Extra-wide mortar joint on the stair steps may show house is shifting.

Siding: Aluminum is a plus. If it's wooden, look for peeling that shows walls hold too much moisture. If windowsills are freshly painted and the rest of the house is not, paint may be covering rot.

Check roof for broken/missing shingles, tar paper bubbles, broken patches. Check metal sheathing around chimney and ventilators. Should be watertight and made of nonrusting material. Look for leaks or breaks in gutters. If possible, check attic for watermarks on underside of roof.

About Home Inspections And Inspectors

• A home inspection covers both structural and mechanical details. Fee: About $1 per $1,000 of the selling price (minimum fee, $150). You'll get an on-the-spot verbal report, with a written assessment to follow. . .and a warranty, plus insurance to cover possible errors or omissions.
Source: *Business Week.*

• Prepurchase home inspections can save you—or cost you—thousands of dollars. An honest inspector can find hidden problems that make the house a bad deal. But. . .beware of real-estate-connected inspectors who will "miss" a problem in order to make the sale. And beware of moonlighting contractors who

find a problem and then offer to fix it. Average cost of a genuine inspection should be about $150. . .more for large houses. Best: Hire an inspector recommended by a truly trusted real estate agent, broker, contractor, or engineer. Alternative: Contact the American Society of Home Inspectors, 655 15 St. NW, Suite 320, Washington, DC 20005, 202-842-3096 for a recommendation. The society is a self-regulated group whose members can't be in real estate and can't repair homes they inspect.

Inspection and the Law

A homebuyer sued the seller when the crawl space drainage system proved inadequate and defective. He recovered $6,750, despite a clause in the contract of sale stating that the buyer had the right to inspect and was buying solely in reliance on his inspection. The court said sellers, by law, give implied warranties of habitability and proper workmanship. These implied warranties can be limited only by clear, specific, and unambiguous language in the contract. . .not by a generalized "right of inspection" clause.
Source: *Tyus v. Resta*, Pa SupCt, 476 A (2d) 427.

When the New House Is a Lemon

A home buyer may be able to get out of the entire purchase contract if the seller has misrepresented a house with many serious defects.

Normally, when defects show up after the buyers move in, they can sue for damages. Some state courts have ruled that two reasons for suing to void the entire sale are: (1) Misrepresentation of an important aspect of the house. (2) The presence of many serious defects.

One case: The builder had assured the

buyer that there would be no water problem. But the house was flooded soon after the closing. The court said the related damage would be impossible to repair.

Source: *Chastain v. Billings*, 570S. W. 2d 866.

Radon and Selling or Buying a House

Radon pollution has been found to be much more widespread than anyone previously believed. Its presence may affect home values and directly affect the pocketbook of any unwary homeowner. In many parts of the country, a radon inspection—or proof that the house has been checked for radon—will become as commonplace as an ordinary pre-purchase structural inspection.

Implications for Sellers

Take the initiative to have your home tested. If you discover unsafe radon concentrations, you can usually remedy the problem easily and cheaply. It is obviously better for you to eliminate the headache before a prospective buyer discovers it during a structural examination—and either refuses to buy or gains a powerful bargaining chip.

The cost for an effective "do-it-yourself" kit is minimal—and is often available from state or local departments of health. In New York, for example, test kits consisting of charcoal canisters cost less than $10 per canister. Two canisters are used. One is placed in a living area, and the other is placed as close as possible to any suspected infiltration point in the lowest level of the structure. The canisters are exposed to the ambient air for a period of days and then forwarded to a laboratory for analysis. The cost of the analysis is included in the cost of the canisters.

There is no need for a professional to conduct the radon monitoring unless you need results immediately. Instant readout equip-ment is expensive and you may pay a fairly stiff fee.

Buyers' Caution

Be cautious when buying a home in a high-risk area, or a home that once had been found to have high levels of radon. Remember, the seller had control over the placement of the detectors. Tests using sophisticated equipment would probably be justified. Some warrantee from the seller would be in order. Even if the problem had been eliminated, it is a good idea to retest every two or three years.

Dealing with Radon

If you discover radon in significant concentrations, the problem is usually easily resolved. Radon is an invisible, odorless radioactive gas that seeps up through the ground and can enter a home through gaps in the walls and foundation slabs, or as a gas dissolved in seeping ground water. In modern, heavily insulated homes, the gas may be trapped and concentrated. Simply sealing the sources of infiltration—cracks in basement floors and walls, gaps around pipes, etc.—and waterproofing the basement may be all that's needed. In extreme cases it might be necessary to install a ventilation system under the foundation slab to let the gas escape into the outside air.

Source: John G. Rossi, president, John G. Rossi P.E., P.C., an engineering consulting firm specializing in home and building inspection services, Box 147, Canton, NY 13617.

Home Warranties

Home warranties that protect against structural defects as well as defects in mechanical systems are increasingly popular for buyers of new and older homes. Typical coverage: Ten years against faults in walls and beams, two years of protection on plumbing, heating, and electrical systems. If defects appear within the covered periods, repairs will be made by the insurer once the deductible, which averages $225, is paid by the homeowner. Cost:

$1.80–$2.75 per $1,000 of purchase price. Older home coverage, costing $270–$345, is limited to mechanical systems and some built-in appliances. Trap: If the warranty is backed solely by the builder, it may negate the implied warranties that apply to new homes purchased in some states.

Source: *Sylvia Porter's Personal Finance.*

How To Buy a House with no Money Down

As real estate prices skyrocket in many areas, the concern of most hopeful buyers is, "How are we going to scrape together the down payment?" As hard as it is to believe, however, it's not only possible to buy property with no money down, it's not even that hard to do—provided you have the right fundamental information.

Note: No money down doesn't mean the seller receives no down payment. It means the down payment doesn't come from your pocket.

• Paying the real estate agent. If a seller uses a real estate agent on the sale, he's obligated to pay the agent's commission. At the average commission of 6%, that can involve a substantial sum of money. The sale of a $100,000 home, for example, would return to the agent at least $6,000.

Strategy: You, the buyer, pay the commission, but not up front. You approach the agent and offer a deal. Instead of immediate payment, suggest that the agent lend you part of the commission. In return, you offer a personal note guaranteeing to pay the money at some future date, with interest. If you make it clear that the sale depends on such an arrangement, the agent will probably go along with the plan. If he balks, be flexible. Negotiate a small monthly amount, perhaps with a balloon payment at the end. You then subtract the agent's commission from the expected down payment.

• Assuming the seller's debts. Let's say, as so often happens, that the seller is under financial pressure with overwhelming outstanding obligations.

Strategy: With the seller's cooperation, contact all his creditors and explain that you, not the seller, are going to make good on the outstanding debts. In some cases, the relieved creditors will either extend the due dates, or, if you can come up with some cash, they'll likely agree to a discount. Deduct the face amount of the debts you'll be assuming, pocketing any discounts from the down payment.

• Prepaid rent. Sometimes you, the buyer, are in no rush to move in and the seller would like more time to find a new place to live—but you'd both like to close as soon as possible. Or, if it's a multi-apartment building and the seller lives there, he may want more time in the apartment.

Strategy: Offer to let the seller remain in the house or apartment, setting a fixed date for vacating. Then, instead of the seller paying the buyer a monthly rent, you subtract from the down payment the full amount of the rent for the entire time the seller will be living there.

• Satisfying the seller's needs. During conversations with the seller, you learn that he must buy some appliances and furniture for a home he's moving into.

Strategy: Offer to buy those things—using credit cards or store credit to delay payment—and deduct the lump sum from the down payment.

• Using rent and deposits. If it's a multi-apartment building, you can use the rent from tenants to cover part of the down payment.

Strategy: Generally, if you close on the first of the month, you are entitled to all rent normally due from tenants for that month. Therefore, you can collect the rent and apply the sum toward the down payment.

• Using balloon down payments. Arrange to give part of the down payment immediately and the rest in one or several balloon payments at later, fixed dates.

Strategy: This technique gives you breathing room to: (1) Search for the rest of the down payment; and/or (2) Improve the property and put it back on the market for a quick profit.

Caution: This move can be risky if you don't make sure you have a fall-back source of cash in the event that time runs out.

• Using talent, not cash. In some cases you may be able to trade some of your personal resources if you are in a business or have a hobby through which you can provide services useful to the seller in lieu of cash.

Strategy: Trading services for cash is, among other things, very tax-wise. Many working people can provide services in exchange for down payment cash. Most obvious: Doctors, dentists, lawyers, accountants. Less obvious: Carpenters, artists, wholesalers, entertainers, gardeners. Note, however, that bartering produces taxable income, and taxes have to be paid on the value of such services.

• Raising the price, lowering the terms. Best applied when the seller is more interested in the price than in the terms of the deal.

Strategy: By playing with the numbers, you might find that you save a considerable sum of money if you agree to a higher price in return for a lower—or even no—down payment.

• High monthly down payments. If you have high cash flow, this could be a persuasive tactic to delay immediate payment.

Strategy: It's not unusual for a seller to be more anxious for steady cash flow after the sale than for immediate cash in hand. An anxious seller might bite at this offer because it gives him the full price. It also offers you the prospect of turning around and quickly selling the property—since you aren't tying up ready cash.

• Splitting the property. If the property contains a separate sellable element, plan to sell off that element and apply the proceeds to the down payment.

Strategy: Perhaps a portion of the land can be sold separately. Or there may be antiques that are sellable. . .the proceeds of which can be applied to the down payment.

Source: Robert G. Allen, a real estate insider and author of the bestseller, *Nothing Down*. He's also publisher of the monthly newsletter, *The Real Estate Advisor*.

Finding the Perfect Mortgage

Getting the perfect mortgage for your home, co-op, condo, second home, ski lodge, etc., can be greatly simplified if you follow a few basic guidelines.

First, take the time to find out about the wide variety of possible financing plans available to you (fixed rate, adjustable, graduated payment, balloon, etc.). Each type of loan is tailored to a specific set of personal needs and expectations. Carefully consider your long-range and short-range goals and your current financial status. It's better to have an idea which type of mortgage you may be interested in before you start speaking to loan officers.

Next, shop the loan thoroughly. Whether you do this through ads or word of mouth, your goal should be to come up with a list of the most competitive lending institutions. A possible alternative is to let a mortgage broker locate the best lending institution for your particular loan. Mortgage brokers track hundreds of different mortgage products from a variety of lending institutions. Some mortgage brokers charge a fee, others are paid by banks.

When shopping for the best loan, contact each bank's main mortgage department first. Executives at branches are sometimes not as up-to-date on the latest mortgage information. Also, do your research quickly; mortgage components can change often. Ask for a simple statement that clarifies the details of any prospective financing package for both parties. Remember, it is required that all usual closing costs (title insurance, legal fees, points, appraisal fee, credit agency fee, etc.) be clearly spelled out before you receive a mortgage commitment. Your objective at this stage should be to avoid last minute surprises.

Don't expect many concessions from a bank on your mortgage financing package. Unless you are a customer who has substantial accounts with the bank, you will probably not be able to negotiate the terms of the loan. On the other hand, if you do have substantial accounts, you may be able to negotiate on points, but probably not on rates.

Mortgage processing takes time. If a full credit package is required by your lender, expect a delay of from four to six weeks to verify all of the information supplied in your application. You can speed up the process by providing the bank with accurate information as quickly as possible.

The problem with processing delays is that the competitive rate that attracted you in the first place to a particular bank may no longer be available. Insure that your contract with the seller gives you ample time to have your mortgage application approved, or you could face higher interest rates than you initially anticipated if your commitment for a mortgage expires before you are prepared to close. As a rule, if a full credit package is required, you'll need a minimum of 45 days; 60 days is preferable.

Source: Jane E. Greenstein, founder and president of Mortgage Clearing House, Inc., 1510 Jericho Turnpike, New Hyde Park, NY 11040, a subsidiary of The Seldin Organization, Inc. The latter is a mortgage brokerage organization that processed nearly $200 million in home mortgages in 1985.

Nonbanking Sources of Mortgage Financing

Most of us associate obtaining mortgage financing with savings and loan associations, commercial banks, and savings banks. But, these don't have to be your only source. There is a wide variety of alternatives you can turn to for help; here is a list of the best.

• Mortgage banking companies. Mortgage banking companies originate mortgages and, in turn, sell them to institutional investors. In the past, mortgage bankers specialized in federal government-insured loans. However, as a result of the significant growth in the secondary market for all types of conventional mortgages, mortgage bankers have become very aggressive in the area of non-government-insured loans as well. Many mortgage bankers work directly with real estate agents, so that would probably be your best place to start your search. They are also listed in the Yellow Pages under mortgages or mortgage banking. A significant number of mortgage banking firms are actually subsidiaries of commercial banks.

• Insurance companies. Also increasing their involvement in the direct origination of residential mortgage loans, insurance companies were formerly a major force in the origination of single-family mortgages, but opted for secondary mortgage market instruments and other investments. For the time being, only the major insurance companies are likely to be a direct source of financing. Check with your insurance agent for prospects. The one major advantage of insurance companies over traditional bank sources is that they are less likely to rely on the income from points.

• Credit unions. Possibly your cheapest source of mortgage financing, there may be a credit union where you work; if not, you can usually join one with little difficulty. Credit unions are becoming more and more popular with a larger cross-section of the population. They have spread beyond private firms and public agencies to include more broadly based social and fraternal organizations.

• Home builders. In many cases, home builders are a source of mortgage financing for the homes they are selling. Some of their sources are traditional lenders, such as savings and loan institutions and banks. However, some of the larger builders have their own mortgage banking subsidiaries, while some large, medium, and even small builders pool their mortgages and sell them directly into the secondary mortgage markets or through investment houses that have specific financing programs for builders. Oftentimes, you can find realtors that will also participate in financing programs through investment houses and organizations that originate, sell, and service mortgage loans.

• Relatives and private individuals. Relatives may not be able to provide you with the entire amount of the mortgage, but often can help with the down payment or a second mortgage to reduce the amount of your first mortgage. Relatives and people you know may accept lower rates of interest than an institution because the rate of return is still higher than many of the investments they can make otherwise.

Professionals such as doctors and lawyers often seek investment opportunities in mortgage financing, providing below-market interest rates as a way of deferring income. In return, they generally require a portion of the rights to the future appreciation of the home. If you pursue mortgage financing from an individual investor, it's smart to hire a lawyer.

• Home sellers. Cheap and readily available financing can be arranged with the seller of a home. Many will have an assumable mortgage with a lower interest rate than is currently available. The major problem with assumable mortgages is that they can require a large down payment if there is a substantial difference between the sales price and the remaining amount of the mortgage. You will also be required to contact the lender to determine if there are any special requirements or fees associated with assumption of the loan.

Home sellers may be willing to finance a prime mortgage or a second mortgage if you cannot obtain a large enough prime mortgage through a lender. Sellers most often interested in this type of arrangement are people who are anxious to sell; may be moving to a cheaper home and want to spread their profit over a long period of time; or, if they are older, may be seeking a steady stream of retirement income.

A seller may also provide a purchase-money mortgage. For example, the seller gives you a short-term mortgage with a term of, say, 10 years. The monthly payments, however, are based on a 25- to 30-year loan. At the end of the loan term, you will be required to negotiate a new loan or find new financing. In most cases, the equity you build up in the home should make it easier to obtain another mortgage.

Source: Robert J. Sheehan, vice president and partner, Regis J. Sheehan & Associates, management and economic consultants, 1606 Wrightson Drive, McLean, VA 22101. He has had 25 years' experience in management and market research in construction and housing. He is a former staff vice president of National Association of Homebuilders.

Qualifying for a Home Loan When You're Self-Employed

If you are self-employed, qualifying for a home loan may be a little more difficult than if you were a salaried employee. Mortgage lenders generally require much more detailed income verifications, tax returns, and company financial data (if you are a business owner). The specific requirements and documentation vary from lender to lender, but there are several basic criteria used by most in determining whether a self-employed individual can qualify for a loan.

The Requirements

Lenders usually require you to have been in business for at least two years. Self-employed individuals with less than two years of business operation do not have a long enough track record to convince lenders of their ability to pay off a mortgage.

Documentation is crucial. All lenders require the following documents: (1) copies of your signed tax returns for the past two years; (2) a year-to-date profit and loss statement signed by you or your accountant, plus a balance sheet; (3) if the business is a partnership—the partnership agreement and partnership tax returns for the last two years, or, if a wholly owned corporation—the last two years' corporate tax returns; and (4) all information regarding your share in the business, major assets, and debts.

The most important item to most lenders is your adjusted gross income figure as it appears on your 1040 tax return. But, don't worry if your gross income figure shows a loss. You may still qualify for a loan. Lenders usually allow certain items to be added back to that figure for purposes of evaluating a loan applicant, including IRA/Keogh contributions, pension or annuity, dividends, all-savers, and non-taxable deductions, plus some depletion and depreciation from Schedule C, the non-taxed portion of long-term gains from Sched-

Self-Employed Case Analysis Sheet

Borrower name _____   Co-borrower name _____

I. Loan overview

Appraised value	_____	Term	_____
Loan amount	_____	Monthly payment	_____
Loan-to-value	_____	Other monthly obligations	_____
Interest rate	_____	Cash required	_____

II. Cash flow

	19___	19___	19___
A. Individual			
1. Adjusted gross income (1040)	_____	_____	_____
2. Dividend interest exclusion (1040)	_____	_____	_____
3. Depreciation (Schedule C)	_____	_____	_____
4. Depreciation (Schedule E)	_____	_____	_____
5. Depreciation (Schedule F)	_____	_____	_____
6. Other (Capital gains, carry-overs, etc.)	_____	_____	_____
Total	_____	_____	_____
Monthly average	_____	_____	_____
B. Additional business cash flow (over 51% owned corporation)			
1. Depreciation	_____	_____	_____
2. Net profit	_____	_____	_____
Total	_____	_____	_____
Monthly average	_____	_____	_____
C. Partnership cash flow (Schedule K-1)	_____	_____	_____
1. Amortization	_____	_____	_____
2. Depreciation (Schedule H)	_____	_____	_____
3. Depletion	_____	_____	_____
Total	_____	_____	_____
Monthly average	_____	_____	_____
Total cash available	_____	_____	_____

ule D, certain real estate depreciation from Schedule E, and certain amortization from Form 4562.

Using the form above you should be able to get a better idea of how a lender will analyze your financial situation.

Source: Ted L. Lyon, branch manager, Merrill Lynch Realty, 3115 W. Parker Rd., Suite 500, Plano, TX 75023. Recipient of the 1985 Merrill Lynch Society of Excellence Award and director of the Texas Association of Realtors, he has taught marketing and finance and has been a speaker for the Institute of Financial Education of Realtor/Lender Relations.

Hidden Mortgage Hazards

The increasing complexity of mortgages can leave a home buyer frustrated, confused, and even angry about negotiations with a lending institution. Yet much of this emotional turmoil can be eliminated if the borrower avoids focusing on interest rates alone and instead looks at the full range of elements in a mortgage program.

Understanding Mortgage Programs

• Mortgage insurance premium (MIP). The MIP insures a lender against a potential loss if a borrower defaults on his mortgage and the lender is forced to foreclose on the property. For a down payment less than 20% of the total mortgage, an MIP is mandated by financial regulatory agencies.

• Points. A lender's fee, one point is equal to 1% of the mortgage amount. The number of points quoted by a lender is not always an accurate reflection of the total fee; "discount points" may not include the origination fee, commitment fee, placement fee, etc. There may also be an additional fee charged to lock in the interest rate.

• Application fee. In addition to points, there is an application fee that normally covers the cost of the appraisal and credit report. In many cases that's still not all you will be charged. A lender may have other fees, such as a documentation fee, attorney's fee, funding fee, etc.

With both points and application fees, be persistent. Always ask the follow-up question: "Do the points and fees that the lender quotes include all the fees of making the loan, including preparation of papers, counsel fees, origination fees, and commitment fees?"

• When the interest rate is set. Your interest rate can be set at the time of application, at the time of commitment, just prior to settlement, or when one of the points is paid as a nonrefundable fee.

• How long the rate is set. The interest rate you are quoted during loan negotiations will be available only for a specified period, varying from seven to 120 days. It is important that you keep the period in line with your settlement date. For example, if your settlement is scheduled for 60 days from the application date, an interest rate set for 45 days won't have an effect on the rate you actually receive. If rates suddenly turn up and your rate is not set, you could get stuck with much higher interest payments than first planned. For the same reason, be cautious of the seller extending the settlement date.

Don't get caught up in processing delays, either. When interest rates are rising, a delay in the processing of a loan can cost you no matter who is at fault. To avoid paying for delays, follow up continuously. Document phone calls, noting the date, time, content of the call, and to whom you spoke. Make sure your employer sends the employee verification, ask the lender if the verification is acceptable, or what else is needed to submit the loan to the underwriter. Your loan processor will probably tell you that everything is fine. Do not accept this answer. Be specific. If everything is fine, ask when it will be submitted for approval. The following checklist will help you track all the common items the lender will need to complete processing.

1. Employment verification.
2. Bank account balance verification.
3. Loan balance verification.
4. Credit report.
5. Appraisal.
6. Title report.
7. Wood infestation report.
8. Well water test certification.
9. With less than a 20% down payment, approval from a mortgage insurance company.

• Amortization. Monthly mortgage payments cover principal and interest; the amount of principal reduction is known as the amortization (positive amortization). A lender may offer a program with a lower than normal monthly payment in the first year or two. This loan may defer interest until a later time, resulting in the smaller monthly payment for the first year. The interest that is deferred is added to the balance of the principal and paid off gradually over the life of the loan. This is known as negative amortization.

Negative amortization can permit a borrower to obtain a loan and house he otherwise could not afford. However, it is not recommended unless you expect your income to rise to cover the higher monthly payments in the second and subsequent years.

• Note rate (accrual rate). On fixed-rate graduated mortgages or on adjustable mortgages, this is the rate on which amortization is based. It differs from the monthly payment rate which is lower and is the rate used to determine how much you pay to your lender monthly.

Adjustable Mortgage Loans

The foregoing elements are common to all loans. Adjustable mortgage loans (AMLs), however, require borrowers to look at even more complex factors.

• The index. An AML is based on an index that is chosen by the lender; the restrictions on this choice are that the index must be readily verifiable by the borrower and out of the direct control of the lender. Find out the index's exact name and whether it is a monthly or weekly average.

• The index's performance. As the index for an AML moves, so does your mortgage interest rate; if the index goes up by 1.25%, your interest rate rises by the same percentage. Every index performs differently, and has a particular bias depending on the financial instrument on which it is based. For example, indexes based on six-month Treasury securities are more volatile than five-year Treasury securities. When market interest rates drop, the six-month Treasury-bill market reflects the change more quickly than the five-year Treasury market.

• Margins. Many mortgage interest rates are expressed as a percentage over the index value. For instance, if one-year Treasury securities are yielding 8% and a lender has a margin of 2.5%, then the home buyer will receive a 10.5% interest rate.

• Teaser rate. A lender may offer a borrower a below-market (discounted) rate for the first year of a loan. The undiscounted rate is the sum of the current index value plus the margin. Confusion about the teaser rate can arise if the borrower does not understand that the rate is for one year only, and that the rate the second year will be higher even if the index remains at the same level.

Your decision about a loan should be based on the undiscounted rate as well as the teaser. To calculate the actual rate, find out the exact name of the index, whether it is a weekly or monthly average, and its current value. Add the margin. If you are comparing two loan programs that give the same total, but one offers a teaser rate, you may decide to take advantage of the discount even if it is only for one year.

Teaser rates usually do not result in negative amortization (i.e., the interest you avoid paying is not added to the balance of the principal). However, increases in the second year from the teaser rate to the undiscounted rate may or may not be affected by a cap.

• Caps. Many adjustable mortgage loans have "caps" or limits on increases and decreases. These protect borrowers if rates go through the roof. If you pick a program with a teaser rate, you should make sure that the cap applies to both your monthly payment rate (the starting discounted rate) and the note rate (for determining your future rates). Otherwise you could see your monthly payments protected while your note rate goes through the roof causing huge unanticipated negative amortization.

• Adjustment period. AMLs can adjust every three months, six months, yearly, every three years, five years, etc. Generally, the shorter the adjustment period, the lower the rate will be.

• Convertibility. In the event that interest rates come down, some AMLs are convertible into fixed-rate mortgages at specified times. This is an attractive option enabling you to lock in a future rate without extensive refinancing costs. (Most convertibility options require some restrictions and additional fees.)

Source: Charles A. Breinig, mortgage analyst, Mortgage Reporting Service, Inc., 602 Washington Lane, Jenkintown, PA 19046, a firm that publishes a weekly report on over 1,500 mortgage programs in the southeastern Pennsylvania and New Jersey area. He also wrote and lectures on *How to Comparison Shop for a Mortgage.*

Adjustable-Rate Mortgage Vs. Fixed-Rate Mortgage

Choosing between an adjustable mortgage loan (AML) and a fixed-rate mortgage requires a risk/benefit decision by the individual borrower. Since the many elements involved affect each home buyer differently, how well they are evaluated can make the difference between substantial savings and an expensive gamble.

Affordability

Fixed-rate mortgages are more expensive than AMLs, because the lender takes on the risk of a possible increase in interest rates in the future. With an AML, on the other hand, the borrower assumes that risk in exchange for a lower initial interest rate.

By choosing an 8½% AML over a 10½% fixed-rate mortgage, for example, you can increase your purchasing power by almost 20%. Assuming interest rates don't rise (making your AML more expensive over the long run), that could mean buying a $130,800 house versus a $110,000 house for the same monthly mortgage payments.

Alternatively, the advantage of a fixed-rate mortgage is that you know exactly how much you will have to pay over a long period of time. This can be very valuable for people living on a fixed income or who don't expect a major increase in their future earnings. In this case, the security of having a fixed monthly payment outweighs the benefit of the potential savings of an AML. However, the extra cost of a fixed-rate mortgage may force a buyer to settle for a smaller house or less desirable neighborhood.

Looking Forward

As a rule, a $100,000 adjustable mortgage (30-year term) at 8.75% interest requires your minimum earnings to be approximately $39,500* (combined family income). How would you handle an increase in interest rates? Assuming the AML had a cap of 2% per year and a 5% maximum lifetime cap, and that the

mortgage increased at the maximum rate permissible, your income would have to grow about 3% for the first two years to cover the increase. (Most AMLs today do have caps or limits on increases in your monthly payments.)

Fixed-rate mortgages also require you to think about the future. Before you take on the mortgage, consider the costs involved in refinancing should interest rates drop and you want to get out of a mortgage that has become very expensive.

Do you plan on living in your home for a long or short period of time? Lenders charge a premium for fixed-rate mortgages because of the risk of increases in interest rates; the longer the term of the mortgage, the more difficult it is to predict interest rate fluctuations—and the greater the risk that interest rates will rise to the point where the loan is not producing an adequate return for the lender.

Don't pay a premium for the ability to keep a fixed-rate loan for 30 years if you plan to sell your home in 3 to 5 years, either because of a job transfer or because the home is a "starter home."

The Best Deal

After you've decided which type of loan is best for you, always shop around for the best rate. Rates between different lenders and different geographical areas can vary widely. Rates on the same type of mortgage loan can differ by as much as 2%. Remember that even a small interest rate savings can mean a significant savings on your overall mortgage payments (for example, a ¾% reduction in the interest rate on a 30-year, $100,000 mortgage would save you $21,000).

Don't rely solely on your real estate agent for advice on the best rates. Real estate agents work with only a handful of mortgage solicitors who provide them with rate quotations on a weekly basis. You may be able to find a better bargain elsewhere. The real estate agent has been hired by the seller to sell a house and cannot be expected to spend his time finding you the best deal.

*Calculation: (Allow 28% of income to pay for mortgage):

$39,500 ÷ 12 = $3,291.67 Monthly income
              X 28%   Allowance
              $921.67

              $781.00   Principal & interest
               120.00   Real estate taxes
              + 20.00   Insurance
              $921.00   Monthly payment

Source: Charles A. Breinig, mortgage analyst, Mortgage Reporting Service, Inc., 602 Washington Lane, Jenkintown, PA 19046, a firm that publishes a weekly report on over 1,500 mortgage programs in the southeastern Pennsylvania and New Jersey area. He also wrote and lectures on *How to Comparison Shop for a Mortgage.*

Questions To Ask Before Signing Mortgage Papers

Because it is such a long-term contract, conditions that may seem minor when signing a mortgage loan contract can end up costing a lot of money during the life of the agreement. Some typical mortgage clauses to negotiate before signing:

• Payment of "points": Percentage of the amount of the loan paid to the lender at the start of the loan. Banks and thrift institutions have no statutory right to charge points. Their presence may reflect competitive local market conditions. And when interest rates are high, points are common. They're inevitable when rate ceilings exist. Recommended: Try to negotiate on points.

• Prepayment penalties: Sometimes as much as six months' interest or a percentage of the balance due on the principal at the time loan is paid off. With mortgages running for 25 or 30 years, the chances of paying them off early are relatively high.

• "Due on encumbrance" clause: Makes the first mortgage immediately due in full if property is pledged as security on any other loan, including second mortgages. Not legal in some places and usually not enforced when it is legal. Request its deletion.

• "Due on sale" clauses: Requiring full payment of loan when property is sold.

• Escrow payment: The popular practice of

requiring a prorated share of local taxes and insurance premiums with each monthly mortgage payment. The bank earns interest on the escrow funds throughout the year and only pays it out when taxes and premiums are due. Amounts to forced savings with no interest.

Have lawyer check state's law to see if interest on escrow-account money is required. (It is, in several states.) If not, try to eliminate escrow—pay taxes and insurance on your own.

Other alternatives to escrow:

Capitalization plan, in which monthly tax and insurance payments are credited against outstanding mortgage principal until they are paid out to the government or insurer, thus lowering amount of mortgage interest.

Lender may agree to waive escrow if borrower opens an interest-bearing savings account in the amount of the annual tax bill.

Option of closing out the withheld escrow payments when the borrower's equity reaches 40%. At that point, the bank figures, equity interest will be a powerful incentive to keep up tax payments.

Source: *The Consumer's Guide to Banks* by Gordon L. Weil, Stein & Day, Briarcliff Manor, NY.

When It Pays To Remortgage

If you bought your home in the past few years, you may now be able to save a bundle by refinancing your mortgage. Rule of thumb: Subtract from the mortgage rate you now pay the rate now available. If the difference is equal to or greater than the points you will be charged to refinance, you should remortgage.

How Refinancing Works

If you have a $100,000 25-year mortgage at 15%, your monthly payment is $1,280.84. If you refinance during the first year at 9½%, your payment will plummet to $873.70. Monthly saving: $407.14. Points (say, $3,000) and other fees (perhaps $750) would be paid off, together with $850 of principal, in less than 10 months.

Even if the drop in interest rates is smaller, you can still benefit.

Example: If the same $100,000 loan dropped from 14% to 11%, you would still save $223 per month, and you would pay off the cost of remortgaging, plus $1,250 of principal, in less than 17 months.

What To Choose

Best deal: Shorter mortgages. Many banks offer loans that can be paid off in as few as 15 years. Don't let the sound of that scare you. Monthly payments are not that much higher.

Installments on a $100,000 mortgage at 11% would look like this:

Mortgage length	Monthly payment
15 years	$1,136.60
20 years	$1,032.19
25 years	$980.12
30 years	$952.33

Bottom line: The difference between payments on a 15-year and a 30-year mortgage is just $184.27/month . . . and you save nearly $140,000 over the life of the loan.

Adjustable-rate mortgages got a bad reputation when rates were high and they were the only type of financing many people could afford. But they bear looking into today.

Source: David Schechner, real estate lawyer, Schechner and Targan, 80 Main St., West Orange, NJ 07052.

New Opportunities (and Traps) in 2nd Mortgages

Second mortgages, often called home-equity loans, are an increasingly flexible and attractive means of raising fairly large amounts of money.

One of the most convenient wrinkles in the second-mortgage business is the ability to write checks against a line of credit secured by the borrower's equity interest in his home. An individual can get a large loan for almost any purpose merely by writing a check.

Moreover, the interest rate on the loan probably will be lower, possibly considerably lower, than it would be if the borrower had obtained an ordinary personal loan. Generally, the interest rate on a second mortgage (because it is secured by residential real estate) is one to two percentage points lower than the interest rate on a personal loan.

Second-Mortgage Risks

A borrower should be aware, however, of some of the dangers inherent in second mortgages. First of all, the borrower is using his home to collateralize the loan. If for some reason the loan cannot be repaid as originally planned, there is the possibility that the house will be lost.

Considering this risk, a potential second-mortgage borrower should think carefully about what he plans to use the loan for. Is it prudent to put a lien on a home to take a vacation paid for by writing a check against a second-mortgage credit line?

When They Make Sense

Second mortgages have a very legitimate role to play and should be carefully considered, especially when large amounts of money are needed—paying for a child's education or an addition to a home, for example, or dealing with a large medical bill.

Potential second-mortgage borrowers should shop carefully. Different institutions offer substantially different kinds of second mortgages and a wide range of interest rates.

A critical element is the amount of money needed. Some lenders set relatively low limits, such as $50,000 or $60,000, while some will go several times higher.

Of course, the amount an individual can borrow under a second mortgage is limited by the equity he holds in his home. That is the appraised value of the property minus the amount owed under the first mortgage. The second mortgage allows the borrower to obtain cash for the increased value of his property and for the amount of principal he has paid on his first mortgage. He thus can "unlock" the frozen cash equity in his home.

Key Consideration

Is the loan fixed rate or variable rate? Usually, the initial interest rate on a fixed-rate second mortgage is higher than it is on a variable-rate loan. Reason: On a fixed-rate loan, the lender is assuming the risk of a rise in interest rates. Even if rates were to rise dramatically, the interest paid by a fixed-rate borrower remains unchanged. On a variable-rate mortgage, however, the borrower assumes this risk, or at least a substantial part of it.

Therefore, an individual should consider the purpose of the loan in deciding whether to opt for a rate that is fixed or variable. If the loan is for a long-term purpose, such as adding an extension to a home, it might be wise to take a fixed-rate loan, viewing the initial higher interest rate as a form of insurance against a sharp rise in interest rates in the future. If interest rates were to drop sharply, the fixed-rate loan could be refinanced. Warning: Check for prepayment penalties, and shop to see which lender's offer is least onerous.

Variable rates usually are better suited for loans that the borrower expects to pay off in a relatively short period. Loans used for investments could be expected to generate enough cash flow to at least keep up with sharply rising interest rates.

Beware of Balloons

Borrowers also should be careful about so-called balloons. These are second mortgages that fall due within a few years, usually three to five. But the repayment schedule might have been calculated on a basis of up to 20 years. Thus, at the end of, say, five years, although very little might have been paid on the principal, the lender could demand immediate and full repayment. If that were to happen and the borrower could not raise the needed money, he might lose his home. It is therefore essential that the contract have a clause requiring the borrower to renew the loan. Note: It is critical that you borrow from a reputable lender. The last thing most well-established financial institutions want to do is take over your home. They will always try to work things out if the going gets tough. That is not always the case with unknown lenders.

If your needs are special, many second-mortgage lenders will try to devise a program that fits your requirements. For example, they might agree to postpone payments for a specified period of time.

Refinancing

An alternative to a second mortgage is refinancing a home. Conceivably, the holder of the first mortgage would be willing to write a new and bigger first mortgage on the home. The interest rate probably would be higher than that on the original mortgage, but the net cost might be lower.

In considering second mortgages or refinancing an existing mortgage, look at all costs. These include taxes and "points" (upfront fees).

Home-Equity Loan Traps

• Most banks are slow in reviewing applications. You may have to wait up to three months before getting a loan commitment. And there's the possibility of an IRS audit. Tax reform allows you to deduct interest on home loans only up to $100,000 (unless used to improve the property). Result: The IRS will be looking closely at equity borrowers to be sure they're not deducting more than they're permitted.

Source: Dr. Michael K. Evans, president, Evans Economics, Inc., 1725 Eye St. NW, Washington, DC 20006.

• Home-equity loans are dangerous propositions—and are often more expensive than other types of credit. Common drawbacks: Excessive up-front point charges and other closing costs, variable interest rates without

471

protective caps, a long payback period (leading to large overall interest charges), large lump-sum balloon payments at the end of the term. A further trap of a long payback period is that the borrower could be deemed "not creditworthy" and lose his line of credit. In this case, the entire balance would be due immediately.

• Home-equity loan traps: (1) Many banks offering equity lines of credit charge an annual fee of $20–$50, whether or not you draw down on the credit line...(2) Several banks have sliding interest scales—the bigger the loan, the lower the interest rate. You may actually save money by taking out a larger loan...(3) Though many banks have stopped charging points, they're now charging "origination fees" that run $100–$450. If you're applying for a relatively small loan (less than $25,000), this fee can add a lot to the total cost of obtaining the loan, which also includes appraisal fees, legal fees, and insurance.

Source: Paul Havemann, HSH Associates, Riverdale, NJ quoted in *Money.*

Mortgage Scam

Fraud is increasing through phony notices of mortgage sales. Beware of notices from an unfamiliar bank or finance company saying that your bank has sold its mortgage—and requesting payments be sent to a new address. Send payments only if (1) Your original bank also sends you a letter giving notice of the sale, the name of the new mortgage company, your outstanding balance, and your account number; and (2) The new mortgage company confirms this information by sending you a book of payment slips with the same account number and the proper balance. Helpful: Call your old bank to double-check.

Source: *Real Estate Investment Digest*, 2111 National Press Building, Washington, DC 20045.

Renovations that Increase Value

Kitchens

Whether you plan a major kitchen renovation (incorporating an entirely new design) or a minor one (mostly cosmetic—refinishing cabinets, new countertops, and a new appliance or two), the emphasis today is the same—new products and sophisticated design concepts. Energy-saving appliances and contemporary European styling are at the top of today's trend list. The following are other trends you may want to adopt in your renovation project.

• Designer-look laminates are very popular in many renovated kitchens, but wood is still holding its own as an accent element on counter edging, beams, and trim treatments.

• Colors are an important selling factor. White, grays, and light wood tones are the most popular. Dark woods and intense colors are losing favor.

• Pay attention to lighting. This is becoming an increasingly important factor in the overall appearance of a kitchen. Options range from high-tech fixtures that illuminate work areas to dimmer switches that provide a more subdued dining or entertaining atmosphere.

• In great demand: Open kitchens that are integrated into living areas. Some homeowners are taking walls out between kitchens and dining areas to achieve an open atmosphere.

In addition to providing energy savings, added convenience, style, and enjoyment value, renovation can boost the resale value of your home. By completely remodeling the kitchen at a cost in the $6,700 to $22,000 range (with a typical cost of $15,000), you can expect to recover 50% to 80% of that expenditure in added value to your home if you sell it within five years.

Bathrooms

Most people have two choices when it comes to bathroom renovation—remodel an existing bathroom or add a new one. Additions often make the most economic sense, because houses with only a single bathroom are usually less salable. Adding a second bathroom at a cost of $4,400 to $10,000 (typically $6,000) can yield a cost recovery of 100% to 130% if you sell your home within five years.

If you decide to remodel an existing bathroom, use care. Total renovation is usually less costly than piecemeal replacement and repairs. But don't go overboard renovating a small or average bathroom; if you plan to sell your home shortly, it's probably not worth your while to spend a great deal of money. On the other hand, expanding an existing bathroom can add considerably to your home's market appeal, as can adding custom features.

If your prime concern is resale, try using lighter, neutral colors and easy-care finishes when renovating. Don't compromise on quality. Brand names may be more expensive initially, but you are guaranteed that replacement parts will be available. Also, try to avoid major shifts in the location of the fixtures (sink, tub, toilet). This only adds unnecessarily large costs to your plumbing bill.

Windows, Doors, and Skylights

Replace windows and doors that are not energy-efficient with ones that are. If you plan to keep your home awhile or want to sell at a higher price, make sure that your window and door replacements are attractive, too.

Important features to look for when replacing windows and doors are richly carved wood doors with double locking devices, deadbolts, peepholes, double-glazed windows, and storm windows and doors.

Skylights are an increasingly popular source of natural lighting that can offer improved ventilation and a feeling of spaciousness. South-facing skylights are potential sources of passive solar heating. Almost any room with a roof directly over it is a candidate for at least one skylight. The one weakness of most skylights—leakage—has been eliminated through better design.

Whether you plan to stay or sell, skylights are a great investment. Their short-term recovery rate is between 60% and 75%, and they are a strong selling point in both cold and warm climates. This is a household addition you shouldn't cut corners on, however. Top-

quality units are easier to assemble and provide savings in installation and over the long-run, maintenance costs.

Fireplaces

Energy-efficient fireplaces are the remodeling project with the highest payback—sometimes offering homeowners up to a 130% return on their investment at the time they sell their home. The main reason for this is the low initial cost of fireplace renovation (normally less than $4,000) compared to other improvements. Another is the increased savings a homeowner enjoys with an energy-efficient unit compared to an open hearth.

Prefabricated units are attractive because of their space-saving features. The most popular models are only 36 inches wide and can be installed in corners to conserve on wall space. The current trend is toward top-quality models finished with floor-to-ceiling stonework, a mantel, and a raised hearth. When you decide to buy, look at three or more different brands and types. And, of course, be sure to have whatever model you select properly installed.

Source: Henry F. Broesche, founder and president, Brighton Homes, Inc., 5450 NW Central Dr., Suite 250, Houston 77092. He is a member and former president of the Home Owners Warranty Corp. and of the Greater Houston Builders Association. In addition, he has served on the executive committee of the Texas Association of Builders.

Home Improvements That Save Taxes When You Sell

You can reduce the capital gains tax on any profit from the sale of your home by adding the documented cost of improvements to the original price you paid. The following is a checklist of improvements that can qualify for this tax benefit.

Improvements to the House

- Additions and finishing: New rooms,

porches, closets, laundry chutes, dumbwaiters, attic and basement improvements.

• Built-in furnishings: Permanently placed units such as chests, cabinets, shelving; installation of permanent floor covering.

• Electrical wiring: Installation of new power lines, outlets, switches, lighting fixtures.

• Equipment: Built-in stereo systems, intercoms, fire alarms, garbage disposal units, dishwashers, stoves, refrigerators, washing machines, dryers, elevators.

Plumbing, Heating, Air Conditioning

• Installation of new or additional plumbing fixtures, sinks, laundry tubs, water softeners; piping, tanks, pumps, wells.

• Upgrading of heating system, air conditioning units, attic fans, humidifiers, dehumidifiers.

• Insulation, solar heating, or other energy-conserving devices (less the amount of energy tax credit claimed).

Structural Work

• Installation of louvers and screen vents in attic.

• Replacement of roofing, gutters, or exterior covering of the house with better materials.

• Installation of awnings, sunshades, shutters, blinds, storm doors, storm windows, screens.

• Upgrading of interiors with major brick, stone, cement, or plastering work.

• New doors or windows; acoustical ceilings; strengthening of structure with steel girders, reinforcing rods, floor jacks.

• Work done on the foundation to eliminate water seepage and settling.

Improvements to the Grounds

• Equipment: Outdoor sound systems, floodlighting, lampposts, barbecue pits, incinerators, mailboxes, underground sprinkler systems.

• Landscaping: Enlargement of lawn area, addition of trees or shrubbery, resurfacing of land areas or installation of drain tiles and other equipment to eliminate drainage problems, addition or redesigning of decorative pools and arbors.

• Paving and surfaces: Blacktopping or other improvements to driveway, laying or extension of walks and curbs, addition or enlargement of patios.

• Recreational facilities: Installation of swimming pool and related facilities, tennis court, children's playground equipment.

• Structures: Addition, improvement, or removal of fences, walls, trellises, garages, carports, toolsheds, stables, greenhouses, or other outbuildings.

Source: William J. Roll, CPA, partner in the CPA firm Herring & Roll, PC, 41 South Fifth Street, Sunbury, PA 17801.

Home-Improvement Mistakes To Avoid

Winter is a good time to turn dreams of adding a bedroom, kitchen, or bath into reality. But that calls for shopping around, simple research, and hard thinking before you convert your dream project into a contract to build.

First of all, don't let a contractor persuade you that putting in a $20,000 kitchen—or any other major renovation—is an "investment" that you'll get back in a higher value on your home when you sell. Most home properties are valued chiefly on the basis of where they're located. A new bath or kitchen may make a home easier to sell, but rarely adds significantly to its value. In some parts of the US a major improvement such as a swimming pool can actually make a home harder to sell to safety-conscious families with young children or to adults who don't want the bother of maintenance.

So the first rule in planning a home improvement is to make sure that you and your family will realize value from the project in convenience and pleasure right now—and that you can afford it right now.

First shop around for the financing you might need. Tell your banker what you're thinking of doing, and ask for the rates and payment terms on second mortgages, home-equity loans, or special home-renovation packages. And if you have a healthy business or personal account at the bank, see what kind of a rate you can get on a straight personal loan. Then, when you start talking with a contractor, you'll be able to compare any financing rates and terms he offers with those from other sources. Sometimes, though not often, he may do enough business with a bank to get lower rates than you can.

Follow the Rules

Once you and the contractor are in serious discussions, don't try to take shortcuts around local regulations. A qualified contractor will know local code standards and can obtain a building permit without delay and without hassle to you.

More and more local communities are licensing contractors. That gives you an opportunity to check them out. Call the local building inspector and ask whether he knows the contractor you're thinking of hiring and whether any complaints are pending. Chances are good that you'll get frank advice to look around further if the contractor has a record of faulty work.

Ask the contractor exactly how he plans to do the work. It's important that you have specific information on how long you will be without a working kitchen . . . or know how the contractor plans to protect your home if he has to open an outside wall. Let him take you step by step through the method he'll use so you'll know what preparations you will have to make: Moving and storing furniture, making alternative living arrangements and the like.

Special precaution: When you're putting an addition on the house, be particularly careful about how the new plumbing lines are installed and protected. Contractors often fail to protect the lines from freezing temperatures. Once the walls and moldings are in place, leaks in these lines will be expensive to repair.

Make clear to the contractor that you expect him to keep the work site clean. Tell him that you expect workers to eat their meals in their cars or on trucks. Reason: Many homeowners find their homes infested with bugs and rodents after a major renovation because the workers dumped their leftover food in the wall spaces.

Good-Neighbor Policy

It usually pays to check your plans for a major renovation with your nearest neighbors before work starts. Put your project in the most positive light, but be alert to signs of opposition, and try to negotiate any differences. A compromise is very likely to be much cheaper than litigation.

Don't rush blindly into even simple projects such as widening a driveway or paving part of the backyard for a basketball court. Many communities restrict the number of cars that can be parked in the front yard, and most zoning codes have restrictions on covering more than a certain portion of the land, which includes the blacktop.

Be careful, too, about when you schedule the work. Most localities have rules about how early in the morning workers can start to use noisy equipment. Many resort communities prohibit major construction during the summer months.

Source: David Schechner, attorney and village counsel for South Orange, NJ, 80 Main St., West Orange, NJ 07052.

Protecting Yourself in Home-Improvement Contracts

Improving a home has become more attractive than buying a new one for many people.

The key to protecting yourself when hiring

a contractor for a major alteration is thoughtful contract negotiation. Even contractors with good reputations sometimes get in over their heads.

• Always do your own financing. Terms of lenders working with contractors are usually stiff. Often they give the lender a second mortgage on your house—sometimes without your realizing it. That can leave you without leverage to force correction of bad workmanship.

• The contractor should show you the document from his insurance company covering workers' compensation. A standard homeowners' policy does not cover workers (except, in some states, an occasional baby-sitter).

• Fix responsibility for repairing wind, rain, or fire damage, as well as possible vandalism at worksite.

• Include a payment schedule in the contract. Typically, a contractor gets 10% of the negotiated fee upon signing a contract, then partial payments at completion of each stage of succeeding work. You should withhold any payment until contract actually begins work. Then hold down succeeding payments as much as possible, so that contractor does not earn his profit until his work is completed.

• Make sure the final payment is contingent upon approval of the work by municipal inspectors.

• Make the contractor responsible for abiding by local building codes. If you assume this responsibility, make the contract contingent on your ability to get all necessary building permits. Be specific about what work you want done, how, and with what materials.

• Don't settle for normal contract language about the project's being done in "a workmanlike manner," because homeowners' standards for work they want done is often higher than common trade practice.

• To avoid misunderstandings, refer in the contract to architect's drawings, where possible, and actual specifications.

• Include a schedule against which to measure work's progress. Use calendar dates: For example, foundation and framing to be completed by March 1; roughing-in by April 1;

sheetrock by May 1; woodwork and finish work by June 1.

• Push for a penalty clause if the work is completed unreasonably late. For example, all work to be completed by June 1. If, however, work is not completed by June 1, the contractor will pay the homeowner $100 a day thereafter.

A Warning on Liens

Tell your prospective contractor right at the start that you want a provision in the work contract that neither he nor any of his subcontractors will file mechanics' liens against your home. If the contractor tells you that he never files liens, respond by saying that he shouldn't mind putting that policy into the contract.

The danger to avoid: Many contractors and subcontractors file notices of intention to do work on your house in the local courthouse. Then, if you hold back payments for the work because of a claim that it is not properly done or finished, they will get a lien on your house for the value of the work they did do. A subcontractor may also get such a lien against your house if the contractor fails to pay him promptly.

Note: Your agreement with the contractor will not be binding as between you and a subcontractor. But if your agreement with the contractor also mentions subcontractors, the contractor will have to wait until the subcontractor's lien is settled before he can receive payment. This is a strong incentive for the contractor to persuade his subcontractors to sign a similar waiver. To protect yourself against a charge of fraud: Whenever you make payment to the contractor, have him sign a statement that he has paid his subcontractors and suppliers. If he refuses, pay them directly and deduct that amount from the contractor's fee.

Source: David Schechner, attorney and village counsel for South Orange, NJ, 80 Main St., West Orange, NJ 07052.

What You Should Know about Real Estate Agents

Knowing your legal rights and responsibilities when selling your home yourself or through a real estate broker can save you thousands of dollars. . .and a lot of worry and frustration over your own possible wrong moves.

Selling your own home is not an easy task. You need to be able to provide buyers with information about zoning laws, community services, and the condition of your home. Also, you have no security against intrusions by unqualified house-hunters—curiosity seekers, potential thieves and the like.

If you decide to sell with a broker, shop around to find one who is knowledgeable about your community and with whom you feel comfortable.

Sellers' failure to read the legal documents pertaining to brokers' contracts causes most misunderstandings. Special points:

Commissions paid by the seller to the broker are no longer established by any state agency or private trade association (by federal law). The individual brokers set fees for their own offices. Some will negotiate a commission rate, others will not. The law does not require them to.

The listing agreement is a legal document that outlines the understanding between you and the broker about how your home will be listed for sale. It includes your name, the broker's name, the address of the property, the asking price and other details about the home, as well as the amount of time you are giving the broker to find a buyer (30, 60, or 90 days is usual). This is a legal document, binding you to its provisions.

Exclusive right to sell is the most common type of listing. The seller pays full commission to the listing broker, regardless of which real estate office brings in the buyer—even if the seller brings in the buyer.

The exclusive agency agreement permits only one broker to offer your property during an agreed-upon time period. However, you may sell the property yourself, with no obligation to the broker, during the same time period. Most agencies will not accept such a listing.

Buyers' cries of misrepresentation or fraud are heard increasingly these days. The seller has a duty to tell the broker about defects in the house that are known to the seller and that might affect a buyer's willingness to purchase the property. Knowing about such defects and not mentioning them invites a suit for misrepresentation or fraud. Honesty may save you future fears and problems.

Lawsuits against sellers and brokers about other problems relating to a house and neighborhood are cropping up. Are you required or is your broker required to disclose that the land beneath the home was once a chemical waste dump, or that you were aware of plans for a sewage-treatment plant down the street? Those kinds of questions are still to be resolved by the courts, but you can see the importance of full disclosure of what you do know.

Signing a contract and accepting a buyer's "earnest" money commit you to the sale—unless the buyer reneges and therefore forfeits the money, or some contingency to the sale negates the contract. If you've signed a contract and then refuse to follow through, you could face a lawsuit should the buyer want to initiate one. In any event, you may still be responsible for the broker's commission.

Source: John R. Linton, vice president, legal affairs, National Association of Realtors, 430 N. Michigan Ave., Chicago 60611.

Ways To List Your House

• Open listing: The owner reserves the right to sell the property himself or to retain brokers.

• Exclusive agency: No other broker will be hired as long as the original broker is retained (usually for a specified period), but this doesn't prevent the owner from selling the property himself.

• Exclusive right to sell: The broker gets his

commission when the property is sold whether by the broker, the owner, or anyone else.

• Multiple listing: Brokers combine to sell properties listed with any member of the brokers' pool. The brokers themselves split commissions between the listing and selling broker.

If no time is specified, the listing is good for a "reasonable" time. The owner can revoke the listing at any time before the broker has earned his commission, provided he acts in good faith and doesn't revoke when negotiations have been substantially completed.

If a time is specified, the agreement will end as stipulated. It would continue only if the owner has waived the time limit by accepting the services of the broker, or if the owner has acted in bad faith (as by postponing agreement with a buyer until after the time limit). In some states, if the listing is for a specified time, the owner can revoke only up until the time the broker has put money and effort into the listing contract.

If nothing is said, the broker will earn his commission on finding a buyer ready, willing, and able to buy on the terms specified. The owner, to protect himself, should ask for a provision under which payment of the commission will depend on closing the deal and full payment.

Getting More for an Old House

An old house (built 1920 to 1950) can be sold as easily as a new one. The right selling strategy and a few improvements may raise the selling price significantly. That's the advice from Mary Weir of Rumson, New Jersey. She has bought, refurbished (on a grand scale), and resold more than 50 houses. Her suggestions:

• Invest in a complete cleaning, repainting,

or wallpapering. Recarpet or have the rugs and carpets professionally cleaned. (Approximate cost for a four-bedroom, three-bath house: $2,500 to $3,000.)

• Get rid of cat and dog odors that you may be used to but potential buyers will notice.

• With trend to smaller families and working wives, it may be desirable to convert and advertise a four-bedroom house as two bedrooms, library, and den.

• Exterior of house is crucial. It's the first thing buyer sees. Paint or replace shutters if necessary. Clean and repair porch and remove clutter. Repaint porch furniture.

• Landscaping makes a great difference and can sell (or un-sell) a house. Get expert advice on improving it. (Approximate cost: Anywhere from $100 to $1,000.)

• Good real estate agents are vital to a quick sale. There are one or two top people in every agency who will work hard to show houses and even arrange financing. Multiple listing lets these supersalespeople from different agencies work for the seller.

Best Color To Paint a House

Yellow houses have the most "curb appeal" and sell faster than those of any other color. Most people associate yellow with sunshine, optimism, and warmth.

Source: Leatrice Eiseman, color consultant and educator in Tarzana, CA, in *Consumers Digest.*

Selling Your House When Credit Is Tight

When mortgage rates are high, homeowners can entice buyers with offers to finance the sale themselves. By offering financing, sellers may make their house so marketable that outside financing will be unnecessary. And the commission saving is substantial.

However, although financing the sale of a house is simple in principle, sellers should have the advice of a lawyer who specializes in real estate.

Four Basic Methods

• First mortgage. If you are trying to sell a $100,000 house that has no mortgage (a rarity), and the purchaser can afford only $40,000 cash down, then the purchaser simply gives you a first mortgage for $60,000, which is paid out over an agreed-upon period, at an agreed-upon interest rate. In case of default, you keep the cash and foreclose on the house.

• Second mortgage. If you are trying to sell the same $100,000 house with an existing $50,000 first mortgage, a second mortgage reduces the cash that a buyer would need. The purchaser assumes the first mortgage and gives you a $20,000 down payment. The purchaser then gives you a second mortgage for $30,000. Interest rate and maturity date are negotiable. But many existing first mortgages held by institutional lenders contain a due-on-sale clause, which prohibits the sale of the house without the consent of the lender. Typically, such consent is given only if the interest rate is substantially increased.

• Wrap-around. Similar to second mortgages. Using the same numbers as in the second-mortgage example, you get a $20,000 down payment, but instead of taking back a $30,000 second mortgage, you take back an $80,000 wrap-around mortgage (the amount of the first mortgage plus the remaining $30,000 of the sales price). One advantage is that defaults are quick to catch because the buyer makes all payments directly to you, and you pay the first-mortgage portion to that lender. Another advantage is that the interest rate on the wrap-around is calculated on the entire $80,000, even though the $50,000 first-mortgage portion may be at a lower interest

rate. Therefore, you receive the interest average, giving you a higher yield on your $30,000 portion.

• Leasing with purchase option. Lease payments may be applied to the purchase price, an amount agreed on when the deal is made. The best approach is to make the term as short as possible. Should another prospective buyer come along with ready cash, you won't be hindered by a long-term contract. And since you are still the owner, you can depreciate the house as a rental unit.

Source: C. Gray Bethea Jr., vice president and general counsel, CMEI, Inc., Atlanta.

Buyers Who Back Out at the Last Minute

Selling a house can be a problem when the potential buyer makes the deal contingent on the sale of his own house. After months of waiting, your deal may fall through.

Solution: Include a kick-out clause in the sales agreement. This enables the seller to keep the house on the market until the sale is completed. If another buyer makes an offer, the original buyer has 48 hours to decide whether he wants to buy the house or not.

If the Seller Has a Change of Heart

The seller of a house said he was canceling his contract to sell, and refunded the down payment. The buyer insisted the seller had no right to cancel. The seller argued that the buyer, by accepting and cashing the check, had agreed to cancellation of the sale. The court ruled for the buyer, and ordered the seller to perform the contract. The return of the down payment, the court said, had no legal effect. It was not a sum of money accepted in settlement of a dispute. It was nothing but the return of the buyer's money, which the seller had no right to keep while refusing to complete the sale.

Source: *Merrill Lynch Realty v. Skinner*, Ct. App., NY, 473 N.E. (2d) 229.

Condos Vs. Co-ops

When you purchase a condominium you own real property, just like when you buy a house. You arrange for your own mortgage with the bank, pay real estate taxes directly to the local government, pay water bills individually, and have an individual deed.

When you buy a cooperative apartment, you are participating in a syndication. A corporation is formed, shares are issued, and people subscribe to the shares. The corporation raises money, takes out a mortgage, and owns the building.

Maintenance charges for a condominium are likely to cost 50% of a cooperative's charges for an equivalent building. The reason: The maintenance on a condominium covers only the common area upkeep. That includes: Labor, heating oil, repairs, and maintenance of the playground, swimming pool, and other community areas. Co-op maintenance fees cover those same items plus mortgage payments, local real estate taxes, utility and water bills.

Capital improvements: If an extensive, major repair needs to be made (such as the replacement of a roof or boiler), the board of managers of a condo cannot borrow funds from a bank unless it receives the unanimous consent of the condo owners. Problem: If a dozen owners are content to live in a dilapidated building, improvements must be funded through maintenance cash flow, which may be very expensive. In a co-op, the board of directors can take out a second mortgage to fix a roof, plumbing, or other major problem. Individual co-op shareholders cannot easily obstruct the board.

Delinquency in paying maintenance fees can be handled more expediently in a co-op than in a condo. In a co-op, an owner who doesn't pay maintenance fees can be evicted almost immediately. The person is served with a dispossess and can be evicted within days. In a condominium, a lien must be placed on the apartment and then a foreclosure proceeding is brought. It could take two years to get the money, and it is a difficult legal proceeding.

Exclusionary rights: Since a co-op is considered personal property, not real property, prospective tenants may be rejected by the co-op's board of directors for any reason whatsoever except race, creed, color, or national origin. Reality: As long as the co-op board members don't state the reason, anyone can be excluded for any prejudice. Problem: A tenant may have trouble subletting a co-op if the co-op board members don't approve of the new tenant. In a condominium, each owner has the right to sell or sublet to anyone the person wants, subject only to the condo's right of first refusal, which is rarely exercised.

From the entrepreneur's point of view, a co-op can be more advantageous if the building at the time of the conversion date has a low-interest mortgage. Reason: When a building is converted into a condominium it must be free and clear of all liens. In a co-op, the former financing can be kept intact.

Source: David Goldstick, senior partner, Goldstick Weinberger, Feldman, Alperstein & Taishoff, 551 Fifth Ave., New York 10017.

When Buying a New Condominium

Before signing any contract for a new condominium, which is harder to check out than an established condominium, buyers should study the prospectus for any of these pitfalls:

• The prospectus includes a plan of the unit you are buying, showing rooms of specific dimensions. But the plan omits closet space.

Result: The living space you are buying is probably smaller than you think.

The prospectus includes this clause: The interior design shall be substantially similar. Result: The developer can alter both the size and design of your unit.

• The common charges set forth in the prospectus are unrealistically low. Buyers should never rely on a developer's estimate of common charges. Instead: They should find out the charges at similarly functioning condominiums.

Common charges include: Electricity for hallways and outside areas, water, cleaning, garbage disposal, insurance for common areas, pool maintenance, groundskeeping, legal and accounting fees, reserves for future repairs.

• Variation on the common-charge trap: The developer is paying common charges on unsold units. But these charges are unrealistically low. Reason: The developer has either underinsured, underestimated the taxes due, omitted security expenses, or failed to set up a reserve fund.

• The prospectus includes this clause: The seller will not be obligated to pay monthly charges for unsold units. Result: The owners of a partially occupied condominium have to pay for all operating expenses.

• The prospectus warns about the seller's limited liability. But an unsuspecting buyer may still purchase a condominium unit on which back monthly charges are due, or even on which there's a lien for failure to pay back carrying charges.

• The prospectus makes no mention of parking spaces. Result: You must lease from the developer.

• The prospectus is imprecise about the total number of units to be built. Result: Facilities are inadequate for the number of residents.

• The prospectus includes this clause: Transfer of ownership (of the common property from the developer to the home-owners' association) will take place 60 days after the last unit is sold. Trap: The developer deliber-

ately does not sell one unit, keeps on managing the condominium, and awards sweetheart maintenance and operating contracts to his subcontractors.

• The prospectus specifies that the developer will become the property manager of the functioning condominium. But the language spelling out monthly common charges and management fees is imprecise. Result: The owners cannot control monthly charges and fees.

Source: Dorothy Tymon, author, *The Condominium: A Guide for the Alert Buyer*, Golden-Lee Books, Brooklyn, NY.

Your Financial Liability When You Sit on a Co-op or Condo Board

It's generally believed that you have "arrived" when you are asked to sit on a board of directors. This applies whether it is a corporation board, bank board, school board, or condo or co-op board. However, along with the prestige goes a high level of responsibility and liability.

Whether you are on the board of directors for a profit-making corporation or a nonprofit organization, never underestimate your obligations. Many people who sit on nonprofit boards and who receive no compensation for their services have little understanding that their legal position is similar to that of someone on a corporate board. In fact, a nonprofit board member may even incur a higher degree of responsibility in the eyes of a court, because he is seen as holding a position of public trust.

The principles of corporate law are applied to most nonprofit boards. The would-be director of any nonprofit organization is therefore wise to check on the state law—which varies greatly—as to the category of directorship and the legal duties that accompany it.

The primary obligations of an individual on a co-op or condominium board are (1) to act within his authority, (2) to exercise "due care," and (3) to fulfill all fiduciary duties. A breach of any of these will result in the following kinds of liability of responsible directors, unless state law specifically exempts nonprofit corporations from statutory proceedings to enforce that liability.

1. If the directors of a co-op or condo do not act within the scope of their authority, a dissenting co-op member may be able to bring suit against the directors to enjoin them or set their action aside, or to render them liable for mismanagement.

2. By law, directors owe their co-op/condo associations a "duty of care." The legislative and judicial definition of this term is not clear as it applies to nonprofit boards. The definition applicable to business corporations, however, is that directors "discharge the duties of their respective positions in good faith and that degree of diligence and care and skill which ordinarily prudent men would exercise under similar circumstances in like positions." A duty of reasonable inquiry and reliance on information provided by others (corporate officers) is also encompassed by the corporate duty of care. The director is liable for dollar-for-dollar damages.

3. Failure to exercise one's fiduciary responsibilities can lead to suits in which a guilty director is liable for dollar-for-dollar damages.

As a fiduciary, a director may not disclose confidential information or use it for personal gain. If a director is ever in doubt about actions taken by management or to the authenticity/accuracy of any or all information furnished, including financial, it is the director's obligation to make known his concern and receive appropriate documentation.

Apart from knowing the applicable law and performing well, what can co-op or condo board members do to protect themselves? Insist on coverage by directors and officers liability insurance.

Source: John M. Nash, president and CEO, National Association of Corporate Directors, 1707 L St. NW, Suite 560, Washington, DC 20036.

The Most Valuable Vacation Homes

For maximum resale value of a vacation home, purchase property on the water, with as much frontage as you can afford . . . a house that faces northwest (for best afternoon sunlight) . . . mildly rolling terrain . . . a rustic exterior . . . a modern kitchen and bath.
Source: *Money.*

How To Save Money When Building Your Own Home

Much can be said for doing things right the first time, especially when it comes to building your own home. It may be financially helpful to cut corners, but make sure you cut the *right* corners. The last thing you want is a shoddily constructed or designed home.

My advice is to treat the building of your home like any other business project. The two most important things you should do before building are to (1) hire a qualified general contractor, and (2) carefully plan your location, design, and budget.

Using a General Contractor

Few people understand the actual number of day-to-day decisions that go into building a house—much less understand the local building rules and regulations. A good general contractor will procure the lowest-priced services, the desired quality, and guarantee the timely completion of your home. Criteria to use when selecting a general contractor:
- Reputation and honesty.
- Financial capabilities.
- Communication skills.
- Business knowledge.
- Provision of a written warranty.

Planning and Budgeting

The best way to insure that your initial investment at least retains its value, but more importantly appreciates with time, is by selecting a good location and marketable design.

Location should always be the first and foremost decision. The main factors to consider:

- Travel time.
- Costs.
- Schools.
- Availability and accessibility of shopping.
- Personal preference.
- Social and economic status of the neighborhood.

The second most important decision is the design and the determination of the specific building requirements of that design. Carefully analyzing each room's size and utilization should help you eliminate or scale down little-used rooms or areas in the house, ultimately saving significant building and maintenance costs (e.g., heating and cooling).

Be sure to select a design that is marketable in the area you have chosen. In other words, avoid building a California home in Vermont. And remember, the design will have a large impact on the total cost of the house. The major factors to consider when selecting a design:

- Two-story designs are the least expensive per square foot.
- Houses with one and a half stories are gaining in popularity, especially those with first-floor master suites.
- Ranches (one-floor plans) are the most expensive per square foot, because the area between the foundation and the roof system is not maximized. It is always cheaper to build up than out.
- Higher-pitched roofs are more expensive and more eye-appealing.
- Vaulted and cathedral ceilings are more expensive than flat ceilings.

Construction Financing

As a property owner, it's better to obtain the construction loan yourself, than to have the builder do it, since you avoid paying double closing costs and construction interest can be written off on your current year's income taxes. When your builder obtains the con-

struction loan, you pay the interest costs and construction loan closing costs in the price of the property, but will have to treat the interest expenses as a capital gain when the property is sold.

Materials

Careful selection and specification of materials can save money without sacrificing quality. Name brand choices drive up costs and add only limited value. Examples: Name brand plumbing fixtures are more expensive than contractor brands but usually no more effective. High-fashion designs and colors increase costs and possibly date the home's appearance. Nationally advertised windows will add 25% to 30% more to window costs.

Pay attention to areas where short-term savings should be weighed against long-term operating and maintenance costs. In particular, note:

- Energy-related items, i.e., extra insulation, high-efficiency furnaces with less than a five-year payback, energy-efficient water heating systems, add-on electric heat pumps for gas and oil heating systems.
- Exterior siding selection:

Material	Initial cost	Maintenance cost
brick	high	low
stone	high	low
wood	high	high
aluminum	low	low
stucco	low	low
hardboard	low	high

Lot Selection and Landscaping

A wooded lot can be very appealing as a place to live, but there are problems when it comes to building. The initial cost of a wooded lot is generally higher than for non-wooded lots. Caution must be used to be sure that all of the trees on a wooded lot are not located where the house will be built. Clearing costs can run as high as several thousand dollars, and you can expect that construction equipment will lose some efficiency when operating in wooded lots, thereby adding more costs.

Landscaping expenses can be reduced by selecting small plants and trees that will grow rather than landscaping with fully grown stock, and by negotiating with the landscaping company on eliminating expensive guarantees for growth. This can reduce your total landscaping bill by as much as 25%–35%. Also, if it is summer or early fall, seeding a lawn rather than sodding will reduce your lawn costs by 40% or more.

Source: Jim Sutliff, president and the owner of Sutliff Builders Inc., 190 S. State St., Westerville, OH 43081, a residential building company with $5 million in annual sales.

Factory-Made Homes

Factory-made homes cost less than comparable conventional homes—as much as 30% less. Reasons: There are no architect's fees (manufacturers rearrange standard floor plans to meet your needs). In addition to the mass-production economies that come with factory-assembled homes, little material is wasted (everything is precut to fit precisely). There is little, if any, cost overrun (labor and materials costs are predetermined).

• Building time is much less. Factory-made homes can be ready for occupancy one week to three months after the order is placed.

• Energy efficiency is better. Many factory-home manufacturers have stricter standards than those set by federal and state governments.

Drawbacks

• There is less variety in floor plans and room layouts.

• Availability is limited geographically. Not every manufacturer sells homes in every part of the country. And some locales have restricted factory-made homes because they pose competition for local unions, contractors, and building-supply interests.

Buying Basics

• Look for manufacturers that have built homes in your area. They should be able to suggest a local contractor or dealer with whom you can work.

• Call or meet with two or three manufacturers that provide the type of home you want. Talk with people who have bought homes from them. Tour one or two finished homes.

• Write to the Building Systems Council (15 and M Sts. NW, Washington, DC 20005) to make sure your proposed manufacturer is a member.

• Show the manufacturer your building site to see if it's compatible with the house you like. If not, the house probably can be modified.

Building Basics

• Ask the manufacturer if any building parts aren't included in the package. If some are not, send a list of them to lumber yards or other suppliers for bids.

• If things like plumbing and wiring are not included in the package, you will have to contract for these jobs. Put everything in writing, and don't pay in full until the work has passed inspection by the local building department.

• Make sure the manufacturer guarantees the house for at least one year—and preferably for five to 10 years.

The Different Types

• Precut homes are good for people who want to help build the house themselves. Parts are assembled at the building site. Features can be custom designed.

Cost: Approximately $40,000 (800 square feet) to $250,000 (5,000 square feet).*

• Panelized homes are made of large factory-built wall panels that are assembled by an installation crew.

Cost: Approximately $40,000 (800 square feet) to $500,000 (10,000 square feet).*

• Modular homes are 95% complete when they leave the factory (in two to four sections). Assembly takes three days.

Cost: Approximately $25,000 (500 square feet) to $150,000 (3,000 square feet).*

*Prices include everything but the land, foundation, and utilities.

Source: A.M. Watkins, a graduate engineer and home-building consultant. He is the author of *The Complete Guide to Factory-Made Houses*, published by The Building Institute, River Rd., Piermont, NY 10968.

When It's Time To Move

Purchasing moving services should be approached the same way you would purchase any other product or service: By becoming informed. A good way to start is by asking your friends and associates which movers they've used. Contact the local Better Business Bureau and review all the literature provided to you by prospective moving companies. If the move will be to another state, check movers' performance records that they're required to provide by the Interstate Commerce Commission.

If possible, try to select a mover six to eight weeks in advance of your ideal moving date to insure availability. The peak season for movers is June, July, August, and September. During these months, vans may be scarce and costs, higher. You can usually save money by moving between October 1 and April 30, when many movers offer lower off-season prices.

It's a good idea to obtain estimates from at least two reputable movers. Determine all of their charges and the types of services they offer. Compare to see which mover best suits your needs and budget. Before reaching a final decision, pay a visit to the mover's place of business to get an indication of how professional the company is. Look for (1) professional and business-like personnel; (2) clean and well-organized offices and warehouse; (3) equipment in good condition.

Getting Accurate Estimates

Unless you get binding estimates, most moving estimates are just educated guesses to help you anticipate your approximate moving expense. The final bill could be very different. To help movers calculate the most accurate estimate, show them every item to be moved. Try to reach a clear understanding about the amount of packing and other services you'll require; services that are not included in the estimate will be added onto the final cost.

Moving costs are usually determined by the actual weight of your possessions or the amount of space they take up in the mover's van. Factored into this total is the distance your possessions are transported and the optional services provided. For example, options may range from guaranteed pickup and delivery dates to a "smokeless" move.

Liability Options

Pay particular attention to the liability options. Moving companies offer a variety of plans:

• Limited liability plan. You can seek recovery on an item at the rate of 60 cents per pound. The protection is minimal, but it costs nothing.

• Added-value protection. Under this plan, you can seek recovery based on the actual cost of the item at current replacement cost, less depreciation. The cost of the option is 50 cents per $100 of valuation.

• Full-value protection. The plan covers the full cost of repair or replacement of items without deductions for depreciation. The costs and extent of coverage of this option vary among movers, so ask prospects for full details.

If any of your possessions are damaged or lost, you have nine months to file a claim. It's always to your advantage to file promptly. The mover is required to acknowledge receipt of your claim within 30 days and within 120 days must make an offer to settle the claim.

Try to plan your packing day one or two days before the actual loading of the van. To save on charges, you may want to pack part of your belongings yourself. Ask the moving company about its policy on liability for customer-packed cartons.

Source: Charles C. Irions, president, American Movers Conference, 2200 Mill Road, Alexandria, VA 22314, the trade association for the interstate household goods moving industry.

Index

488